Modigliani Sculptor

Printed on
GardaPat 13 KIARA - 135 g/m²

Modigliani Sculptor

edited by
Gabriella Belli
Flavio Fergonzi and Alessandro Del Puppo

with the collaboration of
Clarenza Catullo

SilvanaEditoriale

Modigliani Sculptor

Rovereto, Museo di Arte Moderna e Contemporanea
di Trento e Rovereto
18th December 2010 - 27th March 2011

Exhibition Project after an idea and curated by
Gabriella Belli
Flavio Fergonzi
Alessandro Del Puppo

With the collaboration of
Clarenza Catullo

Essays by
Gabriella Belli
Roberta Bartoli
Anna Ceroni
Ilaria Cicali
Alessandro Del Puppo
Flavio Fergonzi
Brigitte Léal
Eike D. Schmidt
Kenneth Wayne

Catalogue Editing by
Massimo De Sabbata

Catalogue and Communication Art Direction
Headline, Rovereto

Translations
Kathryn Lake
from Italian into English
Ilaria Ortolina
from English into Italian
from French into Italian

Installation Project
Caruso Torricella Architett
with the collaboration of
Carlo Appiani
Andrea Cavalletti
and of
Matteo Fiore
Light Design Project

Registrar and Technical Curator
Clarenza Catullo
with the collaboration of
Ilaria Calgaro

Photo Archive
Attilio Begher
with the collaboration of
Serena Aldi
Maurizio Baldo

Installation
Claudio Merz
with the collaboration of
Giovanni Pivato
Giampiero Coatti
Mario Divina
Jorge Daniel Garcia
and of
Arteam Italia

Communication and Public Relations Department
Flavia Fossa Margutti

Press Office and Web Site
Luca Melchionna
Clementina Rizzi

Communication Department
Silvia Ferrari
Carlotta Gaspari
Maria Elena Putz
Lodovico Schiera
Vanessa Vacchini
Francesca Velardita

Technical and IT Department
Giusto Manica
Stefano Manica
Walter Pancin

Educational Texts
Daniela Ferrari

Wall Panels
Serigrafica, Rovigo

Light Design
Idee in Luce di Claudio Cervelli, Vicenza

Mart thanks

Provincia autonoma di Trento

in partnership with

UniCredit

Casa del Vino della Vallagarina

with the support of

Takeda
Takeda Italia Farmaceutici

technical partner

GARDA CARTIERE

for the educational activities

Casse Rurali Trentine

TRENTINO

The exhibition on Modigliani represents the result of years of passionate work and dedication to a project that we are sure will lead to an advancement of the studies devoted to Modigliani as a sculptor. Therefore, the list of thanks could be infinite as it must cover specific people, museums, private collectors, specialists, gallery owners, colleagues, friends and even casual acquaintances who, perhaps unknowingly, have put us on the tracks of important clues to find important data that would help to solve doubts and uncertainties.

A special thank to:
Giorgio Andreatta
Laura Boschini
Anna Ceroni
Annamaria Cescatti
Daniel De Agostini
Margherita de Pilati
Massimo Di Carlo
Chiara Fabi
Leonardo Farsetti
Frances Archipenko Gray
Guido and Silvia Guastalla
Robert Landau
Paolo Manfrini
Claudio Martinelli
Laura Mattioli
Tiziano Mellarini
Werner Merzbacher
Carlo Montanaro
Silvana Pasquin
Amedeo Porro
Giulio Prosser
Dilli Rigamonti
Marcello Salucci
Thomas Sharman
Clara Sforni
Giulio Tega
and to all the directors and curators of international museums and institutions whose contribution to our study has been fundamental:
Elizabeth Armstrong, Minneapolis Institute of Art
Richard Armstrong, Solomon R. Guggenheim Museum, New York
Mariolina Bassetti, Christie's, Rome
Tobia Bezzola, Kunstmuseum, Zurich
Alberto Castaldini, Istituto Italiano di Cultura, Bucarest
Carol Coffin, The Museum of Modern Art, New York
Guy Cogeval, Musée d'Orsay, Paris
Harry Cooper, The National Gallery of Art, Washington, DC
Caitlin B. Corrigan, The Metropolitan Museum of Art, New York
Leah Dickerman, The Museum of Modern Art, New York
Christine Dixon, National Gallery of Australia, Canberra
Vivien Green, Solomon R. Guggenheim Museum, New York
Fiona Grisdale, The British Museum, London
Anika Guntrum and Léonore Vitry, Christie's, Paris
Mattias Herold, The Museum of Modern Art, New York
Joe Holbach, The Phillips Collection, Washington, DC
Richard Koshalek, The Hirshhorn Museum and Sculpture Garden, Washington, DC
Dorothy Kosinsky, The Phillips Collection, Washington, DC
Olga Makhroff, Centre Georges Pompidou, Paris
Maureen McCormick, Princeton University Art Museum
Nathalie Meneau, Centre Georges Pompidou, Paris
Tanya Morrison, Minneapolis Institute of Art
Alain Pasquier, Musée du Louvre, Paris
Christine Moine Patou, Musée du quai Branly, Paris
Catherine Régnault, Musée de la ville de Rouen
Cora Rosevear, The Museum of Modern Art, New York
Timothy Rub, Philadelphia Museum of Art
Sir Nicholas Serota, Tate, London
Paul Schwartzbaum, Peggy Guggenheim Collection, Venice
Simon Shaw, Sotheby's, New York
Maria Sica, Istituto Italiano di Cultura, Moscow
Michael Taylor, Philadelphia Museum of Art
Alicia B. Thomas, National Gallery of Art, Washington, DC
Gary Tinterow, The Metropolitan Museum of Art, New York
Marie-Paule Vial, Musées de la ville de Marseille
Ari Wiseman, Solomon R. Guggenheim Museum, New York
Hirohisa Yoshizawa, Musée Marie Laurencin, Tokyo
and
Library of the Centre Georges Pompidou, Paris
Library and Archive of the Musée d'Orsay, Paris
Library and Archive of the Orangerie, Paris
Library and Fund Nina Kandinsky, Paris
Bibliothèque nationale de France, Paris
Gulbenkian Foundation, Lisbon
Institut National d'Histoire de l'Art, Paris

List of Lenders

Regional Council for Cultural Heritage and Sicilian Identity, Museo Archeologico Regionale P. Griffo in Agrigento
Bearsville, New York, The Archipenko Foundation
Berlin, Ethnologisches Museum
Berne, Kunstmuseum, Hermann and Margit Rupf Foundation
Gianni Mattioli Collection, long term deposit at the Peggy Guggenheim Collection, Venice
Courtesy of Claudia Gian Ferrari Studio di Consulenza per il '900 Italiano, Milan
Courtesy of Galleria dello Scudo, Verona
Courtesy of Amedeo Porro arte moderna e contemporanea, Milan
Courtesy of Guido Guastalla
Courtesy of Galleria Tega, Milan
Copenhagen, Statens Museum for Kunst
Craiova, Muzeul de Arta
Dijon, Musée des Beaux-Arts de Dijon
Düsseldorf, Kunstsammlung Nordrhein-Westfalen
Florence, Museo Archeologico Nazionale
Florence, Museo Nazionale del Bargello
Hamburg, Hamburger Kunsthalle
London, Tate
London, The British Museum
Marseilles, Musée d'Arts Africains, Océaniens, Amérindies
Minneapolis, Minneapolis Institute of Arts
New York, Solomon R. Guggenheim Museum
New York, The Metropolitan Museum of Art
Paris, Centre Georges Pompidou, Musée National d'art moderne / Centre de création industrielle
Paris, Musée de l'Orangerie
Paris, Musée d'Orsay
Paris, Musée du quai Branly
Paris, Musée Guimet
Paris, Musée Zadkine de la ville de Paris
Princeton, Princeton University Art Museum
Philadelphia, Philadelphia Museum of Art
Rouen, Musée des Beaux-Arts
Saint Rémy les Chevreuses, Fondation de Coubertin
Saint Petersburg, The State Hermitage Museum
The Henry and Rose Pearlman Foundation, long term loan to the Princeton University Art Museum
Treviso, Museo di Santa Caterina
Vienna, Belvedere
Washington, DC, Hirshhorn Museum and Sculpture Garden, Smithsonian Institution
Washington, DC, National Gallery of Art
Washington, DC, The Phillips Collection

and all those who have decided to remain anonymous

With Modigliani Sculptor *Mart returns to producing an important international cultural event. In fact, this exhibition can boast a decisive particular: from now on every discussion and study concerning Modigliani will have to take this project into consideration.*
Mart takes on the task of bringing back the attention to a group of works, Modigliani's famous Heads*, which over the last twenty years have disappeared from Italian debates.*
Few artists have been loved by the general public like Amedeo Modigliani. The absence – up to now – of an exhibition like this has succeeded in surrounding the entire sculptural production of the great Italian artist with mystery and ambiguity. Having once again taken up the challenge, defined by most as impossible, shows that Mart has the necessary qualities to impose its prestige and high level scientific authority which places it among the protagonists of the most important international museums.

Lorenzo Dellai
President of the Provincia Autonoma di Trento

Modigliani Sculptor *is perhaps the most ambitious exhibition of those produced by Mart over the years. The event is of great importance for Italian art and culture, because, for however strange it may seem, these marvellous sculptures are very well known but rarely exhibited in our national museums.*
This is not only due to problems connected with the difficulty of obtaining the loans – that Mart has obviously been able to overcome – but also to the fact that in the analysis of Modigliani's work, sculpture has often taken second place compared to painting.
This really far-reaching exhibition lets us take a glimpse at a different and much more fascinating story. The great artist, active and original interpreter of the desire for renewal of his time, confronted stone with inspiration, a passion and a desire to "purify" himself which then played a fundamental role in the genesis of masterpieces on canvas that we all know.
An exhibition that opens up new and unexpected horizons on a critical and pedagogical level which at the same time is clear and fascinating for everyone.
The formula is right and confirms the solidity of the projects of Mart di Trento e Rovereto.

Franco Panizza
Culture Coucillor of the Provincia Autonoma di Trento

Modigliani Sculptor *brings a third of Amedeo Modigliani's sculptures together for the first time in a single exhibition. This is a substantial part of the sculptural production of the artist from Livorno, that still today remains a mysterious and not fully researched chapter of his artistic life.*
This exhibition is a unique event that has taken years of work. Mart needed all its great determination to have these works of art in Rovereto. However, the final result would never have been reached without the help and collaboration of museums and collectors who accepted our requests for loans.
Comparing the famous Heads *and thanks to the contribution of new and fundamental studies concerning the relationships with the artists of the past and present who influenced Modigliani, it is possible to fully understand a key moment of western modernity. For those who are lovers of Oriental and African art it will be enthralling to retrace Modigliani's fascination with ancient and surprising forms of the tribal art of those countries. The meeting between Avant-garde and Archaic art but also that of the Medieval and Renaissance periods which took place in Paris at the beginning of the last century, with the revolutions of geniuses like Picasso, Brancusi and Modigliani himself, have an importance which goes beyond those events.*
A group effort is concealed behind the fascinating linearity and simplicity of the path of this exhibition. A commitment that has the added value of representing a training ground for the professionalism of those who work at Mart and an opportunity for the museum to take the credit as an interlocutor, active and credible yet again on the international art scene.

Franco Bernabè
President of the Museo di Arte Moderna e Contemporanea
di Trento e Rovereto

Contents

Modigliani, Sculptor Rediscovered

Gabriella Belli

For the Sake of Coherency

Modigliani died at 36 years of age on 24th January 1920 and immediately became a legend. The same thing had happened to another great Italian artist, Giovanni Segantini, some years before, he died at forty-one years of age in 1899, an artist that Mart paid a lot of attention to in the 1980's and 1990's.[1]

If it had not been for a very short note in Eugenia Modigliani's diary,[2] from which we can understand that the young boy from Livorno knew the work of the great Segantini, we could say that these two artists had very little in common, apart from that destiny of dying young in tragic circumstances and their way of living beyond and above those conventions dictated by the "respectable" society of that time.

In fact, they were both born in Italy (Segantini was actually still a citizen of the Austro-Hungarian Empire but due to his stay in Milan in his youth he was called Italian), they lived most of their lives outside their country of origin, Modigliani in France and Segantini in Switzerland. They were both famous when they died and were mourned by the international cultural *milieu,* these two painters fomented their own legends not only for their *bohémien* anti-conformism which distinguished the whole of their existence but also, unfortunately, for their sudden deaths, which reserved for the former all the torments of the *mal sottile,* incurable at that time and for the latter, an acute peritonitis, which occurred while he was in the mountains painting one of the panels of his well known *Tryptich of Nature*.[3]

Theirs was a legend, the telling of which has been sustained by testimony, recollections and memories of the *vox populi*, that only by indulging in fantasy and sensation, was it possible to explain that unease of living and that intellectual restlessness, which had marked the increasing fame of their brief season for both of them.

Was it not perhaps Raffaele Calzini who in 1934 told the story of Segantini's whole life in a novelised way, up to that final sigh "I want to see my Mountains," which was in all the artistic literature of the twentieth century, even in the conscience of a shaman like Joseph Beuys, who gave this title to one of his most important works?

And was it not Gustave Coquiot in 1924, so only four years after Modigliani's death, who included him in his *Les Peintres Maudits*, a label which still sticks today and that will continue to classify that sort of artistic extra-territoriality of his work, as an effect of his eccentric way of life, crushed by the saturnine mists of alcohol and drugs?

It would seem that in both cases the critical historiography had availed itself of the interpretation of their respective artistic careers, more with regards to the sorrowful biographic aspects than to a revelation of their life history, free from romanced information. Rather difficult information to forget, also due to the diffused stereotype of the *genius* and *excesses*, which from Alexandre Dumas's *Kean* onwards, badly nourished so much artistic literature during the nineteenth century and the beginning of the twentieth.

If for Segantini the work carried out by the Museum in the mid 1980's, permitted the repositioning in international art history,

from Vienna to Paris, to Munich, of an experience which had been relegated for too long in the narrow valleys of Lombardy or Engadina, as a mere expression of a mainly local culture, for Modigliani sculptor, the studies which started in 2007, had an almost identical aim, that is to transfer his artistic career from myth to history, in particular regarding his sculptural production, which so shamefully occupied the art news in the mid 1980's.
As for Segantini, also for Modigliani the scientific research that we have prepared has emphasised not only an itinerary enriched by international relationships (a fact that has always been ascertained about his painting and that finds confirmation here for sculpture), but above all the uniqueness of the solutions and the results that he achieved in the field of plastic research. This is an important result which thanks to the critical contributions of this catalogue, has brought confirmation of his work from the chaos of models and suggestions, that have always been put forward to justify his inspiration which was so particular, to the certification of a very personal, and original, artistic experience also in the field of sculpture, where if it is possible to find everything it is at the same time legitimate to affirm that nothing is really pertinent, just similar.
This latter is a quite relevant thesis when examining his sculptures, as many will remember they were the object not only of biographic exaggeration which led to the recognition of the authenticity of the fake heads found in Livorno in 1984, but also of a conglomeration of models, today no longer admitted in the critical ordering of his work as a sculptor, this theme has been entrusted to Alessandro Del Puppo[4] in the catalogue with his sound and complete analysis.
What romanticised history has always denied Segantini, has above all been the recognition of his elevated visual culture, of a theoretical and practical knowledge that imbued his painting with good principals and profound aesthetical understanding which derived from his friendships but also and above all from sophisticated reading, even from the Index of forbidden books.
Instead, regarding Modigliani the story called for a fiery and irascible temperament, a good daily dose of alcohol and hashish, fame as a seducer, all the ingredients of a cocktail to which were added, the only true points, the malignant progression of tuberculosis, caught when he was still very young and the story of a life which was certainly miserable from an economic point of view: a mixture of bad living and bad luck from which the young artist seemed to free himself only in the creative gesture.
Yet, it has always been known that Modigliani, dedicated to art since he was young, devoted his intelligence to observing and learning so much, starting from that adolescent journey with his mother in 1900,[5] which saw them crossing the country, to visit the artistic treasures of Naples, Capri, Rome, Florence and Venice and then around 1906, it made him choose Paris as the place where he wanted to live and work, attracted by the cultural climate of the lively French capital at that time.
He was an avid reader of Mallarmé and Lautréamont, which he also suggested to his friend Paul Alexandre, as the young

doctor reported in his recollections,[6] but also with a good knowledge of the Classics, it is certain that Modigliani did not spend his time only in the *bistrots* but also in the museums, from the Louvre to the Trocadéro, the Guimet, from which he gleaned advantage for his sculpture, as Alessandro Del Puppo writes in this catalogue.[7] It is also certain that he made friends with the most innovative artists who were in Paris in those years, from Picasso to Soutine, from Brancusi to Archipenko, from Lipchitz to Zadkine, all brilliant artists from whom he could acquire new stimulations and new experiences.

Just to really get away from the dubious Modigliani mythology, which, on a critical level has conditioned all the judgement on his work, but in particular his sculpture, Mart has wanted to realise a project which right from the start intended to make way for a new story, this time founded on a serious historical-artistic reconstruction and just as systematic philological and stylistic analysis of his work.

Thanks to the retrieval of unpublished or little known historical documents, to the study of sure sources, to the search for new documented relationships with the world of sculptors, who lived or exhibited in Paris during the first fifteen years of the last century, to the stylistic but also precise comparison of the many sources and tribal and oriental models, that have nourished, even with excessive enthusiasm and lack of bibliography on the subject, the Modigliani legend has disappeared during our studies, giving way to a critical report of a completely different nature and interest, above all with regards to that sensational journalistic case, which was the finding of sculptures in the Fosso Reale in Livorno in 1984 (sic!), a late result – seriously penalising according to Italian art critics – of such a widespread legend which was so dear to popular belief, that only accurate and profound scientific studies can today eliminate, we hope forever.

This attempt at cultural moralising of the sources, does not seem however, a brutal intervention on a legend which today is still preferred to the historical reality, as much as a systematic contribution to the interpretation of a crucial passage in Modigliani's artistic career. In fact, as Flavio Fergonzi brings to our notice in his essay published in this catalogue,[8] his sculpture, in the period between 1910-1911 and 1913, represents the interlock between Post-Impressionism filled with the temperament of Cézanne, which characterise his first painting period, and that passionate and seductive, unpublished as much as inimitable iconography of the elongated necks and the porcelain of the powder pink coloured faces, which would distinguish his portraits or the series of his admirable female nudes starting from 1912-1913.

The Idea Was Born in the 1980's

If it had not been for that episode in 1984, this exhibition would not perhaps have been so interesting for the progress of the studies on Modigliani. The impressions that the Livorno "case" aroused in my critical convictions are not important – I was a young art historian then, however already with some museum responsibilities and therefore I was very emotionally involved with what my Professors had to say.

It was at that time that I began considering the importance of an exhibition dedicated to this "delicate" subject. Since that distant 1984 time has gone by without anything really important happening in the studies concerning Modigliani's sculptures and therefore, the void left by the international critics, permitted our museum, twenty-two years later, to start a structured and systematic project on the subject. In 2006, among many difficulties, making the most of the necessary historical prospective and the support of talented art historians, scholars of nineteenth and twentieth century sculpture, but also Modigliani specialists, we started and today we can say have completed our work.

This exhibition and catalogue are a project that we would like to consider as a sort of number zero, which we hope will be followed

by other occasions to proceed towards further critical analysis, perhaps on discoveries that this exhibition of ours could start off.
We have only brought forward one piece of data from 1984, data which today has allowed us to refer to more articulate interpretations of Modigliani sculptor, data which sadly concerns the famous Black & Decker fraud, able to interpret not only the legend of Modigliani, disillusioned by his own art,[9] who throws some freshly hewed blocks into the river, but also that rich repertoire of critical stereotypes that promoted the authenticity of those ugly blocks, turning to an interpretative scheme purely of Primitivist simplification, which at that time seemed made to measure to explain the vocation and suggestions of the young Modì.
A critical parameter so univocal and so reductive for Modigliani as to seem more than ever outdated today,[10] probably the result also of that rediscovery in the 1980's (the Livorno case exploded in 1984, the same year as the excellent exhibition in New York curated by William Rubin on the influence of tribal art on Modernist sculpture[11]), and in many cases perhaps too approximate, leading in a banal way to a primitive influence of plastic experimentations within the historical European avant-garde of the early XX century.
A thesis which in Modigliani's case seemed to be backed by his own biography (or legend?) and his well known friendships and visits to museums.
How would it have been possible for the young Modì, just having finished an extraordinary exhibition of his sculptures at the Salon d'Automne (1912), a great result for his plastic reasoning, expression of a formal synthesis of undoubted Oriental linearity and certainly of pre-cultural warning, yet monumental and classic at the same time, to go back towards that shapeless brutality of those rough casts without any support, dull faces compared to the silent pride and the enigma of a hieratic and fleeting inexpressiveness, already achieved at its maximum in 1912? The comparison with the original blocks – a third of his production is present in the exhibition today – set up in close dialogue with one another but also in relationship with his drawings, in some ways trying to reconsider the scheme of that *ensemble décoratif* that Modigliani had chosen (but not carried out) for his exhibition in 1912 at the Salon d'Automne, finally reopens the critical debate in the presence of the unquestionable authenticity of the works exhibited.
The exhibition offers the possibility to see once again the general catalogue of his sculptures, through new comparative investigations, stylistic and above all through new documents and allows the redesigning of the map of the historical and cultural influences that had some ascendency on the inspiration of the young artist from Livorno. This latter is a theme which has required not only the reordering of a simplification of the many, too many critical hypotheses which have been made in this field – of a merry confusion as Eike Schmidt quite correctly points out in his enlightening essay in this catalogue[12] – but also of a refocusing of the more probable cultural and formal similarity, moving the reference point from tribal art *tout court* to a more reasoned hypothesis of Oriental influences, without however excluding the thorough verifications on the real role played by Greek-Roman and Renaissance sculpture.
If we exclude the exhibition in 1911,[13] in Amadeo de Souza Cardoso's studio in Paris and the one yet again in Paris at the 1912 Salon d'Automne, with Modigliani still alive, this is the first exhibition totally dedicated to his sculptural work, therefore, a completely new exhibition for the Italian and international public.
Differently from painting, that had such a great success at every appearance, up until today his sculpture has been more for the specialists than for the general public, although in these recent years all the

more significant exhibitions can boast the presence of some sculptures,[14] to remember in any case just how important they were, in the general economy of his work, those two years that he dedicated almost exclusively to his chisel.
All the most authoritative sources say that the season Modigliani dedicated to sculpture was as intense as it was brief. The number of works produced in those two years – Ambrogio Ceroni published the first reliable catalogue in 1965 and lists twenty-five – has always been judged as important but residual, a judgement which has perhaps conditioned also that modest interest of his biographers and the great number of critics who were interested i n his pictorial work.
Yet, for a young man who took up the challenge with direct carving (who did not choose modelling and casting according to the fashion of the time), with the effort and energy that the chisel requires, twenty-five sculptures which are all quite noteworthy in size, are not really few, even more so if we think that he dedicated at most thirty months to this work. Perhaps even less, as both the starting and ending dates of the period in which Modigliani almost exclusively dedicated himself to sculpture are uncertain, a period in any case between the middle of 1910 (?) and his return to Paris, after a brief stay in Italy, in June of 1913.
The exhibition and the catalogue ask why the time that Modigliani dedicated to sculpture was so brief, as he declared that it was his first love, and they look for answers both to chronological questions, but also to stylistic problems, that explain a lot also about this sudden abandonment of sculpture, which, as Flavio Fergonzi writes in his essay,[15] can no longer be justified only by his illness, but rather it seems to have a lot to do with the cultural and artistic context in Paris, where not only the Cubist experimentation was appearing, but exactly in June 1913, the sculpture of another great Italian talent, the young Umberto Boccioni, so innovative in his plastic-dynamic research.

The Project Met with Many Difficulties

If the real studies into the problems of Modigliani's sculpture started off between 2007 and 2008, with the involvement of Flavio Fergonzi and Alessandro Del Puppo, who during a long Parisian summer, went through every possible archive and library searching for unpublished or little known documents, investigation which was so fruitful as to build up some reasonable certainties on the theme proposed, and which confirmed their interest in defining a new statute for Modigliani sculptor, the research for the works has kept the Museum busy for almost six years[16] and has been brought to its conclusion thanks to the determination and intelligent work of Clarenza Catullo, who with me has not only followed for all this time the dream of putting next to each sculpture, indicated as private property, the name of a collector but has also shared all the searches in the archives, by joining the fray and personally solving the numerous problems, from the organisation to the conservation, that exhibitions like this entail.
A complex task, which has brought us also many satisfactions above all thanks to the relationship with the European and American public museums, while at the end of the day, when we had to define the list of the works of private property, their undeniable fragility – all the *Heads* were carried out in limestone and have important conservation problems, difficult for a private collector to manage by himself – their rarity and why not, the very recent sale at Christie's auction in Paris, which made the value of one of these masterpieces rocket,[17] have made the presentation of the whole nucleus very complex.
The fact that Modigliani's sculpture has been the object of few thorough studies and that, on the other hand, there are few reliable sources and critical apparatus on the subject, has represented a real puzzle for perfecting the exhibition project, made even more difficult by the 360° dislocation of these works in the world, from America to Australia, to Europe.

Unfortunately Italy does not own any of these sculptures, which confirms – if it were still necessary – how these works were realised in France and most of them remained there until Modigliani's death in 1920, when his art dealer, Léopold Zborowsky, in the wake of the growing international interest, sold them to some important European and American collectors. Paul Guillaume also sold some of the sculptures, like for example the magnificent *Head* given to the Barnes Foundation in Merion (Philadelphia) in 1924. The information on the single works contain the transfer of property, very interesting information, which regards not only the history of Modigliani collecting but also concerns the very tricky question of their authenticity.
Although it is a number zero, as is the catalogue, the exhibition too has been conceived in the light of a very rigorous selection which has changed very little from Ambrogio Ceroni's catalogue, even though the results of the studies have given us some surprises as far as new attributions are concerned, or rather, it has confirmed the hypothesis which had already surfaced in recent studies, like Kenneth Wayne's for example on the occasion of the very important exhibition dedicated to Modigliani held in Buffalo between 2002 and 2003.[18] Despite the countless difficulties regarding the fragility and the rarity of these extraordinary *Heads* – neither of the two *Caryatids* is present for conservational reasons – the exhibition hosts a number which has never been on show before, useful for the redefinition of Modigliani's sculptural catalogue, which if it has had only the above mentioned source of the irreplaceable and infinitely patient work carried out by Ambrogio Ceroni with such seriousness and documentation, today can offer important scientific developments.
In particular it is the numbering of the works that changes, passing from twenty-five sculptures catalogued by Ceroni to twenty-eight, as can be read in the vastly documented essay by Flavio Fergonzi,[19] who not only makes his own the certain authenticity of the Karlsruhe sculpture,[20] proved today by an important photographic document published in a Spanish magazine in 1914,[21] but also puts order in Ceroni's numeration, where the former Lévy *Head*, which went up for auction in the spring of this year, was identified by Ceroni with the old photograph taken by Amadeo de Souza Cardoso in 1911 and wrongly considered to coincide with the work that is Chester Dale's property.
Instead these are two different sculptures. A third sculpture must be added of unknown ownership, which Flavio Fergonzi identifies in a photograph which shows Paul Guillaume in front of a fireplace where two of Modigliani's sculptures can be seen, one can be identified with the work which belongs to the Barnes Foundation and the other is still unknown today. During the phase of reconstruction of the various ownerships and collocation of the works, the consultation of the Perls Galleries archive in New York has been extremely interesting, this is now conserved in Washington,[22] where it has been possible to find interesting connections between Perls, the most important American dealer in Modigliani's works – the precious Canberra *Caryatid* passed through his gallery – and the private American collectors.
During the consultation in Washington it was disappointing to find the absence of documents proving the various transfers of property regarding the sculpture which is now at the Metropolitan Museum of Art in New York, bought by the American museum directly from Perls, a work which is not published in Ceroni and therefore not included in the exhibition, like the one from Karlsruhe. Also the consultation of the Amadeo de Souza Cardoso Archive, conserved in Lisbon,[23] revealed to us the presence of interesting documents and we were permitted to look at not only the original photographs of the Modigliani sculptures presented in 1911 in Amadeo de Souza Cardoso's studio, images which were very probably taken by the Portuguese

artist, but we also saw a very interesting photogram, with particular reference to one photographic image which is testimony to the presence in the Parisian artists' studios (but it is known that this diffusion was common all over Europe) of copies of Classical sculpture, a question which comes very close to the theme of the influence that the plastic Renaissance tradition had on Modigliani's works, a theme dealt with in the catalogue both in the above mentioned essay by Eike Schmidt and in Kenneth Wayne's.[24]

However what mostly enriched our knowledge was what we learnt during those many and repeated visits to a great part of the private collections and to nearly all of the public ones, where there was a *direct* verification of the works. It goes without saying that the observation of the original sculptures has allowed some very interesting thorough examinations that regard not only the stylistic aspects, easier to pick out in photographic images, but all the precious and irreplaceable information, that comes from a direct inspection of the chisel work on the block, from the measuring of the pressure that transpires from the marks, from the rhythm and direction of the chisel movements visibly carved into the material, from the pressure that changes according to the parts that the hand and tool are working on, from seeing back and front: all observations of method, but also of authenticity, that only the original could reveal.

Happiness Is an Angel with a Strict Face

With these words, written down by Modigliani on the back of a postcard from Lucca addressed to his friend Paul Alexandre on 6th May 1913, the circle surrounding the question of Modigliani sculptor could be closed. In May of that year Modì was in Italy, where he probably arrived about mid April, as a postcard from Livorno addressed to Paul Alexandre shows, dated 15th April 1913. This was his second return home, after 1909. Also on this occasion he only stayed briefly: in a letter dated 13th June, sent from Lucca, he already announced his return to Paris to his friend Alexandre. So this second and last stay in Tuscany was only for two months.[25] A trip which, thanks to the documents and testimonies, we know represents the most intense phase of his passion for sculpture, at least in words, but also that of the sudden loss of this same passion. On 23rd April, a few days after his arrival, Modigliani informed his friend Paul that he had rediscovered the blinding lights of the Carrara quarries: "The village where I would also literally pitch my tent, a field tent, there is such a blinding light of the most blinding limpidity of air and light that exists."[26] Nothing more true, for those who know those clear breaks in the body of the mountain set in a semi-circle above Carrara, that show their white, ample surfaces which are almost indecent, like reflecting diamonds. "I would do everything in marble,"[27] he could not help promising himself in front of those stones inundated with light, of such absolute purity to make him forget that poor limestone, which he had worked on in Paris with direct carving to give life to the fantastic *imagerie* of his aristocratic *Heads*. There was no follow up to this enthusiasm. In contrast with what he proposed and as Paul Alexandre testifies in the copy of a letter addressed to Ambrogio Ceroni in 1953 "in Italy in 1913 he had a flare of enthusiasm which did not last long as he never dedicated himself to sculpture again, that I know of, once he returned to Paris."[28] From June 1913, the traces of his work as a sculptor are lost, even though some of his works appear reproduced in magazines or exhibitions like *Twentieth Century Art: A Review of Modern Movements,* organised in 1914 at the Whitechapel Art Gallery in London, where the magnificent *Head* that is now in the Tate Gallery was presented. However, this work was already known, it was not carried out especially for the exhibition, it belonged – as Kenneth Wayne informs us[29] – to the South African painter Roworth, who had probably bought it in 1911, during his honeymoon in Paris, and

who had evidently lent it to the Whitechapel exhibition.
Also in the case of the exhibition held in New York at Marius de Zayas's Modern Gallery in 1916,[30] an exhibition dedicated to international sculpture, the two works which were exhibited, that Wayne identifies with the *Head* in the Philadelphia Museum of Art and the one in Karlsruhe, were not new works. They very probably already belonged to Paul Guillaume, who had been a close friend of Modigliani's since 1914 and he bought and sold his work.
It is therefore evident that from 1913 onwards, the chapter regarding sculpture was closed, even if the growing international interest from collectors increased in an opposite trend compared to his radical choice. However, let us return to the note written on the postcard in 1913.
It was very probably a poetic exercise, perhaps the noting down of a thought or an emotion that he felt when close to a frescoed chancel in a Tuscan apse. However, the tension that characterised those days of his stay in Italy, when he placed that idea of sculpting in the centre of his thoughts and projects, that had catalysed all his creative energy for two years, makes us think that this may in some way be connected to his particular plastic concept.
The theme is fascinating: already in 1912 his exhibition project of the seven *Heads* at the Salon d'Automne foresaw a kind of group, an *ensemble décoratif*, as he himself called it. We can think of a sort of choir, as Lipchitz seems to see it, who would later describe his project as an ensemble of "organ reeds." In any case, they are two images that have something to do with a sort of sacred memory. If happiness is an angel with a strict face, where the attribute strict sounds like a Latin *gravis*, authoritative, serious, majestic, solemn, perhaps this is the path that Modigliani thought about and found joy in imagining his battle with stone or marble? Or was it perhaps a way of his own of re-reading the work he had done up to then, thinking about that *ensemble* again, like a chorus of cherubs, of classic recollection, with solemn faces, those messengers whom God, in the Genesis, placed in the east of the Garden of Eden to guard the path to the tree of life? History does not give us an answer: however the strong impression remains that in this simple note Modigliani has left us a key to the interpretation which is anything but banal.

---

1 In Trento in the Palazzo delle Albere, where Mart had its original centre, two important monographic exhibitions dedicated to Giovanni Segantini were organised, one in 1987 dedicated to his painting and the second one in 1999 to his work on paper. In 1990 a large exhibition was dedicated to Italian Divisionism, which brought the attention of the specialised studies back to the question of divided painting, imported into Italy by Vittore Grubicy de Dragon, dealer and artist, a great friend of Segantini's, to whom he introduced, the first among the Divisionist painters, the techniques used by the Impressionists in France.

2 As referred by Paul Alexandre's son, Noël Alexandre, Eugenia Modigliani had dictated to her daughter Margherita, who knew French well (in fact, she was a French teacher), a long biography about her son, a very detailed text, which carries the date of 10th December 1924. This long note is published in Alexandre 1993. In 1898, a year marked by Modigliani's serious illness, his mother recalled: "He used to talk during the long delirium of his fever. He continuously spoke about paintings glimpsed in reproduction, that there were none of in Livorno. One of his nightmares: he missed the train that was to take him to Florence to see the Uffizi. He spoke about the painter Segantini who was then very successful and all this with such insistence that his mother who was taking care of him decided to please him." Cf. Alexandre 1993, p. 29.

3 The news of that time tells us that the painting Segantini was working on was that part of the triptych entitled *Death*, a large canvas today conserved at the Segantini Museum in Saint. Moritz, showing a landscape of the high mountains covered in snow, with a small mountain

hut on the far right of the painting, that a horse-drawn funeral hearse is setting out from. The theme could not have been more tragically symbolic and in some aspects not a good omen for the painter.

4 Cf. pp. 62-75 in this catalogue.

5 Alexandre 1993, pp. 28-32. In the text Eugenia recalls the long journey to the south, financed by her brother Amédée Garsin, to help her son's delicate health, see pp. 30-31.

6 Alexandre 1993, p. 62.

7 Cf. pp. 62-75 in this catalogue.

8 Cf. pp. 21-61 in this catalogue.

9 Traces of this event remain in Modigliani's bibliography. Among all the sources that deal with the question, his daughter Jeanne's is considered the most interesting. In her book Modigliani 1958, written with the aim of clearing away all the many fantasies surrounding her father, she mentions this episode. Jeanne writes that Modigliani had probably sculpted during his last trip to Livorno, but none of his friends had ever seen the sculptures he carried out. The doubt about where Modigliani had put these sculptures added to the legend about his great rejection of those works and his throwing them into the Fosso Reale. In fact, Jeanne recalls, only the painter Romiti seemed to have seen a sculpture (p. 69). It is however certain that his friends had jokingly suggested to Modì to throw them into the ditch. Silvano Filippelli wrote (Filippelli 1954, pp. 224-239): "What he did in that big room with those stone blocks, none of us ever knew. He never took us up there, we never saw the room nor the blocks. Who knows what he was planning during those days. He certainly must have done something. Because when he decided to go back to Paris he asked us where he could put some of his sculptures that had remained in the big room. Did they exist then? Who knows? Modigliani took them with him, or he followed our friendly and hasty advice: we all told him, in fact: throw them in the ditch [...]." This was in the 1950's and nobody could have foreseen that due to this badly interpreted testimony, the Superintendence of Pisa and the Galleria Nazionale d'Arte Moderna in Rome would have authorised the excavation of the Fosso Reale (sic!) in 1984.

10 Cf. note 14.

11 Rubin 1985.

12 Cf. pp. 86-95 in this catalogue.

13 This is Modigliani's first exhibition of sculpture which is known and photographically documented; the exhibition was held on 5th March 1911 in the studio of his Portuguese friend, the painter Amadeo de Souza Cardoso in Rue Colonel Compes. Cf. Lisbon 2006-2007, p. 27; it was on that occasion that Modigliani gave or swapped a drawing of a *Caryatid* (dated 1911) with Cardoso. For the relationship between Cardoso and Modigliani see also the catalogue *Amadeo de Souza Cardoso 2007*, pp. 139, 293.

14 It is important to notice that after 1984 there were many reviews dedicated to Modigliani painter; exhibitions where sculpture was treated thoroughly have been few. For this specific subject see the exhibition Düsseldorf 1991, an exhibition which gave the opportunity to see some important sculptures, six of which catalogued in Ceroni 1965 and another two which are not present in the Ceroni 1965 catalogue. We can also recall, for the importance of the documents exhibited and published, the exhibition Venezia 1993, a fundamental exhibition to know his work on paper and therefore the great number of drawings carried out before and during the realisation of his sculptures; the exhibition Buffalo 2002-2003 is also of great importance, this exhibition then went to Fort Worth, Texas and Los Angeles.

15 Cf. pp. 21-61 in this catalogue.

16 The project began with a team that included, apart from myself, Tomas Sharman and Margherita de Pilati. In 2008 the project came to a halt due to the many problems posed by the lenders. After that, with the collaboration of Clarenza Catullo the work started again and despite many difficulties it has come to a conclusion, thanks also to some changes in the scientific leadership of institutions such as the museums of Philadelphia, Princeton and Minneapolis.

17 Cf. Christie's Paris, auction of 14th June 2010, Lot 26, Sale 6525, work estimated 4-6 million Euro, sold at 43,185 million Euro. The work belonged to the Gaston Lévy Collection (1893-1977) founder of the chain of Monoprix department stores.

18 Buffalo 2002-2003, then Kimbell Art Museum, Fort Worth, Texas (9th February-25th May 2003), then Los Angeles County Museum of Art, Los Angeles, California (29th June-28th September 2003).

19 Cf. pp. 21-61 in this catalogue.

20 Karlsruhe, Staatliche Kunsthalle.

21 The work is reproduced in Dumond Wilden 1914, p. 12.

22 Washington, Archives of American Art, Smithsonian Institution, Perls Galleries Fond.

23 Lisbon, Centro de Arte Moderna José de Azeredo Perdigão, Fundação Calouste Gulbenkian, espolio Amadeo Souza Cardoso.

24 Cf. pp. 76-85 in this catalogue.

25 In her diary his mother recalls Modigliani's desire to return to Livorno in 1920: "Then he announced his dear Jeanne's second pregnancy and, at the same time, the project to bring to Italy his first born and her mother, in the spring of 1920, after his partner had given birth, to let them meet the family. This desire to see his country and family again, was the last one he could express." Reported in Alexandre 1993, p. 32.

26 Alexandre 1993, p. 104.

27 Alexandre 1993, p. 104.

28 Copy of a letter from Paul Alexandre to Ambrogio Ceroni dated 4th August 1957, reported in Alexandre 1993, p. 104: "In April 1913 – wrote Paul Alexandre – before leaving for Italy, Modigliani signed this selection of his drawings. This choice included only studies destined for his sculpture. It was then that he deposited all his sculptures at 13 avenue Malakoff (except for those that had already been bought by Mr. Augustus John from Chelsea, London). He took them back when he returned. All the authentic pieces that I have seen since then were part of this group. He did not add any [...] Modigliani dedicated himself to sculpture only in 1912. He used up all his strength until 1913. In Italy, in 1913, he had a short-lived flare of enthusiasm as he never dedicated himself to sculpture again, as far as I know, once he returned to Paris."

29 Buffalo 2002-2003, p. 56.

30 Wayne 2002, pp. 58-59.

Preliminary Issues for Modigliani Sculptor

Flavio Fergonzi

The Information Known Today, the Present Situation of the Studies

At the beginning of the essays in the catalogue, I think it is worth gathering together the little certain information about Modigliani that can be obtained from documents of that time (letters, photographs of his works, exhibition catalogues, critical reviews); and follow them, distinctly separate, with some recollections which are considered reliable, as they are from people who knew the artist and spent time with him at the beginning of the second decade.

After exhibiting paintings and drawings for three years (1907-1910) at the Salons des Indépendants and d'Automne in Paris, Modigliani presented an "ensemble décoratif" of seven sculptural heads[1] (fig. **1**) at the Salon d'Automne in October 1912. The photographs, the drawings (press coverage or caricatures) and the reviews published by magazines of the time enable us to identify them with works that are known to us today:

- the *Head* catalogued by Ambrogio Ceroni at No. XV[2] (from here on referred to as *Head* XV; today in Saint Louis, private collection, fig. **2**) is recognisable in the photograph of room XI of the Salon published in *L'Illustration* on 12th October (it is the second head from the left); it was also reproduced in the London magazine *The Sketch* on 16th October 1912 and in *Comœdia Illustré* on 20th October with the same photograph (fig. **3**);
- *Head* XXI, today in New York, Solomon R. Guggenheim Museum (fig. **4**), is recognisable in the last on the left of the photograph published in *L'Illustration* on 12th October (fig. **5**);
- *Head* XXII, today in a private collection (fig. **6**), can be recognised in the drawing published

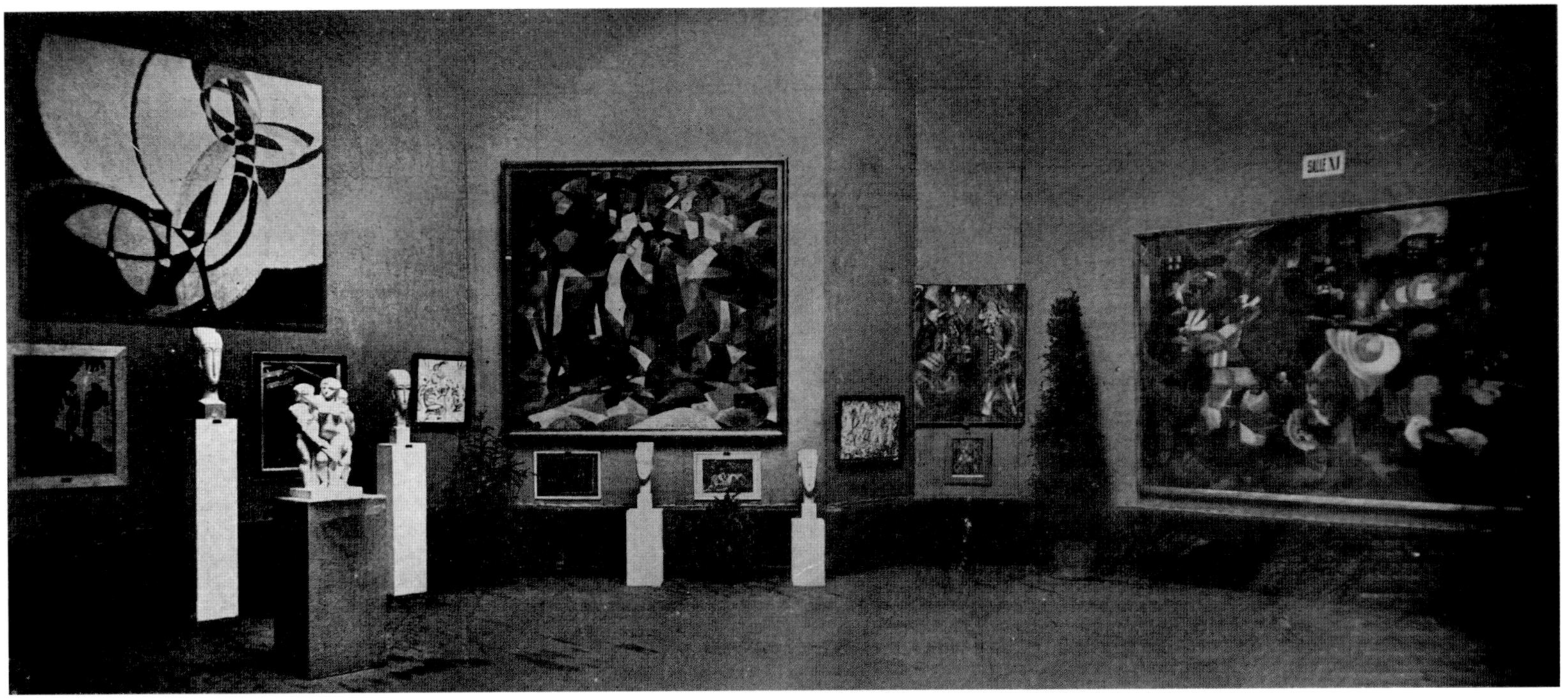

1. Paris, Salon d'Automne 1912, room XI, in *L'Illustration*, 12th October 1912

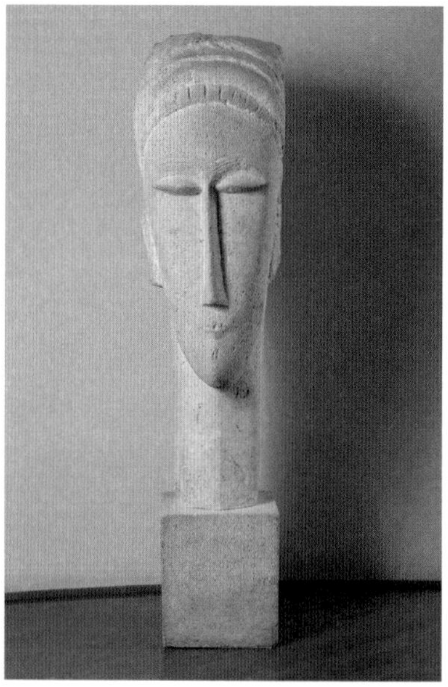

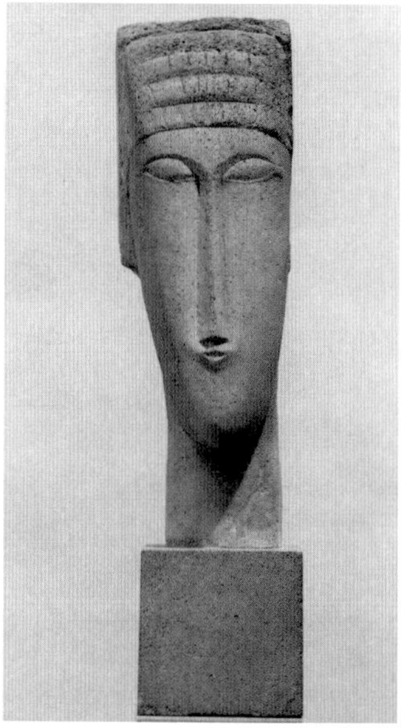

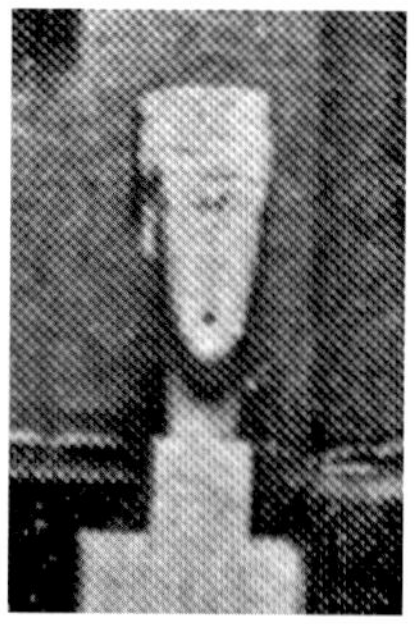

4. Amedeo Modigliani
Head, 1911-1912. New York, Solomon Guggenheim Museum. Ceroni XXI

5. Amedeo Modigliani, *Head*, in *L'Illustration*, 12th October 1912 (detail of fig. 1)

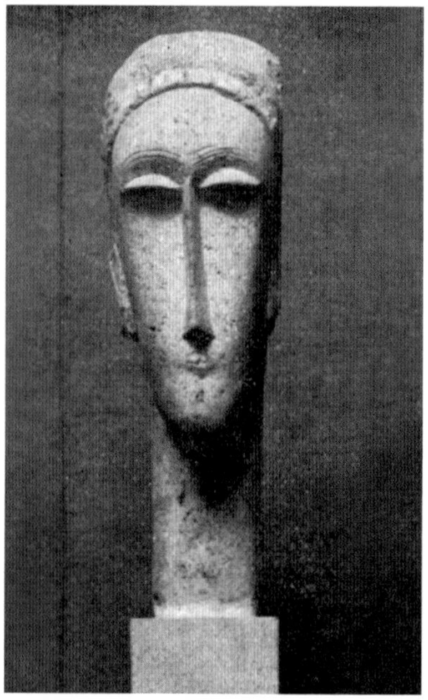

2. Amedeo Modigliani
Head, 1911-1912.
Saint-Louis, private collection.
Ceroni XV

3. Amedeo Modigliani
Tête cubiste, in *Comœdia Illustré*, Paris, 20th October 1912

in *La Vie Parisienne* on 5th October; and in the first head on the left in the photograph in *L'Illustration* of 12th October (fig. **7**);
- the *Head* from the former Lévy collection (fig. **8**), auctioned at Christie's in Paris on 14th June 2010, (not catalogued by Ceroni: Sculpture "A" according to Kenneth Wayne[3]) can be recognised in a second drawing that appeared in *La Vie Parisienne* on 5th October; and published in *The Sketch* on 16th October 1912 and in *Comœdia Illustré* on 20th October with the same photograph (fig. **9**);
- the third sculpture from the left in the photograph in *L'Illustration* (fig. **10**) cannot be identified with certainty due to the condition of the reproduction: the similarities that can be seen, in the proportions between hair, face and neck, with the head today in the Museum of Karlsruhe (from here on *Head* "B") seem to be confirmed by a comparison with an old photograph of the *Head*, belonging to the Archive de Zayas, this photograph can only be traced today in the form of a photocopy preserved at the Butler Library of Columbia University[4]; the identification seems to find definite plausibility in the first, known reproduction of the *Head* which up to now had eluded the studies carried out, in a magazine on Catalan Modernism, *Revista Nova*, 20th August 1914 (fig. **11**).
Before this date, the information that can be documented with certainty about Modigliani's sculptural activity is practically inexistent. We cannot be sure that in the personal exhibition opened by Modigliani on 5th March 1911 in a private room (evidenced by a letter from Brancusi to Paul Alexandre[5]) any sculptures were included; nor that this exhibition corresponds to the one, which according to later recollections, Modigliani held in Amadeo de Souza Cardoso's studio. The four photographs (figs. **12-15**) of five sculptures (these are Ceroni XIII, XIV, XV, XVI and *Head* "A") which were found among Cardoso's papers by Paulo Ferreira[6] and sent by the latter to Jeanne Modigliani who first published them in 1958,[7] according to the popular idea, document the exhibition in the Cardoso atelier, these will be the subject of analysis in this text. However, the incompleteness of the heads documented by the photographs compared to those that we know today, the positioning of one of the heads on the floor and, above all, the presence of a drawing hanging behind one of the heads would make us think of a photograph of an ongoing work in a studio, rather than an exhibition, for however much semi-private, organised in someone else's studio. Among other things, Modigliani's calling card (with the address in Cité Falguière 14) which he sent to Alexandre through Brancusi, would favour the idea of

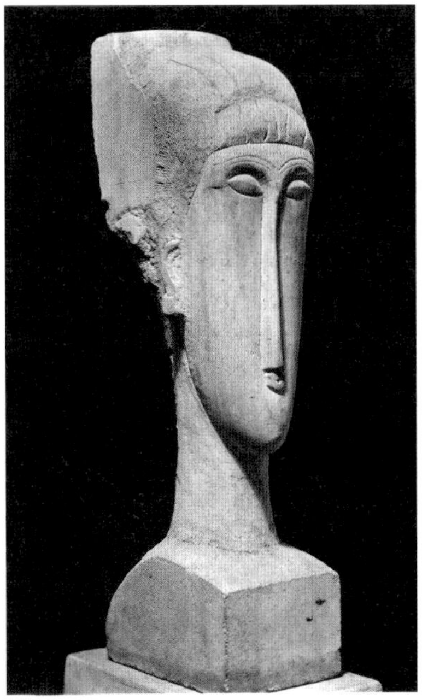

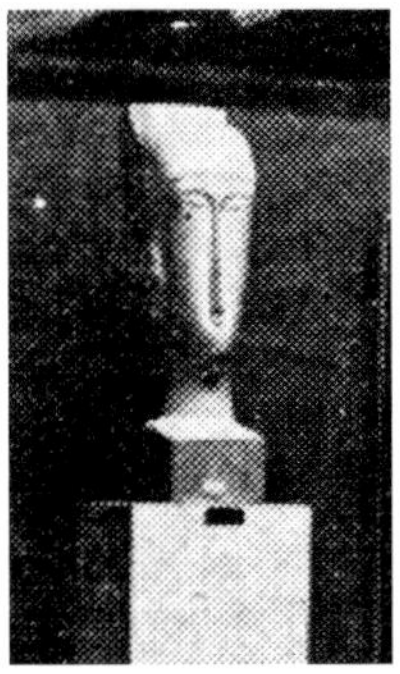

6. Amedeo Modigliani
Head, 1911-1912.
Private collection. Ceroni XXII

7. Amedeo Modigliani
Head, in *L'Illustration*,
12th October 1912 (detail of fig. 1)

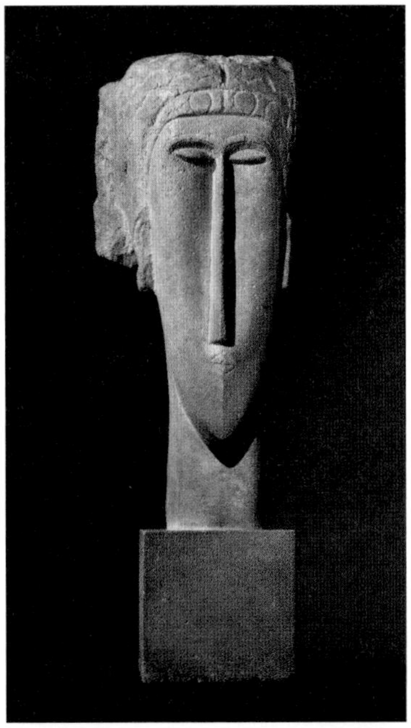

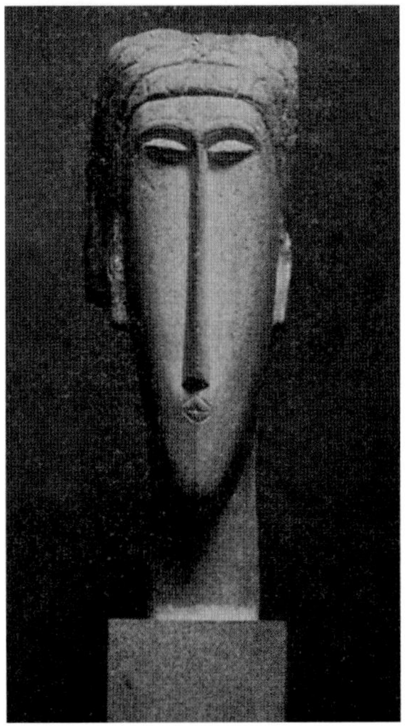

8. Amedeo Modigliani
Head, 1911-1912.
Formerly Paris, Lévy Collection.
Not in Ceroni (*Head* "A")

9. Amedeo Modigliani
Tête cubiste, in *Comœdia Illustré*,
20th October 1912

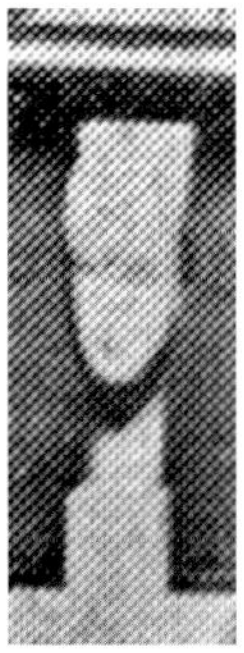

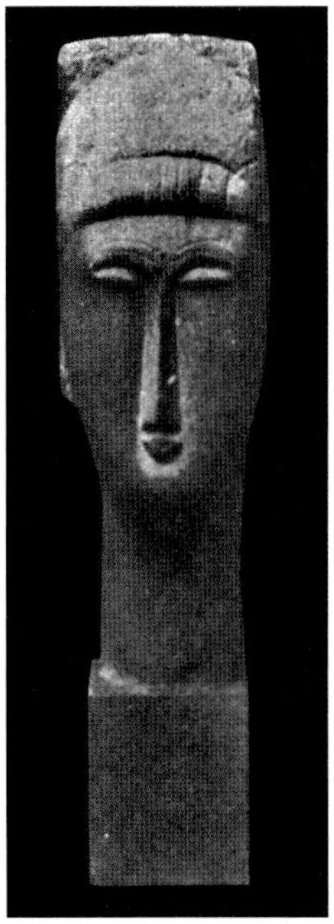

10. Amedeo Modigliani
Head, in *L'Illustration*,
12th October 1912 (detail of fig. 1)

11. Amedeo Modigliani
Bust, in *Revista Nova*,
Barcelona, 20th August 1914.
Not in Ceroni (*Head* "B")

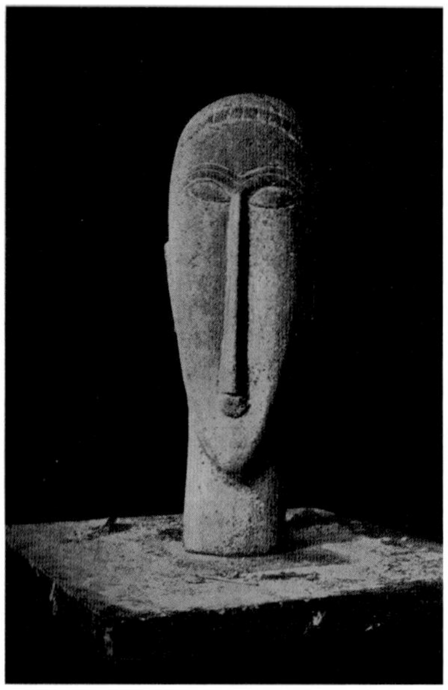

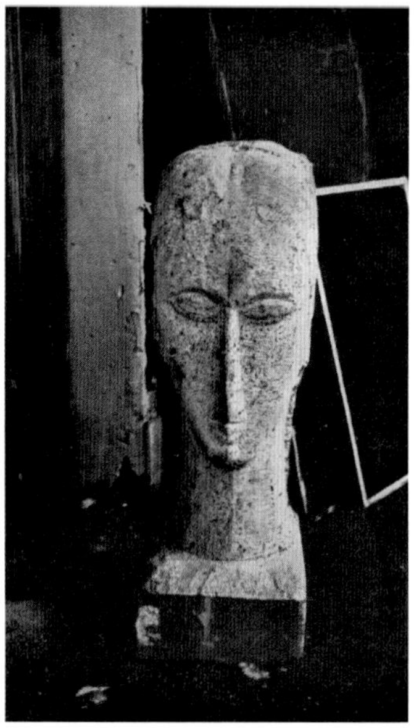

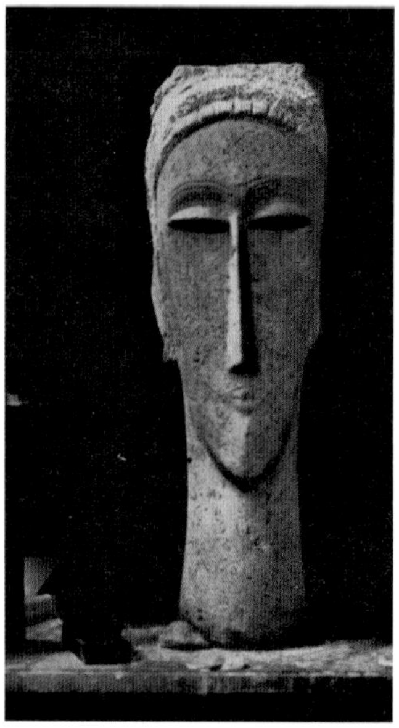

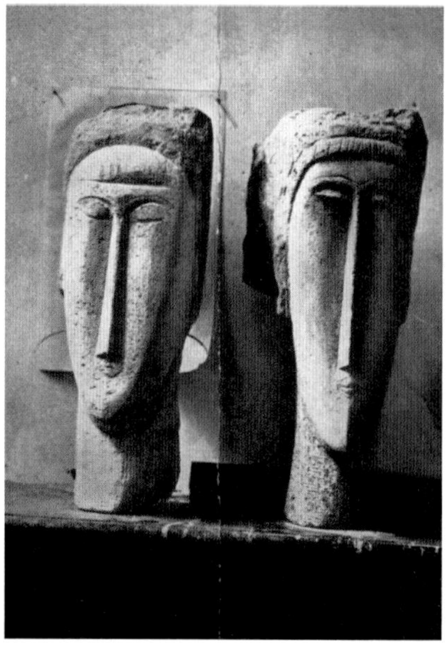

12. Anonymous photographer
Head, 1911-1912,
by Amedeo Modigliani (Ceroni XIII).
Lisbon, Fundação Calouste
Gulbenkian, Amadeo de Souza
Cardoso Archive

13. Anonymous photographer
Head, 1911-1912,
by Amedeo Modigliani (Ceroni XIV).
Lisbon, Fundação Calouste
Gulbenkian, Amadeo de Souza
Cardoso Archive

14. Anonymous photographer
Head, 1911-1912, by Amedeo Modigliani
(Ceroni XV). Lisbon, Fundação
Calouste Gulbenkian, Amadeo de
Souza Cardoso Archive

15. Anonymous photographer
Heads, 1911-1912, by Amedeo
Modigliani (Ceroni XVI and *Head* "A").
Lisbon, Fundação Calouste
Gulbenkian, Amadeo de Souza
Cardoso Archive

an exhibition held in Modigliani's own studio. The *Caryatid* and the *Head* exhibited at the Indépendants in April 1911[8] should not be considered as two sculptures but probably as two tempera paintings: in fact, in the catalogue, the specification of any work exhibited as a sculpture was always added after the title, as with drawings (and *Dessins*, for Modigliani, were the four numbers that followed). However, a margin of doubt remains due to the fact that his works appear in the addenda of the catalogue, evidently put together in a hurry before going to print. If we accept the signature and the date as written by Modigliani, then two studies, graphical and pictorial, of caryatids that can be connected to his sculptural activity could be placed in 1911. In a drawing published (fig. **16**) by Noël Alexandre we can read, with some difficulty, the date "2 juillet 911"[9]; furthermore Paulo Ferreira's studies evidence Modigliani's offer to Souza Cardoso of a fine caryatid, an oil on cardboard 82 x 51 cm, signed and dated "novembre 1911" (fig. **17**).[10]
In a not very well known undated letter that Modigliani sent to his brother Umberto, he defined his presence at the Salon d'Automne (apparently the one in 1912) "relatively successful", especially for the "acceptance of the block" of his work and he said he was motivated to "work and exhibit," convinced that "if I clinch the Indépendents I will have made a good start."[11] Then any certain news about him during the last months of 1912 and the first of 1913 is very scarce, until his departure for Italy: contradicting the commitment he made to himself just a few months earlier, the artist did not send anything to the Salon des Indépendants, which opened in March 1913.
Two drawings for sculptures can be placed in 1913, dated by the artist "21 mars 1913" (fig. **18**) and some, which are stylistically similar and dated only with the day and month (fig. **19**) can reasonably be situated in those same days[12]. It is also probable that three drawings from Paul Alexandre's same collection, dated 20th and 22nd August (figs. **20-21**), should be referred to 1912, following the recollections of the owner's son[13]: these are in fact very similar (for the proportions of the face and decorative motifs of the hair) to two of the sculptures definitely exhibited at the Salon d'Automne in 1912, *Head* XXII and *Head* "A"(figs. **22-23**).
There are also few positive testimonies regarding 1913: from Italy, in April, Modigliani wrote to Paul Alexandre, asking him to pick a sculpture up for him which was momentarily deposited with a "Serbo-Croat" (a term which, according to Alexandre, he used jokingly to indicate his friend Brancusi) and to deposit it with Alexandre himself in Avenue Malakoff; he expressed his intention, in sculpture, to "do everything in marble."[14]

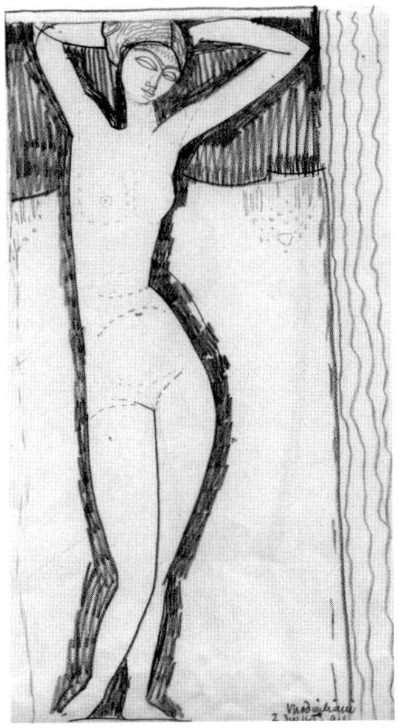
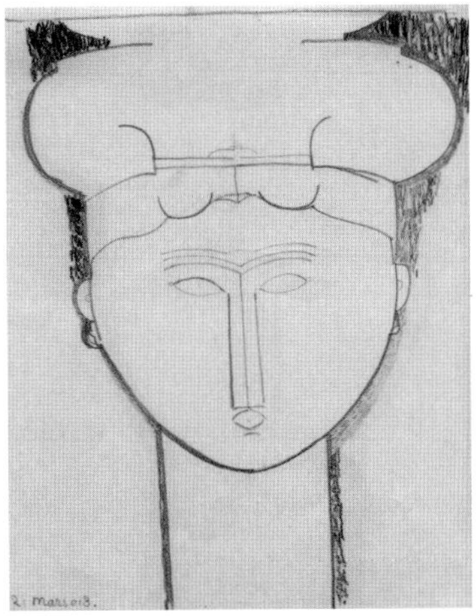
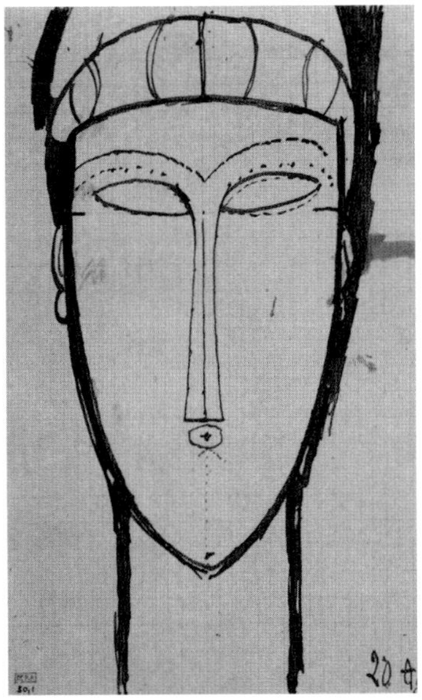
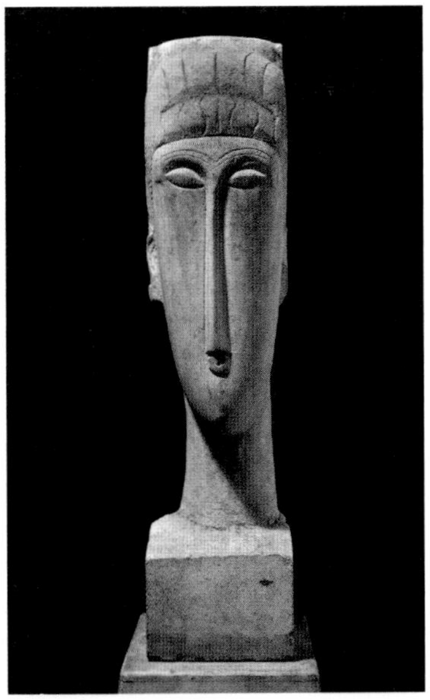
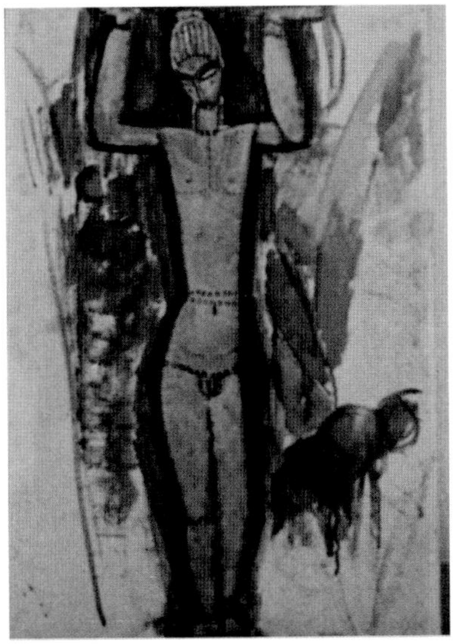
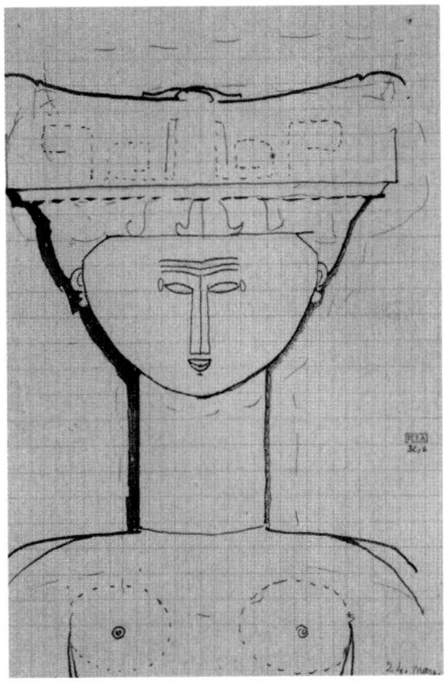
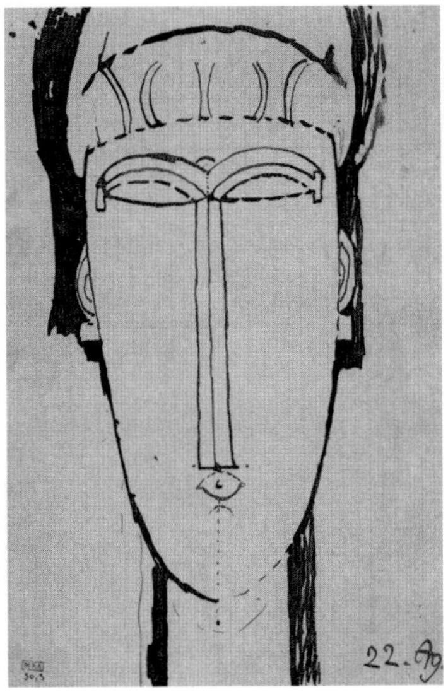
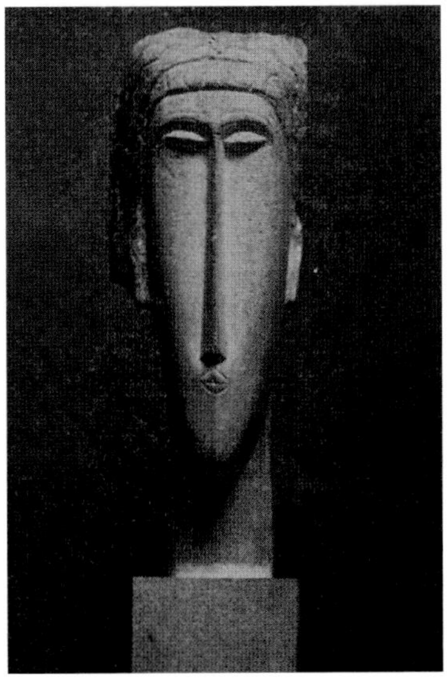

16. Amedeo Modigliani, *Caryatid*, 2nd July 1911, pencil on paper. Private collection

17. Amedeo Modigliani, *Caryatid*, November 1911, oil on cardboard, in D. de Macedo, *Les deux Amadeo. Amadeo Modigliani et Amadeo de Souza Cardoso*, Lisbon 1959

18. Amedeo Modigliani *Head-capital*, 21st March 1913, blue pencil on paper. Private collection

19.. Amedeo Modigliani *Head-capital*, 24th March 1913, ink on squared paper. Private collection

20. Amedeo Modigliani, *Head*, ink on squared paper, 20th August 1912. Private collection

21. Amedeo Modigliani, *Head*, 22nd August 1912, ink on squared paper. Private collection

22. Amedeo Modigliani *Head*, 1911-1912. Private collection. Ceroni XXII

23. Amedeo Modigliani *Head*, 1911-1912. Private collection. Not in Ceroni (*Head* "A")

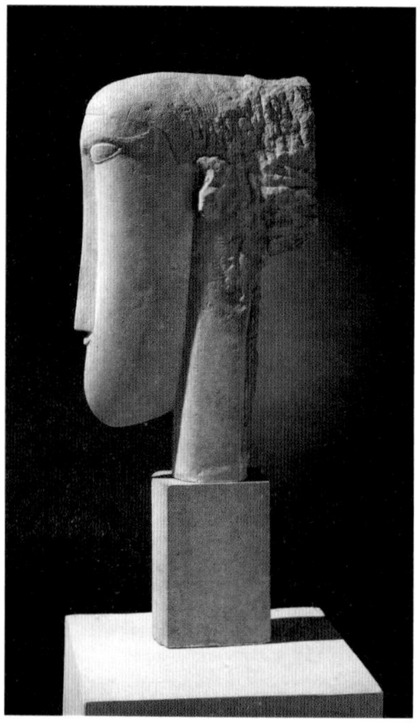

24. Amedeo Modigliani
Head, 1912-1914.
London, The Tate Gallery.
Ceroni XXIV

25. Amedeo Modigliani, *Head*
Ceroni XX,
in *Revista Nova*, 20th August 1914

26. Amedeo Modigliani, *Head*
not in Ceroni (*Head* "B"),
in *Revista Nova*, 20th August 1914

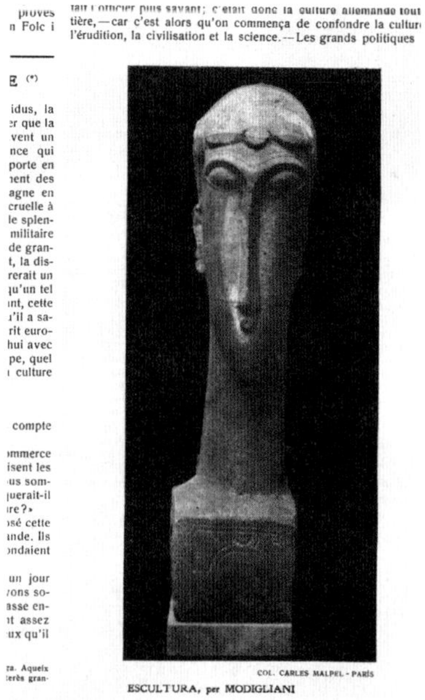
proves
n Folc i
E (*)
idus, la
er que la
vent un
nce qui
porte en
nent des
agne en
cruelle à
le splen-
militaire
de gran-
t, la dis-
rerait un
qu'un tel
nt, cette
u'il a sa-
rit euro-
hui avec
pe, quel
culture
compte
mmerce
isent les
us som-
querait-il
re?»
sé cette
nde. Ils
ndaient
un jour
vons so-
asse en-
t assez
ux qu'il
a. Aqueix
erès gran-
tait l'officier plus savant; c'était donc la culture allemande tout
tière, — car c'est alors qu'on commença de confondre la cultur
l'érudition, la civilisation et la science. — Les grands politiques
COL. CARLES MALPEL - PARÍS
ESCULTURA, per MODIGLIANI

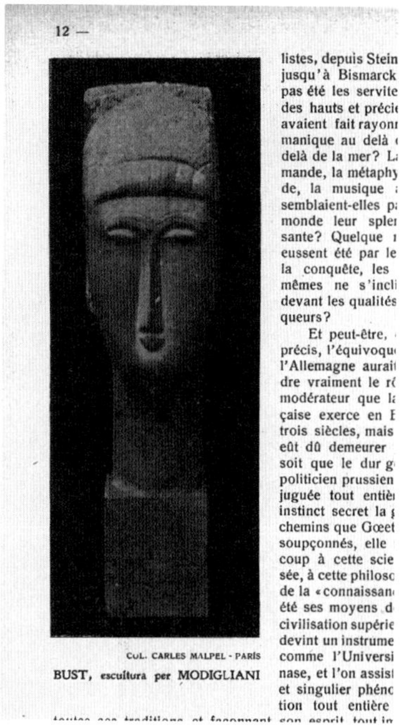
12 —
COL. CARLES MALPEL - PARÍS
BUST, escultura per MODIGLIANI
listes, depuis Stein
jusqu'à Bismarck
pas été les servite
des hauts et préci
avaient fait rayonn
manique au delà
delà de la mer? La
mande, la métaphy
de, la musique
semblaient-elles pa
monde leur splen
sante? Quelque
eussent été par le
la conquête, les
mêmes ne s'incli
devant les qualités
queurs?
Et peut-être,
précis, l'équivoqu
l'Allemagne aurait
dre vraiment le r
modérateur que la
çaise exerce en E
trois siècles, mais
eût dû demeurer
soit que le dur g
politicien prussien
juguée tout entiè
instinct secret la
chemins que Gœet
soupçonnés, elle
coup à cette scie
sée, à cette philoso
de la «connaissan
été ses moyens d
civilisation supérie
devint un instrume
comme l'Universi
nase, et l'on assist
et singulier phéno
tion tout entière

In a later letter he announced that he was sending two small pieces of marble "en eclaireurs."[15]
During Modigliani's life his sculptures were never exhibited again in Paris.[16] Some of them, however, were sent to two important exhibitions outside of France. In chronological order the first was a collective exhibition on modern artistic movements held with the title *Twentieth Century Art* at the Whitechapel Art Gallery in London in May-June 1914. A *Head* in stone belonging to Edward Roworth appeared in the catalogue, he was a South-African painter who studied in London and travelled through Paris in those years[17]: according to the precise research carried out by Kenneth Wayne, Roworth bought it between 1911 and 1914[18] and it is identified as *Head* XXIV, today at the Tate Gallery (fig. **24**). The second one was an exhibition of modern sculpture held in 1916 in New York at the Modern Gallery by Marius de Zayas; two photocopies of photographs from the Archives de Zayas have permitted Kenneth Wayne to identify them with *Head* "A" (former Lévy Collection) and "B" (Kunsthalle in Karlsruhe).[19] Furthermore, in the summer of 1914 in the Catalan *Revista Nova*, *Heads* XX and "B" were illustrated for the first time (indicated as belonging to the Parisian Charles Malpel collection) to accompany an article by the Belgian writer Dumont Wilden on the comparison between the French and German feelings about the war which had just begun (figs. **25-26**).[20] It goes without saying that an activity which was limited in time, rarely mentioned in the Parisian press apart from some mocking comparisons with the Cubist deformations, had a significant market, a precocious international appreciation and was placed on the same level as the Modernist proposals of Brancusi, Gaudier-Brzeska Epstein, Nevinson.
There are, however, two photographs that show the existence of at least two other sculptures while Modigliani was still alive. In one photograph (fig. **27**) that shows the art-dealer Paul Guillaume in his apartment-gallery in Avenue de Villiers (where the works bought by him were visible from 1916 until October 1917, when he inaugurated his new gallery in Faubourg St. Honoré[21]), it is possible to recognise *Head* XIX on the mantelpiece and, above all, another *Head* which stands out in high relief from a background just hewed, and this does not correspond to any of the sculptures in the Ceroni catalogue: we will call this sculpture "C". Another photograph[22] (fig. **28**) shows Modigliani wearing summer clothes (lightweight trousers and shirt), with every

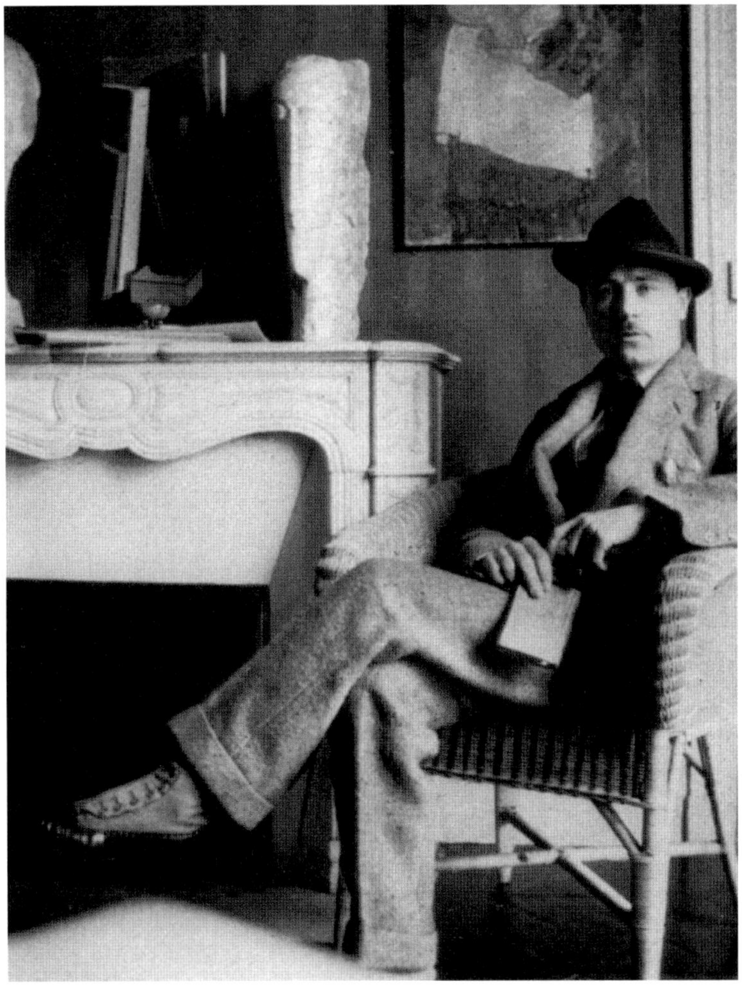

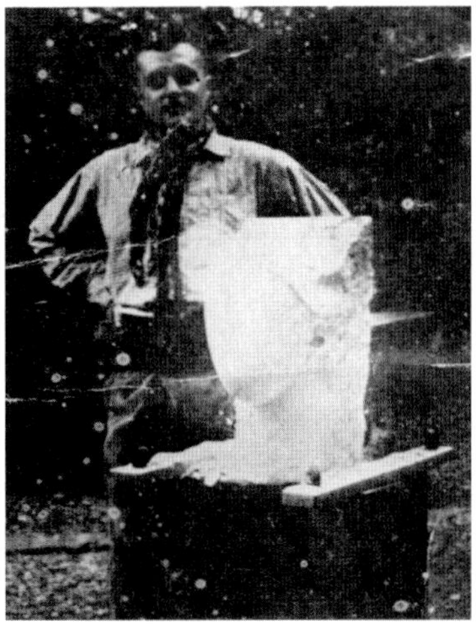

27. Paul Guillaume in his apartment in Paris, Avenue de Villiers (1916-1917): on the mantelpiece the *Heads* Ceroni XIX and a *Head* not in Ceroni (*Head* "C")

28. Amedeo Modigliani in the courtyard of his studio in Paris, Cité Falguière (1911-1913): in front of him *Head* Ceroni I

probability in the courtyard of his studio in Cité Falguière, working on Ceroni I.[23]
It was necessary to wait for the death of the artist to have a document that would give the visual proof of a Modigliani sculpture: after the war in the renewed "Kunstblatt" in Berlin, edited by Paul Westheim, *Head* XV[24] is reproduced in an issue of 1921 with the specification that it belonged to the Köhler collection in Berlin. This showed a lively market, managed with care and good timing: but systematic research into the exhibitions during the two years following Modigliani's death which presented, in a whirling succession, the works of a an artist in a continuously increasing commercial ascent, has still not been carried out: the result of some of my first research into this question would seem to regard successful exhibitions connected to paintings and drawings, not to sculptures, with only a few, and dubious, exceptions.[25]

In the abundant literature of memories regarding Modigliani there are not many recollections about the season of sculptural research that can be used for their reliability. Noël Alexandre has collected memories, written or tape-recorded, of his father Paul (the dermatologist who was the first collector of Modigliani's work, having a close relationship with him from 1907 to 1914) and has published some extracts from his correspondence with later Modigliani scholars. Paul Alexandre gives a picture of Modigliani sculptor which is useful for at least three aspects. The first aspect is that of the chronological extension of the artist's sculptural activity. In a letter to Ambrogio Ceroni dated August 1957 Alexandre wrote that, before leaving for Italy in the middle of April 1913, Modigliani left him all his sculptures (apart from one already bought by the English painter Augustus John from Chelsea) that were stored at his home in

Avenue Malakoff, with the intention of picking them up on his return; and that still before his departure for Italy, he left him the drawings relative to the sculptures,[26] signing them for the occasion. His sculptural activity was collocated in a brief season, from 1912 to the spring of 1913, without being taken up again after his return to Paris in June 1913. The second aspect is that of his technical apprenticeship. Modigliani is said to have been initiated to sculpture by Brancusi and Maurice Drouard, who gave him some advice on working stone and the choice of materials, he would sculpt by directly attacking the block, after a long graphic preparation and without any corrections, therefore, starting on a new block if there was an error; he carried out more than twenty statues, abandoning the sculptural activity due to the fatigue of direct carving; he dreamed of being able to afford someone to do the hewing for him. The third aspect is that of the formal references: Modigliani is said to have gone above all to the Ethnological Museum at the Trocadéro, he was keen on tribal art and even more on the "Angkor exhibition," the selection of ancient Oriental art on the first floor of the museum: it is a little surprising that given all this he admired the work, to our eyes elegantly academic, of Elie Nadelman.[27]
The only conclusive correction that can be made to this information is about the early buyer cited by Paul Alexandre, Augustus John. In a later recollection he spoke about his visit to Modigliani's studio (he was impressed by the state of the floor which was full of heads that were all very similar to one another for their narrow and elongated form[28]), he bought two sculptures from Modigliani not one. Kenneth Wayne's research has allowed a positive identification of these sculptures with *Heads* XXI and XXII[29]: this is particularly precious information as it permits us to conclude that the heads were bought by John after the inauguration of the Salon d'Automne, October 1912, where both of them were certainly exhibited. In this way David Bomberg's recollection would become more credible, that he was in Paris with Jacob Epstein in the spring of 1913 to organise the exhibition of modern art at the Whitechapel Gallery in 1914, for the occasion he would have convinced his friends Roworth and John to buy Modigliani's sculptural heads.[30]
As far as the chronological extension of the carrying out of Modigliani's sculptures is concerned, the information from his contemporaries is quite diverse. Paul Guillaume, who had known him since 1914, remembered in 1920 that Modigliani only abandoned sculpture in 1915, when he moved to the studio in Rue de Ravignan.[31] Adolphe Basler refers to a long graphic apprenticeship which began in 1909; and only at a much later date (also later than that of the watercolour caryatids) did he start on stone, to then stop in 1914.[32] André Salmon, without giving any explanation, collocates Modigliani's last sculpture in 1919.[33] According to Jacques Lipchitz in 1912 the Italian artist was working on five of the seven stone heads which were to be exhibited at the Salon d'Automne[34] several months later. After his return to Paris in June 1913, Modigliani took back the sculptures which were stored with Paul Alexandre, they remained for some time in the artist's studio: from the collector André Level we know that, in the meeting between himself, Pablo Picasso and Léonce Rosenberg in Modigliani's studio at the beginning of the war (so, summer-autumn 1914) these stone sculptural heads could still be admired.[35]
The information is very interesting and usually convergent, about the technique, the plastic intentions and in general, the meaning that the presence of those sculptures had in his studio. Jacques Lipchitz recalled Brancusi's direct influence, from which Modigliani derived the firm conviction of the necessity for directly carved sculpture, able to show the hardness of the material and the unnaturalness of the carving. In his recollections Modigliani drew compulsively, then instinctively sculpted works which were conceived not to be seen individually but as a single whole: when he

exhibited them at the Salon d'Automne, he wanted them to be "placed according to height, almost as if they were the reeds of an organ with the purpose of producing the music he wanted."[36] Jacob Epstein, who spent time with Modigliani between 1912 and 1913, spoke about his studio full of "nine or ten" heads ("noses like razor blades which often broke off and needed to be reattached") and the sculpture of a figure: "at night he would place candles on the top of each one and the effect was that of a primitive temple."[37] The sense of ensemble ("his sculptures were to form a whole"); I believe that the particular of the candles lit at night, in an almost magical ritual, derived from nocturnal visits organised by Canova in his studio for high ranking visitors ("he sprinkled [the heads] with water to make them shiny, and went all round them with six other lighted candles in one hand, so as to make the shadows and magical lights play on their surfaces") is remembered by Diogo de Macedo, a Portuguese sculptor who had arrived in Paris in October 1911 and had become friends with Modigliani and Souza Cardoso.[38] Ossip Zadkine remembered the existence of polychrome caryatids, but he might have been confused by the pictorial caryatids, painted in bright red.[39] With regards to his method of impulsively confronting the stone we have Curt Stoermer's recollection.[40]

Instead, there are many divergences among the various testimonies about Modigliani's visual passions, a determining point for positioning the artist in the currents of Parisian Modernity. To confirm Paul Alexandre's testimony about his attention to tribal art there are Adolphe Basler's memories (he admired the African tribal masks in the Frank Burty Haviland collection and their "pure and simple architectonic forms"[41]); Jacob Epstein's (a vision "influenced but not dominated by art nègre"[42]); the English painter Nina Hamnett's,[43] whom Modigliani met in 1914; those of Gustave Coquiot.[44] However it is the important testimony of the Russian poetess Anna Achmatova, who had an affair with Modigliani from 1911, that reveals his passion for Egyptian sculpture (of which he admired "majesty and decoration"), studied at the Department of Antiquities in the Louvre[45]; while Lipchitz insisted on Modigliani's particular attention to early Renaissance painting.[46]

The questions which still remain unanswered from a philological point of view, are not therefore without importance: if there was an extensive sculptural research over a period of time lasting several years,[47] therefore interfering with the paintings 1914-15, or instead just a few months (1912-13, according to Paul Alexandre); if there was a temporal relationship of consequentiality between *Heads* and *Caryatids*, even though the two surviving caryatids, the one in Canberra (XI) and the one in New York (XXV), seem not to be very chronologically close to each other, stylistically referable to two different seasons; what the story is, and the meaning of those heads not exhibited or not otherwise documented, especially those that present evident characteristics of incompleteness (here the Ceroni *Heads* III, V, VII). Then it is not certain where Modigliani's sculptures were physically situated once the artist stopped sculpting: if they all went to Paul Guillaume, after the latter started buying his works in 1914 (the two heads on the mantelpiece were certainly his property, and the two sent to de Zayas in November 1915), or if a part of them, transported during the winter of 1916 and 1917 from the studio in rue Ravignan to the one in rue Joseph Bara, remained property of the artist and their sale was managed by Léopold Zborowski, who from 1916 was Modigliani's official dealer.

There are other questions to add to these that regard the style and formal references of the sculptures. However, the first question to face, seeing the great number of surviving drawings, is to wonder what was the meaning of the persistent and abundant graphic preparation of the heads and the caryatids.

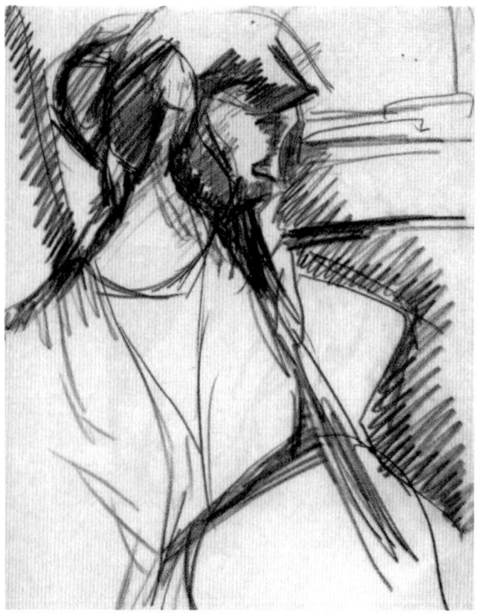

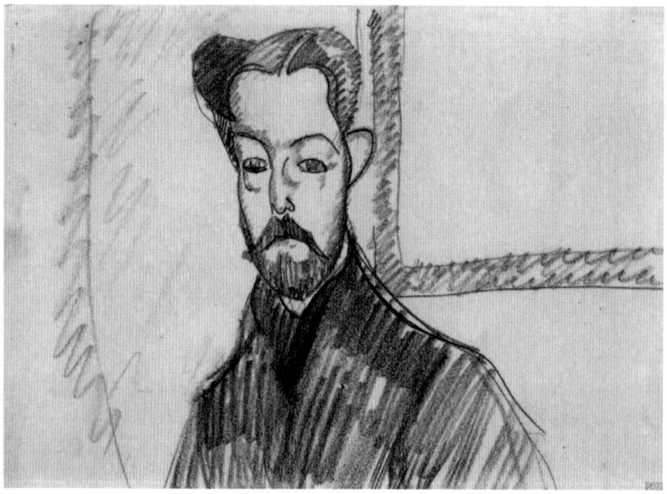

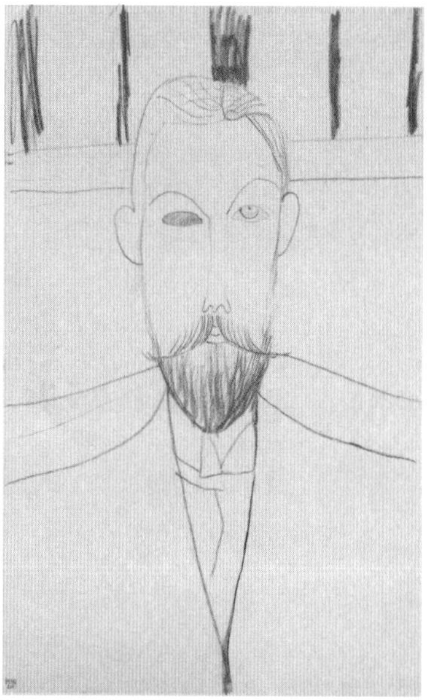

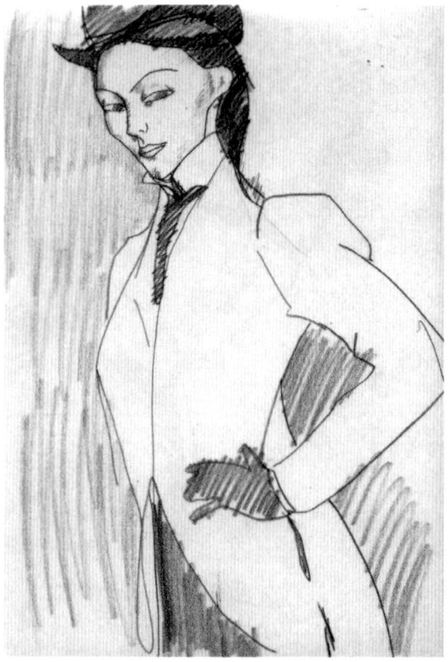

29. Amedeo Modigliani, *Study for the Cellist*, 1909, pencil on paper. Private collection

30. Amedeo Modigliani, *Study for the Amazon*, 1909, pencil on paper. Private collection

31. Amedeo Modigliani, *Study for a Portrait of Paul Alexandre*, 1909, pencil and charcoal on paper. Private collection

32. Amedeo Modigliani, *Study for a Portrait of Paul Alexandre*, 1913, pencil on paper. Private collection

Drawings for sculptures: Modigliani's mark

Modigliani's change towards sculpture, at the beginning of the second decade, was swift and unexpected; and the reason for this change at the present stage of the studies, is still not very clear.

In fact, Modigliani was a painter who until 1910 had wagered a great part of his stylistic identity on the chromatic tone. Even in *Cellist*[48] painted in Livorno in the summer of 1909 and exhibited at the Salon des Indépendants in the spring of 1910, he had committed himself to searching for a range of shades able to harmonise the painting. Cézanne's lesson, learnt about for the first time at the retrospective of the Salon d'Automne in 1907, had given him the key to be a modern painter: that is to study the tonal colour, that particular quality of colour that permits, without (or almost) the use of chiaroscuro, giving the correct luminous and spatial collocation to the people, the objects and to the voids between them.

In the drawings and preparatory studies for the paintings carried out before 1910, Modigliani was above all searching for the character of the person posing, the thoughtfulness of Jean-Baptiste Alexandre, the subtle, elegant melancholy of Paul Alexandre, the knowing glamour of the *The Amazon* (fig. **30**), the silent concentration of the *Cellist* (fig. **29**), the fatalistic satisfaction of *The Boy*[49]; and his mark seemed perfectly functional to the rendering of this character. The stylistic knowledge the draughtsman had acquired was typical of the modern international style: abrupt and segmented lines alternated with other sinuous ones; some particularly accurately focused and others neglected; dense charcoal backgrounds, where a vigorous mark could be seen, and areas of the drawing left artfully blank. Over all these solutions, and not always coherently, another one overlaps, more up to date with the progress of the Parisian modernity: sometimes the outline widened and the charcoal and pen were substituted by ink used with a brush, certainly not to search for pictorial effect but to concentrate the figure in its individuality. The painting then, with the repertoire learnt from Cézanne, would have to harmonise the figure with the environment using tones. Few examples explain so well the meaning that the experience of sculpture had on Modigliani the painter as the comparison between a graphic study for the portrait of Paul Alexandre in 1909 and one for the portrait of the same Alexandre in 1913 (figs. **31-32**), a drawing, the latter Alexandre dated 10th November 1913[50]: what seemed a shift from Post-Impressionist realism to "portrait of the soul" is instead a progress towards the exclusion of spatial connections. In the 1913 sheet there is no longer a connection suggested by the draughtsman between

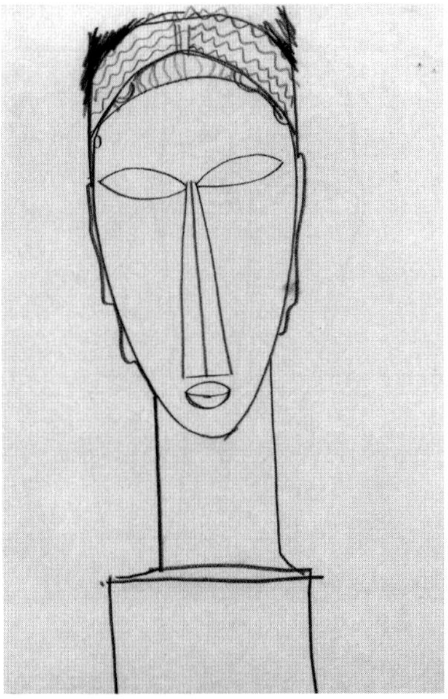

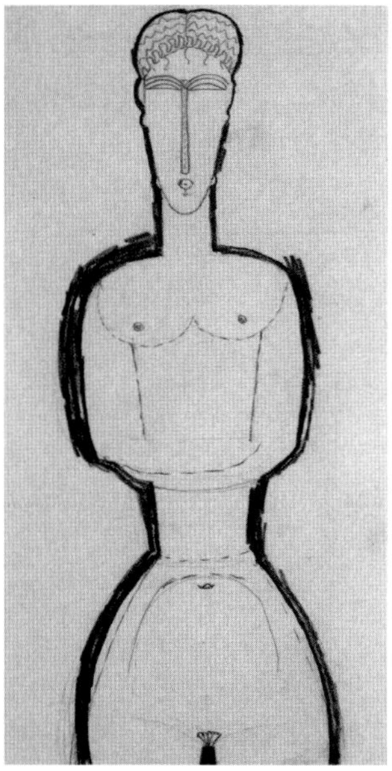

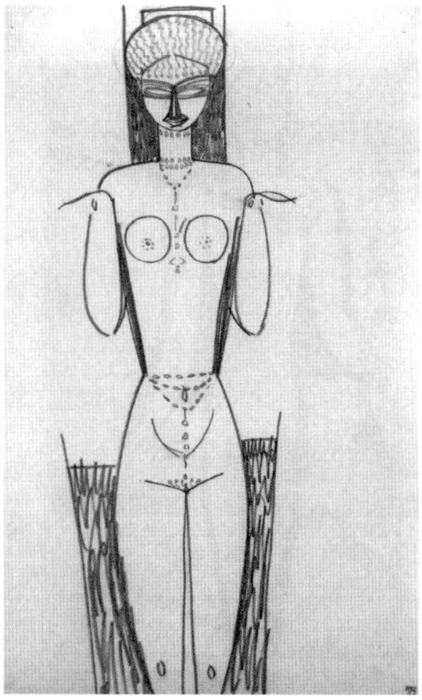

35. Amedeo Modigliani, *Standing Nude Figure, with Folded Arms*, 1911-1912, pencil on paper. Private collection

36. Amedeo Modigliani, *Standing Nude Figure, with Offering Gesture*, 1911-1912, pencil on paper. Private collection

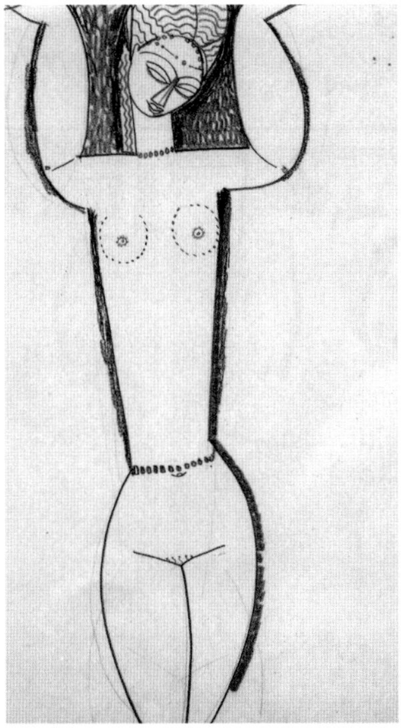

33. Amedeo Modigliani, *Study for Sculptural Head on Base*, 1911-1912, pencil on paper. Private collection

34. Amedeo Modigliani *Standing Caryatid with Necklace and Pearl Belt*, 1911-1912, pencil on paper. Rouen, Musée de Beaux-Arts, Cabinet de dessins, donated by Blaise Alexandre

the various depths of the representation: the spectator's eye is required to three-dimensionally recompose what seems to be a simple surfacing of lines.

When Modigliani began studying themes that then flowed into his sculpture (heads, busts, nude standing or kneeling figures, caryatids) his graphic lines were surprising in their certainty and simplicity. It was often a mark in grease pencil with a clear, uniform contour, standing out perfectly etched against the whiteness of the sheet (fig. **33**), which defined the general profile and some particulars (fig. **34**, sometimes very accurate and others with a discontinuous line). The result seems to be an almost overwhelming bi-dimensionality and decorativeness: the chiaroscuro is nearly always absent; when the pencil thickens the dark marks repeating the profile of the head or figure it does not do so to suggest a shadow as in a bas-relief (the dark shadow is in fact distributed equally along the whole profile) but it obtains a strange effect of delineating this profile even more precisely against the whiteness of the sheet (fig. **35**). The proportion between the general line and the details is favouring the latter, often obsessively repeated: the sequence of the curls on a head: the motif of small circles (which from one time to another represent a jewel, a tattoo, or the symmetric circle of the two nipples) increase the impression of an aristocratic and decorative elegance (fig. **36**). The heads, busts and bodies drawn on paper by Modigliani have no relationship with the space that contains them, mysteriously self-referential. When the surroundings are suggested (a setting with drapes, or candles or columns for the figure of a woman [fig. **37**]; the base and pediment for the caryatids [fig. **38**]) the indication is nearly always allusive: this presence of a setting is never in relationship, with chiaroscuro or space, with the substance of the statue conceived on paper.

This is the mark that would least be expected from a sculptor and particularly from a sculptor between the first and second decade of the XX century. The significance of the drawing, for a modern sculptor, had been summarised by Rodin (in the introduction to *L'Art,* the long conversation he had with Paul Gsell) in these rather authoritative words: "remember this: there are no lines, only volumes. When you draw, never worry about the outline but about the relief. It is the relief that carries the outline."[51] Rodin entrusted only a functional role to the outline from a body it was possible with pencil in hand, to prise out "la vie" through "l'espression complète des profils:"[52] only the profiles as a whole gave, in synthesis, the plasticity of the figure. In Rodin's drawings after 1900 (fig. **39**) the profile, even when it was reduced to a simple outline, was

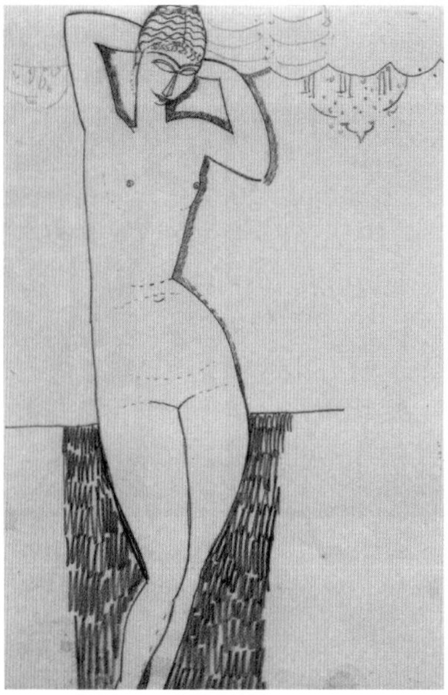

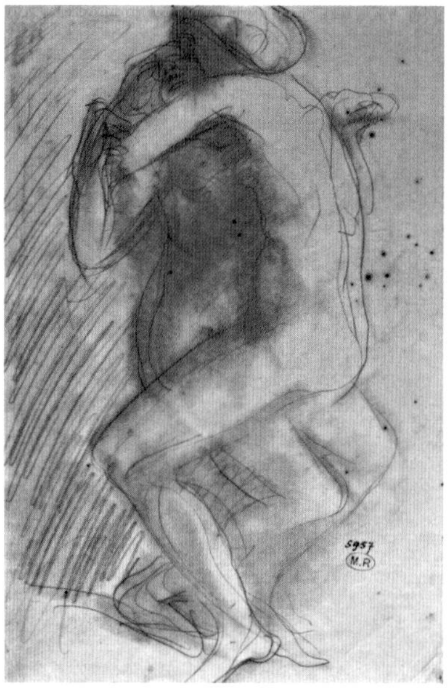

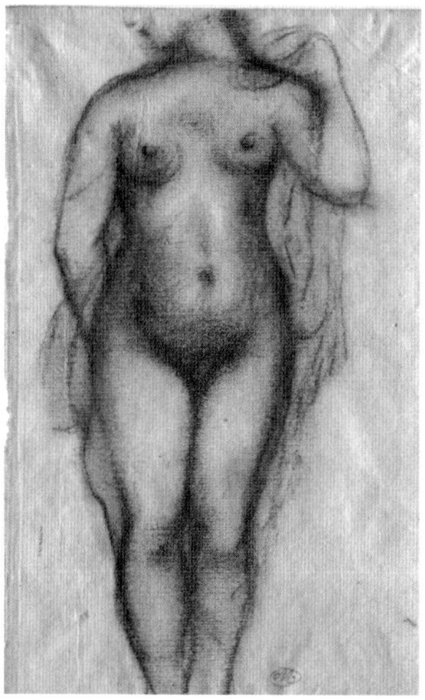

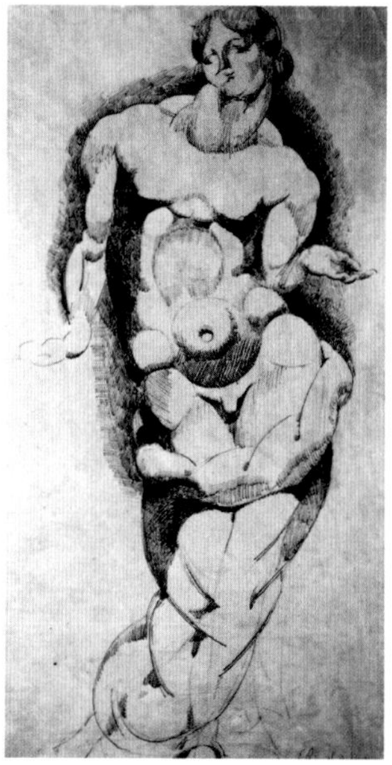

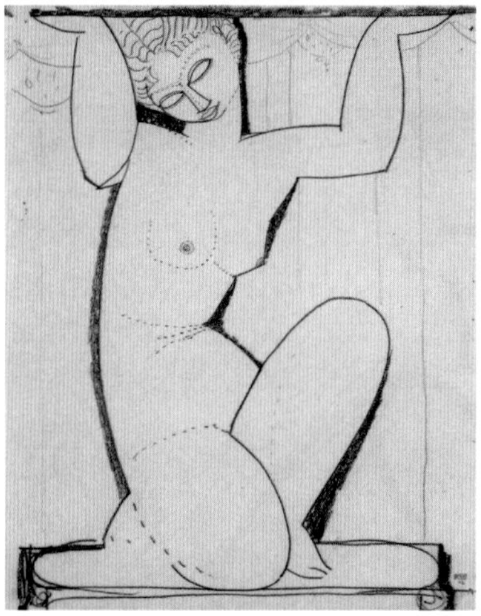

39. Auguste Rodin, *Two Women Embracing*, 1900-1910, pencil on paper. Paris, Musée Rodin

40. Aristide Maillol, *Standing Female Nude*, circa 1910, sanguine on paper. Cleveland, The Cleveland Museum of Art

41. Elie Nadelman *Standing Male Nude*, circa 1909, ink and pencil on paper. Washington DC, Hirshhorn Museum and Sculpture Garden

37. Amedeo Modigliani, *Standing Nude Figure, Arms behind the Head*, 1911-1912, pencil on paper. Private collection

38. Amedeo Modigliani, *Kneeling Caryatid*, 1911-1912, pencil on paper. Private collection

able to express tension and tragic vitality. The following generations contested this theory. In 1904 Maillol, for example, declared that he studied the figure in drawing starting "from the great decorative line."[53] His drawings reveal a patient analysis of the chiaroscuro texture of the bodies (fig. **40**), as if the search for a new synthesis, for a new Classic style had stimulated in him a more detailed review of the reciprocal ratio between the plastic planes. The relationship between drawing and sculpture in all the greatest French sculptors of the post-Rodin generation (Bourdelle, Bernard, Despiau) reveals a great desire to imagine on paper the effects of the volume that they wanted to obtain in sculpture: and this was true also for who, like the painter André Derain, was discovering sculpture as a way of giving a different solidity to the nude in painting. Even who drew with a different style from these artists seemed to be dominated by the same worry. Elie Nadelman, who in his ink studies seemed close to a certain stylisation of profiles in Modigliani style, knowingly recuperated historical graphic styles: he shaded the figures by means of an intense network of cross hatching, in XVII century fashion (fig. **41**); or he stood them out against the background turning to a Neo-eighteenth century mark, made of up grafts of comma shaped marks.
Constantin Brancusi, who was certainly a reference for Modigliani in his early days as a sculptor, used a drawing that meant to hint, due to the particularity of the mark itself (non sharpened charcoal or pastel that leaves a large blurred mark on the paper) at the

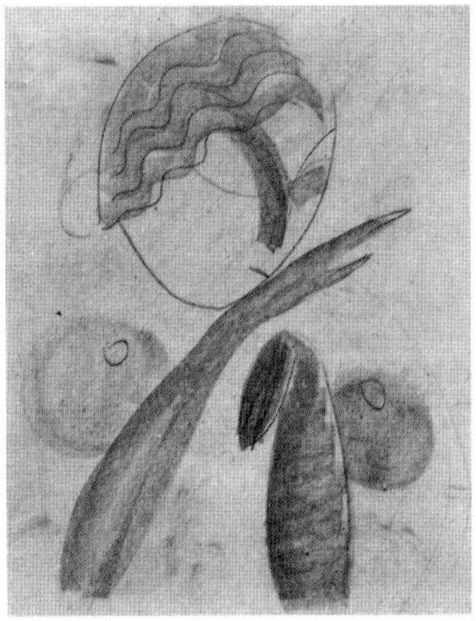

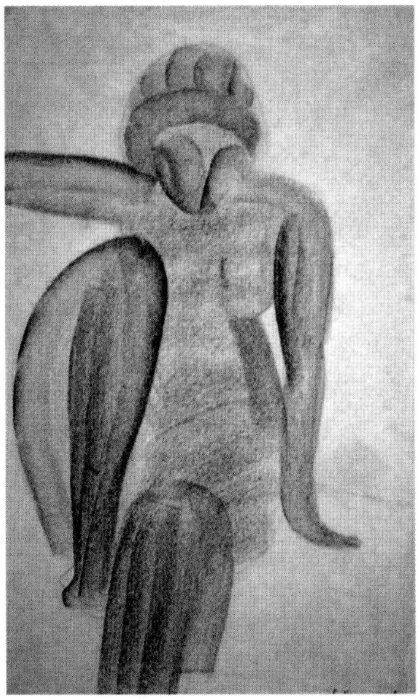

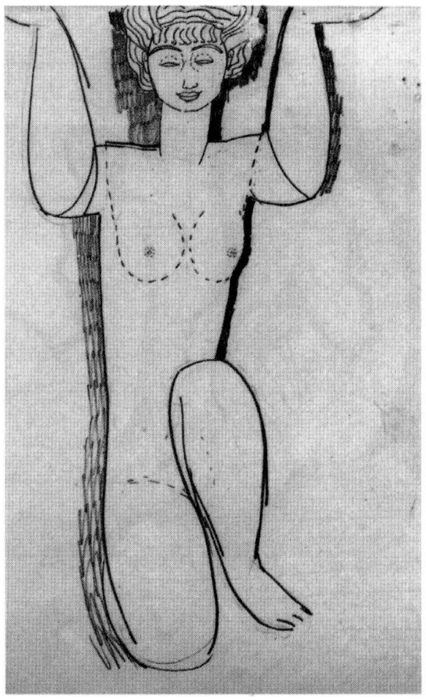

42. Constantin Brancusi, *Mademoiselle Pogany*, 1912, pencil and charcoal on paper. Stuttgart, Staatsgalerie, Graphische Sammlung

43. Constantin Brancusi, *Seated Nude*, circa 1912, blue and yellow pastel on paper. Elmira, New York, Arnot Art Museum, Gift of Charles Rumsey

44. Amedeo Modigliani, *Kneeling Caryatid*, 1911-1912, pencil on paper. Private collection

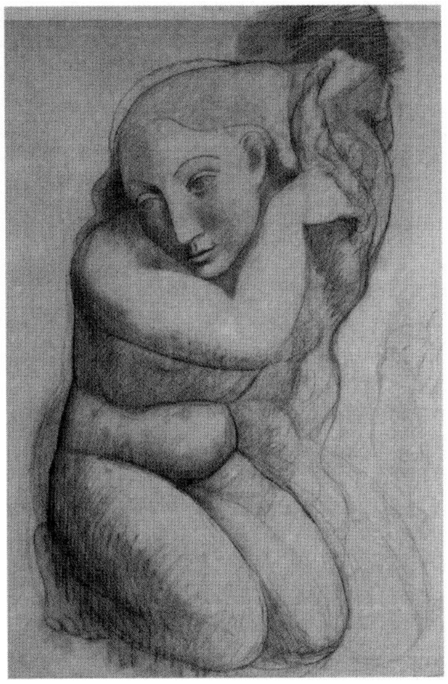

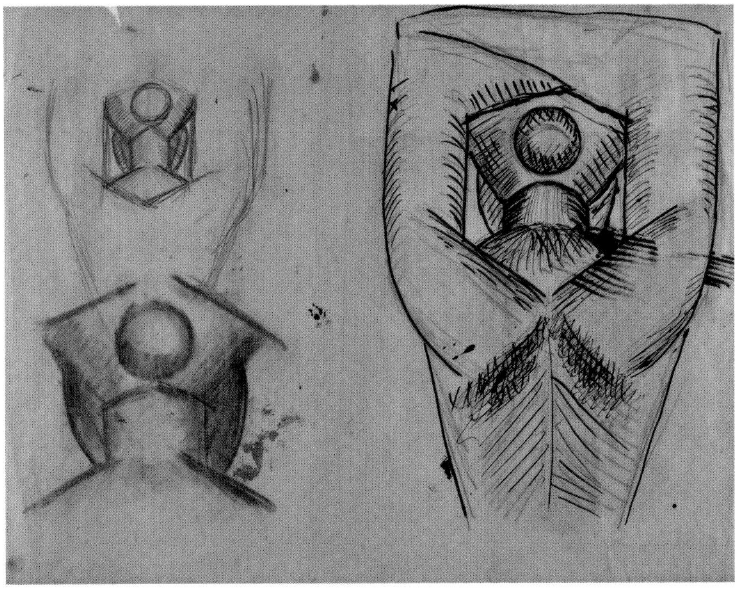

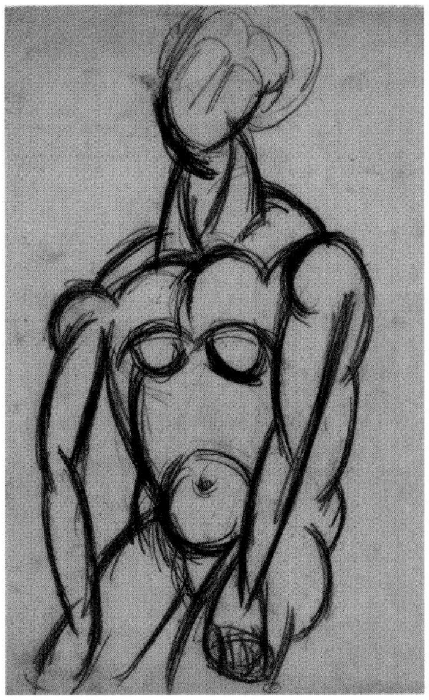

45. Pablo Picasso, *Woman Combing Her Hair*, 1906, pencil and charcoal on paper. Sainsbury Centre, Norwich, England, Robert and Lisa Sainsbury Collection

46. Pablo Picasso, *Three Studies of a Woman with Raised Arms*, 1908, pencil and ink on paper. Paris, Musée Picasso

47. Pablo Picasso, *Standing Nude Woman (Fernande)*, 1909, charcoal on paper. Paris, Musée Picasso

surfaces he imagined in sculpture. In the not very many drawings of his that are known of during the period in which Modigliani devoted himself to sculpture[54] the role that the drawing assumed in the process of progressive isolation of the volumes is evident (the transition, in 1912, from the drawing for *Mlle Pogany*, today in the Museum of Philadelphia to the more advanced one, today in the Staatgalerie in Stuttgart [fig. **42**] is a fine example). If we compare his *Seated Nude* dated 1912 (fig. **43**) with Modigliani's drawings of kneeling caryatids (fig. **44**) then it is obvious how Brancusi, contrary to Modigliani, thought about his figure in precisely three-dimensional terms (a figure never carried out in sculpture), anticipating on paper the potential plastic effect of marble or bronze. Also Picasso, who was the first to revolutionise the representation of the body through reference not to the live model but to the stability of sculpture, attributed a primary role to the representation of the volume using chiaroscuro. In his first studies of "Iberian" heads and nudes (1906) (fig. **45**) he had tried to suggest the unheard of simplification of their plastic planes by means of a precise cold registration of the play of shadows; this was a practice that, extended to nudes, would hold still, with the evolution towards the geometric planes of Cubism, until 1908 (fig. **46**). Only in a later phase, around 1909

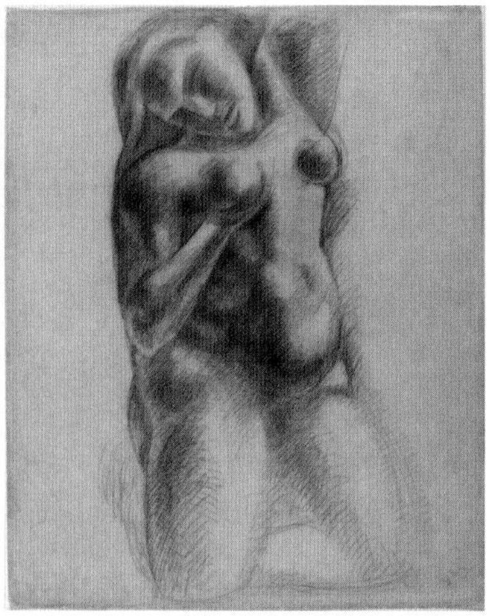

48. André Derain, *Bather*, pencil on paper, 1908-1910. Paris, Centre Georges Pompidou, Musée National d'art moderne

(fig. **47**), the pure contour would take on a new meaning, of extreme synthesis of the various plastic planes.

The sculptural drawing of Modigliani's contemporaries mainly had the meaning of translation of the forms from the live model to the synthesis of the sculpture; this is particularly evident in the drawings of a painter, André Derain, who experimented with sculpture during the same years for his own need for clarity and expressive firmness (fig. **48**). Henri Matisse, a companion of Derain's in his research during the heroic years of the "Fauves" Salon, had this new need for synthesis in mind when he suggested to his pupils how to look at a body and, through drawing, transfer it to a different entity, a sculpture: "Express yourselves with proportions of mass related to the great linear movements. You must determine the characteristic shapes of the different parts of the body and the direction of the contours it will result from. In a standing man, all the parts must be organised directionally so as to contribute to giving this impression. The legs ascend towards inside the torso, which in turn closes onto them. You must have a vertebral column. You can divide the work putting in opposition the lines (or axles) that indicate the directions of the parts, building the body so as to immediately suggest the general character and movement."[55]

The main difference between Modigliani and nearly all his contemporaries (with the exclusion of Picasso) is that he wanted to draw not a figure but a sculpture. To do this, having reached a mysterious turning point in 1910 (the conviction that it was necessary to close with Post-Impressionism if you wanted to be a modern artist) he tried to use, in his drawing, the resources elaborated by Picasso around 1909, shooting ahead of what Picasso had already done between 1906 and 1909: finding once again a strange convergence between conceptual simplification of the Picasso-style drawing and an almost Liberty style elegance which was sophisticated and archaic at the same time.

In Modigliani's catalogue, those few pictorial studies of heads and figures similar to the sculptures are fundamental[56] (figs. **49-50**). It is even possible that the artist had begun experimenting pictorially, in reddish tones with uniform backgrounds like Matisse's, a series of solutions (simple outlines, archaic and alienating gestures, more Egyptian-like than primitive) before starting the cutting of the stone. Already in these studies he wanted to represent sculptures, not figures. Studying Egyptian sculpture at the Louvre must have been the key to this phase.

Modigliani learnt from Egyptian models not only extreme plastic simplification, that included geometric basics of representation; not only did he import that impending frontality that increased the magical and hieratic nature of the figure. Above all he learnt to use that decisive division between the mark and the living model: the mark, now, defines not a body but a sculpture, an object extracted from space and unrelated to it: in a relationship with space which is not of logical continuity but of magic discontinuity.

In this way Modigliani came into contact with a theme which had been debated in sculpture for half a century. Charles Baudelaire, in the statues reviewed in a Salon in 1859, had recognised a singular anti-modern fascination: that of sculpture was "Inevitable barbarity, synthetic, childish, that often transpires even in a perfect art (Mexican, Egyptian or Assyrian) and that descends from the need to see things on a large scale, considering them above all in the effect of their whole."[57]

Charles Blanc, in his treatise on the arts which became fundamental for the visual ideology of Post-Impressionism, had underlined the intrinsically synthetic nature of sculpture: "The style in sculpture consists in returning forms to their original and general nature, removing insignificant details that usually occlude them."[58]

Artists who were close to Modigliani would have loved, in his sculpture, his distance from the live model he referred to ("There is a plastic life and a life of human beings" – Nadelman was sure[59]); and together with the ability to disturb the spectator in irrational and mysterious ways: Zadkine claimed that the statue had to "exhaler un 'quelque chose' qui subjugue le spectateur, qui lui entrouve un chemin insoupçonné au sein de sa propre âme."[60] This same and rather particular short circuit destined to be created between the statue and its observer was spoken about, with some ingenuity, by Augustus John, one of the first buyers of Modigliani's heads: after seeing them in his studio, he was "obsessed for days with meeting the models for the statues in the streets"; and he wondered if he had not, with his unrealistic and stylised heads, "discovered a new, unknown aspect of reality."[61]

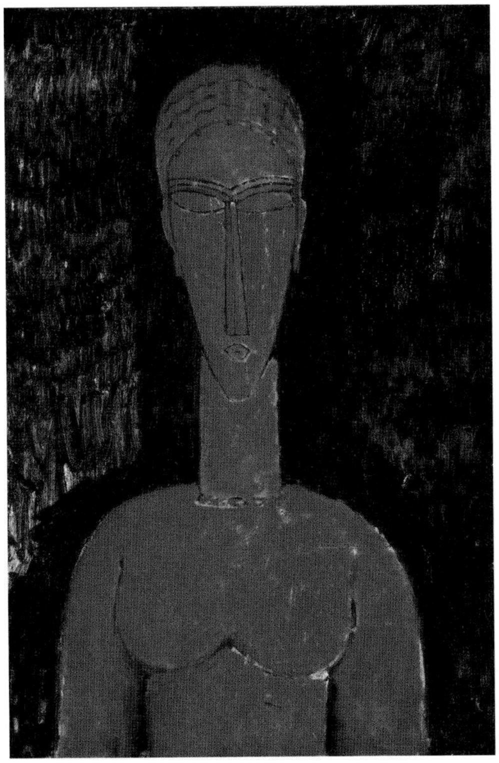

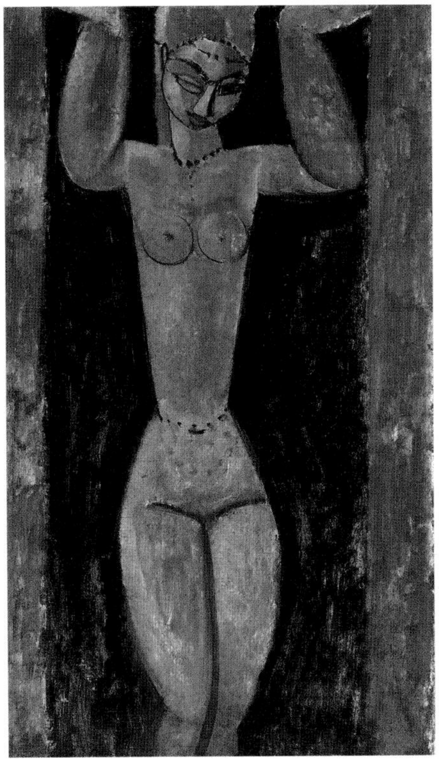

49. Amedeo Modigliani
Female Bust, 1911-1913, oil on cardboard. Private collection

50. Amedeo Modigliani, *Standing Caryatid*, 1911-1913, oil on canvas. Nagoya, Aichi Prefectural Museum of Art

The Sculptural Heads and Their Preparatory Drawings

If the sculptural *Heads* documented while Modigliani was alive were lined up together (those certainly exhibited, or evidenced by photographs of the time, or purchased: I, XIII, XIV, XV, XVI, XIX, XX, XXI, XXII, XXIV, "A", "B", "C") and those which today have reached a more advanced state of completion (IX, XII, XVII, XVIII, XXIII) it would be obvious how Modigliani carried out his research on a repertoire of minimum variations, testing a limited number of proportions. Each time the sculptor studied a perfectly symmetric head, without any trace of expressive movement (the only exceptions are asymmetry of the nose in *Head* IX and the slight misalignment of the eyes in *Head* XVII). From time to time the shape of the head varies (a more or less accentuated oval, the chin more or less pointed); the shape and length of the nose (which could be almost parallel to the planes of the face or a "slice of Brie"; a pure geometric solid or widened at the nostrils); the shape above all of the cut of the eyes (lunettes cut at the base in IX, almond shaped variedly slanted in others); the shape and jut of the mouth (from a simple cylinder grafted onto the face to the archaic smile of XII; from a just a hint of a line to the strong protrusion of XX); the height of the positioning of the ears; the shape, the size and the decorative motif of the hair. Furthermore, he worked on the proportions of size and distance between the hair, the forehead, nose, upper lip, mouth and chin. A formal proportion that has a different meaning is the one between the finished parts of the head and the non-sculpted parts of the block. However, it is difficult to draw any conclusions about this as we do not know how long Modigliani intended to carry on with the finishing: XXI and XXII, exhibited at the Salon d'Automne in 1912 seem to exploit the resource of the unfinished block with clear plastic intentions: it is more difficult to judge its function in XV, XVI or XIX.
All these variants do not testify to the search

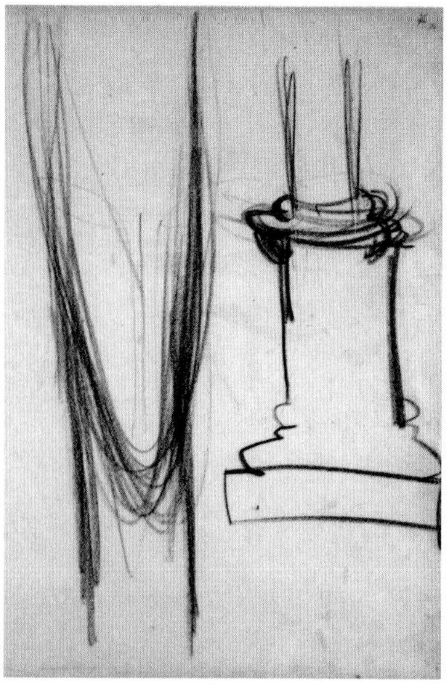

51. Amedeo Modigliani, *Study of Head with Column Pedestal*, 1911-1912, blue pencil on paper. Basle, Kunstmuseum, Kupferstchkabinett, Fund Karl A. Burckhardt-Koechlin

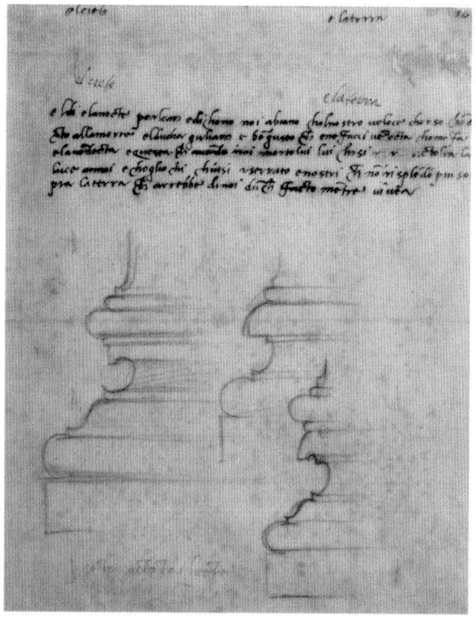

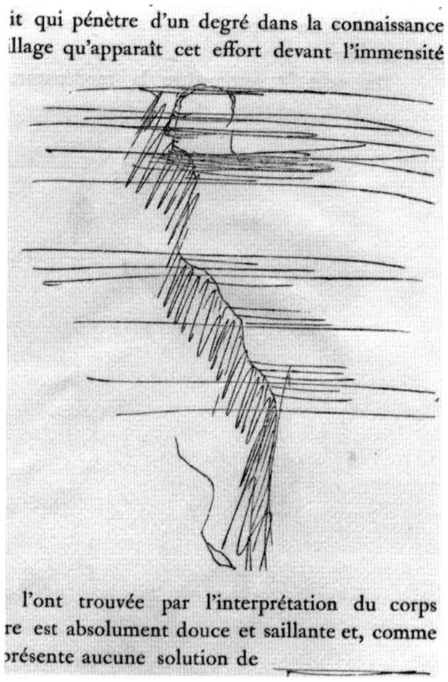

52. Michelangelo Buonarroti *Profiles of Base of Column with Grotesque Head*, circa 1520-1525, sanguine and pen on paper. Florence, Casa Buonarroti

53. Drawing by Auguste Rodin in J. Cladel, *Auguste Rodin. L'œuvre et l'homme*, Brussels 1908

for an ideal head neither do they search for diversification of an expressive nature among the various heads. What we read today as elegance or grotesque lives happily together in Modigliani sculptor. In the same way that different stylistic references live together: the everted cylinder mouths of the Etoumbi tribal masks and the archaic smile of the pre-Phidian masks or the Oriental ones; the perfectly rounded mass of the heads of Egyptian sculptures in the Louvre, the pure ovals of the Italian Renaissance and the extreme elongation of the Guro heads. We are faced with purely proportional research, decorative with abstract shapes. Just as an architect studies the reciprocal ratios that govern the base of a column, capital or the cornice of a window, so Modigliani studied the proportions of the head and, sometimes, of the torso. There are even drawings that show this assimilation of the head to a column, or a capital,[62] or that indicate the play of reciprocal relationships between the profile of a head and that of a moulding[63] (fig. **51**).

This is a fundamental passage in understanding the substantially architectonic sense that Modigliani attributed to his sculpture. During the last decade of his life Rodin returned to the beloved Michelangelo drawings (fig. **52**) that played on the anthropomorphic ambiguity of the profile of the base of a column and re-proposed in some drawings the equivalence (fig. **53**) between human shapes and architectonic shapes: in his opinion it was the nude that determined the forms of architecture (the architects of Gothic or Renaissance had invented "la belle moulure onduleuese qui confère à [...] l'architecture sa souplesse, sa qualité de vie, qui, en quelque sorte, l'illumine" by means of "l'interprétation du corps humain"[64]). Modigliani did the opposite, he started off from the rather alienating severity of architecture and found the rules for the proportions of the body and the face.

I believe it is some writing which gives a sure foothold to this observation. At the bottom of one of his drawings from March 1913 (it is dated 24th March) where the head stands out frontal and rounded becoming the central element of a capital (fig. **54**), Modigliani wrote with the same grease pencil, in the same blue that he used for the drawing, *Le panier fleuri*. The flower basket that Modigliani refers to (but that is not represented, as there are no hints of flowers or vegetation on the sheet) leads back to the invention of the Corinthian capital as told to us by Vitruvius in the fourth book of Architecture: the sculptor Callimachus seems to have been inspired by a basket of flowers left on the grave of a dead person by his loved one: the vegetation was bigger than the basket and created, intertwining with its coils, an extraordinarily

54. Amedeo Modigliani
Head-capital, 24th March 1913,
blue pencil on paper.
Private collection

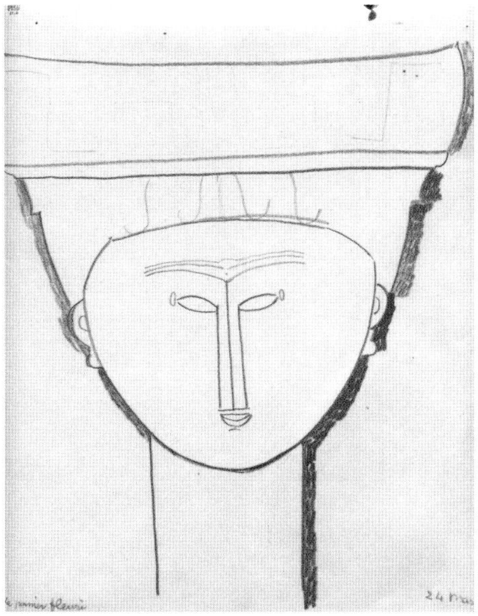

55. Amedeo Modigliani, *Study for Sculptural Head*, 1911-1912, pencil on paper. Private collection

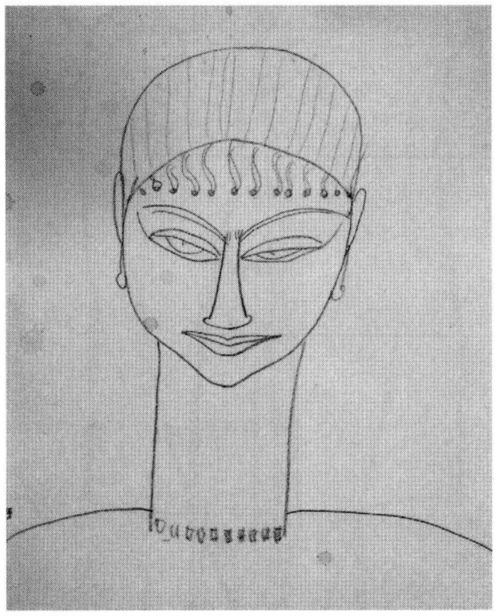

56. Amedeo Modigliani, *Head* [1911-1912]. Harvard University, Fogg Art Museum. Ceroni VIII

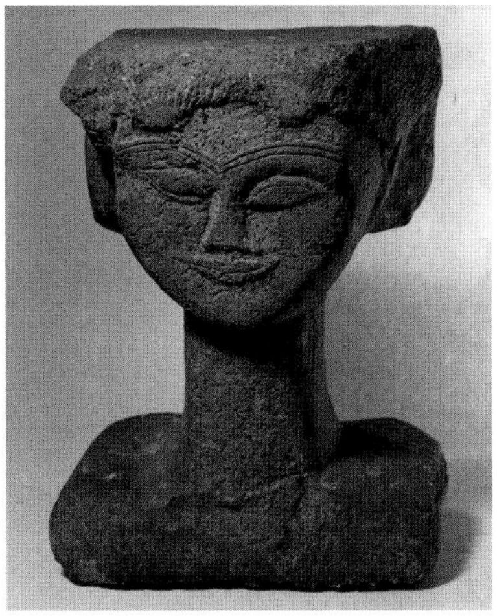

harmonic motif. With this writing Modigliani was alluding, in a game with himself, to the interchangeability between the form of the face (wide and graceless, almost grotesque if looked at for itself) and the shape of the capital: not a face that can be glimpsed in a capital, but rather a capital that determines the shape of the face.
If it was a compositional rule, architectonic, that governed the inspiration for Modigliani's heads then it becomes crucial to know something more about how he worked them. The different states of the finishing of the heads allows us to draw some conclusions about Modigliani's technical procedure.
He carved, on one side of the block, a rough outline of the features of the face and continued, as if for a bas-relief, removing little by little, the layers of stone until he reached the edges of the block, with an action and vision that was absolutely frontal. The last finishing, as can be seen from the small differences between the heads photographed in his studio and those we know today, regarded decorative or proportional variations: the modification of the ornamental motif of the fringe, the depth of the incision for the profile of the eye, the nose more or less protruding.
Unfortunately, these photographs do not tell us much about Modigliani's sculptural invention, especially about the question concerning the proportions that existed between the various heads. Instead, the drawings are determining in helping us in this regard. With the drawings at hand we can understand how Modigliani's plastic reasoning proceeded; and we can even make some hypotheses about the groups to be formed within the 26 catalogued *Heads* (Ceroni's 23, plus the other three that are documented) and perhaps propose some sequences of execution. This question which I think is crucial, has never been faced, even after the availability of the main part of Paul Alexandre's collection: a corpus of certain origin and according to the recollections of the owner, carried out almost completely within a *terminus ante quem,* that is April 1913, when Modigliani left for Italy and gave Alexandre a large number of studies of heads and caryatids.
For this analysis, it seems useful to start off from one of those few drawings that shows a head, in its general proportions and its details, in a state very near to that of the stone known today: or from those drawings that study with certainty only one sculpture, even though with significant variations compared to the sculpture known today.
In some cases these sheets do not reveal elements that are particularly useful for an attempt at serialising or grouping amongst the sculptures; however, they are useful for understanding some aspects of the single sculpture. Sheet 103[65] (fig. **55**) shows us

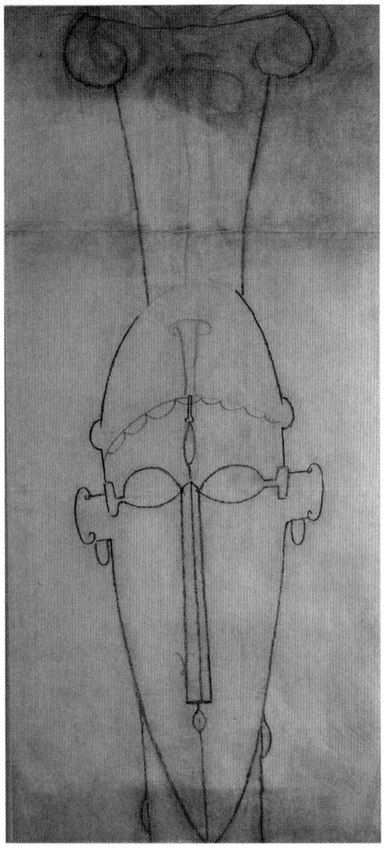

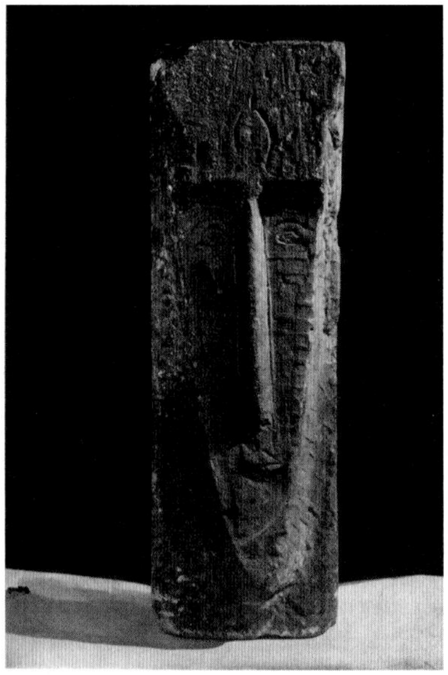

57. Amedeo Modigliani
Study for Sculptural Head Crowned by Ionic Capital, 1914, pencil on paper. Private collection, deposited in Rouen, Musée des Beaux-Arts, Cabinet de dessins

58. Amedeo Modigliani
Head, 1911-1914.
Toronto, Latner Family Art collection. Ceroni IV

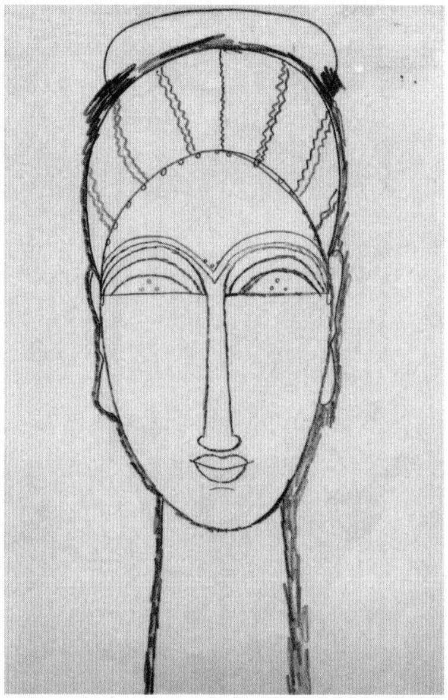

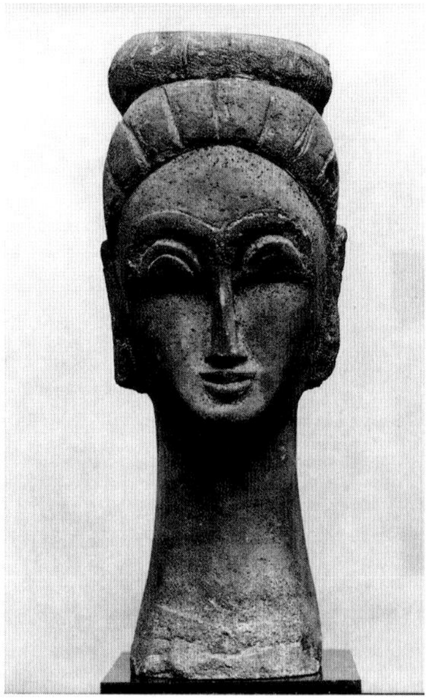

59. Amedeo Modigliani
Study for Sculptural Head, 1911-1912, pencil on paper. Private collection

60. Amedeo Modigliani
Head, 1911-1912.
Küsnacht, Werner Marzbacher collection. Ceroni IX

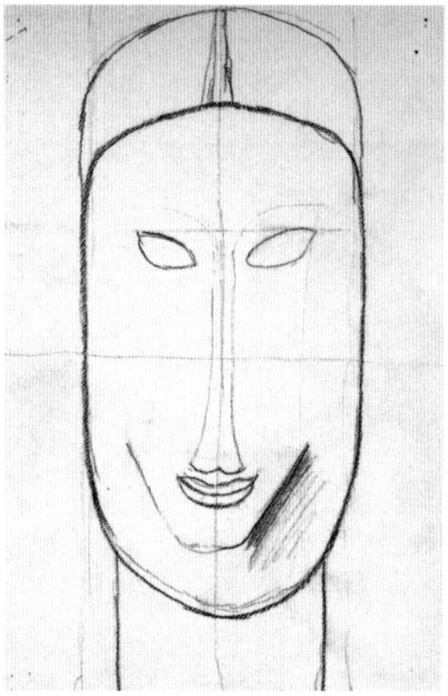

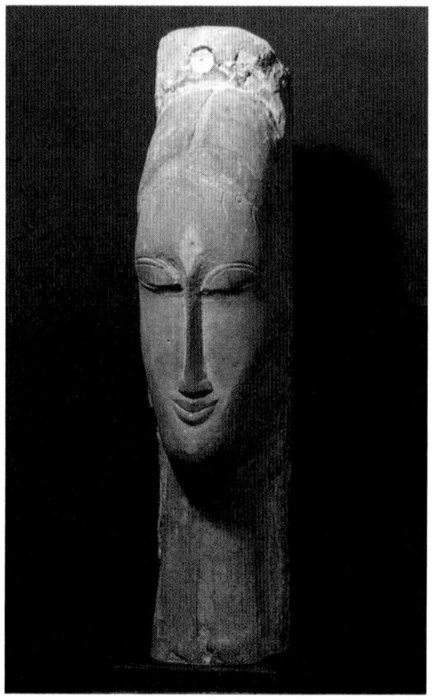

61. Amedeo Modigliani
Study for Sculptural Head, 1911-1912, pencil on paper. Private collection

62. Amedeo Modigliani
Head, 1911-1912.
Paris, Centre Georges Pompidou, Musée National d'art moderne. Ceroni XII

what the final intention was for *Head* VIII (fig. **56**) before Modigliani gave up carving the stone: some solutions take on a more readable meaning like the widened face, the wide carved mouth, the particular pointed profile of the chin. Sheet 183[66] (fig. **57**) explains the meaning of the strange motif carved on the hint of a forehead for *Head* IV (fig. **58**); this is an elongated jewel, that creates, joining up with the features of the face, an uninterrupted central graphical axle between the top of the hair and the point of the chin; but it also explains the extreme geometric schematism of the head, originally thought of as being crowned by a tall capital. Sheet 104[67] (fig. **59**) and two others that belonged to the Alexandre collection[68] almost literally study *Head* IX (fig. **60**), except for a few simplifications found on the stone (the single line of the eyebrows instead of the double one in the drawing; the abolition of some decorative details on the pearls beneath the hair and those of the necklace): placing them near numbers 66 and 67[69] shows us that many of the solutions for this head had derived from the heads of the standing figures or the caryatids (and on the other hand *Head* IX, with the chignon that is transformed into an entablature, is the one that more than the others shows its architectonic function). Sheets 111 and 112[70] (fig. **61**) , drawn on both

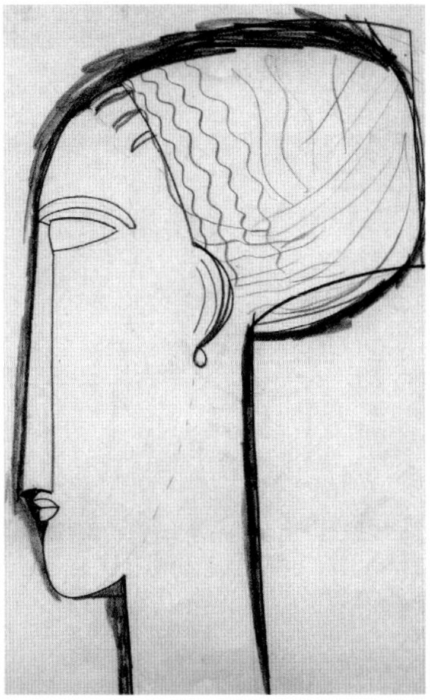

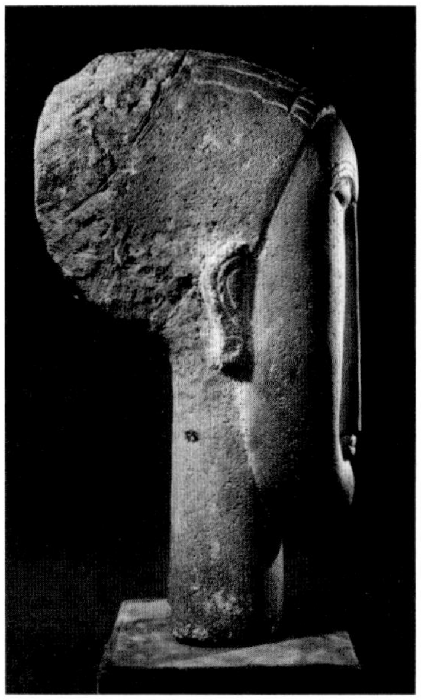

63. Amedeo Modigliani
Study for Sculptural Head,
1911-1912, pencil on paper.
Private collection

64. Amedeo Modigliani
Head, 1911-1912.
Rupert Burgess collection. Ceroni XIII

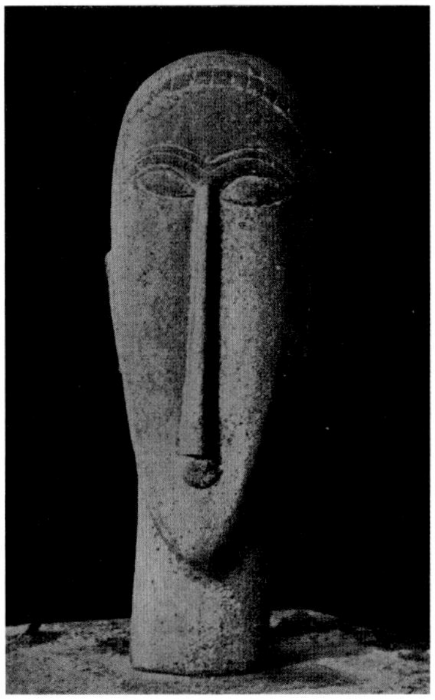

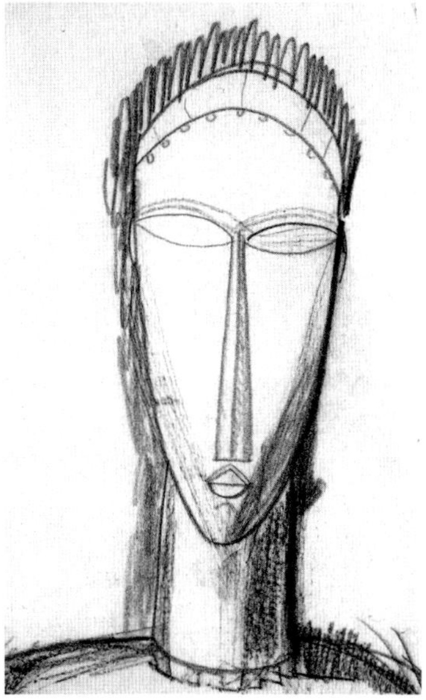

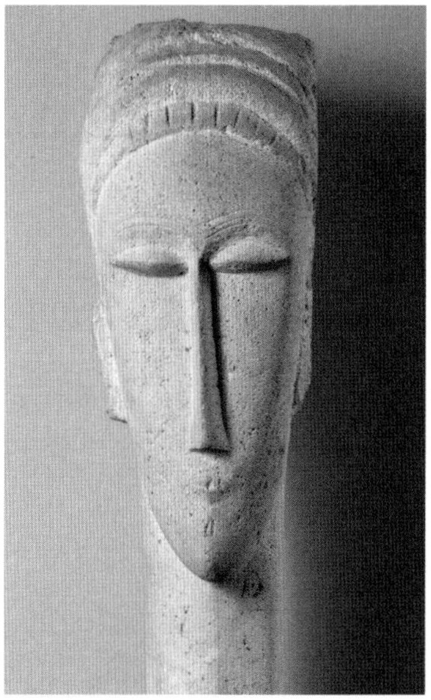

65. Amedeo Modigliani
Head, 1911-1912.
Rupert Burgess collection. Ceroni XIII

66. Amedeo Modigliani, *Study for Sculptural Head*,
1911-1912, pencil and charcoal on paper. Private collection

67. Amedeo Modigliani
Head, 1911-1912.
Saint-Louis, private collection.
Ceroni XV

sides, explain where the invention of *Head* XII (fig. **62**) started from, with the unusual shape of the elongated but almost oblong head, as if the angles had been rounded off, and its archaic smile: in the passage from the drawing to the stone Modigliani had toned down these too clearly Oriental aspects of his starting point.
Instead, two examples supply some keys of a different nature, and create a network of references among several sculptures. A pencil drawing, the 153[71] (fig. **63**), almost literally studies *Head* XIII in profile (fig. **64**): the few differences concern the decorative motif of the hair and the profile of the lower part of the chin (even though in the drawing Modigliani seems to consider the alternative of the sharp horizontal cut, that he would later use on the stone). In a smaller sheet measuring 274 x 227 mm, number 108[72] (fig. **66**), drawn on the front and the back with frontal heads, Modigliani seems to be directed, starting from *Head* XIII (fig. **65**), towards solutions that are similar to *Head* XV (fig. **67**): the perfect oval in XIII widens out at the eye level; the lips take on a diamond shape, the lines of the eyebrows increase from two to three; the eye begins to be thought of in relief and is cut halfway along the line of the eyelid. The more geometric scheme of *Head* XV will be grafted onto a bust of a caryatid, and livened

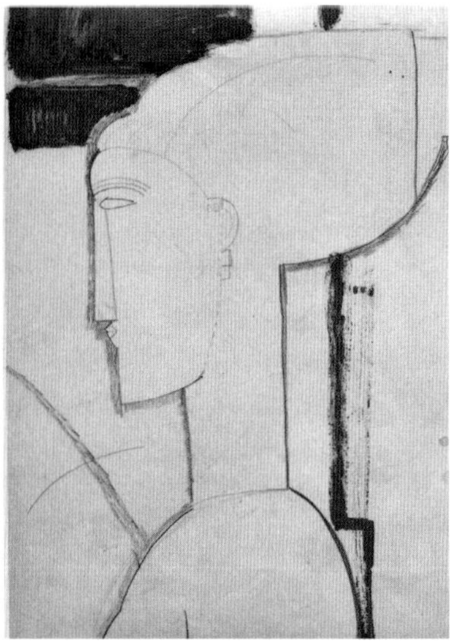

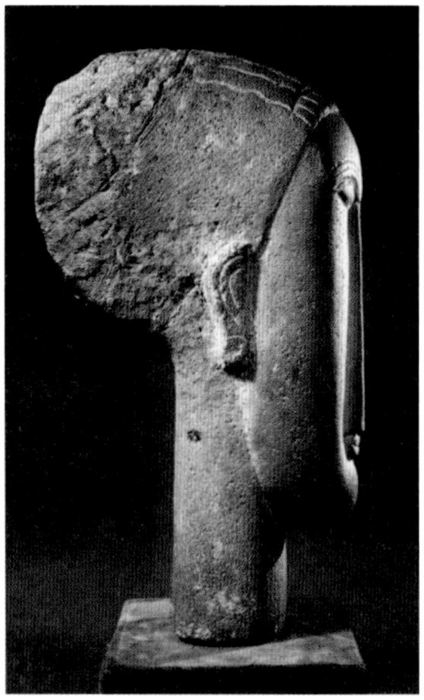

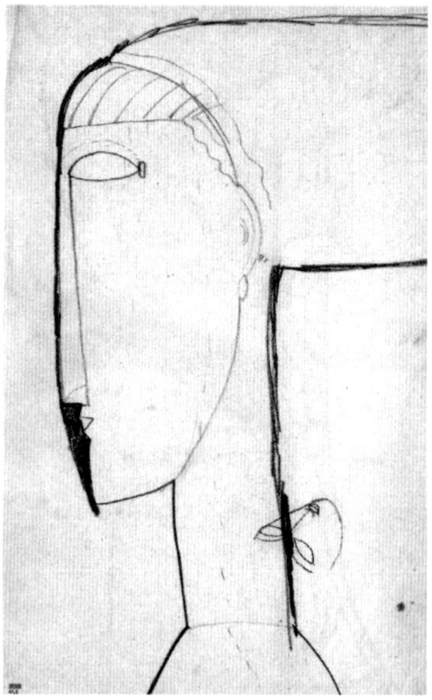

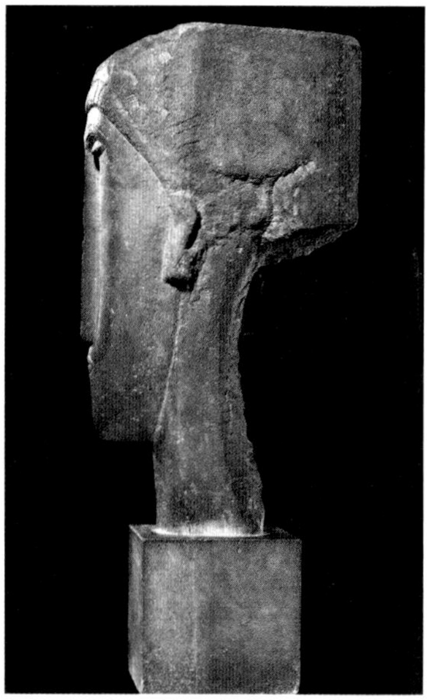

68. Amedeo Modigliani
Study for Profile of Sculptural Bust, 1911-1912, blue pencil and white lead on paper. Private collection

69. Amedeo Modigliani, *Head*, 1911-1912. Rupert Burgess Collection. Ceroni XIII

70. Amedeo Modigliani, *Study for Profile of Sculptural Head*, 1911-1912, pencil on paper. Rouen, Musée des Beaux-Arts, Cabinet de dessins, donated by Blaise Alexandre

71. Amedeo Modigliani, *Head*, 1911-1912. Formerly Lévy Collection, Paris
Not in Ceroni (*Head* "A")

up with red gouache, in 147[73] (fig. **68**). This was not the only direction that his work took. In a series of drawings of profiled heads (145, 148, 149,[74] fig. **70**), Modigliani started from the scheme of *Head* XIII (fig. **71**) to fix the characteristics (longer and pointed chin, thinner mouth, bulging eyes with half closed eyelids, in No. 145) of *Head* "A" (fig. **71**), the one reproduced in *Comœdia Illustré* on 20th October 1912. However, in another drawing, number 97[75] (fig. **73**), one of the rarest cases in which the head is studied in three quarters, the starting point for *Head* XIII (fig. **72**) the oval of the face, the proportions between nose, mouth and chin, with a hint at relief of the chin just under the mouth) evolves towards solutions that lead to *Head* XVI (fig. **74**). For example, the solutions are the same for the eyebrows and the eyes, with a short segment in relief at the side; the fringe is still missing that will substitute the circular motif of the hair in *Head* XIII (but a comparison with *Head* XVI [fig. **75**] while being worked and the final version shows us that the hair was the last characteristic to be defined). In a profile drawing, 154[76] (fig. **77**), the solutions that lead from XIII (fig. **76**) to XVI (fig. **78**) are nearly all present: the fringe, the eyebrow arch, the mouth, the curve of the chin are literal. However, the eyebrows with the short sloping relief transit into studies that lead to *Head* XIX (fig. **81**): in a sheet like 121[77] (fig. **80**) it is clear that Modigliani is keeping his options open between *Heads* XVI and XIX (where he literally repeats the proportions of the face) and *Head* XV (fig. **79**), where he repeats the shape of the mouth. In the sequence of profile drawings 144, 150 and 156[78] (figs. **83-85**), the artist studies a vast range of solutions that, again starting from XIII (fig. **82**), will transit into XV, XVI, XIX and above all, *Head* "A" (fig. **86**, 156 is the closest study). The passage between *Head* XVI and *Head* "A" (figs. **87-88**) is documented in a series of frontal studies (123-124[79];

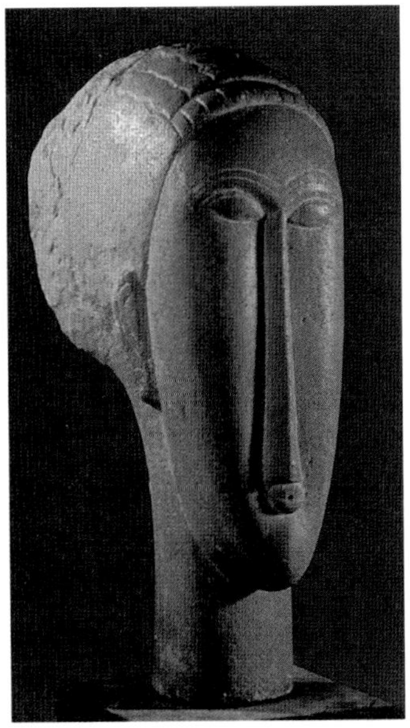

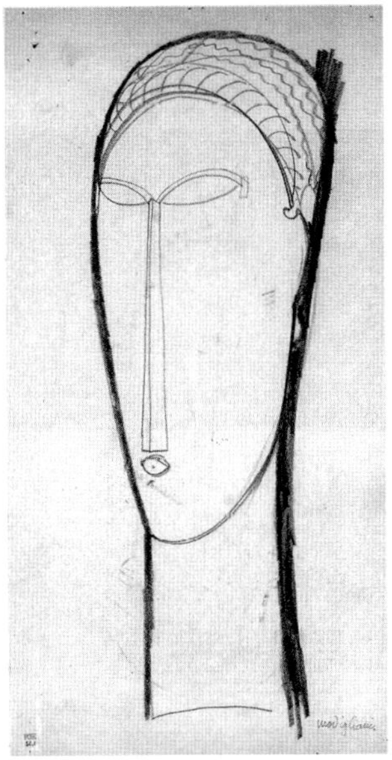

72. Amedeo Modigliani
Head, 1911 1912.
Rupert Burgess Collection. Ceroni XIII

73. Amedeo Modigliani,
Study for Three Quarter Sculptural Head, 1911-1912, pencil on paper.
Private collection

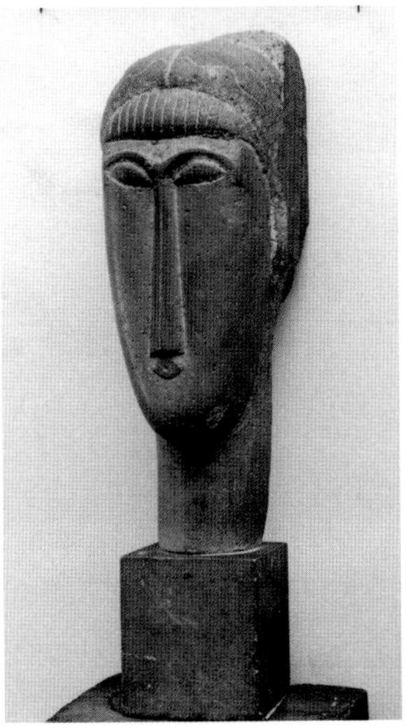

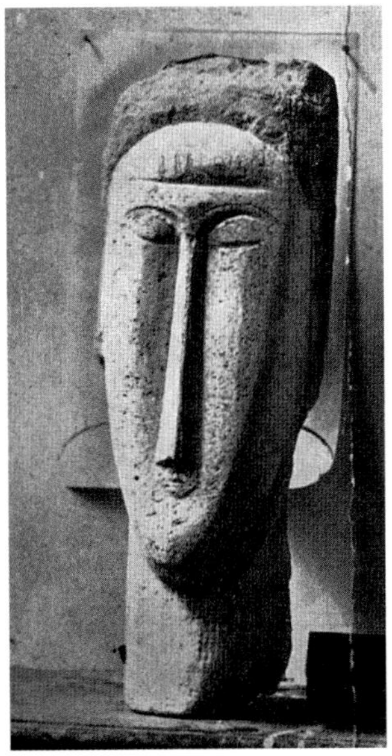

74. Amedeo Modigliani
Head, 1911-1912. Minneapolis,
The Minneapolis Institute of Arts.
Ceroni XVI

75. Anonymous photographer
Head Ceroni XVI while being worked on
(detail of fig. 15)
Lisbon, Fundação Calouste
Gulbenkian, Amadeo de Souza
Cardoso Archive

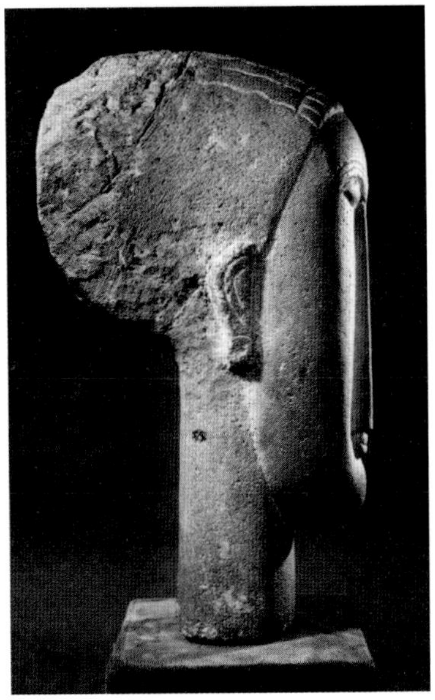

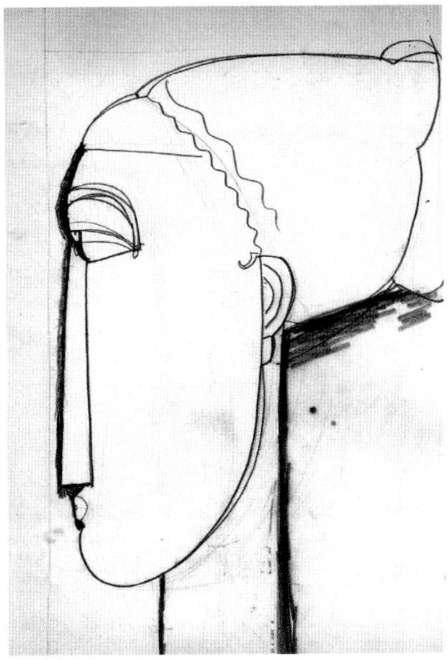

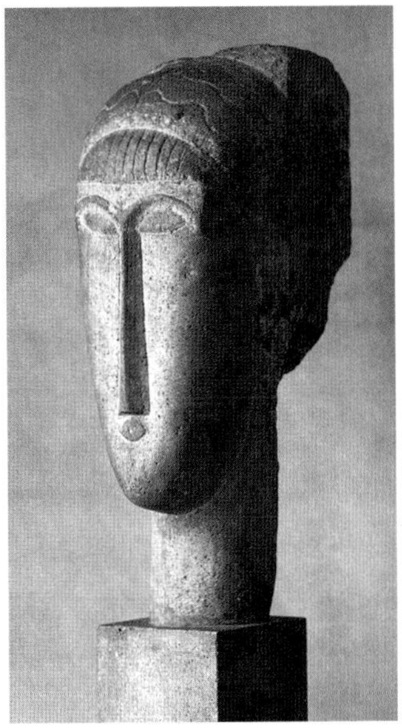

76. Amedeo Modigliani,
Head [1911-1912].
Private collection. Ceroni XIII

77. Amedeo Modigliani, *Study for Profile of Sculptural Head*,
1911-1912, pencil and charcoal
on paper. Private collection

78. Amedeo Modigliani,
Head [1911-1912]. Minneapolis,
The Minneapolis Institute of Arts.
Ceroni XVI

79. Amedeo Modigliani
Head, 1911-1912.
Saint-Louis, private collection.
Ceroni XV

80. Amedeo Modigliani
Study for Sculptural Head,
1911-1912, pencil on paper.
Private collection

81. Amedeo Modigliani
Head, 1911-1912.
Merion, Pennsylvania,
The Barnes Foundation.
Ceroni XIX

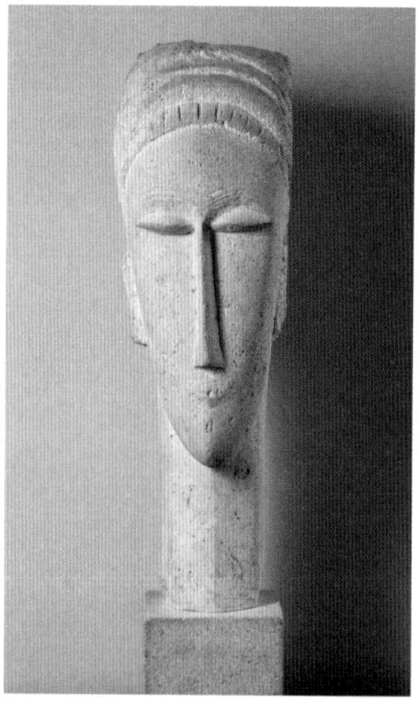

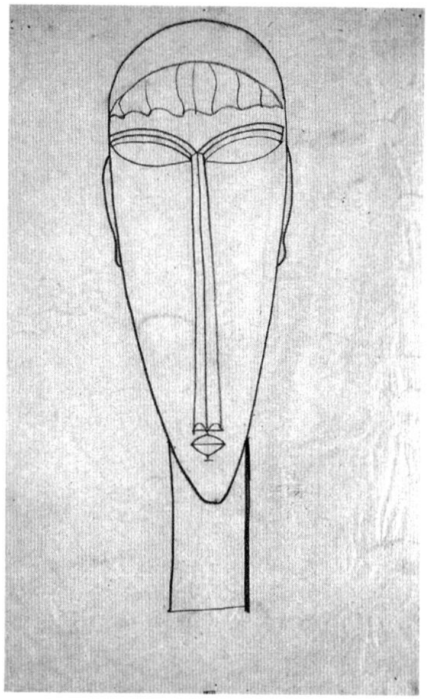

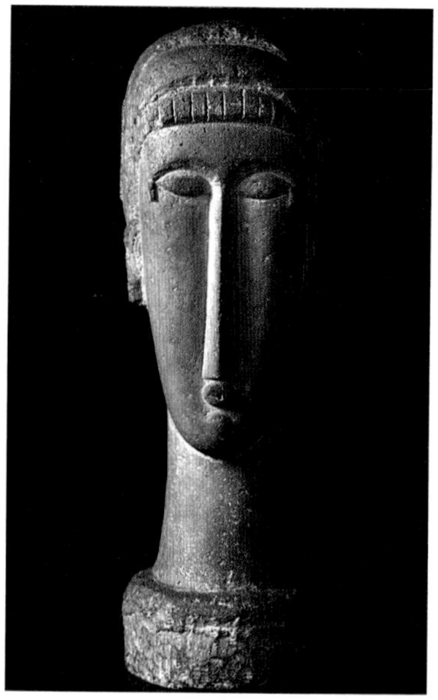

82. Amedeo Modigliani
Head, 1911-1912.
Rupert Burgess collection. Ceroni XIII

83. Amedeo Modigliani
Study for Profile of Sculptural Head,
1911-1912, pencil on paper.
Private collection

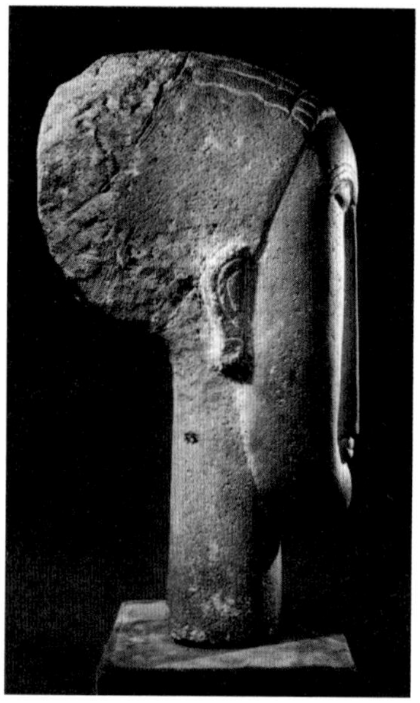

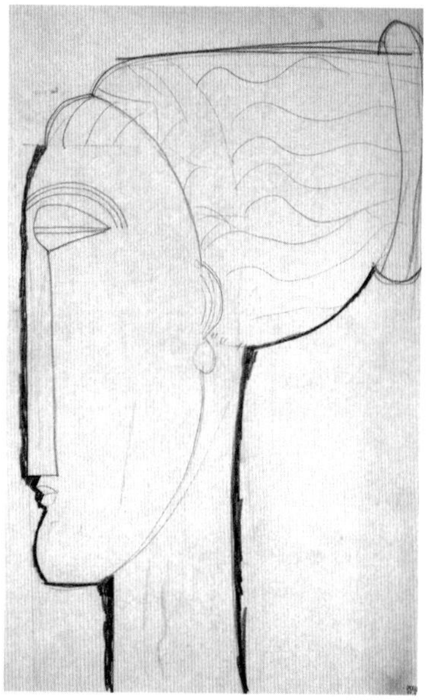

84. Amedeo Modigliani
Study for Profile of Sculptural Head,
1911-1912, pencil on paper.
Private collection

85. Amedeo Modigliani
Study for Profile of Sculptural Head,
1911-1912, pencil on paper.
Private collection

86. Amedeo Modigliani
Head, 1911-1912.
Formerly Paris, Lévy collection.
Not in Ceroni (*Head* "A")

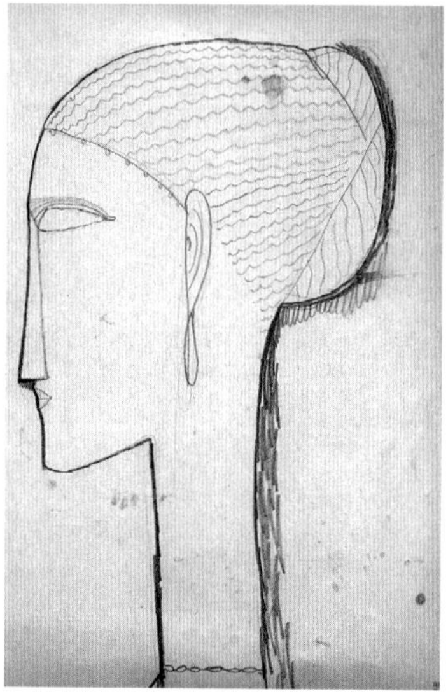

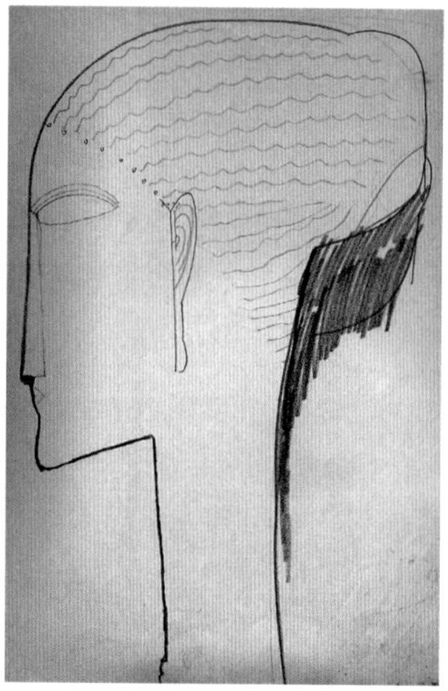

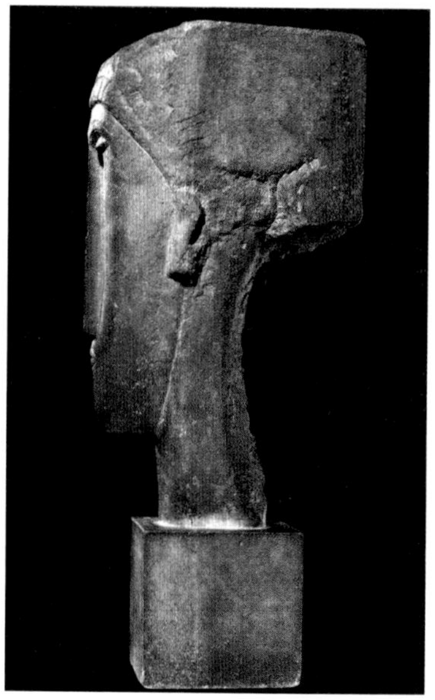

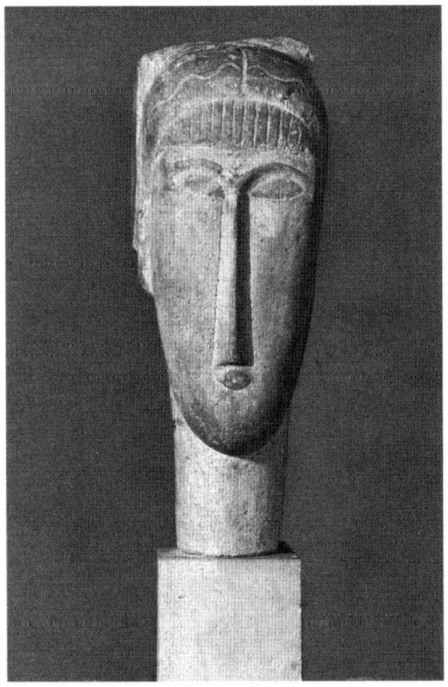

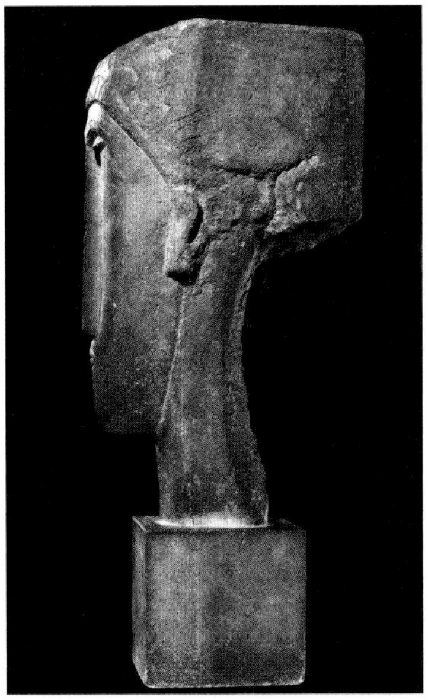

87. Amedeo Modigliani
Head, 1911-1912. Minneapolis,
The Minneapolis Institute of Arts.
Ceroni XVI.

88. Amedeo Modigliani
Head, 1911-1912.
Formerly Paris, Lévy collection.
Not in Ceroni (*Head* "A")

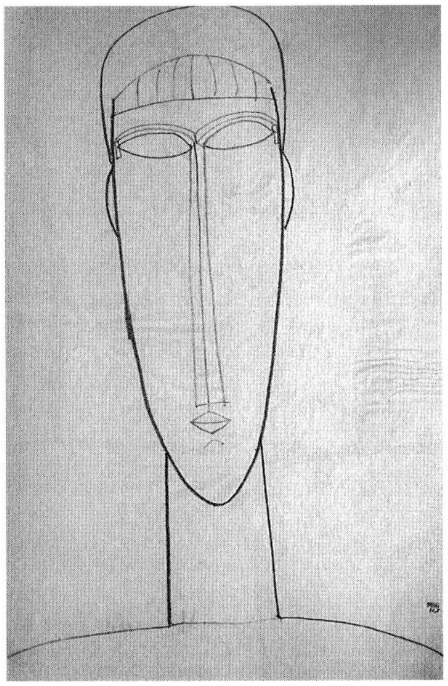

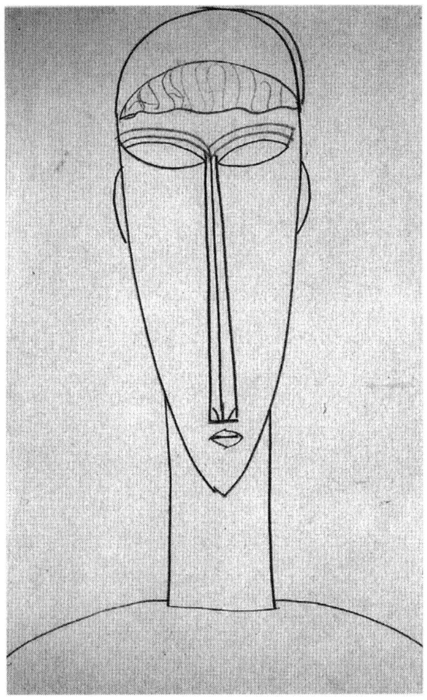

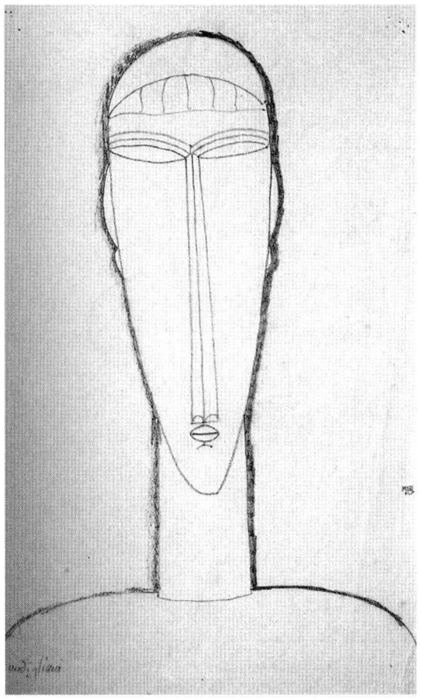

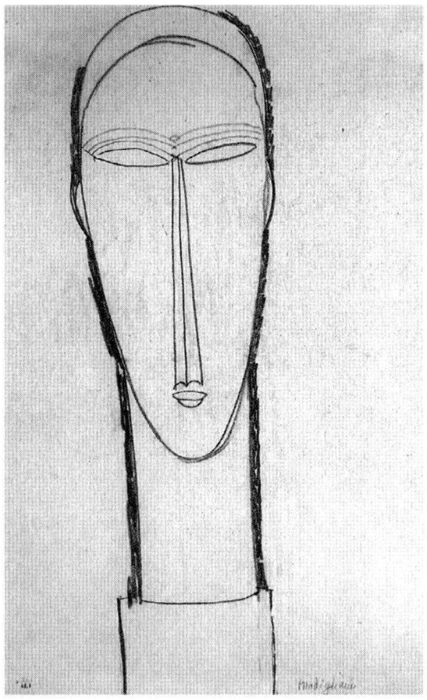

89. Amedeo Modigliani, *Study for Sculptural Bust*, 1911-1912, pencil on paper. Rouen, Musée des Beaux-Arts, Cabinet de dessins, donated by Blaise Alexandre

90. Amedeo Modigliani, *Study for Sculptural Bust*, 1911-1912, pencil on paper. Private collection

91. Amedeo Modigliani, *Study for Sculptural Bust*, 1911-1912, pencil on paper. Private collection

92. Amedeo Modigliani, *Study for Sculptural Head on Base*, 1911-1912, pencil on paper. Private collection

93. Anonymous photographer
Heads, 1911-1912 by Amedeo Modigliani (Ceroni XVI and *Head* "A"). Lisbon, Fundação Calouste Gulbenkian, Amadeo de Souza Cardoso Archive

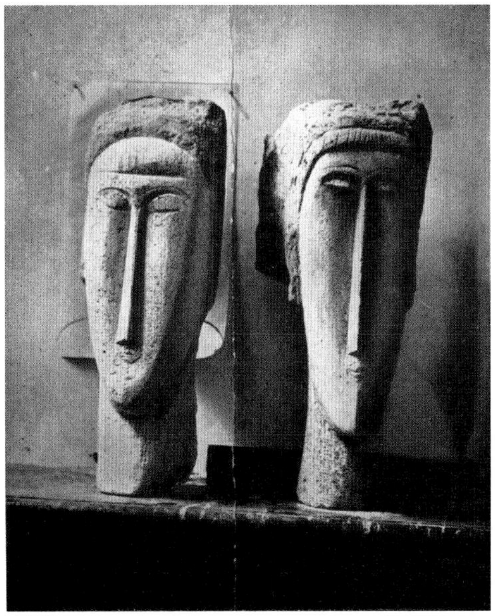

94. Amedeo Modigliani
Study for Sculptural Bust, 1911-1912, pencil on paper. Private collection

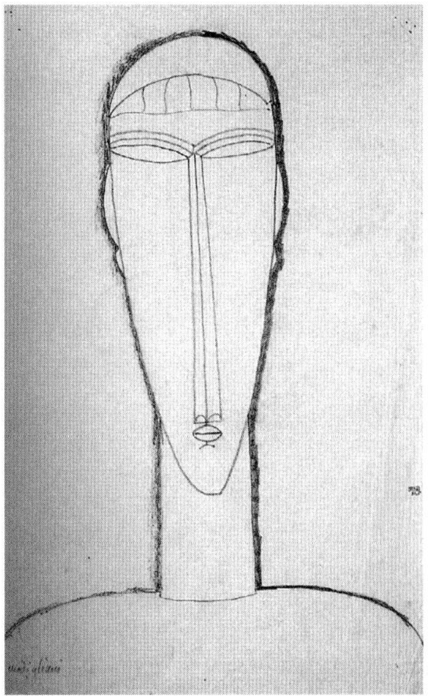

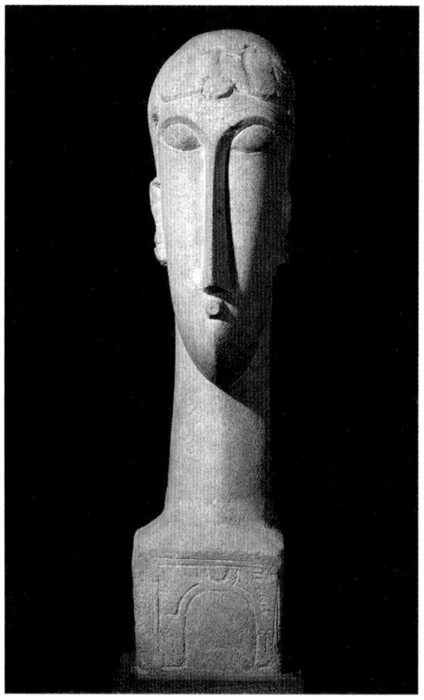

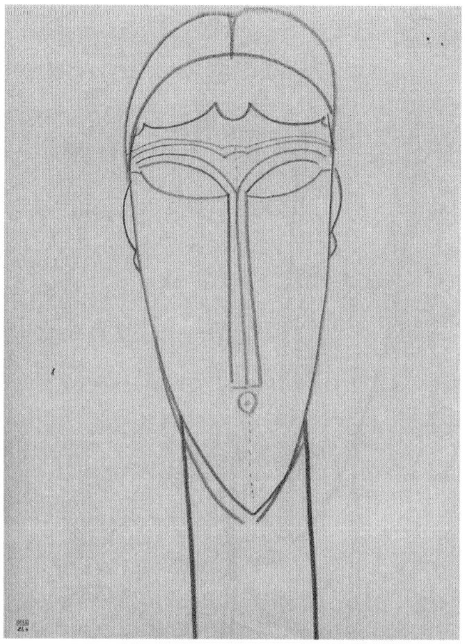

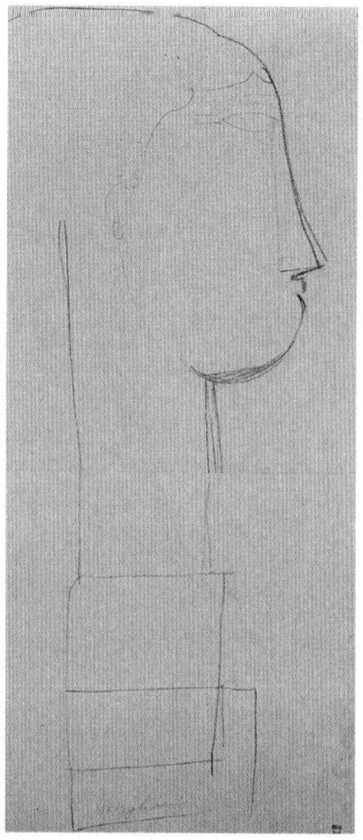

95. Amedeo Modigliani
Head, 1911-1912. Philadelphia, The Philadelphia Museum of Art. Ceroni XX

96. Amedeo Modigliani
Study for Sculptural Head, 1911-1912, pencil on paper. Private collection

97. Amedeo Modigliani
Study for Profile of Sculptural Head on Base, 1911-1912, charcoal on two sheets glued together. Private collection

120-126,[80] figs. **89-92**). In the photograph (fig. **93**) that shows, during the working phase, *Head* XVI and *Head* "A" next to each other, a drawn sheet of paper can clearly be seen hanging behind the sculpture on the left: it is possible to recognise a bust, the line of the shoulders and perhaps the top of the head. It could be identified in 126[81] (fig. **94**), the drawing that already establishes precise details of sculpture "A" (the double carved line of the eyebrows, the very long nose, the tapering of the chin, the lips) but maintains the solution for the hair of Ceroni XVI.
A frontal study of *Head* XX (fig. **95**) exists, without any afterthoughts, number 157[82] (fig. **96**), which shows it literally up to the point of the neck. We also have a study of this *Head* (139,[83] fig. **97**) with a particular solution for the base with an entablature: on the sheet that shows the head in profile Modigliani had glued another sheet where he experimented the elongation of the neck and added a base with two entablatures, one on top of the other. For those who reason on the genesis of the sculptural heads through the graphic studies that have survived, *Head* XX has the benefit of having an unmistakeable advantage, the fringe has a wavy motif against the forehead. In the other two heads that have forms and proportions similar to *Head* XX, this profile is nearly always straight or draws just a hint at a simple curve; when the profile is wavy (*Head* VI, with the clear central parting, *Heads* XVIII and XXIII) the shape of the head is very different to XX, so much so that there can be no confusion. The wavy motif was found by Modigliani developing the archaic theme of the round jewel hanging in the middle of the forehead (and the roundness carried on to the stone head): it can be seen well in the small frontal ink study No. 162[84] (fig. **98**); and its later development, the profile study – also in ink, No. 167[85] (fig. **99**). Both of these studies have a slight difference compared to *Head* XX (the trace of a single eyebrow); in the second one the solution of a mass of hair going to the back of the head is foreseen. However, the first one (No. 162) is the most interesting as the squared kind of paper and the ink mark make it very similar to another three (Nos. 164-166,[86] figs. **100-101**) that study the same head in profile (the jewelled pendant in the middle of the forehead is very evident) with the detail of the jutting out mass of hair, above which there is a geometric element, like an abacus: in No. 165 the motif of the eyebrows has doubled, as in the final stone *Head*. In another three drawings (159-161,[87] figs. **102-104**), identical in the size of the sheet (212 x 134 mm), for the kind of squared paper and the ink technique to number 162, Modigliani wrote the dates of 20th and 22nd August. In these three drawings Modigliani studied variants that are clearly related to

98. Amedeo Modigliani
Study for Sculptural Head,
1911-1912, ink on squared paper.
Private collection

99. Amedeo Modigliani
Study for Profile of Sculptural Head,
1911-1912, ink on squared paper.
Private collection

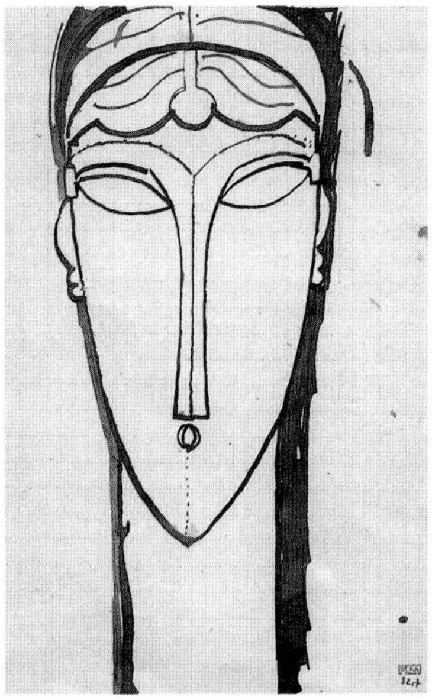

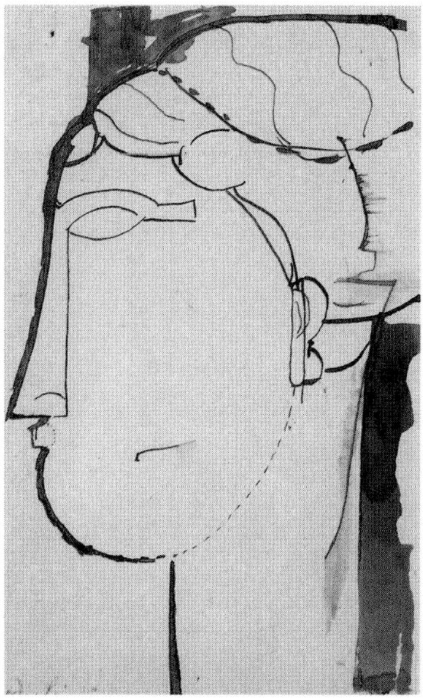

100. Amedeo Modigliani
Study for Profile of Two Sculptural Heads, 1911-1912, ink on squared paper. Rouen, Musée de Beaux-Arts, Cabinet de dessins, donated by Blaise Alexandre

101. Amedeo Modigliani, *Study for Profile of Sculptural Head*,
1911-1912, ink on squared paper.
Private collection

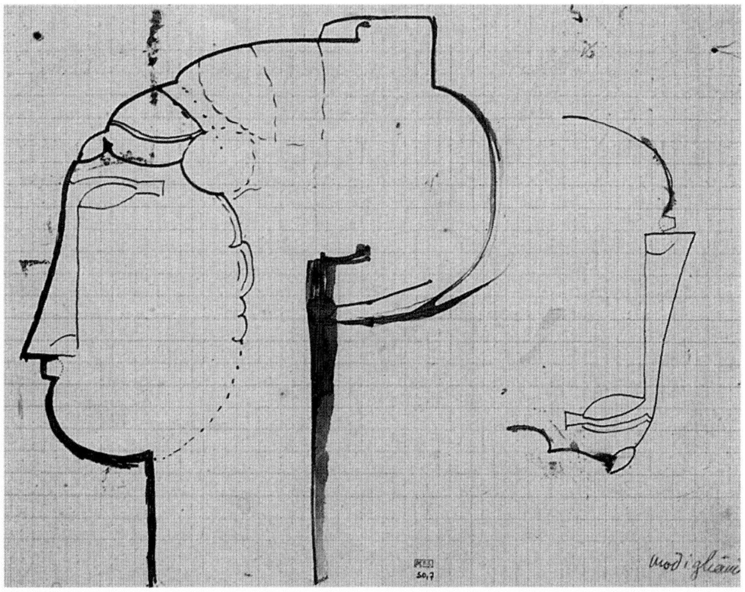

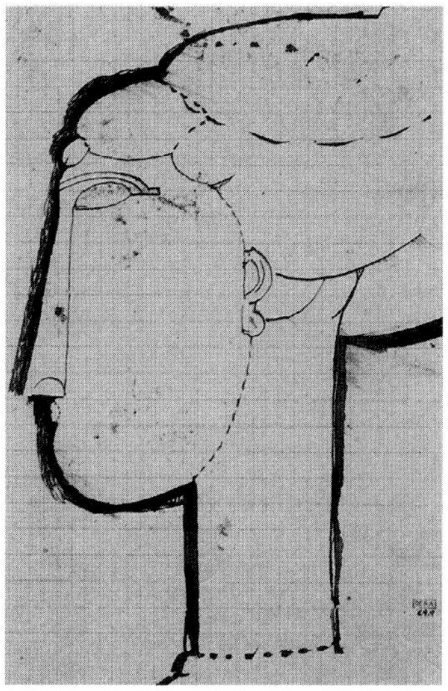

102. Amedeo Modigliani, *Study for Sculptural Head*, 20th August 1912,
ink on squared paper.
Private collection

103. Amedeo Modigliani, *Study for Sculptural Head*,
22nd August 1912, ink on squared paper. Private collection

104. Amedeo Modigliani
Head, 1911-1912.
Private collection. Ceroni XXII

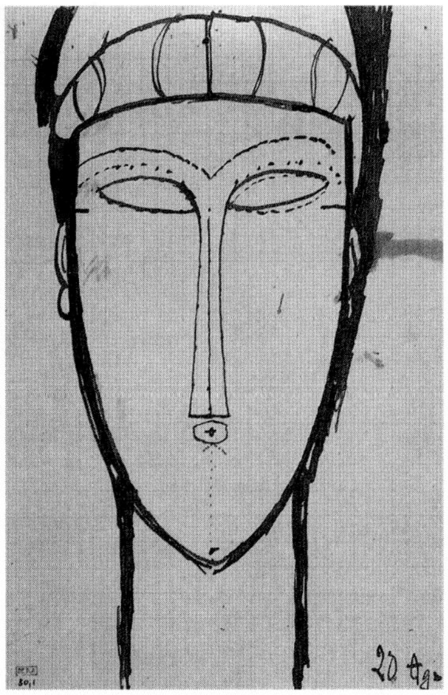

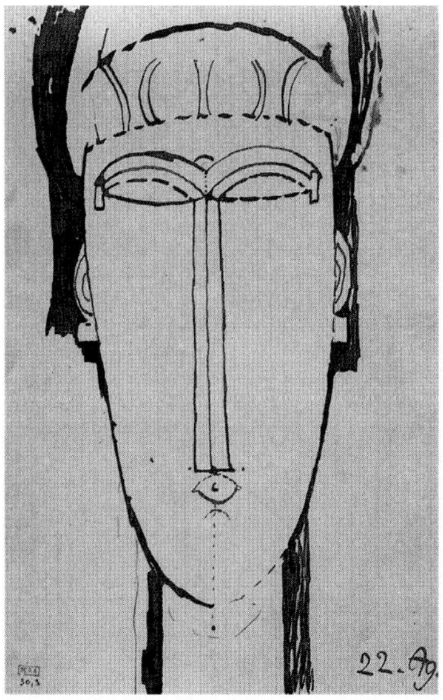

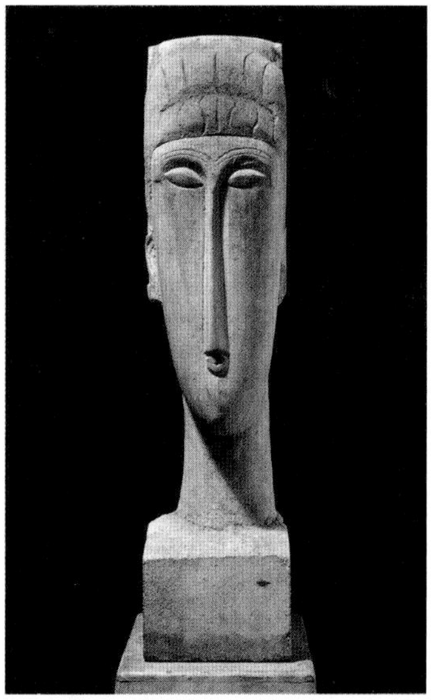

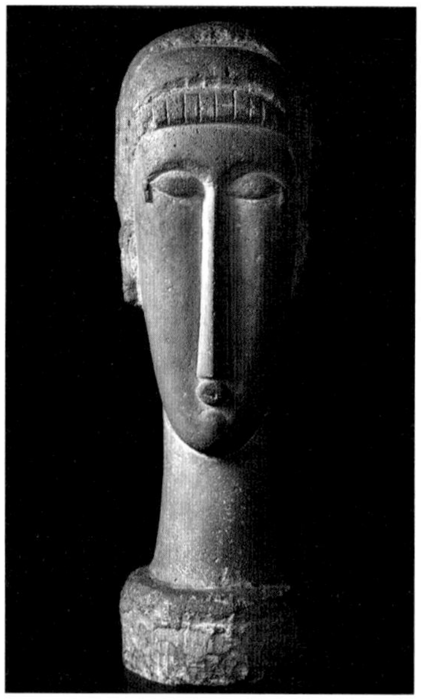

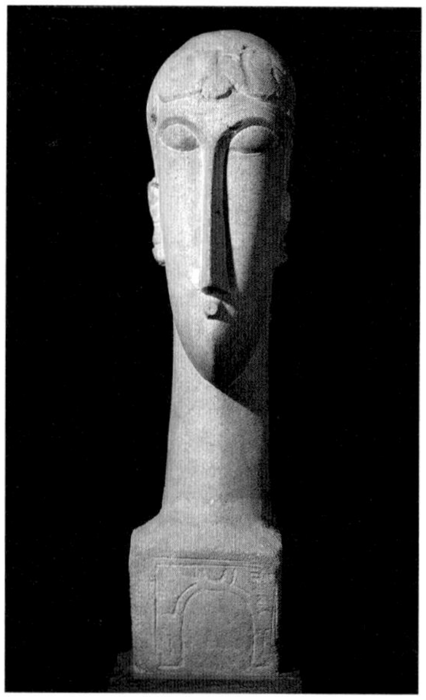

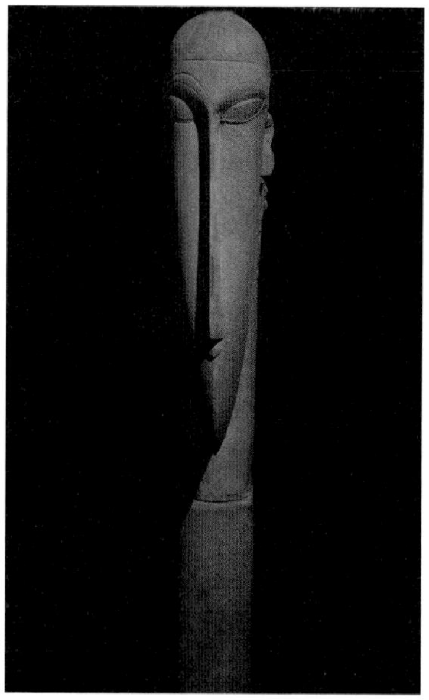

105. Amedeo Modigliani
Head, 1911-1912.
Merion, Pennsylvania, The Barnes Foundation. Ceroni XIX

106. Amedeo Modigliani
Head, 1911-1912.
Philadelphia, The Philadelphia Museum of Art. Ceroni XX

107. Amedeo Modigliani
Head, 1911-1913.
London, The Tate Gallery.
Ceroni XXIV

Head XXII (fig. **104**): the sickle-shaped motif is present in counterpart on the fringe; other analogies are the rounding of the chin, the oval shaped mouth, the elongated nose. At a certain point of the work Modigliani reached the joint of *Head* XIX (fig. **105**). Starting from this, in two different ways he found the solutions that led to one side of *Head* XX (fig. **106**, from which XXIV developed, fig. **107**: sheet No. 138[88] illustrates this passage perfectly); from the other (fig. **108**) to *Head* XXII (fig. **110**, its accurate study is the drawing 182[89] fig. **109**). From this latter sculpture a successful, very elegant deduction is *Head* XXI (fig. **112**), with its geometric tower of Egyptian hair, of which only a very preliminary study remains, No. 177[90] (fig. **111**): this shows how a well found solution has no need for too many elaborations on paper in order to be translated onto stone.
That Modigliani realised the excellence of the points that I have tried to reconstruct is evidenced by the documented presence, in the room at the Salon d'Automne 1912, of the Ceroni *Heads* XXII, XXI, "A" and XV: these were not a casual choice of his sculptural production that year but, as he wrote to his brother Umberto, a compact group of works that had been accepted.[91]
The sheets dated 21st and 24th March 1913 remain that (Nos. 169-171,[92] figs. **113-114**) create some problems in the sequence of the work on the sculptures, if we accept the authenticity of the date (the writing seems to reveal Modigliani's hand, with the refined, decorative italics, and the very closed "3"). They show heads-caryatids all rigorously frontal with a rounded face (or even oval widthways) that forms the body of a capital and the mass of hair becomes the base for a trabeation. If we accept March 1913 as the date they were carried out on then there is the reference to two of Modigliani's *Heads* (I and II, figs. **115-116**), left incomplete, that present an almost spherical face. Modigliani did not search for the motif of the capital in the stone, but he proposed the same short and linear nose, slightly upward slanting eyes, small heart-shaped mouth. These would close and not open the series of stone heads: the photograph of the artist in the courtyard of his studio working on *Head* I could be moved to 1913, perhaps after his return from Italy.
The drawings of sculptural heads were not only studies to focalise on the motifs to use in his work on stone; or *d'après* to set the achievements of a sculpture on paper, perhaps to use as a starting point for a new, different sculpture. They entered the sculptor's laboratory in a direct way, like projects that were to lead the work: and the size of most of the sheets, about two thirds compared to those for the heads in stone, is good evidence of this. The old photograph

108. Amedeo Modigliani
Head, 1911-1912.
Merion, Pennsylvania,
The Barnes Foundation.
Ceroni XIX

109. Amedeo Modigliani
Study for Sculptural Head, 1911-1912,
pencil on paper. Private collection

110. Amedeo Modigliani
Head, 1911-1912.
Private collection. Ceroni XXII

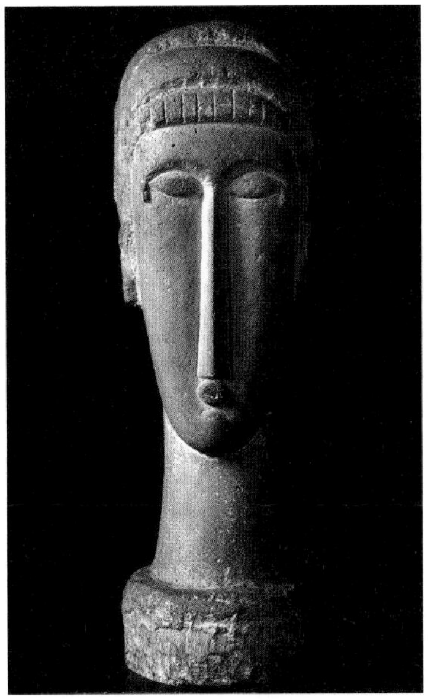

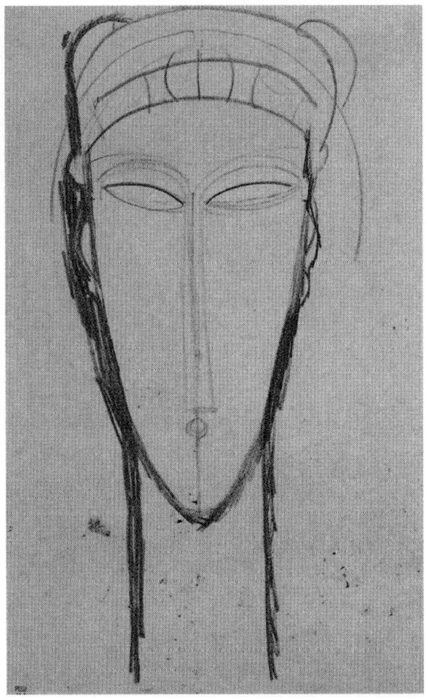

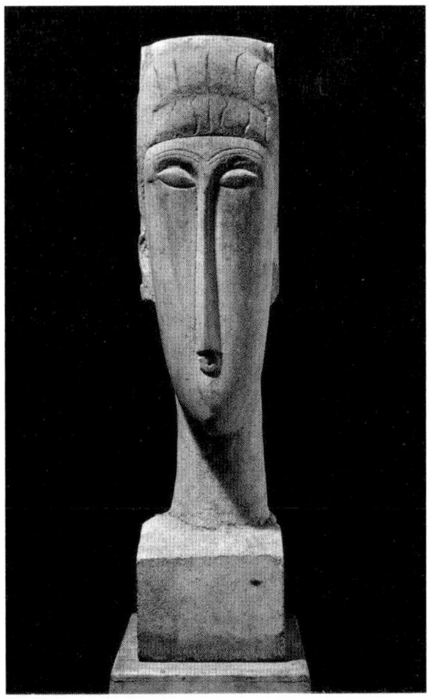

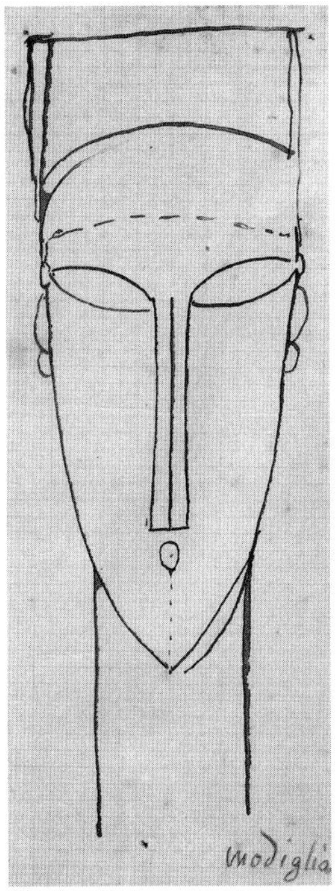

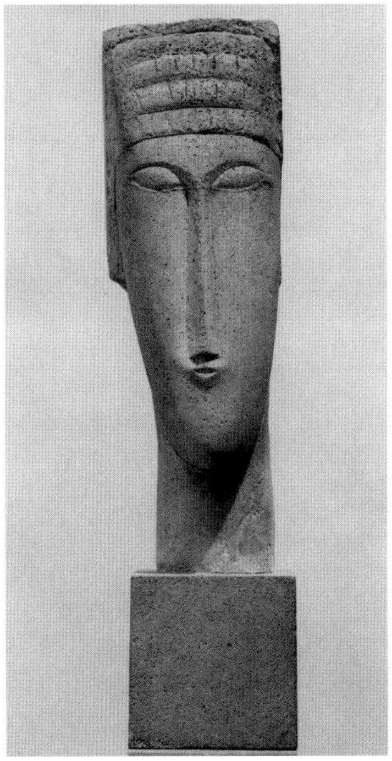

111. Amedeo Modigliani
Study for Sculptural Head, 1911-1912,
pencil on paper. Private collection

112. Amedeo Modigliani, *Head*, 1911-1912.
New York, Solomon Guggenheim Museum.
Ceroni XXI

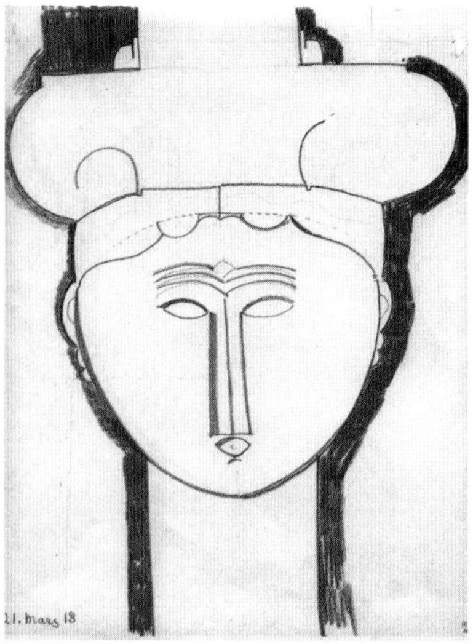

115. Amedeo Modigliani
Head, 1911-1913.
Gwendolyn Weiner
Collection. Ceroni I

116. Amedeo Modigliani
Head, 1911-1913.
Private collection. Ceroni II

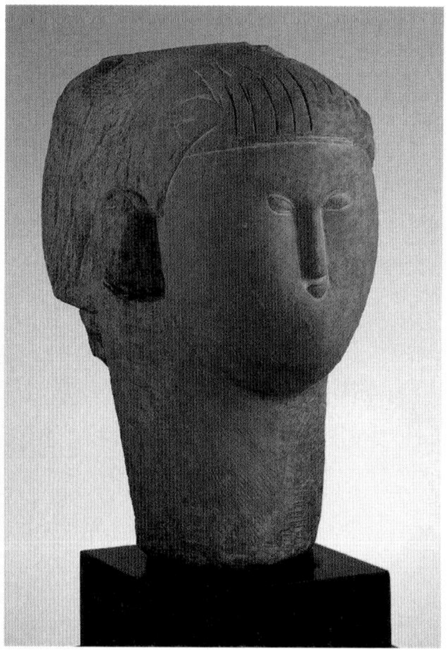

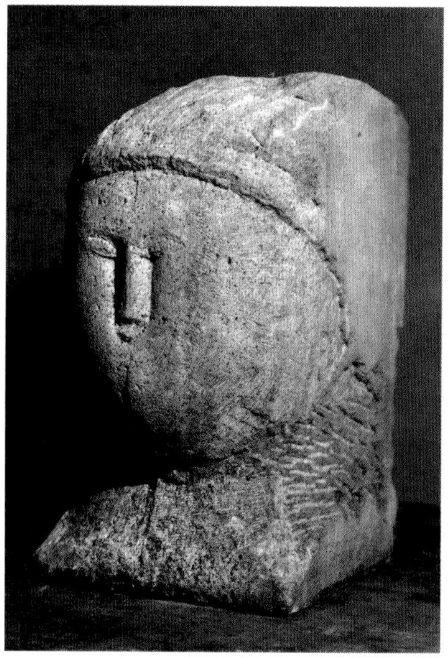

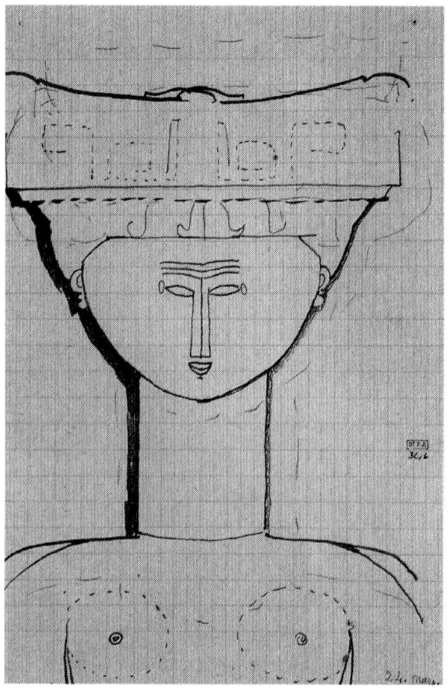

113. Amedeo Modigliani
Head-capital, 21st March 1913,
blue pencil on paper. Private collection

114. Amedeo Modigliani
Head-capital, 24th March [1913],
ink on squared paper. Private
collection

where we can see *Heads* XVI and "A" in his studio and while they were being worked shows behind them, as has been mentioned, a drawing fixed to the wall: this method is not very different to Joseph Bernard's "academic" one, in a famous photograph, he places the graphic study of a detail of *La Danse* (1910-12)[93] in front of the marble and carves the relief, carefully following the indications (also in chiaroscuro) contained in the drawing.

The Caryatids: Two Stones, a Lot of Studies on Paper and the Abandoning of Sculpture

It is, in fact, impossible to separate the heads from the caryatids. Many heads (some in stone, many on paper) were considered as details for the caryatids: sometimes, there is a geometric entablature on top of the hair to support a trabeation; furthermore, their visibility, which is always foreseen from the front or in profile, removes them from the statute of sculptural head in the traditional meaning (when the spectator can move around them and discover suggestive angles and chiaroscuro) but they are similar to a shape having an architectonic function. That both researches, heads and caryatids, came to light linked very closely together is well demonstrated by their first exhibitive appearance that, as we have seen, came about in parallel (with graphic studies or, more probably, in tempera) at the Indépendants in 1911.
Modigliani's two sculptural *Caryatids* that are known to us today (XI and XXV figs. **117-118**) are however so different from each other as to lead us to believe there were two phases of chronologically distinct research and there is general agreement in placing first the rigid volumes of the *Standing Caryatid* in the Museum of Canberra (XI), before the rounded planes of the *Kneeling Caryatid* at the Museum of Modern Art in New York

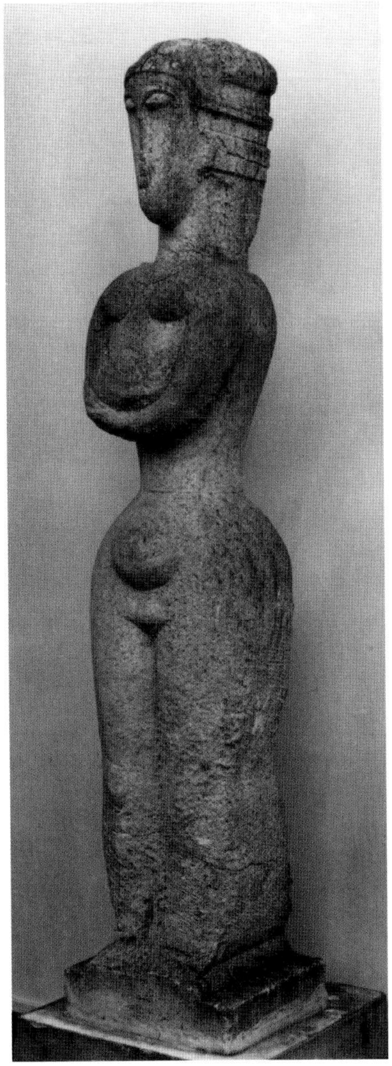

117. Amedeo Modigliani, *Caryatid*, 1912. Canberra, The National Gallery of Australia. Ceroni XI

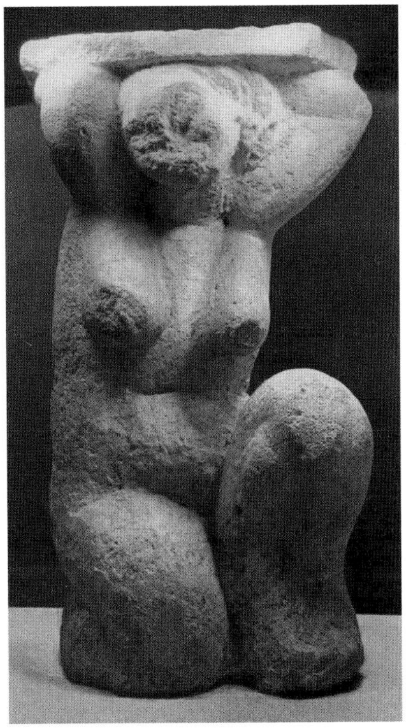

118. Amedeo Modigliani, *Caryatid*, 1913-1914. New York, The Museum of Modern Art. Ceroni XXV

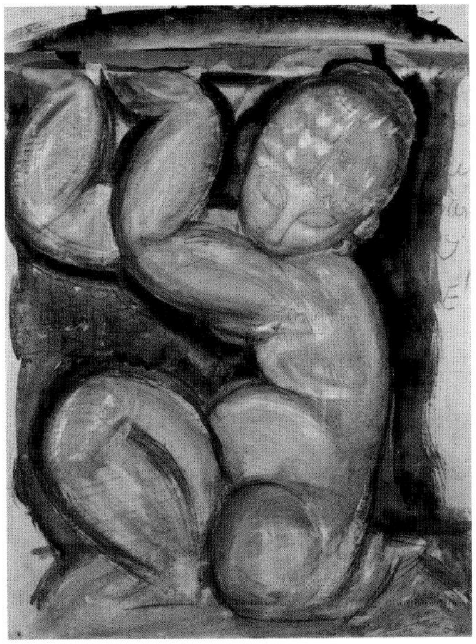

119. Amedeo Modigliani, *Caryatid*, 1913-1914, gouache and pencil on paper. Private collection

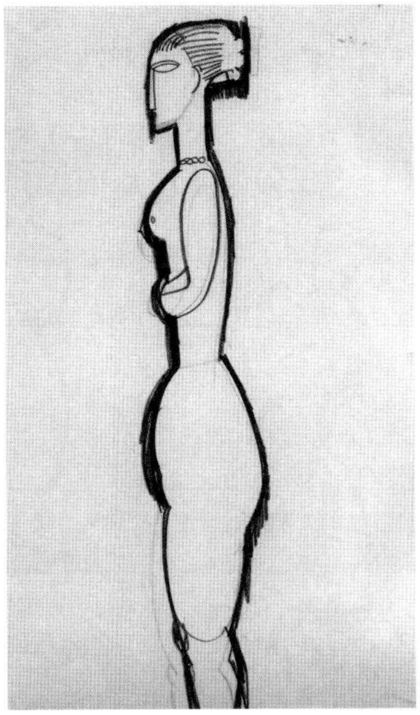

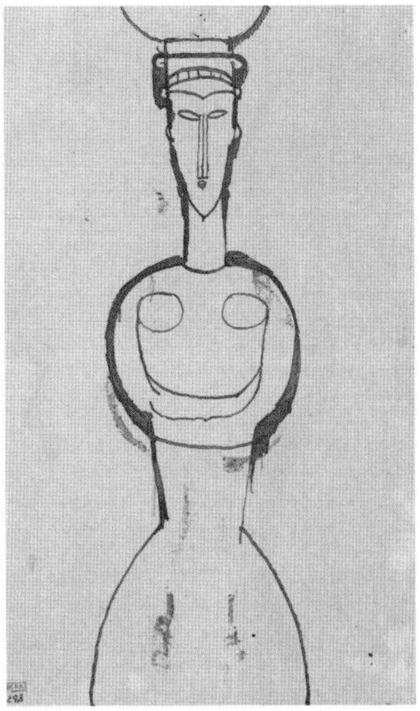

120. Amedeo Modigliani, *Study for Profile of Standing Sculptural Figure*, 1911-1912, pencil on paper. Private collection

121. Amedeo Modigliani, *Study for Sculptural Caryatid*, 1911-1912, ink on paper. Private collection

(XXV). There is some unquestionable evidence regarding this. If it is true, as Paul Alexandre claimed in his above mentioned letter to Ambrogio Ceroni in 1957, that the preparatory studies for the sculptures in his collection were entrusted to him by Modigliani before he left for Italy in April 1913, then all the drawings where the body of the caryatid is obtained by assembling rounded volumes (fig. **119**), in the shape of spindles fitted to one another and characterised by chiaroscuro should be after that date: none of these drawings are documented among those belonging to Alexandre. The pose and volumetric research of *Caryatid* XXV can be closely referred to this latter cycle of drawings and watercolours,[94] while other drawings from the Alexandre collection[95] (figs. **120-121**), (so before April 1913) evidence the very close link to *Caryatid* XI (fig. **117**). There is not much solid evidence for the dating of the caryatid studies. After the first two mentioned with the date 1911, there is a sheet dated and dedicated by Modigliani in

123. Amedeo Modigliani, *Kneeling Caryatid*, 1911-1912, pencil on paper. Rouen, Musée de Beaux-Arts, Cabinet de dessins, donated by Blaise Alexandre

124. Amedeo Modigliani *Caryatid*, 1911-1912. oil on canvas Düsseldorf, Kunstsammlung Nordrhein Westfalen

125. Amedeo Modigliani, *Study for Standing Figure with Arms Folded,* 1911-1912, pencil on paper. Private collection

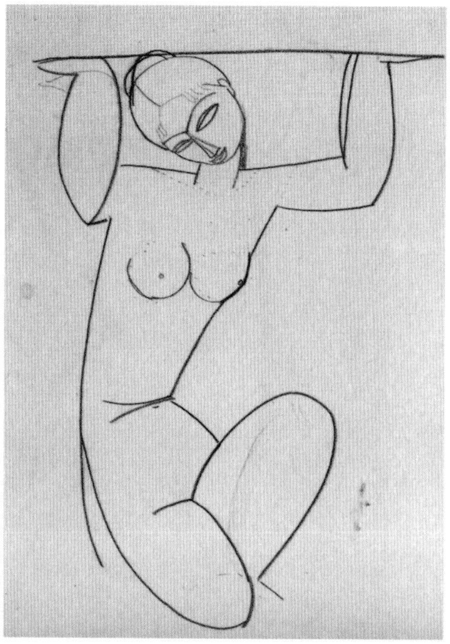

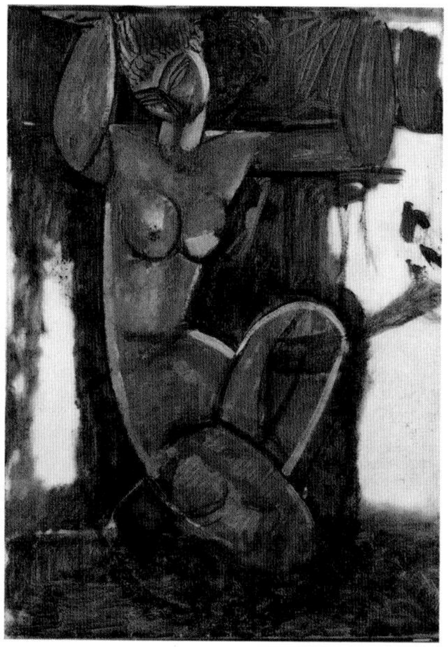

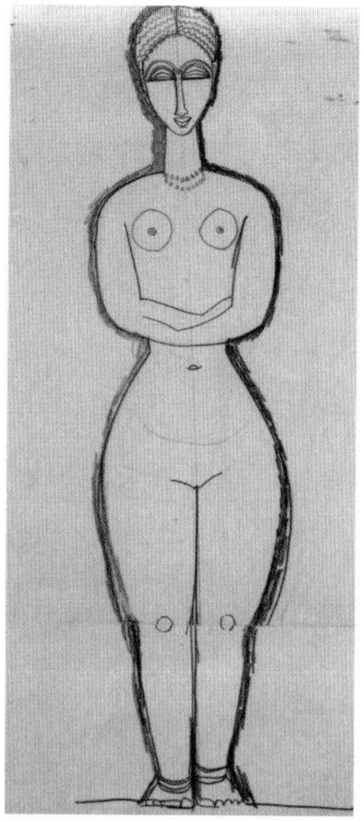

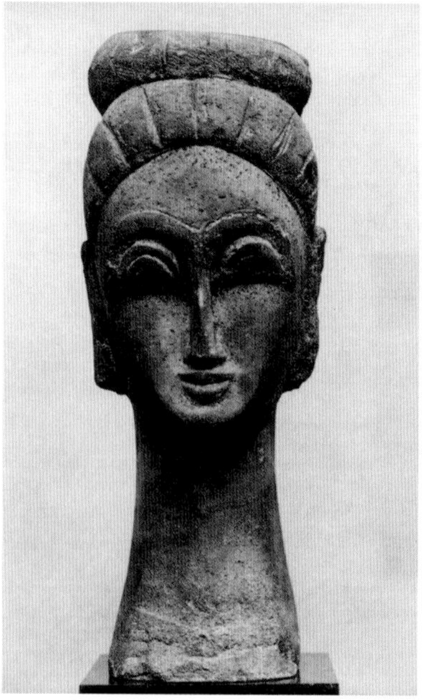

122. Amedeo Modigliani *Head*, 1911-1912. Küsnacht, Werner Marzbacher Collection. Ceroni IX

April 1912[96] and one, in September 1914.[97] It would seem, therefore, that the caryatid studies were chronologically ahead compared to the studies of heads and the style is a little removed from the typical geometric stiffening common to all the sculptural heads.
In substance, there are two overlapping areas between the drawings of heads and those of caryatids in the Paul Alexandre collection.
The studies that can be referred to *Head* IX (fig. **122**, with the perfect oval of the face, the not too elongated nose, a slightly smiling mouth, big eyes, often cut in lunette shape with a straight base) are used indifferently for painted caryatids[98] (fig. **124**), graphic caryatids (standing,[99] or kneeling,[100] fig. **123**) and, finally, for standing figures (fig. **125**) that are not exactly caryatids: in fact, they do not support an architrave with their heads or arms, instead they present arms either folded, or outstretched or raised to shoulder level.[101] The preparatory drawings for the more elongated heads (fig. **126**), with a longer straight nose (wavering between XIII and XIX) were instead used only for the standing caryatid type (fig. **127**), with folded arms[102]: this is the only figure that would be carried out in stone (XI), completed with a head very similar to XXII. However, these similarities give us few answers: only that Modigliani must have considered *Head* IX studied on paper (which is finished in the stone version) as an important achievement, to be inserted into a wider range of solutions and postures; and that the more elongated and abstract heads must have been thought of as a completion of more elongated, rigid caryatids, similar to columns. As the *Heads* exhibited at the Salon d'Automne 1912, among which XXII, were very probably carried out during the summer of the same year, it can be argued that *Caryatid* XI was carried out in that period of time, or shortly after: perhaps when Modigliani hoped, as we know from his letter to his brother, to exhibit a new group of sculptures at the Salon des Indépendants in March 1913. To be honest, there is a third similarity, that between the face of *Caryatid* XXV and the later graphic and watercolour caryatids that are usually collocated at the end of the path[103]: but the damage suffered by the stone which is in the MoMA today[104] does not allow a very certain link.
As many graphic studies and only two stones of the caryatids have survived (as we have seen they are very different from each other), the reasoning will concentrate above all on the range of research evidenced by the drawings.
The difficulty here in finding a guideline is almost insurmountable. In fact, drawings

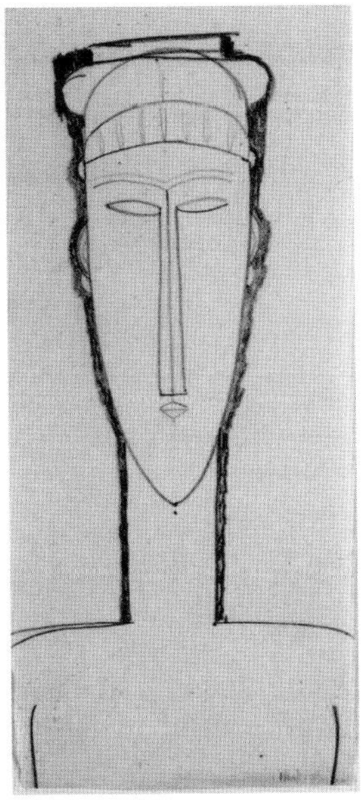

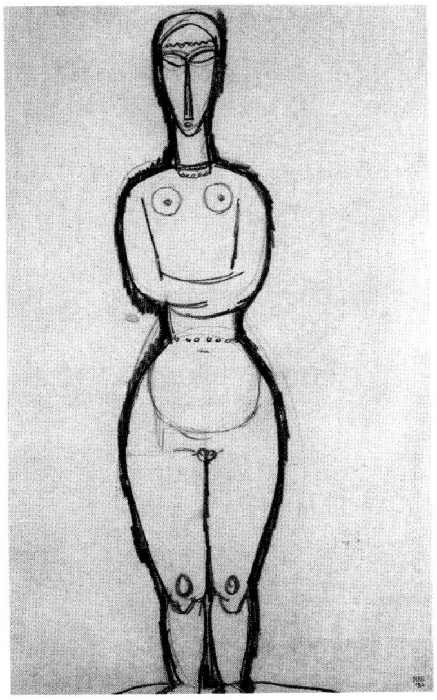

126. Amedeo Modigliani
Study for Sculptural Head,
1911-1912, blue pencil on paper.
Private collection

127. Amedeo Modigliani
Study for Sculptural Standing Caryatid,
1911-1912, ink on paper.
Private collection

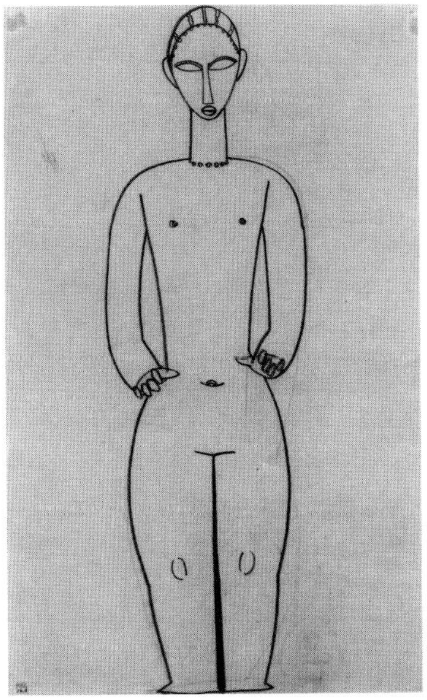

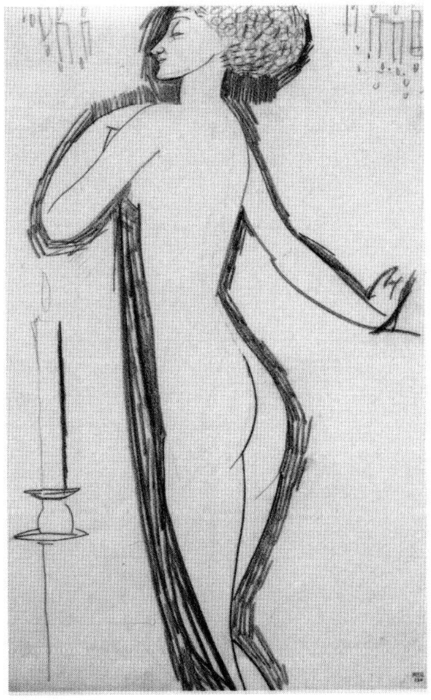

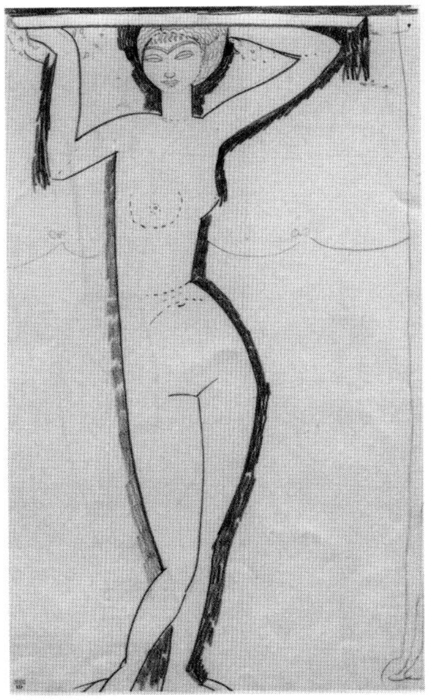

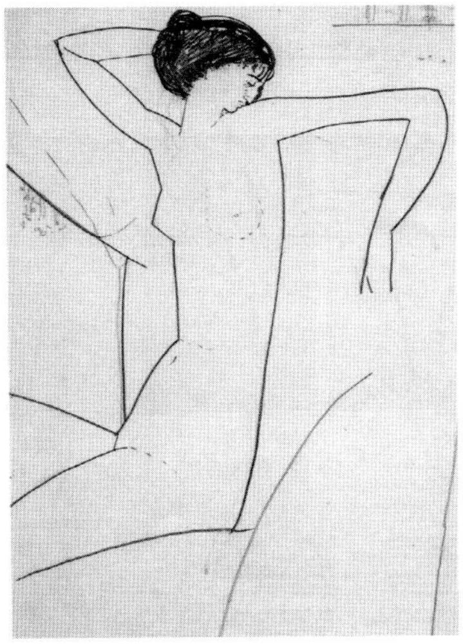

128. Amedeo Modigliani
Standing Hermaphrodite, 1911-1912,
pencil on paper. Private collection

129. Amedeo Modigliani
Standing Caryatid, 1911-1912,
pencil on paper. Private collection

130. Amedeo Modigliani
Standing Female Nude in an Internal,
1911. Private collection

131. Amedeo Modigliani
Anna Achmatova Nude, seated on a sofa, 1911. Private collection,
deposited in Rouen, Musée
de Beaux-Arts, Cabinet de dessins

with standing figures of an extraordinary, brutal Primitive synthesis (the one exhibited here at No. 46, fig. **128**) and others[105] of an almost affected elegance: in some of them (fig. **129**) the gestures carried out by the caryatids in supporting the trabeation seem more like a dance gesture than one produced by the effort of holding up a weight. Drawings like the latter descend, in the pose of the figures and even more in the style, from a series considered for a "theatrical" environment (fig. **130**): drapes, candles, curtains (that may allude to the stage curtain being raised or not) surround nude female figures, standing or kneeling, with a refined Liberty style grace. When

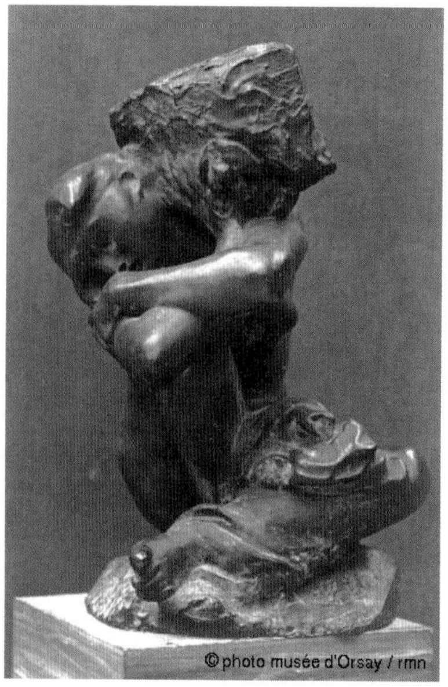

132. Auguste Rodin
Caryatid Holding a Stone, 1883.
Paris, Musée d'Orsay

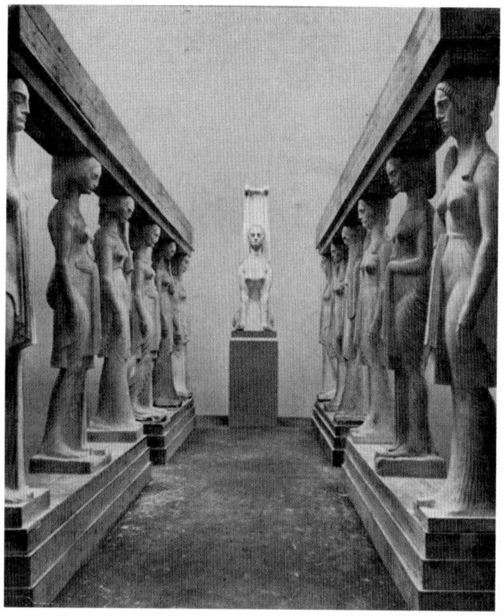

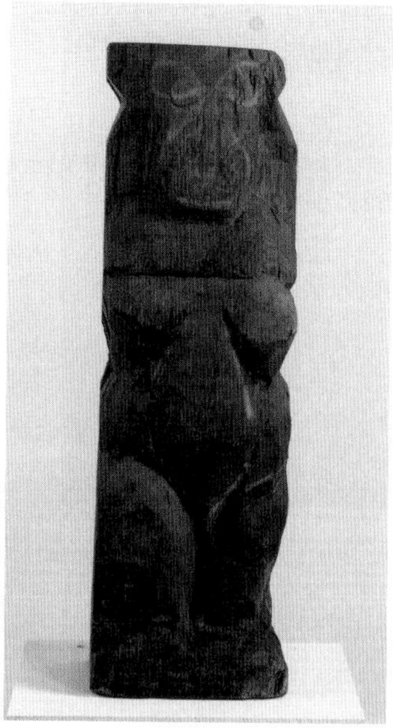

133. Ivan Meštrović
Temple Dedicated to the Heroes of Kosovo, arrangement at the Esposizione Internazionale of Rome, 1911, in *Die Kunst für Alle*, Munich, 1911-1912

134. Pablo Picasso
Caryatid Figure, 1907.
Paris, Musée Picasso

these figures are not kneeling, their filiation to the studies (fig. **131**) of Anna Achmatova posing nude in an armchair is very clear.[106] A survey has never been carried out to find a context for these mysterious figures, in the direction of sketches of scenes and drawings of contemporary theatrical costumes as documented in the news and entertainment magazines: leafing through *Comœdia Illustré*, from 1910 to 1912, sometimes holds some surprises, with similarities not only of style. In Paris a world of sophisticated, stylised exoticism with uncommitted decoration was in fashion, of which the scenery projects for the Russian Ballet are only one of the many possibilities. At a certain point Modigliani decided that for his hypothetical group of statues that he had in mind to carry out, the caryatid figures had to play a decisive part. The theme of the caryatid, in the culture of that time, was not unusual. Among the developments of the figures considered for *The Gates of Hell*, Rodin had been studying a *Caryatid Carrying a Stone* (fig. **132**) since 1883, intertwining the two plastic themes of compression and torsion in ways that must have appealed to Modigliani: it was sent to the Salon d'Automne in 1909, in bronze, bought by the State and immediately exhibited at the Musée du Luxembourg.[107] However, also the new architectonic sense which was pleasing to the post-Rodin generation had made the caryatid an important theme. I do not know if Aristide Maillol's event was already known, during his visit to Greece in 1908 he was so enthused by the caryatids of the Erechtheum, for the balance between the effort and elegance, that the guardians of the Acropolis had to hold him back from climbing up to kiss them.[108] Modigliani cannot have missed the two *Caryatids* that Ivan Meštrović exhibited at the Salon d'Automne in 1909[109]; certainly his memory was strengthened by the discussions that his *Temple* dedicated to the Heroes of Kosovo (fig. **133**) had aroused when a part of it was exhibited at the Esposizione Internazionale in Rome in 1911,[110] Modigliani must have been fascinated by something in the function of those figures, admonishing in their repetitiveness and their archaic imperturbability.[111] Caryatids were also invading the more radically Primitivist and Modernist research. Brancusi, tied to Modigliani by a close friendship, had hewed (but never finished and exhibited) two Assyrian style caryatids that today are used at the MoMA, as bases for *Maiastra*.[112] Also Picasso had given the figure of a woman the attitude of a caryatid, roughly carved in wood (fig. **134**) that was an explicit homage to the expressive brutality of tribal art[113]. In these last two examples showing the figure as a caryatid means reducing it to its purely plastic function: referring to the solid, stone

135. Amedeo Modigliani
Standing Nude Figure Interior, 1911-1912, pencil on paper. Rouen, Musée de Beaux-Arts, Cabinet de dessins, donated by Blaise Alexandre

136. Egyptian Art, *Statuette of Nude Woman*, III intermediate period, XI-VII century BC. Paris, Musée du Louvre, Department of Egyptian Antiquity

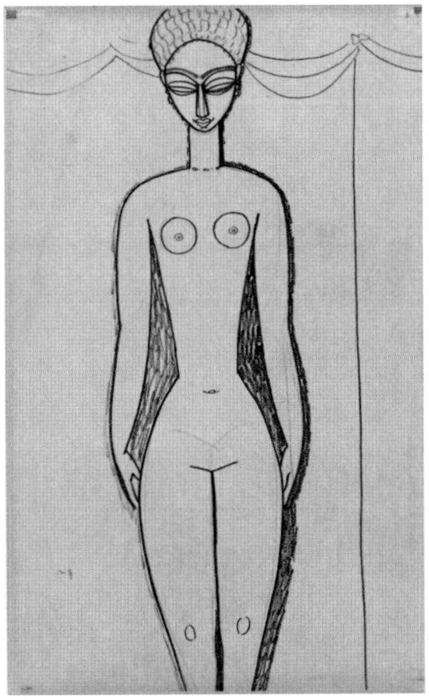

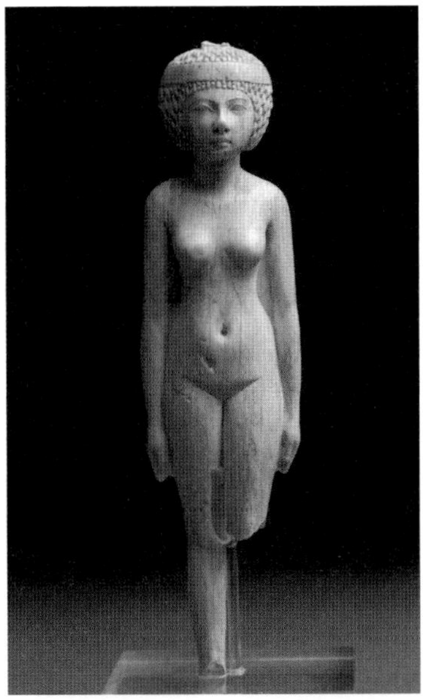

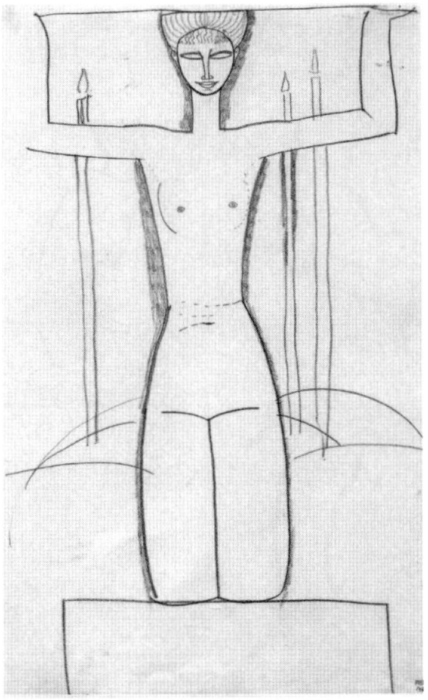

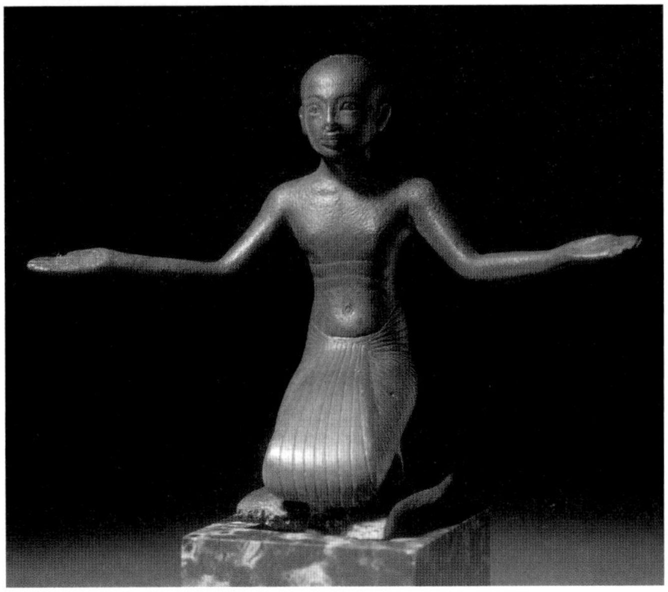

137. Amedeo Modigliani
Kneeling Caryatid, 1911-1912, pencil on paper. Private collection

138. Egyptian Art, *Priest Praying*, 19th dynasty, XIII-XII century BC. Paris, Musée du Louvre, Department of Egyptian Antiquity

or wood, that they emerged from and the architectonic function of resistance they were subjected to.
In the moment that Modigliani began studying the caryatids on paper, his sources intertwined in a surprisingly free way. Through these drawings he had to take into account, for the first time, those formal themes of modernity that, in a vast range of fashions that were not always coherent with one another, were passing through the studios of the Parisian artists around 1910. It was apparently the Egyptian collection in the Louvre that also here offered the most captivating solutions; and the reflections on the subject by Edith Balas[114] and Alessandro

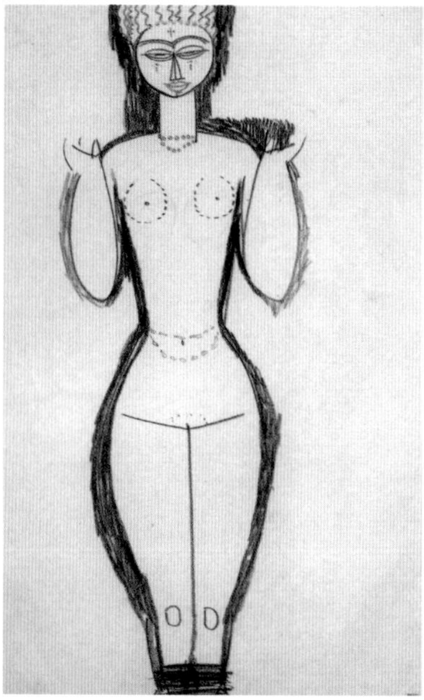

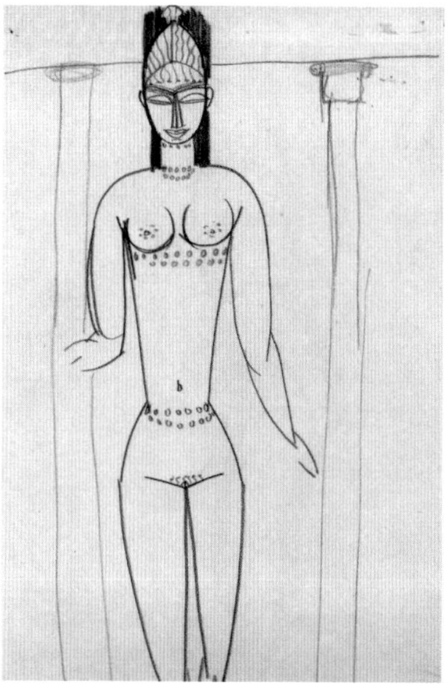

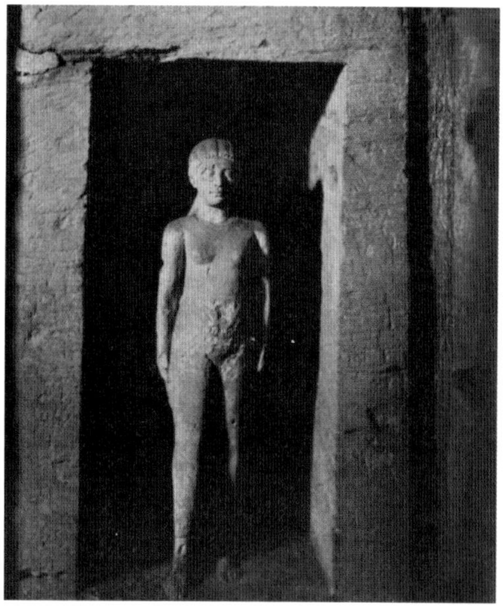

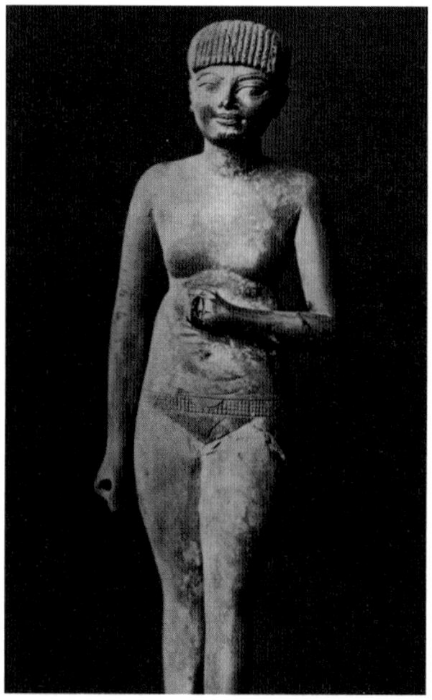

139. Amedeo Modigliani
Standing Nude Figure, 1911-1912, pencil on paper. Rouen, Musée de Beaux-Arts, Cabinet de dessins, donated by Blaise Alexandre

140. Egyptian Art, *Statuette of Young Girl*. Paris, Musée du Louvre, Department of Egyptian Antiquities

141. Amedeo Modigliani
Figure Standing in front of a Colonnade [1911-1912], pencil on paper. Private collection

142. The Excavations of Kom-El-Chougafa, in *L'Art Décoratif*, 1911

Del Puppo in this catalogue have given very convincing testimony. I will try to propose here some other comparisons. Modigliani had admired that archaic, inexpressive intentness in the standing statuettes (figs. **135-136**); or, in other statuettes, he had studied the kneeling pose, starting with the profile to set off either the torsion of the bust towards the spectator or the underlining of the mysteriously ritual gesture of the raised arms (figs. **137-138**); or, yet again, he had made his own the decorative motifs of the thin belts that encircled the waist of the nude female figure, transforming them into mysterious tattoos (figs. **139-140**). It must not be excluded that, to collocate the statues in an architectonic niche that housed them or in front of a colonnade,[115] Modigliani might have been impressed by a photograph of recent archaeological digs of Egyptian underground tombs (figs. **141-142**), with the figures hieratically silhouetted against the entrance to the pronaos, photographs published with some prominence even in magazines that followed modern art like *L'Art Décortif*.[116] However, for some solutions that he experimented in the same series of drawings, Modigliani contaminated that Egyptian model with others. In the offering gesture of a female caryatid with her arms outstretched (fig. **143**), he looked at Piombino's Apollo in bronze from the Louvre (fig. **144**), the same one that Maillol referred to for his *Pomona* which was so much admired at the Salon d'Automne of 1910. The kneeling caryatids (fig. **145**) refer, without too much concealment to the Hellenistic kneeling Venus from the Vatican Museum (fig. **146**) or the Galleria di Firenze.[117]
It is a world, that of Modigliani's caryatids drawings, archaic and hieratic, proudly anti-modern. However, also conscious that every Primitivist synthesis, or every archaeological allusion, had to be translated into stylised elegance, very pleasing to modern tastes. The styles of the ancients had to undergo a knowledgeable reduction to the rules of modern linear harmony.
This research, at a certain point, was interrupted, this could coincide with the abandoning of the project for a decorative ensemble where head and caryatids co-existed. After his return from Italy in June 1913, Modigliani started working again on an important series of pencil and watercolour studies of caryatids (figs. **147-148**) that had very little to do with those taken into consideration so far here and that are mainly the development of a single posture, not by chance the most elegant among those he had studied the year before: the kneeling female figure in profile and turned towards the observer, with both arms raised either joined behind the head or

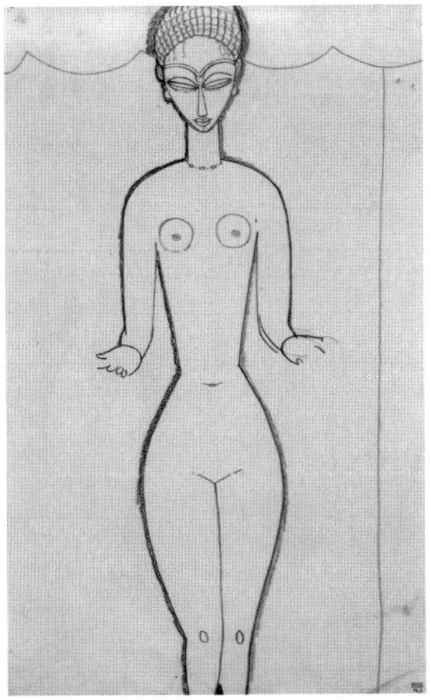

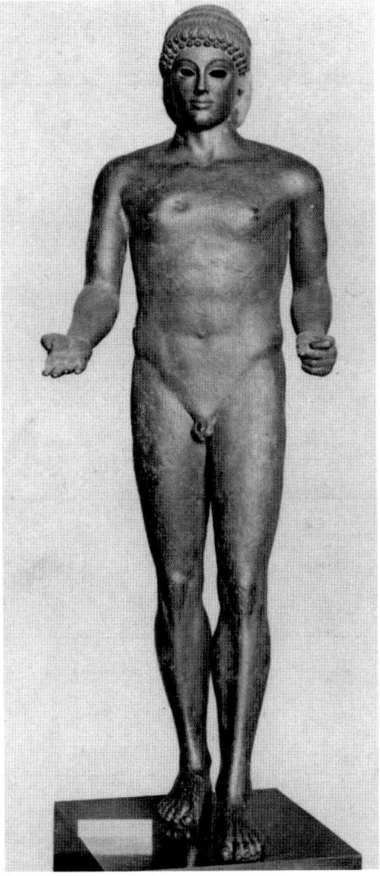

143. Amedeo Modigliani
Standing Nude Figure, with Offering Gesture, 1911-1912, pencil on paper. Private collection

144. Roman art, *Apollo of Piombino*, I century BC. Paris, Musée du Louvre (photo Munich, Bruckmann 1888)

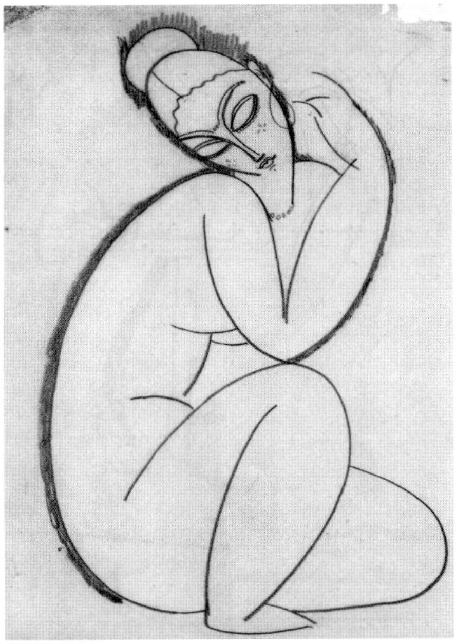

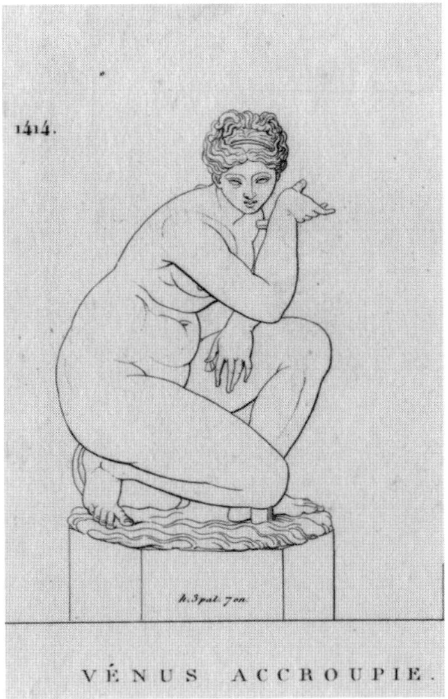

145. Amedeo Modigliani
Kneeling Nude Figure, 1911-1912, pencil on paper. Private collection

146. *Crouching Venus*, in S. Reinach, *Répertoire de la Statuaire Greque et Romaine*, Paris 1906

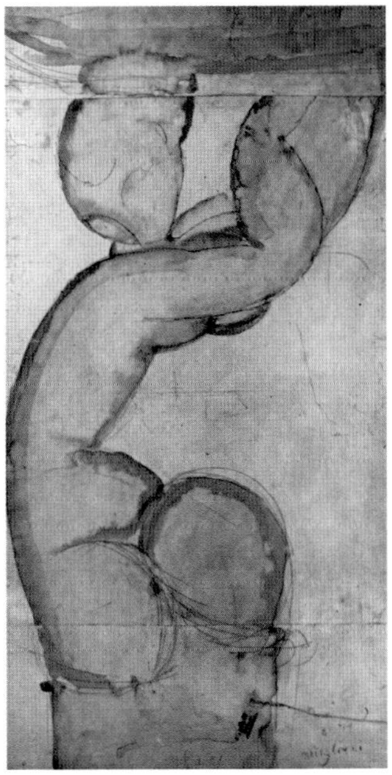

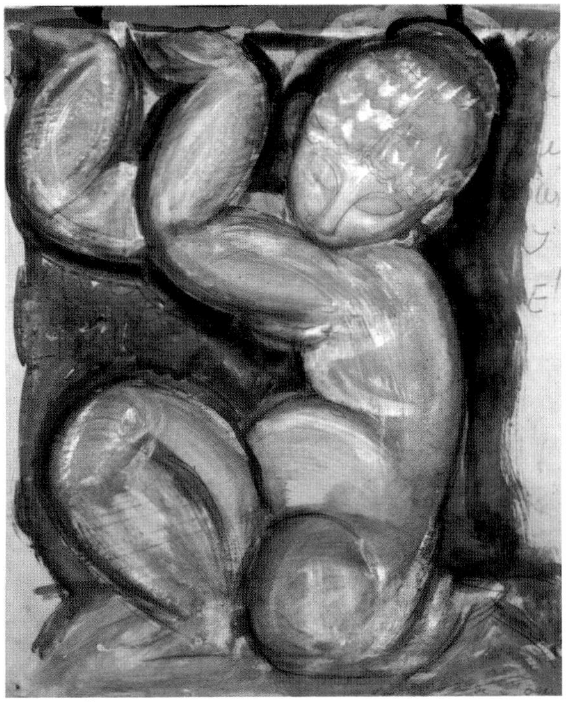

147. Amedeo Modigliani, *Caryatid*, 1913-1914, water colour and pencil on paper. Private collection

148. Amedeo Modigliani, *Caryatid (Audacious)*, 1913-14, gouache and pencil on paper. West Palm Beach, Florida, The Norton Gallery of Art

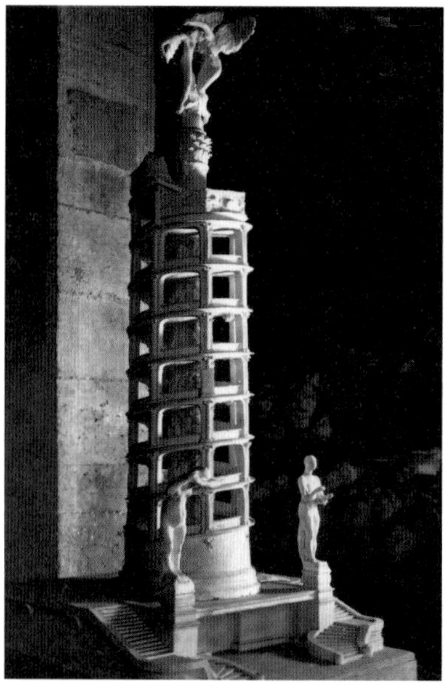

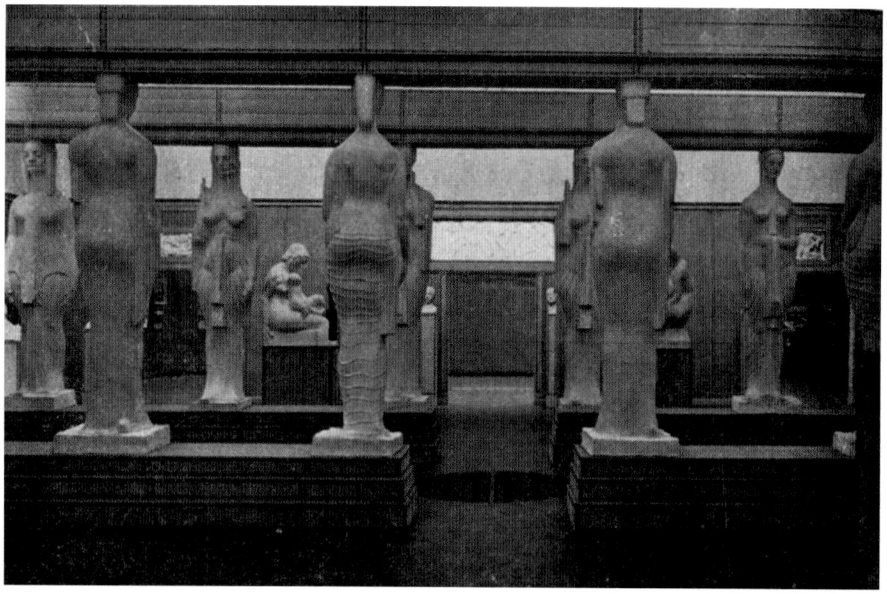

149. Auguste Rodin, *The Tower of Work*, in *Vita d'Arte*, Siena, 1908

150. Ivan Meštrović *Temple Dedicated to the Heroes of Kosovo*, arrangement at the Vienna Secession in 1910, in *Emporium*, Bergamo, 1910

outstretched, in the gesture of supporting a trabeation or vase.
For Modigliani this cycle of studies constituted his farewell to sculpture and some final words must be spent on it. When, at the beginning of 1911, Modigliani thought about sculptural themes (the *Head* and *Caryatid* at the Indépendants of that year) he was in fact, placing himself in no man's land. On one hand there was the sculpture of the sculptors. Some years before, they had established the necessity for a new Classic order, in a range of possibilities extended from the pre-Phidian archaism of Bourdelle to Nadelman's Neoclassic and decorative elegance. They were, with some weariness, discovering the poetry of direct carving, in a clear anti-Rodin function. On the other hand there was the more experimental sculpture, that of the painters. The wood and stone carved by Derain and Picasso, the figures modelled by Matisse were the results of a research aimed at reformulating the grammar of the figure in the light of the new rules of "non-cultured" art, pre-cultural or exotic as it may have been.
Modigliani placed himself in no man's land between these two positions; he did so thinking he could unite sculpture with architecture, even though an artificial architecture like that "temple of love" that he hoped to carry out according to Paul Guillaume's recollections.[118] That of a sculptor who planned and carried out a total work of art where sculpture and architecture could live together was one of the myths of his time: Rodin's *Tower of Labour* (fig. **149**, celebrated, among others, by an Italian, Ricciotto Canudo, in an Italian magazine *Vita d'Arte*, in 1908[119]) or the temple to the Serbian heroes of Kosovo by Ivan Meštrović (fig. **150**) re-launched with some strength the theme of a superior unity of style between the statue and the architectonic frame, a theme of antique and noble tradition (Michelangelo and the tomb of Giulio II or the New Sacristy). In those days there were many who said that sculpture should be renewed through intersection with architecture: in an important review at the Salon d'Automne in 1912 where Modigliani's heads were exhibited, Fernand Roches claimed for the sculptors, "la possibilité d'architecturerer leur travaux"; in his thoughts, "seule l'architecture sculpturale leur [the sculptors] permettra d'exalter les formes par le jeu de leurs groupements et dans des proportions qu'elle commande."[120]
Modigliani thought about an ancient temple populated by sculptures, obsessing in their hieratic quality, lack of expression and above all repetitiveness of a module with minimum variations. However, he did not conclude the project: it was too ambitious due to the time

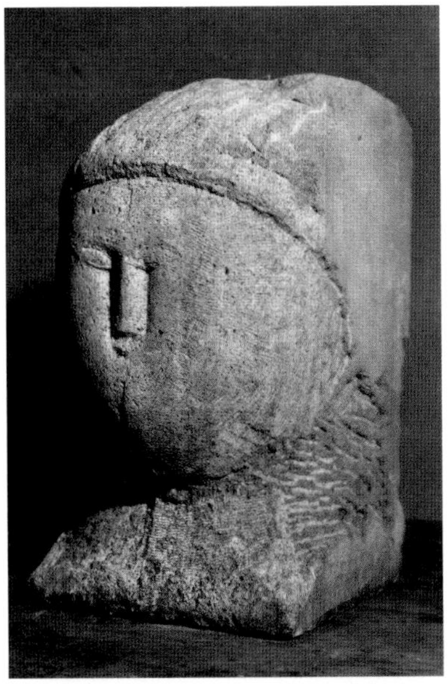

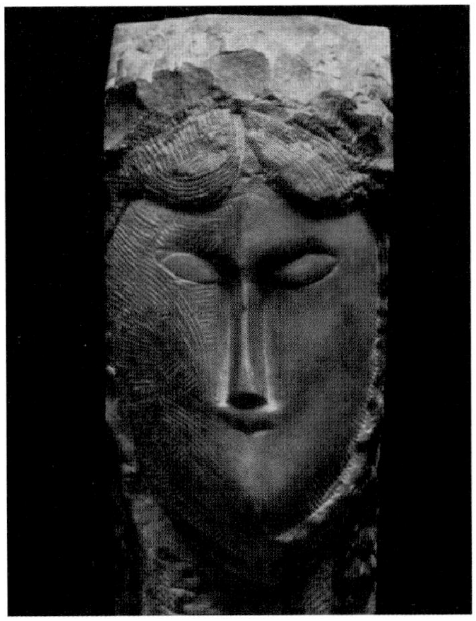

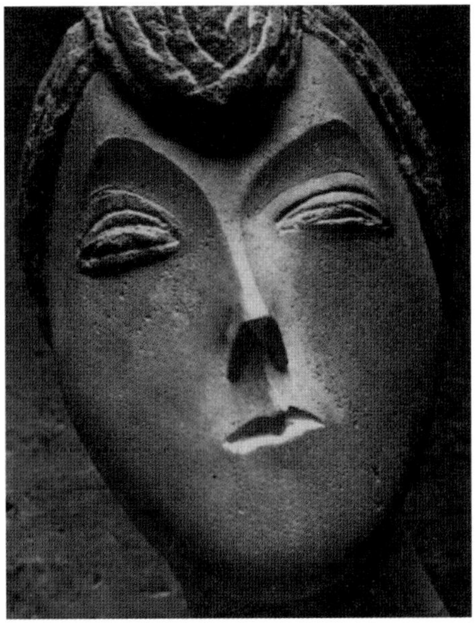

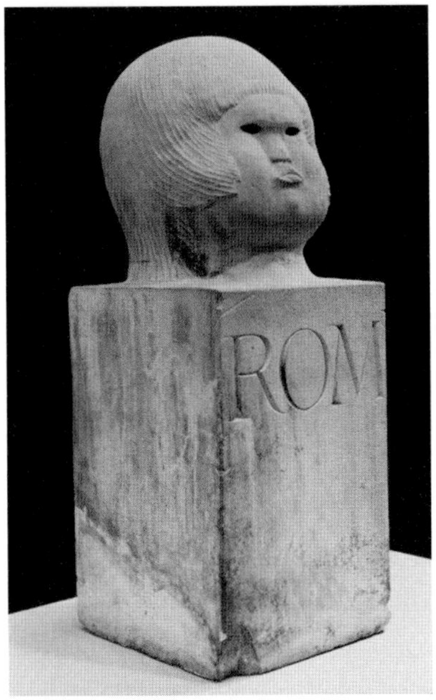

151. Amedeo Modigliani
Head, 1911-1913.
Private collection. Ceroni II

152. Jacob Epstein
Rom (Head of Romilly John), 1910.
Cardiff, National Museum of Wales

153. Amedeo Modigliani
Head, 1911-1912.
Villeneuve d'Ascq, Musée d'Art Moderne. Ceroni VI

154. Constantin Brancusi
Portrait of Baroness R.F., 1909.
This work has been lost

needed and the costs. Furthermore he was suffering from tuberculosis which did not permit him to breath in the dust that was produced by working on stone for long periods of time. Together with the project of "temple of love", he in fact, abandoned sculpture.

Besides his health reasons, I believe there were two causes for this abandonment. The first, inside Modigliani's thoughts, is that the distance from the sources (that fine line between the allusion of a style and re-transcribing it in a superior elegance), one of the artist's real obsessions, is more difficult to reach in sculpture than in painting. Sculpture obliges the declaring of one's debts more openly to that huge catalogue of proposals that are museums, and the Parisian ones in particular (Louvre, Musée de Cluny, Musée des Monuments Français, Musée Guimet, Musée Etnographique). A deformation, a linear emphasis, a decorative accentuation directly recall the sources they refer to. Through painting, and the pictorial portrait in particular, Modigliani was able to absorb in an intricate mixture the most varied models (Italian XIV and XV century, International Mannerism, even Ingres) and render them in a personal way that is seductive and perfectly recognisable as his.

The second reason could be the interpretation that Modigliani, around 1913, gave to the sculptural research of his time. Up to then he had been able to move around learnedly within his contemporaries' range of stylistic models. Comparing his *Head* II (fig. **151**) to Jacob Epstein's *Romilly John* (1910, fig. **152**), or his *Head* VI (fig. **153**) to Brancusi's now lost *Baronne R. F.* (1909, fig. **154**) or, even, his *Caryatid* XXV (fig. **155**) to Henry Gaudier-Brzeska's *Sepulchral Figure* (1913, fig. **156**) means collocating Modigliani within a system of visual inter-culture that appropriated archaic or variedly museum-like themes and translated them into modern styles. From 1913 onwards, however, more radical choices were imposed on sculpture in Paris. The main example came from his friend Brancusi: his Egyptian or ancient-Oriental passion that had made him realise, at the end of the previous decade, a work of sophisticated allusion to sources like *Wisdom of the Earth* in Bucharest (fig. **157**) or the *Ancient Figure* today in Chicago (fig. **158**) was making way for a new attitude: the search for a pure volumetric abstraction, as can be seen in *Maiastra* (fig. **159**), in *Muse* and *Mademoiselle Pogany* (fig. **160**) and even more so in his drawings (fig. **161**). Modigliani did not want to follow him down this path.

In this sense, it is necessary to consider the impact on Modigliani of the exhibition of the Futurist sculptor Umberto Boccioni at the Galerie La Boëtie in June 1913. Modigliani, who felt the value of the assertion of Italianism in Paris very strongly, on his

155. Amedeo Modigliani
Caryatid, 1913-1914.
New York, The Museum of Modern Art. Ceroni XXV

156. Henry Gaudier-Brzeska
Sepulchral Figure, 1913.
London, Tate Gallery

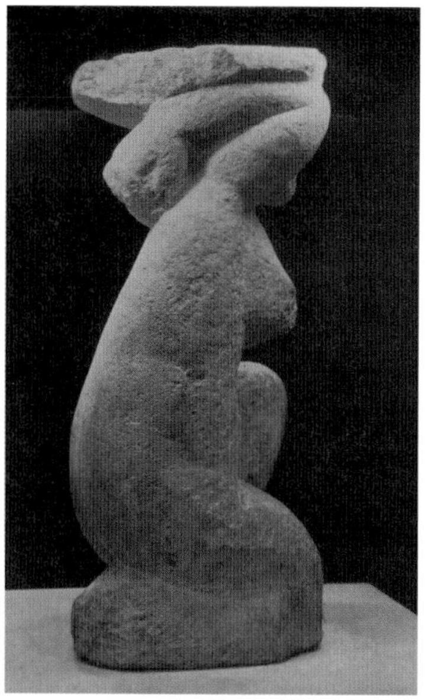

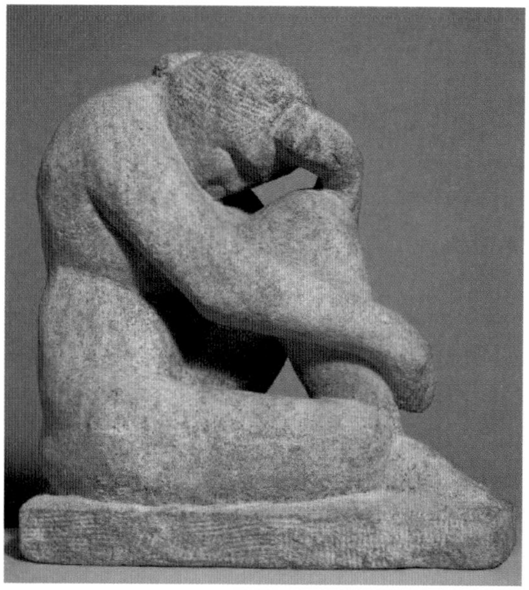

157. Constantin Brancusi
The Wisdom of the Earth, 1908.
Bucharest, Muzeul National de Art al României

158. Constantin Brancusi
Ancient Figure, 1908.
Chicago, The Art Institute of Chicago, Ada Turnbull Hertle Fund

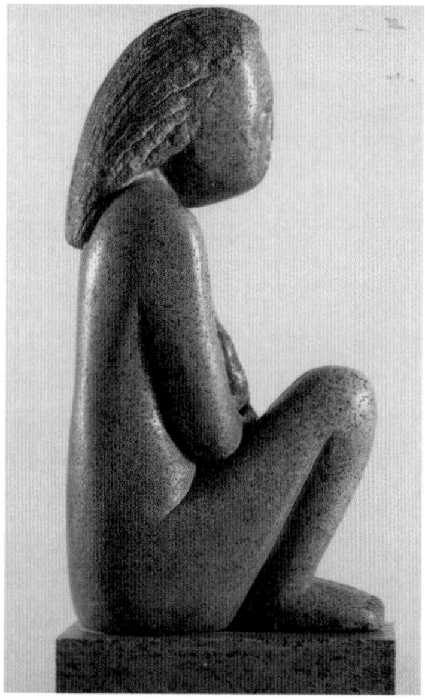

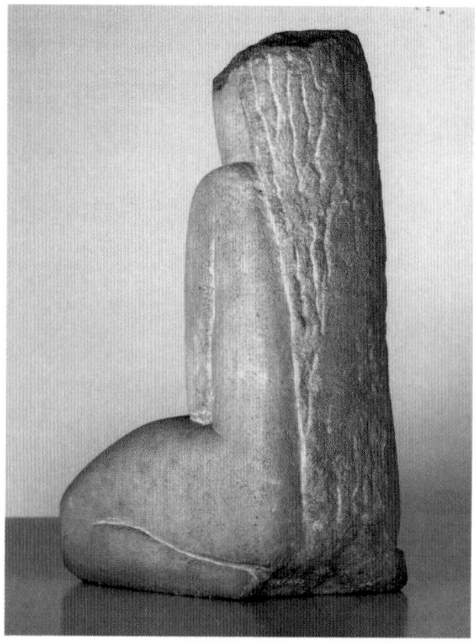

159. Constantin Brancusi
Maïastra, 1912, silver salt print.
Paris, Centre Georges Pompidou, Musée National d'art moderne

160. Constantin Brancusi
Mademoiselle Pogany [I], 1912, silver salt print.
Paris, Centre Georges Pompidou, Musée National d'art moderne

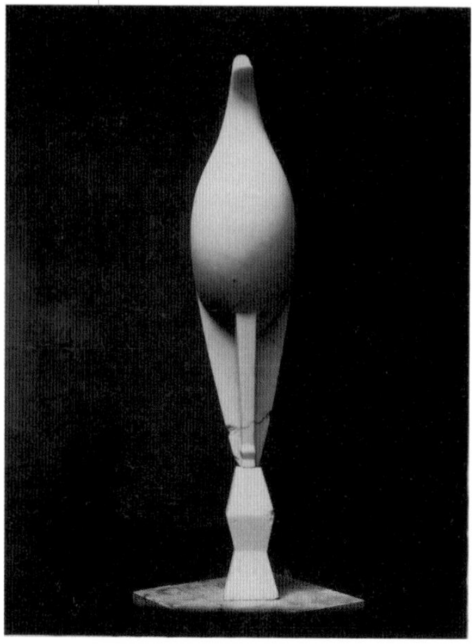

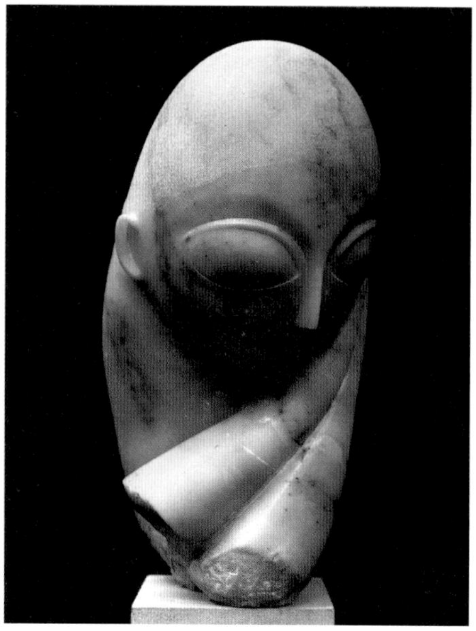

161. Constantin Brancusi
Study for The First Step, 1913, pencil and charcoal on paper. Washington DC, Hirshhorn Museum and Sculpture Garden

162. Amedeo Modigliani
Kneeling Caryatid, 1913-1914, pencil and gouache on paper. Private collection

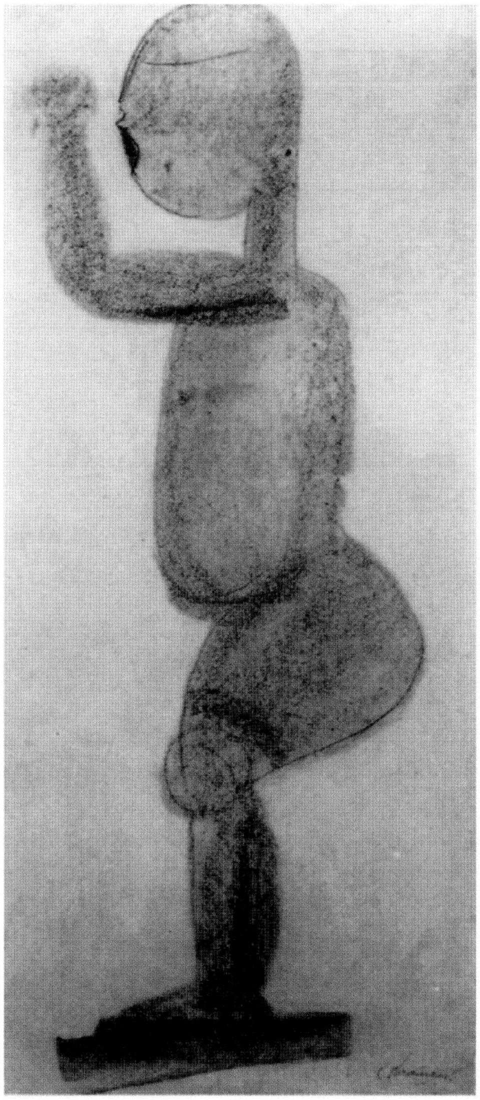

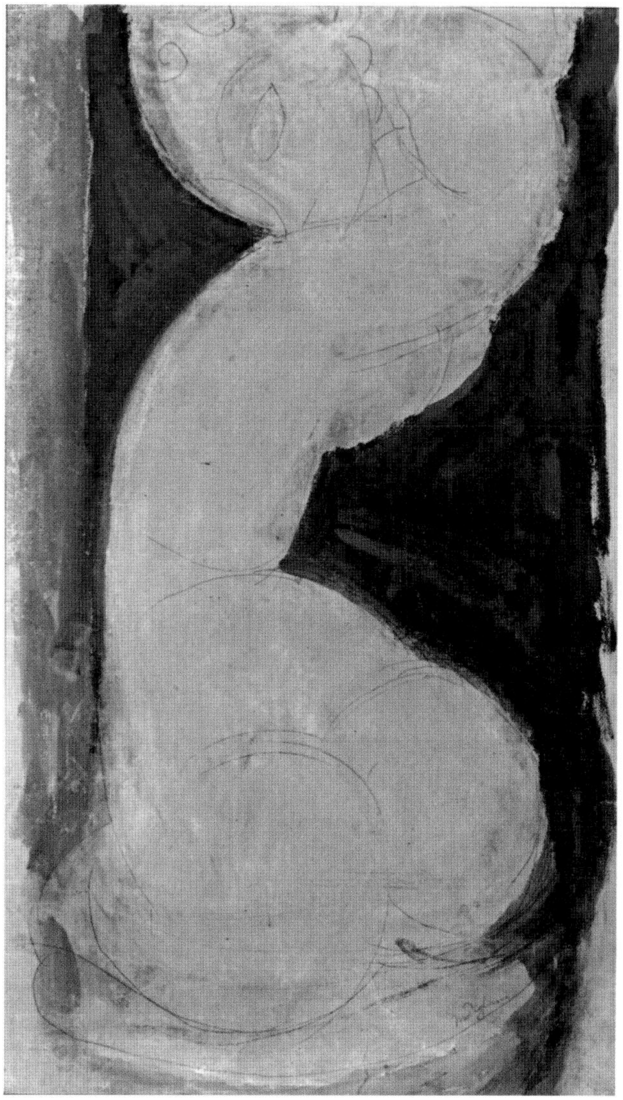

return from Italy certainly visited the rooms with Boccioni's plasters and drawings. Boccioni's way of composing bodies, especially on paper, by means of ellipsoids, could not have left him with indifference: and beyond the destructive proclamations contained in his *Manifesto tecnico della scultura futurista*, Boccioni practised a linear elegance that was strangely seductive. Perhaps Modigliani found, starting off from Boccioni's drawings, an urge to research, in drawings and above all in watercolours of caryatids, purer forms (simple solids grafted on to one another), volumes with a clearer plastic evidence, able to express an idea of torsion and tension in space. However, he realised that for this aim Boccioni's sculpture was more suitable and advanced than his.
The last caryatids carried out by Modigliani in watercolour (fig. **162**) cannot be explained as being preparatory to stone XXV, but more like an autonomous research: for linear harmonies in the direction of plastic rarefaction and arabesque flatness. Their result would not be sculptural: as François Carco acknowledged for the first time, already in 1919,[121] we would see their elaboration in the painted nudes in 1917.

1 Paris 1912, Nos. 1211-1217
2 Ceroni 1965, No. XV, p. 25, figs 70-71
3 Wayne 2002, p. 61.
4 I owe the knowledge about the photocopy of this photograph to Kenneth Wayne, it was pointed out by him in Wayne 2002, pp. 62 and 194, note 65.
5 Letter from Constantin Brancusi to Paul Alexandre sent 4th March 1911: "Mon cher docteur C'est demain Dimanche que Modigliani ouvre son exposition. Je joint (sic) la cartte (sic) qu (sic) il vous envoy (sic). Bien cordialement a (sic) vous. C. Brancusi", in Alexandre 1993, p. 100. Modigliani's calling card was with the letter giving his residence as 14, Cité Falguière.
6 Ferreira 1995, p. 73; today the originals are kept in the Amadeo de Souza Cardoso Archive, at the Fundação Calouste Gulbenkian, Lisbon.
7 Modigliani 1958, after p. 48, Nos 15-18.
8 Paris 1911, Nos. 6655-6656.
9 Alexandre 1993, No. 44, fig. 104.
10 Ferreira 1995, p. 80. Today the caryatid belongs to a Portuguese private collection.
11 Letter from Amedeo Modigliani to his brother Umberto Modigliani, undated, published in Modigliani 1958, p. 62, then in Guastalla 2006, p. 65. The letter was accompanied by the drawing of a sculptural head, here at cat. 70, and on p. 143.
12 Alexandre 1993, Nos. 168-169, figs. 258, 259; dated "24 mars".
13 Alexandre 1993, p. 237: these are the drawings at Nos. 159-161, figs. 179-181, dated "20 ag" and "22 ag".
14 Letter from Modigliani to Paul Alexandre sent from Livorno on 23rd June 1913, in Alexandre 1993, pp. 104-105.
15 Letter from Modigliani to Paul Alexandre sent from Lucca on 13th June 1913, in Alexandre 1993, p. 106. I am not certain that I understand the meaning of "petits moreceaux de marbre en *eclaireurs*": perhaps in the military use of "explorers", that is forerunners, small examples of the marble that Modigliani was thinking of using, certainly not "in the shape of an endoscope, " as in the (involuntarily) comic Italian translation of the letter.
16 In fact, there is no trace at all that the three untitled numbers (22, 23, 24) indicated in the catalogue of the exhibition Paris 1916 can be referred to three sculptures, as hypothesised in Schuster-Pfannstiel [1986], pp. 88, 90; where two of them are identified, without giving any sort of proof, as XXIII and one that is not present in the Ceroni catalogue, illustrated there with the number XXVIII.
17 London 1914, No. 287; the whole subject in Wayne 2002, pp. 55-56 and 201.
18 Roworth was in London from 1911 to 1914, the sculpture would have been bought in Paris during the artist's honeymoon, that his daughter dates in a letter to Kenneth Wayne as 1911-12: Wayne 2002, p. 56.
19 Wayne 2002, pp. 59-62.
20 Dumond Wilden 1914.
21 Giraudon 1992, pp. 28-40; photograph p. 28.
22 Published for the first time in Werner 1960-61, p. 70 as a copy of an older photograph conserved at the Museum of Modern Art in New York: in Schuster-Pfannstiel [1986] the original is said to come from an English private collection; in Ceroni 1970, p. 106 the photograph is dated 1911, without giving any reason.
23 The photograph of a presumed Modigliani caryatid "in Ruches garden" published in Venice 2000, p. 17 is difficult to interpret, and therefore too problematic for discussion here: it would seem to be *Head* XXV in New York, during the working phase or, perhaps, before being damaged.
24 Westheim 1921, p. 291.
25 What follows are the testimonies that I have found, in the press of that time, of the exhibitions with works by Modigliani from the three year period 1920-1922. Before his death, eluding Wayne's 2002 register, pp. 198-203, a collective exhibition of modern painting at the Galeries Branger, rue Cambon 5, presented some of Modigliani's work as shown in *Journal des Débats*, on 26th April 1919, p.3. Some of Modigliani's paintings were added to the anthological *La Peinture Moderne* at the Galerie Devambez, 22nd February 1920. One of Modigliani's nudes is remembered in an exhibition of nudes at the Galerie Crès, in *Le Petit Parisien*, 22nd March 1920. A retrospective of Modigliani's paintings was organised within the exhibition *La Jeune Peinture Française* held at the beginning of summer 1920 (closing on 4th July) at the Galerie Manzi et Joyant as indicated in de Colombier 1920 and in Hamel 1920, p. 24; and in the column *Expositions et Concours* 1920, p. 108. Some of Modigliani's paintings were presented in a collective exhibition at the Galerie Brunel (*Salons et Expositions, Le Petit Parisien*, 28th November 1920). A retrospective exhibition inaugurated on 8th December 1920 at the Galerie Montaigne (managed by the new director Jaques Hébertot) was announced in *La Rampe* on 28th November 1920 and was reviewed in Sarti 1921; in Fels 1921, pp. 92-94; in Vanderpyl 1920. Some nudes were exhibited in the exhibition of 60 nudes at Bernheim –jeune in May 1921 (*Le Petit Parisien*, 15th May 1921). A selection of Modigliani's works at the Galerie Paul Guillaume was announced in *La Rampe*, 19th November 1921. A large exhibition of paintings and drawings organised by Modigliani's friends at the Galerie Bernhaim-Jeune was said to be underway in February 1922 in *Les Arts, Modigliani*, 1922, p. 234; and it was mentioned in *Les beaux-arts. A travers les expositions*, 1922, p. 185; violently criticised by Alexandre 1922; and reviewed in *Coup d'oeil aux Expositions* 1922, p. 2. In March 1922 paintings by Modigliani appeared in a collective exhibition at the gallery G.L. Manuel Frères according to the news which appeared in *Les Potins de Paris*, 3rd March 1922, p. 13. In September 1922 an exhibition of engraved copies of Modigliani drawings realised by G. Gorvel at the Galerie Tremois was announced in *Revue Moderne des Arts et de la Vie*, 28th February 1922, p. 15. The purchase of works by Modigliani made by Albert Barnes at Paul Guillaume's gallery (among which perhaps also *Head* XIX) is pointed out in *Le Petit Parisien* 1st February 1923. Auctions held at the Hotel Drouot with paintings by Modigliani were announced in *Journal des Débats* of 15th May 1920, p. 4 (Louis Libaude Collection), in *Le Figaro* of 5th June 1920, 30th March 1921 (and *Le Gaulois*, 30th March 1921), 13th February 1922, 16th March 1922 in the *Journal des Débats* dated 6th February 1922, p. 3 (Collection MM. Bine et Chaigneau); in *Le Figaro* 15th November 1922; in *Journal des Débats* 21st November 1922 (André Costurier and Durand-Ruel Collections).
26 Draft of Paul Alexandre's letter to Ambrogio Ceroni dated 4th August 1957, in Alexandre 1993, pp. 104-106.
27 Alexandre 1993, pp. 60-67.
28 John 1954, p. 130.
29 Wayne 2006, p. 68 and note 17 p. 73.
30 Cork 1988, p. 48; if we accept

the credibility of this memory, Roworth's purchase of *Head* XXIV would be moved forward by at least one year compared to his daughter's recollections.
31 Guillaume 1920, p.1.
32 Basler, 1931, p. 52.
33 Salmon 1926, p. 15; the date is rejected in Werner 1962, p. 22.
34 Lipchitz 1954, pages not numbered.
35 Level 1959, p. 41, quoted in Wayne 2002, pp. 38-39.
36 Lipchitz 1954b, pages not numbered.
37 Epstein 1940, p. 38; the particular of the noses being reattached in Epstein 1931, p. 120.
38 de Macedo 1959 in Ferreira 1995, p. 66.
39 Zadkine's recollection is reported in Werner 1962, p. 26
40 Stoermer 1931, pp. 13-14.
41 Basler 1931, pp. 10-11.
42 Epstein 1931, p. 129.
43 *Laughing torso* 1932, p. 54.
44 Coquiot 1924, p. 104.
45 Achmatova 1973, p. 146; regarding the whole question Balas 1981.
46 Lipchitz 1954, pages not numbered.
47 Even nine years (1906-1915) according to Schuster-Pfannstiel [1986]; six (1909-1915) according to Werner 1962; five or six (1910-1915) according to Modigliani 1958, p. 147; three-four (1910-1913) according to Ceroni 1965 and Patani 1992.
48 Ceroni 1970, No. 23.
49 Alexandre 1993, figs. 406-435.
50 Alexandre 1993, No. 334, fig. 410 and No. 366, fig. 448.
51 Rodin 1911, p. 11. The introductory chapter (*Testamento*) that the quotation is taken from, was not present in the first edition but only in the second (Paris, Grasset 1912).
52 Dujardin-Beaumetz 1913 p. 16; for the discussion regarding the topicality of these opinions among French sculptors Le Normand Romain, 2009, pp. 105-109.
53 Declaration by Aristide Maillol to Harry Kessler in Kessler 2004, p. 701.
54 Rowell 1995, pp. 286-299.
55 Matisse 1908, p. 26.
56 Ceroni 1970, Nos. 32-38.
57 Baudelaire 1859, pp. 290-291.
58 Blanc 1867, p. 66; for discussion of this part Messina 1994, p. 16.
59 Nadelman 1974, quoted in Elsen 1974, p. 122.
60 Zadkine 1968, p. 66.
61 John 1954, p. 130.
62 Patani 1992, No. 241.
63 Livorno 1984, p. 83.
64 Declaration by Auguste Rodin in Cladel 1908, p. 143.
65 Alexandre 1993, fig. 243.
66 Alexandre 1993, fig. 163: this sheet is the only one of a series that is dated after Modigliani's return from Italy "2.4.1914".
67 Alexandre 1993, fig. 186.
68 Petani 1992, Nos. 50 and 86: show the stamp of the collection with the numbers 28,4 and 21,7.
69 Alexandre 1993, figs. 152-153.
70 Alexandre 1993, figs. 215-218.
71 Alexandre 1993, fig. 197.
72 Alexandre 1993, figs. 177-178.
73 Alexandre 1993, fig. 194.
74 Alexandre 1993, figs. 207-209.
75 Alexandre 1993, fig. 164.
76 Alexandre 1993, fig. 206.
77 Alexandre 1993, fig. 233.
78 Alexandre 1993, figs. 196, 193, 195.
79 Alexandre 1993, figs. 234-235.
80 Alexandre 1993, figs. 241-242.
81 Alexandre 1993, fig. 241.
82 Alexandre 1993, fig. 239.
83 Alexandre 1993, fig. 187.
84 Alexandre 1993, fig. 182.
85 Alexandre 1993, fig. 189.
86 Alexandre 1993, figs. 201-203
87 Alexandre 1993, figs. 179-181.
88 Alexandre 1993, fig. 192.
89 Alexandre 1993, fig. 173.
90 Alexandre 1993, fig. 184.
91 The letter in Guastalla 2006, p. 65.
92 Alexandre 1993, Nos. 257-260.
93 The two photographs are next to each other in Parigi 1986, p. 123.
94 Approximately Patani 1992, Nos. 133-247
95 Alexandre 1993, Nos. 142-148.
96 Patani 1992, No. 137 ("Dimanche 5 avril 1912 à Schencke, très amicalment").
97 Patani 1992, No. 137 ("12 Sept 014 / à mon ami Coria")
98 Ceroni, 1970, Nos. 32-37.
99 Alexandre 1993, figs. 104-112; Patani 1992, Nos. 104 and 126.
100 Alexandre 1993, figs. 113-129; Patani 1992, Nos. 100, 101, 102, 111, 112, 113, 138.
101 Alexandre 1993, figs. 148-160; Patani 1992, Nos. 90, 91, 95, 105
102 Alexandre 1993, figs. 143-147; Patani 1992, Nos. 64, 97, 106.
103 Patani 1993, Nos. 141, 155, 163, 164, 191-193, 221, 226.
104 The story of the damage suffered by the stone and the restoration by Jacques Lipchitz at the request of the architect Pierre Chareau who kept it in his garden in Paris until 1939 is summarised in Werner 1962, p. 28.
105 Alexandre 1993, No. 45, fig. 109.
106 The drawing is discussed, but without a date (it should be around 1911, when the love story between the two took place) in Alexandre, Bakhuÿs 2002, No. 38, p. 75.
107 This news in A. Beausire 1988, p. 82 and 312-313; the sculpture arrived at the Salon d'Automne on the day of the inauguration and there was no time to insert it in the catalogue.
108 The notice in Werner 1962, p. 32.
109 Paris 1908a, No. 1214 (*Une cariatide*, fragment plâtre) and No. 27 (*Etude de cariatide*, plâtre).
110 For the whole discussion 2009, pp. 465-490.
111 Braun 2006, pp. 51-52 has quite correctly insisted on this reference.
112 Miller, *Brancusi. A survey of his work*, Oxford, Oxford University Press 1995, pp. 74-76 and fig. 56.
113 Spies 1983, No. 19.
114 Balas 1981.
115 Alexandre 1993, No. 160.
116 d'Ivray 1911, pp. 250-251.
117 Alexandre 1993, pp. 206-207; Reinach, 1897, p. 339 table 629 (*Vénus accroupie* in the Vatican Museum); No. 630 (*Vénus accroupie* in the Uffizi).
118 Guillaume 1953, p. 34.
119 Canudo 1908.
120 Roches 1912, p. 342.
121 Carco 1919, p. 206: the quotation of the passage in this catalogue on page 181.

Worldly Primitivism, Orientalism for Museums

Alessandro Del Puppo

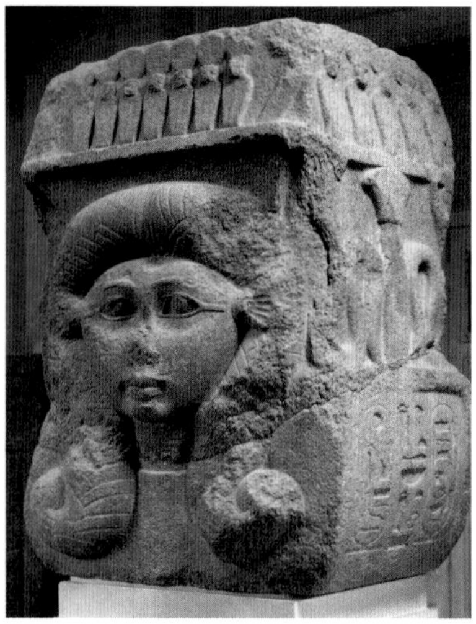

1. *Egyptian art*, middle kingdom. *Capital with the Goddess Hathor*, from Bubastis. Paris, Musée du Louvre

The Labyrinth of the Sources

Delving into the critical bibliography that regards Modigliani means facing, among numerous other problems (signature, dating, provenance), the question of the sources. There are numerous proposals, the suggestions, the more or less significant "affairs," the brilliant *trouvailles* and the more or less justified attempts, to find the proof for a style that has always seemed to be very recognisable but elusive at the same time. Even the most fragmentary of the examples within the large amount of critical studies concerning Modigliani can only confirm this. In a monograph dated 1929, actually more dangerous than useful, Arthur Pfannstiel mentioned Brancusi's sculptures and those from the Ivory Coast, Egyptian, Hindu and Khmer art, without neglecting the Classical lesson and Cézanne's starting point: a judgement where the vastness of the possible references showed respect for the logic of a linear path ("Tout en lui résulte d'une évolution") as well as deference for the real passwords of the visual culture of that time (so the "recherche d'un grand style, c'est-à-dire d'un style éternel").[1] On the occasion of the Biennale in 1930, which would become legendary for a whole generation of Italian artists (who, however, presented only two sculptures), Lionello Venturi was able to confirm that "la scultura negra, la scultura gotica francese, i primitivi italiani [...], l'arte giapponese, il Greco, queste ed altre voci discordanti del passato giunsero a lui."[2] In the first study in the French language, Adolphe Basler noted the importance of a sculptor like Elie Nadelman, and through him, Greek art; however, he did not conceal, once again, possible references to Khmer and African art. Furthermore, Basler admitted that the most recognisable stylistic traits that passed from sculpture to painting (the elegant stylisation, the well elongated lines, the unvaried and geometric nose, the architectonic simplification, some intended deformations that broke up the rigid symmetry) derived from the fetishes coming from the French colonies, re-conducted to an almost too carefully observed homogeneity of style ("en somme, toute la production de Modigliani se ressemble").[3] On those rare occasions of specific interpretation carried out in the 1920's and '30's when Modigliani's sculpture was completely or almost unknown, it was overshadowed by his pictorial production – object, as we know, of great success with the critics and of continuous market revaluation – with the result of creating real critical substance. Widening the range of comparisons is always dangerous, when not supported by historical conscience; and so dangerous hypotheses were quickly reached, like Schaub-Koch's in 1933 ("Il la force stylisée de Greco et de Mantegna, leur acité de vie et leur puissance"),[4] or Wilenski's who, some years later, in one of his books on sculpture ventured to hypothesise possible Byzantine and Chang figure sources.[5]

For however well carried out, visual philology can only take relationships into account, not loves. Modigliani's case is exemplary from this point of view. He has been attributed with countless visual passions; it is much more difficult to vouch for verisimilitudes and intensity of contributions. Even more so when you move within a canon which is debated and questionable because it is problematic, like the one vouched for by Ambrogio Ceroni.

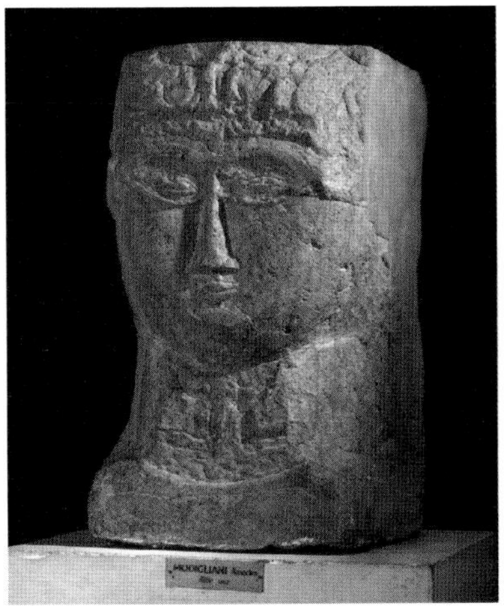

2. Amedeo Modigliani
Head, 1911-1913.
Paris, Centre Georges Pompidou,
Musée National d'art moderne.
Ceroni III

Modernist Primitivism

If the repertoire of the possible sources can still today seem like an intricate knot of influences, it is also true that all the observers agreed on recognising the role of Primitive art. Actually this term was quite generic; it often included the whole range of non-European figurative traditions: Egyptian and African tribal art, Chinese, Japanese and Tibetan painting, Javanese and Indochinese sculpture, Oceanic and Meso-American art. In the critics' opinion it was the actual significance of these sources that was modified, not their existence.

The German painter Ludwig Meidner, who met Modigliani very early in Paris, remembered how Paul Gauguin's retrospective at the Salon d'Automne in 1906 had aroused the souls of the young painters not so much for the allure of Tahitian exoticism but rather for the "barbaric" use of Polimateric sculpture, with its brutal impact; however, he acknowledged that the influence of African art on Modigliani was almost negligible.[6] The sculptor Jacques Lipchitz was also among those who played down the role of primitive objects. He believed that Modigliani "although he admired negro-African art and the other primitive arts like the rest of us, he was never deeply influenced, in the same way that he was not influenced by Cubism. He derived certain stylistic elements but was never touched by their spirit."[7]

Those few pages dedicated to Modigliani's relationship with primitive sources were characterised for many years by an attitude that was almost nonchalant. So, Waldemar George's "certain analogies" must be noted,[8] Giovanni Scheiwiller's concession in terms of "youthful boldness"[9] and the simple allusion to the "souples arabesques" of the caryatids that can be found in Basler's study of modern sculpture, a scholar who also recognised how much the barbaric reduction of the African fetishes, with their instinctive balancing of the composition, had been important for the elimination of the Classic *poncif*.[10]

It was even easier for archaeologists and ethnologists to play down the interpretation of the primitive objects carried out by Modigliani, and even more generally the artistic avant-garde at the beginning of the century. During the *Exhibition of Negroid Art* at the Biennale of Venice in 1920 in a room very close to the rather limited retrospective of Modigliani, a wise observer like Carlo Anti could write without too much reticence: "Tutti questi artisti videro nelle sculture negre non quello che vi era veramente, ma piuttosto quanto sentivano in sé o andavano affannosamente cercando. Il loro non era un giudizio, ma una interpretazione troppo soggettiva dell'arte negra."[11]

The perception of an unbridgeable distance, to approximate as much as possible with the forms of one's own individuality, was shared by the most attentive among the poets and artists. In his splendid *Essai sur l'exotisme* Victor Segalen had fully understood how much the power of exoticism lay in the possibility of understanding the distance of the other from oneself, measuring the distance: "L'exotisme n'est pas donc une adaption; n'est donc pas la compréhension parfaite d'un hors soi-même qu'on étreindrait en soi, mais la perception aigue et immédiate d'une incompréhensibilité éternelle." [12]

The definitive contribution for a more correct dimensioning of the question began arriving

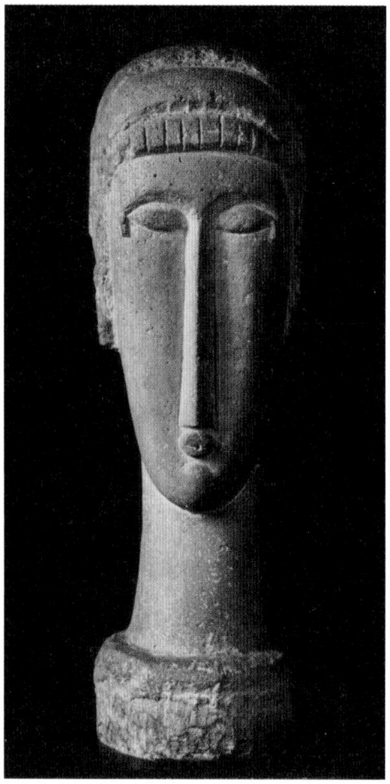

3. Amedeo Modigliani
Head, 1911-1912. Merion, Pennsylvania, The Barnes Foundation. Ceroni XIX

from the first modern studies of Primitivism. During an exhibition at the Museum of Modern Art in New York, James Johnson Sweeney drew a clear line between the phenomena of real similarity and that of interpretation or critical appreciation, a category within which he could collocate, together with the first works of Picasso and Brücke, also Modigliani's work.[13]
This position was maintained by Robert Goldwater, in what is considered the text which started off the study of Primitivism. Describing Modigliani's works, Goldwater had the possibility to object how in his stylistic results (the slanted oval eyes, the long concave noses, the tilting of the head, the flat planes) the sculptor had never reached that overbearing effect of cubic mass that appeared, at least in the reductive aspect of Modernism, as the primary influence of African art. Both in his drawings and his heads, the charm of the arabesque ("his sentimental linear rhythms") seemed very distant from the more rudimental forms of volumetric syntax.[14]
Therefore, it was not surprising when Alfred Werner, in the first serious attempt to put some order into the question of Modigliani sculptor, concluded that the idea of a prevailing influx of African art should be rejected, as it was exaggerated.[15] However, I think that this consideration quite easily can be extended even further, to the whole range of suggestions that nourished the birth, the development and the conclusion of Modigliani's sculptural reasoning. What André Salmon wrote a few years after Modigliani's death is important, word for word: "archaïques et du dernier jour, marquée d'une instinctive volonté de grande stylisation de l'élément naturel immédiat."[16] An instinctive desire for great stylisation: it is difficult to say so much in so few words. This consideration really adapts itself well not only to the naturalistic external information (that Salmon obviously thought referred to the painted portraits), but also to the process of decantation and purification of the sources. In the construction of Modigliani's sculptural style, the contribution of Classical, Primitive and Oriental art models seems therefore to be able to arrange itself according to two opposite positions: syncretism and elusion. Syncretism explains why it was so easy to succeed in proposing such a vast range of sources, real or presumed; elusion – or rather the accurately dosed mixture of it, up to the point of dissolving the models inside the work – explains why it has always been so difficult to adequately motivate these relationships.

Forms of Primitivism

The reasons for this difficulty can be quickly explained. Modigliani left no written proof, or documents about the subject. According to the data we have at our disposal, it does not seem that Modigliani ever possessed tribal objects (while instead Picasso, Derain, Matisse and many others did), or kept studies or monographs on the subject, or even only photographs.[17]
His name never appeared in the many and important pages that his main art-dealer, Paul Guillaume, dedicated to Primitive art throughout his life.
The relationship between Modigliani and Primitivism is therefore: 1) acknowledged after his death; 2) without any direct sources; 3) conjectural. It has therefore always been reconstructed indirectly, due to how the brush strokes were applied, or stylistic deduction, in the same way that has been done also for this exhibition.
For each of Modigliani's sculptures grouped here the attempt has been made to show the elements accepted or derived from possible Primitive or extra-European sources, evaluated on the two-fold level of stylistic congruence and the reliability of the sources (that is, the contemporaneity and the accessibility of the objects proposed). First of all these elements were studied in the surviving drawings and in the many others, we may think, that have been destroyed or lost. Concentrating only on the Alexandre catalogue, many drawings present studies of profiles with elements that can be traced back to tribal masks

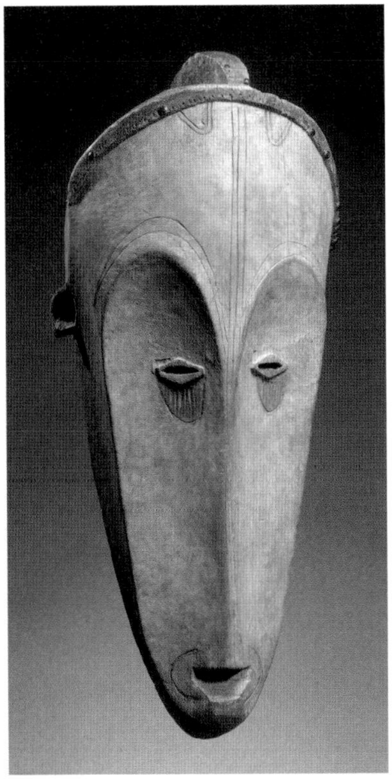

4. *Fang Mask*, Gabon.
Paris, Musée du quai Branly

(Nos. 187 and following, plus 168-170 in the male version); sometimes, they are contaminated by "Egyptian" heads (like the seventeen studies Nos. 193-209; cat. **17**). Two studies on the back and front sheet showing a tribal head (210-211), can be more certainly connected to a type of Fang head-reliquary that Modigliani knew well and which was also in the Paul Guillaume collection (today in the Musée du quai Branly; refer to Section 6 for this). Other frontal studies of heads seem referable to prototypes of a nègre kind, for the development of the elongated nose and the grafting on the almond eyes (these are the sequences: 171-185, with the latter being contaminated by Egyptian influence; 220-227, with accentuation above all of the full lips and flattened nose; 230-242, a *suite* of folios with an almost unvaried scheme (cat. **15**).
In the drawings, the side view is planned in the elementary logic between semi-circular curves of chin and skull – the two extremes of the block – and the hyperbolic ones of the nose, with the addition of decorative graphic elements of the contour of the eyes, of the eyebrow arches (often doubled or tripled), the hairline, the profile of the lobes (cat. **16**).
A whole series of frontal caryatid female heads (244-260), can be referred to possible Egyptian and archaic Cypriot sources of the head-capital bearing the features of the goddess Hathor (fig. **1**), one of the first and more well known examples of decorative symbolic heads associated with an architectonic structure.[18] This suggestion seems valid for the idea of a sculptural block where the head is nested, in fact, taken up once again in sculpture III (fig. **2**) while certain graphical motifs of the face seem to derive more from the physiognomic details – which in the Egyptian heads are modelled in relief – of the wood carvings of some African masks. From this point of view, one of the most typical problems of Modigliani's sculptural work was that of converting in the direct carving of the stone, formal motifs which were originally used on wood.
The development of the subject head-caryatid can be followed well on certain drawings (like number 193 and following; but see Fergonzi's essay here), among the most refined and elaborate, with extended chiaroscuro and chromatic interventions, almost as if foreseeing the future pictorial transition. Finally a small group of drawings must be connected to the study (or, perhaps more exactly, the reminiscence) of archaic Greek and Oriental art preparatory to *Head* XII (for this, see Section 5 and relative details).
Summing up, until today slightly fewer than 60 studies of the typology of the elongated face can be documented (plus 23 catalogued by Patani), with various contaminations of Egyptian and archaic motifs; 17 Alexandre (plus 5 Patani) drawings, are clearly referable to the Fang mask prototype, with some generic mannerism in Oriental style.
At the same time as the studies on paper (but it is very difficult to establish the timing with certainty), these same elements were translated into the rough hewing and finishing of the block. First of all, with a certain difficulty, in roughly the first ten of the works in the catalogue; then, with greater confidence in the work of carving and smoothing of the stone, these materials were led to a unifying and stylistically impeccable synthesis, even though formally slightly cold, which maintained a visible trace of these contributions. Here, in order, drawing up a summary of the reasons discussed in the various reports in the catalogue (and having three important sculptures like *Heads* XVIII-XX as terms of comparison) they can be listed like this:
- the frontal and hieratic position of the head (figs. **3-4**);
the elongation of the face up to proportion base/height of one to four (instead of the conventional three to four), derived particularly from Fang masks;
- the bilateral symmetry, maximum in the later heads, with the symmetrical axis underlined in the drawings with a discontinuous line;
- the small, thin and everted cylinder-shaped

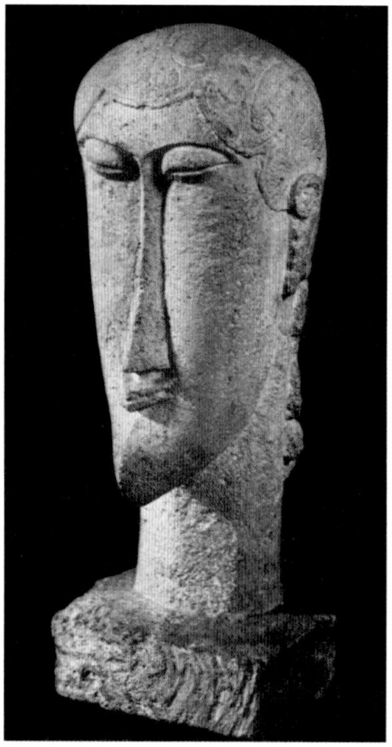

5. Amedeo Modigliani
Head, 1911-1912.
Private collection. Ceroni XVIII

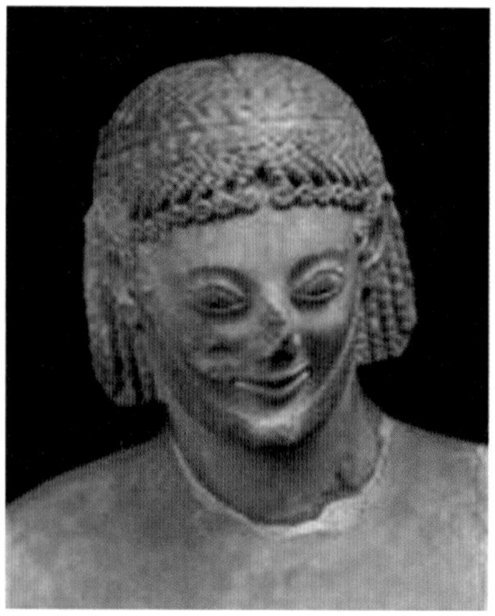

6. *Rampin Horseman*, marble head integrated with moulds of a torso of a horseman and the neck of his horse conserved at the Museum of the Acropolis in Athens, just after 545 BC. Paris, Musée du Louvre

mouth (a form which can be traced to the Nimba and Grebo masks, figs. **7-8**), or with the corners turned in a stereotype smile (turning to Greek-Cypriot-archaic art, or, that is, Oriental, difficult to dissolve; figs. **5-6**; cf. cat. **24**);
- the nose with trapezoidal, slightly convergent planes, pointed and protruding chin;
- elongated lobes, both as a formal solution with joining of ear and earring, and as reference to the corresponding motif in Buddhist statues;
- full and dilated eyeballs;
- arabesque hairline, which in accordance with the solution used can be traced back to Egyptian head-capitals or Etruscan statues.

In Modigliani's sculpture not everything appears to be symptomatic and nothing seems to be traceable to an essence. There is not one sculpture where all these traits are integrally present; however, all of them as a whole participate in various ways to the recognisability of the single sculptural work. The attempt to find an extreme stylisation, is common to all the single elements, even though not continuous.

The first numbers in the catalogue (III-IV, V, VII-VIII) show rather rudimental carving on the stone. If we compare a clearly unfinished head like *Head* IV with one of the finished ones (like XXIV), we can understand something about this process. First of all the forms were organised according to the brutal planes of the jutting elements that emerged with the first work of hewing the stone (figs. **9-10**). A process of elaboration that leaves no difficulty in considering it rather long and difficult, led to a result which was closer to modelling than carving. The distinction between full and void was in fact, integrated, or completely substituted by a more fluid linearity of the profiles. Extreme rarefaction was achieved In this way, as well as complete anti-naturalistic abstraction of the more completed heads (fig. **11**).

These last works, displaying undaunted statics of Classical sculpture, succeeded in representing the point of greatest balance between two extremes: the substrate in formal Modernist language and the Primitive brutality of the double-sided stone.

Faced with these results, it is very difficult to admit a direct study of the sources; it is more probably a re-elaboration, very casual and carried out from recollection, of rather formal themes common to sculptors and painters of that time. Leaving to one side the problem of the caryatids and full figures (studied in Fergonzi's essay here), what could Modigliani's reasoning have been for the sculptural heads? In his drawings he isolated two fundamental types: the Egyptian head-caryatid and the "nègre" elongated head, with the relative studies of profiles: he integrated these two basic schemes with detailed solutions (almond eyes, straight nose, repeated lines of the eyebrows that meet at the bridge of the nose, the tiny mouth) and he developed them like a composer, once the idea of the melody had formed, he kept it within a defined structural scheme, researching the formal developments (fig. **12**).

This conclusion may seem even too generalised, elusive in itself; however, perhaps it enables us to propose some other observations regarding one of the few things that are certain about Modigliani's sculpture, the only one to be confirmed by definite photographic documentation: the organisation of his work at the Salon d'Automne in 1912. We should remember that apart from the occasional exhibitions of sculpture (there were only two, one in London in 1914 and another two years later in New York), virtually held without the author having any control, Modigliani exhibited his sculptures only on that occasion (the exhibition in the studio of Souza Cardoso, like many other things and as Fergonzi discusses here, contributed more to the myth of the author than a historiographic reconstruction).

Modigliani decided to exhibit his works all grouped together as a "decorative ensemble," possibly based on the model, as Emily Braun suggested, of Ivan Meštrović's display in the temple of Kosovo at the

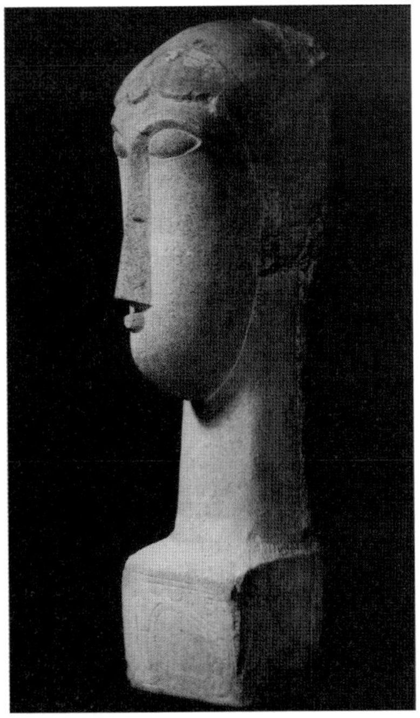

7. Amedeo Modigliani
Head, 1911-1912.
Philadelphia, The Philadelphia Museum of Art. Ceroni XX

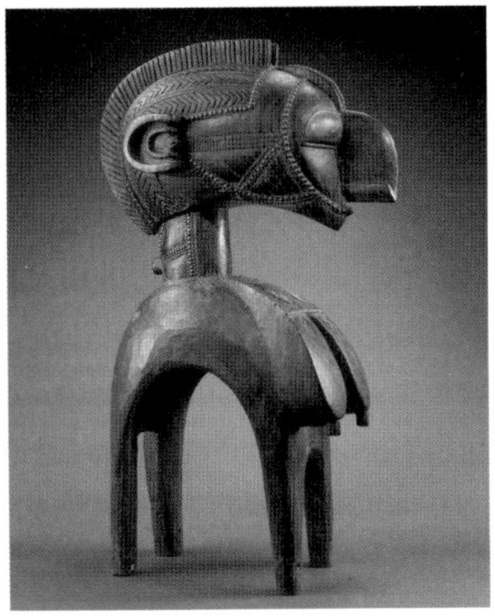

8. *Nimba Shoulder Mask*, Guinea.
Paris, Musee du quai Branly

Esposizione Internazionale in Rome in 1911, which caused such a sensation.[19]
The sculptural heads should have been exhibited on bases next to one another, as Lipchitz recalls with a nice image ("come le canne di un organo," that is, at different heights). However, this intention cannot be confirmed by the few photographs at our disposal. In fact, these show only four of the works (and not seven), and furthermore they are distributed around the room following a logic of filling in the gaps between one canvas and another, more than as an "ensemble décoratif." It is very probable that, from this point of view, Modigliani's intentions were denied by a practice of organisation of the rooms that made the collocation of sculptures just like simple ornaments. This habit became such that it urged, right at the closure of the 1912 Salon, the presentation of an order of the day at the general Assembly of the Salon d'Automne with the aim of guaranteeing sculpture with "some rooms where it can have a dominant position."[20]
However, considering the data available to us, beyond what seems to have been a complete failure of the exhibition project, why would Modigliani have wanted to present his works in that way? I propose two possible reasons. The first aimed at a sort of new proposal of the linear sequence of the sculptural heads. A coordinated order that was common practice in the antique art collections in the museums of the Trocadéro, at the Guimet, at the Louvre itself. In my opinion, the second reason is that in the repetition of the heads the author tended to privilege the process of formal rarefaction of the substance, rather than his amazing gestural elaboration of a sculptural theme, condensed into only one work, perhaps (if he had really wanted to imitate Meštrović, or Rodin) a full figure, a colossal size, overpoweringly placed in the middle of the room making an absolute focus point for it. The organisation that Modigliani wanted does not seem to suggest a gesture of categorical rebellion or contrast; rather to offer, in the sequential presentation of the works, the reasons for his work with minimum variations.
Modigliani undertook the serial mechanism as an integral structure, founded on parsimony and reduction of the synthetic links. Seven heads, only one face, no expression. The dissolving of one into the multiple. This is the sense that I would give to "decorative ensemble." A lavish moment, in the number, but ambiguous in the result. It was the price to pay for having a sculptural idea, faced with the decomposition of traditional sculptural art, of the anatomic disarticulation of Expressionism, of the corrosion of the principles of Classical sculpture.

Abstractions and Misunderstandings
In some ways the organisation of his works was thought out coherently with the fore-chosen models for the stylistic research. This problem can be corroborated by the evidence of the comparisons mentioned so far, and by two collateral questions: the first relative to a problem of style, the second to a problem of iconography.
Modigliani certainly observed Primitive art, recognising in it – even though indirectly – those values of pure form invented in those same years by the critics to establish an interpretation of Primitive art suitable for the expectations of Modernism.
Modigliani's most influential art-dealer, Paul Guillaume, was amongst the first and most convinced promoters of Primitive art. However, Guillaume's preferences, also for clearly commercial reasons, right from the beginning turned to tribal objects with the most reassuring and pleasant qualities, sculptures and masks with elegant elongated forms and shiny smooth surfaces.[21] It was not important if this interpretation was founded on partial knowledge, not to say wrong, of the primitive objects. We can, in fact, give some examples of the mistaken interpretation regarding the sources of tribal art that we have studied in Sections 6 and 7.
The Fang reliquaries that so much impressed Modigliani and Guillaume were

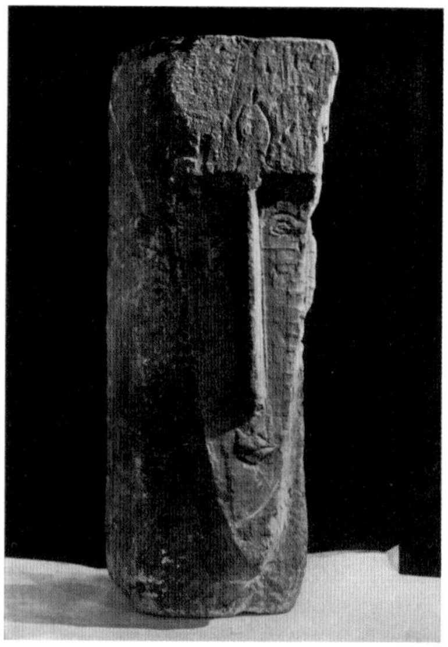

9. Amedeo Modigliani
Head, 1911-1912.
Toronto, Latner Family Art Collection.
Ceroni IV

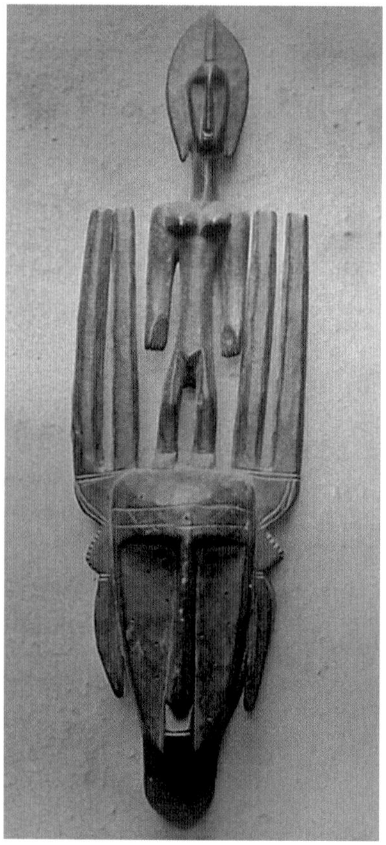

10. *Ritual Mask*, Guinea,
in *Sculptures nègres*,
Paris, Paul Guillaume 1917

present on the Parisian market after being banned by French officials at the beginning of the century. Up until then, they had been used before every significant event by various communities to consult the relics of their ancestors. The head that surmounted the container, so much appreciated for its composed volumes, was originally decorated with necklaces and fake hair made out of straw, raffia or grass; metallic discs were nailed to the eyes. The Nimba (or D'mba) statues, from northern Guinea – object of a ritual suppressed only a few years ago by the Muslim government – represented the figure of a strong, mature and monumental woman, with sagging breasts that identified her as a mother who has breast fed. The whole body was covered in horse-hair or vegetable fibres, with an elaborate hairstyle and metallic inserts (fig. **13**).[22]
The Fang culture had contributed to kindling the primitive western imagination thanks to its softwood masks, painted with kaolin, like the very famous one owned by André Derain. However, also here, a real process of colonisation had removed the original ritual and anti-evil influence of the masks, handing them over instead to the field of European visual arts. These works arrived in the museums and western collections nearly always unadorned; the admiration that the artists had for them was encouraged by a purely aesthetic perception, rather than the understanding of the ritual nature of the object. The presumption went even further in believing that these works had no real author – substituted by the myth of the unknowing author – and substantially without any stylistic developments.
In fact, the victims of these processes of appropriation could be weak, but rarely passive. One of the most widespread masks in the Parisian avant-gardes, which relives today, so to speak, in some paintings by Matisse and Picasso, can be traced back to the Ngontang type ("young white woman": a female spirit that returns from the land of the dead; fig. **14**). These works were introduced into the Fang culture at the beginning of the twentieth century, as an answer to the presence of the Europeans, who due to their white skin were understood to be like the spirits of the dead that return.[23]
In nearly all the cases that we have studied, the tribal objects were always interpreted out of context, without any ceremonial adornments, removed from ritual practice and manipulation of the performer.
Every characteristic that could seem incompatible with this extreme and rarefied formalism could quite easily be removed, without any embarrassment regarding the real function of the tribal work.
An aesthetics of primitive purification strengthened these prejudices with a convenient phraseology. What Guillaume acknowledged as the "grande audace du goût,"[24] which had been able to interpret the African idols as real works of art, was really an act of pride.
However, around 1910, studies of primitive cultures began to radically change; the concepts of degeneration and Eurocentricity made way for relativism and objectivisation of social sciences. Franz Boas's studies rejected the connection between mental and racial types and showed that every cultural and linguistic product was determined by cultural, rather than genetic causes.[25] However, in the art world, these ideas were late in developing. The mediation of authors like Gauguin favoured drawing on aestheticism to interpret Primitivism, which from potentially subversive became conciliatory, conservative and acceptable.[26]
Carl Einstein's work (*Negerplastik*, 1915), dismissed by Clouzot and Level as "un livre allemand de métaphysique transcendantale"[27] was in fact, the first serious contribution to the Modernist interpretation of African art. The book brought to light some commonplaces (for example, the simplest forms are not the oldest) and was an invitation to pass from the ethnographic logic of inventory to that of the stylistic description, substituting the classification of objects with the study of forms. It is clear that this direction on the one hand freed the studies from the heavy

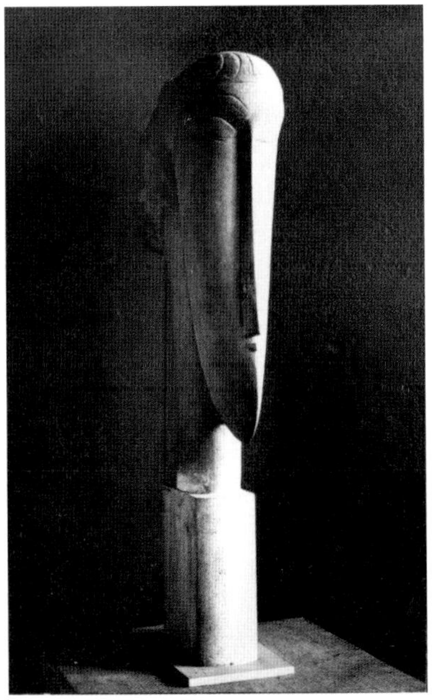

11. Amedeo Modigliani
Head, 1911-1912.
London, Tate Gallery. Ceroni XXIV

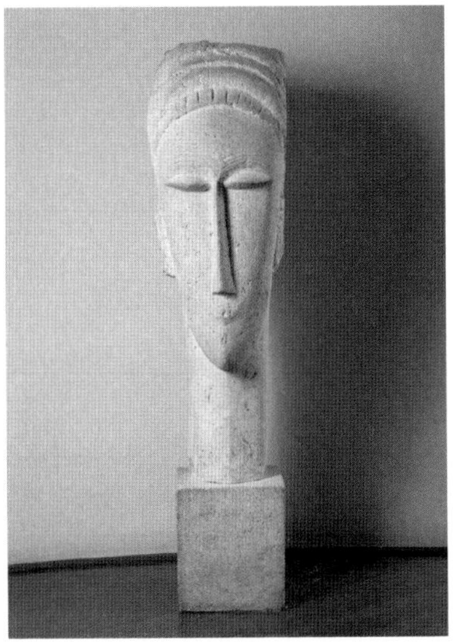

12. Amedeo Modigliani
Head, 1911-1912.
St. Louis, private collection.
Ceroni XV

nature of nineteenth century classifications but on the other ratified the possibility of a purely aesthetic interpretation of the primitive object, confirming the myth of a pure and authentic creation.
Influent British art critics, like Roger Fry and Clive Bell, in the same way spread definitions such as "pure plastic form" or "significant form." The whole range of Primitive arts – an expression which here included every non-Classic and non-western tradition – had three distinct characteristics in their opinion: the absence of meaning, the absence of disdainful qualities, a sublime impression of form.[28] The Primitive artist seemed to be guided only by the necessity to create form. This was clearly an extreme interpretation, of obvious reduction of the whole experience of tribal art to the conscious formalism of European avant-garde: a theoretical position which was more suitable for clarifying the movements of one rather than the effective reasons of the other. From an iconographic point of view Modigliani was always ready, both in painting and sculpture, to defend the classic and traditional quality of his subjects (portrait heads, caryatids, nudes). For this reason, he was always distant from that study of primitive forms which instead allowed, in another order of intentions, the creation of an efficient language, a mixture between noble and trivial repertoire. The painting and sculpture of Picasso, Derain, Matisse used caricature stylisation and deformation of expression to undermine traditional schemes and iconographies, not to confirm them in a more or less courteous way.[29]
The extreme formalisation led Modigliani to an opposite position compared to Primitivist Expressionism that we can find in the works of Picasso or Kirchner from just a few years earlier. His search for anti-psychological stylisation led him to rarefied forms of an abstract and timeless representation, without symbolic values or explicit expressive tensions. Taken individually, these untitled heads seem like faces-images: but they are portraits without people. Taken collectively, like a population of an *ensemble décoratif*, these sculptures belong to a monument without any architectonic system and without memory. In modern sculpture, the material was establishing itself as substance of the form. Maintaining the human figure and the traditional stone material meant therefore, placing oneself *naturaliter* outside the processes of plastic revolution. The choice of carving stone kept Modigliani away from the most radical volumetric experiments. His homage to the most noble material tied him to a reasoning on the sculptural block, when it seemed that new spaces were opening up in the diversification of materials. Brancusi was searching for the luminous effects outside of Impressionist modelling, side by side with the various materials (stone and marble, but also wood, brass, glass); Picasso and Archipenko were trying, not without some difficulty, to interpret the complex Cubist spatiality into polimateric and polychrome constructions (see Section 7 about this).
Modigliani's attention towards an archaic style seems, at least in the logic of Modernism, like a passive form of timeless Classicism and without any potential development.
Confronted with the unbridled resort to Primitive art which characterises the work of those artists mentioned, Modigliani's sculptural work can therefore seem arbitrary, if not weak. However, to draw a negative opinion from his moderation would mean reflecting the prejudices of Modernism.[30] In fact, this allegiance of his can be motivated by the fact that the Primitive radical stylisation coexists with other less striking possible forms of retrospective taste, equally present in the agenda of artists and critics of the time.

Oriental and Primitive Syncretism

For however well carried out, in fact, the main historical narrations about Orientalism and Primitivism have the defect of one beginning when the other seems to end,[31] in this way losing the sense of a continuity that

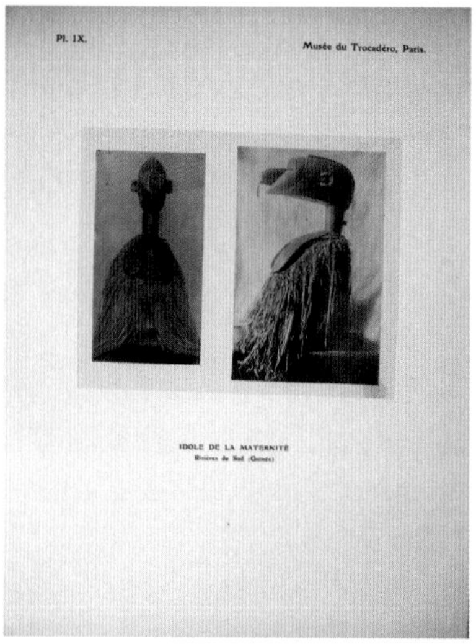

13. *Nimba Shoulder Mask*, Guinea, in *Sculptures nègres*, Paris, Paul Guillaume 1917.

joins the heroic phases (the *japonisme* of the Second Empire, led by the Goncourt brothers, by Manet, Whistler, Renoir and all the others) with those of a prolonged decline which intercepts, without ever completely exhausting itself, the growing passion for tribal arts.

Besides the official chronologies, there exists a longer period for these phenomena of taste, which still has its ramification in the years when Modigliani found himself having to reason about painting and sculpture. In fact, in some ways, the years that he spent in Paris (1906-1920) coincided with at least three crucial phases: the long decline of the passions for Oriental art and their progression into museums; the constitution of a line of "moderate" Primitivism in accordance with the most extreme stylistic options; its reformulation, finally, in social and commercial terms that would lead to the so-called *déco nègre* of the 1920's.

All three cases have something to do with Modigliani's work, and later, led the acceptation of the works. We will briefly analyse them in these last three paragraphs, starting with the most interesting problem: the Oriental and Primitive syncretism of the first decade of the century. It is a context which I think is useful for trying to understand something more about the genesis of sculptures like IX and XII. Two events had crossed paths in 1904, offering new terms of valuation and a radical subversion of consolidated judgements to those who followed art. The exhibition of French Primitives at the Louvre had shown the existence of a historical-artistic substrate that could strengthen the idea of a national school and of a specific "Gothic" tradition also in painting and sculpture.[32]

Having shaken off the *grandeur* of the Exposition Universelle of 1900, the correspondence from French journalists at the St. Louis World's Fair did not hide their admiration, and sometimes surprise, for the formidable cultural and commercial rise of the United States and the effects of that particular melting-pot (even if lowered in the usual frame of racism. "presque tous les nègres – observed Paul Adam – ont l'oreille juste").[33] The sense of distance in time and distance in space could always rely more heavily on new cultural phenomena and products.

In the meantime, however, the objects which fifty years earlier had started off the fashion of exoticism were acquiring a solid collocation in museums. In 1903, the purchase of important works at the Hayashi sale was just the starting point of the nucleus of Japanese works in the Musée Guimet, enriched by the legacy of prints and above all, with the lot of Dunhvang paintings offered by Paul Pelliot in 1907, on his return from an expedition to Central Asia. There followed more than six hundred ceramics from China, Japan and Vietnam from Paul Grandidier's legacy in 1911 and Jacques Bacot's collection of Tibetan painting in 1912.[34]

The dispersion of the first historical collections soon became the prerogative of the most powerful gallery owners. In 1906 Durand Ruel put Siegfried Bing's collection of Chinese art up for sale and, Madame Langweil's collection of antique Chinese painting in two *tranches* in 1911; that same year at the Hôtel Drouot he put Alexis Rouart's collection up for auction. The Levesque gallery, which later had the possibility to exhibit some of Modigliani's work, put on the market in 1913 the 481 pieces of Chinese, Japanese, Korean, sculpture, painting and ceramics, Persian miniatures and finally, seen as similar to them, some examples of "art nègre," from Charles Vignier's collection.[35]

These occasions were interwoven in commercial practice, with the recovery of French eighteenth century art, particularly promoted with Georges Petit's lots of Chardin and Fragonard in 1907, a gallery owner who had no qualms about promoting a *suite indienne* of fifteen decorative panels by the painter Albert Besnard, on his return from India.[36]

All in all, these circumstances helped to reformulate the categories of high society collections in Paris in the first and second

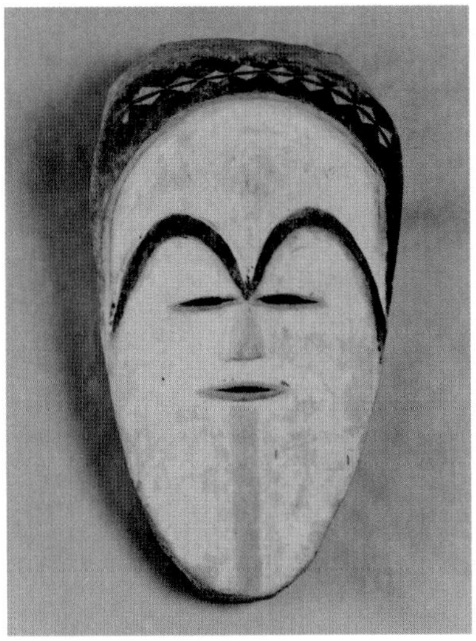

14. *Fang Funeral Mask*, Ivory Coast. Former Alberto Magnelli collection. Paris, Centre Georges Pompidou, Musée National d'art moderne

decades of the century: a taste in which the symbols of the *grand tradition* and "Egyptmania" mixed with extended boundaries of *japonisme*, not to call them extremely nonchalant and completely consolidated.

The programmes of the museums confirmed this open and sincere syncretism with a lively exhibition activity. In 1905 the Musée des Arts Décoratifs was installed at the Pavillon de Marsan at the Louvre; here a series of Japanese art exhibitions began which were held yearly. One of these, *Le goût chinois en Europe au XVIII siècle,* was judged as a "leçon de goût français"; another of a Japanese kind, was admired for "le charme d'un art délicieux" by Paul Guillaume himself.[37]

The Musée d'Ennery was inaugurated in May 1908 in Avenue du Bois de Boulogne, thanks to Clemence d'Ennery's legacy to the French state, his drawing room had been a meeting place for the Goncourt brothers and the theatrical world. The collection included more than six thousand Oriental objects, most of them bought after 1890. In 1909 Albert Kahn very successfully opened a Japanese garden in Boulogne full of pavilions, paths and bridges. An exhibition of antique Chinese painting, held at the Cernuschi Museum in 1912 had the names of an influential high society *milieu* among the lenders: besides Émile Guimet, Léonce Rosenberg, Henri Rivière, Lucien Henreaux, Jacques Doucet, Roger Fry.[38] Thanks to the renewal of the museum collections, the idea of an Oriental art made up of enamels, lacquers and polychrome ceramics left room for conspicuous examples of noble and severe statues.[39]

Next to this rich and constant activity of exhibitions, there were some scholarly studies,[40] some popular works by experts on the subjects,[41] and art editions.[42]

Scientific historiography and archaeological digs were opening up spectacular new sources, these were followed with much attention by the art magazines. The spreading of "Greek-Buddhist" art from Gandahara seemed to foresee a development of Hellenistic Classical art towards oriental regions, in a surprising, and often disturbing mixture of Christian motifs and Buddhist subjects (that we have tried to discuss in Section 5).

Alfred Foucher discussed the question of Classical influence in the Middle East, that from Gandhara seemed to reach India and from there Java, with words that brought back the figurative prejudices of European traditions.[43] However, not rarely, such a vast panorama was able to increase the claims, never appeased, of the nationalist critics, who faced with the risks of drifting towards xenophobia, obscured the function of saving local tradition, able to fortify the even too hybrid styles of the avant-garde (fig. **15**).[44]

In any case, as the studies progressed and modern knowledge increased, Oriental and Primitive art were redeemed by their mythical dimension and aesthetic approach which was rare and marvellous, it was led into a scheme of historical development, not without some parallels with western tradition. This deep rooted historicity was able to substantiate a wider range of comparisons, re-drawing the geography of trade and history of the forms.[45]

An agréable *Primitivism*

During the years between 1904 and 1914 an intensive activity of exhibitions was recorded that saw the intertwining of different currents: French Medieval art, seventeenth century Flemish art, eighteenth century French art, Chinese art (or more in general, Asian), and finally the *dernier cri* of *art nègre*. These activities were followed both by magazines and by publishing houses, that were in turn stimulated by the exhibitions in the museums. It was an official panorama, but not academic, which placed itself between the conflicting experiences of the avant-garde and the Salons. This picture formed the background against which the movements of many artists were drawn, those who, like Modigliani arrived in Paris not in order to form immediate relationships, exclusive to the most radical groups of the avant-gardes (as

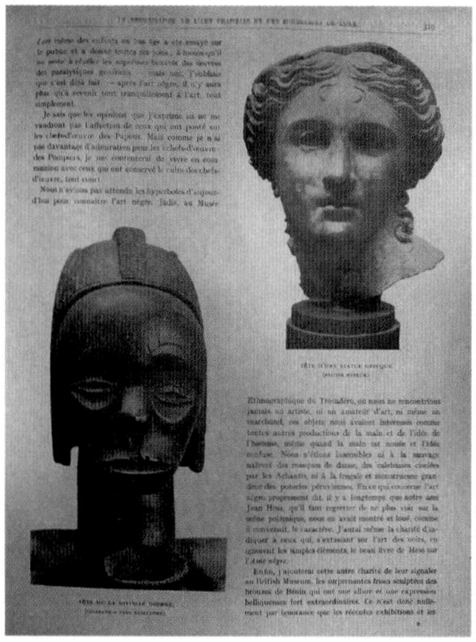

15. Arsène Alexandre
Black and White, in *La Renaissance de l'Art Français et des industries de luxe*, II, 1919

often happens with a historiography too concentrated on confirming the Modernist myths), but rather to get their bearings and try to understand. Not therefore the presumed purity of Modernism, but rather an ecumenical "having a look around."
When Guillaume Apollinaire wrote – in a monograph promoted by Guillaume himself – about African art in terms of "curiosité" and with his own nonchalance, of its "indubitable parenté avec l'estétique égyptienne", he contributed to this atmosphere.[46] If we are willing to put to one side the image of the alcoholic *bohémièn*, and we consider Modigliani for what he was (a cultured, educated artist with a sharp intelligence), that panorama that we have presented, even though just a glimpse, is what he could observe during his fine days in Paris: an uninhibited mixture of traditions and modifications, a cultured and academic substrate, a commercialisation of styles that went hand in hand with an astonishing speculation (when Guillaume began his commercial activity, a Parisian newspaper observed with hyperbolic taste "certain faciès particulièrement hideux se vendent au prix d'un Bonnat").[47]
From this point of view, I think that the accurately reduced use of African and Oriental sources makes an exemplary case of Primitivism for Modigliani, borrowing a category used in the studies of the late eighteenth century, we could define as *agréable*.[48] This tendency could find confirmation in the widespread taste of the Apollinaire group with the unconditioned admiration – in fact, the real invention – of the "modern primitive" Henri Rousseau (fig. **16**). It also seems to resound in the decorative fluid rhythms and in the pastel tones of the delicately styled figures of Marie Laurencin, of Luc-Albert Moreau or Jean Émile Laboureur, or in the "normalised" reception of painters like Derain and Braque.[49] It is what happened in the social *côté* that can be found in Henri-Pierre Roché's notebooks: a sublime nonchalance, aesthetics of *blasé* conversion. The idea itself of "decorative ensemble" was considered by the critics of the time as more or less the quintessence of a level-headed ideology of bourgeois ornament: the Modernist version of a *grand goût* that never really died out.[50]
On this level, the African barbarization in *Demoiselles d'Avignon* was more the exception than the rule.
Therefore, Modigliani's Primitivism seems like a form of calculated syncretism of styles. It was his will to build his own sculptural world, inside the apparent cultural cosmopolitanism in Paris. Modigliani used only heterogeneous materials for his heads: however, he favoured the more graceful Primitive stylist elements, refusing the explicitly tribal roots and the more exotic echo of Oriental art. Images of contemplated beauty were mixed with vocabulary of popular or child-like innocence. A cultured context interwoven with a plurality of subaltern styles, filled with reminiscent characteristics; an allure of bourgeois grand style coexisted with more ordinary styles, scattered in numerous traces, sometimes with signs of commercial use. The famous letter written in June 1913 where Modigliani announced to Paul Alexandre that he was sending "deux petits morceaux de marbre"[51] also impresses me, I should say above all, for the seaside exoticism of the headed paper: "Del Chirac Giulio. Viale Margherita, Viareggio, Bar egiziano, pasticceria e gelateria."

Worldly Appropriation
Tribal art was not able to escape the destiny that had seen "Egyptmania" pass in less than a century from museum to *bal tabarin*. In fact, it took even less time. From the first rudimental fetishes that had appeared in the Montmartre studios at the beginning of the century, in just a few years there was the lively business of the *jazz age*. Modigliani's great success after his death does not seem out of place in a social and cultural context that was stimulating the conversion of *nègre*, Oriental and Classic motifs into the festive and innocuous subjects of art déco.[52]
Even before the Modernist appropriation, which later made it the object of

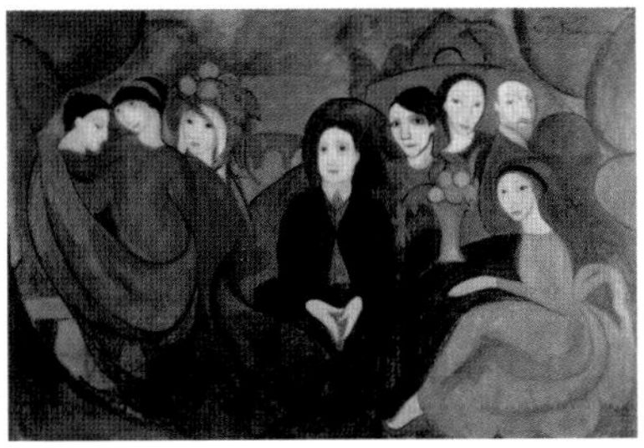

16. Marie Laurencin
Apollinaire and his Friends, 1909.
Paris, Musée Picasso

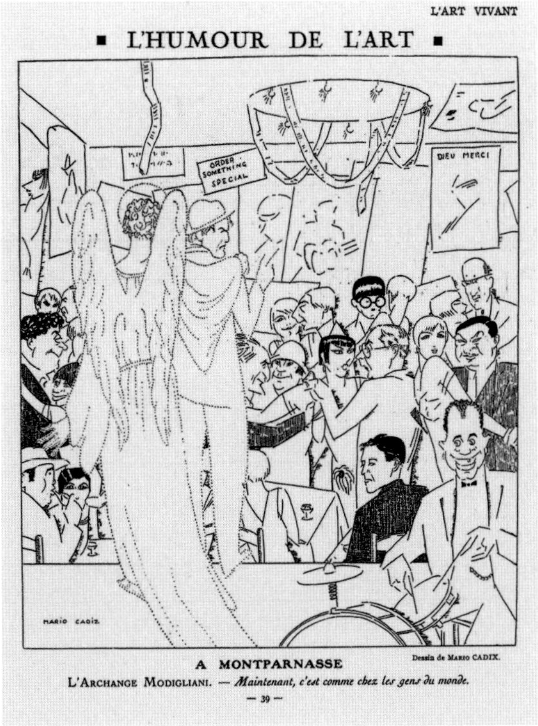

17. *L'Art vivant*, 15 avril 1925

instrumental interpretation, when not a term of confirmation for its own interpretational sophism, Primitivism was becoming a habitual phenomenon, not unknown to the outcome of merchandising as triviality.
The merchants of tribal objects, from Ernest Brummer to Paul Guillaume, were turning to, *et pour cause,* the more cultured and influential classes of the cultural *élites.*
The redemption of the neglected savage did not cancel out either the presumption of European taste or the commercial heteronomy. There soon appeared a form of trivialisation of what was phenomenal and a process of making what was magic and mysterious become carnival-like.
At the cry "L'art négre est à la mode" in 1919 Guillaume organised a memorable *fête nègre,* with the two-fold objective of spreading the passion for tribal arts ("l'art nègre est le sperme vivificateur du XX^{è} siècle spirituel", he proclaimed)[53] and creating an audience of clients for his rather substantial stock of fetishes. Some pointed at the phenomenon as a dangerous subversive drift: "Que cette fumisterie, que cette apothéose de mamanboulisme inégral ait réussi le *nègre plus ultra* de la terre, voilà un signe éclatant de l'esprit charentonnesque qui règne actuellement. Cubisme, art nègre jazz-band, bolchévisme, tout cela se touche".[54]
Other newspapers, with more progressive positions, objected instead, that for all the worldly ostentation at the Champs Elysées theatre, no negroes had in fact been seen. It was only a question of time. Josephine Baker's body was needed to incarnate the fantasies of liberation and, with them, the definitive slide of the Primitive repertoire to a thunderous fashionable word. A reporter of the same era as Picasso (and we can add even more so of Modligliani's) wrote that we should speak about "nègrerie" in the same way as we speak about *chinoiserie* regarding some of Boucher's arabesques.[55]
To end with, let us change place. We are in a *bistrot* in Montparnasse, in 1925 (fig. **17**). Modigliani has come down to earth with his angel and observes, in his usual crumpled corduroy suit, the fame and revels of the Parisian avant-gardes. Marcel Duchamp, Gertrude Stein, Jean Cocteau, Picasso, André Derain, Foujita and all the others are eating and dancing noisily, enjoying a jazz orchestra where you can see the demoniac coloured *batteur* in the foreground.
Now, Modigliani sighs, it is like being with the rich.

1 Pfannstiel, 1929, pp. 12-13, 82.
2 Venturi, 1930, p. 117. Translator's note: "negro sculpture, French Gothic sculpture, Italian Primitives [...], Japanese art, Greek, these and other discordant voices reached him from the past."
3 Basler, 1931.
4 Schaub-Koch, 1933, p. 49.
5 Wilenski, 1932, p. 18
6 Meidner, 1943, p. 87, 91: "Influenced by negro art he started a kind of cubist portrait sculpture which, however, within his life-work, does not seem very important."
7 Lipchitz, 1958, p. 3.
8 George, 1925 (later in Ceroni 1965, pp. 15-21): "Ses sculptures aux profils saillants et accusés présentent parfois certaines analogies avec les masques nègres"; while he writes about the paintings: "le réalisme si rude des portraits, dont l'armature géométrique rigide cède sous la pression d'un couleur dramatique fait songer à ces masques du Gabon qui, sous une construction prismatique, rigoureuse, révèlent un telle somme de mystère!"
9 Scheiwiller, 1927 pp. 6-7: "First he did sculpture. With youthful boldness he carved works directly from the stone that were influenced by Cubism which was in fashion then, and, even more by the nègre sculpture which gave birth to it." The text remained identical in the following editions in 1932 and 1950, where due to the increase in the bibliography and the illustrated tables there was a total absence of sculpture; the lack of success of his sculpture in Italy is reaffirmed by the Milanese retrospective in 1968, where not even one was exhibited (while three sculptures, Ceroni III, XII and XXIV were exhibited in Rome in 1952: cf. Carli, Rome, 1952, p. 16 and Nos. 26-28). There also exists a whole line of criticism that ventured to offer various hermetic or existentialist interpretations of Modigliani's Primitivism; this goes for the all the Ungaretti style interpretation given by Franchi, 1947, p. 17.
10 Basler, 1928, pp.51, 55.
11 Anti, 1922, p. 41. The selection of what was the first exhibition of tribal art together with contemporary art was rather obscure in Italy; the objects, which came from ethnographic collections in Rome and Florence, reflected more the geography of Italian explorations than real evidence of the models which the artists appreciated most. Works from the Congo, Angola, Cameroon were very different from those of Gabon or the Ivory Coast, so famous in Parisian circles; and so, despite the proximity of the groups of exhibits, there was no way to be able to establish any connections. Translator's note: "All these artists saw in negro sculpture not what there really was, but rather what they felt inside themselves or what they were anxiously searching for. Theirs was not a judgement but a too subjective interpretation of art nègre."
12 Segalen, 1995, p. 25.
13 Sweeney, 1935, p. 11: "In the early work of Picasso and his French contemporaries, as well as in that of the German 'Brucke' group, frank pastiches are frequently to be found. But these, like the adoption of characteristically negroid form-motives by Modigliani and certain sculptors, appear today as having been more in the nature of attempts at interpretation, or expressions of critical appreciation, than true assimilations." The name of Modigliani often appears, and with some relevance, in the pages of Afro-American criticism: cf. Locke, 1924, pp. 134-138; Porter 1937, pp. 8-9.
14 Goldwater 1938, p. 238. It is clear that the problem of the "primitive" sources regarding Modigliani appears to refer to a vaster circulation of models between painting, sculpture and graphics. If the evidence denies or changes the perspective of art nègre, there are, however, more probable forms of pictorial contamination with Derain's archaic-like language around 1909, or with the synthetic calligraphy started by Matisse with works like *Luxury*, that find useful terms of comparison with the faces in *The Conversation* 1909-1912 and *Portrait of Madame Matisse*, 1913, (cf. Messina 1994, p. 199).
15 A. Werner 1960-1961, p. 77.
16 Salmon 1926, p. 22.
17 However, I must point out that in the catalogue of an exhibition with the promising title *Modigliani e la spiritualità africana* (Rome 2007), on p. 82 a detail of a female goddess figure was published with the following caption, that I transcribe as an example of (involuntary?) philological humour: "Foto del 1911-12 di *Busto* [*sic*] *di donna*, in pietra di proprietà di Amedeo Modigliani (coll. Paul Guillaume) esposta a Parigi e alla Biennale di Venezia (foto proveniente dagli Archivi della Biennale di Venezia)."
18 Balas 1981, p. 87.
19 Braun 2006, pp. 45-63.
20 The information is in *Comœdia*, 8th December 1912, p. 3.
21 Rubin 1985, vol. 1, p. 17.
22 Cf. for this Blackmun Visonà et al., 2001, pp. 179, 355, 361.
23 Two examples can be seen in *Sculptures nègres*, 1917, No. VI and Clouzot, Level, 1919, No. XX, as well as in *Les Arts à Paris*, No. 6, November 1920.
24 *Sculptures nègres* 1917, (without page numbers).
25 Boas 1911.
26 Cf. for this aspect Bullen, 2003, pp. 3-12; P. Kropmanns 1999, pp. 24-31.
27 Clouzot, Level 1919, p. 13.
28 Fry 1910, pp. 334-338 and Fry 1920, pp. 65-68; useful on this theme, Torgovnick 1990, pp. 85-104.
29 Gopnik 1983, p. 375.
30 As happened in George E. Downing's review of Werner's monograph (Downing 1963, p. 90): "Nobody doubts the provocative authenticity of Modigliani's art. At the same time, perhaps, we have to admit the troubling conviction that it is dated in a way that great works by some of his predecessors and contemporaries are not."
31 The exemplary case is Rubin 1985, about Paris 1988.
32 The obligatory reference is to the exhibition Paris 2004.
33 Adam 1906, p. 311.
34 Bégain 1995.
35 *Collection du M. Charles Vignier* 1913.
36 Jamot 1912, pp. 437-449, on the fifteen large panels exhibited by Petit, 23rd April - 16th May, on themes of Indian fantasy following his journey (which he had told personally *Le Figaro*, 9th February 1912; an article also in *L'Art et les artiste*, "L'Inde vue par M. Albert Besnard").
37 Paris 1910, (the judgement is taken from a cutting of *Comœdia*, undated but signed "Tout-Paris" which is in the Louis Vauxcelles fond, Institut National de l'Histoire de l'Art, Paris); Paris 1911b Paul Guillaume's review, *L'Intransigeant*, January 1911 (press cutting, Paul Guillaume Fond, Musée de L'Orangerie, Paris); Paris 1912a ; 1911a; (it was the French stop of a tour which had already been to London and Stockholm). I think the Guimet-Cernuschi line was only obscured by C.L. Ragghianti 1959 and, as often happened with regards to this important art historian, neglected for too long.
38 Paris 1912b. Here is what was observed by a Parisian magazine close to the avant-garde about the season of

exhibitions of the *annus marabilis* 1912: "Voilà une année vraiment féconde en manifestation d'art! Nous avons fini la saison avec la rétrospective de David et ses élèves, avec les expositions de Matisse, du sculpteur Nadelman, avec les admirables exhibitions d'art d'extrême-Orient au musée Cernuschi et de la collection Vignier qui, outre les merveilles de la statuaire chinoise nous à montré des sculptures nègres, dont la beauté n'était comprise jusqu'a maintenant que par des artistes comme Picasso, Derain, Wlaminck [sic]", *Les Arts Plastiques* 1913, p. 12.

39 Gronkowski 1920, p. 466: "nous révèle un art très inattendu, et qui posait des problèmes d'un extrême intérêt [...] tout simplement un département nouveau dans le royaume de la Beauté, ignoré jusqu'ici ,fait de sévère grandeur et d'une noblesse inégalée – celui de la Chine primitive".

40 Chavannes 1913, two volumes dedicated to Han sculpture and Buddhist sculpture.

41 Maspero 1908, Maspero 1912; Maspero 1913; Fenellosa, 1914; Bushell 1910, a very rich repertoire with 240 tables out of text, translation from the original English by H. D'Ardene de Tizac, keeper at the Musée Cernuschi; De Seidlitz 1911.

42 I only quote Migeon, 1908.

43 Foucher 1905, 2 vols. P. 767: "A l'Inde elle doit sans doute, d'après tout ce qui nous avons vu, ce que la critique européenne s'impresserait d'appeler le manque d'accent des lignes, l'insuffisance du détail anatomique et l'absence d'action dramatique, sans s'arrêter un instant pour se demander si ce n'est pas notre goût occidental qui est corrompu par une recherche excessive du mouvement, du muscle et de l'expression pathétique". Cf. also Vogel, 1908, pp. 487-500. P. Guillaume would later point out "des divinités bouddhiques et helléniques" which gave Roger Fry's home in Camden Town "un pittoresque inattendu" (Guillaume 1920b, p. 2).

44 Hourcade 1912a, "Il est incontestable, nous semble-t-il [...] que notre mentalité actuelle qui s'intéresse à la fois à l'art des Grecs, des Primitifs italiens ou espagnols, et à celui des Chinois, retrouve en eux le génie occidental qui est en nous"; Dimier 1912b, p. 4.

45 This phenomenon is not exclusive to the Parisian situation; other reports that can be documented allow the positioning of the Jugendstil culture close to such an extended Primitivism. The most important example is undoubtedly the Folkwang Museum in Hagen, where the ethnographic collections were offered in a Liberty setting. Here, in 1907 Kirchner saw Gauguin's work for the first time. Karl Ernst Osthaus (who had been to Tunisia in 1897), founder of the museum, in 1904, ordered an exhibition of Oriental objects (Java, Japan, India) in comparison to industrial textile products designed by Peter Behrens. Osthaus's attention to non-western art was to be a model for contemporary art and for the local industrial production of silverware, ceramics and textiles. From 1909 onwards the works in the museum accumulated, deliberately avoiding the historical and typological distinctions. Buddhist and early Christian works were mixed with the works of Gauguin, Cézanne, Le Fauconnier, Bernard, Matisse, Kandinsky and Nolde, they were placed next to Balinese paintings, Bavarian products, Egyptian, Korean, Congolese sculptures. Cf. Lloyd 1991, p. 15.

46 G. Apollinaire, in *Sculptures nègres 1917* without page number.

47 *La Vie Parisienne*, 27 April 1912, p. 289: "Un marchand de tableau sceptique et ingénieux, vient de lancer le 'dernier cri' en matière d'art: ce sont les bois nègres. Il s'agit de morceaux de bois grossièrement sculptés et peints de couleurs violentes, qui représentent généralement des têtes grimaçantes. C'est affreux, mais c'est cher [...]. En tout cas nos fauves, cubistes et futuristes sont dans la désolation. Ils se sentent amèrement que leurs plus abracadabrantes compositions ne sauraient lutter contre la concurrence noire".

48 The reference is obviously to Rosenblum 1970.

49 The example of Laboureur's thirty vignettes is emblematic for the edition of the *Chanson Madécasses*, in the translation by Évariste Parny (*Chanson Madécasses 1920*); and what Clive Bell wrote in view of a similar reception Bell, 1922, p. 114.

50 Vildra 1913, pp. 175-178: "La tare fondamentale de bien des tentatives artistiques modernes, c'est qu'elles visent la clientèle du jeune millionnaire émasculé, de la princesse russe, de l'Argentin, de l'excentrique Américaine et de toutes ces bêtes et bécarres trop nourris qui constituent 'le monde'".

51 Alexandre 1993, p. 140.

52 Regarding the Primitive, archaic and Oriental sources scattered in déco, the essays collected in the volume Benton et al.,are fundamental.

53 *Opinions sur l'art nègre* 1920, p. 24.

54 *La Patrie*, 5th July 1919.

55 Levinson 1925: "je dis 'nègrerie' en parlant de l'époque Picasso comme j'aurais parlé de 'chinoiserie' pour expliquer certains arabesques de Boucher". In the same booklet a recollection of Modligliani was written by Maurice de Vlaminck. The comparison had already been introduced by Bell 1922, p. 115: "touch one of these African figures and it will remind you of the rarest Chinese porcelain."

Modigliani, Modern Sculpture and the Influence of Antiquity

Kenneth Wayne

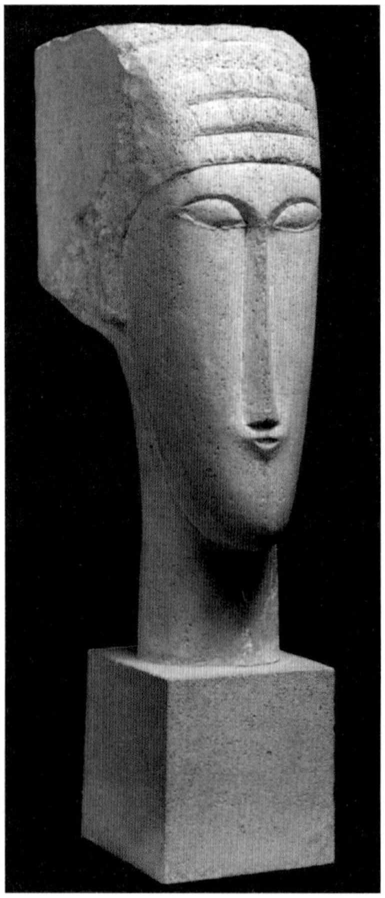

1. Amedeo Modigliani
Head, 1911-1912. New York, Solomon Guggenheim Museum. Ceroni XXI

Modigliani's sculptures (fig. **1**) share many characteristics with the Egyptian art that he loved so much and visited regularly at the Louvre: a quiet solemnity, a profound air of mystery and spirituality, blocky forms, blank almond-shaped eyes, a beatific smile, an imposing frontality and forward stare, and decorative elements in the hair and the forehead (fig. **2**). The blank eyes in Modigliani's sculptures also recall Greek and Roman sculptures as they have come down through time, with the painted elements worn off. Even the rough, unfinished quality of some of Modigliani's sculptures gives them the look and feel of bruised ancient Egyptian, Greek and Roman sculptures. Modigliani's favored material too, limestone, was the same used to make the Great Pyramid and Great Sphinx in Giza and some Egyptian and Greek sculptures. With his use of limestone, Modigliani was tying himself into a long and distinguished tradition. His love of the caryatid, a Classical Greek architectural element that he portrayed as an independent form in sculpture and on paper with great exoticism, is especially notable. By infusing his sculpture with the mystery and allure of ancient art, Modigliani was helping to revive European sculpture, which many critics felt had become stale and sterile in the hands of academics.

Despite these visual kinships, many recent art historians have asserted that modern sculptors in the 1900-1914 period broke with the ancient past and that the vanguard quality of their work lies in this fact.[1] However, this was "the age of great excavations" when antiquities from Egypt, Greece and Rome streamed into museums like the Louvre, and were studied with great devotion by contemporary sculptors. The artists also learned of antiquity's importance through their training in the independent academies of Montparnasse and through the writings of Adolf von Hildebrand. Modern sculptors were encouraged to look at ancient art for guidance as they developed a sculpture that was reflective of their own time.

In the literature at the turn of the XX century, one does not find sculptors or critics referring to a rupture, break or repudiation of the classical past. On the contrary, one finds discussions of antiquity's importance to this generation of modern sculptors.

Looking at the works of Alexander Archipenko, for example, art critic Guillaume Apollinaire proclaimed: "One perceives in his art a total adaptation of tradition... Archipenko was reared on the best that tradition had to offer... he was reared on Greek sculpture."[2] Another critic said that Archipenko's cubist sculpture, *Family Life* (fig. **3**), which was exhibited at the Salon d'Automne of 1912 and was destroyed a few years later during the war, reminded him of the *Laocoön*, the famous Hellenistic Greek work (fig. **5**).[3] Indeed, notes by Archipenko and photographs in periodicals indicate that both were life-size and contained three figures, suggesting that Archipenko did use the ancient sculpture as a model. A 1911 drawing by Archipenko called *Laocoön* further supports the point that this ancient sculpture was on his mind.[4]

There are many other connections between modern sculpture and the classical past. In a 1914 article on Elie Nadelman, André

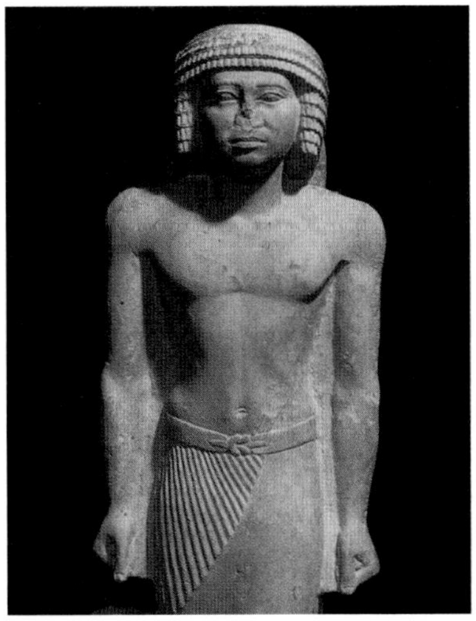

2. Tomb of Irukaptah and his family at Saqqara, detail, circa 2300 BC. New York, Brooklyn Museum of Art

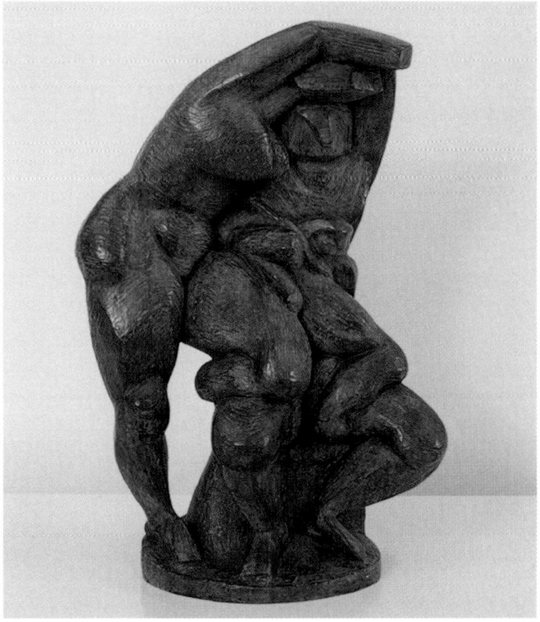

3. Alexander Archipenko
Family Life, 1912. Saarbrücken, Saarland Museum

Salmon discusses at length that artist's relationship to antiquity, saying for example: "This is how Nadelman joins the Greeks – he goes back to them in order to make a new departure."[5] Indeed, Nadelman was nicknamed "Praxitelman" or "Phidiashon"– a reference to the sculptors Praxiteles and Phidias – because of his attachment to the Greeks.[6] This characterization is significant, for Nadelman was known as a leading modern sculptor during the *avant-guerre*. To Salmon's eyes, Wilhelm Lehmbruck represented the best of classicism:

> If I maintain that the art of Lehmbruck proves to be authentically Rhenish, I would add that it tends first and foremost toward the pure virtue of classicism. Classicism is order and equilibrium; indeed Lehmbruck possesses this trait to the highest degree.[7]

Like Archipenko's *Family Life*, Jacques Lipchitz's first cubist work *Woman with a Snake* was based on the *Laocoön* as well, as Lipchitz states in his autobiography.[8] Raymond Duchamp-Villon's masterpiece *Torso of a Young Man* (fig. **6**) is based on two figures from the Temple of Aphaia at Aegina (fig. **7**).[9] Boccioni's chef d'œuvre *Unique Forms of Continuity in Space* (fig. **8**) is clearly indebted to the *Victory of Samothrace* (fig. **9**) at the Louvre as both represent a figure striding forward with clothes blowing in the wind. As John Golding remarked, '[Boccioni's] use, even if it were partially unconscious, of some of the conventions and forms of a classical past was to give the sculpture of its power and beauty."[10] Joseph Csaky's cubist figure, *Standing Woman* (1913, fig. **10**) and Elie Nadelman's *Standing Nude Figure* (c. 1907, fig. **11**) are in the position of the "Venus Pudica" (fig. **12**), a classical Venus type. Matisse's *The Thorn Extractor* (1906, fig. **13**) is an obvious homage to the famous Hellenistic *Spinario* (fig. **14**). Furthermore, Rodin, Modigliani, Brancusi, Zadkine and Meštrović carved caryatids, an element from classical Greek architecture, while Archipenko and Zadkine sculpted Venuses. In addition, Archipenko, Manolo, Lipchitz and Henri Laurens produced bas-reliefs. All of the Greek sculptures mentioned above come from the Classical and Hellenistic periods, not the "primitive" archaic period of ancient Greece, which has often been mentioned as a primary inspiration to the development of modernism in sculpture. Brancusi provides a particularly strong case study. Discussion of the artist's possible relation to primitive art has overshadowed his debts to classical Greece. His main materials at this time were bronze and marble, the favored media

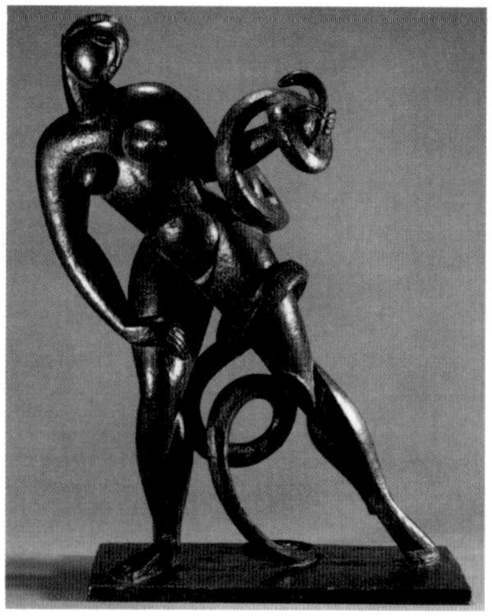

4. Jacques Lipchitz, *Woman with a Snake*, 1913. Jerusalem, Israel Museum

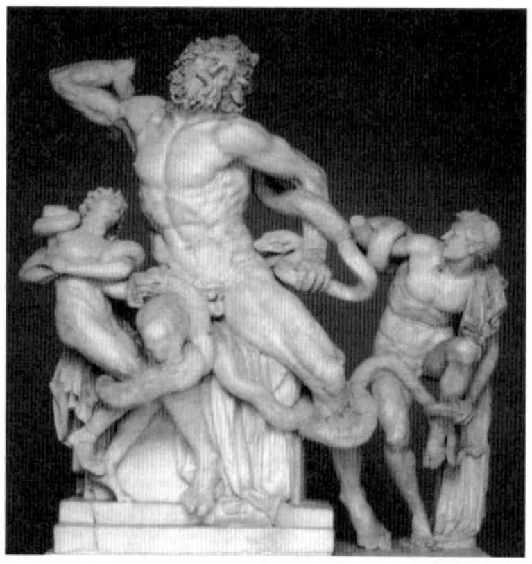

5. *Laocoön and His Two Sons Fighting with Snakes*, I century BC. Rome, Musei Vaticani

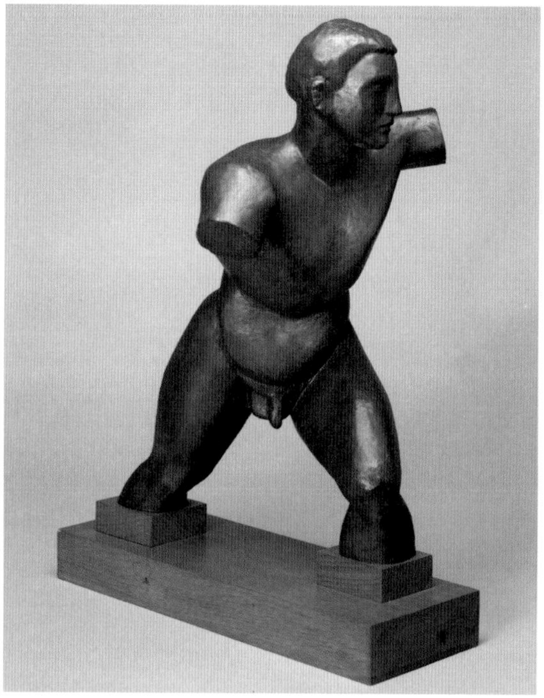

6. Raymond Duchamp-Villon, *Torso of a Young Man*, 1910. Private collection

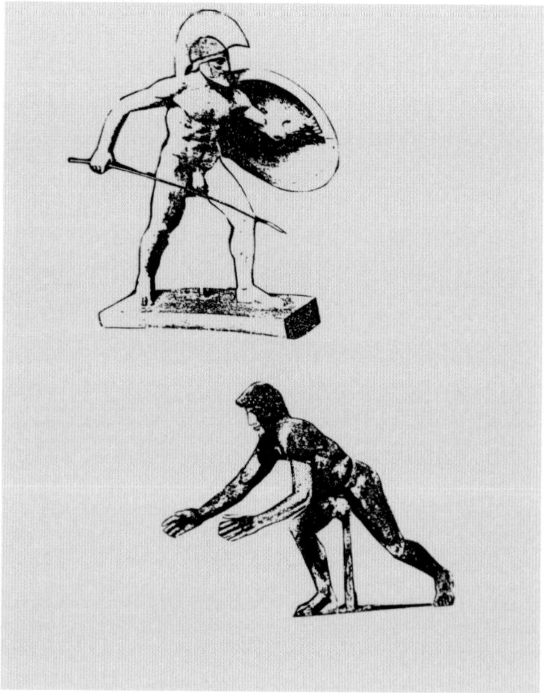

7. Two figures in relief on the eastern pediment. Temple of Aphaia, Aegina

of antiquity. In addition, virtually all of his early titles allude to mythological Greek or ancient subjects: *Prometheus* (1911), *Danaide* (1907-09), *Narcissus* (1909-10), *Ancient Figure* (c.1909), *Double Caryatid* (ca.1912, fig. **17**), *Muse* (1912), and *Maiastra* (1912).

In the period 1890-1930, when modern sculptors were producing their works, a burst of ancient Greek, Roman and Egyptian objects came on the market in France and started swelling the museums thanks to new excavations around the Mediterranean.[11] The excavations of Troy and Mycenaea by Heinrich Schliemann were among the best publicized digs, as was the uncovering of the legendary labyrinth of Minos on the island of Crete in 1900. All of this activity led Andreas Rumpf, the noted classicist, to call the period 1870 to 1914 "the age of the great excavations."[12] Many of the antiquities being unearthed were sculptures and, thus, had special relevance for contemporary artists in this medium. Indeed, several sculptors collected antiquities, including: Rodin, Bourdelle, Epstein, Maillol, Picasso and Lipchitz.

Ancient sculptures have lived a long, rich and influential life, more so than works in other media. In antiquity, sculptors were discussed and recorded in literature for posterity. Pliny called the *Laocoön* "of all paintings and sculptures the most worthy of admiration."[13] By contrast, according to Robin Barber, a scholar of ancient art, there are "no original works of the great painters named in ancient literature."[14] Made of impermeable bronze and marble, ancient sculpture could last for centuries. Further, it was easy to make molds of the works to duplicate and disseminate them. Greek painting had no such luck, according to Barber: "There are no examples of classical Greek painting in European museums and very few in Greece itself."[15] Given this background, we can understand why "for centuries it was accepted by everyone with a claim to taste that the height of artistic creation had been reached in a limited number of antique sculptures."[16]

As articles in the *Gazette des Beaux-Arts* and the *Revue Archéologique* from 1890-1914 attest, the Louvre was continually being enriched with ancient pieces from excavations in Greece, Rome and Egypt. New rooms seemed to open up annually. Thus, rather than being a dull repository of objects, the Louvre was actually an exciting, growing institution. It was especially

8. Umberto Boccioni
Unique Forms of Continuity of Space, 1913.
Milan, Civico Museo d'Arte Contemporanea

9. *Victory of Samothrace*, II century BC.
Paris, Musée du Louvre

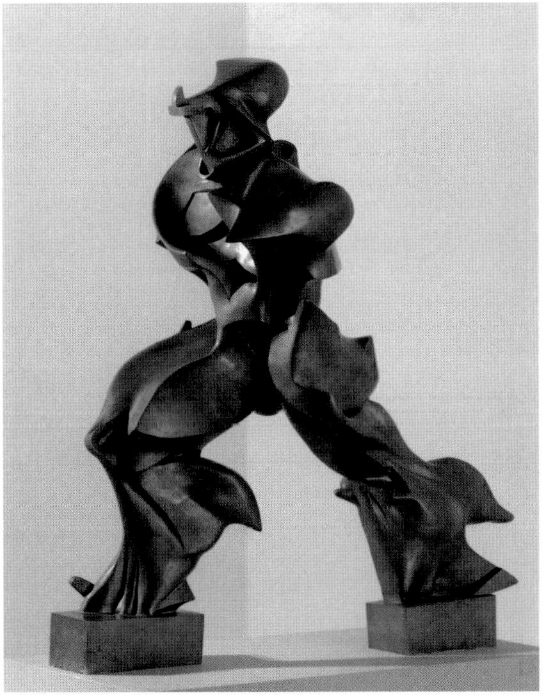

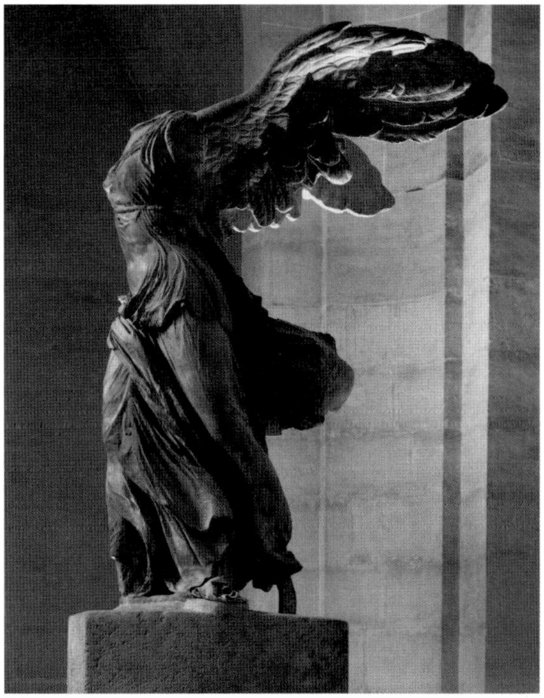

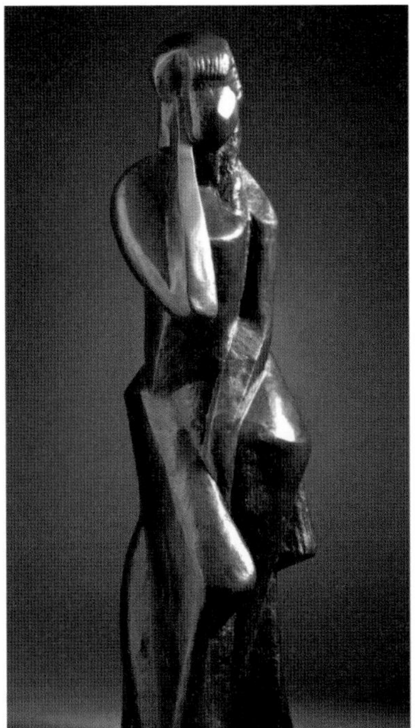

10. Joseph Csaky,
Standing Woman, 1913.
Los Angeles, Los Angeles County Museum of Art

important to sculptors, since it was above all in their medium that the museum was expanding.

I include Egypt in my definition of "classical" antiquity because at the turn of the last century it was seen that way (fig. **19**). Egyptian art was not a "new" source or influence in art, as defenders of primitivism have suggested, but rather one of the three fundamental areas outlined by Charles Blanc in his 19th-century academic manual on sculpture.[17] He specified that "we can reduce to three main categories that which a sculptor must be able to recognize: the Egyptian style, the Greek style and the Roman style." When artists and writers at the time invoked "masters of antiquity," they meant Egyptian, Greek and Roman artists. An Egyptian revival had swept through France in the nineteenth century following Napoleon's Egyptian campaign, and manifested itself in art. France's longstanding interest in Egyptian culture resulted in a major exhibition at the Louvre in 1994 titled *Egyptomania*.[18]

At the Louvre, Modigliani became especially attached to the *Venus de Milo* (fig. **20**) and to Egyptian antiquities as certain friends and acquaintances of his recalled. The poet Anna Akhmatova, who knew and posed for Modigliani in 1910-11, later recalled:

> [Modigliani] used to rave about Egypt. At the Louvre he showed me the Egyptian collection and told me there was no point in seeing anything else, 'tout le reste.' He drew my head bedecked with the jewelry of Egyptian queens and dancers, and seemed totally overawed by the majesty of Egyptian art... Commenting on the Venus de Milo, he said that women with beautiful figures who were worth modeling or drawings always seemed unshapely when clothed.[19]

In a letter to his brother Emanuele of 1912, Modigliani included a drawing of an Egyptian idol, thus demonstrating that Egypt was on his mind at the time.[20] Edith Balas, in her article, "The Art of Egypt as Modigliani's Stylistic Source," draws specific stylistic parallels between Modigliani's sculpture and Egyptian art. She cites the following shared characteristics:

Frontal hieratic position of the head, rounded chin, blank almond eyes, sharply defined rectilinear volumes of the nose, double eyebrow lines which meet at the bridge of the nose, low forehead, geometrically patterned hair style, well-

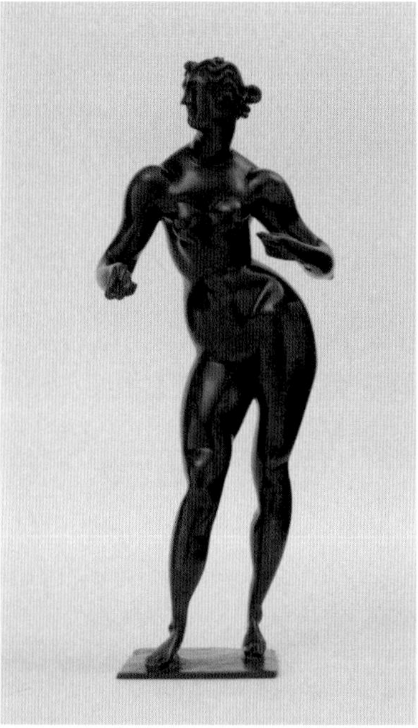

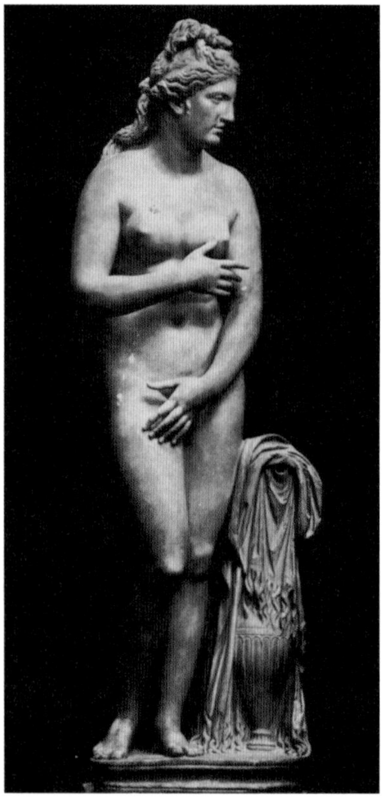

11. Elie Nadelman,
Standing Nude Figure, circa 1909.
New York, Museum of Modern Art

12. *Capitoline Aphrodite*.
Roman copy. Rome, Musei Capitolini

defined ears, and both heads are surmounted by an abacus.[21]
In addition, virtually all of the hundreds of Modigliani drawings owned by Dr. Paul Alexandre, who was close to the artist from 1907-1914, show the artist's infatuation with Egyptian art in their flatness, stylization and exoticism.[22]
Modigliani also liked to see the Italian and Greek works at the Louvre. According to his close friend Marevna Vorobev, "His thorough knowledge of Italian art made him an excellent guide at the Louvre, and he acquainted Soutine with...all the masterpieces he himself most admired."[23] Modigliani acquired this erudition from visiting museums in his native Italy during his childhood. According to his mother:

> In the museum in Naples Amedeo spent hours contemplating antique bronzes. A Silenus, a child lifting its foot to pull out a thorn, but above all a Hermes—perhaps an Aphrodite with numerous breasts—held his gaze longest.[24]

Modigliani may have had a mystical intention for his sculptures, some of which he exhibited in the 1912 Salon d'Automne as an ensemble. Jacob Epstein described seeing Modigliani's studio filled with nine or ten long heads and one figure: "At night he would place candles on the top of each one and the effect was that of a primitive temple. A legend of the quarter said that Modigliani, when under the influence of hashish, embraced these sculptures."[25] According to his dealer Paul Guillaume, Modigliani dreamed of creating a temple to mankind, which would be surrounded by hundreds of "columns of tenderness."[26]
Rodin was another one of the passionate visitors to the Louvre, where he studied antiquities. Speaking about his youth, Rodin reminisced that each afternoon, after school, his fascination with ancient art led him to frequent the Louvre to make drawings after the antique.[27] Speaking of his early years in Paris, Archipenko exclaimed, "My school was the Louvre, which for a few years I visited every day. There I principally studied archaic art and the great dead styles."[28] A cartoon review of the Salon des Indépendants in *La Vie Parisienne* of March 30, 1912 underscores Archipenko's debt to the Louvre at this time. It depicts two women standing in front of Archipenko's *Venus*, then on view. One asks, "Really? You think she's the sister of the one at the Louvre?" The other responds, "Yes, but they're not from the same father" (fig. **21**)
At the Louvre, Archipenko would have also seen *Tanagras* (fig. **22**) to which his own figurines are clearly indebted. Indeed, Archipenko made a painted terracotta in 1915 called *Tanagra Motif*. Among the subjects depicted by these small Hellenistic figurines are draped ladies. They were first found around 1870, and many were discovered by archaeologists from the Louvre. According to a tourist guide book of 1900, the *Guide Joanne*, the Louvre possessed "[a] marvelous series of Greek terracottas from Tanagra." The 1910 edition of the same guidebook referred to these works as: "Greek terracottas, ravishing figurines from Tanagra." In 1909, a long article was devoted to Tanagras in the *Gazette des Beaux-Arts*.[29] Regarding Tanagras: Maillol's earliest sculptures resemble them, Matisse was interested in them and Rodin owned some. Elie Nadelman later made some works that were clearly based on Tanagras as well. Bernard Dorival has singled out certain sculptures by Archipenko as having been influenced by specific works at the Louvre, saying that the artist was drawn above all to Classical, Hellenistic and Roman sculpture rather than to Archaic sculpture.[30]
He demonstrates, for example, that Archipenko's famous *Torse* of 1909 is based on the *Aphrodite dans l'attitude de la Venus de Medicis*. Archipenko's *Negres* of 1910 was not based on an African work of art but rather, according to Dorival, on an ancient *Génie funéraire* at the Louvre. Likewise, Archipenko's *Repos* of 1910, depicting a classically reclining figure, is "without a doubt" based on the famous

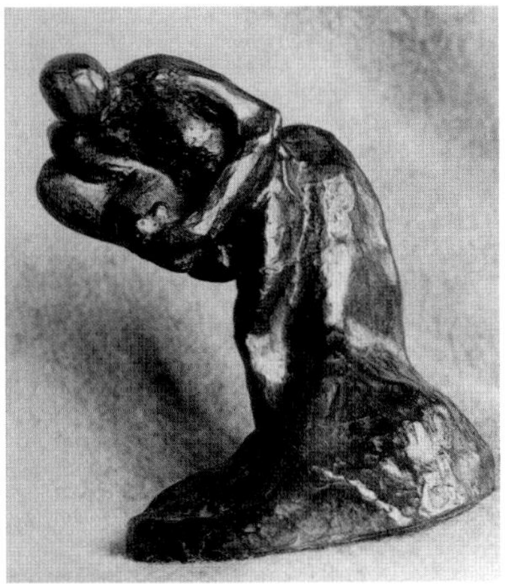

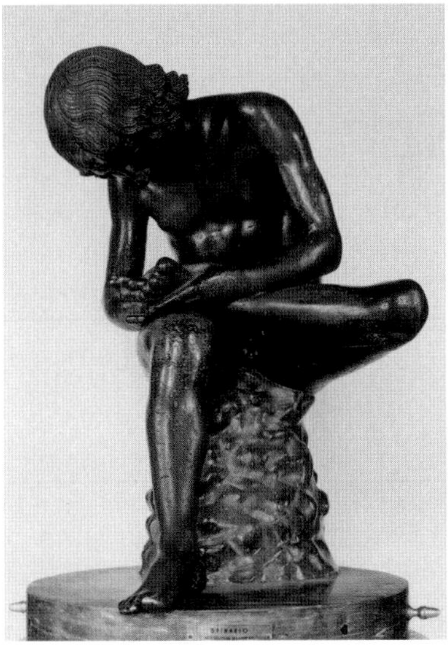

13. Henri Matisse, *The Thorn Extractor*, 1906. Private collection

14. *Spinario*, Hellenist. Rome, Musei Capitolini

Ariane endormie at the museum. In a particularly surprising yet compelling analogy, Dorival compares Archipenko's important *Carroussel Pierrot* with the famous *Borghese Gladiateur*, saying that the two share the same stance.

Henri Gaudier-Brzeska loved museums, especially the Louvre. In fact, his first date with his companion Sophie Brzeska was a visit to that museum, where he purportedly removed his hat out of respect in front of the *Victory of Samothrace*.[31] Gaudier seemed to be fond of portraying animals in his sculpture, particularly cats. Archipenko shared this interest, as his sculpture *Woman with Cat* attests. These portrayals are undoubtedly indebted to the Egyptian section at the Louvre where there are dozens of sculpted cats, a theme which had a special significance and power in Egyptian culture.

Visits to the Louvre were also important to Picasso, Matisse, Epstein, Zadkine and others.

The teaching of art in the independent academies of Montparnasse – where Modigliani lived and studied – stressed the importance of looking to antiquity for inspiration. A devoted student, Modigliani is known to have studied at two institutions on rue de la Grande Chaumière: the Académie de la Grande Chaumière and the Académie Colarossi (at nos. 14 and 10 respectively). He later lived at no. 8, from 1917-1920. He also studied at the Académie Russe and perhaps at the Académie Julian and the Académie Ranson. Among other modern sculptors who studied in the independent academies of Montparnasse were Lipchitz, Epstein, Nadelman, Zadkine, John Storrs and Chana Orloff. Archipenko was part of the circle of the Académie Russe and taught in his own academy at 169 bis, boulevard du Montparnasse. Antoine Bourdelle started teaching sculpture at the Académie de la Grande Chaumière in 1909, and his teaching notes are now conserved in the Musée Bourdelle. In practically every lecture, he pointed to sculptural practices and works from

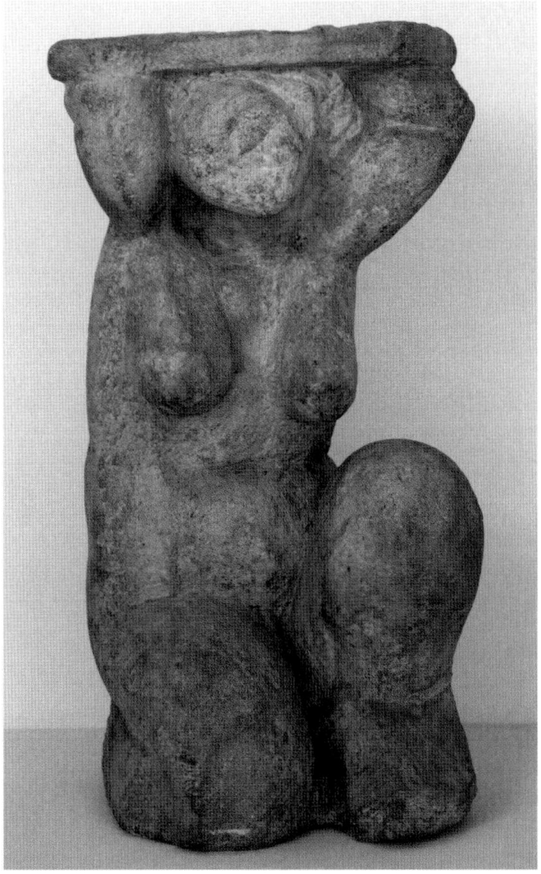

15. Amedeo Modigliani, *Caryatid*, 1913-1914. New York, The Museum of Modern Art. Ceroni XXV

antiquity as examples to emulate and strive for. In one lecture, he remarks:

> The great ancient works that we see as having been made by artists were created by people who were above all, scholars. A masterpiece is a work of logic and simplicity: something true. The Greeks left us works that seem have been made by demi-gods, rather than by men. (Class of April 7, 1910)

In another lecture, he develops this idea:

> Greek sculpture, as is well known all over the world, comes out of the great masterpieces of Antiquity, especially from Egypt. That is the result of a very high level of culture. There had to be decadences in the greatest cultures on Earth in order for Greek art to flourish. This proves that nothing happens spontaneously. (Class of December 30, 1909)

The teaching philosophy of the Académie Russe was equally indebted to antiquity:

> While working from nature the student is guided above all by the greatest examples of ancient and modern art

16. Amedeo Modigliani, *Caryatid*, circa 1913. France, private collection

17. Constantin Brancusi, *Caryatid* or *Double Caryatid*, 1912. Cambridge (USA), Fogg Art Museum

18. Caryatids from the lodge of the Erechtheum, circa 415 BC. Athens, Acropolis

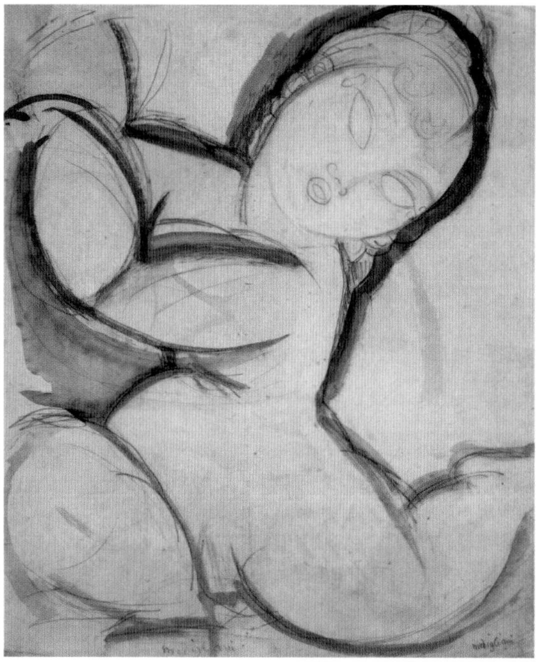

as well as by the general principles derived from all the theoretical premises of both painting and sculpture.[32]

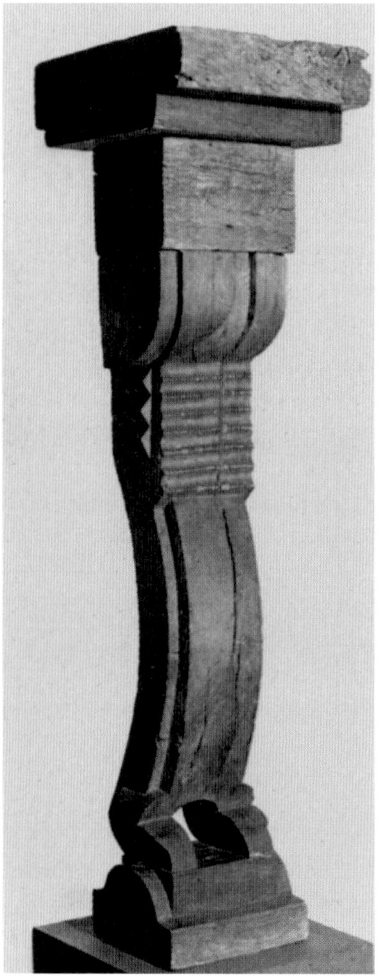

Another influence on progressive sculptors in Montparnasse before World War I was the Munich-based theorist Adolf von Hildebrand. His book, *Das Problem der Form in der bildenden Kunst*, first published in Strasbourg in 1893, was republished nine times by 1914, and translated into several languages. Previous scholars have suggested that Hildebrand influenced this generation of sculptors, but have not explained how a theorist in Munich had an effect on a group of artists working in Paris, aside from mentioning the 1903 publication of the French version of his book, *Le Problème de la Forme dans les Arts figuratifs*. There are several likely channels. Hildebrand's influence may have been transmitted through the sculptor-turned art dealer Joseph Brummer, who studied in Munich in 1903 before establishing himself in Montparnasse. Brummer, an antiquities dealer who also sold some African art, was in turn in contact with many of the sculptors in this study, especially Modigliani who was close friends with Brummer's shop assistant Martin Wolf.[33] Elie Nadelman also spent a few months in Munich in 1904 en route from Warsaw to study in Paris, and in his library had Hildebrand's book.[34] It is quite likely that this young sculptor, known for his classicizing works, would have become aware of Hildebrand while in Munich. Indeed, a review of Nadelman's 1913 one-man show at the Galerie Druet claimed that Nadelman interpreted antiquity "in the way it is seen in Munich."[35] Gaudier-Brzeska visited Munich just before settling in Montparnasse in October of 1909.[36] Thus there was a fairly direct connection between Parisian sculptors and Munich. Hildebrand's ideas would have been available to progressive sculptors in the heart of Montparnasse at the Café du Dôme, which was dominated by a large group of German artists precisely during this *avant-guerre* period.[37] Most of these German artists in Paris had in fact studied in Munich.[38] One German writer said that the Café du Dôme was "Munich transported to Paris."[39] These German artists were so numerous and conspicuous that they acquired a name: "Dômiers."[40] Alfred Flechtheim held an exhibition of twenty-three of these artists at his Dusseldorf gallery in June 1914.[41]

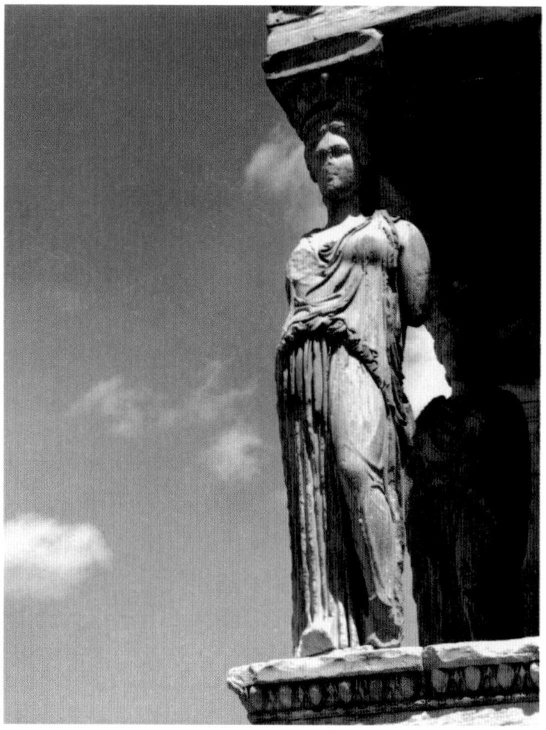

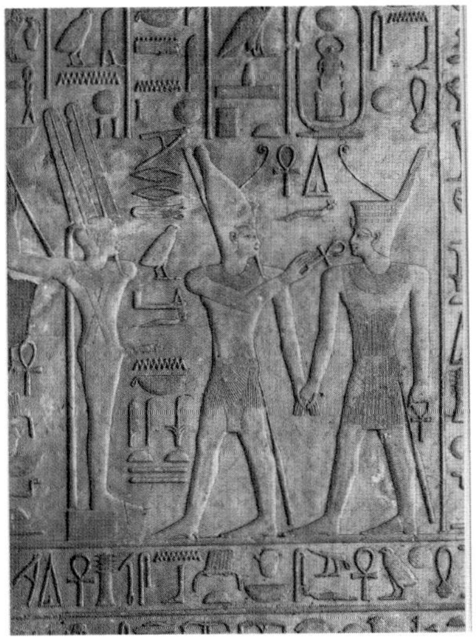

19. *Senwosret I led by Atun towards Amon-Ra*, circa 1930 BC. Thebes, White Chapel

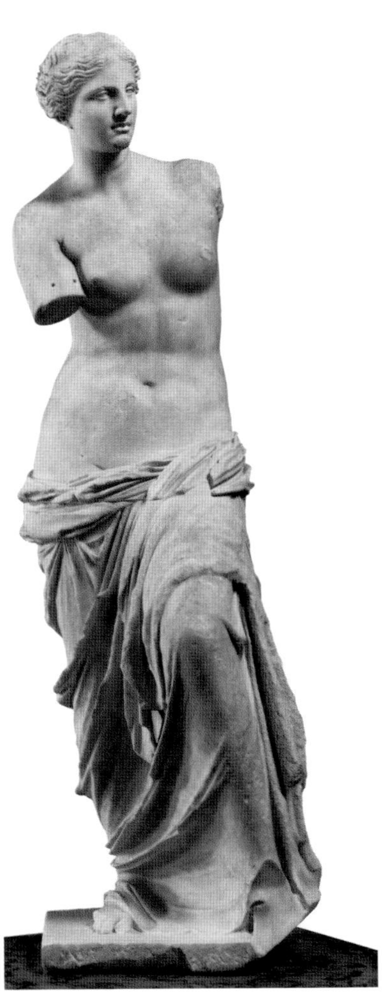

20. *Venus de Milo*, II century BC. Paris, Musée du Louvre

One of the Dômiers was the sculptor Wilhelm Lehmbruck.
All of the progressive sculptors—from Archipenko to Zadkine—frequented the Café du Dôme, which is located within a couple of hundred yards of most of the private academies discussed above, as well as most of the studios and homes of these artists. Modigliani spent considerable time at the Café du Dôme and made many of his portrait drawings there. From 1910 to 1913, Nadelman was a regular habitué of the cafes du Dôme and de la Rotonde. According to Ernest Brummer: "He was part of the décor then in that period."[42] Jacob Epstein even used the Dôme as his mailing address in Paris.[43] Indeed, the importance of café life in the development of modernism has often been mentioned by scholars.
The matriculation of large numbers of Germans in the Montparnasse academies before the war would have helped further spread Hildebrand's ideas among the avant-garde sculptors in Paris. German presence seems to have been especially substantial at the Académie de la Grande-Chaumière, for example, located across the street from the Café du Dôme.[44] German interest was so significant, in fact, that Bourdelle was approached by German officials to see if he would open a studio that would only accept students from the art schools of Munich and Berlin.[45]
Hildebrand was a modern sculptor who was obsessed with antiquity. He offered a model to modern sculptors of how to make an art for their day by looking to antiquity for guidance. He argued that contemporary sculptors should look to antiquity to learn how to get beyond "the poverty of sculptural art today" and make an art in sync with their times.[46] As he remarked, "a comparison of the Art of earlier times with that of today must reveal the undoubted fact that the logic of visual representation was far more highly developed then than it is now; and upon this fact is founded the superiority of earlier Art over ours."[47] He supplements such remarks with numerous illustrations of what he calls simply "ancient sculptures" – all of which are Classical or Hellenistic Greek works. He notes in the beginning of the book that he intends for his ideas to be used, not just discussed; in other words, he hopes that his book will serve as instruction manual.[48]
Hildebrand's influence may also account for the sudden and curious proliferation of sculptures of caryatids, an ancient Greek architectural element, around 1910. Picasso, Modigliani and Brancusi made caryatids as independent objects (i.e. not attached to architecture). In a sense, all of Modigliani's sculptures can be linked to caryatids given the regular suggestion that they had some sort of architectural connection.
In addition, Modigliani made dozens of drawings of caryatids. These drawings deserve special mention, for they are among the most beautiful images ever put on paper. In these graphic works, Modigliani takes the caryatid, a classical architectural feature, and gives it an Egyptian feel: the figure is shown in profile or frontally in a flat graphic style that makes it seem like a hieroglyphic. He also imbues his caryatids with a quality that one does not normally associate with this static, solid architectural feature, namely that of emotional intensity. Instead of presenting them in their standard erect stance, he depicts them buckling under the weight of an unseen burden. They seem to push on the top of the paper. He gives them further appeal, and modernizes them, by depicting them often in red or blue crayon or watercolor. He also alludes to Cambodian or Khmer sculpture – which he had seen with his friend Dr. Paul Alexandere – by giving them serene smiles and thick lips. Modigliani has made the Greek caryatid more exotic and even non-Western.
Rodin was a major example to this new generation of sculptors in his love of antiquity. He expounded on this passion in interviews with Paul Gsell in 1907, which have been published and re-republished many times. He also wrote several articles

21. Cartoon commenting the Salon des Indépendants in 1912 (with the *Venus* by Alexander Archipenko), in *La Vie Parisienne*, 30 mars 1912

22. *Tanagra*, Greece, III century BC. New York, The Metropolitan Museum of Art

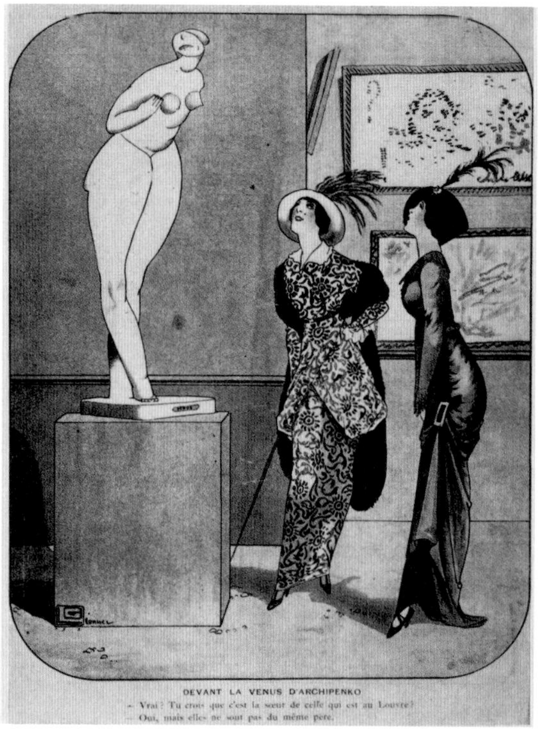

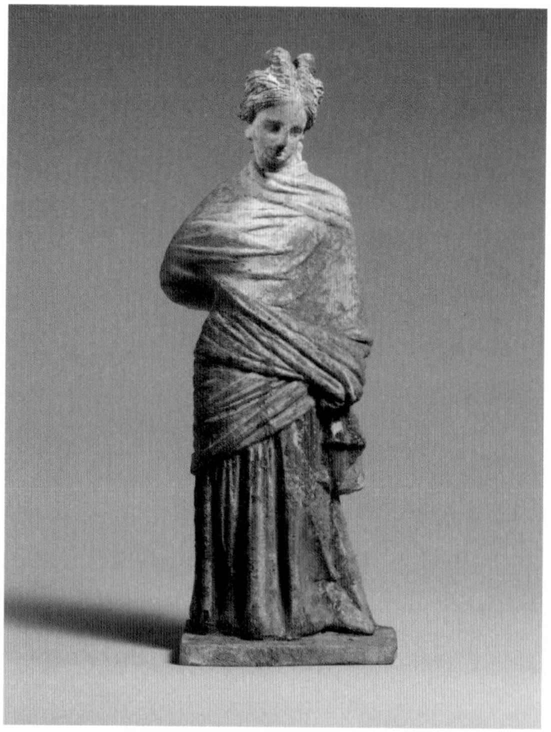

during the first decade of the century on ancient works: "Vénus, à la Venus de Milo"; "La leçon de l'Antique"; "Le Parthenon et les Cathédrales"; "Une statuette de femme au Musée de Naples"; and "La Tête Warren" (a well-known ancient head).[49] The timing of the Gsell interviews and Rodin's articles corresponds not only with the artist's voracious collecting of antiquities, but also with his decision to exhibit partial figures as complete works, which was anathema to academic sculptors.

Many of Rodin's signature elements came from his interpretation of ancient sculptures, as he makes clear in his writings. His greatest legacy was perhaps his appreciation of partial figures, for that is the way that many ancient sculptures were seen after history had taken its toll on them. If we can celebrate ancient partial figures like the *Venus de Milo* (no arms) and the *Victory of Samothrace* (no head) for their mystery and beauty, Rodin's reasoning went, then why not make modern partial figures?[50] Thanks to Rodin's validation, it was in the area of partial figures that ancient sculpture had perhaps its biggest impact on modern sculpture. When it came to ancient art, modern sculptors responded to what they saw, not to the works as they were made. Modern sculptors used ancient art to inject mystery and appeal to their works as a way to revive European sculpture.

1 See, for example, the writings of M. Rowell, H. Read, F. Licht, A.M. Hammacher and R. Krauss.
2 Apollinaire 1988, p. 360.
3 Allard 1912, p. 5.
4 This drawing was exhibited in December 1912 at the Museum Folkwang in Essen, Germany. It too is now lost. However, an Archipenko drawing titled *Lacoön*, ca. 1900, was sold by the Nagel auction House in Stuttgart, Germany, on April 21, 2009, lot 365.
5 Salmon 1914, pp .107-114.
6 As recalled by Ernest Brummer and quoted in Kirstein 1948, p. 26.
7 Galerie Levesque, *Exposition des oeuvres de Wilhelm Lehmbruck*, preface by A. Salmon, Paris, June 20-30, 1914, n.p.
8 Lipchitz, H.H. Arnason, 1972, p. 11.
9 Pach 1924, p. 16.
10 Golding 1985, p. 27.
11 Most of the material for this section is drawn from Robin Barber, "Classical: Discovery, Research and Presentation, 1890-1930", in Tate Gallery 1990, pp. 391-411.
12 A. Rumpf, *Archaeologie, I*, 1953, quoted in *On Classic Ground*, p. 392.
13 Haskell, Penny 1981, p. 2.
14 Barber 1990, p. 395.
15 *Ibid.*
16 Haskell, Penny, 1982, p. xiii.
17 Blanc, n.d., p. 173.
18 Humbert 1994.
19 A. Akhmotova, *Poem without a Hero, 1940-62*, in Schmalenbach 1990, p. 184.
20 Modigliani 1990, p. 80. The letter is undated, but internal evidence allowed the artist's daughter to date this letter to 1912.
21 Balas 1981, pp. 87-94.
22 See Alexandre 1993.
23 Marevna [Vorobev] 1974, p. 18.
24 Cited in Alexandre 1993, p. 30.
25 Epstein 1940, pp. 38-39.
26 Paul Guillaume to Gotthard Jedlicka in Jedlicka 1953, pp. 33-4. For more on this, see Balas 1987, pp. 181-90.
27 Elsen 1965, p. 146.
28 Wiese 1923, p. 4.
29 Pottier 1909, pp. 21-33.
30 Dorival 1974, pp. 201-220.
31 Ede 1971 (1931), pp. 12 & 16.
32 "Russkaja Akademija," [L'Académie Russe], in Marcadé 1979 (2), pp. 174-183.
33 For more on Brummer see Wayne 2002, pp. 26-29.
34 Kirstein 1973, p. 164.
35 Anonymous, "Eli Nadelmann," *Gil Blas*, June 1, 1913, p. 3.
36 Ede, Messiah 1987 (1931).
37 See Wilhelm Lehmbruck Museum, Pariser Begegnungen, 1904-1914, Duisburg, Germany, 1965 and Ahlers-Hestermann, 1918.
38 See also Gautherie-Kampa 1993.
39 Hausenstein 1918, p. 8 in Gautherie-Kampa 1993, p. 76.
40 Wilhelm Lehmbruck Museum, *Pariser Begegnungen*, 1904-1914.
41 *Ibid.*
42 Brummer quoted in Kirstein 1948, p. 26.
43 See Epstein letter to Rodin, September 12, 1912, Musée Rodin.
44 Dormoy 1922, pp. 684-702.
45 *Ibid.*
46 Hildebrand 1907, p. 116.
47 *Ibid.*, p. 121.
48 *Ibid.*, p. 15.
49 Auguste Rodin, "La Léçon de l'Antique," *Le Musée*, vol. I, 1904, pp. 15-18; "Le Parthenon et les Cathédrales," *Le Musée*, Vol. II, 1905, pp. 66-68; "Une statuette de femme au Musée de Naples," *Le Musée*, vol. I, 1904, pp. 116-120; "La Tête Warren," *Le Musée*, vol. I, 1904, pp. 298-301; "Vénus, a la Vénus de Milo," *L'Art et les Artistes*, March 1910.
50 For more on this topic, see Elsen 1969.

Modigliani: Lights and Shadows from the Past

Roberta Bartoli, Eike D. Schmidt

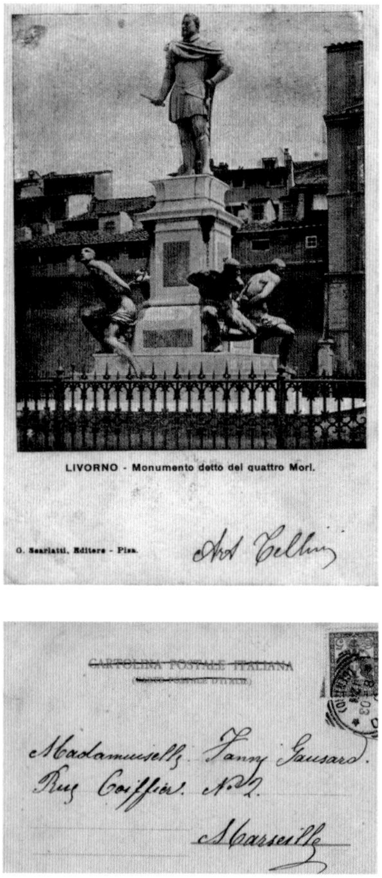

1-2. Postcard showing the *Monument to Ferdinand I de' Medici* by Giovanni Bandini with the *Four Moors* by Pietro Tacca, belonging to Amedeo Modigliani. Front and back. Paris-Rome, Modigliani Institut Archives Légales

The monumental literature that has overwhelmed the figure of Modigliani over the last ninety years, that is to say from the moment of his death and the immediate wave of commotion – and attention for the artist – that followed, can rarely be separated from the temptation to find in the Old Masters of Italian art the predecessors, the figurative stimulants, the most suggestive references for his formation as an artist. However, the game has become so heavy going that, wanting to sum up the presumed or real sources of inspiration, you lose count, and include the protagonists of nearly every current, of every period from Medieval art to the Renaissance to Baroque, in a cheerful confusion. Without taking into consideration the perhaps more reliable influence of *art nègre,* the suggestions of Khmer sculpture and of the Indian Buddhas, then the Egyptians, the Etruscans (for the quota of "Tuscanity" particularly corresponding to the artist) and Greek sculpture: from archaic because of the smooth ovals and mysterious smiles,[1] to the Periclean for the thematic invention – the *Caryatids.* There is the serious risk of presenting the Modigliani recipe as the outcome of such an exaggerated and heterogeneous series of ingredients, that it loses its taste and becomes uneatable.[2]
First of all, there are the moments of formation as a boy: in his native Livorno, the *Four Moors* in bronze by Pietro Tacca, in the monument to Ferdinand I in Piazzetta della Darsena (figs. **1.3**), would have been his companions from a very young age, and almost honorary members of the figurative family that little by little was fashioning his sensitivity (not least, it would have had a role of some kind in forming the idea of imprisoned figures, so similar to the principles of the *Caryatids*), then his journeys to warmer climate to cure his tuberculosis, to Rome, Naples and Capri at the beginning of the century. The little evidence that has remained is not enough to really solve the legend of the artist's imprinting. His letters to his friend Oscar Ghiglia[3] are adolescent outbursts, sometimes a little exaggerated due to the books Modigliani had read, about the emotions of his first contact with the great monuments of Rome ("I won't talk to you about Rome. About Rome, that as I speak to you is not without but within me, like a terrible jewel set above its seven hills, like above seven imperious goddesses [...]"[4]), and of his first approaches to the opposite sex. Then there are his mother's memories,[5] above all in a second account that she sent through her daughter Margherita, many years later, to Amedeo's friend, Paul Alexandre in Paris.[6] During a journey that lasted many months to cities like Rome and Naples, it is obvious that a young boy with a quick, grasping mind would have filled his eyes with every work of art, of every shape and colour. However, of those many months of study and rest and visits to museums and churches, up to now above all the name of Tino di Camaino, the XIV century sculptor from Siena, has been put forward (fig. **4**).
In our opinion this would seem in open contrast with the cosmopolitan atmosphere that was breathed in the Modigliani-Garsin home. It does not really seem plausible that the young Amedeo in those cities, that he was seeing for the first time – and it was an authentic immersion into antiquity, his first contact with Bernini, with Fanzago, and certainly also the contemplation of

3. Pietro Tacca, *Moor*, detail of the *Monument to Ferdinand I*, 1607-1626. Livorno, piazza Micheli

4. Tino di Camaino, *Virtue*, 1333. Naples, Santa Chiara, from the tomb of Carlo di Calabria, in W.R. Valentiner, *Tino di Camaino. A Sienese Sculptor of the Fourteenth Century*, Paris 1935

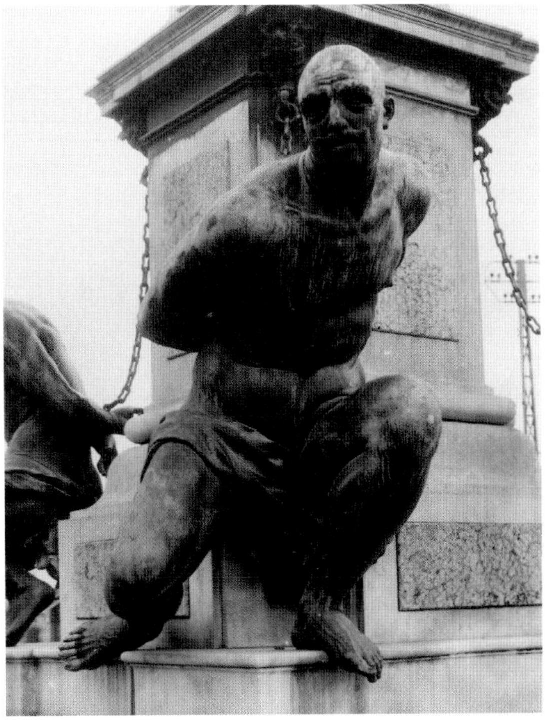

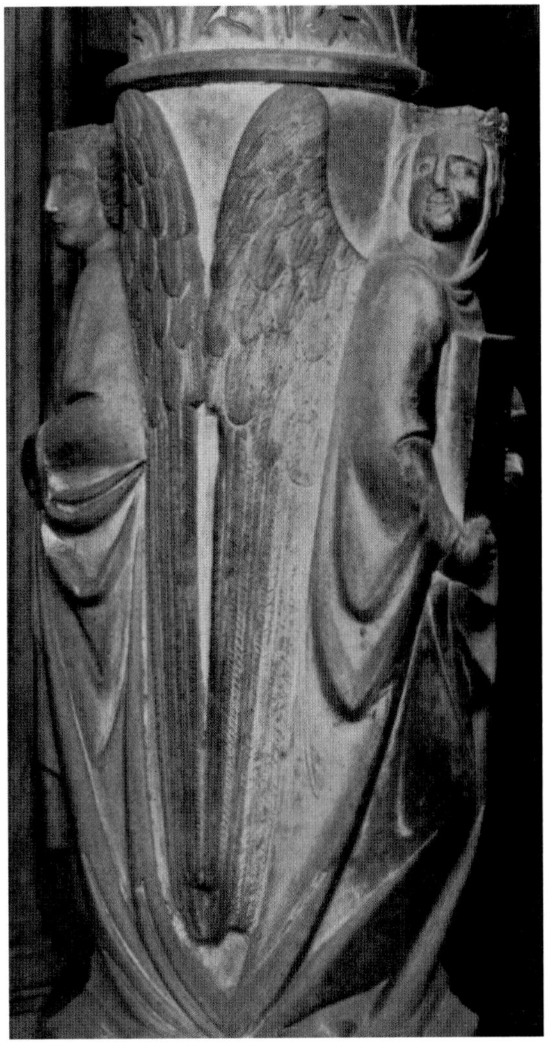

Donatello and Michelozzo in Sant'Angelo a Nilo (figs. **5-6**) – should especially single out a Tuscan artist among the many he came across, that he was dazzled by him and later on nourished himself obstinately with those distant memories. Investing Tino di Camaino with such a role, pointing out similarities with Modigliani's multiform and huge cultural knowledge, is an exaggeration that has been created almost idly by historiographic word of mouth. The first person to offer the name of the XIV century artist from Siena was Enzo Carli in 1952, but it was a suggestion advanced in very bland and mitigated tones: "it is equally probable that in the Tuscan Modigliani – we do not know how knowingly – the memory of an old Tuscan sculptor whose works he must have admired during his visits to Siena, Florence and Naples as a young boy" came into action, and this is also true for the affinity with the theme of the caryatids, that in the Angevin monuments in Naples are "blocked by strong contour lines like the torsos in the Modigliani style caryatids." Regarding the Sienese sculptor "it would be no surprise if a good quarter of a century ahead of us critics and scholars, it would have been up to a great artist to rediscover his importance and modernism, an artist sensitive to the value of Sienese linearism not only in his well

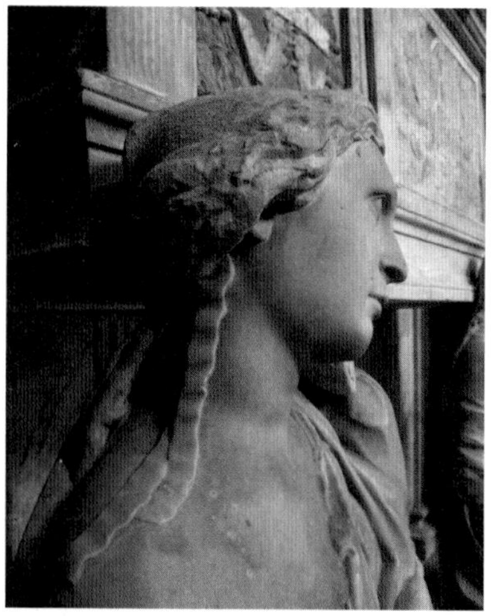

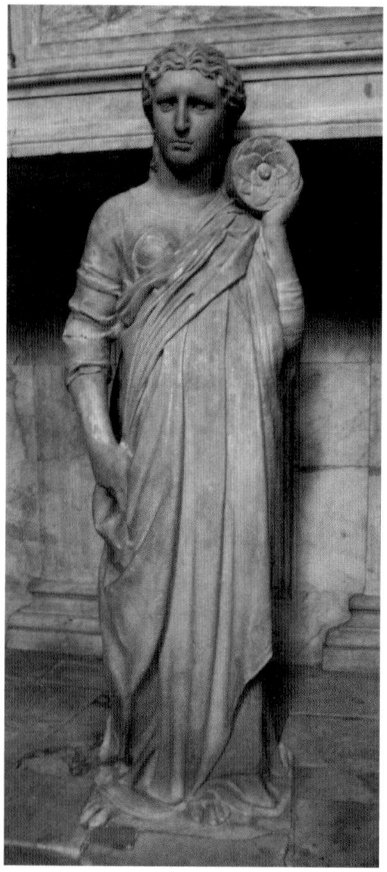

5-6. Michelozzo, *Caryatids*,
detail of cardinal Rinaldo Brancacci's tomb, circa 1426-1433.
Naples, S. Angelo a Nilo

known pictorial manifestations, but also in his then much ignored sculpture."[7] However, we shall return later to the real possibility of unreservedly accepting these affirmations, above all regarding the stylistic derivations. The fact is that Amedeo's daughter, Jeanne, pupil of Enzo Carli, also due to a sense of affection and respect towards the professor, amplified and glorified the idea, often repeating it in her biography of her father, published for the first time in 1958.[8] In our opinion, this is in the wake of the attention to Tino di Camaino aroused by Carli's monograph, published in 1934 almost at the same time as Valentiner's, which appeared in 1935, and then through publications concentrated on the works of the Sienese in Naples, by Luisa Becherucci (1935) and Ottavio Marisani (1945). However, at this point, every XIV century sculptor could be invoked as being part of the brigade of personalities who inspired Modigliani, if the simplified purity of the volumes was sufficient, the almond shaped eyes of the figures and a decorative line seen in the elongations and in the sinuosity. Art has always supplied examples of caryatids, telamones in every era and in every city. Therefore one wonders: is it necessary to dwell on Tino? How much influence might Nicola Pisano (fig. **7**) have had, as well as Giovanni, with their crowds of figures, of heroes-telamones, scattered to support the pulpits in Pisa (fig. **8**), Siena and Pistoia?[9] How much time would the young Dedo have spent observing the undulating and slim figures by Andrea and Nino Pisano? In several cases, in the most recent literature, some polychrome wooden sculptures of the XV century begin to appear among Modigliani's Sienese ascendants, hovering in the images of comparison – see the *Annunciate Virgin* at the Museo di Buonconvento, attributed to Maestro Angelo, that Lea Mattarella compares to *Portrait of a Red Haired Young Woman* in a private collection.[10] It would have been easy to go on trips to Siena (and Pistoia, figs. **9-10**) from Livorno, and in any case the artist himself speaks about it, in 1909, in a letter to his friend Paul Alexandre: "I have sent you a postcard from Pisa where I have spent a *divine* day. I want to see Siena before I leave."[11] Pisa and Siena: one can immediately sense an ideal "path of pulpits" by Pisano father and son, but in Siena for sculptures there would also have been many painted wooden statues, in the Museum, in the churches. Jacopo della Quercia (fig. **11**), Francesco di Valdambrino (fig. **12**), even Domenico di Niccolò dei Cori (figs. **13-14**), in their angels and Madonnas, in extremely elegant elongated figures, supplied multiple examples of a controlled geometry of the faces, of eyes stretched towards the temples, of towering necks.[12] And colour. It is known that Modigliani experimented with polychrome statues (Ossip Zadkine referred to it for the first time in 1930).[13]
If the trip to Siena took place in 1909, it can easily be inferred how much his imagination would have been changed by all these stimulations in the following years in Paris, almost entirely dedicated to sculpture. In this continuous change of ideas about the highest and most sublime forms of Gothic art we find Modigliani's passion for Dante's universal texts (that he could recite by heart) and Petrarch's, a passion that might also have invested the figurative arts. Elena Pontiggia correctly reminds us that "the 'long necks' were not invented by Modigliani and did not come to light only from his meditation on African masks. Also the contemplative Sienese Madonnas had them, hidden in the soft folds of their veils. All their retinues had them, the white guard of the angels and saints that escorted them, because the clarity of the line, impressing itself on the ivory of their skin, did not permit the face to blend into the neck [...]."[14] The artist's relationship with Sienese Gothic art would not therefore have been limited to the evident similarities – fittingly remembered by the historiography – in his portraits and the pure ovals of Simone Martini's Madonnas, and above all that of the Virgin in the *Annunciation* in the Uffizi, who knows how many times admired during the Florentine years, in the hours stolen from

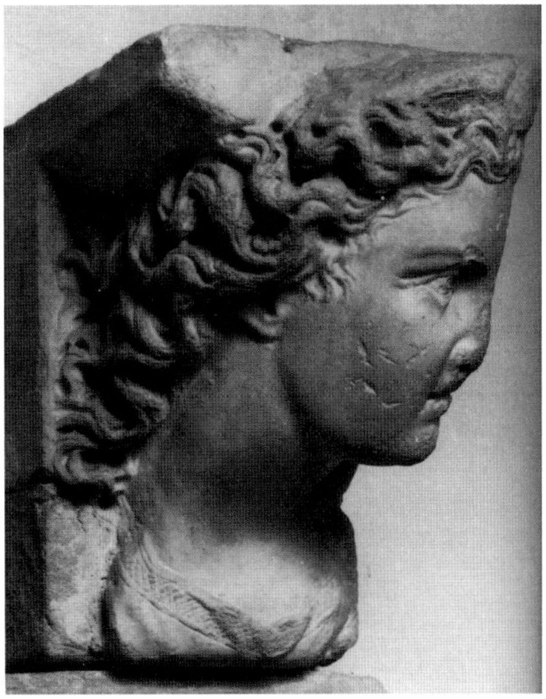

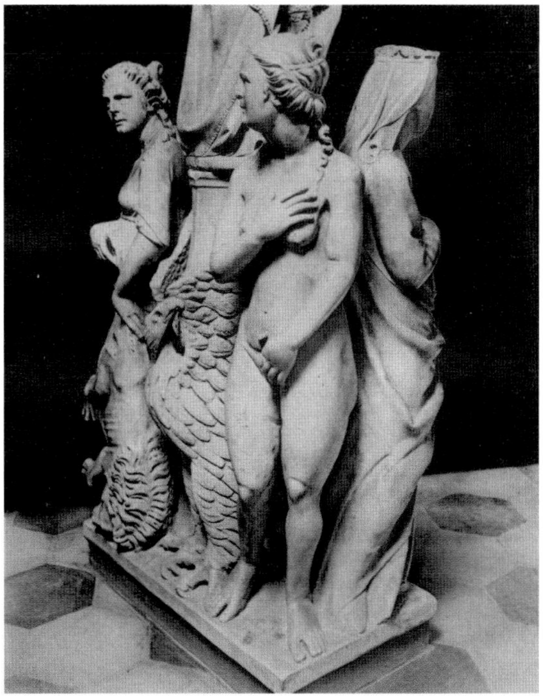

7. Nicola Pisano
Shelf with Head of a Woman, 1260-1265. Florence, Museo Bardini

8. Giovanni Pisano
The Cardinal Virtues [Caryatids], detail of the pulpit, 1301-1310. Pisa, Cathedral

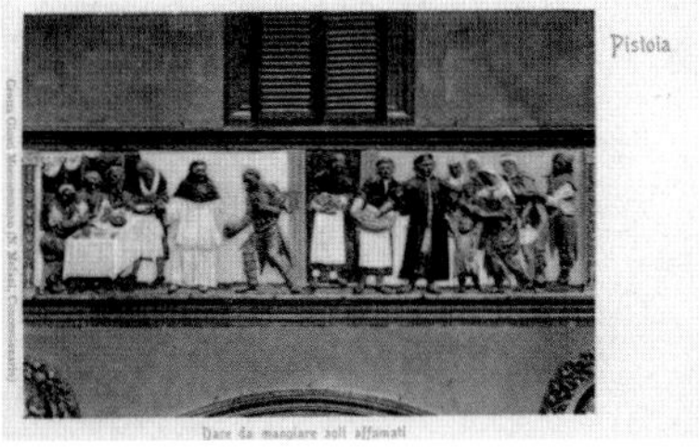

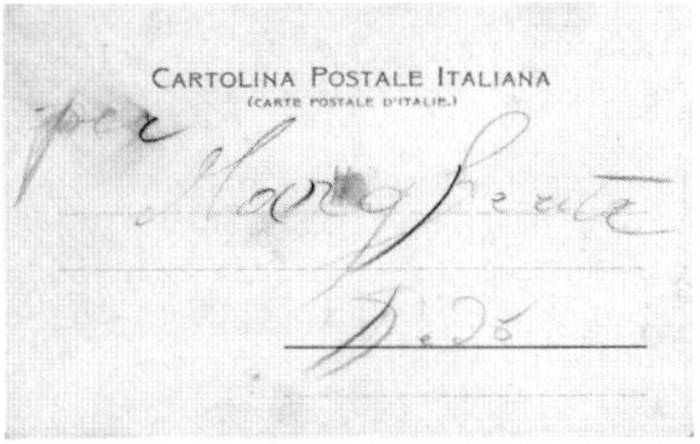

9-10. Postcard from Pistoia showing the frieze by Santi Buglioni on the façade of the Spedale del Ceppo (1514). Front and back. Paris-Rome, Modigliani Institut Archives Légales

the Scuola Libera di Nudo. The all Tuscan tradition of drawing after the "good masters" advised by Leonardo, and continued in the following centuries (remember Santi di Tito's "matitatoio"[school of pencils]), or assiduously copying the works of the great artists onto paper, until prising out the intimate essence, was also practiced in the schools and Academies that Dedo attended.[15] However, the boy went further and his visits to churches and museums were not only aesthetical experiences or merely intellectualistic operations. The Sienese refrain continued during the years in Venice (1903-1906), where he started as a well-balanced middle-class boy and then continued under the banner of genius and loose living. In the beginning – we are in 1903 – there was the meeting with Ardengo Soffici, on a journey to Venice for the Biennale. The latter remembered that Modigliani "was in Venice, he told us, to study the graceful manner of Giovanni Bellini, of Carpaccio and some Sienese artists who could be found in that Academy, or in other galleries and churches; above all to learn from them the secrets of their pictorial technique [...]."[16] Modigliani then neglected the courses at the Academy to dedicate himself to enjoyment, séances, women, without omitting a detailed and a complete reconnaissance of the city, accompanied by his very young friend Guido Cadorin. At that point the "secrets of the pictorial techniques" must have been deciphered not only thanks to the assiduous observation of the Sienese but also to that of the Venetians (as can be seen in the *Nudes*, warm and tonal, 1916-17) and the artists present in the Galleria dell'Accademia, which he visited frequently and with great attention. It is true that his friendship with Fabio Mauroner, painter and engraver from Friuli, introduced him to the knowledge of Vittorio Pica's *Attraverso gli albi e le cartelle,* judged by Mauroner himself as "the first and perhaps only interesting Italian study on modern engravers and draughtsmen."[17] However the interest for engraving (even though never practised) must have gone back to even more remote times: for the magnificent and sensual *Reclining Nude (on Her Left Side)*, from 1917 (private collection), it actually seems as if Modigliani had taken as his model an engraving by Giulio Cesare Campagnola from 1510, showing a sleeping Nymph.[18] How many engravings, prints, old papers must the omnivorous Amedeo have seen in

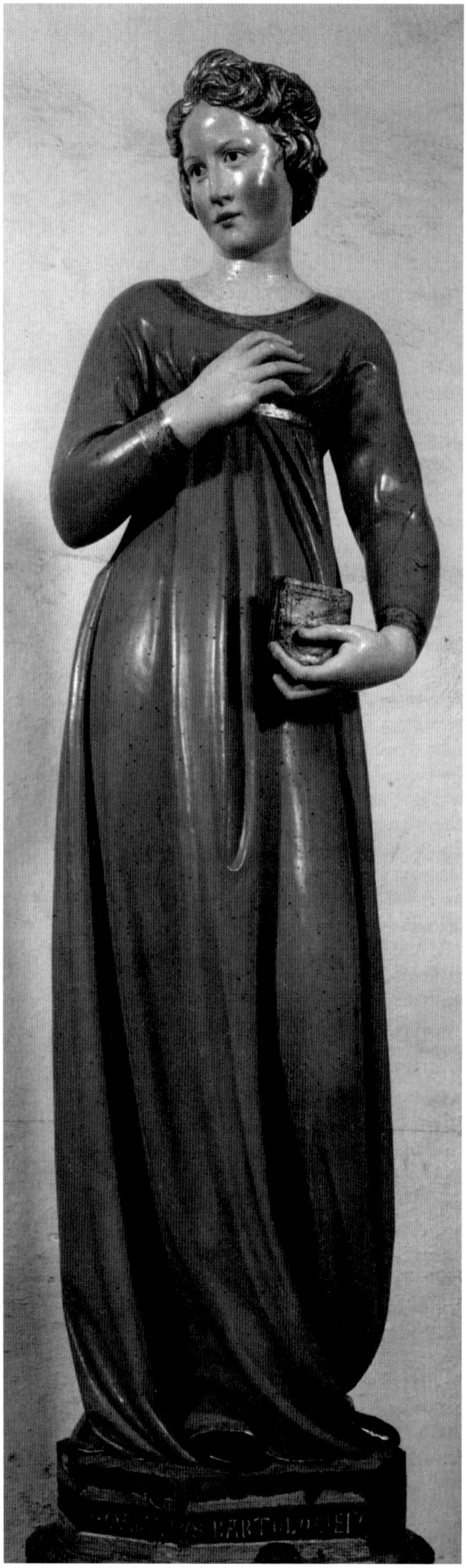

11. Jacopo della Quercia
Announcing Virgin, 1421-1426.
San Gimignano, Collegiata

the Venetian workshops and during his walks through the *calli*? Certainly it is necessary to wonder if the survival of the images, that ran through his mind and then emerged after more than a decade, was a conscious fact (would the artist have kept the image of the famous XVI century engraving in his mind while he traced the lines of his *Nude*?) and not the natural sedimentation of a vast and prehensile culture, the stocking up of a figurative collection of samples recomposed from time to time in unusual, and at the same time, "classic" solutions. In some cases, the reference is obvious (see, for example, the sheet with *Portrait of Chana Orloff*, private collection, on which the artist wrote in Hebrew "Raphael's daughter").
So in the literature that regards him, among the names of Duccio and Paolo Uccello, Simone Martini and Titian, Antonello da Messina, El Greco and Filippino and Pollaiolo, and all the host of other names that appear to explain the Modigliani phenomenon – and that would explain substantially his absolute "Italianism"[19] – one of the most recurrent is Botticelli. He would certainly have offered a fine repertoire of female images to meditate on, and dream about, with long willowy necks once again, like stems, surmounted by the elongated and noble ovals. However, Botticelli-style drawing has a decorative and engraving-like flow, like a goldsmith's, Botticelli's drawing is sublime calligraphy, while from Modigliani's thick, dark lines the full volume gushes out. This superficial similarity between the two artists, of their respective female exponents, does not reflect, on the other hand, a similarity of spirit, and Sandro's blonde, vain beauties will never be able to lower their gaze towards the painful and haughty humanity of Amedeo: but haughty due to the privilege of an atavic sufferance, the depth of meditation, the proud solitude in which it is immersed. Another beauty, the Nefertiti in Berlin, despite the suggestiveness of the comparison, should be removed from the repertoire hitherto proposed to trace Modigliani's artistic family tree.[20] Because

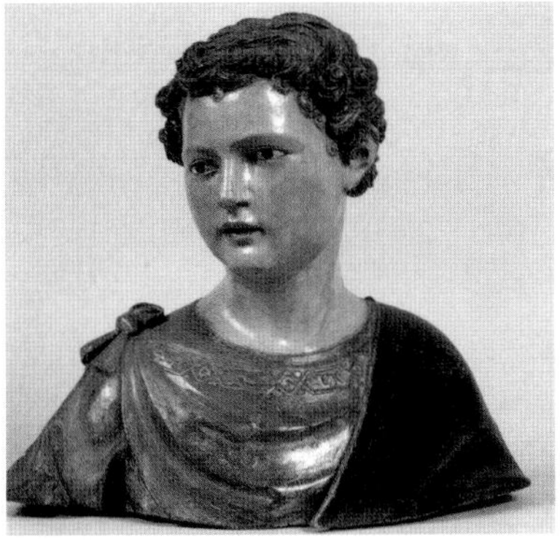

12. Francesco di Valdambrino
Saint Crescenzio [or Ansano?], 1409.
Siena, Museo dell'Opera

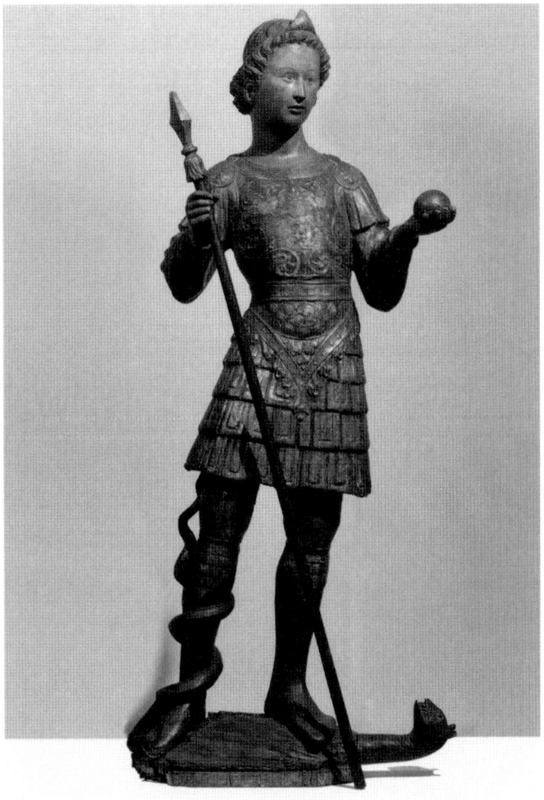

13. Domenico di Niccolò dei Cori
Saint Michael the Archangel,
circa 1415-1425.
Florence, Villa La Pietra

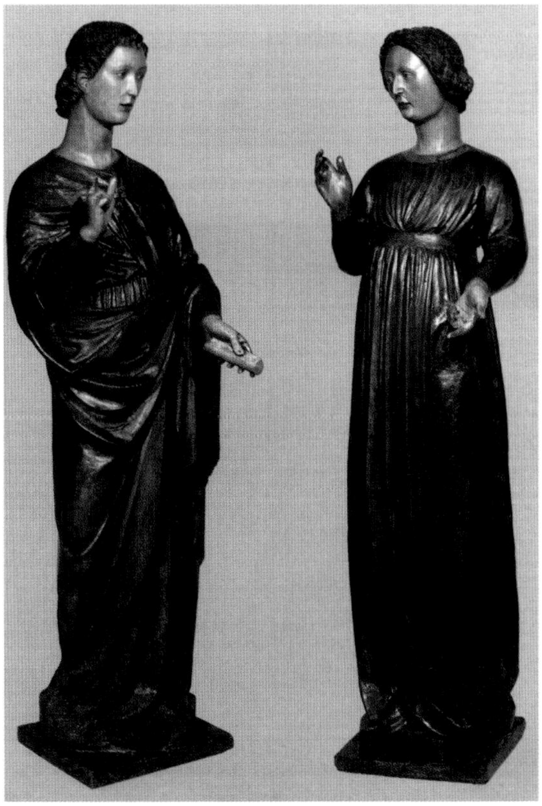

14. Domenico di Niccolò dei Cori
Announcing Angel and Announcing Virgin, circa 1415-1425.
Florence, Polo Museale Fiorentino

Modigliani did not go to Berlin, and the bust of the Queen, found by the archaeologist Borchardt in 1912, left Egypt illegally to be delivered to the banker Simon who financed the excavation: given the very delicate situation and the possibilities of a scandal, the very few reproductions existing at those dates were second hand and certainly not made public. The work was exhibited only after 1921 – Modigliani had just died – when Simon donated it to the museums of the German capital.[21] Amedeo discovered Egyptian art in Paris, in the rooms of the Louvre when he dragged along the poetess Achmatova: "At that time [1911] Modigliani dreamt about Egypt. He took me to the Louvre to visit the Egyptian section; he affirmed that all the rest "tout le reste," was not worthy of his attention. He drew my head with the hairstyle of an Egyptian queen, or dancer, and seemed completely overawed with the great art of ancient Egypt."[22] "Tout le reste", all that Paris and the Louvre offered, had on the other hand already been seen and assimilated in the previous years, because it is impossible to think that the Sienese that he had searched for and studied in Venice could have lost all interest for him just because he had crossed the Alps; and then Pisanello, and the slender neck in his *Portrait of a Princess of the House of Este*,[23] or Giotto, finally Leonardo, who he had already admired for hours in Naples, according to his sister's account[24] (and we do not give in, we who are sceptical about all this name dropping, to the temptation of a comparison with the *Belle Ferronière* to some portraits of Hébuterne[25]). It will perhaps be surprising to remember that among the reproductions that he had fixed to the walls in his studio there was one of Leonardo's drawings, in ink: a head of San Giovannino for the *Virgin of the Rocks* in the Louvre (fig. **15**). The small drawing, with quick, very mobile strokes, from a graphic point of view is an anti-Modigliani manifesto *par excellence*[26], it is also further proof of how he absorbed every possible figurative source, perhaps also – like this one – of a not obvious kind. The paintings in the Grande Galerie at the Louvre must have been not only an opportunity for Dedo to "study the technical secrets" of the ancients, as he did in Venice, but also a meeting with

15. Leonardo da Vinci
Head of Saint John, 1483.
Reproduction belonging to Amedeo Modigliani. Paris-Rome, Modigliani Institut Archives Légales

16. Michelangelo Buonarroti
Brutus, ca. 1550. Florence, Museo Nazionale del Bargello

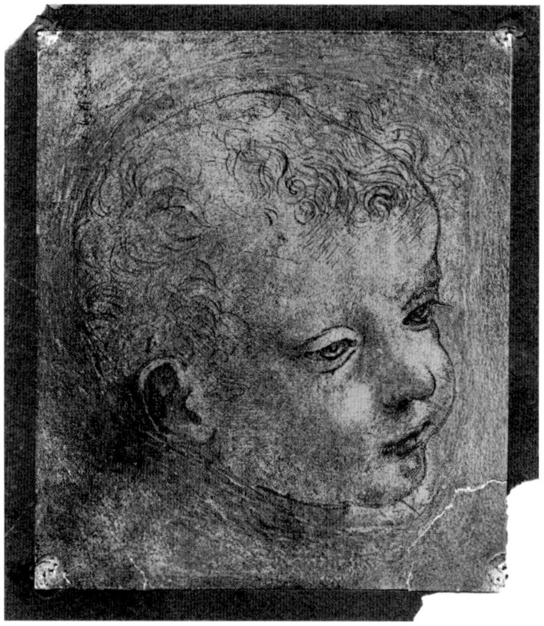

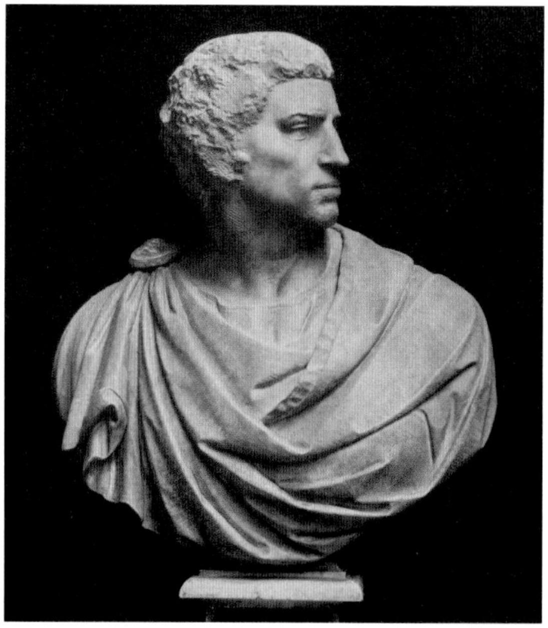

the roots of his humanistic formation. Lipchitz claimed that the early Renaissance had strongly refined his sensitivity,[27] and perhaps it also marked that disdainful exactingness that led him to destroy all the works of his youth. The early Renaissance was that which Modigliani was able to assimilate, with freedom of choice and time, during his years in Florence, in who knows how many visits to churches, the Uffizi, to that mine of sculpture that is the Bargello – where certainly the bust of *Battista Sforza* by Laurana was a useful object of contemplation for the times to come, in painted portraits but above all in the facial stylisation and the static regality of the figure. However, from Laurana's style of purified realism nothing passes to Modigliani's sculpted statues, to his timeless and homeless masks, magical emissions of hard material and above all "stony" to the highest degree. There is nothing of Laurana's silky surfaces in these extremely solid figures armed with long and sharp noses, we would look in vain for the buttery volumes and the undulating sweetness of a Tino di Camaino. There is however, a tactile particularity (shared also by his painting, where the weave of the brush-strokes can be perceived[28]) that could be described as "porous," rough, unfinished: a particularity in a certain way reminiscent of Michelangelo. Of course, as has been pointed out before, Modigliani carefully studied Michelangelo's works in Florence[29] (and probably read him and Vasari too), but not so much the perfectly smooth *David* or *Bachus*, but *Brutus* (fig. **16**), and the *Prisoners*, then in the Grotta Grande of the Boboli Garden (figs. **17-20**). He understood the sense of those marks on the stone, the traces of the scalpel, the tactile effect and the absorption of the light by the rough material just freed from its shapeless wrapping. The figures encased in the block, the sculptors "know how to free them that are inside that piece of marble" claimed Anton Francesco Doni about Michelangelo.[30] The intense graphic projection of every formal proportion in the figures, is to be understood perhaps – in a procedure similar to that used by Michelangelo – as a sort of mental "x-ray" of the block of stone, on which Modigliani worked directly without any preliminary models. The very thematic choice of the Caryatids (fig. **21**) further ties the shapes to the initial rough block and animates the relationship sculpture/architecture with a deeper meaning: the architectonic structure to be supported is the image of the material itself, of the magma from which to free the bodies, exactly like Michelangelo did with his Prisoners/Telamones. For this reason, to exalt the creative process, comes the

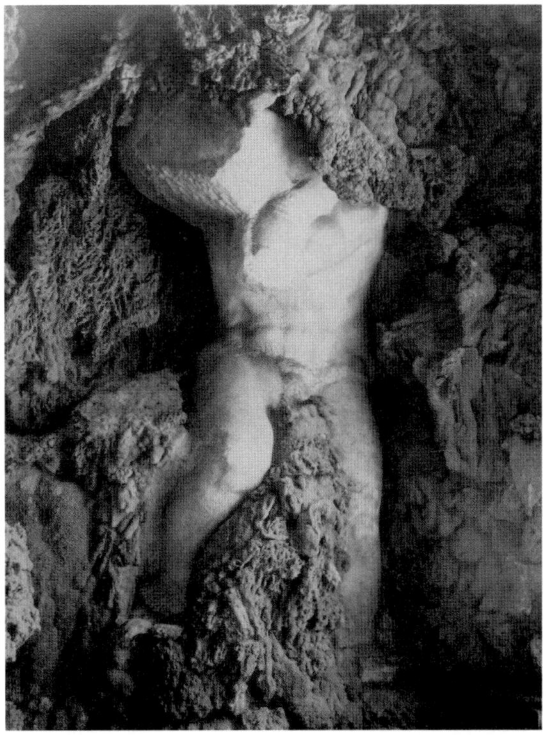
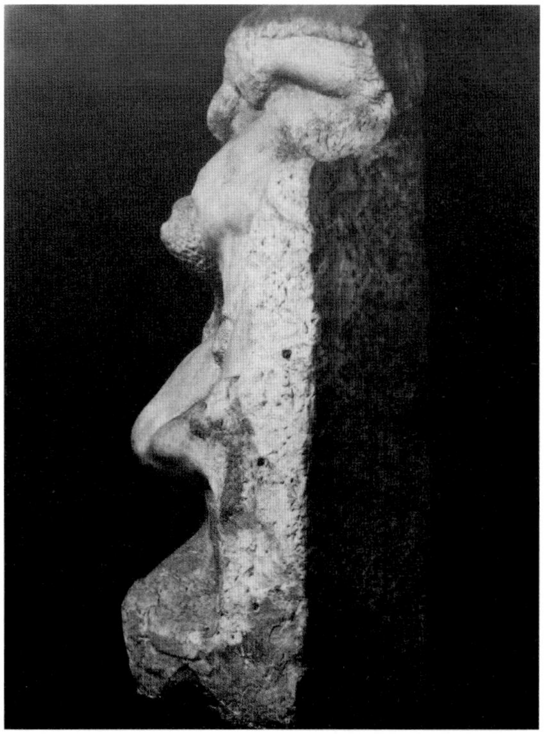
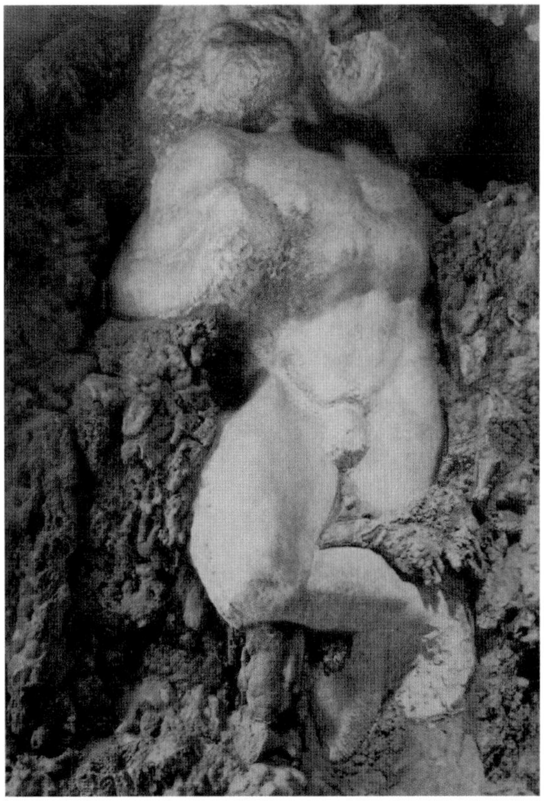
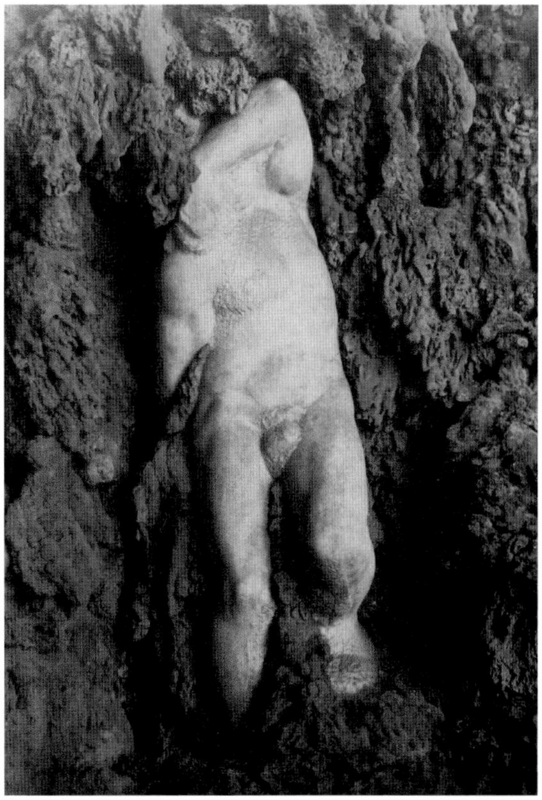

17-20. Michelangelo Buonarroti
Prisoner,
probably soon after 1516. Florence, Polo Museale Fiorentino, Galleria dell'Accademia. (Photo taken in the Grotta Grande, Boboli Garden, before 1911).

necessity of that "hardness," which the artist so ardently searched for; Lipchitz recalled that Modigliani claimed that the stone in itself (or rather its material quality) made little difference; the important thing was to give the sculpted stone the impression of that hardness.[31] For example, observing the head in Washington (Hirshhorn Museum), the one in Toronto (Latner Family Art Collection), or the one in Minneapolis (Minneapolis Institute of Arts, fig. **22**), on the back of which the architectural component

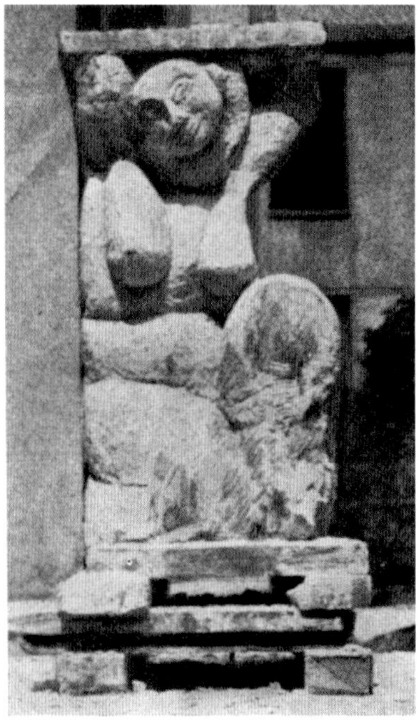

21. Amedeo Modigliani
Caryatid, 1914. New York, Museum of Modern Art (from A. Salmon, *Amedeo Modigliani: Sein Leben und sein Schaffen. Seine Briefe und Gedichte*, Zurich 1960, p. 39)

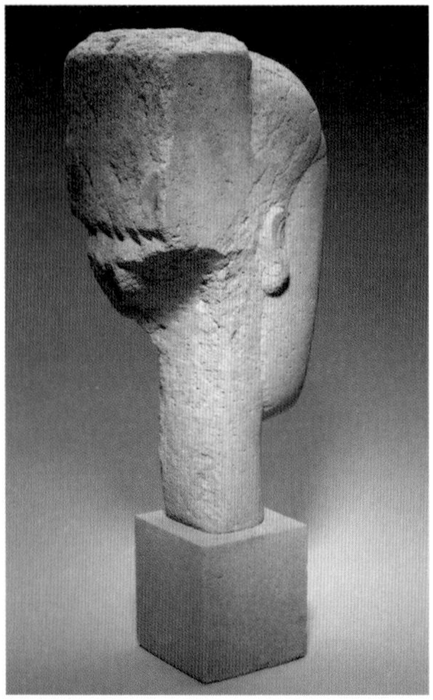

22. Amedeo Modigliani
Head of a Woman, ca. 1911. Minneapolis, Minneapolis Institute of Arts. Gift of Mr. and Mrs. John Cowles

is clearly roughed out, the rendering of the stone "skin" and of its most intimate structure and consistency is evident in dramatic contrast with the intention of making the "colonnes de tendress" of his "Temple of Beauty" out of them. Due to the choice of limestone out of necessity, of the construction stones that cost little or nothing, the weave of the material with its riddled surface and sponginess became an element of style, battling with the strength of the elements. The result stands, programmatically, in opposition to Rodin's ideal of the Unfinished, as yeast of softness, which Modigliani openly rejected as decadence of sculpture[32]. In the Italian artist, the pathos of the setting and disposition of the sculpture, – "temples" and "columns" – together with the attitude of creative fury that accompanied their genesis, cannot fail to make us think about the approach of another "damned" artist of some centuries before, Benvenuto Cellini. The scene narrated by Epstein about his visit to the studio in Montparnasse is significant: "his study at that time was a miserable hole within a courtyard, and here he lived and worked. It was then filled with nine or ten of those long heads which were influenced by African masks, and one figure. They were carved in stone; at night he would place candles on top of each one and the effect was that of a primitive temple."[33] The flickering light of the candles fell onto the sculptures from above, exalting the volumes and creating an almost mystic effect, a miraculous suggestion: the same spirit had urged Cellini to give life to his silver Jupiter for Francesco I, lighting a torch camouflaged by a thunderbolt. "The Jupiter was raising his thunderbolt with the right hand [...]. Among the flames of the thunderbolt I had very cleverly introduced a torch of white wax. Now Madame d'Etampes detained the king till nightfall [...] either to prevent his coming, or else to spoil the effect of my work by its being shown off after dark; but as God has promised to those who trust in Him, it turned exactly opposite to her calculations; for when night came, I set fire to the torch, which, standing higher than the head of Jupiter, shed light from above and showed the statue far better than by daytime."[34]
Cellini's satisfaction about the effect of his sculpture illuminated from above is the same as that which urged Modigliani to contemplate his own caryatid heads in a similar "mysterious" stage setting (fig. **22**), vaguely evocative of the séances that he had attended since his youth and especially in Venice. A satisfaction that urged the artist – truth or hearsay? – to even embrace the stones that he had sculpted.[35]
However, nothing precise – no "copying" – tied Modigliani to his Latin origins, no relationship of real filiations from the Italian figurative traditions, even though loved and studied with patriotic pride. It is in this cultured but at the same time mindful independence that his relationship with the antecedents of Gothic and the Renaissance must be read: the revelation of affinity, at the most, conceptual, in his attitude towards his creation. However always in solitary independence: in Paris in 1917, during the war, his friend Osvaldo Licini remembered him claiming: "in art there is no turning back or being born again. I adore Raphael but the idea of the coming of another Raphael makes me laugh, it is Baroque. As if there could two suns in the sky."[36]

* The authors are deeply grateful to Christian Parisot, director of the Modigliani Archives Légales (Rome-Paris) for generously allowing us access to the material conserved at Palazzo Taverna in Rome. His help, suggestions and collaboration have made the writing of this essay possible. We also wish to thank Eleonora Chiolo and Ilaria Banni for their precious collaboration.

1 Cf. most recently Strinati 2010, pp. 20-23 and Parisot 2010, pp. 25-38, *passim*, (in both essays, the comparisons are established mainly through the illustrations in the text).

2 An example of how Modigliani's figurative culture has been probed can be found in the catalogue to the exhibition *Livorno 1984*, where Matti Megged comments the artist's nudes in a crescendo of references: "the line can easily be followed that leads from Botticelli to Titian and from these to Rubens, Ingres, Courbet, and on to Manet and Matisse [...]" (p. 57). To these names could be added (cf. Schmalenbach 2006, p. 40) those of Pontormo, Parmigianino and El Greco and many others.

3 Now in Modigliani 2006, pp. 9-17.

4 Modigliani 2006, p. 12.

5 In Alexandre 1993, now in Parisot 2006, pp. 291-311.

6 In Alexandre 1993, pp. 28-32.

7 Carli 1952, p. 18.

8 Modigliani 2005, pp. 63, 96, 97. It is particularly significant, instead, that also in the latest monograph regarding Tino di Camaino, by Francesca Baldelli (Baldelli 2007), the chapter on the XX century success of the artist (pp. 3-24) does not mention the name of Modigliani, while there is no lack of more pertinent comparisons with Barlach (also discussed in Valentiner 1935, p. 2), Arturo Martini, Carlo Carrà, Federico Papi.

9 The name of Giovanni Pisano was also put forward by Piccioni 2004, p. 7. Pistoia was also, among others, a certain destination of one trip. In the Modigliani – Archives Légales in Rome, Palazzo Taverna, a postcard is conserved sent to his sister Margherita and signed "Dedo", showing the frieze in polychrome terracotta from the Ospedale del Ceppo, by Santi Buglioni (figs **9-10**).

10 Mattarella 2006, p. 108. Comments on the stylistic analogies with the ancient wooden sculpture had already been made in di San Lazzaro 1957.

11 Cf. the most recent Modigliani 2006, p. 19.

12 Christian Parisot arrived at the same conclusion, independently. We thank him for this cordial exchange of information.

13 Ossip Zadkine in *Paris Montmartre*, 1930 (issue dedicated to Modigliani), in Werner 1960-1961, p. 74. C. Douglas quoted by Patani 1992, p. 11.

14 Modigliani 2006, pp. 52-53.

15 Cf. Parisot, 2008, p. 33, note 2. "the professor [...] then made them copy portraits and compositions of the past, above all Raffaello's work. He advised reading the treatises of fifteenth and XVI century painting, written by Cennini, Alberti or Vinci [...]".

16 Soffici 1954, pp. 486-487.

17 Remembered among other things by Modigliani 2005, pp. 68-69; see most recently Tagliapietra 2002, pp. 234-235. The scholar also points out that at the Biennale of 1903 a room was dedicated to Modern portraits, and decorated with a frieze by Cesare Laurenti , which extended for more than fifty metres along the perimeter of the room and showed from Giotto to Tiepolo, the most important and famous examples of portrait painting of the past. "it was not very important that they were reproductions: Modigliani found himself in contact with the history of the portrait, perhaps unaware that he would have to continue it [...]" (p. 236).

18 Bertelli 1989, p. 59.

19 On this point see also Schmalenbach 2006, p. 34. A certain scepticism regarding this infinite fishing among the artists of the Middle Ages and the Renaissance, by now quite common in Modigliani critics, is also expressed by Piccioni 2004, p. 8: "many names put together end up forming nothing more than an indication of origin, we certainly cannot go any further."

20 Caprile 2006, p. 213.

21 Montserrat 2002, pp. 3-8

22 Achmatova 2004, p. 12.

23 Paris, Musée du Louvre: Bertelli, 1989, p. 60.

24 In Alexandre 1993, p. 31: "In the Museum in Naples [...] he spent many hours admiring an incomplete painting by Leonardo da Vinci." Perhaps it was instead the *Madonna with Child* by Bernardino Luini (Naples, Museo di Capodimonte, inv. Q 92) which was attributed to Leonardo da Vinci for a long time.

25 Modigliani carried out numerous portraits of women which were vaguely inspired by the Renaissance model, especially Florentine or Leonardo-style. There could be a reference to the *Belle ferronière* in the askance glance and the serious expression of the woman portrayed in *Portrait of a Woman with Necklace* or *The Café Singer* (New York, private collection; cf. Milan 2003, cat. no. 51, pp. 280-281).

26 Paris, Département des Arts Graphiques, inv. 2347 (by Leonardo according to Marani 1999, p. 125, considered a copy instead by Zöllner 2004, p. 180). We are grateful to Christian Parisot for putting the image at our disposal and for having permitted the reproduction. The sheet still carries the marks of the pins, and the tears at the corners probably testify to the artist's continuous moves to his various studios.

27 Hammacher 1984, p. 46.

28 Cf. Modigliani 2005, p. 162, "the colour is spread directly onto the surface, then it is taken up, 'scratched' by the brush poor in colour, to the point that sometimes the pictorial material shows a glimpse of the brush strokes that design a weave."

29 Parisot 2006, p. 53; Parisot 2008, p. 41.

30 Doni 1552, p. 128.

31 Lipchitz 1953, p. 2; Patani 1992, p. 18, who however refers to this information as having been personally communicated to André Salmon.

32 Cf. most recently Parisot 2006, p. 102.

33 Epstein 1995, pp. 46-47, quoted also in Parisot 2006, p. 120.

34 Cellini 1558-1566, 1983, p. 143. "Aveva il ditto Giove in nella sua mano destra accomodato il suo fùlgore [...] in fra le fiamme avevo con molto destrezza commisso un pezzo d'una torcia bianca. E, perché Madama di Tampes aveva intrattenuto il re insino a notte [...] o che lui non venissi o sì veramente che l'opera mia, causa della notte, si mostrasse manco bella, e come Iddio promette a quelle creature che hanno fede in lui, ne avvenne tutto il contrario perché, veduto fattosi notte, io accesi la ditta torcia che era in mano al Giove e, per essere alquanto elevata sopra la testa del ditto Giove, cadevano i lumi di sopra e facevano molto più bel vedere che di dì non arien fatto" (Cellini 1558-1566, p. 348.)

35 Epstein 1955, p. 47: "A legend in that district said that Modigliani, when he was under the effect of hashish, embraced these sculptures".

36 Licini 1934, p. 106.

The Complex Identity of Sculpture: Comparisons and Debates in Paris between 1910 and 1912

Ilaria Cicali

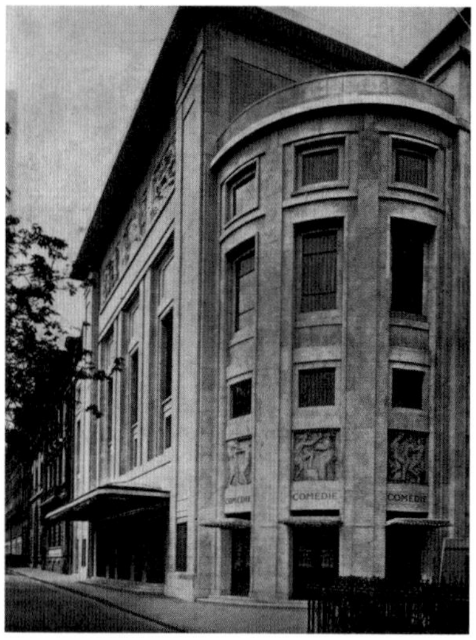

1. Auguste Perret
Théâtre des Champs-Elysées, façade, 1912-1913. Paris

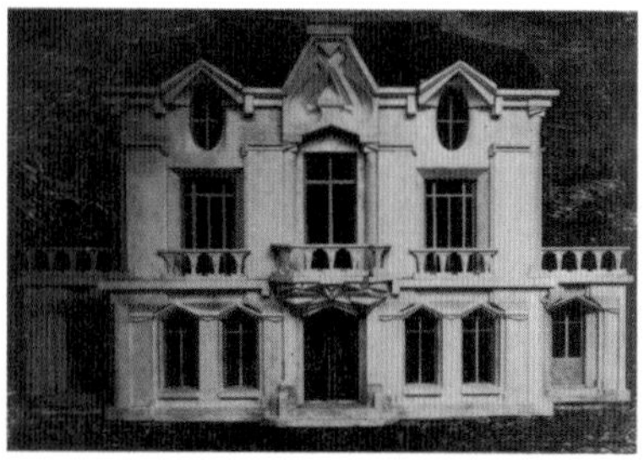

2. Raymond Duchamp-Villon
Cubist House, 1912.
Paris, Centre Pompidou, Musée National d'art moderne

Autumn 1912: Enquiry into Decorative Sculpture

In Paris the autumn of 1912 was a moment full of important events for sculpture and the way in which possible developments in a "modern" sense could be perceived. The season was inaugurated by an enquiry into decorative or *plein-air* sculpture, promoted by the art critic Louis Vauxcelles and published in the daily newspaper *Gil Blas*.[1]

In the wake of the debate sparked off by the proposal to substitute Jean-Baptiste Carpeaux's original *The Dance*, the decoration on the front of the Théâtre de l'Opéra, with a copy so as to avoid the progressive deterioration, Vauxcelles asked various artists to express their opinion about it and more in general to contribute to the definition of a decorative sculpture.

The answers published in the newspaper during the month of September converged on various points. The idea that the Carpeaux group should stay where it was, was almost unanimous; there was a certain agreement in claiming that the "decorative" nature and the "architectonic" one were the two essential qualities not only of *plein-air* sculpture but more generally of sculpture *tout-court*; everyone hoped for a clear organisation of the volumes, aimed at making it easy to read the sculptural work also from a distance and a consequent simplicity of gestures, with the correct division of the main planes and a harmonic alternation of shadow and light.

In the case of sculpture connected to architecture, an organisation of the lines was required so as not to destroy the harmony and the visual balance of the whole. As an example of this concept models were mentioned that ranged from Assyrian and Egyptian art to Ancient Greek and reaching the decorative cycles of the Medieval cathedrals.

That an enquiry was underway in Paris in 1912 about the possible forms that decorative sculpture could assume and the relationship between sculpture and architecture is proved by the projects which at that moment were involving two sculptors drawn into the question by Vauxcelles: Emile Bourdelle and Raymond Duchamp-Villon. The former was already well known by then and was working on a series of bas-reliefs for the decoration of the façade of the Théâtre des Champs-Elysées (fig. **1**). The latter who was younger and linked to the research of the pictorial avant-garde, would present his project for a façade for a Cubist house (the *Cubist House*) at the Salon d'Automne of that year together with some other sculptures destined for internal decoration (fig. **2**).

The theatre in Avenue Montaigne was the subject of great attention from the press throughout 1912, it was planned by Auguste Perret and integrated by decorations carried out by the painter Maurice Denis and Bourdelle. The choice of reinforced concrete as the construction material showed the modernity; the general appearance, linear and without any decorative elements, and particularly the pictorial and sculptural decorations set it in that "return to style" current which developed in France during the first decade of the twentieth century of which Maurice Denis was a convinced upholder.[2]

The painter's theoretical writings, like the debate developed by various critics between 1910 and 1912, about the "rebirth of a Classic ideal," had in fact brought to light the necessity to bring back a clear and structured language to artistic expression, connected to nature and at the same time able to

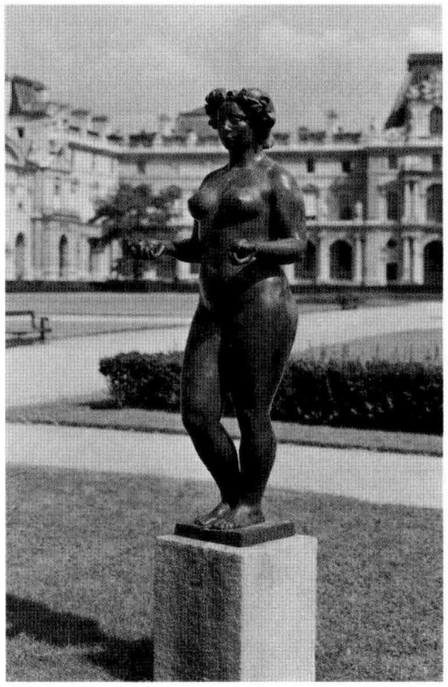

3. Aristide Maillol
Pomona, 1910.
Paris, Jardin des Tuileries

synthesise variety in a simple form, aimed at communicating with the spectator. "The ideal of art is to condense, to summarise in a few clear and concise forms those infinitely varied relationships that we perceive in nature," wrote Denis in an essay dedicated to the sculptor Aristide Maillol, explaining that the prerogative of Classic art of all times was precisely that of proceeding by means of synthesis until reaching a harmonious balance between "nature and style."[3]
Also the *Cubist House*, set up in the decorative arts section of the Salon d'Automne, saw the participation of many artists, in this case belonging to the avant-garde group, gathered around the figure of André Mare. On the basis of a similar desire for simplification, the path indicated by Duchamp-Villon in his project for the façade was that of a "mise en valeur" not included in those rules that regulated the internal structure of the building. Although scarcely innovative in the final result, Duchamp-Villon's proposal, in the same way as the response to Vauxcelle's enquiry, indicated a desire for abstraction that continued over the next two years also in sculptural research.[4]
The attention given to a simple and well structured configuration, rather than to the figure represented, emerged as a distinctive trait of the pictorial and sculptural works presented at the Salon d'Automne in 1912. The journalist and critic Olivier Hourcade in the pages of *Paris-Journal* spoke of the revenge of "intelligence over the natural gift and effort over negligence," indicating Cézanne and his "desire for writing" as an example followed by the young artists: "it is a return to style" he declared, naming Joseph Bernard, Wield and "still some others" among the sculptors who were representatives of this tendency.[5]
This analysis was also suitable as the interpretive key to the Cubist works if, in a brochure published a few months later for the Armory Show – the first large exhibition organised in New York to show the public the latest artistic trends that were developing in Europe – Walter Pach, one of the organisers of the Show, indicated Cézanne and his way of "organising a work like a structure" as an example followed by the young innovatory artists. Pach wrote: "That was the death-blow of the anecdote that was formerly thought necessary. With this new system of using simply the volumes, lines and colours of nature, the men called "Cubists" are showing that, somewhat as in music, important facts about nature and sensations derived from it can be registered in a work of art without giving the physical appearance of nature.
It must be clear even from this short description – unaided by reproductions from the works of these artists, that a very probable fruition of their tendencies would be architecture."[6] He continued showing how Duchamp-Villon's sculptural research was based on the same architectonic principle of shape.

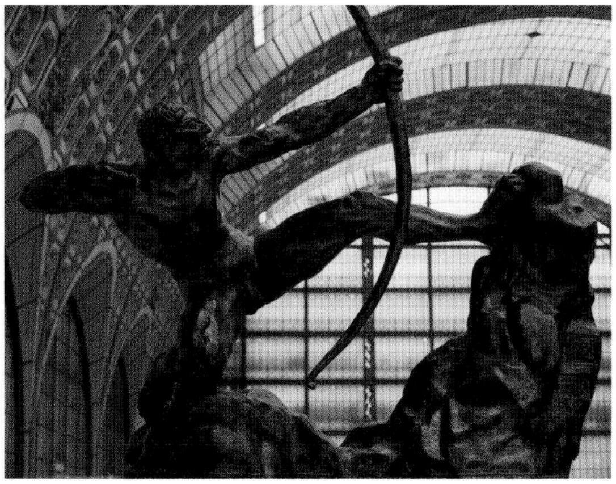

4. Émile-Antoine Bourdelle
Herakles the Archer, 1909.
Paris, Musée d'Orsay.

5. Charles Despiau, *Paulette*, 1910.
Paris, Centre Pompidou,
Musée National d'art moderne

6. André Derain, *Crouching Man*, 1907.
Vienna, Museum Moderner Kunst
Stiftung Ludwig

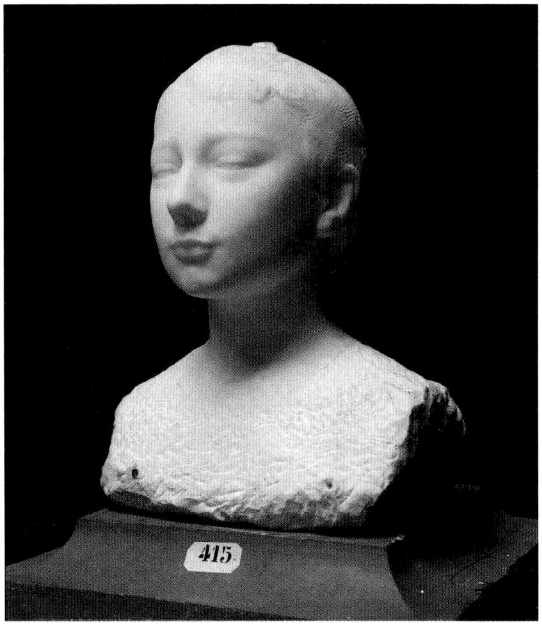

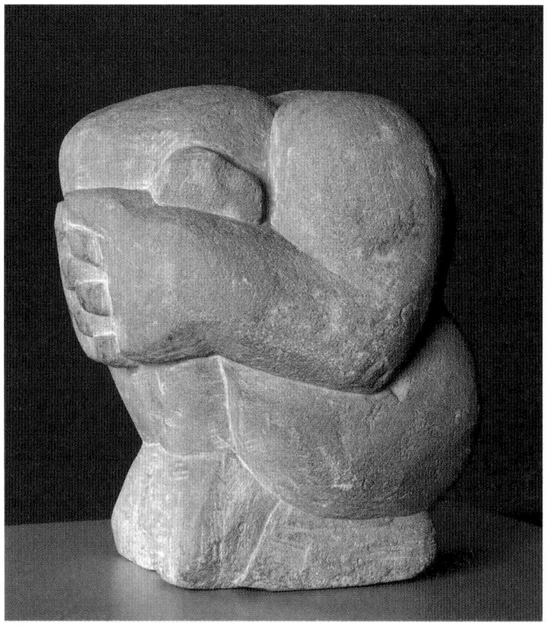

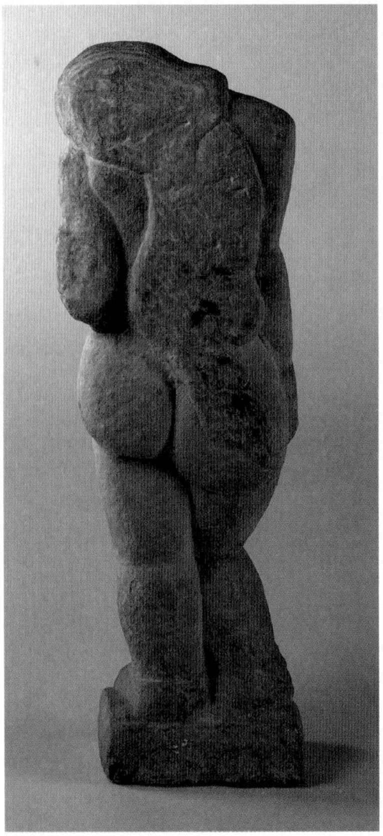

7. André Derain
Standing Figure, 1907.
Paris, Centre Pompidou,
Musée National d'art moderne

Return to Style and Cubist Sculpture: Analogies and Differences

On one hand the fact that a similar interpretative key was used to speak about research which could have led to different results is symptomatic of the artists sharing the same interests, on the other, of the difficulty for the critics to read and interpret the different tendencies that were being defined.[7] The phenomenon was particularly evident in sculpture, where since 1910 an all French school had been placing itself in the public attention, starting from what was called Rodin's "second manner," referring to some full and linear modelled torsos, claiming to be "harmonious and disciplined", a complete realisation of that return to style hoped for in all the arts.[8] Both Maillol and Bourdelle were present at the Salon d'Automne in 1910 with two works *Pomona* and *Herakles* (figs. **3-4**), to indicate the possible solutions for a sculpture that was desired to be first of all a strong construction but balanced in masses and volumes.

The former according to a line of Greek-Mediterranean tradition, the latter with elements from archaic and Roman-Gothic languages. Other artists like Charles Despiau, Albert Marquet, Jeanne Poupelet and a group of sculptors who assembled around the brothers Lucien and Albert Schnegg, advocated the same kind of research, presenting some portrait busts and simple, well-constructed female figures[9] (fig. **5**), above all at the Salon de la Société Nationale des Beaux-Arts et des Artistes Français which were held every year in spring, and sometimes at the Salon d'Automne. Some foreign artists who arrived in Paris during the first decade of the twentieth century turned their attention to those artists. During their early years Brancusi, Csaky, Lipchitz, Zadkine participated in these "official" Salons, with works that were influenced by Rodin and the above mentioned aesthetics of the "return to style."

However, as Brigitte Léal indicates in her contribution to this catalogue, already in 1910 – in a less official exhibition place than the Salon des Indépendants – Agéro, Archipenko, Brancusi and Duchamp-Villon were present with their works. In particular, Archipenko and Brancusi indicated research that sprang from the study of other sources, more primitive and archaic-like, the same that the pictorial avant-garde such as Matisse, Picasso and Derain had examined during the previous years, in the attempt to reformulate the traditional pictorial language codes. All three of the artists had used sculpture as a supplementary means of inquiry, achieving results that, although not shown in public exhibitions, except for some of Matisse's sculptures that had already been

8. Alexander Archipenko
Woman with Cat, 1910.
Saarbrücken,
Saarland Museum

9. Raymond Duchamp-Villon
Baudelaire, 1911-1948.
Paris, Centre Pompidou,
Musée National d'art moderne

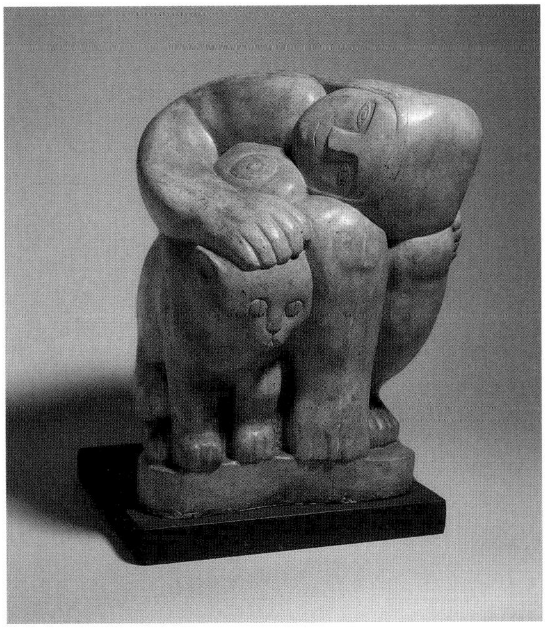

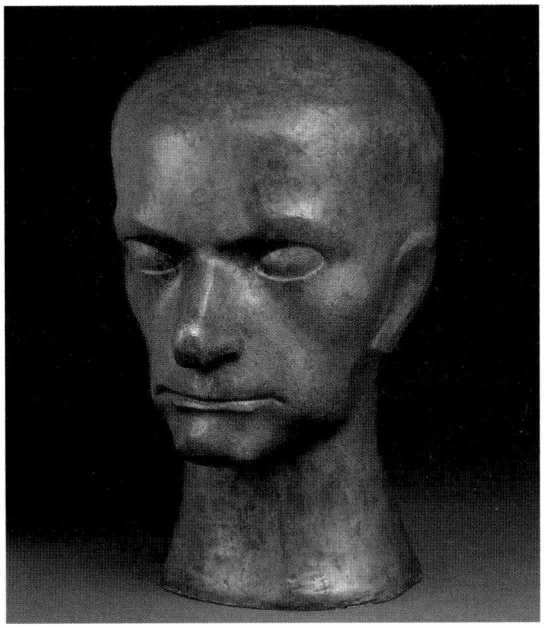

present at the Salon d'Automne in 1908, were however visible in their studios and the gallery of the German art dealer Daniel-Henry Kahnweiler.

Derain in particular and the attention that he gave to archaic languages – from the volumetric synthesis of Egyptian and pre-Colombian art, reflected in the compact mass and the motif of the entwined fingers of the *Crouching Man* (fig. **6**), to that in a synthetic key of the *Standing Figure* (fig. **7**), with the compact and sinuous profile, similar to Gauguin and the examples of art from the Indonesian area – seemed to find an immediate comparison in the works presented by Archipenko at the Salon des Indépendants in 1910, such as *Adam and Eve* and at the Salon d'Automne in 1911, *Motherhood* and *Woman with Cat* (fig. **8**), as also in the genesis of Brancusi's *The Kiss*.

It was in the autumn of 1911 that some critics, poets and journalists such as Gustave Kahn, Roger Allard and André Salmon tried to read the works presented by Archipenko, Nadelman and Duchamp-Villon at the exhibition organised by the Société Normande de Peinture moderne, in terms of a Cubist elaboration of sculpture. It was the first time that the Cubists, who had already shown their work together in room 41 of the Salon des Indépendants of that same year, exhibited together in the limited and private space of a gallery.[10] Of the works presented by the three sculptors, only Duchamp-Villon's bust *Baudelaire* (fig. **9**) is presently identifiable and it was certainly not the most innovative if André Salmon wrote in a contribution for the occasion: "Archipenko is Russian, and even more original, a Cubist sculptor. At this present time it is the least required profession, but it will not be like that for long. I am not exaggerating and, compared to Archipenko, Duchamp-Villon is no other than a Pompier artist.[11] This judgement was confirmed by Roger Allard who spoke about the Ukrainian artist's sculpture as "daring realisations," characterised by a "modelling on the surface" yet able to achieve "an extreme delicacy."[12] Kahn's interpretation was also interesting, he instead hoped for a sculpture without the "multi-faceted brutality" of pictorial Cubism, and that starting from "Rodin's second manner," there would be a softening of "the corners, the edges and less attention to the synthesis of the volumes."[13]

The sculptors' participation in the movement for the renewal of painting was confirmed by Roger Allard regarding the works exhibited by Archipenko, Brancusi and Lehmbruck at the Salon des Indépendants in 1912. Each of them, in accordance with the rules that permitted a limited number of three entries for every artist, presented three sculptures.

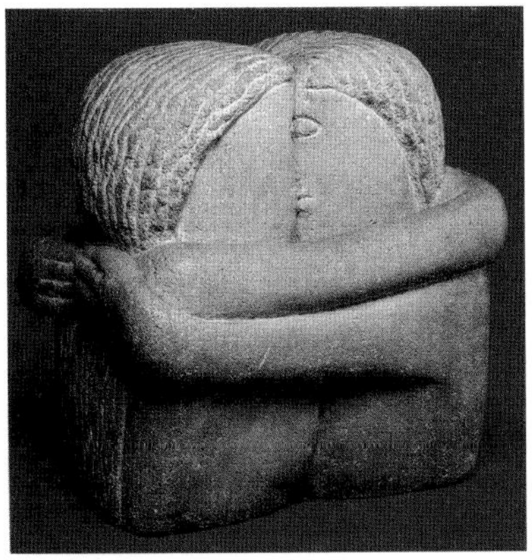

10. Constantin Brancusi
The Kiss, 1909-1910.
Craiova, Muzeul de Arta
(cat. **6**)

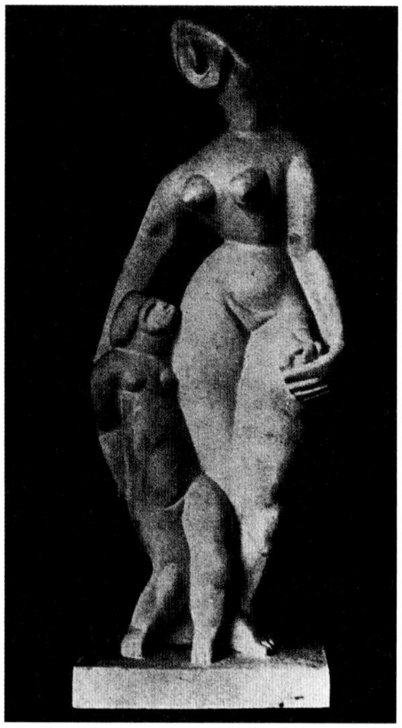

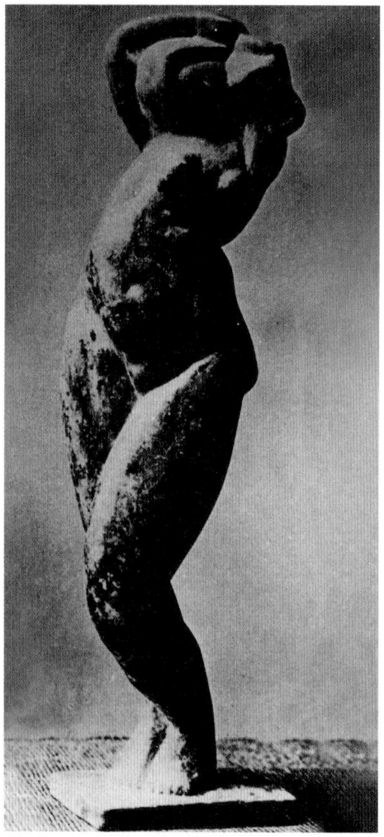

11. Alexander Archipenko
Mother and Daughter, 1909-1910.
New York, Archipenko Foundation

12. Alexander Archipenko
Negress, 1910-11. New York,
Archipenko Foundation

Brancusi exhibited two in marble, *Sleeping Muse* and *Prometheus* and one in stone, *The Kiss*, "of calm and strong architecture"[14] (fig. **10**); Archipenko two plasters, *Venus* and *Mother and Daughter* (fig. **11**) and a statuette in cement, *Negress* (fig. **12**), while Lehmbruck presented a *Torso of a Woman* in stone, another work not better identified and seventeen engravings. Allard spoke about these works in terms of "finished, noble and sensitive aspect, pure in style, with strength and expression," and a sincerity unknown to those artists who although committed to the search for "style" were moving away towards "archaism, curiosity and imagery."[15] This observation takes on greater importance if compared to the comment that Alfred Serstevens, critic of the *Comœdia* newspaper, made about the works presented at the Salon de la Nationale of that same year where a "predominant taste for archaeology and art of the past, expressed by means of a strange return to archaism," was considered, "beautiful in itself, but unable to express the modern thought."[16] So, at this moment, a delineation began between the research connected to a neo-traditionalist taste and that concerned with the pictorial avant-garde. Although still in the common interest of a work that was to be the plastic equivalent of reality and architecture of volumes, in the first case the importance given to "expertise" emerged, the links with nature and a plastic characterised by "massive allure" and a certain "lourder archaique"[17]; while in the second case a predominance of the intellective dimension of the executive aspect and a boldness turned towards abstraction.[18] Agéro, a Catalan sculptor, friend of Picasso, also participated at the same Salon with a portrait bust of Braque and some statuettes in wood and bronze, the former probably of tribal inspiration,[19] and Ossip Zadkine, with two studies for a *Heroic Head* and a *Heroic Fragment* in marble.

It was in this context that Amedeo Modigliani, installed in the south-western district of Montparnasse, in an area strongly characterised by the presence of both French and foreign sculptors, decided to dedicate himself to sculpture. Initiated in the technique of direct carving by Brancusi, from 1910 onwards he gave life to a series of heads accompanied by their preparatory drawings that betrayed "a variety of generically primitive suggestions,"[20] according to the path already indicated by Derain about 1908-1909, of an "archaic-like Mannerism" translated into a stylised elongation of the features, into an incisive and linear mark, into a language that isolated the figures represented in a rarefied and remote dimension.[21] These characteristics, already visible in the paintings that he carried out during his first years in Paris, such as *Seated Nude* in 1908 (fig. **13**) or *Beggar Woman* in 1909, returned with great strength to his sculptural production, between 1910 and 1914, in the same way as the painted portraits that followed.

Modigliani was present at the Salon des Indépendants in 1910 and 1912, with some paintings and drawings but he did not show his sculptures publicly until autumn 1912, apart from an exhibition organised in the studio of his painter friend Amadeo de Souza Cardoso of which there are few documentary traces.

In the months before the exhibition, the Italian artist frequently met the English sculptor Jacob Epstein, author of the funerary monument to Oscar Wilde, present in Paris to follow its installation in the Père Lachaise cemetery. The event was the object of numerous discussions, following the decision made by the Keeper of the cemetery to cover with plaster the too clearly exhibited intimate parts of the winged sphinx that decorated the sepulchre.[22] There were many affinities between the two artists, they were both exclusively dedicated to direct carving on stone and shared the project of giving life to a sculptural ensemble in accordance with the idea of an ancient temple.[23] Another foreign artist who had only arrived in Paris a few years before, Jacques Lipchitz, would remember Modigliani in the spring-summer of 1912 in the courtyard of his studio, in the Cité Falguière, busy placing

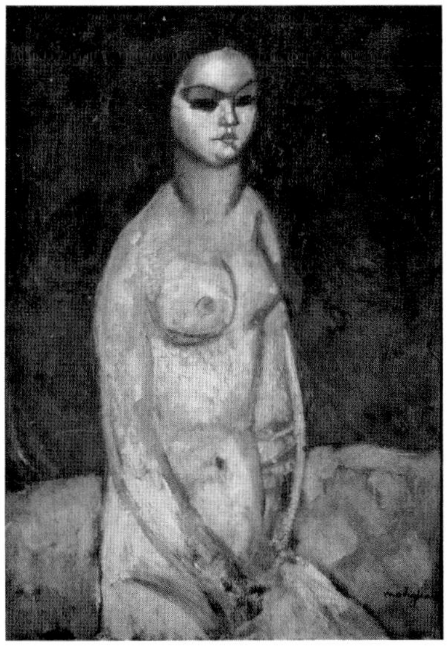

13. Amedeo Modigliani
Seated Nude, 1908.
Paris, private collection

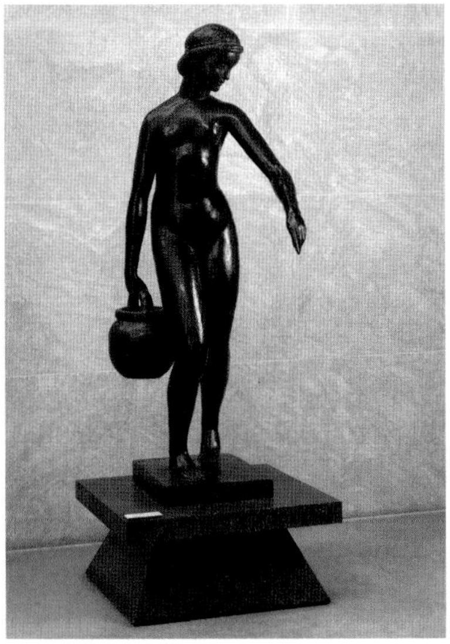

14. Jopeph Bernard
Water Bearer, 1908-1912.
Paris, Musée d'Orsay

together some of the statues he was working on: "It seems as if I can still see him" – wrote Lipchitz – "bent over these heads, he explained to me, that his idea was that they should form an ensemble. I think I remember they were exhibited some months later, the same year, at the Salon d'Automne, arranged according to their height as if they were organ reeds to realise the music that sang in his spirit."[24]

The Salon d'Automne in 1912: Presence and Comparisons

The Salon d'Automne opened its doors on 1st October 1912, set out in the spaces on the first floor of the Grand Palais. The inauguration was welcomed with great excitement by the critics: the works presented in room 11, the *salle cubiste*, were the subject of a parliamentary discussion on the state of French art and the necessary precautions that had to be taken to safeguard its identity from the danger of a foreign invasion. Echoes and words of a growing nationalist policy invested the artistic scene.

A photograph which appeared on 12th October in the newspaper *L'Illustration* offers evidence of the works that were exhibited and their collocation: the large canvases by Frantisek Kupka, Francis Picabia, Henri Le Fauconnier, next to those by Albert Gleizes, Fernand Léger, Jean Metzinger and Amadeo de Souza Cardoso. Close to the walls there were four of the seven sculptures presented by Modigliani, each with the title *Head: Decorative Ensemble* and, nearer to the centre of the room, a work by the Hungarian Joseph Csàky, a *Group of Women* not mentioned in the catalogue and re-proposed at the following Salon des Indépendants.

There was a large presence of sculptors at the Salon. In the space surrounding the *Rotonde* of Avenue d'Antin the visitors were welcomed by Joseph Bernard's thirteen sculptures, among which at the centre there was the imposing monument to Michel Servet, or to the Victims of the Inquisition, commissioned by the municipality of Vienne, the artist's birthplace, and all around a varied ensemble of female figures, groups or single heads, characterised on one hand by a still symbolic allure recalling Rodin's example, on the other by a plastic simplification and a *gaucherie*, for some time indication of that "return to style" that had first involved sculpture and then found affirmation also in painting at the Salon d'Automne in 1912 (fig. **14**).

A comparison between the catalogue of the Salon and the reviews that appeared in the newspapers allows a reconstruction of the presence of sculptures in the Cubist room, of which the photo in *L'Illustration* shows a partial image. Alexander Archipenko exhibited a group in plaster, *Family Life* (fig. **15**), and a figure in cement, *Bather* (fig. **16**), works reproduced in photographs and also drawn in two newspapers of the time next to Modigliani's heads.[25]

Joseph Csáky presented his plaster *Group of Women* (figs. **17-18**), a female figure, *Dancer* (fig. **19**), and an unidentified portrait; Elie Nadelman, three sculptures in bronze: a head of a woman and two nudes, *Female Nude* and *Juggler*[26] (fig. **20**).

If in the reviews a lot of space was dedicated to the work of Joseph Bernard and Ernest Wield, read in terms of a "great plastic and voluminous sentiment," recalling "archaic modellers, of the great Mycenaean art and the stone cutters of the Middle Ages,"[27] only few words, if not silence were dedicated to the foreign sculptors present in room XI. To Nadelman's bronzes an antique ascendency was attributed: "inspired by the Renaissance" according to Apollinaire, "c'est du joli faux-vieux"[28] added Hourcade, who limited himself to mentioning Archipenko saying that behind his group "of strange shadows" a small Basque landscape by Tobeen was hidden.[29]

A more interesting indication came from Vauxcelles' pen, for the whole month of October he had kept up a lively debate against Cubism and its followers, warning the young artists "full of badly digested literature, and of science and philosophy written by primates" of the danger in distancing themselves from nature.[30] In his cutting review of the Cubist room he observed: "To increase the interest of this room, various bizarre sculptures have been added to the *bariolages* thanks to a good man who undoubtedly believes he is continuing [the tradition] of the Assyrian or Egyptian stone cutters while he has simply looked at his models in the mirrors of a Fair Ground."[31] Putting in doubt the ascendance of the archaic languages in the works exhibited by the Ukrainian sculptor, Vauxcelles offered another interpretation, that of deformation and more generally of grotesque, already attributed to tribal art and indication of a plastic which was alien to every intention of reality.

Modigliani's group of heads, presented as "ensemble décoratif," like the two groups belonging to Archipenko and Csaky, *Family Life* and *Group of Women*, seemed however to take the line of the debate on the agenda in Vauxcelle's inquest which was echoed by the two projects of *Cubist House* and the Champs-Elysées theatre. It is possible to think that a modern elaboration of decorative sculpture and the problem in the relationship between sculpture and architecture was one of the subjects circulating in the sculptors' studios in the Montparnesse district. The collocation of Modigliani's heads on parallelepiped rectangular bases seems to recall on one hand Brancusi's entry in the previous Salon des Indépendants, that *Kiss* which Roger Allard had interpreted as a "symbolic capital," whose architecture gave the look of a "stable and strong character" to the form of the column it crowned[32]; on the other hand the image with which Bourdelle had symbolised the relationship between sculpture and architecture in one of the bas-reliefs for the theatre in Avenue Montaigne (fig. **21**). Closed in a static and remote linearism the Italian artist's heads (fig. **22**) remained tied, however, to an "archaic-like" language, according to a decorative style that was distant from the plastic research carried out by the other three sculptors, who, in the elaboration of the group or the single figure, had privileged baring the compositional architecture of the form. The flat and linear surface was therefore substituted by a dynamic assembly of closed in volumes set in contrast, particularly in the case of female nudes, in a decorative arabesque of Ingres-like influence.[33]

It is interesting to note about this what was written in a short column dedicated to Joseph Csaky in *Paris-Journal* on 27th

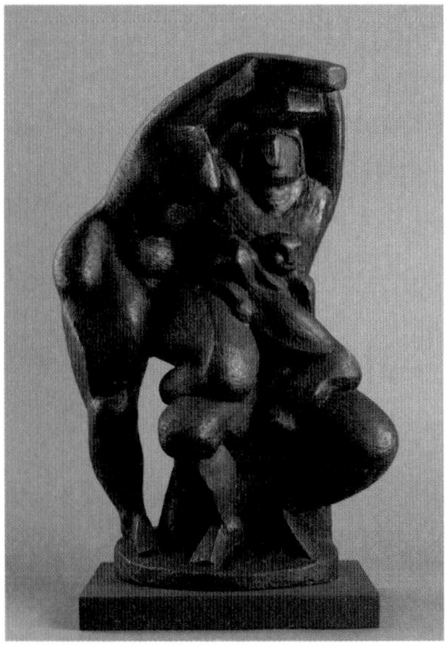

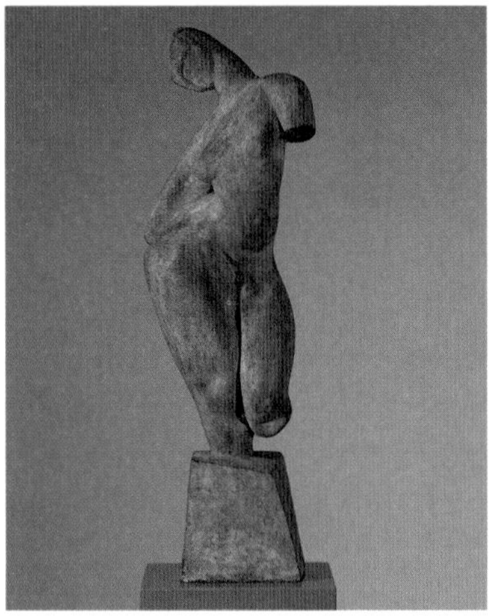

15. Alexander Archipenko
Family Life, 1912.
Saarbrücken, Saarland Museum

16. Alexander Archipenko
Bather (*Salome*), 1912.
New York, Archipenko Foundation

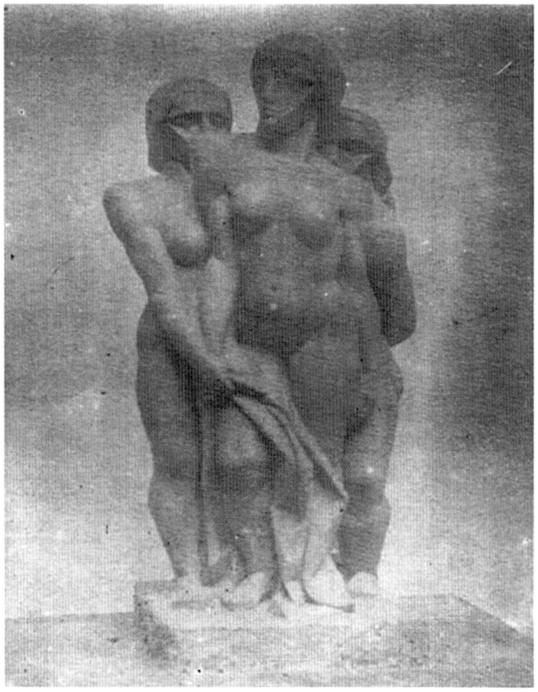

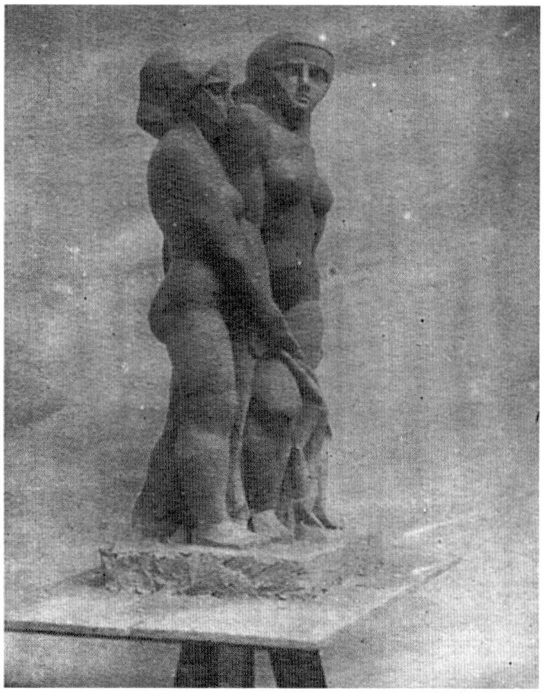

17-18. Joseph Csaky
Group of Women, 1912.
Work has been lost

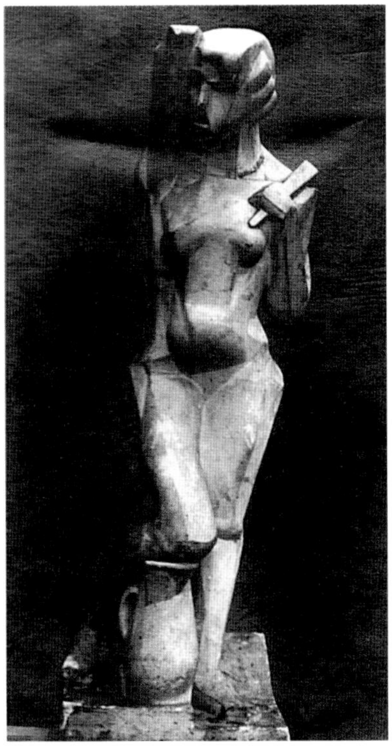

September 1912, just a few days before the opening of the Salon: "The works of Mr. Csaky, a young Hungarian sculptor, show a new effort and a studied science of the form. He is particularly interested in the construction. One of our friends told us this: 'His *Dancer* is an important group that represents the mechanism of the human body in a rather strange way.'"[34] It is the idea of the human body as a mechanism, as an assembly of distinct parts (and materials) , or architecture of pure volumes that in the immediately following years interested the research of the avant-garde sculptors. To accelerate such a change, and the consequent efforts of the critics to keep up with sculpture that measured itself against the aesthetics of a technical and scientific modernity,[35] it was another Italian, Umberto Boccioni, whose *Manifesto of Futurist Sculpture* was published and circulated in France precisely in the autumn of 1912.

At that time, especially in the public opinion, the history of another type of sculpture still had to be written: "Marinetti launches the manifesto of Futurist sculpture. 'It will model the environment. It will abolish the closed statue. It will open the figure like a window and will close inside it the space in which it lives. We will have plastic areas and the traditional sublime will be killed'. It seems to have been Boccioni who signed the manifesto. Let us wait for the first works before we start laughing. However, we think that all this will not have the value of Bourdelle's works, nor Rodin's, nor those of Duchamp-Villon."[36]

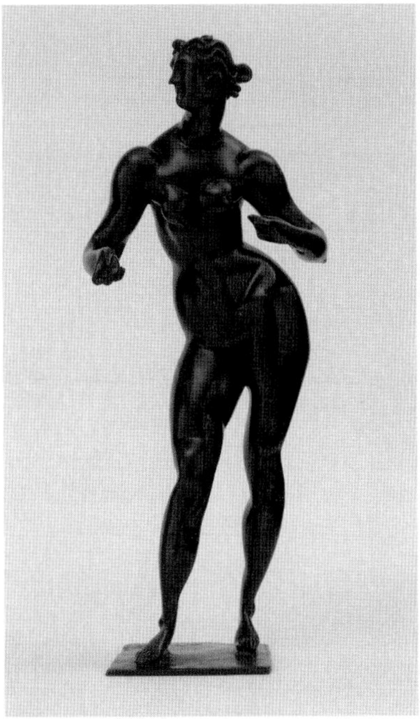

19. Joseph Csaky, *Dancer*, 1912. Work has been lost

20. Elie Nadelman, *Standing Female Nude*, 1909 ca. Washington, D.C., Smithsonian Institution, Hirshhorn Museum and Sculpture Garden

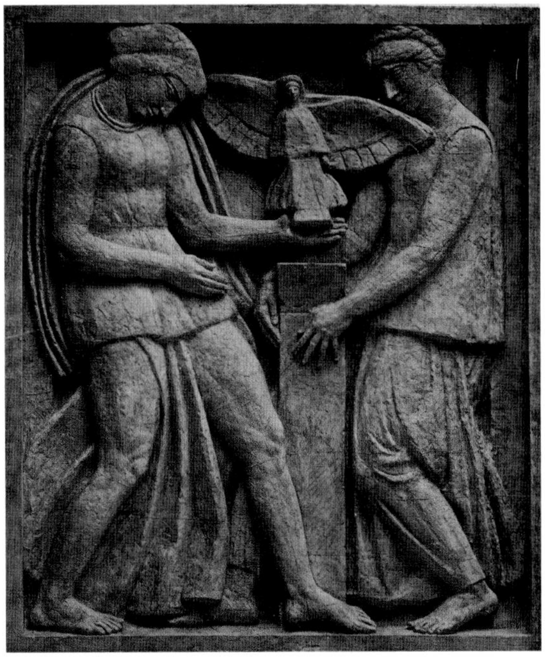

21. Émile-Antoine Bourdelle *Sculpture and Architecture*, bas-relief for the façade of the Théâtre des Champs-Elysées, 1910-1913. Paris, Musée Bourdelle

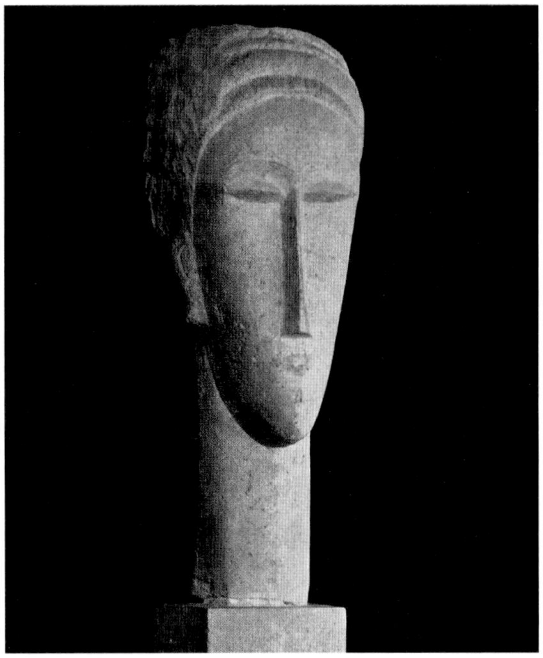

22. Amedeo Modigliani *Head*, 1911-1912. Saint Louis, private collection. Ceroni XV

1 Vauxcelles 1912a, the enquiry began on 7th September on the fourth page of the newspaper and developed throughout the whole month of September.

2 The documentation in the Musée Bourdelle has an interesting collection of prints of the time regarding this. Cf. *Le Théâtre des Champs-Elysées* 1912, newspaper cutting, without page number, noted as document No. 172; Serstevens 1912b, pp. 1-2. There were also many visits to Bourdelle's studio and interviews with the sculptor, for example *Silhouettes-Emile Antoine Bourdelle* 1912, p. 4.

3 Denis, 1905, p. 228: "L'idéal de l'Art c'est de condenser, de résumer en un petit nombre de formes claires et concises les rapports infiniment variés que nous percevons dans la Nature." Denis's writings, published between 1890 and 1910 were the object, in 1912, of a new edition that saw them all assembled in a single volume and they had a strong influence on the critical debate of that period. The enquiry into the rebirth of a "Classic ideal" was promoted by Charles Morice in the pages of *Paris-Journal* in April 1910 and continued with various contributions until the autumn. It is interesting to note how many critics saw a firm affirmation of this tendency in sculpture, cf. Vauxcelles 1910, p. 3: "La sculpture, sous l'impulsion formidable de Rodin, a déjà, à vrai dire, sa voie toute tracée."

4 R. Duchamp-Villon's answer, published on 17th September in the pages of *Gil Blas*: "L'œuvre doit vivre à *distance*, decorativément, par l'harmonie des volumes, des plans et des lignes, le sujet important peu, ou pas de tout" (Duchamp-Villon 1912, p. 4). Duchamp-Villon was present at the Salon d'Automne the following year in André Mare's decorative ensemble with four bas-relief medallions representing animals and the bas-relief *Les amants*, exhibited in room number VI, next to works by Gleizes, La Fresnaye, Kupka, Metzinger and Picabia. For an analysis of the relationship between Cubism, architecture and decorative arts see Cottington 1997, pp. 17-40.

5 Hourcade 1912b, p. 1: "Une première remarque s'impose cependant: la revanche, chaque jour plus importante, de l'intelligence sur le don naturel, de l'effort sur la négligence: le retour au style."

6 Pach 1913, pp. 17-18.

7 For a further analysis of the complex situation of sculpture in Paris between 1905 and 1914 see the catalogue to the exhibition Paris 2009. In particular the Chevillot essay 2009, pp. 159-165.

8 Salmon 1910, p. 2: "C'est peut-être à la sculpture que le visiteur qui saura voir goûtera les plus hautes joies d'art. Pour la première fois, depuis dix ans, un heureux mouvement s'affirme, une école harmonieuse et disciplinée nous est née. Tandis qu'Auguste Rodin triomphe justement avec ses torses de femmes aux modelés pleins [...], de jeunes artistes [...] s'apprêtent à nous livrer l'œuvre nouvelle."

9 In the review written about the Salon de la Nationale in 1910, André Salmon grouped together in this line of research: Charles Despiau, with his portrait of *Paulette*, whose "pure and strong structure left the vital freshness of the young face intact," Arnold, Wlerick and Cavaillon, artists who were close to Despiau in their formation and style; Bourdelle, who presented works which were "strong, finished and complete" (*Herakles Killing the Birds of Lake Stymphalis* and the *Bust of Rodin*); Desbois, whose patience and discipline in his work he admired; and still, Niederhausem-Rodo, Jeanne Poupelet and Lucien Schnegg who had died the year before and to whom a retrospective was dedicated (Salmon 1910, p.2).

10 The exhibition took place at the Galerie d'art ancien et d'art contemporain in Rue Tronchet in Paris, particularly thanks to the interest of the Duchamp-Villon brothers and Pierre Dumont who was president of the Société Normande. This marked the union of different groups of artists and is considered the forerunner to the exhibition of the Section d'Or (Paris 1912).

11 Salmon 1911b, p. 4.

12 Allard 1911.

13 Kahn 1911, p. 846.

14 Allard 1912a, p. 71.

15 *Ibid.*

16 Serstevens 1912, p. 2: "Il n'y a pas un art aujourd'hui, où se manifestent des tendances aussi multiples. On abandonne la figure allégorique, le groupe est en baisse. [...] D'autre part, l'éclectisme contemporain, le gout de l'archéologie et de l'art rétrospectif nous apportent un fort curieux retour à l'archaïsme, beau en soi, parce qu'il était l'expression d'un instant et d'une croyance, mais qui ne peut exprimer la pensée moderne".

17 *Ibid.*

18 Not by chance Apollinaire recognised in Archipenko the elegance of certain "imagiers gothiques," reading from the point of view of the Primitives and therefore an art which privileged a "reality of conception" over the "reality of vision," the elongation of the anatomic parts and the visual *raccourci* present in his sculptures. Apollinaire 1912a: "[...] Archipenko, qui a la sentiment de l'élégance comme l'avaient certains imagiers gothiques".

19 There are few images of Agéro's work, some were reproduced in the catalogue to the exhibition Châteaurous 2000. A. Salmon in the column *Courrier des ateliers*, (Salmon 1912, p. 2) mentioned about Agéro a "Buste de Georges Braque," a "Homme accourpi" and a "vitrine de petites tailles en bois."

20 For a reading of the elaborations of the primitive sources in the avant-garde language see Messina 1994. Quoted here in chapters VII, *Le Tracce di una via italiana*, pp. 193-203, in particular pp. 198-199; and chapter V, *La revisione dei linguaggi. I Fauves. Il ritorno all'ordine de Derain*, pp. 143-155.

21 See A. Derain *La Toilette* exhibited at the Salon des Indépendants in 1908 and the following studies of *Bathers*.

22 In an article that appeared in *Comœdia* on 9th October 1912 the artist is photographed beside one of his sculptures, *Motherhood* while to the side another image reproduces the censored monument, cf. Bazile 1912, p. 2.

23 Silber 1986, pp. 23-26.

24 Lipchitz 1954a: "Quand j'arrivais chez-lui – c'était le printemps ou l'été – il travaillait dehors. Plusieurs têtes de pierre – cinq peut être – étaient posées sur le sol cimenté de la cour devant l'atelier. Il était en train de les réunir. Il me semble que je le vois encore: penché sur ces têtes, il m'expliquait que, dans son idée, elles devaient former un tout. Je crois me rappeler qu'elles furent exposées quelques mois plus tard, la même année, au Salon d'Automne, échelonnées comme des tuyaux d'orgue pour réaliser la musique qui chantait dans son esprit".

25 *Le Salon d'Automne* 1912b, p. 713; *Au Salon d'Automne* 1912b, p. 62. A photograph of *Family Life* also appeared on the front page of *Comœdia* on 30th September 1912.

26 It is not possible to affirm with certainty that Csáky's three works were exhibited in room XI. The same for Nadelman's entries: Apollinaire lists *Juggler* together with the Cubist canvases that were exhibited but Allard indicates her *Head of a Woman* in room number three (Apollinaire 1912b, p. 332; Allard 1912c, p. 3).

27 Vauxcelles 1912c, p. 3: "Vous aurez l'impression d'un art plus intellectuel que sensible, et tout parfumé de réminiscences, mais d'une véritable noblesse et d'un grand sentiment plastique et volumineux. M. Joseph Bernard est hanté par les modeleurs archaïques, l'art grandiose de Mycènes lui est familier. Et sa dilection n'est pas moins grande envers les tailleurs de pierre et imagiers gothiques".

28 Apollinaire 1912b, p. 332; Hourcade 1912d, p. 3.

29 Hourcade 1912c, p. 2: " caché derrière un groupe aux ombres curieuses de *Archipenko*, voilà un petit paysage basque de Tobeen".

30 Vauxcelles 1912f, p. 4: "truffés de littérature mal digérée, et de science ou de philosophie compilées par des primaires".

31 Vauxcelles 1912d, pp. 2-3: "Pour corser l'intérêt de cette salle, on a adjoint aux bariolages diverses essais de sculpture loufoque dus à un brave homme qui croit sans doute continuer les tailleurs de pierre d'Assyrie ou d'Egypte et a bonnement regardé ses modèles dans les miroirs de Luna Park".

32 Allard 1912b, p. 3: "Le Baiser, sorte de chapiteau symbolique, emprunte à l'architecture de la colonne qui'il couronne un caractère puissant et stable".

33 For an interpretation of Ingres' work in the sphere of the French avant-garde see the path investigated by Messina 2004, pp. 23-26.

34 La Brosse 1912, p. 4: "Les œuvres de M. J.A. Csaky, jeune sculpteur hongrois, montrent un effort nouveau et une science étudiée de la forme. C'est à la construction que M. Csaky s'attache surtout. Un de nos amis nous disait à son propos. Sa *Danseuse* est un groupe important qui nous représente curieusement le mécanisme du corps humain".

35 Salmon 1919, pp. 10-11.

36 *Sculpture futuriste* 1912, p. 3: "Marinetti va lancer le manifeste de la sculpture futuriste. 'Elle modèlera l'ambiance. Elle abolira la statue fermée. Elle ouvrira la figure comme une fenêtre et y renfermera le milieu où elle vit. Nous aurons des zones plastiques et le sublime traditionnel sera tué'. Il parait que c'est Boccioni qui doit signer le manifeste. Attendons les œuvres avant de rire. Nous pensons cependant que cela ne vaudra ni les œuvres de Bourdelle, ni celles de Rodin, ni celles de Duchamp-Villon".

Invisible Sculpture

Brigitte Léal

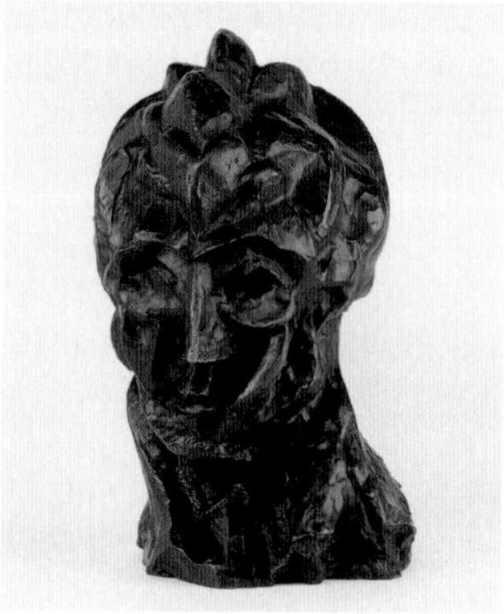

1. Pablo Picasso
Head of a Woman (Fernande), 1909.
Berlin, Staatliche Museen,
Nationalgalerie, Museum Berggruen

"What have sculptors done after Rude? Neither good nor bad. They have remained in the social role of the photographer-*retoucher* or the upholsterer or the cake-confectioner. The grocer from Tours who sculpts loaves of lard or *rilettes* has done more for the progress of sculpture than the great funerary Rodin!"[1]

These provocative phrases pronounced by Guillaume Apollinaire, the greatest representative and defender of the avant-garde in Paris, during a conference at the Academy of modern sculpture on 7th June 1913, sounded the funeral march for traditional sculpture. This had remained relegated to imitation at the moment when, as the poet pointed out, concept and abstraction were gaining ground.

In some prophetic pages Apollinaire was able to draw up a first balance sheet of the victories of the sculptural avant-garde and to imagine future sculpture. In 1913 the poet had already understood the great importance of the *Impressions of Africa* by Raymond Roussel,[2] who would become the fermenting agent of all Marcel Duchamp's production and of art *nègre* as a new source of inspiration.[3] He also insisted on the "considerable role" of "sculpture of the painters" in modern art, and foresaw all the phases of twentieth century sculpture: the object, the machine, kineticism, bricolage, the shapeless, the anti-form, the happening and also the connection between art and life, imagined with lyrical inspiration: "Which sculptor will put over us a sculpture similar to a pneumatic bell? Which sculpture will chase its terrorised admirer through the streets? Which sculpture will free itself into the air like a star more beautiful than the stars? Which sculpture will pour over us like a jar of oil? Which sculpture will spill itself on this parquet like hair cut by the hairdresser? Where are your sculptures as transparent as carafes?"[4]

Apollinaire's trust was founded on the spectacular upheavals he had seen and commentated on since the beginning of the century. In 1909 it was Picasso who "exploded the homogenous form" – these are the words of his art-dealer and critic Daniel-Henry Kahnweiler – with *Head of a Woman (Fernande)* (fig. **1**) which is today considered the first Cubist sculpture and in which the poet immediately perceived the dynamic qualities.[5] In 1912 it was Georges Braque who, in the secrecy of his study, built an evanescent paper sculpture, similar to a butterfly pinned into space: then it was Picasso again who cut out a large *Guitar* from a sheet of iron, bent and pulled with metallic wires, and hung it on the wall: the first assemblage in the history of sculpture.[6] Then, the following year Marcel Duchamp took the path of no return by combining a ready-made bicycle wheel and a stool, deprived of their original function, the multiplication of the work, in the form of signed editions, accentuated the anonymity.[7]

Faced with this unprecedented attack of the object against sculpture, that was incarnated in the scandalous *Fountain* (a urinal in painted ceramic)[8] created by Duchamp in 1917 – the year of Auguste Rodin's death – the unfortunate Salon sculptors, faithful to traditional materials and techniques but also to an ideal of eternal regulation which was outdated, seemed immediately old-fashioned and anachronistic. A new generation had appeared, convinced about "what was

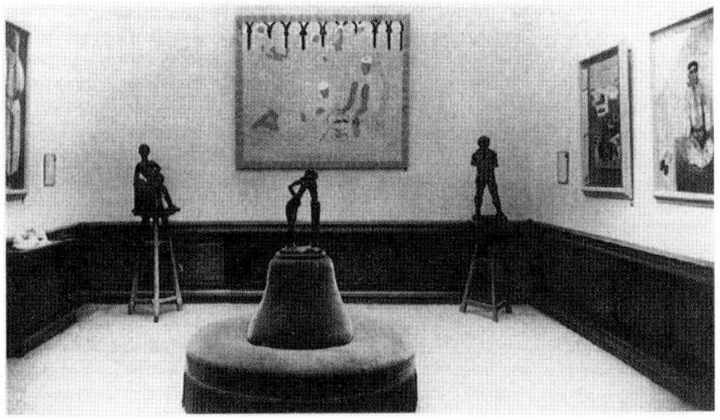

2. Exhibition of Matisse at the Galérie Bernheim-Jeune, Paris, 1913

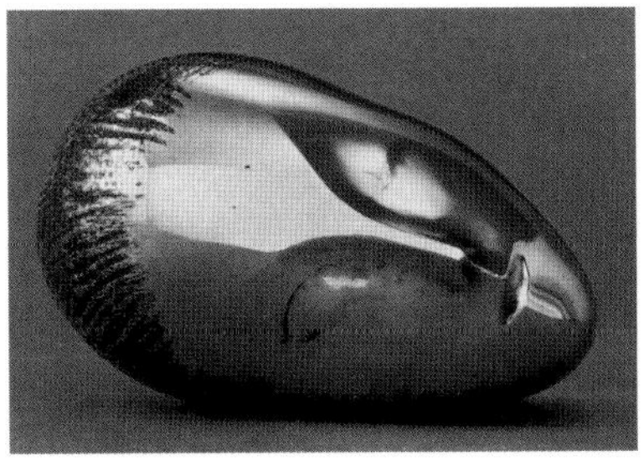

3. Constantin Brancusi, *The Sleeping Muse I*, 1910. Paris, Centre Georges Pompidou, Musée National d'art moderne

no longer possible" (Roland Barthes) but helpless in front of the general indifference and hostility. If today it is the Classics that are not seen well in the eyes of the modern, yesterday it was the avant-garde who had to go through a long purgatory before they were able to impose their autonomy and freedom.

Wrongdoers and Hooligans

In the period from 1905 to 1914, modern sculpture, Cubist or Futurist, did not exist for the contemporaries. At the editions of the Salon, that Gustave Kahn maliciously defined as a "sort of rectangular Père-Lachaise,"[9] modern sculpture went unobserved, buried by the thousands of academic or figurative works that were crowded into the Quai d'Orsay or the greenhouses of the Grand Palais. Only three debutantes, Raymond Duchamp-Villon, Constantin Brancusi and Alexander Archipenko, played the game of the official shows participating at the Salon d'Automne, the first until 1905, with works mainly inspired by Rodin,[10] then exhibiting more or less every year until the Great War against the Société Nationale des Beaux Arts and the Salon des Indépendants (where Archipenko participated for the first time in 1910). At the Salon des Indépendants of 1911 (that coincided with the first appearance of four sculptures by Ossip Zadkine) it was the first time for Amedeo Modigliani, who exhibited a *Caryatid* and a *Head* and would then compose, for the Salon d'Automne of the following year, a "Decorative ensemble," as it was defined in the catalogue, of seven heads.

In 1912 the Salon d'Automne could boast about accepting a *Project for a House* by Duchamp-Villon, with furniture by André Mare, which entered into the history of art as *The Cubist House*, and represents the first attempt at integration of the arts. On the other hand sculpture cut a poor figure at the polemic Salon de la Section d'Or in 1912, which only had ten works by the Spaniard Auguste Agéro, a cement statuette by Archipenko (*Dancer*, 1912) and a group of sculptures by Duchamp-Villon, who with his recent head, *Maggy* (1912, clay) expressed his conversion to Cubism.[11] If we exclude Picasso, segregated by Kahnweiler, Duchamp-Villon, also crowned Vice-President of the Salon d'Automne in 1910, was the only modern sculptor who could count on the support of the market, thanks to the Societé Normande de Peinture Moderne, to the dealer-photographer Eugène Druet and the André Groult gallery, which in 1914 (6th April-3rd May) organised a real retrospective of his work in the ambit of a collective exhibition that united his brother Jacques Villon and the painters Albert Gleizes and Jean Metzinger. It is necessary to consider that Modigliani, despite the support of his patron, Dr. Paul Alexandre, was obliged for lack of anything better, to exhibit his sculptures for one day only, 5th March 1911, in the studio of one of his friends, the Portuguese painter Amadeo de Souza Cardoso,[12] and that even Henri

4. Exhibition of Umberto Boccioni's Futurist sculpture at the Galerie La Boëtie, Paris, 1913

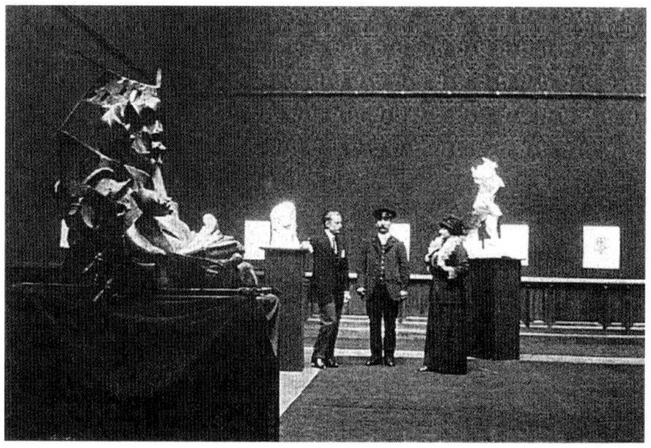

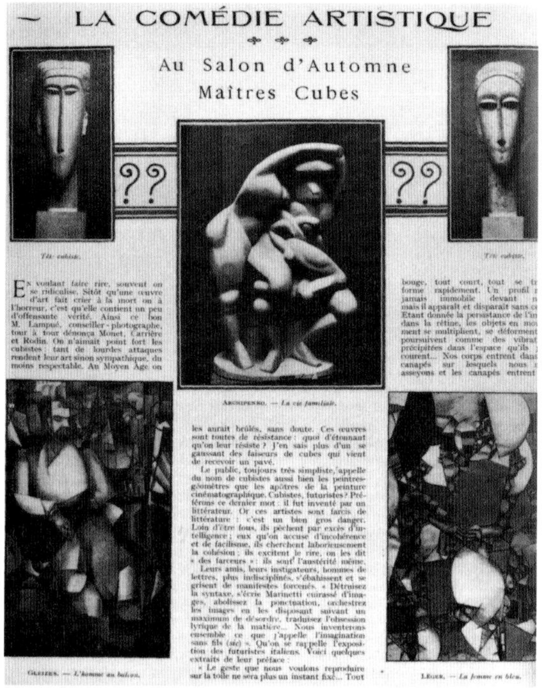

LA COMÉDIE ARTISTIQUE

Au Salon d'Automne

Maîtres Cubes

??

Tête cubiste.

En voulant faire rire, souvent on se ridiculise. Sitôt qu'une œuvre d'art fait crier à la mort ou à l'horreur, c'est qu'elle contient un peu d'offensante vérité. Ainsi ce bon M. Lampué, conseiller-photographe, tour à tour dénonça Monet, Carrière et Rodin. On n'aimait point fort les cubistes: tant de lourdes attaques rendent leur art sinon sympathique, du moins respectable. Au Moyen Âge on

Archipenko. — La vie familiale.

les aurait brûlés, sans doute. Ces œuvres sont toutes de résistance: quoi d'étonnant qu'on leur résiste? J'en sais plus d'un se gaussant des faiseurs de cubes qui vient de recevoir un pavé.

Le public, toujours très simpliste, appelle du nom de cubistes aussi bien les peintres-géomètres que les apôtres de la peinture cinématographique. Cubistes, futuristes? Préférons ce dernier mot: il fut inventé par un littérateur. Or ces artistes sont farcis de littérature: c'est un bien gros danger. Loin d'être fous, ils pèchent par excès d'intelligence; eux qu'on accuse d'incohérence et de facilisme, ils cherchent laborieusement la cohésion; ils excitent le rire, on les dit « des farceurs »: ils sont l'austérité même.

Leurs amis, leurs instigateurs, hommes de lettres, plus indisciplinés, s'ébahissent et se grisent de manifestes forcenés. « Détruisez la syntaxe, s'écrie Marinetti cuirassé d'images, abolissez la ponctuation, orchestrez les images en les disposant suivant un maximum de désordre, traduisez l'obsession lyrique de la matière... Nous inventerons ensemble ce que j'appelle l'imagination sans fils (sic) ». Qu'on se rappelle l'exposition des futuristes italiens. Voici quelques extraits de leur préface:

« Le geste que nous voulons reproduire sur la toile ne sera plus un instant fixe... Tout

bouge, tout court, tout se tr
forme rapidement. Un profil
jamais immobile devant n
mais il apparaît et disparaît sans ce
Étant donnée la persistance de l'im
dans la rétine, les objets en mo
ment se multiplient, se déforment
poursuivent comme des vibrat
précipitées dans l'espace qu'ils
courent... Nos corps entrent dans
canapés sur lesquels nous
asseyons et les canapés entrent

5. Salon d'Automne (with the sculptures by Amedeo Modigliani and Alexander Archipenko), in *Comœdia Illustré*, 20th October 1912

Matisse, whose early sculptural production still wisely recalled Antoine-Louis Barye, Pierre Puget and Rodin, had to wait until a personal exhibition in 1913 at Bernheim-Jeune to exhibit a series of thirteen early bronzes (fig. **2**).

Still at the Salon des Indépendants, Parisian manor of Modernity and one of the models of the New York Armory Show, three great masterpieces of Modern sculpture made their first appearance in 1912, that is Brancusi's *The Sleeping Muse* (fig. **3**), the *Prometheus* – both in marble – and *The Kiss* in stone. It was yet again in that Salon that the debutant Henri Laurens started his career in 1913 exhibiting a *Sepulchre* and a *Head of a Man* of a completely Roman purity that he would end up destroying.

Finally the Italian Futurists, skilful strategists, hit the mark with a great stroke – that left the Cubists open mouthed – with the manifestation in 1913, presenting at the Galerie La Boëtie eleven *Plastic Ensembles* by Umberto Boccioni (the word sculpture itself was excluded from their radical vocabulary), among which *Unique Forms of Continuity in Space* (1913 fig. **4**), accompanied by groups of drawings which have programmed and declamatory titles *I Want to Synthesise the Unique Forms of Continuity in Space* or *I Want to Transfix the Human Form in Movement*. These titles correspond to the theories of simultaneity and dynamism so vigorously expressed in the *Technical Manifesto of Futurist Sculpture,* published in Paris, 11th April 1912, but Apollinaire was not at all convinced and as he was completely dedicated to the opposing cause, he did not waste the opportunity to be ironic about this "real cemetery of athletes."[13]

If these occasional manifestations are evidence to the fact that, as Dominique Bozo remembered, "it was in Paris that the essence of Modern sculpture developed,"[14] its history went almost unnoticed in the newspapers or art publications of that time, which instead dedicated passionate pages to arguments about the development of Cubist painting, whose actions of penetration at the Salon were the object of heated discussions. A handful of pages was sufficient to establish the critical success and the reception of Cubist sculptures in Paris.[15] They focused around two exhibitions in 1912, the Salon des Indépendants (20th March – 16th May) and the Salon d'Automne (1st October – 8th November), where the Modern sculptors attempted an incursion. Today there could be a certain amount of surprise in discovering that the most popular and reproduced sculptor was Archipenko, whose group *Family Life*, presented at the Salon d'Automne in 1912, appeared for better or for worse on the front pages of the newspapers, as did also Modigliani's *Heads* in stone, included in a positive sounding article by Claude Roger-Marx for *Comœdia Illustré* (fig. **5**),[16] but

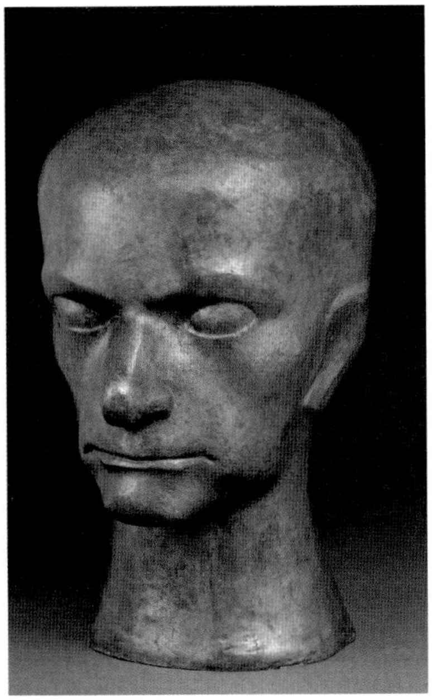

6. Raymond Duchamp-Villon
Baudelaire, 1911.
Paris, Centre Georges Pompidou, Musée National d'art moderne

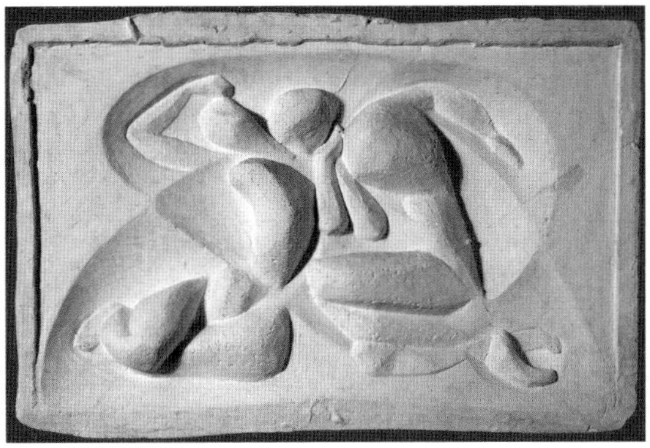

7. Raymond Duchamp-Villon
The Lovers III, 1913.
Paris, Centre Georges Pompidou, Musée National d'art moderne

object of sarcasm from the conservative critics in *L'Illustration* or the caricaturists in *Le Figaro*.[17] Alexandre Mercereau, admired Duchamp-Villon's *Baudelaire* (fig. **6**) in *Vers et prose* in 1911,[18] Roger Allard, was the only one apart from Apollinaire to notice the importance of Brancusi, Archipenko and Lehmbruck at the Indépendants in 1912 and to point out that at the Salon d'Automne, with his *Cubist House*, Duchamp-Villon "opened up a new way,"[19] or even further André Salmon, praised and reproduced Duchamp-Villon's relief, *Lovers* (1913 fig. **7**) in *Montjoie!*,[20] one of the instruments of the avant-garde. Despite all these rare illuminated spirits, how much blindness and how many insults, where the mixture could be found of xenophobic based politics, anti-Semitism and exaggerated nationalism, aiming at discrediting the avant-garde. The crucial point was the open letter addressed by M. Lampué, member of the Commission for Fine Arts of the city of Paris, to M. Bérard, Undersecretary of State to Fine Arts, after the inauguration of the Salon d'Automne in 1912: "Have I really the right to lend a public monument to a group of wrongdoers who behave in the world of art like hooligans in everyday life?" (fig. **8**).

Faust's Laboratory
Even in the eyes of Apollinaire, a true passionate supporter of innovations, these manifestations often did not merit more than a few lines in his articles in *L'Intransigeant*, in *Soirées de Paris* or in *Paris-Journal*,[21] that reveal a more eclectic taste than his *Aesthetic Meditations* could let us suppose, consecrated to the defence of Cubist painting[22]. If at the end of the text the poet dismisses the subject with a calming phrase – "Among the sculptors who want to unite with the Cubist school we mention, besides Duchamp-Villon, M. Auguste Agéro, M. Archipenko and M. Brancusi" – he remedies by adding an appendix dedicated to the work of Duchamp-Villon, whose architectonic and decorative ambition he admires.
At the Salon des Indépendants in 1912, distinguished by the surfacing of Cubist painting represented by Fernand Léger and Robert Delaunay, the poet articulated this comment: "Brancusi, delicate and very personal sculptor whose works are amongst the most refined, Archipenko, who has a sense of elegance as certain Gothic masters had, Lehmbruck,[23] whose talent allows us to overlook all that is ordinary and affected transmitted to him by sculptors from Düsseldorf, Agéro, who this time has carried out a fine bust, simple, dignified and of noble sentiment with a very new technique."[24]
This rather lukewarm attitude seems even more surprising because it is in contrast with the lyricism with which he greets Rodin, "the greatest living sculptor," or the "mighty" Émile-Antoine Bourdelle. His enthusiasm, perhaps aroused by his admiration for Duchamp-Villon regarding the maestro from Dijon, is above all addressed to François Rude's "simple, strong and live" work, he considered him the real forerunner of French modern sculpture.[25]
In fact, according to Apollinaire other Cubist sculptors apart from André Derain and Picasso did not exist, they admitted him – together with a few other privileged poets or artists – into the recesses of their studios-laboratories, as witnesses of experimental

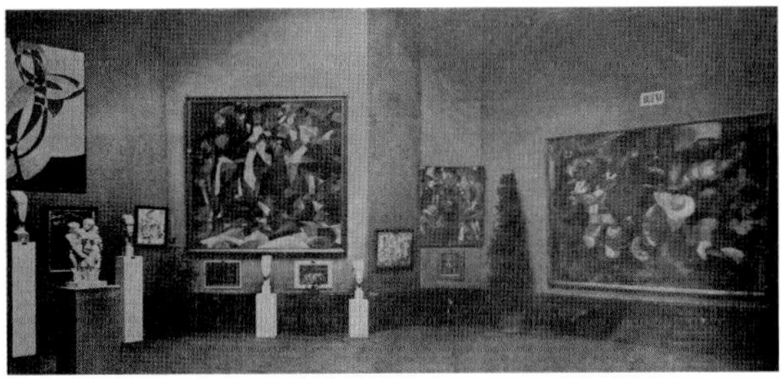

8. Paris, Salon d'Automne 1912, room XI, in *L'Illustration*, 12nd October 1912

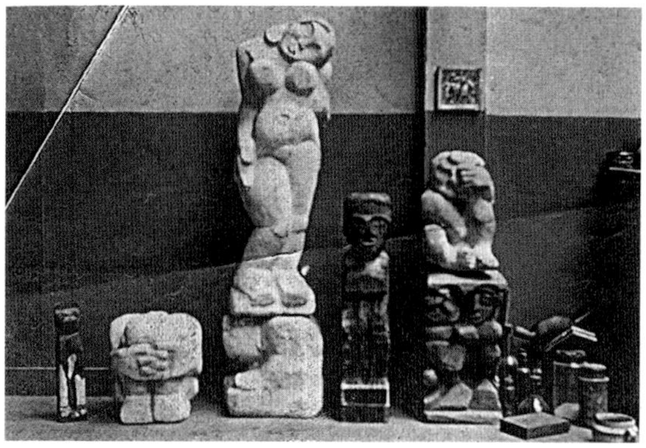

9. L'atelier di André Derain in Montmartre, 1908. Geneviève Taillade Archives

creations destined to remain secret, when not destroyed by their own creators. Apollinaire was the only critic for a long time, followed by André Breton, to highlight the importance and particularity of Derain, the first to see exotic art (the Maori sculptures in the British Museum in 1906) as an art in its own right and not just as an ethnological curiosity. In his conference in 1913 on Modern sculpture, which aroused some envy, Apollinaire did not hesitate in stating that "among the artists who are at the beginning of modern sculpture, it is necessary to mention André Derain [...] here he is finally armed with a sculptor's chisel and makes synthetic forms of a completely new harmony emerge from the really hard slab of stone."[26]
With that he referred to the five directly carved sculptures taken from the stairs of the family home in Chatou, between the end of 1906 and the autumn of 1907, of which only one photograph, taken in his studio in Rue Tourlaque in Montmartre in 1908, maintains the memory, as only three of these sculptures have been preserved, one of which is the voluptuous *Standing Nude* from the Musée National d'Art Moderne, while the two wooden sculptures which were inserted in the line of Paul Gauguin's wooden works have been lost[27] (fig. **9**). How can the impact of a not very visible work be judged? Who will have seen the impressive block of *Crouching Man*[28] (1907), exhibited in September 1907 in Rue Vignon by Kahnweiler and then forgotten, like the other work in sandstone, *Man and Woman*[29] (1907), which remained in the studio in Chambourcy until Alice Derain's death? Perhaps Brancusi was inspired by this work, as Sidney Geist suggests, for his legendary *Kiss* in stone[30] (1907-1908), rehabilitating the technique of cutting the block as opposed to the Rodin style of "l'art du beefsteak" ["the art of the beefsteak"]?[31] However, perhaps Derain himself had realised his attempts at direct carving under the influence of the revelation of the Iberian heads by Cerro de los Santos, stolen from the Louvre in 1907 by Apollinaire's secretary and kept by Picasso, who was inspired by them for his first version of the *Demoiselles d'Avignon?*
How is it possible to reconstruct the history of modern sculpture in its relationship with Primitivism, or Gauguin's late sculptures, presented at the Salon d'Automne in 1906 (*War and Peace, Be Mysterious, Love and You Will Be Happy* as well as the *Oviri* ceramic) without the actual presence of those sculptures? How can the latter be evaluated and collocated compared to Picasso's twelve works in wood, that he started working on in Gósol in 1906 and continued in Paris in 1907[32], in the studio in Bateau-Lavoair, that another photograph, probably taken in 1908, shows us fully imbued with African sculpture?
In fact, for however surprising it may seem in the case of the twentieth century artist who has had the greatest exposure in the media, all Picasso's Cubist sculptures were invisible to the eyes of most of his contemporaries except for a handful of elite authorised to enter the bohemian studio – that André Salmon defined as "Faust's laboratory" – belonging to the one who refused the official baptism at the Salon to inaugurate a parallel story, that of the triumph in the private galleries and the spreading of the treasures from the studios on an international level by means of photographs: in his case the famous "cliché Kahnweiler."[33] In fact, before the revelation of most of these works to the public – including the *Guitar* in sheet metal dated 1912[34] (fig. **10**), often considered the first sculpture of the XX century! – at the exhibition *Hommage à Pablo Picasso*,

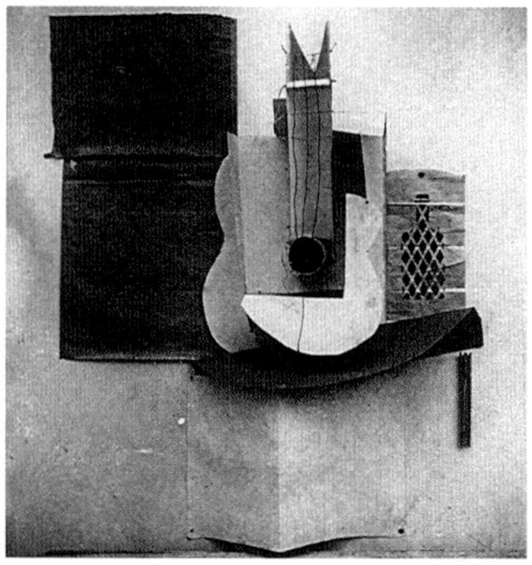

10. Pablo Picasso, *Guitar, Bottle*, 1913, in *Les Soirées de Paris*, 1913

organised at the Petit Palais in 1966-1967,[35] most of his Cubist constructions had never been shown, except for *Still Life*[36] (1914), presented at the *Exposition surréaliste d'objets* held in 1936 at the Galerie Charles Ratton in Pari,[37] with one of the examples of *Glass of Absinthe* dated 1914.
Perhaps Picasso had been upset for a long time on account of the disappointment of his friend Apollinaire, who in November 1913, when he dared to publish the photographs of five of Picasso's recent still life works, among which a painting and four Cubist ensemble,[38] in the first issue of a new series of *Soirées de Paris*, had provoked such protests from the subscribers to the magazine that he was obliged to justify himself? Or must we believe like Louis Vauxcelles, declared enemy of Cubism but with a very fine instinct, that "the mystery that Picasso surrounds himself with is functional to his legend"[39]? The fact remains that the artist contented himself with guaranteeing the spreading of some of his works in a limited and qualified circle by means of the reproductions present in the catalogue of his production edited by Christian Zervos, that was published, regarding the Cubist part, in an era – 1942 – not very favourable to the history of art![40]
So it is possible to understand how André Salmon could have written in 1919. "I have seen what a man had never seen. [...] I have seen Picasso's studio, more hallucinating than Faust's laboratory, this studio – someone would swear – it did not contain a single work of art, in the old meaning of the word, it was full of absolutely new objects. [...] What is this? Does that rest on a pedestal? Does that hang on the wall? What is this, painting or sculpture? – Picasso [...] It is nothing, it is El Guitare!"[41]
The myth of works that did not exist apart from in the memory of a few observers quickly grew. The fragility of the materials they were made from and their quality as studies, if not of iconoclastic games invented by *bricoleurs* artists,[42] could easily justify acts of self-destruction or negligence by their authors, strengthened by the saying, of a Dada-like violence, of Louis Aragon, who in 1930 claimed: "The greatness of Cubism in this era dwells in this: anything, without worrying if it is perishable, is useful [...] to express oneself and even better if it has no value, if it disgusts its world."[43] In 1965, John Golding, author of a history of Cubism which had become an important reference point, could still write, under the image of the *Guitar* in cardboard at the Museum of Modern Art, defined "currently lost": "The role carried out by these constructions by Picasso and Braque in the development of Cubist painting is difficult to define; most of those works were too fragile to survive."[44]
Small cardboard boxes tied up with string, simple nailed boards, fragile ensembles of paper that surprisingly, as another sculptor, Julio González, had understood, "they give the impression of things carved out of rock."[45] These works have invented a modern beauty, convulsed, in front of which only an "eye in the wild state" could be enchanted: "I find once again the eyes of my youth when I recall my first encounter with Picasso's art thanks to an issue of Apollinaire's *Soirées de Paris*, that offered the rather confused reproduction of five of his recent still life productions (it was 1913). Four of those works consisted of assemblies of materials of a residual nature, like boards, bobbins, fragments of linoleum, ropes, borrowed from everyday life. The shock provoked by what had never been seen before was replaced by the sensation of a sovereign balance of the finished work, promoted – whether you like it or not – to organic life and that justified its necessity. Almost half a century has gone by since then: according to what Picasso told me one day, those constructions were dissembled, but the image that remains is sufficient to show up to what point he anticipated the forms of expression which today are considered the most daring. Up to what point, very often, those works dominate over these latter thanks to the authority of the testimony they hold, and that immediately dissolve every suspicion of gratuitousness."[46]

1 Apollinaire 1913a.
2 "Two or three years ago we believed in a great novelty, which manifested itself in a *pièce* of uncertain success: *Impressions of Africa*. The author, whose name I have forgotten, had imagined a statue made of whalebones that rolled along the tracks of the brain of a calf: so prodigious as to move those who loved art and its sublime monsters; it was all only made of cardboard, wretched theatrical accessories! Perhaps it was the first time that an attempt was made to renew sculpture. But it was renewed only in words." (Apollinaire 1913a). Roussel's *pièce*, taken from his novel *Impressions of Africa*, was shown more than once in Paris, in September and October 1911.
3 Backing Baudelaire, "who had foreseen this arrival in our aesthetics of the Savage aesthetics," Apollinaire saw this influence in a faded way: "Art *nègre* [...] has only confirmed in the spirit of the young sculptors what they already thought about the future of their art"(Apollinaire 1913a).
4 Apollinaire 1913a.
5 "Already for three years a bronze by Picasso, where the artist has gathered all that could be gathered in terms of light, has partly contained this dynamism" (Apollinaire 1913b, p. 410).
6 New York, Museum of Modern Art.
7 Marcel Duchamp, *Bicycle wheel*, ready- made, 1913; metal bicycle wheel on a painted wooden stool, the original has been lost, replica in edition of 13 units.
8 Marcel Duchamp, *Fountain*, ready-made, 1917, urinal in white ceramic, glazed and painted, signed "R. Mutt," the original has been lost, replicated by the artist in an edition of 12 units.
9 Gustave Kahn made a precise reference to the rooms of the Salon d'Automne: "The Salon d'Automne is not very rich in sculpture: the space conceded by the State is partly the reason, because the sculptors do not enjoy themselves with this sort of rectangular Père Lachaise, lined up for the event along Avenue Alexandre II." (Kahn 1912, pp. 178-182).
10 Paris 1905, Duchamp-Villon: No. 494, *Woman Reading*, marble; No. 494, *Football Players*; clay model; No. 496, *Bust by M.D.*, bronze. Paris 1906, Brancusi: No. 218, *Portrait of M.S. Lupesco*, bust in varnished clay; No. 219, *The Child*, bust in clay; No. 220, *Pride*, bust in clay; Duchamp-Villon: No. 498, *Silence*, bronze; No. 449, *Aesop*, bust in clay.
11 The two works by Archipenko and Duchamp-Villon are conserved at the Musée National d'art moderne in Paris.
12 The exhibition received a visit from his friend Brancusi. Modigliani did not find a dealer until 1916, date of his meeting with Léopold Zborowski.
13 Apollinaire 1913b, p. 410.
14 Bozo 1986, p. 6.
15 My thanks to Ariane Coulondre for her research on the critical success of Cubism between 1908 and 1919.
16 Roger-Marx 1912.
17 *Au Salon d'Automne* 1912; Faivre 1912.
18 Mercereau 1911.
19 Allard 1912a, Allard 1912b.
20 Salmon 1911a.
21 As a journalist for various newspapers, Apollinaire was obliged to react quickly to the manifestations, and he was also obliged to come to terms with the artistic groups that he defended and met with. To know more about this subject: Apollinaire 2009.
22 Apollinaire 1913c (*Baudelaire, Detail of an Ornamental Pond, Sketch for the Sun, Project for a House*).
23 He dedicated a few ambiguous lines in the same way to Lehmbruck in Apollinaire 1914, p. 500.
24 Apollinaire 1912, p. 294.
25 In his reply to Louis Vauxcelles's enquiry (Vauxcelles 1912b), Duchamp-Villon proclaimed his interest for Rude's work. In the notes of *Œuvres en prose complètes* by Apollinaire, Pierre Caizergues and Michel Décaudin maintained that the poet's admiration for Rude, that he expressed in two conferences held in Pairs in 1913, was connected both to his nationalistic ideology and Duchamp-Villon's text.
26 Apollinaire, *Œuvres en prose complètes*, op. cit., p. 596.
27 Another document, a photograph which shows Derain posing in his studio with a wooden cat beside the three sculptures in wood and stone, was published by the American journalist Gelett Burgess to illustrate his famous article Burgess 1910, pp. 401-414, dedicated to the studios of the Parisian avant-garde in 1910.
28 Vienna, Museum des 20. Jahrhunderts.
29 Duisberg, Stiftung Wilhelm Lehmbruck Museum.
30 Craiova, Muzeul de Arta.
31 On 17th October 1963 Kahnweiler confirmed to Sidney Geist, via courier, the presence of *Crouching Man* in the gallery at that date (New York, the Guggenheim Museum, Archives Brancusi). For Derain's sculptures and the few documents about his existence that have been conserved, see Simon 1994, pp. 313-321.
32 *Nude with Raised Arms* 1906, *Bust of a Woman (Fernande)*, 1906; *Head of a Woman*, 1906-1907; *Mask*, 1907; *Figure*, 1907; *Standing Nude*, 1907; *Three Nudes*, 1907; *Figure* 1907; *Standing Man*, 1907; *Standing figure*, 1907; *Doll*, 1907; see numbers from 6B to 21 in Paris 2000.
33 For the impact of the "Kahnweiler cliché" – the photographs of the works of Braque and Picasso taken by Émile Delétong for the Daniel-Henry Kahnweiler gallery, sent by Kahnweiler to Vicenc Kramàr in Czechoslovakia – see Klein 2000.
34 The *Guitar* of 1912 left Picasso's studio only two years before his death, when he gave it to William Rubin, in 1971, for the Museum of Modern Art in New York.
35 Paris 1966.
36 London, Tate Gallery.
37 The construction *Nature morte le casse-croûte*, given to Paul Éluard by Picasso, was also exhibited at the Surrealist exhibition in London, curated by Roland Penrose in 1947, it was then bought by the Tate Gallery in 1969, the first museum to buy and exhibit one of Picasso's constructions while he was still alive.
38 On this subject see Parigoris 1988, pp. 61-74.
39 Vauxcelles 1912e.
40 Zervos 1942.
41 Salmon 1919, pp. 103-104.
42 In particular we can think about the surprising *Construction au jouer de guitare* [*Construction with Guitar Player*], 1913, an assembly made from a *papier collé* on which a real guitar is hanging, held by arms made out of newspaper, of which only a photograph exists taken in Picasso's studio in Boulevard Raspail and published in *Cahiers d'art* in 1950. The document was re-published by Daix 1979, No. 578, p. 299.
43 Aragon 1930, p. 47.
44 Golding 1959, pp. 228-229.
45 González 1931-1932.
46 Breton 1965, pp. 116-118.

Ambrogio Ceroni.
Short History of a Passionate Connoisseur

Anna Ceroni

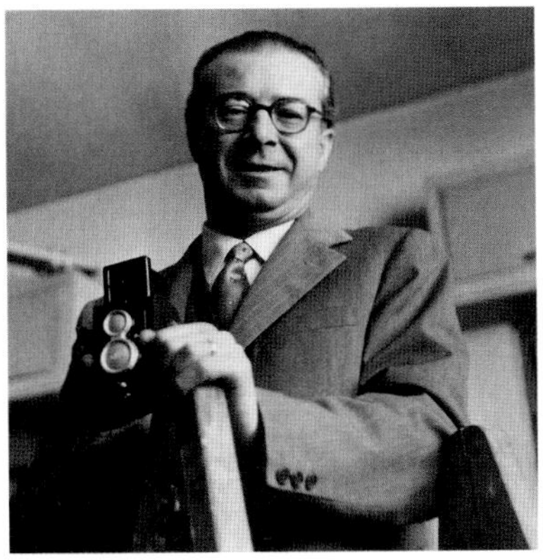

Ambrogio Ceroni with his Rolley.

Ambrogio Ceroni was born in Milan on 29th August 1907 at 13 Via Santa Maria alla Porta, where there was also the headquarters of the business, founded by his grandfather, dedicated to stuccos and decorations. To carry out the wishes of his father, Ambrogio attended courses of a commercial nature that led him to get his degree in the academic year 1928-1929, in Economy and Commerce at the Luigi Bocconi University. His university years were characterised by travels and stays in France and England, Ambrogio knew the languages of those countries and made a lot of friends. His interest in contemporary art and valuable books, which he would collect for the rest of his life, was already being cultivated in an amateur way during this phase of his life.
According to the will of his family and in line with his studies, Ceroni's working activity took place first in a commercial environment and then in the industrial one in Milan, until the end of the Second World War. On 31st October 1945 he left the company "Ercole Marelli" where he had been working since January 1936 to enter, as artistic collaborator, the Galleria del Milione together with Gino Ghiringhelli, with whom he had been connected for some time owing to their common cultural interests and a sincere friendship that started when they both frequented the Milanese artistic ambient, of the art galleries and teachers from the Accademia di Brera. A fundamental element for their human and cultural association was also Giuseppe Ghiringelli, whom everyone called Peppino, Gino's ingenious brother who took care of the the Edizioni del Milione, the publishing house of art connected to the art gallery. Ambrogio collaborated assiduously with him during the preparation of the two catalogues dedicated to Modigliani's work, published by the Edizioni del Milione in 1958 and 1965. Peppino was also a significant go-between with the publishing house Rizzoli for the publication of the third catalogue in 1970. During his activity carried out at the Milione for twenty-five years, his passion for Modigliani took shape right from the beginning in a task of assiduous research into paintings and drawings to be examined and studied as well as a careful comparison of them. The systematic study of Modigliani's work, in view of the publication of the catalogue in 1958, can be traced back to 1950 as Ceroni himself recalled when writing to a gallery owner in New York: "In fact during my personal study on Modigliani's works, started in 1950, only once I met such [...] a small book, and occasionally in Paris during 1957" (to J.S. Knafou, 5th December 1969). Perhaps because it was a real passion, this activity knew no outcome of an economic nature and in fact he was never paid, as is evident from many letters where he underlined the gratuity of his opinion, whether it was for private collectors or famous auction houses that, with increasing frequency after the publication of the first catalogue, turned to the then widely famous expert. "I never charge when requested on my opinion, but obviously I always keep the photograph sent to me in examination for expertise" (to Mr. Irving Lunts, director of the Irving Galleries, Wisconsin, 2nd April 1968); "For my assistance on Modigliani and Italian Artists, can I ask to let me have, admiring it, the catalogue concerning the English Pottery?" (to Sotheby's and Co., London, 21st January 1969); "Please take note that my opinion is always given free of charge, but I always keep the photograph of the work

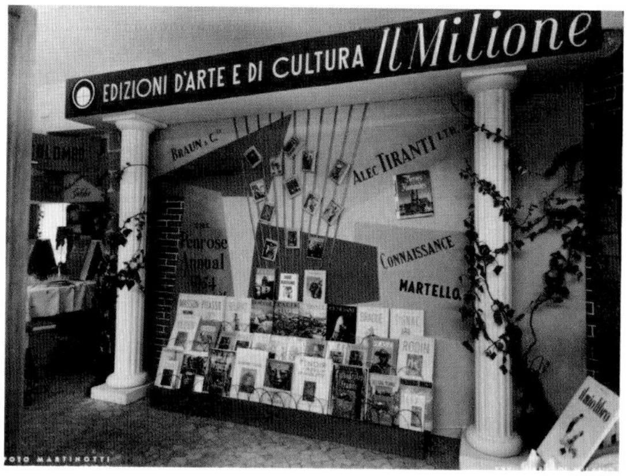

Stand of the "Edizioni d'arte e cultura Il Milione", XXXII Fiera di Milano, 1954.

judged for my archive" (to Mr. J. W. Bjorneby, 3rd April 1970).
The study of Modigliani's production was therefore based on the analysis and systematic collection of a continuously increasing number of works attributed to the artist from Livorno which led to a vast collection of photographic material, regarding the quality of which there are numerous letters that contain precise indications for their realisation: "for a good transparency is necessary a day-light pose. A large size of the transparency is necessary to obtain a good colour reproduction" (to Sydney R. Barlow, 4 July 1967).
The preparation of the painting catalogue, the number 6 of the series *Monographies des Artistes Italiens Modernes*, in 1958, determined the creation of a rich and vast series of epistolary contacts with collectors and galleries, both concerning the search for authentic unpublished works and photographic material of known works, necessary for the volume where all the 156 paintings are reproduced on full pages in black and white or colour with rare editorial care. In this phase there were frequent trips to Paris, sometimes to Switzerland, to examine unknown works; sometimes it was the collectors themselves who went to Milan, especially if the question concerned drawings, so that they could be examined. Many relationships were formed in this way, and in time even became friendships, like that with Dr. Paul Alexandre, with whom Ceroni had already begun corresponding in the mid 1950's, and with his son Blaise, from 1965 onwards.

The Alexandre family acknowledged Ambrogio Ceroni as the editor of the planned catalogue of the many drawings in their possession that later, due to Ambrogio's death in November 1970, was edited by their son Noel Alexandre and published, in Italy, by U. Allemandi in 1993. Such trust had its first official confirmation in the letter that Paul Alexandre wrote to Ambrogio Ceroni on Sunday 8th February 1959 to show his appreciation for the volume he had just received that reproduced all the oil paintings he owned. Among the friends made during the course of this long and passionate research we can include the gallery owner Henri Bing from Paris, to whom Ceroni first showed the second catalogue, still in preparation: "Naturellement je porterais mon dossier sur Modigliani, pour vous montrer les oeuvres que je pense reproduire dans mon prochain livre, et surtout pour avoir votre opinion sur l'originalité de l'ensemble"[1] (to Henri Bing, 3rd September 1962). It was Henri Bing who put him in touch with Waldemar George, the critic of the previous generation most highly esteemed by Ambrogio who asked him if he could include, in the introduction to the 1965 volume: "votre essai vraiment unique, toujours valable et digne d'etre reportè integralement"[2] (to Waldemar George, 28th March 1963). Among those who had the luck of living in Paris in the years that saw Modigliani's activity, the Polish refugee, Lunia Czechowska, became friend with Ceroni, she was a friend of the Zborowsky's, immortalised by Modigliani in at least ten oil paintings from 1917 onwards. Lunia, with whom the friendship became such as to have her as his guest in the family home on Lake Maggiore, was full of memories and precious evidence concerning the artist's pictorial activity: "L. Czechowska told me that Modigliani, who always carried out portraits with a posing model, always finished his paintings in two or three sittings at the most. He usually worked in the afternoon. The sittings were three or four also for the nudes. Apart from one or two occasions he never carried out portraits on commission: perhaps due to his character or the lack of

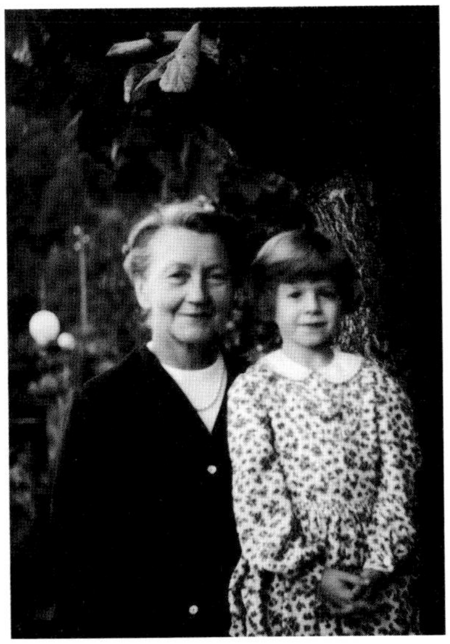

Anna Ceroni, Ambrogio's daughter,
with Lunia Czechowska
in the family home on Lake Maggiore,
summer 1959.

understanding of his style. He painted portraits of common people, artists and his favourite [...]" (to C.L. Ragghianti, 3rd May 1965).
In the artistic and cultural ambient of Paris around 1910 many figures revolved around Modigliani among whom his friend and dealer Zborowsky, and he must be credited with "le mérite d'avoir reconnu le premier le génie de Modigliani"[3] (from "Les souvenirs de L. Czechovska," Ceroni 1958). However he was probably the first to put into circulation, immediately after the artist's death, the fakes carried out by painters who already painted "in the manner of," like Henri Hayden, husband of Odette (Dedie), who was painted by the artist from Livorno. It was Lunia again who remembered this: "During the years from 1918 to mid 1919 he produced very little [...] to the point that Zborowsky became interested in portraits carried out in Modigliani style by the painter Henri Hayden [...] (for Henri Hayden see table 152, 1965)." Ceroni commented: "Hayden used to go to Zborowsky's house [...] when Modigliani was in Nice for health reasons [...] and naturally he took his canvases [...] not signed then; [...] I have classified many Haydens" (to C.L. Ragghianti, 3rd May 1965). Still connected to Zaborowsky the figure of Arthur Pfannstiel emerged who, following the suggestions and indications of the still active dealer, published the artist's first catalogue in 1929 (without images), to later dedicate himself to that work for the rest of his life, signing a high number of expertises, writing articles, compiling (1956) or promising other catalogues. As Ceroni observed in several letters to private collectors or well known auction houses: "I am not convinced as Mr. Pfannstiel says in his recent article appeared in *The Connoisseur of May* that: 'Do not people in Paris and in Italy say that Modigliani never did the same portrait twice? Yes people say so. But they are in error in doing so. At Dr. Paul Alexandre's house in Paris I have seen oil paintings in reds and blues on boards measuring about 36x26 inches representing caryatides which resemble each other so closely as to confuse one.' [...] I have reproduced in my first book all the oil paintings owned by Dr. Alexandre and there are none that resemble each other so closely. Mr. Pfannstsiel as usual says too many things [...] without proving with photos. [...] There are some drawings executed for sculpture's purpose that repeat the poses but always [...] you find some variations" (to Mr. Ellis-Jones, Sotheby's and Co. London, 14 May 1965); "What Mr. Pfannstiel is doing with his catalogue raisonné I don't know, being not in touch with him, as we have different opinions on the Modigliani works. Since 1957 I have seen many of his certificates with the notice 'such work will be included in my forthcoming catalogue raisonné' " (to Mr. T. Norton Parke-Bennet Galleries, New York, 6th April 1966).
The preparation for the second catalogue was even more articulated and complex, again published by the Edizioni del Milione in 1965, that reproduced 66 oil paintings, added to the 156 in 1958, 156 drawings and 25 sculptures. In the wake of the success of the previous volume, his contacts extended to gallery owners across the Ocean, among whom stand out, for the frequency of their letters, the owners of the Perls Galleries of New York and Beverley Hills: "I have of course your book in my library, as I have followed the Modigliani market and literature for many years. And we have an extensive photographic documentation which, please note, is entirely at your disposal, should you ever wish to take advantage of it" (K.G. Perls, 23 March 1962).
Among the most important private collectors, Anne Netter opened her house in Paris to Ceroni in 1963 and he did not fail to visit her on every following trip to the French capital. The friendship between them consolidated to such a point as to entrust Ceroni with the delicate task of dividing the Modigliani canvases in her collection between her two heirs. "Ma mère aviez pour vous une réelle amitié et me parlait souvent de vous en termes chaleureux et je sais egalement toute la sympathie que vous avis pour elle."[4] (G. Netter to A. Ceroni, 1970). The double list, result of later re-elaborations, was prepared

and sent within only five days of her unexpected death: "Me referant a la votre gentille demande, ci inclus je vous donne la liste des deux ensembles que je retiens équanime soit pour le choix que pour leur valeur intrinseque "[5] (to G. Netter, 7th November 1970).
Also Jeanne, Modigliani's daughter, became a regular correspondent of Ambrogio's, whom she often asked also as a friend, for advice and suggestions about her own activity as a painter, so much so that in 1962 she wrote to him: "My desire to work secretly for another few years seems to be difficult to fulfil and I am assailed by the strangest proposals. So why not discuss the possibilities with a serious person – and friend – like you? (20th November 1962)."
The research, the comparison, the analysis of the work of the artist from Livorno were realised once again in the publication, in May 1970, of a third catalogue (*Modigliani - I Classici dell'Arte Rizzoli*) enriched with 337 paintings and 25 sculptures but not exhaustive, neither concerning Modigliani's activity nor the study, by then of more than twenty years, carried out by Ambrogio Ceroni. If the appearance of the publication cannot be compared to the two refined volumes edited by the Milione, the Rizzoli catalogue, although with its typographical limits of a low cost edition and wide circulation, offered a new possibility for the comparison of the artist's pictorial work that, in the end, for some aspects went beyond the expectations of the author, who accepted to realise the volume only after an initial refusal and many perplexities. It was Ceroni himself who declared to his friend Lunia in a letter dated 1st October 1970: "Je vous expedie mon dernier travaille [...] Pour Modigliani j'ai jamais eu de benefices, mais seulement la satisafaction de faire quelque chose pour les autres et pour le plaisir de m' approcher à la verité [...]. Les reproductions en couleur sont mauvaises, mais la suite de noirs avec sa sequence presque cinematographique m'a beaucoup plu, et explique beaucoup[6]".
Regarding this last volume, another two letters, written just a few days before his death, take on the character of an almost spiritual testament: "Une année après, à l'occasion d'un voyage à Paris,causant Modigliani avec Mr. Huisman, j'ai lui dit de mon refus et en méme temps sachant leur mauvaise conduite envers vous j'ai domandé son avis. Il m'a repondu: [...] c'était mieux accepter pour la simple raison qu'un autre le faira, et comme d'habitude il y aura un'autre mauvais catalogue[7]" (to D. Wildenstein 29th October 1970). "Dear friend, towards me you have been so kind, so faithful, always satisfying my requests without suggest or requesting anything in occasion of my Modigliani's passion and work, that I feel to consider you as a real friend. With great pleasure I receive your letter dated 6 instant. As foreword I will tell you that I have accepted to work at such art serie, also if I didn't like their absurde color reproductions and the small size of the black ones [...]. At present I am satisfied to have done it for a result not considered at the beginning. The reproductions in black printed as a strip or better as a micro-film sequence, have given me a new personal favorable impression. It is possible to obtain a new vision of the painted works of Modigliani; a good impression for a comparison and time succession of their execution" (to K. Perls, 30th October 1970.
However the publication of the volume edited by Rizzoli, with its various limits and unexpected virtues, did not satisfy Ambrogio's research or passion, so much so that, on 31st October, expressing a negative opinion on two works, after having traced a synthetic but detailed history of the group of fakes that they belonged to, already known as such in the 1960's, he wrote to Henri Bing's widow who had moved to Cannes: "En effet, ayant en projet un troisième livre sur Modigliani, je voulais vous rencontrer pour avoir la possibilité de consulter à nouveau les albums de photographies que M. Bing m'avait montré à son temps, chez lui rue Cresson. Les avez vous encore? J'espère que oui. Mon livre est paru, et separemment je vous en envois un exemplaire. Mais il ne s'agit d'un catalogue definitif: et dans le texte je le precise."[8] Unfortunately, the meeting which never took place would have been "à Nice pour les fêtes de fin d'année" 1970[9].

Ambrogio Ceroni's writings are quoted in their original version.

1 "Of course I will bring my material on Modigliani with me to show you the works that I am thinking of reproducing in my next book, but above all to have your opinion on the originality."
2 "Your essay is really unique and is worthy of being published in full."
3 "The merit of being the first to acknowledge Modigliani's genius."
4 "My mother felt that she had a real friendship with you and often spoke about you in such a friendly way and I also know of the great affection you had for her."
5 "In accordance with your kind request, I am attaching here the list of the two groups that I think are the same both for the choice and their value."
6 "... I am sending you my latest work... I have never had many advantages from studying Modigliani, but only the satisfaction of doing something for others and for the pleasure of getting close to the truth... the colour reproductions are very bad quality, but I really liked the sequence of the black and white ones, almost cinematographic. It lets you understand a lot."
7 "A year later, during a trip to Paris in a conversation with Mr. Huisman about Modigliani, I told him about my refusal, and knowing about their very bad behaviour in your regards, I asked his advice and he replied:"[...] it was better to accept for the simple reason that someone else would do it, and as usual, there would be another bad catalogue."
8 In fact, as I have a third book on Modigliani in mind, I wanted to meet you to be able to consult the photograph album once again that M. Bing already showed to me once, at his home in rue Cresson. Have you still got it? I do hope so. My book has come out, I will send you a parcel under separate cover. This is not the definitive catalogue however, and that is pointed out in the text."
9 "In Nice for the new year celebrations."

Catalogue

Modigliani's Sculptures

I.
Head, 1911-1913
Stone
52.4 x 24.8 x 37.5 cm
Gwendolyn Weiner Collection

II.
Head, 1911-1913
Sandstone
h. 45 cm
Private Collection

III.
Head, 1911-1913
Stone
47 x 25 x 30 cm
Paris, Centre Pompidou, Musée National d'art moderne / Centre de création industrielle

IV.
Head, 1911-1912
Stone
73 x 23 x 31 cm
Toronto, Latner Family Art Collection

V.
Head, 1911-1912
Limestone
41.8 x 12.5 x 17 cm
The Henry and Rose Pearlman Foundation, long term deposit with Princeton University Art Museum

VI.
Head, 1911-1912
Marble
58.3 x 20.5 x 27 cm
Villeneuve d'Ascq, Musée d'art moderne

VII.
Head, 1911-1912
Stone
49.5 x 18.4 x 22.8 cm
Washington, DC, Hirshhorn Museum and Sculpture Garden, Smithsonian Institution, gift by Joseph H. Hirshhorn, 1966

VIII.
Head, 1911-1912
Sandstone
39,4 x 31.1 x 18.7 cm
Cambridge, Harvard University Art Museum

IX.
Head, 1911-1912
Sandstone
57.2 x 21.9 x 23.5 cm
Küsnacht, Werner Merzbacher Collection

X.
Head, 1911-1912
Sculpted stone
H. 23 cm
Madrid, Abelló Collection

XI.
Standing Nude, 1911-1912
Limestone
162,8 x 33,2 x 29,6 cm
Canberra, National Gallery of Australia

XII.
Head, 1911-1912
Stone
58 x 12 x 16 cm
Paris, Centre Pompidou, Musée National d'art moderne / Centre de création industrielle

XIII.
Head, 1911-1912
Sandstone
50 x 19.6 x 19 cm
Rupert Burgess Collection

XIV.
Head, 1911-1912
Sandstone
50.8 x 16 x 19 cm
Private collection

XV.
Head, 1911-1912
Sandstone
H. 66 cm
Private collection

XVI.
Head, 1911-1912
Sandstone
65.4 x 17.1 x 21.3 cm
Minneapolis, The Minneapolis Institute of Arts, gift by Mr. and Mrs. John Cowles

XVII.
Head, 1911-1912
Limestone
65 x 19 x 24 cm
Washington, DC, National Gallery of Art, Chester Dale Collection

XVIII.
Head, 1911-1912
Sandstone
H. 51 cm
Private collection

XIX.
Head, 1911-1912
Stone
65 x 17.1 cm
Merion, Philadelphia, The Barnes Foundation

XX.
Head, 1911-1912
Limestone
70.5 x 23.5 x 7.6 cm
Philadelphia, Philadelphia Museum of Art, donated by Mrs. Maurice J. Speiser in memory of her husband, 1950

XXI.
Head, 1911-1912
Limestone
71.8 x 18.4 x 20.6 cm
New York, Solomon R. Guggenheim Museum

XXII.
Head, 1911-1912
Sandstone
H. 73 cm
Private collection

XXIII.
Head, 1911-1912
Sandstone
56.5 x 12.7 x 37.4 cm
New York, The Museum of Modern Art, donated by Abby Aldrich Rockefeller in memory of Mrs. Cornelius J. Sullivan

XXIV.
Head, 1912-1913
Limestone
89.2 x 14 x 35.2 cm
London, Tate: Transferred from the Victoria & Albert Museum in 1983

XXV.
Caryatid, 1912-1914
Sandstone
92.1 x 41.6 x 42.9 cm
New York, The Museum of Modern Art, Mrs. Simon Guggenheim Fund (1951)

Head A
Head, 1911-1912
Limestone
H. 64 cm
Private collection

Head B
Head, 1911-1912
Stone
H. 64 cm
Karlsruhe, Staatliche Kunsthalle

Head C
Head, 1911-1912
Unknown location

The Roman number refers to Catalogue Ceroni 1965

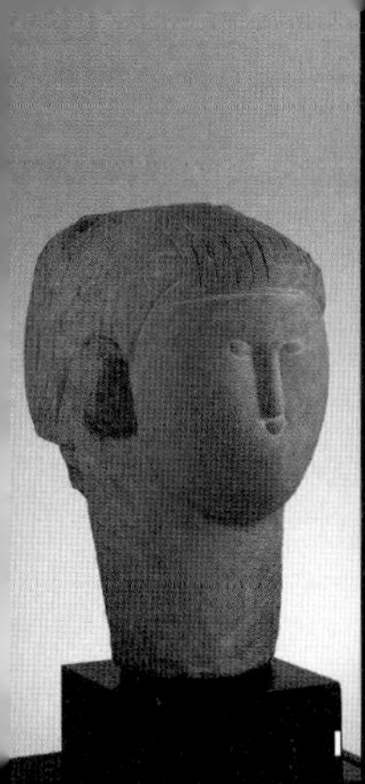
I

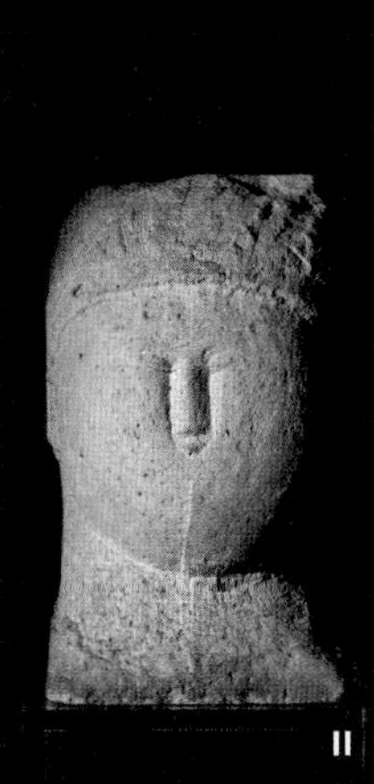
II

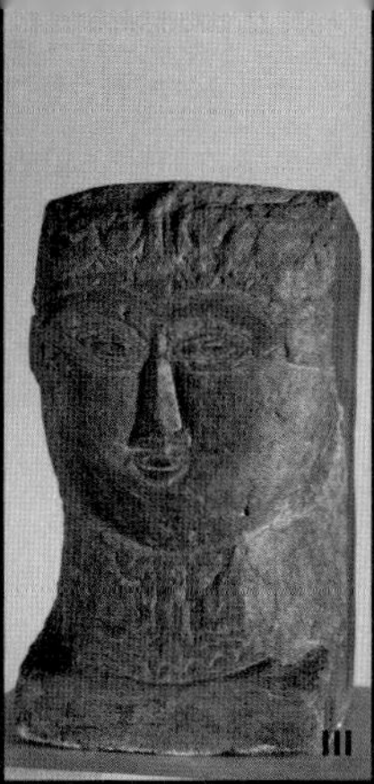
III

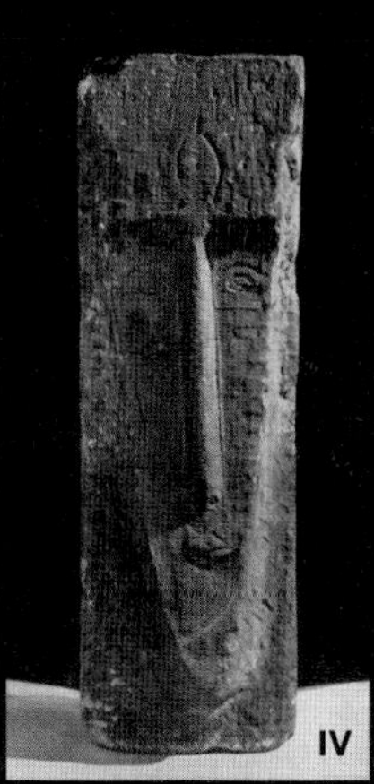
IV

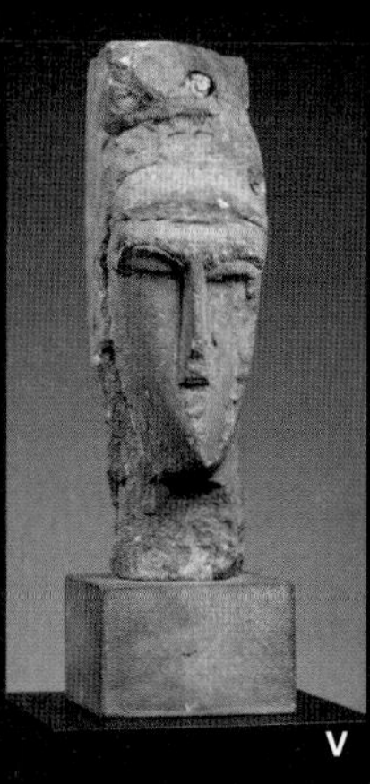
V

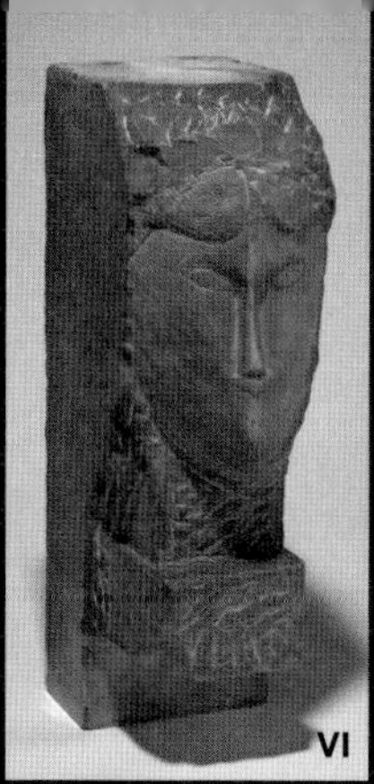
VI

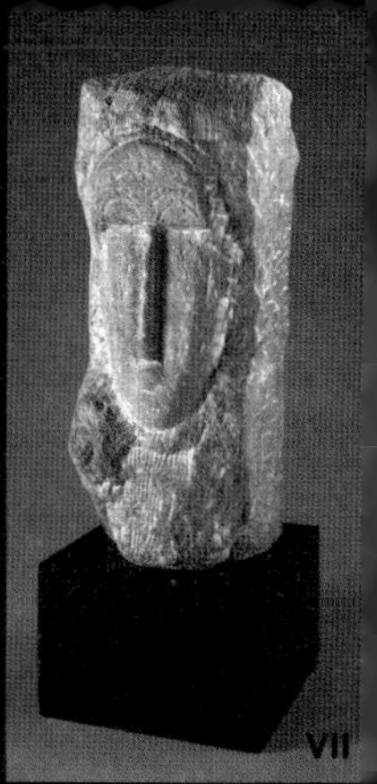
VII

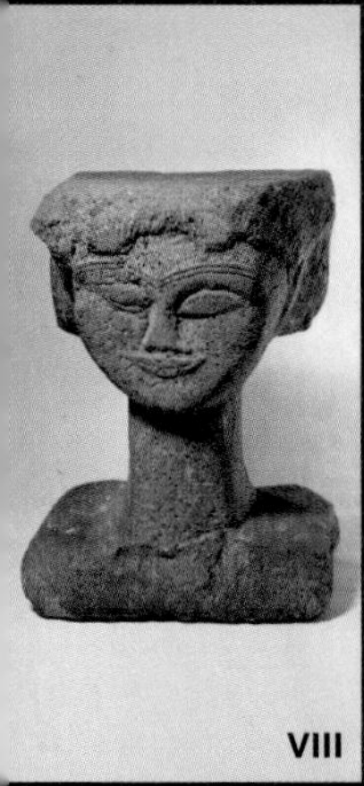
VIII

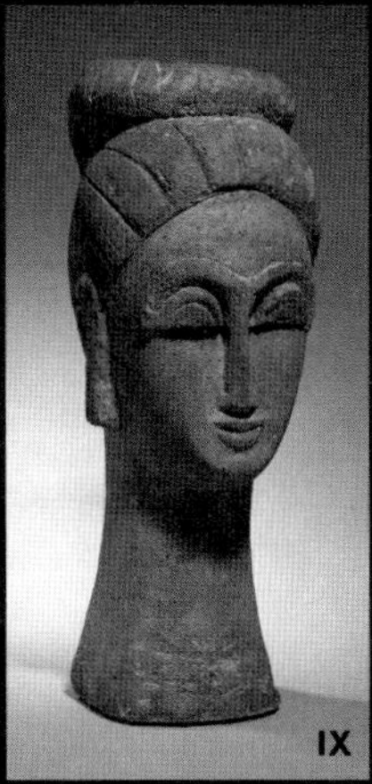
IX

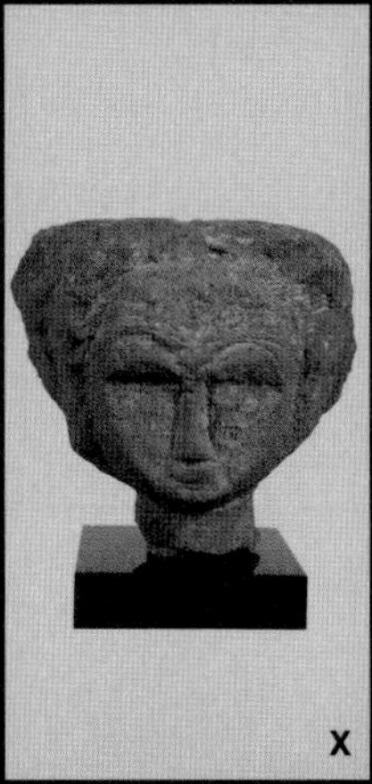
X

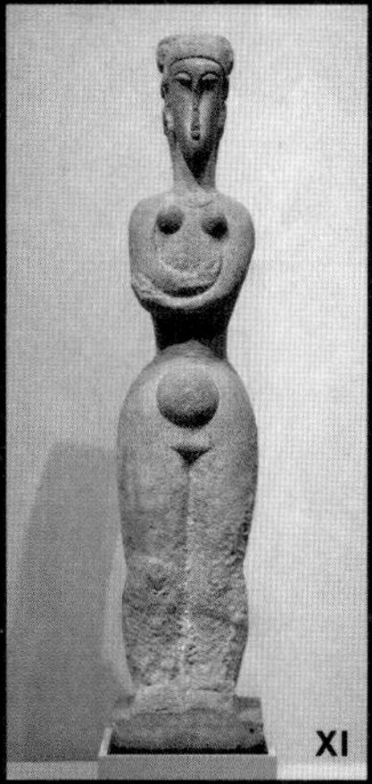
XI

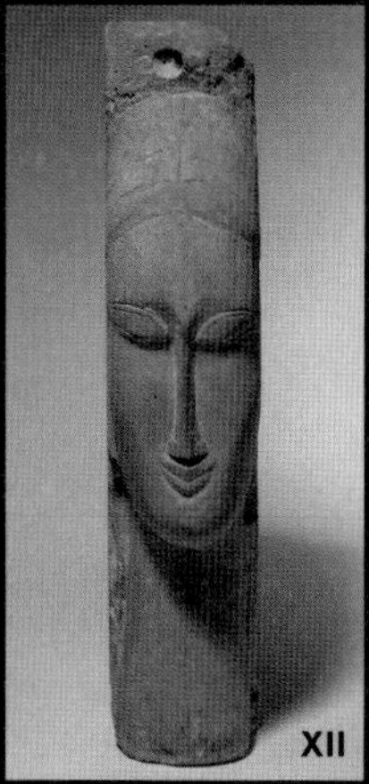
XII

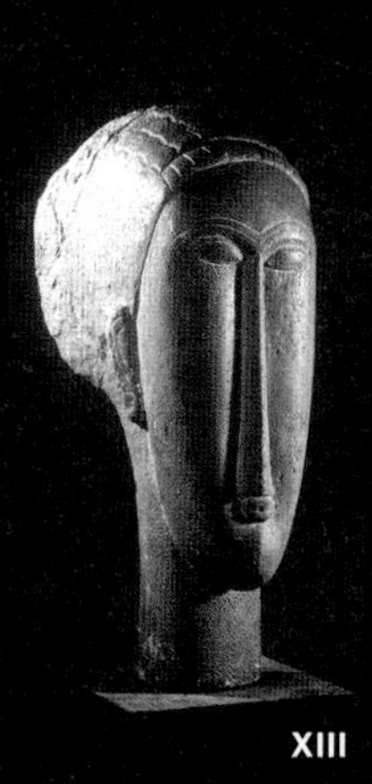
XIII

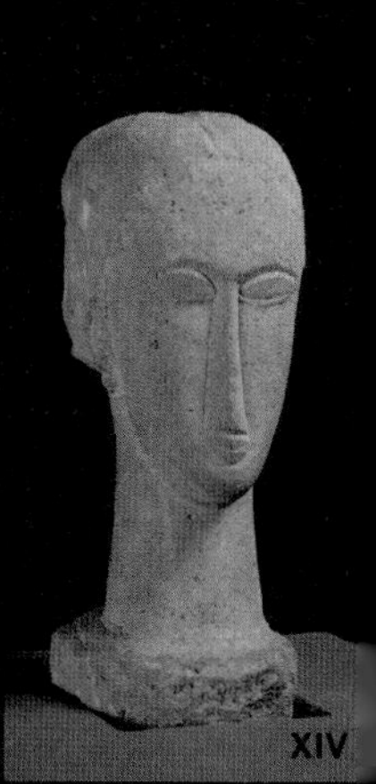
XIV

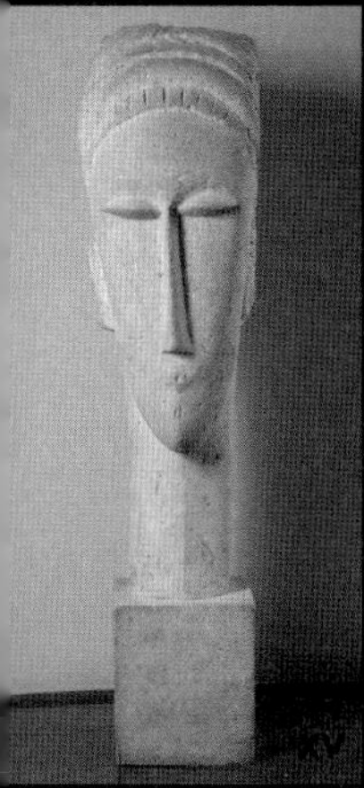
XV

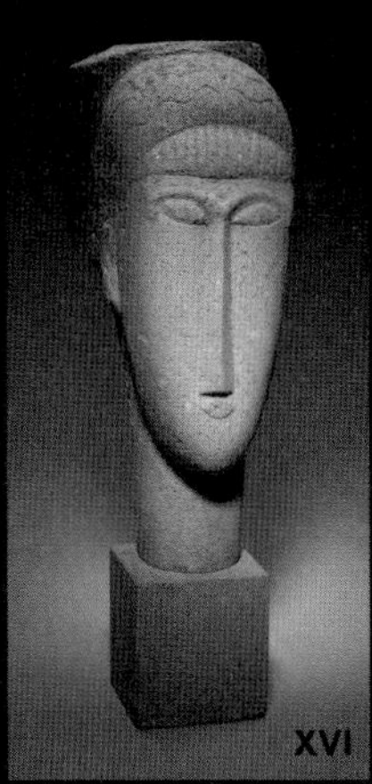
XVI

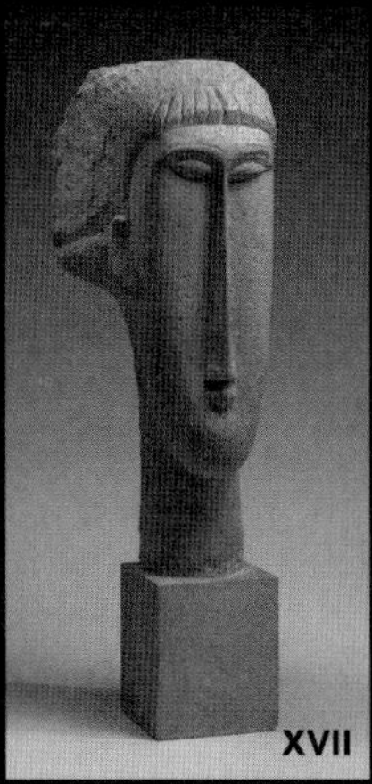
XVII

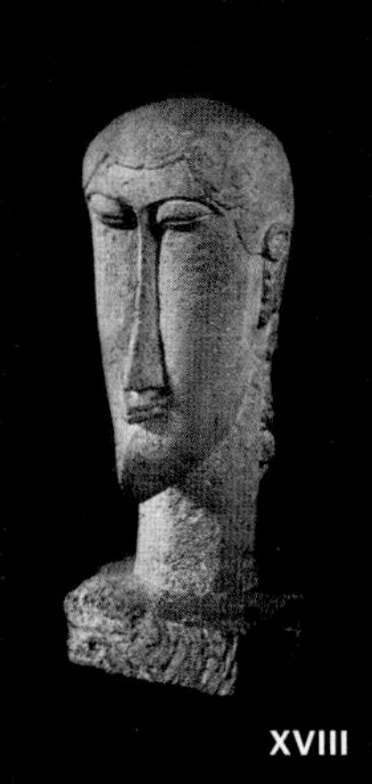
XVIII

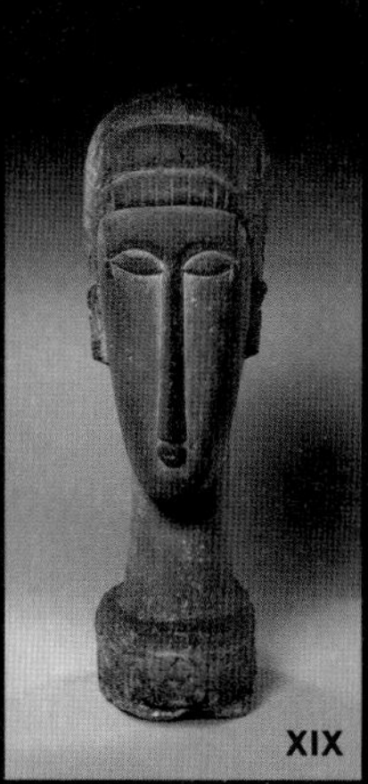
XIX

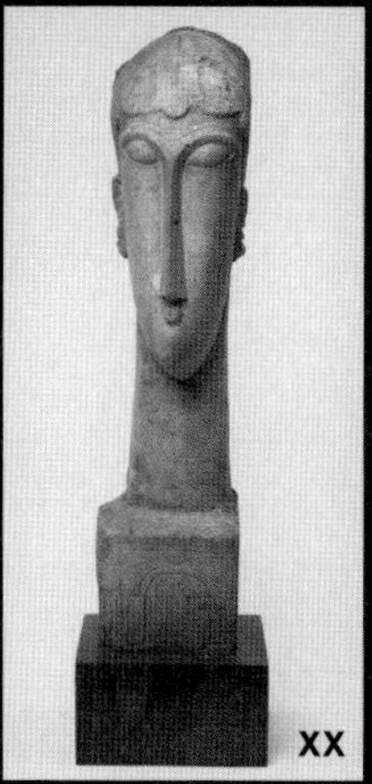
XX

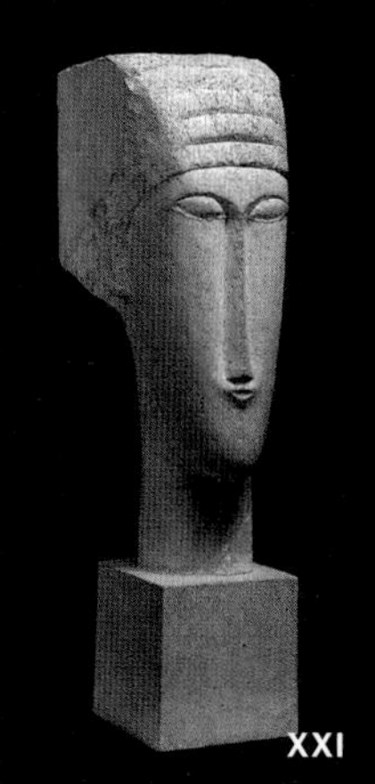
XXI

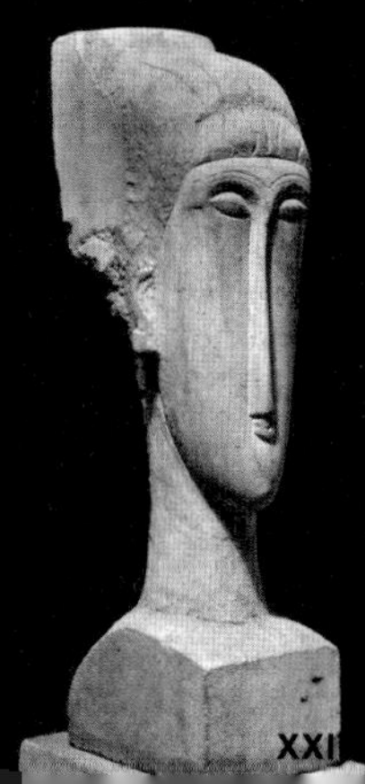
XXII

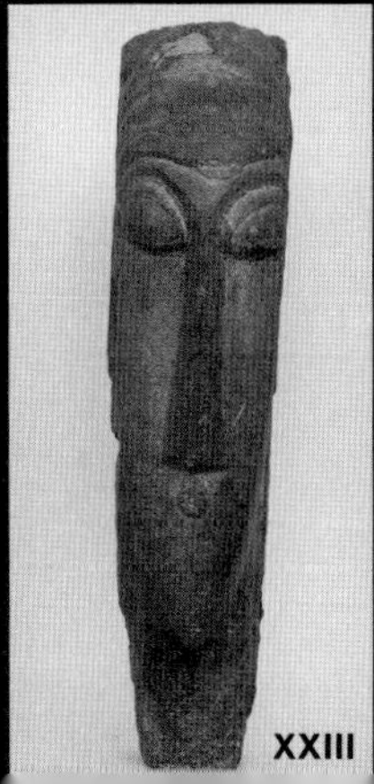
XXIII

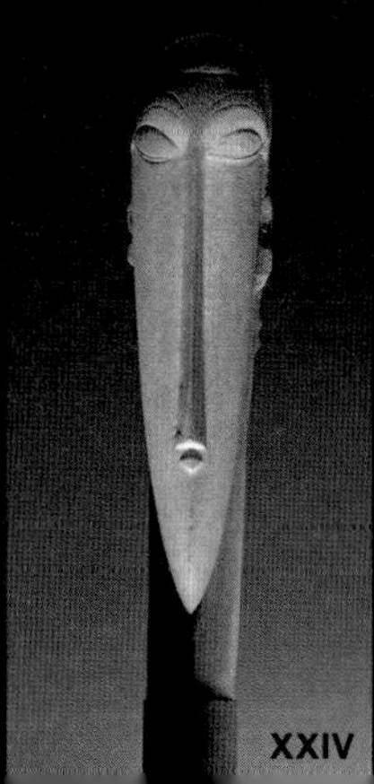
XXIV

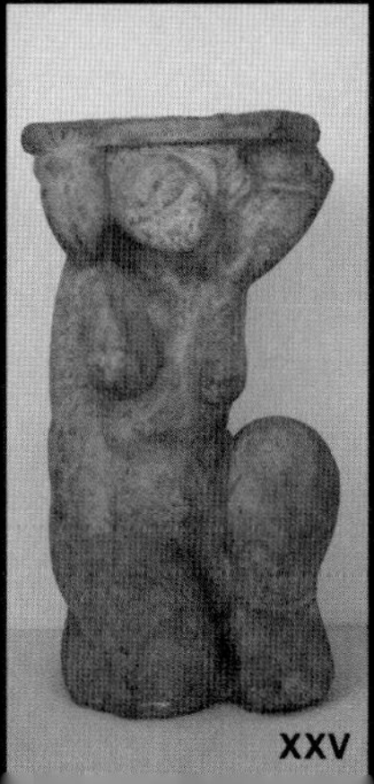
XXV

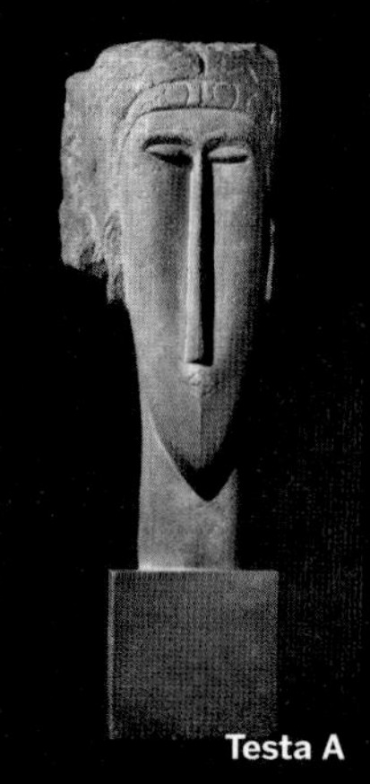
Testa A

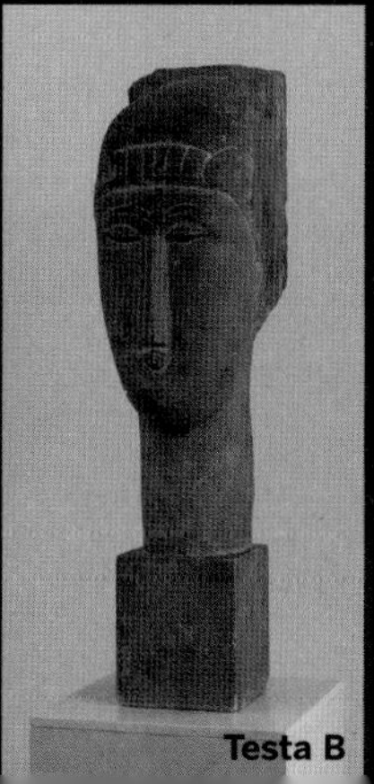
Testa B

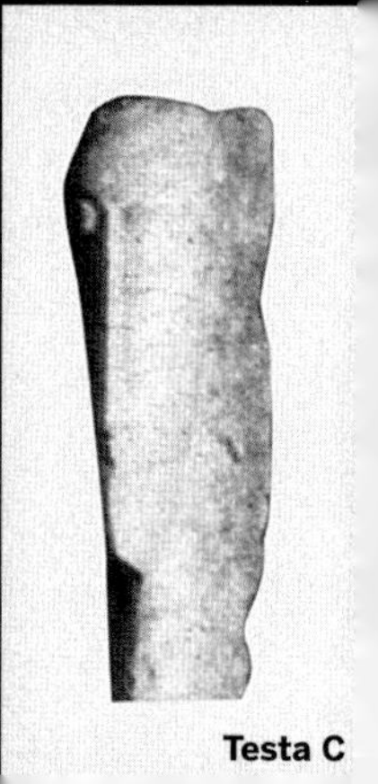
Testa C

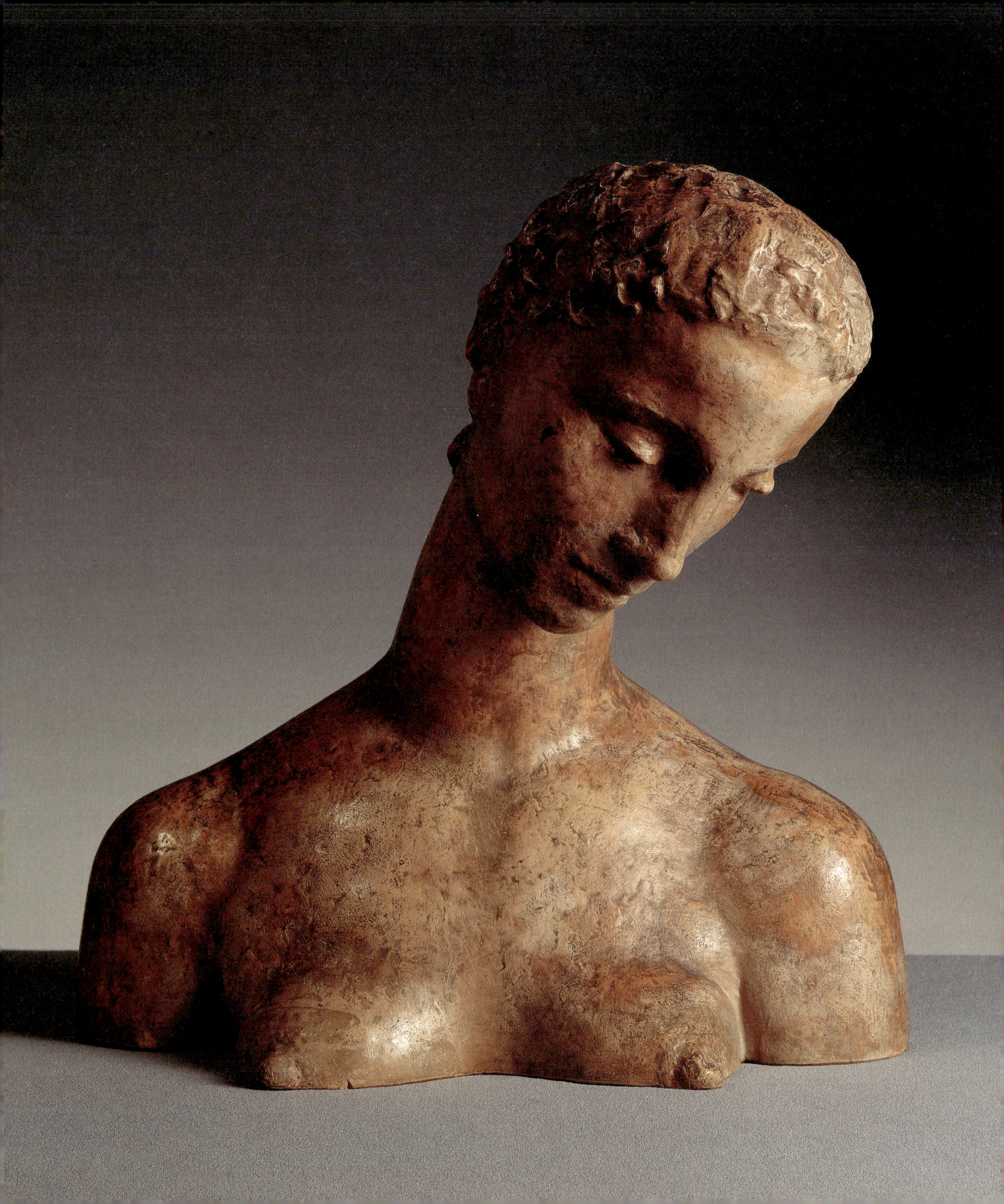

Section 1

Post-Rodin Options for the Sculptural Head in Paris

The European figurative culture of the first decade of the twentieth century was characterised by a two-fold movement of historical recapitulation of the legacy of the great Impressionist and Post-Impressionist masters and attempts at liberation from the shapes and styles imposed by them. The *suite* of retrospective exhibitions at the Salon des Indépendants and the Salon d'Automne, between 1904 and 1910, allowed a rich and punctual review of the events regarding French painting, from Ingres to Manet, up to the astonishing personal exhibitions that contributed to establishing the Post-Impressionist principles of van Gogh, Cézanne, Gauguin and Seurat. For the sculptors, the term of comparison was almost exclusively directed towards the name of Auguste Rodin: the retrospective at the Exposition Universelle of 1900 (with the first showing of *The Gates of Hell*) brought him fame as the greatest sculptor of the nineteenth century, as well as being the most sought after and well paid artist of his time, continuously increasing the mythicism of the Prometheus like figure of the artist, that the subsequent phases only helped to increase (the inauguration of *The Thinker* in front of the Panthéon in 1906; the attainment, from the French state, of the sumptuous Hôtel Biron two years later; the long interview with Paul Gsell published in 1911; Rodin 1911).

Modigliani arrived in Paris at the beginning of 1906 and it is probable that he did not escape from the general admiration for such an institutional escalation; however, it is also true that he quickly made friends with the first really dissident Modernist, in the shape of Constantin Brancusi (who, as it is known, had abandoned his role as *practicien* at Rodin's atelier in 1907) and with the group of Montparnasse poets and writers, from Adolphe Basler to Blaise Cendrars to Guillaume Apollinaire, through these people he was able to obtain first-hand information about the work (just as much sculptural as pictorial) that Picasso was carrying out on the *Demoiselles d'Avignon*.

Already in this phase it was possible to see the signs of sensitivity for the hieratic forms of pre-Classic art and for the disconcerting formal composition of primitive masks; however, less radical lines of research were being followed, beyond the feelings of the more passionate avant-garde that should not be overestimated, in the sculptures of the first decade and particularly in the official representations of the autumn Salons.

In a statement made during the year of the 1912 exhibition, a very attentive observer like Léon Rosenthal pointed out two directions that sculpture could take. One direction followed Rodin in realistic-naturalist research. Its objective was to fix the direct sensation of the bodies. Making it possible for the muscular masses to filter through the skin and emphasise the articulation of the figures, this school aimed at an intense restitution of the structure of the human body, making the most of the rhetoric of movements in space and the virtuous use of the materials, with the aim of creating sculptures to be perceived *en plein air*: that is, isolated in an exceptional abundance of life. The other direction tended, on the other hand, to lead the living being into a geometric structure. Such an "esprit de stylisation" did not belong to the Classical tradition, but rather, it was recognisable in Egyptian culture and, arriving in modern times, in the ways that were instituted by the German secession and the Slavic areas. The most complete expression was found In Ivan Meštrović's severe modelling, able to lead the anatomic complexity of bodies inside the material and inside the architectonic partitions of the volumes, rather than excluding them or going against them (Rosenthal 1912, 40-41).

Wilhelm Lehmbruck
Bust of a Kneeling Woman, 1911
chamotte, 48 x 48 x 36 cm.
Vienna, Belvedere
(cat. **4**)

Joseph Antoine Bernard
Straining Towards Nature, ca. 1907,
Lens stone, 32 x 29 x 31.5 cm.
Paris, Musée d'Orsay
(cat. **1**)

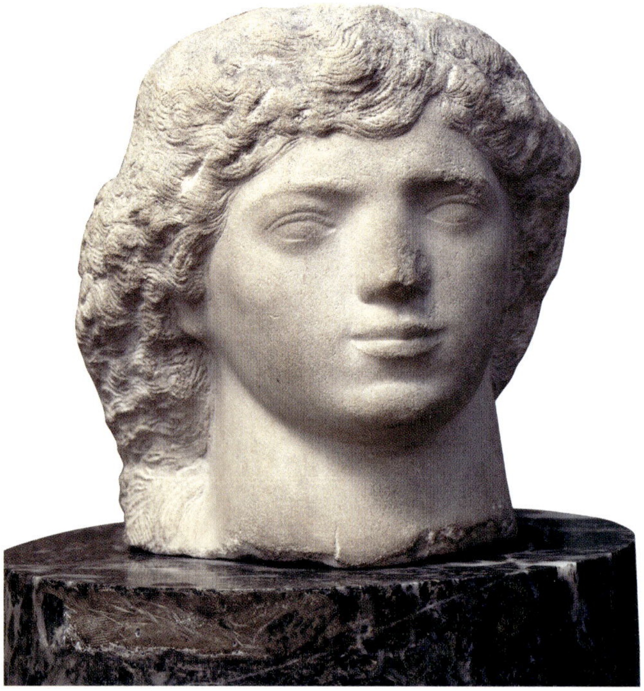

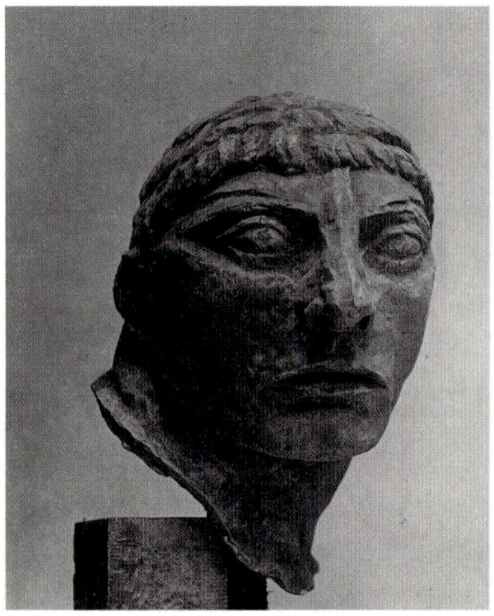

1.1. Émile-Antoine Bourdelle
Head of Herakles the Archer, 1909

It seems that two paths were open to go beyond Rodin's lesson and not to fall into the conformist disguise of the imitators. The retrospective at the Salon d'Automne in 1904 had recognised the statute of Modern Classicism in Auguste Renoir's work also in sculpture, thanks to the "Mediterranean" Classicism of his figures. Auguste Maillol had proclaimed an act of faith in the monumentality of the figure, leading it back to a compositional stability and a formal shapeliness which recomposed Rodin's vibrant modelling in full and symmetric volumes, smooth surfaces, in balanced masses. On the other hand, Emile Antoine Bourdelle exasperated the archaic-like features of the face and anatomy, emphasising architectonic values and the bi-dimensionality of the profiles. Faced with his *Heracles the Archer*, presented at the 1910 Salon (fig. **1.1.**), a critic like Charles Morice could admire "ce type à la fois fin et brutal, sauvage et rusé, qui fait songer à la race aztéque" (Morice 1910, 159).

The naturalistic respect for the full body, instead of the symbolic cult of the fragment, the composure of the figures, rather than the melodramatic and exasperated *pathos*; the use of stone, as opposed to the manageable materials of plaster, terracotta and wax seemed like clear anti-Rodin gestures. The search for a simplified form substituted the predominance of the expression; there was an attempt to eliminate every form of theatricality of gestures in the austerity of the figures.

The return to direct carving (as will be seen in section 2 of the exhibition), after many years of exasperated neo-Michelangelesque modelling and Luminist ingenuity, meant using a procedure of audacious control of the sculptural block. In this way the head in stone or marble became one of the most widespread types used for a sculpture that aspired at affirming, more than a sensational cultural fracture, a bland dissidence, tempered by faithfulness to traditional materials and techniques.

In this first section, the works of the Frenchman Emile Bernard, of Elie Nadelman and the German Wilhelm Lehmbruck (the name of the Englishman Jacob Epstein could also be added) document the European diffusion of this sensitivity, in the specific genre of the sculptural head, as immediately preceding Modigliani's work.

Joseph Bernard (1866-1931) is well known for female figures, of a composed and measured Classicism (*Woman with Jug*, 1910; *Woman with Child*, 1912), that achieved great success in the Parisian Salons, supplying numerous replicas on a smaller scale. His production also included figures and heads in marble, with a clear Rodin-like tone, both in the themes and the titles which

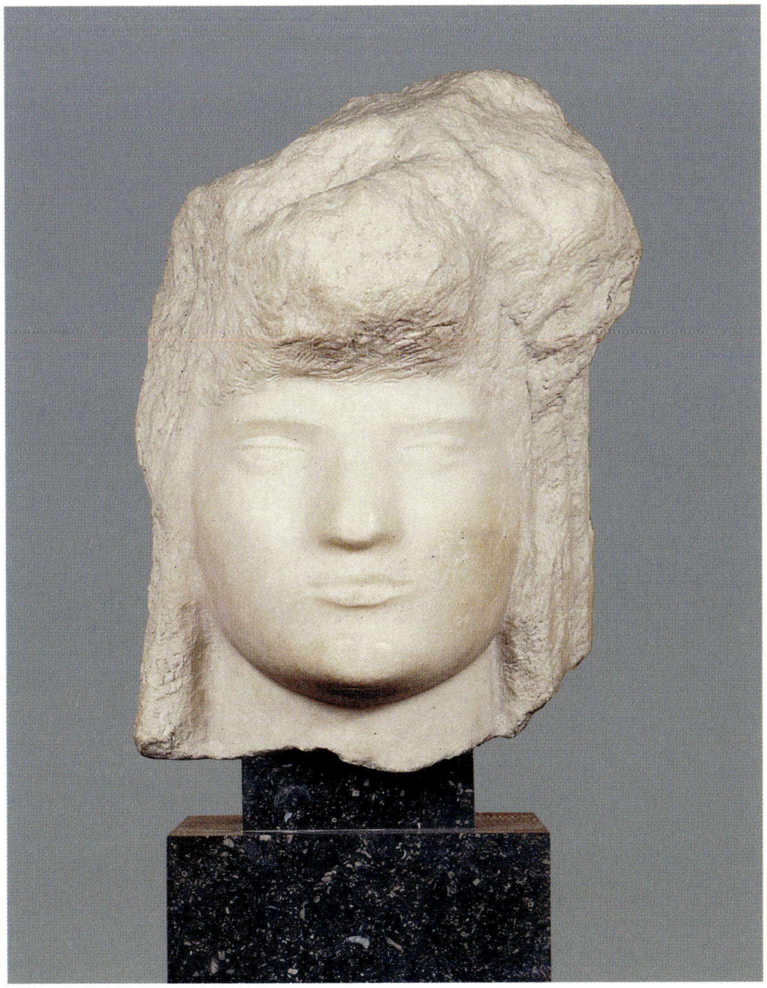

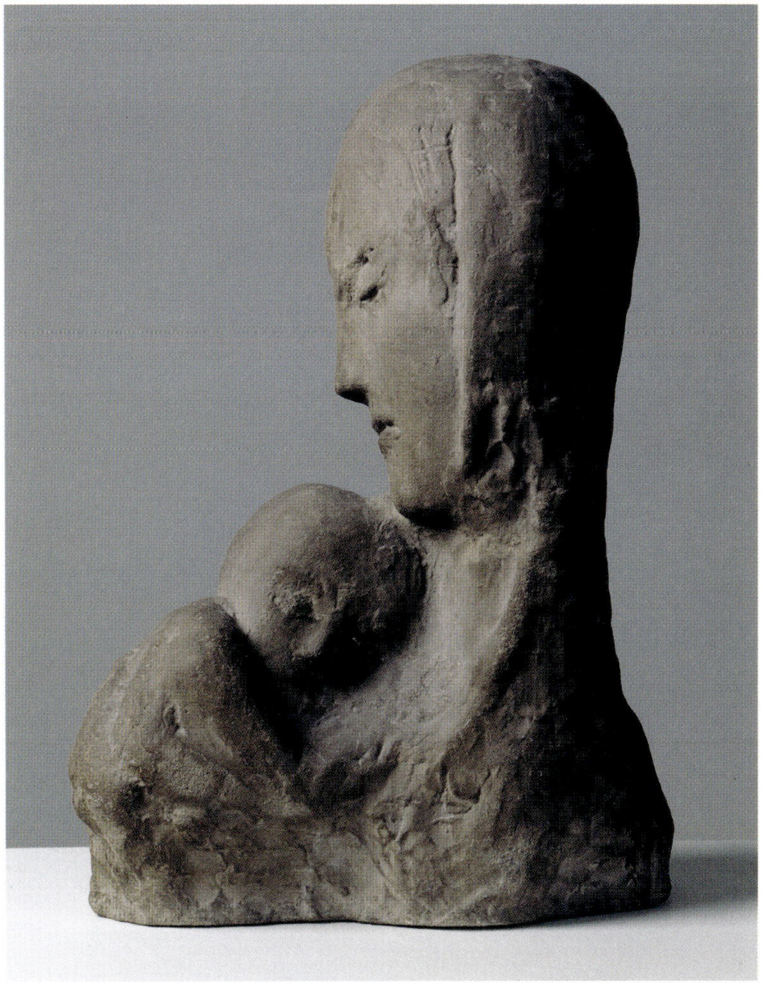

Joseph Antoine Bernard
Modern Sphinx, 1908,
Asian marble, 34 x 21.5 x 30 cm.
Saint Rémy lès Chevreuses, Fondation de Coubertin, donated by Jean Bernard 1985
(cat. **2**)

Wilhelm Lehmbruck
Mother and Child, 1917-1918,
artificial stone, 53 x 34 x 17.5 cm.
Hamburg, Hamburger Kunsthalle
(cat. **5**)

were still of late-Symbolist taste (as in *Straining towards Nature,* cat. **1**), and the sculptural technique which counterpoised the extreme and scrupulous accuracy of the female figure with the deliberate harshness of the sculptural block, following a solution that recalled the idealist division of coarse material and formal ideal, made famous by Rodin's *La Pensée* (1886). The head entitled, also with literary traces, *Modern Sphinx* (cat. **2**) was exhibited, together with an explicit, stone *Thinker,* at the Salon d'Automne in 1912, that same one where Modigliani presented his heads. The cautious mediation between post-Rodin continuity and a formal Neoclassical style, idealised in pleasant archaic-like tones, formed a significant solution without too many difficulties.
Still in the 1920's, Bernard was praised by Waldemar George (George 1922) both as a supporter of direct carving, also with a nationalistic intention, and as the author of faces that incarnated a grace which was particularly French.
On the contrary there was another protagonist of Parisian sculpture to whom Modigliani paid particular attention, Elie Nadelman. Nadelman (1882-1946) was born in Poland and educated in the Classic models of the Glyptothek in Munich. He arrived in Paris a couple of years before Modigliani, in 1904, and began exhibiting regularly in the annual Salons, making friends with Apollinaire, Leo and Gertrude Stein, Picasso. His first exhibition, held at the Galerie Druet between April and May 1909 with thirteen figures (among which the *Classical Head* 1909, cat. **3**) and a hundred or so drawings, immediately had a controversial result: the radical simplification of the form, with complacent and rather mannered Attic and Praxitelian tones, clashed with the much more radical tastes of the Apollinaire *clan*, but they must have aroused Modigliani's admiration. In fact, Nadelman insisted on ideal forms taken from real life, following an abstract figuration instead of conferring specific individual features. These elements drew away from the

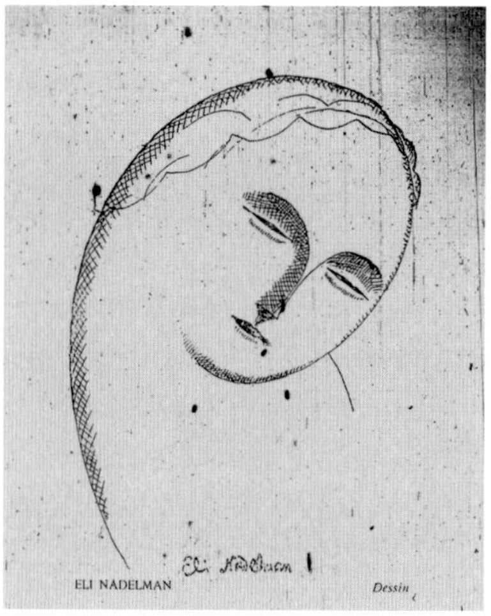

1.2. Elie Nadelman, *Drawing*, in *Montjoie!*, No. 4, 29th March 1913

temporariness of sensorial perceptions, giving way to a purified and idealised beauty, even though quite cold. Even if he always remained a little unrelated to that elegant Neoclassic and Mannerist stylisation which became the author's recognisable style, Modigliani acquired the idea of a plastic reasoning from Nadelman which proceeded through the ideal type, of Classical derivation, of the sculptural head and its order in homogenous series.

In his almost exclusive use of this solution and in the timeless and anti-naturalistic idealisation of the sculpted face, Modigliani, however, showed a consonance with Nadelman's work, which went as far as the explicit quotation of the hair on some of his marble sculptures on *Heads* XIII, XV and XVII (preferably to be compared to the other *Classical Head* 1911-1912, fig. **1.2**).

This mysterious turn towards classical forms, re-elaborated and condensed into a static and irrevocable style, has also been interpreted as a deliberate sharing of a common language among certain *transplanté* authors (Haskell, 2003). Excluded from national prizes, from the aid of the École des Beaux Arts and public commissions, foreign sculptors like Nadelman and Modigliani could free themselves from the Neoclassical revival which local artists were often bound to. It was easier for them to adopt a style which was unimpeded by national language, elaborating instead a neutral Classicism, more appropriate for the international community they lived in.

In fact, Leon Stein's patronage rapidly imposed Nadelman into a circle of collectors from around the world who were overcome by the precise and clear Classicism of his works (Helena Rubenstein's purchase of all the works in a personal exhibition in London in 1911 was memorable). His second personal exhibition took place in 1913 and was dedicated to a series of figures in bronze which had a decidedly Mannerist character, by then distant from Modigliani's style; however, the two sculptors found themselves together once again at the exhibition *Twentieth Century Art: A Review of Modern Movements* at the Whitechapel Art Gallery, in London in 1914, where the painter Edward Roworth lent his *Head* XXIV (cat. **32**) which he had just bought at Modigliani's studio in Paris.

The third term of comparison for the typology of the sculptural head leads to Wilhelm Lehmbruck's work. Considered the most important German sculptor of the early twentieth century, Lehmbruck (1881-1919) was influenced by a great deal of information in the fundamental texts concerning Italian sculpture (he studied the Medici Chapels in Florence) and nineteenth century European sculpture (Meunier, Rodin, Maillol) in repeated visits to Paris, where he established himself permanently from 1907, remaining in contact with Derain, Brancusi, Archipenko and Modigliani himself.

If the works presented at the Salon d'Automne in 1910 confirmed the adhesion to the modes of Rodin, mediated by his German academic culture, there was a significant shift with the *Kneeling Woman,* that the bust in Vienna takes its origin from (cat. **4**; cf. Schnell 2009). When this work was exhibited at the Salon des Indépendants in 1912, the critic Roger Allard observed that: "sans être d'un caractère aussi personnel, est d'une délicatesse et d'une pureté rares" (Allard 1912a, p. 73).

In this sculpture the fullness of the volumes of the Maillol style contracted into an expressive tension which to many seemed to be quite clearly in "gothic" taste. The sculptural forms were more slender and tense; the body was dramatically tapered; without any residual sensuality, the face maintained naturalistic features, with a sweet meditative note. This was a psychological significance which was almost unique in the panorama of sculpture of that time and that Lehmbruck, after his first personal exhibition at the Parisian Galerie Levesque in 1914, was able to keep alive in the years to come, when his proposal could flow freely into the culture of Expressionism. A work like *Mother and Child* (1917-1918, cat. **5**) testifies to the continuity of the specific genre of the sculptural head and the technique of carving on stone, as well as documenting the extreme phase of the author, linked to Modigliani also for his tragic existential epilogue as he committed suicide in 1919.

Alessandro Del Puppo

Elie Nadelman
Classical Head, ca. 1909, marble, 32.1 x 21.3 x 22.7 cm. Washington DC, Hirshhorn Museum and Sculpture Garden, Smithsonian Institution, donated by Joseph H. Hirshhorn, 1966 (cat. **3**)

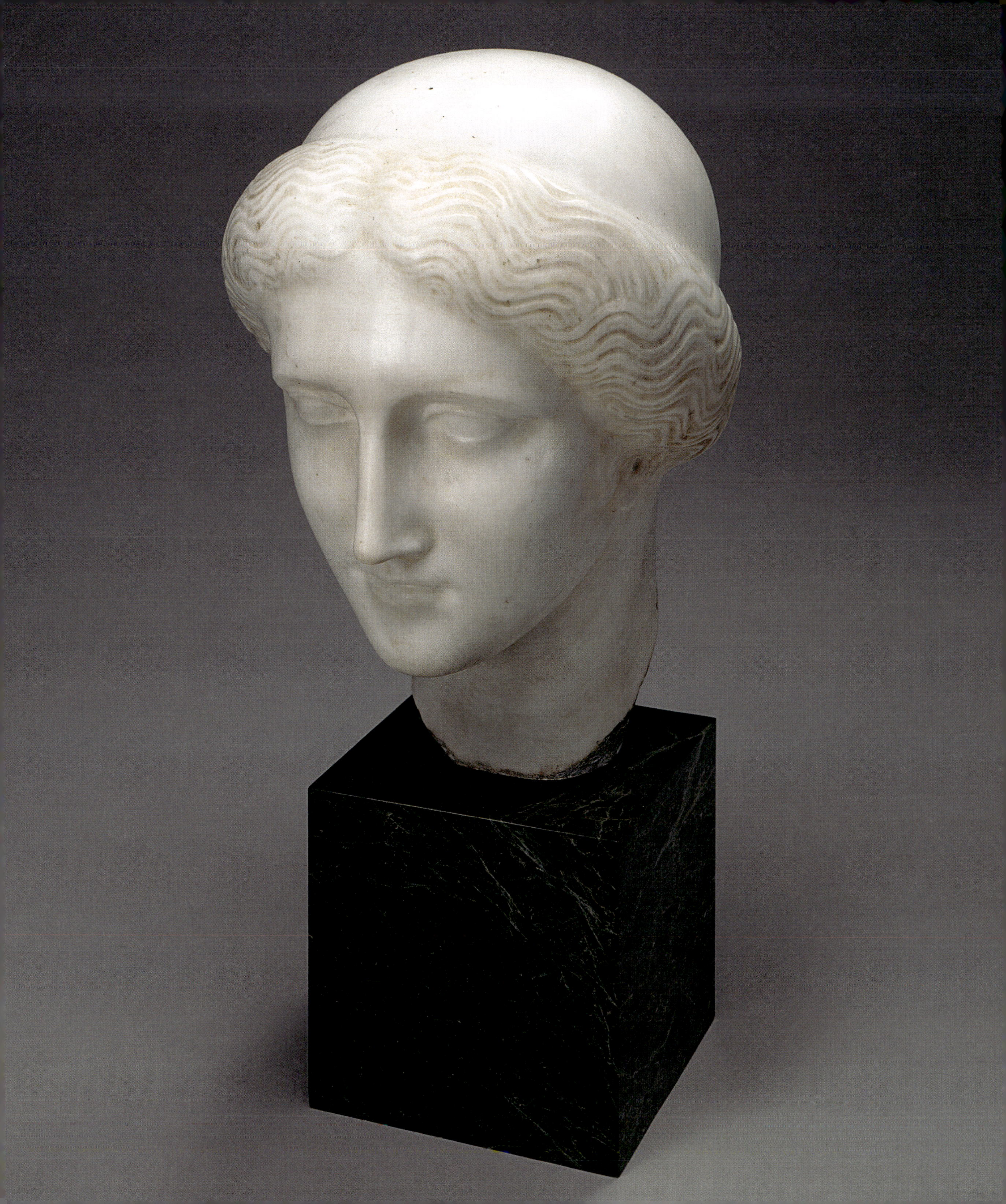

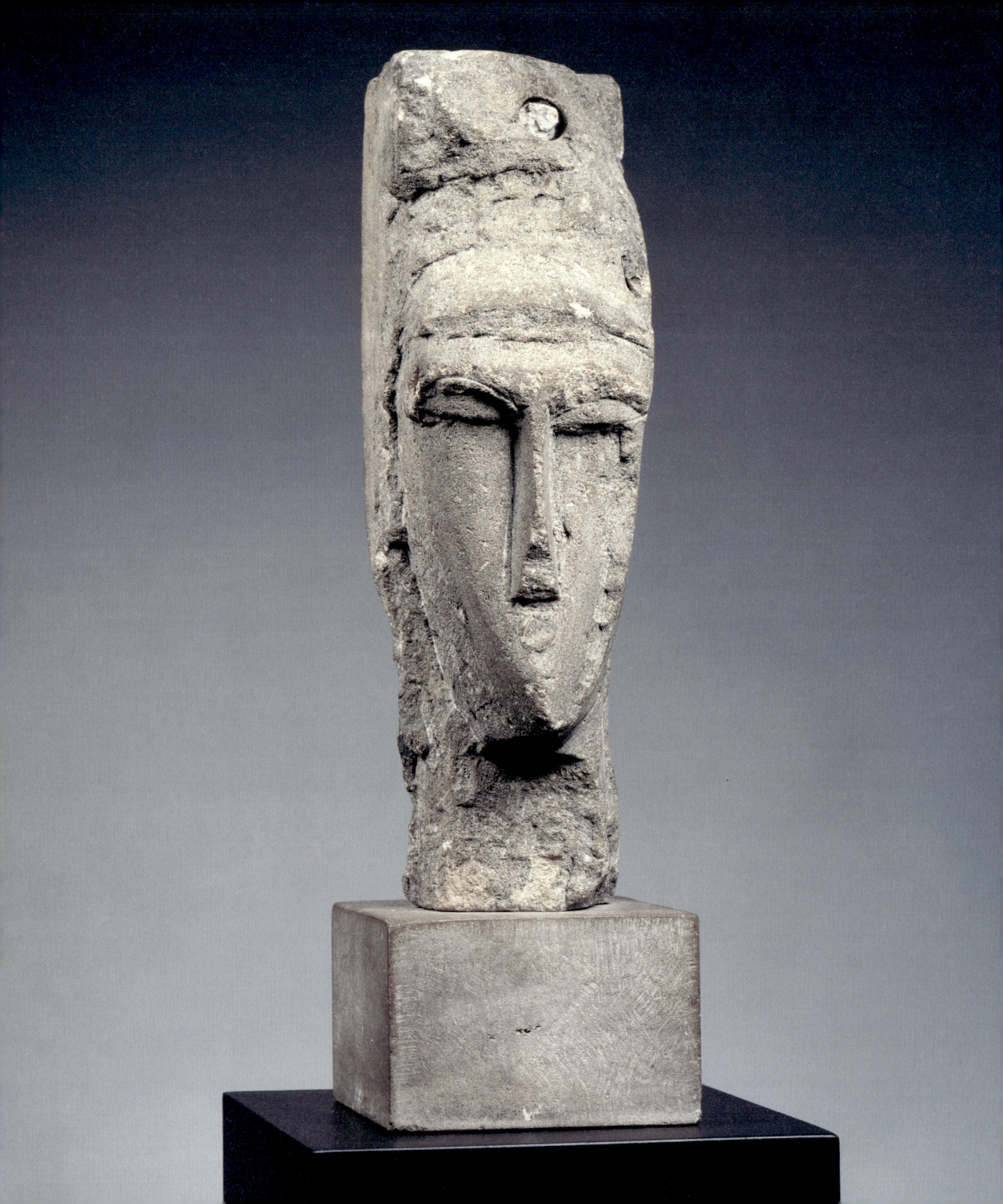

Section 2

Modigliani's Beginnings as a Sculptor. Direct Carving on Stone, Precedents and Continuations

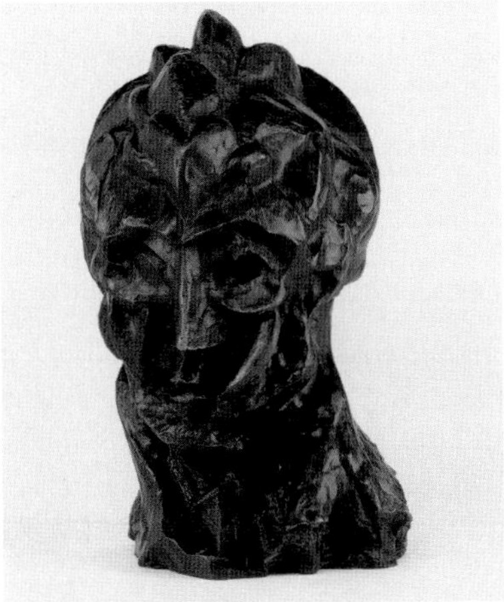

2.1. Pablo Picasso
Woman's Head (Fernande), 1909.
Paris, Musée Picasso

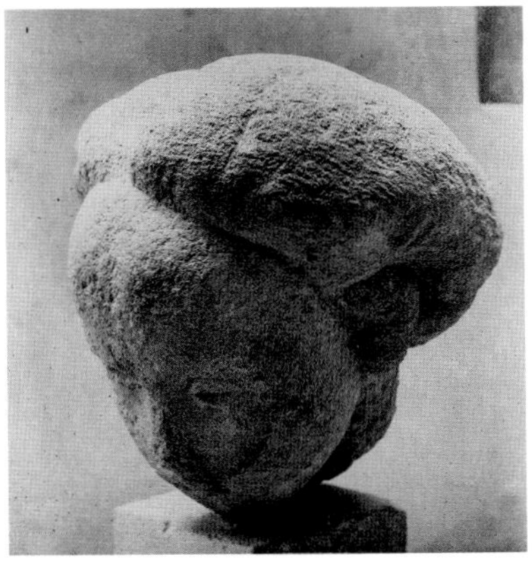

2.2. Constantin Brancusi
Danaide, 1908-1909. Paris, Musée National d'Art Moderne, Centre Georges Pompidou

Amedeo Modigliani
Head, 1914, limestone,
41.8 x 12.5 x 17 cm.
The Henry and Rose Pearlman Foundation on long term loan to Princeton University Art Museum
(cat. **9**)

Brancusi's abandoning of Auguste Rodin's studio, that of the most important and famous living artist, generated a *boutade* which became part of the sculptor's mythology ("nothing grows in the shade of a tall tree"), however, it was also a gesture of great symbolic value. Rejecting the rigid organisation of Rodin's atelier and its nature as a real artistic enterprise, Brancusi took on the role of the artisan who, by refusing the forms of industrial specialisation in bronzes, was able to salvage a direct and individual relationship with the sculptural subject. From a practical point of view there were at least two consequences: the possibility to complete a unique work of art, worked on up until the point of obsession (instead of the routine of moulds, copies, mechanical renderings in marble); and the possibility to recuperate the technique of direct carving (in Rodin's atelier this was delegated to specific rather marginal figures).

Brancusi's work from 1907 onwards was followed and admired by many sculptors. They shared the same impatience when faced with a language which was continuously more wearily tied to virtuosic modelling, to expressive emphasis, to the loss of architectonic stability of the block, searching for a luminous sensation and epithelial effects of the surface. That the difficulty of breaking free from the language of Rodin and Medardo Rosso, and more in general, from the tradition of Impressionist sculpture, was inherent to maintaining traditional modelling, is evidenced by Picasso's most important sculpture of that time: the *Woman's Head (Fernande)* (1909, fig. **2.1**) where the faceting of the face was more the exasperation of an old language than the opening up of a new one. It is for this reason that, for many sculptors, the technique of direct carving became the most pleasing form in the exploration for less predictable expressive modes. Works like Brancusi's *Danaide*, 1908 (fig. **2.2**) or *The Kiss* (cat. **6**) show how much the archaic technique of carving of the block could efficiently respond to a new plastic synthesis. Rather than a fluctuating and asymmetric articulation in space, the stone block offered an architectonic stability and a plastic uniformity. The sense of gravity, sobriety and simplicity of the forms were reflected by the rough stone which, absorbing the light, confirmed its monolithic nature; in this way the details could be traced with great formal economy, using a sort of engraved writing on the surface. Brancusi then followed these direct experiments on stone with an admirable *tour de force* on various different materials (brass, wood, marble, plaster), exploiting the different qualities of luminous reflection and absorption. His role in the development of Modigliani as a sculptor is recognised as decisive.

Modigliani was introduced to Brancusi by Paul Alexandre already at the end of 1907; the relationship became stronger when the painter moved to Montparnasse, not far from Brancusi's studio, starting off on a systematic activity as a sculptor. According to the testimony of Alexandre himself, both Brancusi and Maurice Drouard (a traditionally formed sculptor, pupil of Antonin Mercié at the École des Beaux Arts, a companion of Brancusi's in his atelier) gave him advice on the technique of cutting the stone and on the use of gravestone materials (Alexandre 1993, p. 60). The memory of the collector is precious for some of the technical details: "Before painting, he drew (often in blue) the outline that he had meditated on for a long time. Then he put down the highly diluted oil

Constantin Brancusi
The Kiss, 1907-1908,
Marne stone, 28 x 26 x 21 cm.
Muzeul de Arta, Craiova – Romania
(The Art Museum of Craiova)
(cat. **6**)

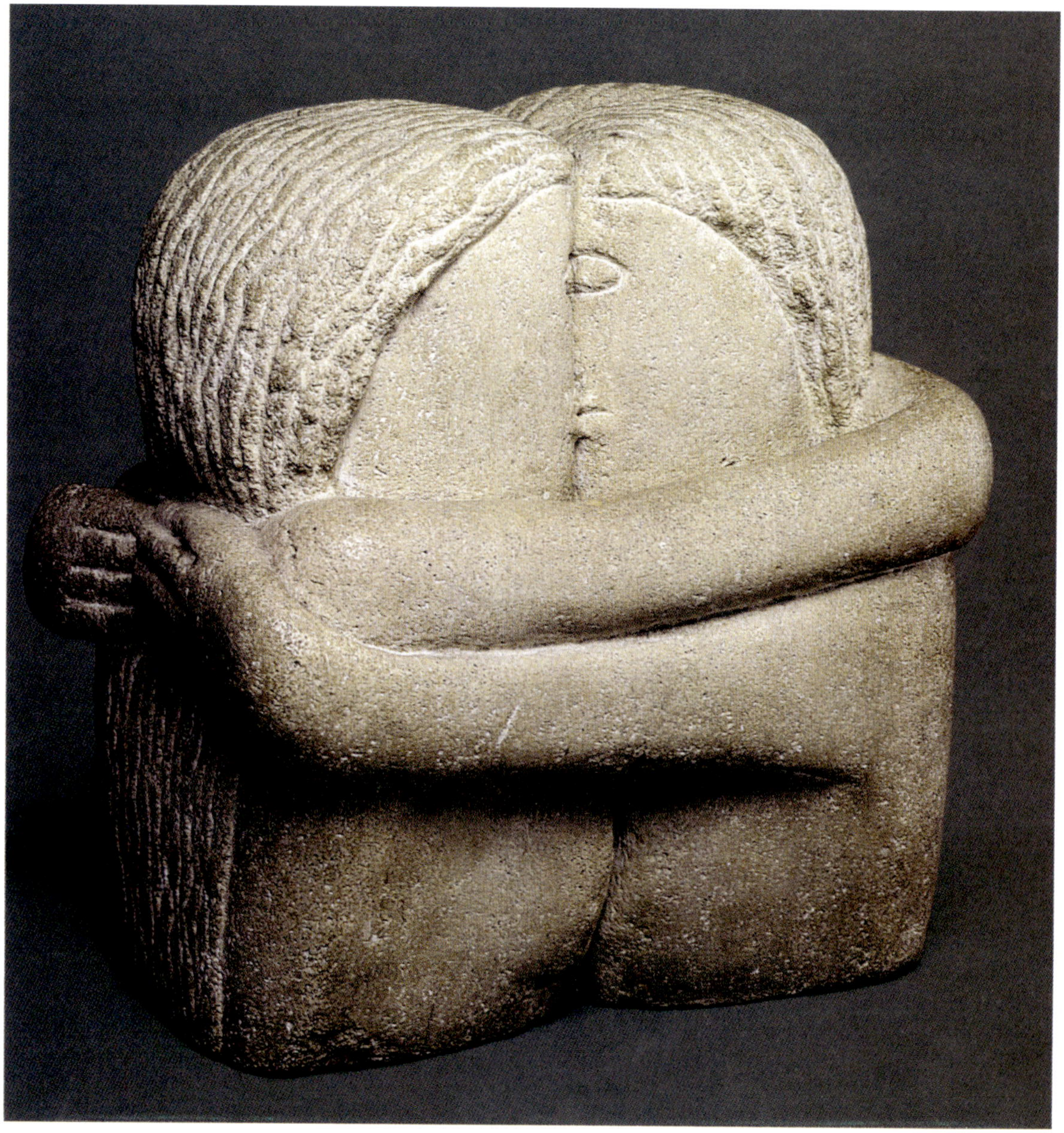

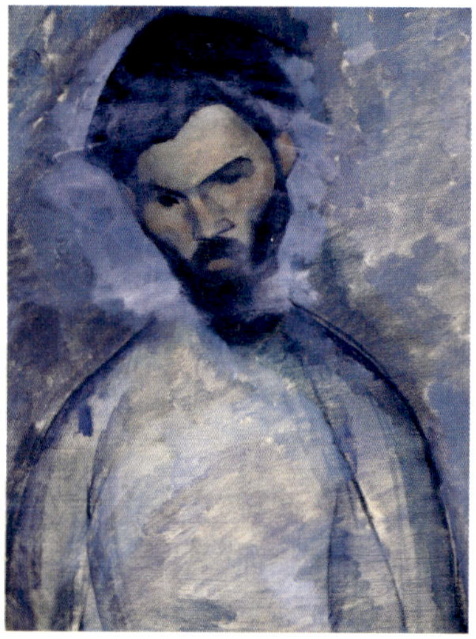

2.3. Amedeo Modigliani
Portrait of Brancusi, 1909.
Madrid, Abelló Collection

paints [...] He sculpted in the same way: he drew for a long time and then he worked directly on the block. If an error occurred, he took another block and started again. The rough hewing tortured and exasperated him" (Alexandre 1993, p. 67).
If the effort of the sculptural work did not delay in becoming one of the many motives of the legends about Modigliani it is also true that it was the most satisfying technique for the author's aims. During years in which sculptors worked around problems of translation of the Cubist space (Archipenko, Duchamp Villon, Lipchitz, Csáky, Gutfreund), of dynamic renewal of the forms (Boccioni, who in June 1913 presented his plasters to the Futurists in Paris), when not of polymateric aggregations (Picasso as well as Archipenko and Boccioni), wavering between modelling and construction, in fact, Modigliani maintained a firm trust in the most classic of technical procedures.
Apart from teaching him the basics of direct carving, Brancusi was able to transmit to him the crucial problem of the mass repetition of a subject. Two fundamental works are examples of this, like the *Sleeping Muse,* presented at the Salon des Indépendants in 1912, then repeated in marble for the Armory Show in 1913; and the six variations in stone and plaster of *The Kiss* which followed the stone one presented at the Indépendants in 1912.

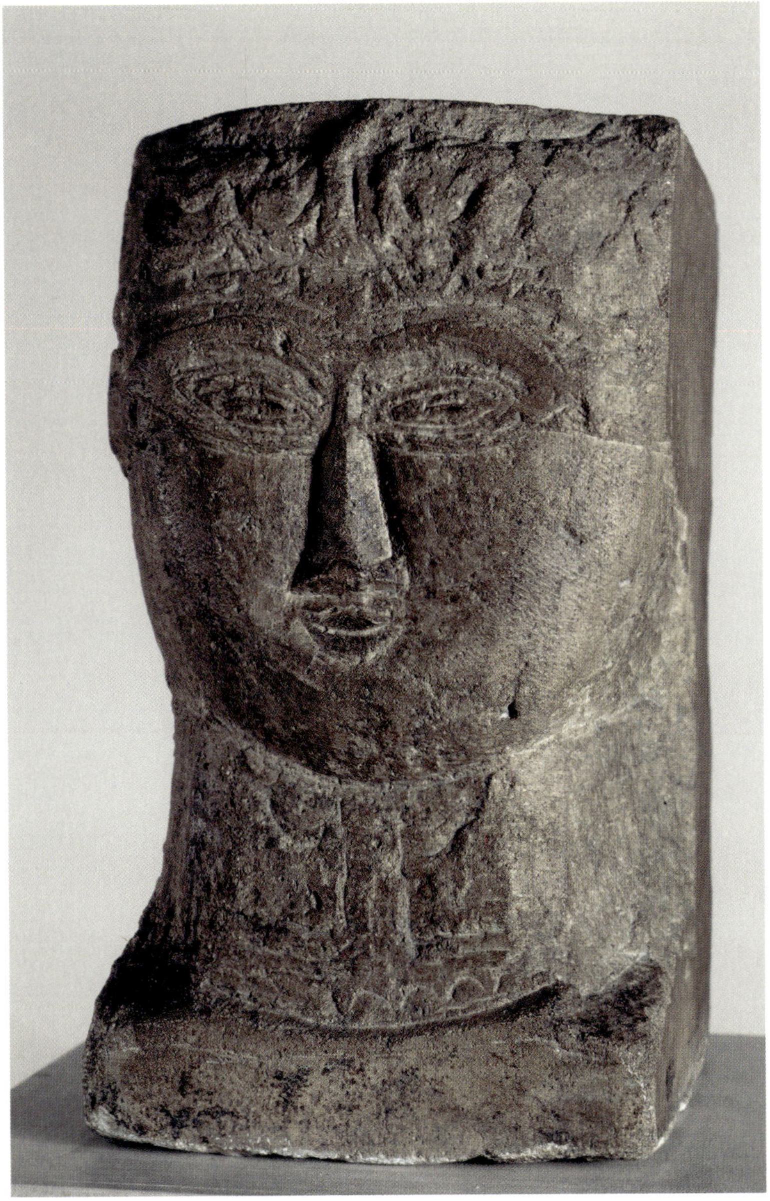

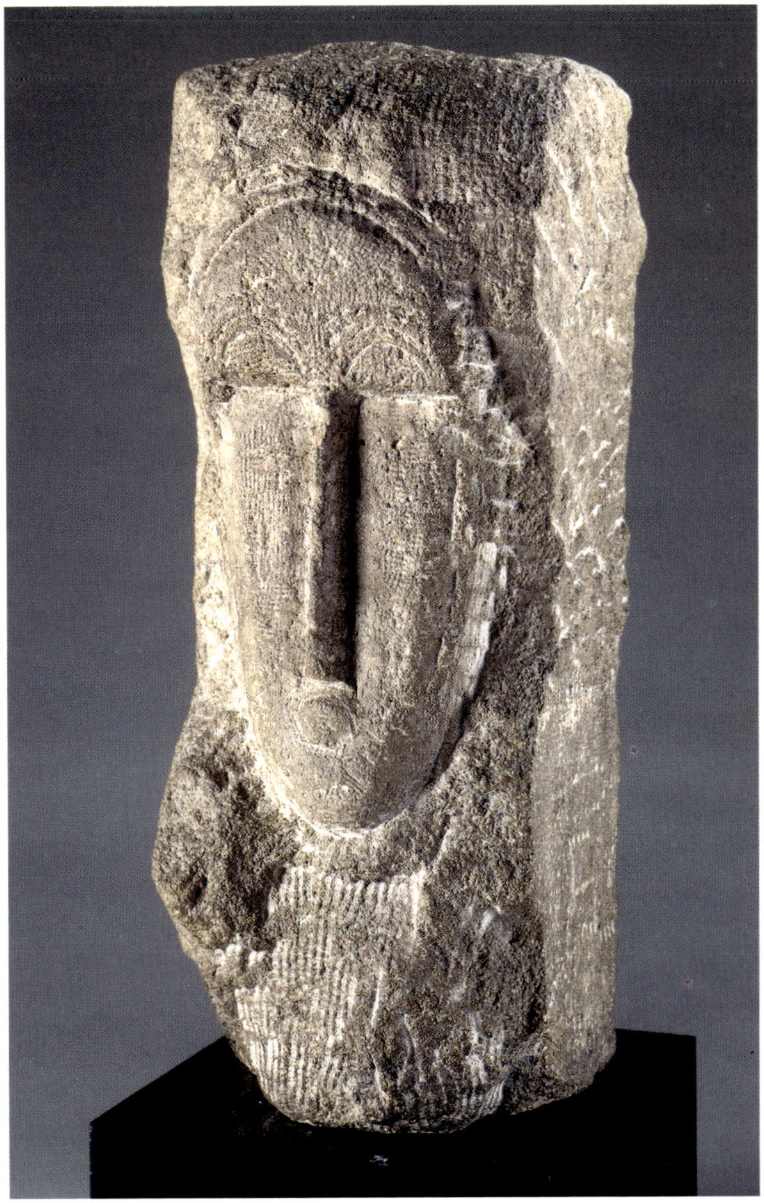

Amedeo Modigliani
Head of a Woman, 1911-1913,
stone, 47 x 25 x 30 cm.
Paris, Centre Pompidou, Musée National d'art moderne / Centre de création industrielle
(cat. **7**)

Amedeo Modigliani
Head, 1911-1912,
stone, 49.5 x 18.4 x 22.8 cm.
Washington DC, Hirshhorn Museum and Sculpture Garden, Smithsonian Institution, donated by Joseph H. Hirshhorn, 1966
(cat. **8**)

In some ways, the Modigliani heads appeared to be like a vertical version of Brancusi's ovoids. Lined up on their bases, grouped "comme des tuyaux d'orgue," in 1912 (according to the memory of Jacques Lipchitz which was proved to be false, however, by the photographic documentation of the time), they offered the testimony of a definite theme arranged in multiple variants.
Furthermore, Brancusi's work could suggest some stylistic expedients to Modigliani, like the deformation of the eyeballs in *M.lle Pogany* which can be found, for example, in *Head* XXIII. From this point of view, the portrait of Brancusi that we can see sketched on the back of the *Cellist* (fig. **2.3**) is a singular document, in its reversibility: an act of faith in late Cézanne language the *Cellist* (exhibited at the Indépendants in 1910); an opening towards a new season of sculpture, a homage to the Romanian.
The most decisive innovators of modernist sculpture were converging from different directions on the technique of direct carving on stone, or carving on wood (London 2009). Solutions of this kind were very widespread in British sculpture, both in mainstream collecting and in avant-garde thinking. From this point of view, *Hieratic Head of Ezra Pound* by Henry Gaudier-Brzeska, fundamental text of British modernism (1914) can be

Ossip Zadkine
Head with Lead Eyes, 1919,
stone encrusted with original lead,
50 x 23 x 23 cm.
Paris, Musée Zadkine de la Ville
de Paris
(cat. **10**)

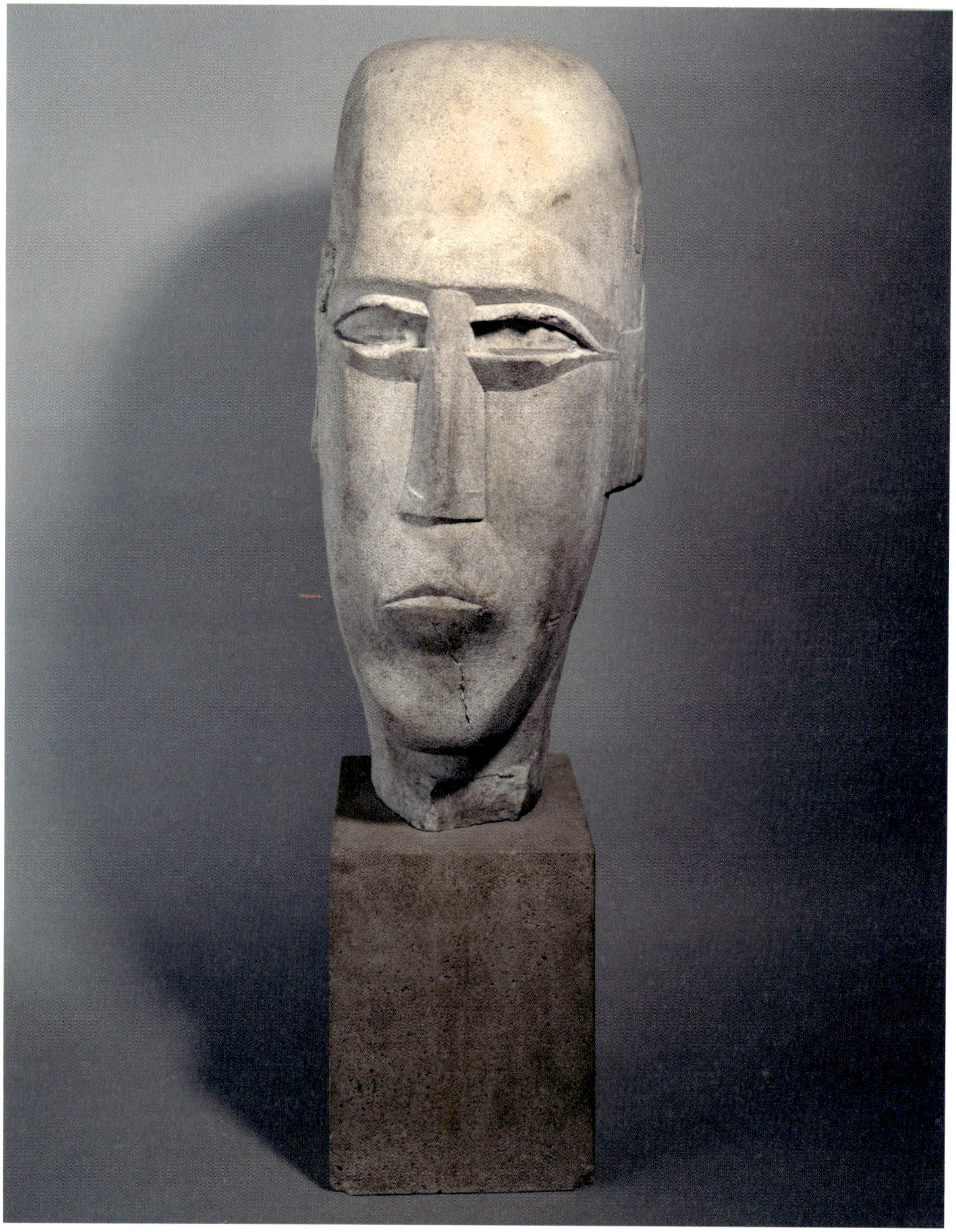

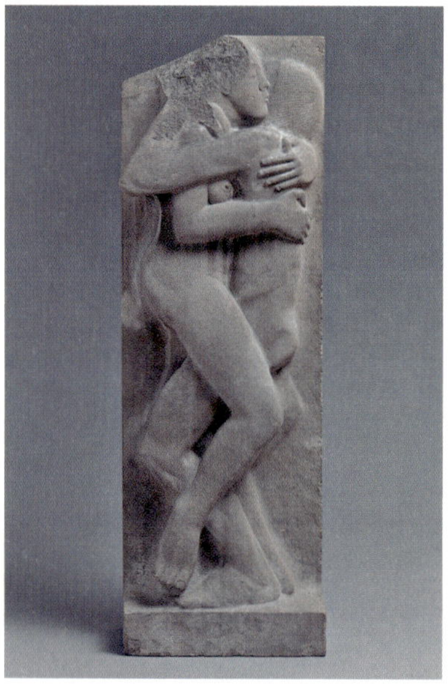

2.4. Eric Gill, *Ecstasy*, 1910-1911.
London, Tate Gallery

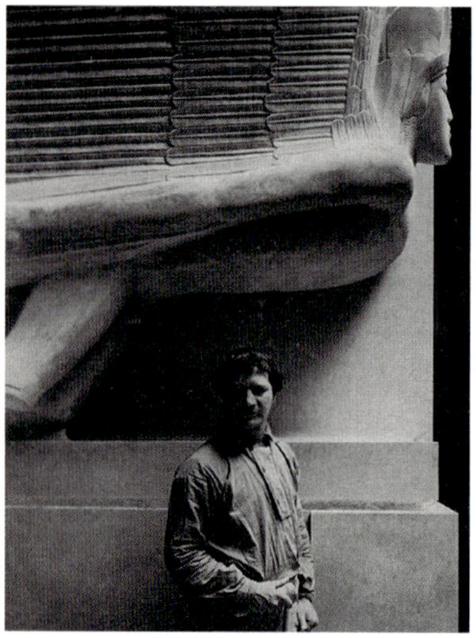

2.5. Jacob Epstein in his studio in front of the Tomb of Oscar Wilde, 1909

counterpoised to Eric Gill's (1881-1940) bas-relief known as *Ecstasy* (fig. **2.4**): a work which was influenced by sculptures in Indian temples and carried out on the request of Edward Perry Warren, who had already commissioned a version of Auguste Rodin's *The Kiss*. The renewed spreading of direct carving sculpture was reflected by sensational cases, like the unveiling, in June 1912, of the monument to Oscar Wilde carried out by Jacob Epstein at the Père Lachaise (fig. **2.5**). The cenotaph added the rigour of the sculptural block to a distinct taste for synthesis and Egyptian linearity. Epstein was recognised by the local press as "un sculpteur audacieux dont les ouvrages sont empreints d'un archaïsme un peu voulu, ma qui ne va pas sans une certaine grandeur" (*La tombe d'Oscar Wilde* 1911).

Henri Laurens
Woman with Earrings, 1921
stone, h. 40 cm, 13 x 9.3 cm
Berne, Kunstmuseum, Hermann and Margit Rupf Foundation
(cat. **11**)

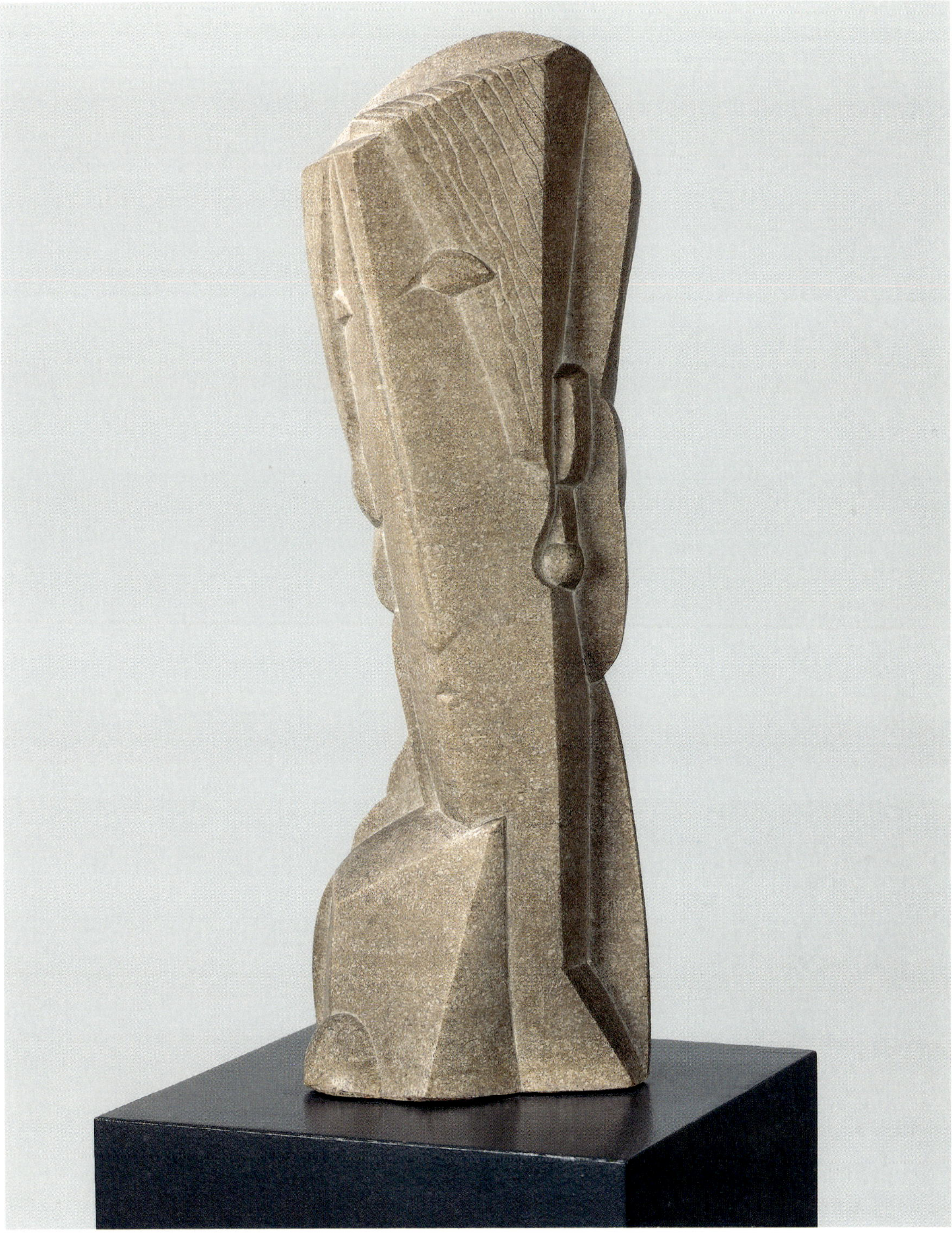

However, the controversy did not regard the stylistic choices, but rather the decorum of the cemetery, as the statue showed the male genitalia. In a magazine which was not distant from the tendencies of the Parisian avant-garde like *Montjoie!*, however, the author – who refused to attenuate the realism of the work – was defended against the threats of the Comité d'Esthétique of the Prefecture of the Seine (where there was, among others, Mercié) and he was found guilty only of having "excessivement stylisé sa médiocre statue" (Le Journal, 28 September 1912; Lariot 1913).
In Modigliani's Paris, in fact, much more radical paths were being trod. In 1907 Picasso had sculpted in wood a *Standing Nude* (Spies 2000, n. 17; fig. **2.6**) which, condensing all the

Ossip Zadkine
Head of a Man, 1918,
stone, 34 x 19 x 18 cm.
Paris, Musée Zadkine de la Ville
de Paris
(cat. **13**)

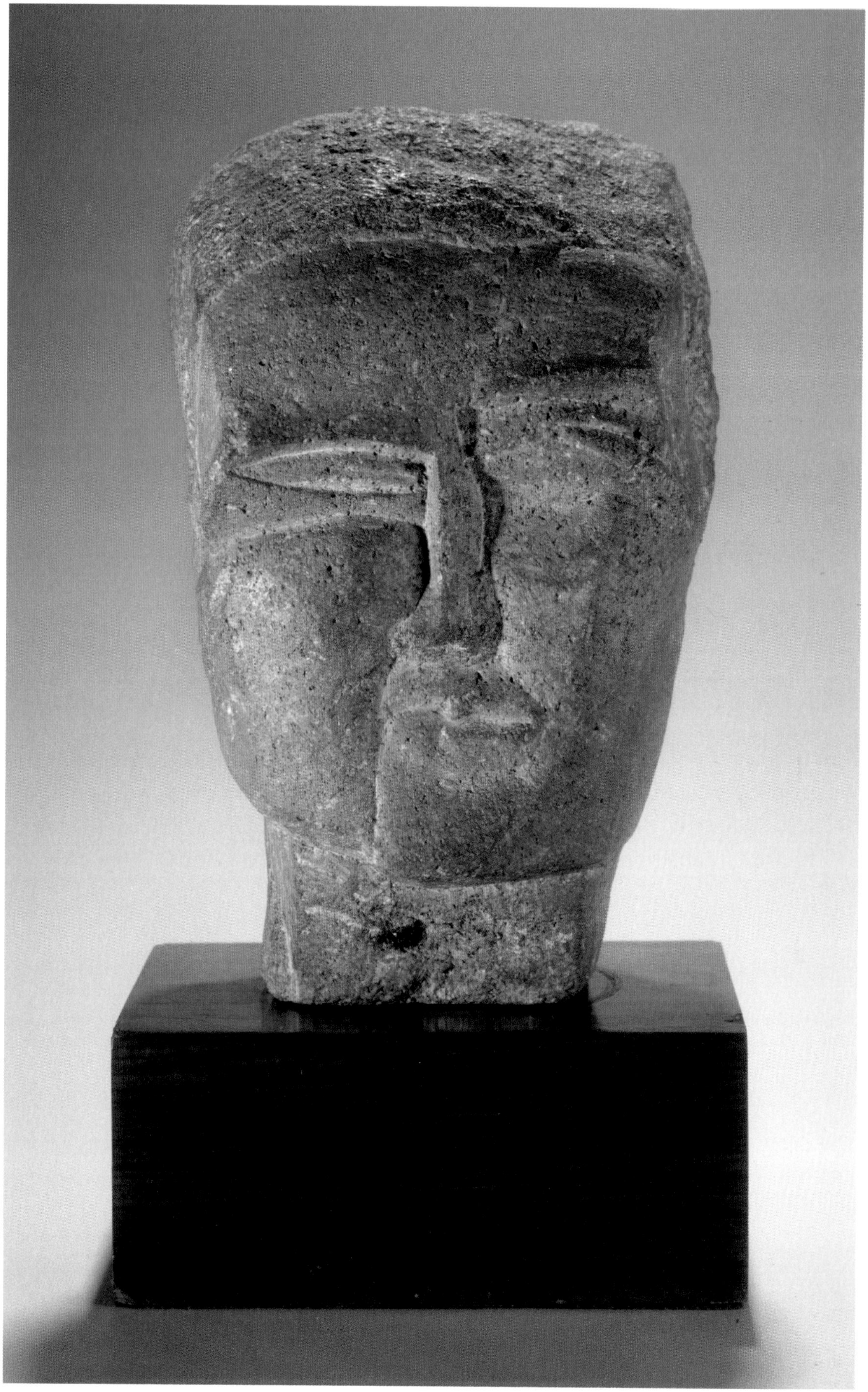

studies of simplification that had taken place up to then, radically put into discussion the proportions of the human body, as well as offering a prototype of *nègre* stylisation, followed by Modigliani himself, as can be seen in *Head* VII (cat. **7**). At that same time, André Derain carried out a series of stone sculptures (fig. **2.7**) where the vicinity to primitive models permitted an extravagant rudimental gesture, of primordial simplification and clearly archaic taste, not without reminiscence of wood carvings by Gauguin which were re-launched with the 1906 retrospective (Ferrara 2006, n. 25). Working on the block in this way, the three-dimensional modelling left room for a synthetic volume. The proportion between the full and void spaces and the dialogue between surface and depth was led back to one of the most elementary contrasts of plastic surfaces.

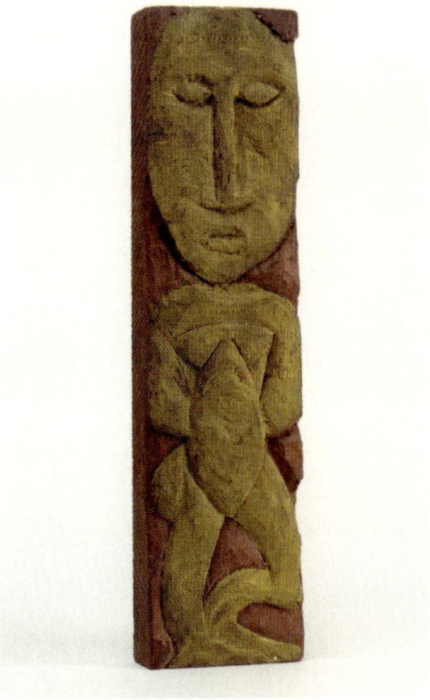

2.6. Pablo Picasso
Standing Nude, 1907.
Paris, Musée Picasso

Modigliani's early sculptures were influenced by this rebirth of direct carving on stone sculptures and the author's clear impatience with clay modelling: he complained to the sculptor Jacques Lipchitz who visited his studio while the heads were being made, that in sculpture of the Rodin tradition there was "too much mud." It was not difficult, during the years of the sensational recovery after Modigliani's death, to obscure in this preference of his the stigma of an expressive urgency veined with existential anxiety, reverberated in the Prometheus like figure of the artist caught in a creative fit. The German Curt Stoermer, who visited his studio in 1909, gave the image of an artist who, abruptly putting away canvas and brushes, started off with great hammering to extract figures from the stone blocks (Stoermer 1931); Arthur Pfannstiel, who is certainly among the least credible of the commentators, went so far as to write, in his monograph of 1929: "Le ciseau lui devenait un crayon qui ne faisait que suivre docilement son rêve entérieur. Et c'est ce qui explique ces formes si expressives jaillies directement de la profondeur de la pensée"(Pfannstiel 1929). The first works in the Ceroni catalogue, in particular, are eloquent documents on the technique of the attack and rough hewing of the block. A cross comparison with the most certain drawings makes it able to distinguish two essential types of sculptures: first the rounded caryatid heads, cut from an almost cubic block (and which can be referred to the first studies of female caryatid heads, documented by the Alexandre 1993 sheets Nos. 130, 245 and following; cf. also Patani 1992, Nos. 52 and 53), in preparation for the first incomplete three heads. These were followed by the development of the longer face typology, with progressive additions of primitive stylistic elements, oriental and archaic, direction in which the uncompleted *Heads* VII and V (cats. **8** and **9**) seemed to be moving. In his early phase Modigliani still appeared to be working on visual memories of pictorial derivation; so *Heads* I and III (cat. **7**) can be compared to the rounded face, short nose, small full mouth of *Nude* 1908 exhibited at the Salon des Indépendants in 1908; and in a sort of continuous circle between plastic and pictorial pattern, this solution would later find a further elaboration in *Portrait of Picasso* 1915 (cat. **12**) as confirmation of the role of sculpture as a bridge between two pictorial phases.

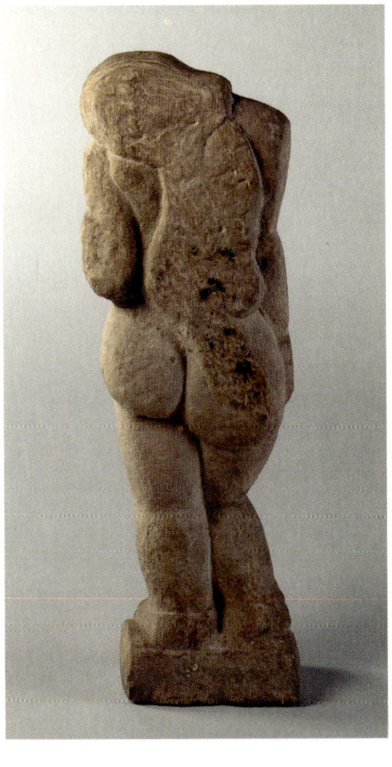

2.7. André Derain
Standing Nude, 1907.
Paris, Musée National d'art moderne, Centre Georges Pompidou

The fascination of direct carving would continue to nourish the thoughts of those who having endured the experience of Cubism, preferred to restore simplicity and explicitness to the figures. From this point of view, Ossip Zadkine's work (cats. **10** and **13**) and Henri Laurens' (cat. **11**) contributed to the Post-Cubist redefinition of sculpture.

A proletarian, Laurens (1885-1954) initially started working in the decorating trade; he began reasoning on the possibilities of transferral of Cubist pictorial syntax to the three dimensions, directly inspired first by Georges Braque and then by Juan Gris. After his first experiments with the use of polychrome, Laurens reached the point of condensing the Cubist facets to flattened and elegantly decorative volumes, translated into terracotta and stone, in a constant flow of figurative themes from modelling to carving and vice-versa. Zadkine's training was more regular, a Russian sculptor (1890-1967), nationalised French. After his studies at the École des Beaux Arts, Zadkine approached modes of an archaic-

Amedeo Modigliani
Portrait of Pablo Picasso, 1915,
oil on cardboard, 34.2 x 26.3 cm.
Russia, private collection
(cat. **12**)

Primitivist simplification of the form, as a direct consequence of his decision to always want to favour the formal rules of the chosen materials. In the following years, the stylistic solutions changed in extreme ways, according to the media chosen (from time to time stone, bronze, iron), however, remaining faithful to the principle of the expressive deformation of the physiognomy. Zadkine met Modigliani in the studio in Boulevard Raspail, just when he was concentrating solely on sculpture; many years later he recalled that he was impressed by the deliberately unfinished character of many heads, and the presence of some painted heads, of which there is no trace today (Werner 1960-61, p. 74).

Alessandro Del Puppo

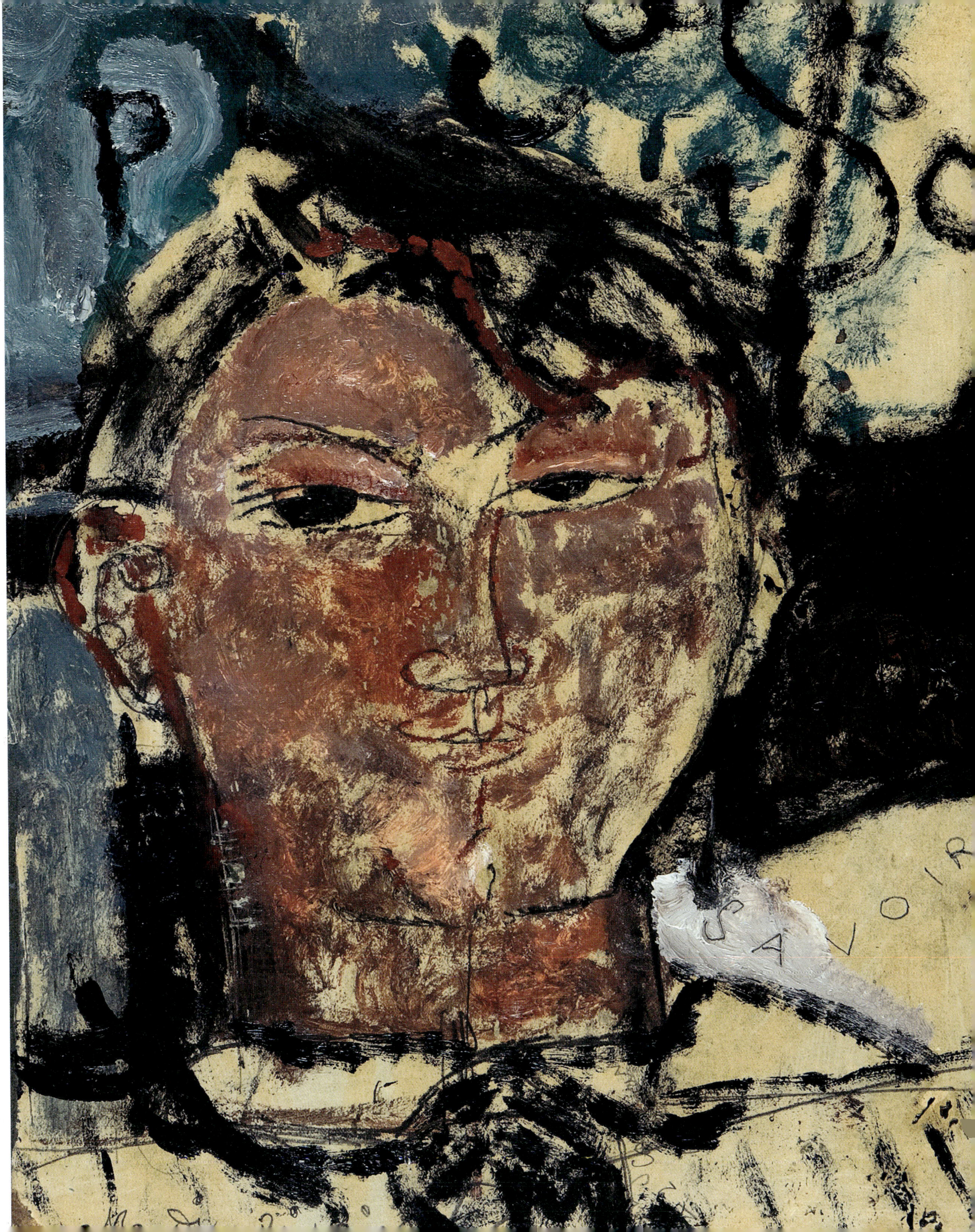
SAVOIR

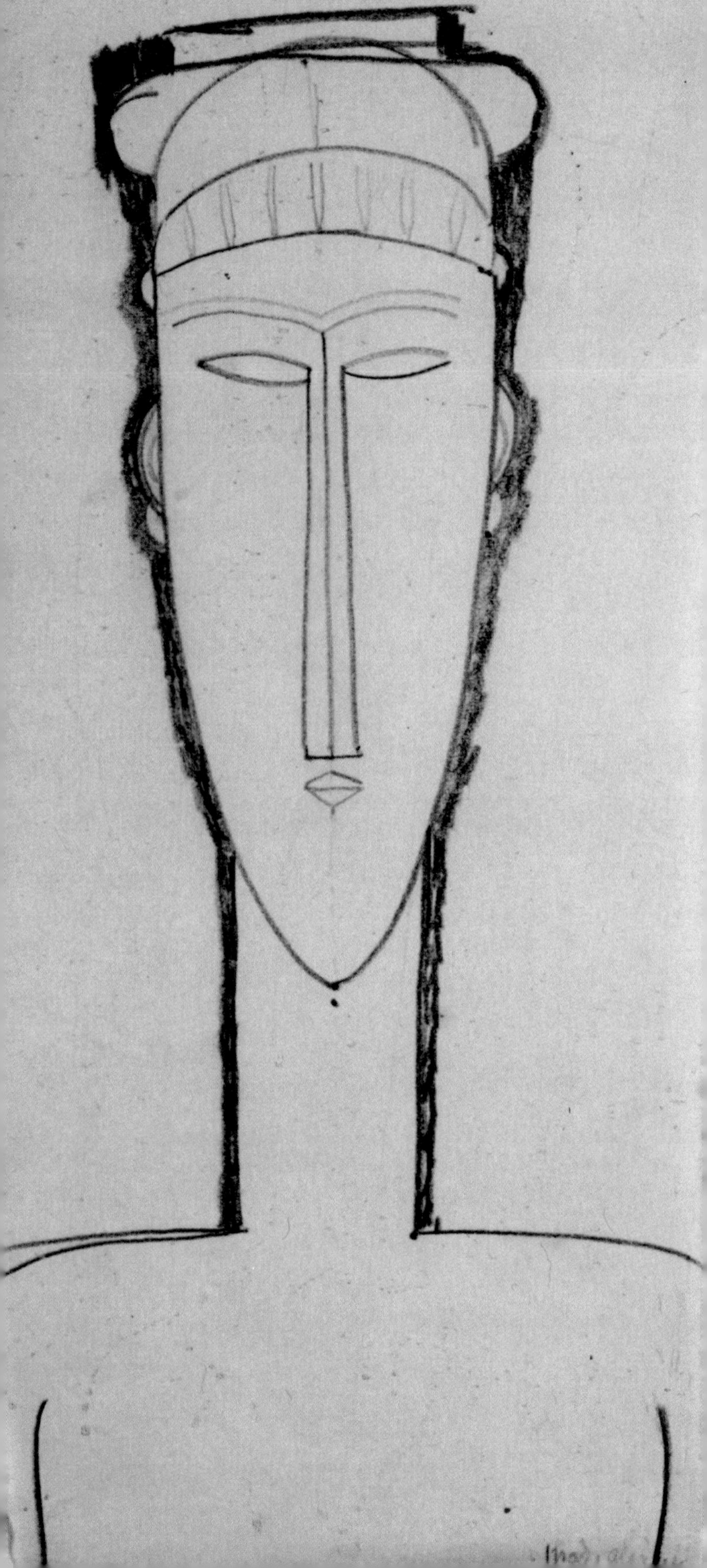

Section 3

Modigliani. The 1912 Salon d'Automne Heads: the Graphical Studies

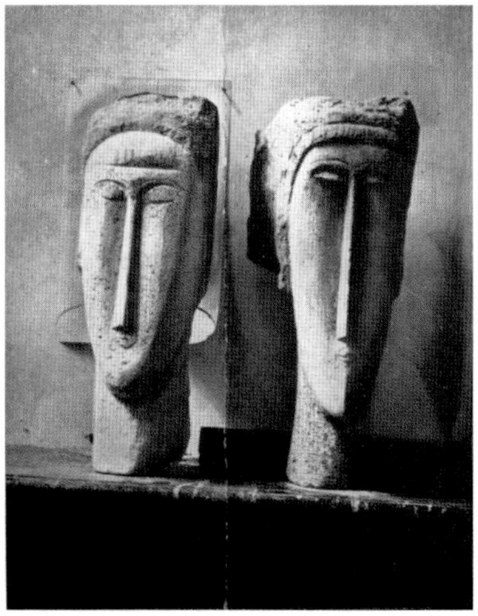

3.1 Anonymous photographer
Head [1911-1912] by Amedeo Modigliani (Ceroni XV and *Head* "A"). Lisbon, Fundação Calouste Gulbenkian, Amadeo de Souza Cardoso Archive

A series of drawings which study the sculptural heads carried out in stone by Modigliani have been known about since 1965. These drawings present some unusual characteristics when compared to those by some of the sculptors who were Modigliani's contemporaries. The first characteristic is the large quantity of them, compared to the rather small amount of surviving sculptures: there are 111 studies (limiting ourselves only to those that belonged to the Paul Alexandre collection: to those published in Alexandre 1993, numbers, 95-183 must be added for the presence of the collector's stamp, the Patani numbers 49, 50, 52, 53, 55-57, 70-76, 78, 80, 81, 84, 86, 92, 93, 117, 119) which prepare a group of only 26 sculptures (the 23 *Heads* in the Ceroni catalogue, plus those that are called "A," "B" and "C" in this catalogue). The second characteristic is the regularity of the size of the paper: the majority are sheets measuring 43 x 26 centimetres, with some rare sheets, sometimes squared, 21 x 13 centimetres, evidently the result of halving the former. However, the most particular characteristic regards the significance of Modigliani's graphic work that these studies reveal. These drawings, in fact, do not seem to consider the plastic problems that we would expect from a sculptor of the post-Rodin generation (analysis of the chiaroscuro, sharply angled view points, emphasising the plastic articulations); instead, they study inexpressive female heads, or, more rarely, male heads, always and only from the front or profile, in an impressive sequence of proportional variations and decorative solutions. The relentless regularity of the lines (nearly always a charcoal stroke which does not vary in thickness on the single sheet and when it returns over the same line again and becomes thicker, it does so to isolate the outline of the head from the whiteness of the background) shows a precise purpose. Once he had established a few clear starting points for the head he intended to carry out in stone (elongated shape, or round; flat hairstyle or over the forehead), Modigliani experimented the harmony of the proportions, he sounded out the balance between the whole and the decorative details: his reasoning was mainly of an architectonical nature, completely detached from the expressive nature of the head.
A good demonstration of the purpose of these drawings can be gleaned from the photograph (fig. **3.1** in Modigliani 1958, p. 48) that, presumably taken in 1912 and in Modigliani's studio, shows *Heads* XVI and "A" behind which a sheet of paper is fixed with two pins on which the curve of the shoulders of a drawn head can be distinguished (it could be the Alexandre 1993, No. 123 or 126). The similarity of the format (roughly a two to three proportion) between the drawn head and the sculpted one makes it seem as though the drawings are executive projects, aimed at closely guiding Modigliani in carving the stone, an activity for which he did not have a specific preparation.
For the drawings and watercolour studies of caryatids we have the possibility of an imaginary hypothesis regarding his initial starting point. Modigliani began transforming other standing or kneeling figures into caryatids, in various poses, often in theatrical surroundings. The drawing of heads, however, in Modigliani's catalogue are like a sensational *ex abrupto*: if we accept Paul Alexandre's statements that those owned by him passed into his hands before Modigliani left for Italy (April 1913), most of them should be collocated during those months from 1912 (the dates 20th and 22nd August written on the

Amedeo Modigliani
Head of Caryatid, 1910-1911
blue pencil on paper, 43 x 17 cm
Verona, courtesy Galleria dello Scudo, private collection
(cat. **14**)

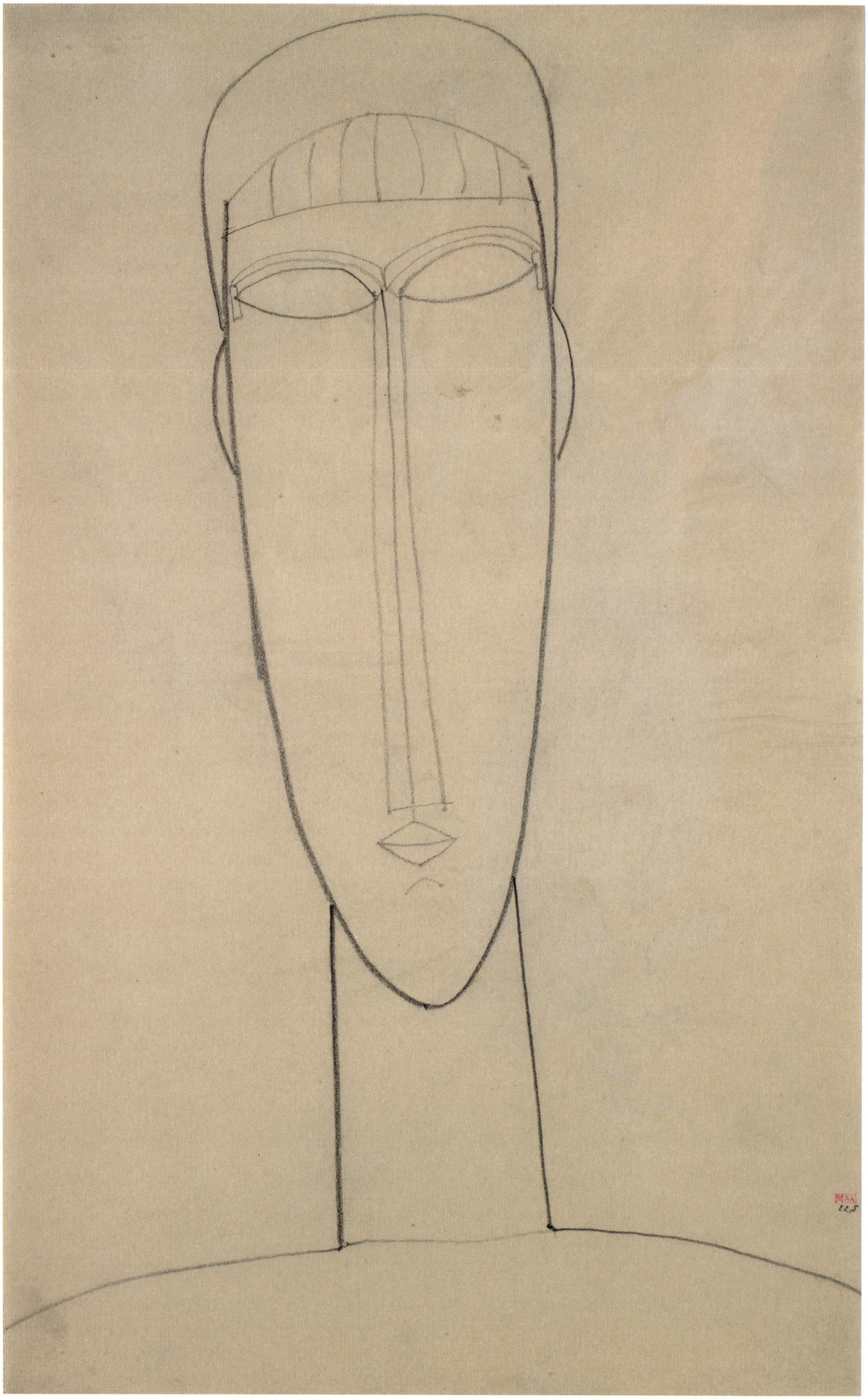

Amedeo Modigliani
Head and Shoulders from Front, Fringe
black pencil on paper, 42.8 x 26.5 cm.
Rouen, Musée des Beaux-Arts,
donated by Blaise Alexandre, 2001
Musées de la Ville de Rouen.
Photograph Catherine Lancien
(cat. **15**)

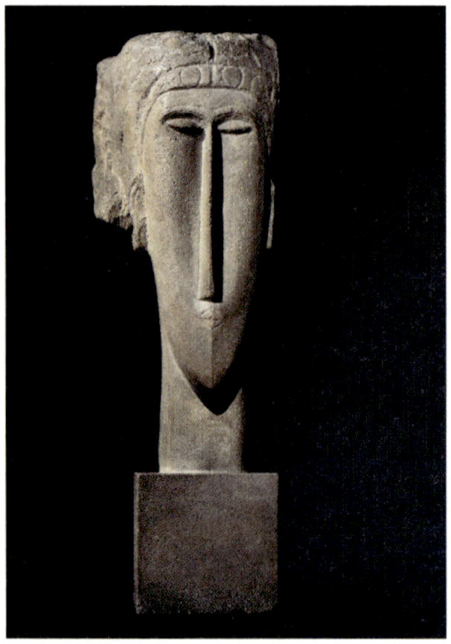

3.2. Amedeo Modigliani,s
Head, 1911-1912. Formerly Paris, Lévy Collection. Not in Ceroni (*Head* "A")

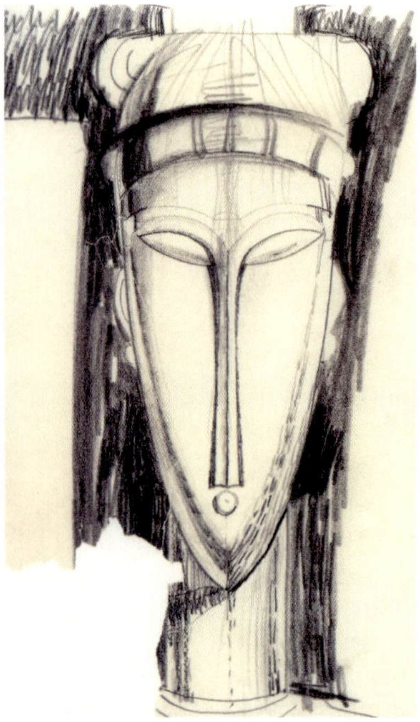

3.3. Amedeo Modigliani
Study for sculptural Head, 1911-1912, pencil and charcoal on paper.
Private collection

Amedeo Modigliani
Head surmounted by architectural element – sketch for the same figure upside down, 1911-1912
pen and black ink on paper,
20.9 x 26.7 cm.
Rouen, Musée des Beaux-Arts,
donated by Blaise Alexandre, 2001
Musées de la Ville de Rouen.
Photograph Catherine Lancien
(cat. **16**)

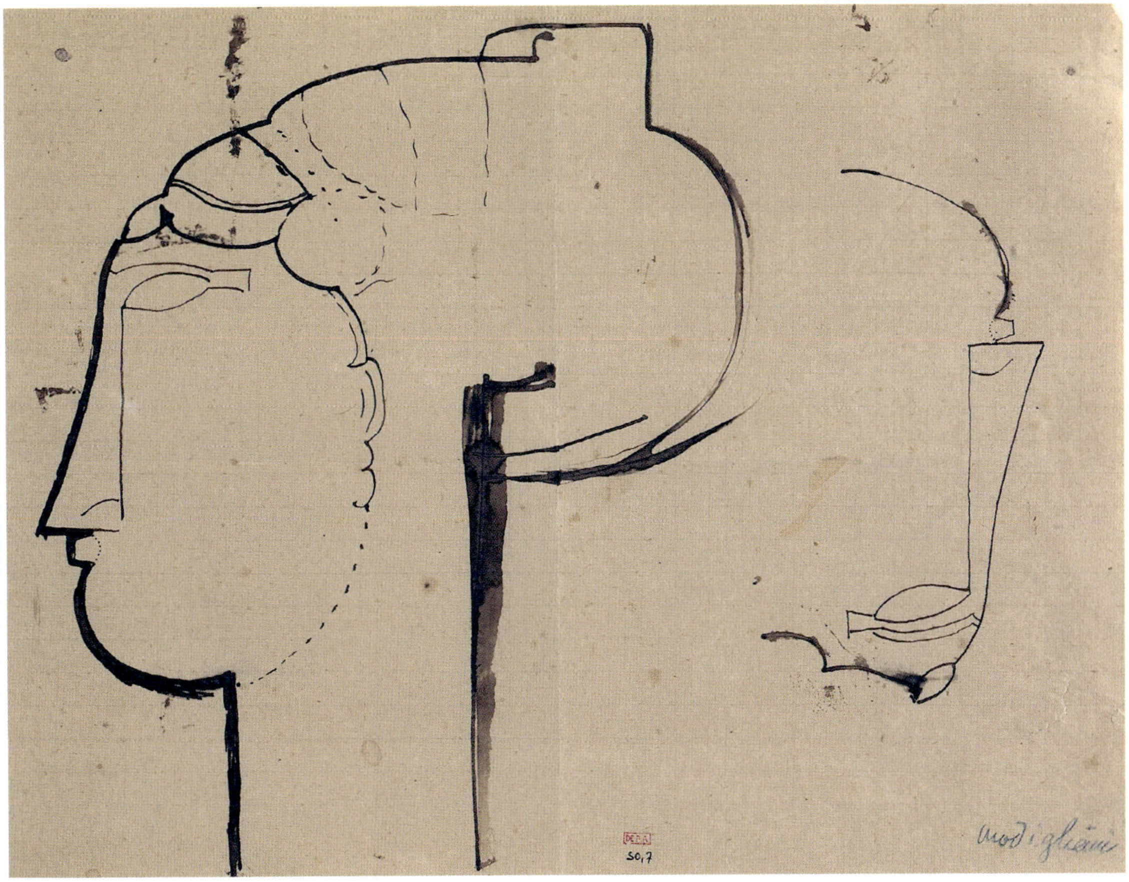

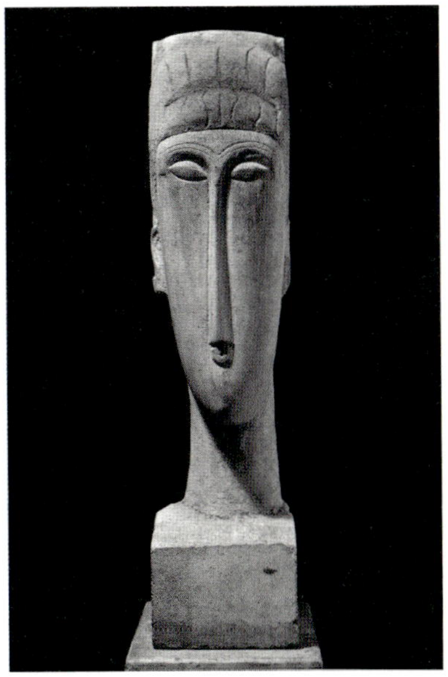

3.4. Amedeo Modigliani
Head, 1911-1912.
Private collection. Ceroni XXII

Alexandre sheets 1993, numbers 159-161 could be a reference) and March 1913 (date written on sheets numbers 168-170): the only exception is the head with capital (Alexandre 1993, No. 183) dated 2nd April 1914. The temptation to try and read these drawings as a particular development of the caryatid theme, which had certainly begun in 1911, finds however, an important pitfall. At the Salon des Indépendants in April 1911 Modigliani exhibited a *Head* and a *Caryatid* (Paris 1911a, numbers 6655 and 6656): they could have been two paintings like those catalogued in Ceroni 1970, No. 38 (*Head*) and 35-37 (*Caryatids*); certainly not sculptures (which were always specified in the catalogue, after the title of the work) and perhaps not even drawings (the specific "dessin" belongs, in fact, to the following numbers, from 6657 to 6660). However, the Indépendants catalogue proves that the two genres, *Heads* and *Caryatids,* were objects of a parallel study which was already underway in the spring of 1911.
The drawing shown here (cat. **14**) represents a head whose hair, from the ample lateral locks is transformed into a capital, at the top of which even an entablature is foreseen aimed at supporting a trabeation. Therefore, it is a particular study of the head of a caryatid, whose architectonic function is also affirmed by the perfect stereometry. The elongated shape of the face, the proportions between the part of the forehead which is not covered and the fringe and some details (the form of the eyes and the eyebrows, the diamond-shaped profile of the lips) show an evident similarity between this drawing and *Head* "A" (fig. **3.2**) which Modigliani sent to the Salon d'Automne in 1912. The photograph of the sculptural head being worked on (fig. **3.1**) shows the same ornate fringe and parallel motifs that can be read in these drawings: it was substituted, during the finishing of *Head* "A" by the more sparse and sickle shaped motifs shown in the photograph of the *Head* at the Salon d'Automne and in the present state of the stone. During this phase of the work Modigliani wavered between the solutions of *Head* "A" and those of another sculpture. A

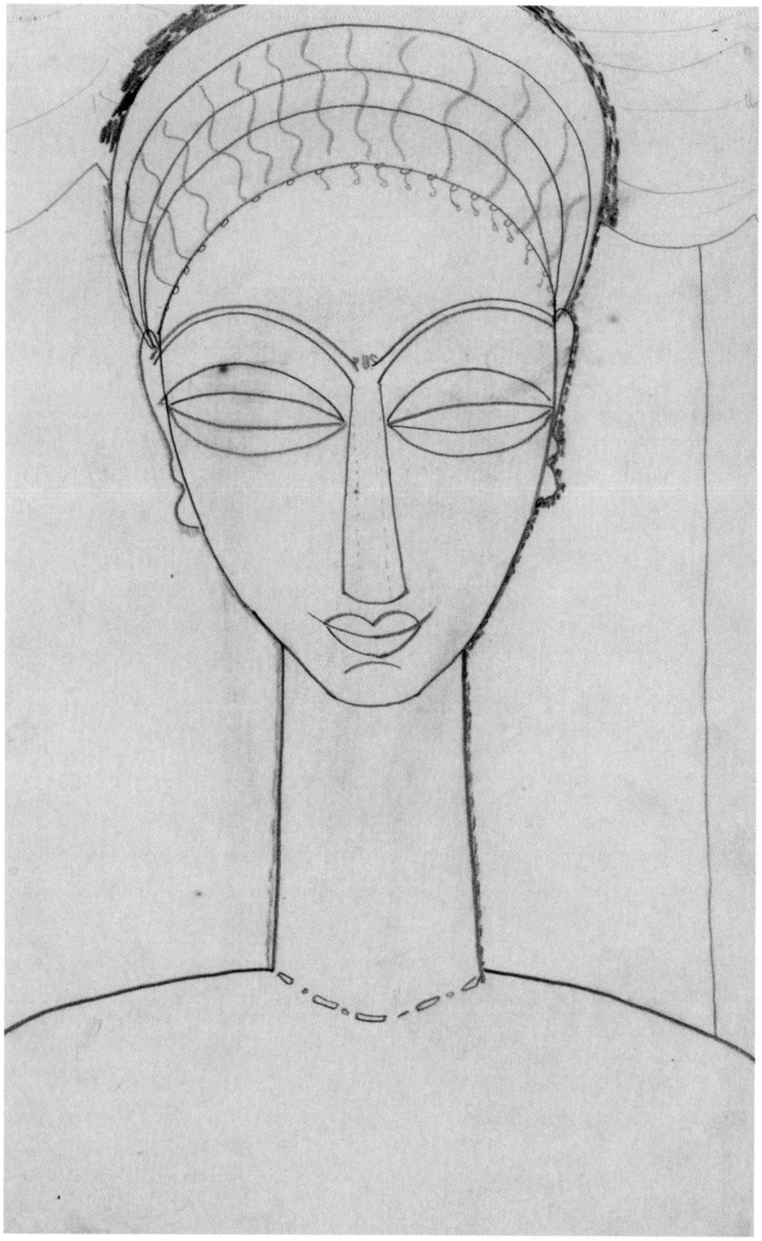

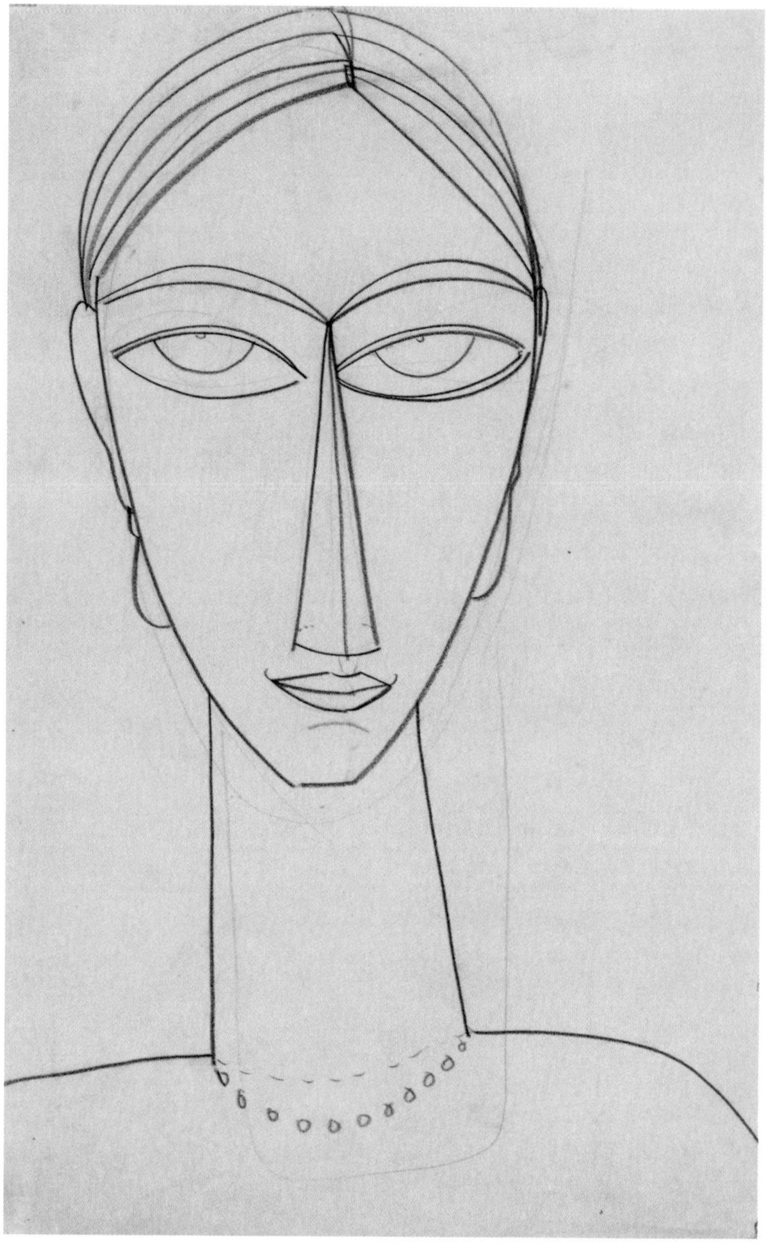

Amedeo Modigliani
Head, 1910-1911,
pencil on paper, 43 x 26.5 cm.
Private collection
(cat. **17**)

Amedeo Modigliani
Head, 1912,
pencil on paper, 43 x 26.5 cm.
Private collection
(cat. **18**)

drawing which was part of Paul Alexandre's collection (Alexandre 1993, No. 182 fig. **3.3**) shows, in fact, a progression towards a more deforming stylisation (the oblique shape of the eyes, the everted mouth which can also be found in *Head* XXII (fig. **3.4**), the only one among the very elongated heads to have an architectonic termination, a flat entablature, on top of the hair. The drawing here at number (cat. **19**) which studies the elegant profile of a head brings together some characteristics which would then flow over into *Head* XXII (the pointed chin, the nose perpendicular to the face, the moon shaped ear, decorated with concentric circles) and in *Head* "A" (above all the low cut of the fringe and the curve at the nape of the neck). The *Head* here at number (cat. **15**) would instead seem to refer to a phase of study between *Heads* XVI and XIX (with the linear motif in relief which continues the eyebrows lower down), with the anticipation of a greater elongation which would appear in *Head* "A." The squared sheet here at number (cat. **16**) is very interesting for its value of the details of a head in an advanced phase of definition which certainly refers to *Head* XX. The drawing here at number **18**, seems to have a different stature, a small graphic detail for *Head* XIV.

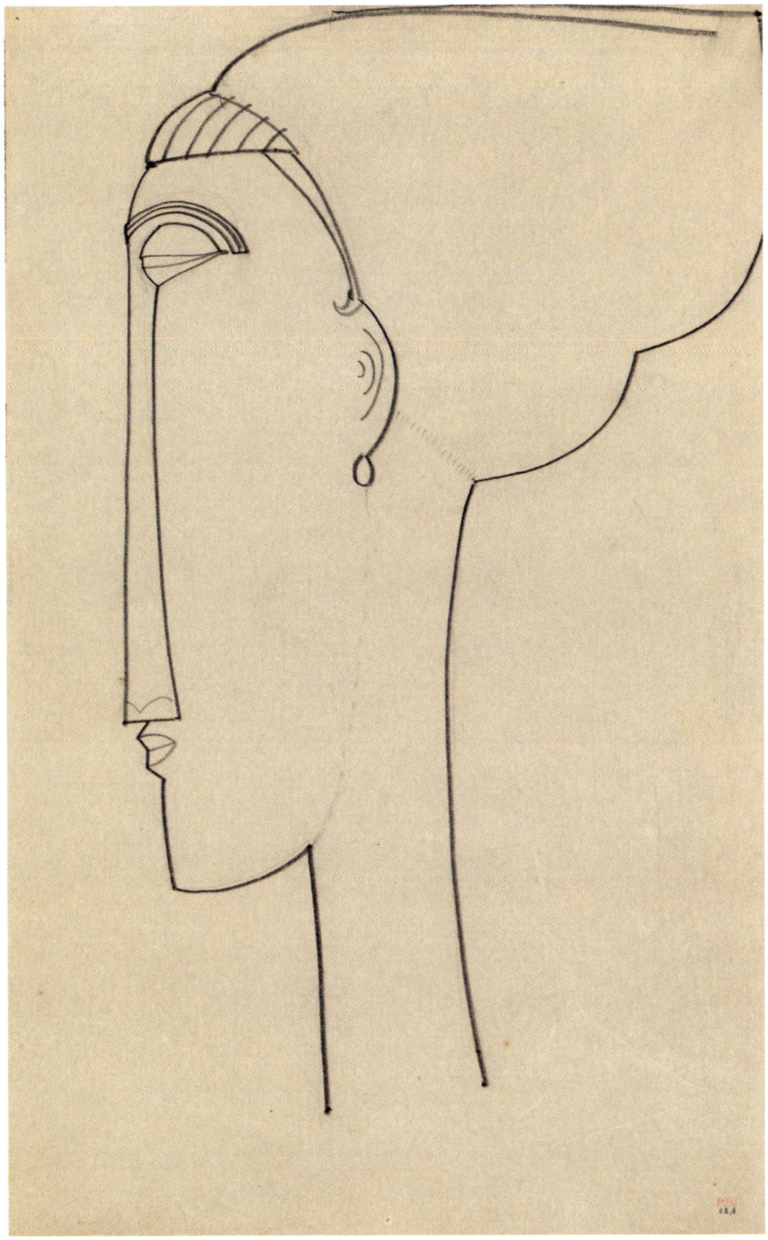

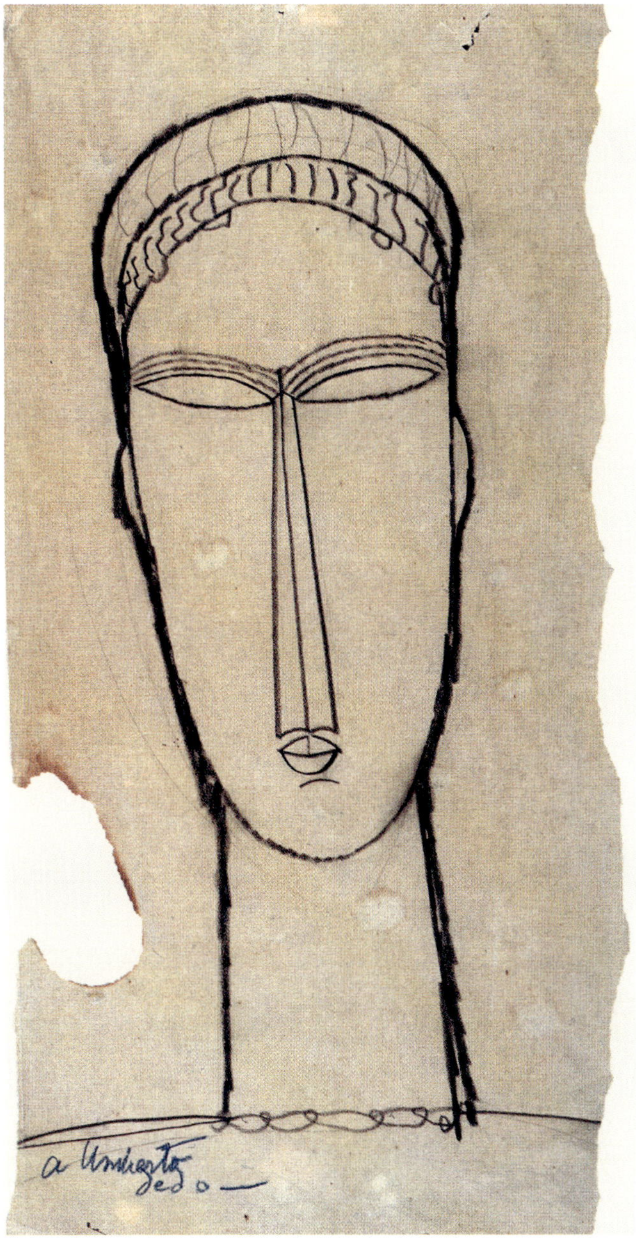

Amedeo Modigliani
Profile of Head, 1911
grease pencil on paper, 43 x 26.5 cm.
Private collection
(cat. **19**)

Amedeo Modigliani
Sculptural Head, 1910-1911
grease pencil on paper, 43 x 19 cm
Courtesy Guido Guastalla
(cat. **70**)

On the contrary to these drawings, which all seem to search for solutions for a series of heads to be exhibited as a group, with variations which are only appreciable when seen together, another drawing (cat. **17**) seems to be the study of the characteristics of *Head* IX, which stands out from all the others for the particular style of its features, between Negroid and Egyptian: in this drawing Modigliani approached the theme of its incumbent frontality and hints at an ambient, like a sort of stage complete with curtain and wings, as he was doing in some studies of standing figures and caryatids.

Flavio Fergonzi

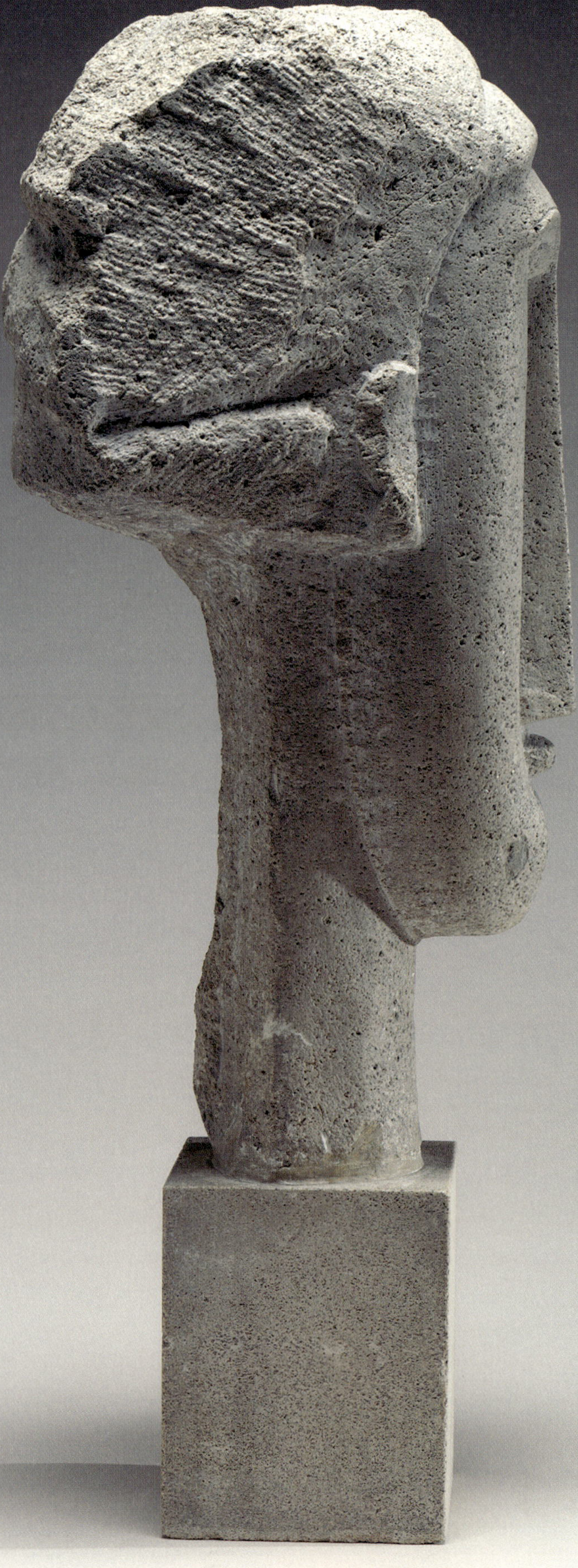

Amedeo Modigliani
Head of a Woman, 1911-1912
limestone, 65 x 19 x 24 cm
Washington DC, National Gallery
of Art, Chester Dale Collection 1963
(cat. **20**)

Section 4

The 1912 Heads, between the Renaissance and Cubism

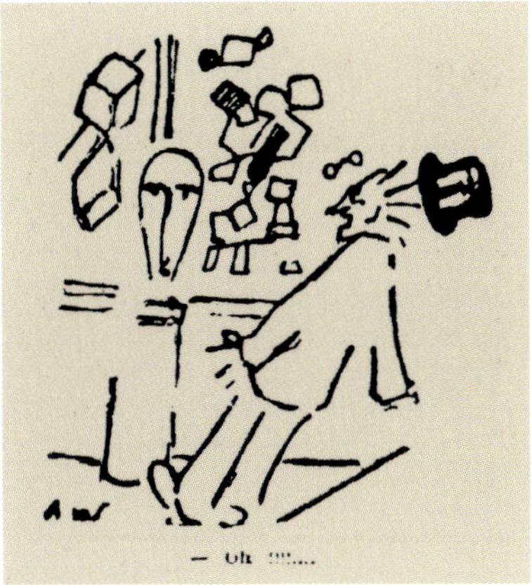

4.1. Caricature of room XI of the Salon d'Automne 1912, in *Comœdia*, Paris, 1st October 1912

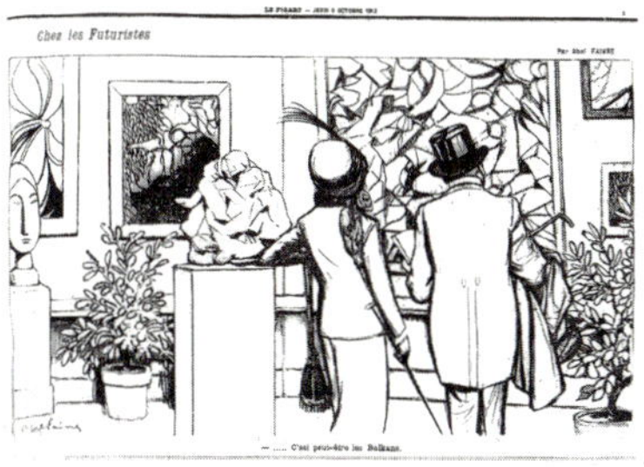

4.2. Caricature of room XI of the Salon d'Automne 1912, in *Le Figaro*, Paris, 3rd October 1912

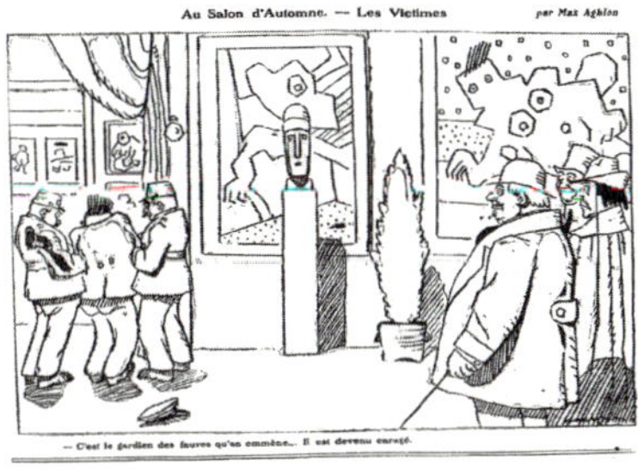

4.3. Caricature of room XI of the Salon d'Automne 1912, in *Gil Blas*, Paris, 7th October 1912

Of the 26 sculptural heads known to be by Modigliani (the 23 in Ceroni's catalogue and *Heads* "A," "B" and "C" as they are called in the beginning of this catalogue) only 10 of them (XIII, XV, XVI, XVII, XX, XXI, XXII, XXIV, "A," "B") stand on a stone base, either a cube or a prism, rightly considered today as an integrated part of the sculpture. The only time that Modigliani personally took care of the exhibition of his sculptures, as can be seen in the photographs of room XI at the Salon d'Automne in 1912, they were arranged on cubic stone bases of various heights. These were not part of the original sculptural invention: the photographs which reveal five while they were being made, show the heads worked up to the neck level. The bases were therefore added before the exhibition, with the precise purpose of standardising what was declared as an "ensemble décoratif" in the catalogue.
Today four of the seven heads exhibited by Modigliani at the Salon d'Automne in 1912 can be identified with certainty (XV, XXI, XXII, "A") and, with some probability, a fifth one (*Head* "B" in Karlsruhe). So, only two remain unidentified: choosing between those that have preserved the cubic base, there is the hypothesis, with a wide margin of probability, of the presence of one of the two exhibited here, *Heads* XVI and XVII (cats. 22, 20): I would be inclined towards *Head* XVI from the Museum of Minneapolis, because it was photographed while work was underway next to *Head* "A" which was sent to the Salon d'Automne. For the identification of the seventh head, excluding XXIV which had probably already been bought by Roworth (Wayne 2003, p. 56), the field seems to narrow down, between XIII and XX. Therefore, Modigliani did not choose to send heads which were too similar to one another, intending to document a research which was open to the widest range of inventions within those rules (frontality, stereometry, inexpressiveness, geometrizing) that he had so severely imposed upon himself.
The attitude of the critics, and especially the caricatures (figs. 4.1-3), that commented Modigliani's exhibits, was particularly mocking due to the relationship between the heads and the Cubist paintings that were hung on the walls (Kupka, Le Fauconnier, Gleizes, Metzinger) or sculptures exhibited in the room (two by Archipenko and one by Czáky out of catalogue). This was due to the schematic geometric reduction of the shape of the heads but also to the strange cube shaped bases which linked Modigliani's impersonal and Antigraceful style to that "Cubism," painting of cubes, which by then had been the subject of scandal for a year in Paris, fluctuating between critical debates and social controversy. The absurdity of putting Modigliani and the Cubists on the same level is that in some aspects of deformational synthesis and formal reduction, Modigliani turned not to the Cubist works that could be admired at the Salon d'Automne in 1912, but rather to the older Cubist works. That is, he turned to Pablo Picasso's faces and busts of 1907-1908, unknown to most of the visitors to the Salons, known only to those few visitors to the Galerie Kahnweiler: due to the contract drawn up with the dealer who put their art on show, Picasso and Braque were not allowed to send their work to collective exhibitions, with the aim of stimulating the myth that it was difficult to have access to them and the exclusiveness of the gallery that dealt with them.
Modigliani had known Picasso since 1906. In 1912 he did not seem interested in his latest evolution, that had led him to the destruction of the visible through the multiplication of the planes of the objects and the re-composition of a different reality, no longer optical but

Francesco Laurana
Bust of Battista Sforza
marble, h. 49 cm
Florence, Museo Nazionale
del Bargello
(cat. **21**)

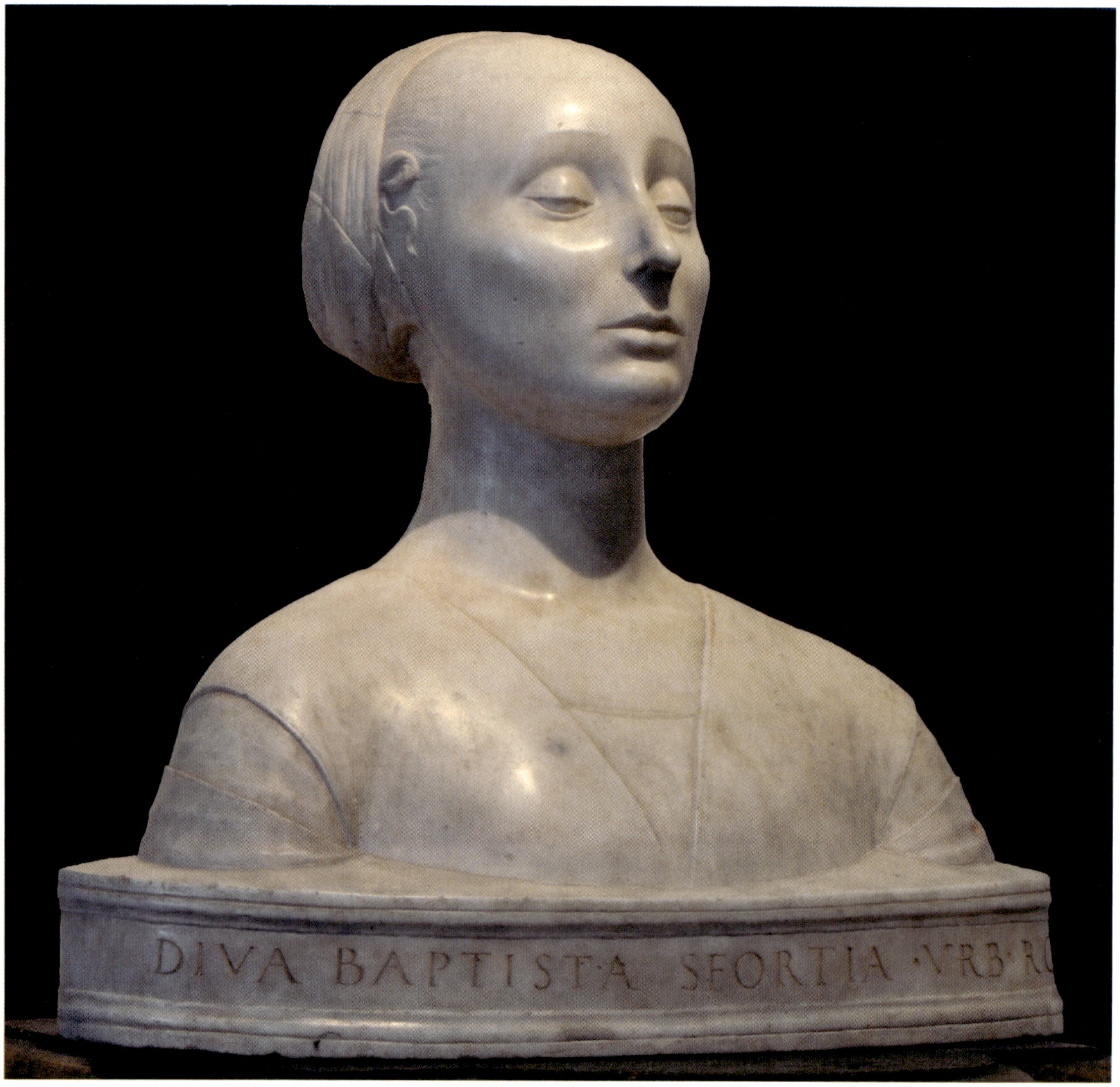

conceptual, through the fragments of the collage. Picasso's graphic and pictorial research in the very early Cubism was useful to Modigliani. In these works, the face, the bust and whole human body had been standardised and dehumanised thanks to their assimilation into sculptures: to obtain that lack of expression Picasso had found help in distant civilisations, geographically (tribal sculptures) or chronologically (Egyptian modelling). In the *Bust of a Woman*, 1907, exhibited here (cat. **23**), we can find characteristics which are present in Modigliani's sculptures in this section: the approximate plasticity of the oval of the face and its inexpressive stereometry: the features determined by rigid, thick profiles: the empty eyes, without eyelids or pupils: the nose just suggested by a geometric shape which reminded the French of a slice of Brie cheese. Even greater similarities can be found with this painting in *Head* IX, that Modigliani studied graphically for a long time, and to which he added explicit Egyptian and Negroid recollections. From one of Picasso's paintings dated 1907, like the *Bust of a Woman* (fig. **4.4**, Daix 1979, No. 38) in the Musée National d'art moderne in Paris, Modigliani certainly appreciated the aristocratic lack of expression: while in another *Bust of a Woman* (Daix 1979 No. 134), in the Narodni Galerie in Prague, he could find the rules concerning the reduction of the body to a purely architectonical function which would be useful for him in the series of standing caryatids. However, it was not the literal correspondences which certainly made Picasso 1907-1908 a model for Modigliani in 1911-1912. What counted for Modigliani was that, for Picasso, the relationships between the single

Amedeo Modigliani
Head of a Woman, 1911 ca.,
limestone, 65.4 x 17.1 x 21.3 cm.
Minneapolis, Minneapolis Institute
of Arts, donated by Mr. and Mrs. John
Cowles
(cat. **22**)

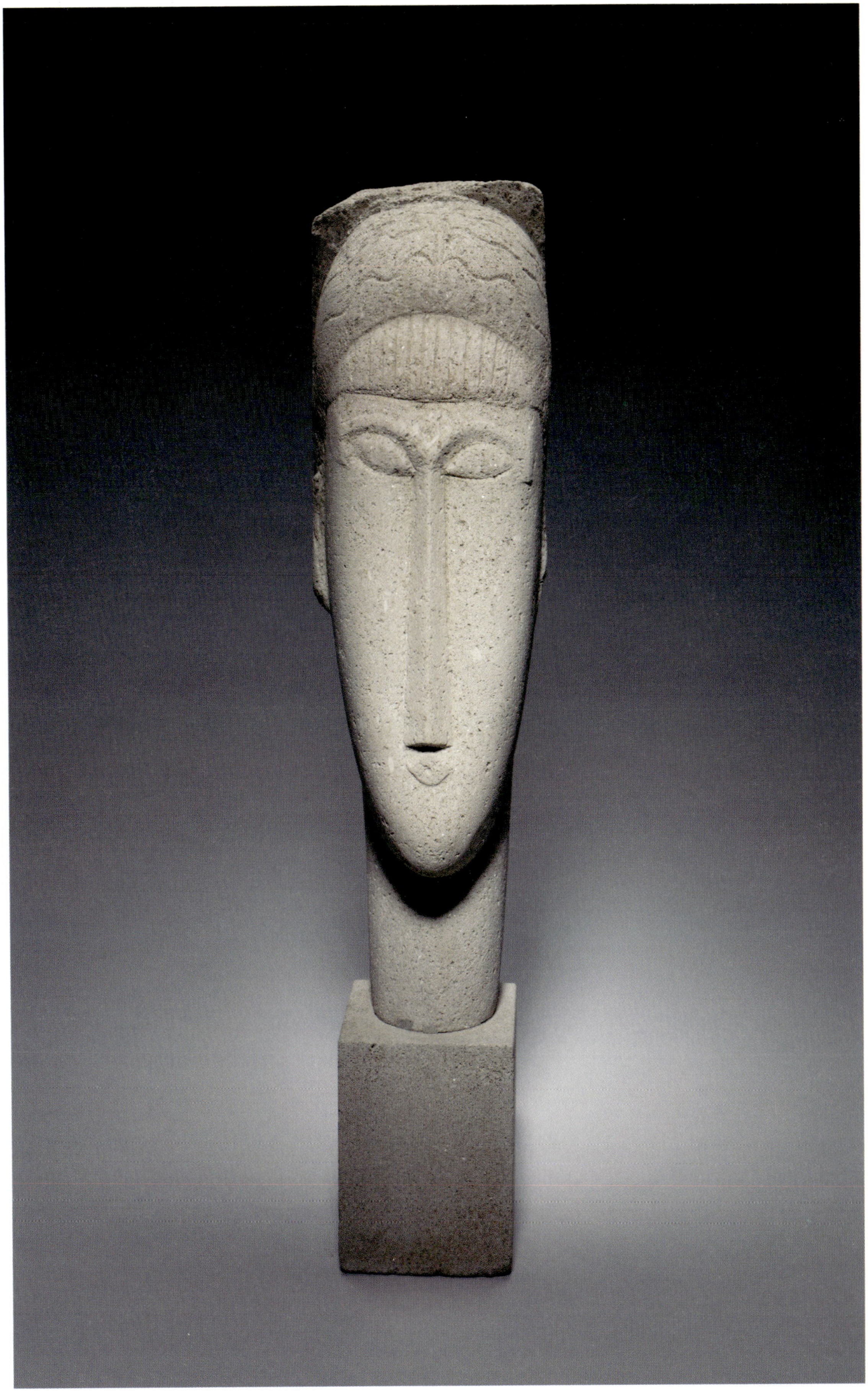

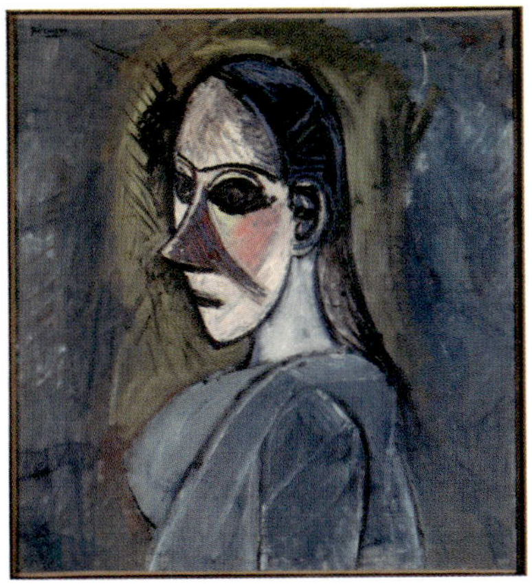

4.4. Pablo Picasso
Bust of a Woman, 1907.
Paris, Centre Georges Pompidou,
Musée National d'art moderne

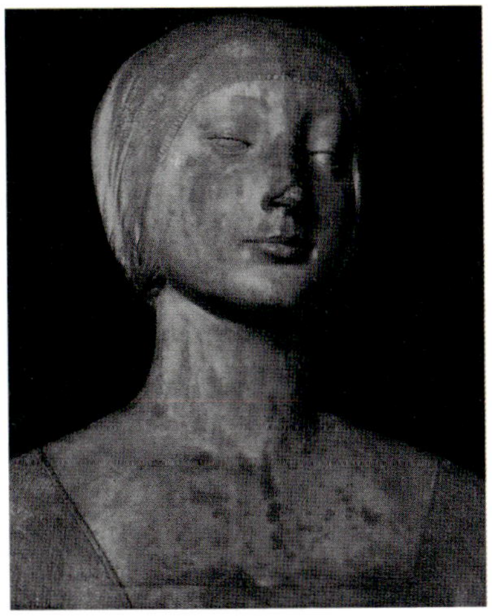

4.5. Francesco Laurana
Bust of Isabella of Aragon,
in *Les Arts*, Paris, 1902

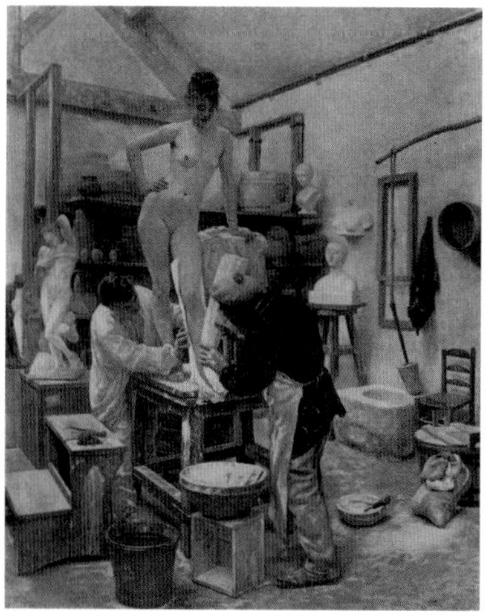

4.6. Edouard Dantan
The Mould of the Natural Model (1888),
in *Salon Illustré*, Paris, 1888

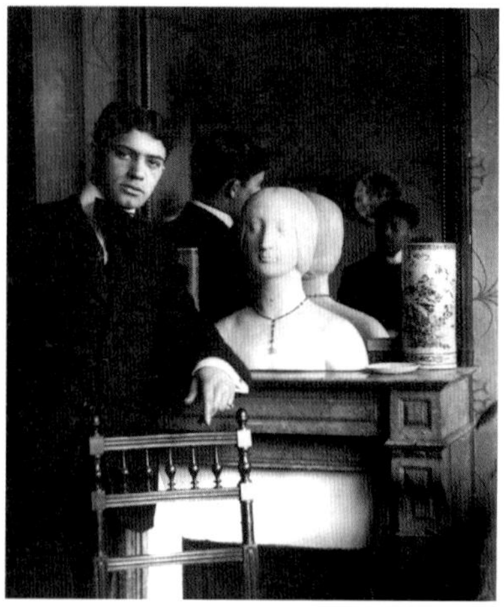

4.7. Anonymous photographer
Amadeo de Souza Cardoso in his apartment in Paris with the mould of the *Bust of Isabella of Aragon* by Laurana (circa 1910). Lisbon, Fundação Calouste Gulbenkian, Archivio Amadeo de Souza Cardoso

Pablo Picasso
Female Nude, 1907
oil on canvas, 61 x 47 cm
Saint Petersburg, The State Hermitage Museum
(cat. **23**)

volumes of the head were governed not by laws of expressive verisimilitude but by pure formal logic.
The fascination for Modigliani's heads which was felt by the first buyers (Augustus John, Edward Roworth, Paul Guillaume) was not only due to this Modernist revolution. In those stones there was something harmonious, balanced and stylistically attractive. Right from 1929 Arthur Pfannstiel called attention to the Classic nature of Modigliani sculptor, derived from the study of fourteenth century and Renaissance Italian masterpieces while later studies (Schmalemback 2006, pp. 53-63) have proposed new similarities (Braun 2004, pp. 34-35) or historically explained the reason for the existence of this critical attitude.
In this exhibition there is the desire to propose a perhaps unexpected comparison, that between *Heads* XVI and XVII and the *Bust of Battista Sforza* by Francesco Laurana, conserved at the Museo del Bargello (cat. **21**). The reasons for a stylistic similarity are obvious: the aristocratic detachment, the absent gaze, the perfect stereometry and the pure geometry of the face. However, there are also some historical reasons which determine this comparison. Laurana was a much debated sculptor during the first decade of the twentieth century and the restoration of Alfonso of Aragon's triumphal arch in Naples, finished in 1908, had favoured a return to the study of his works. In Paris, in particular, a long debate concerning the attribution of work concentrating on the names Laurana and Desiderio da Settignano had appeared in *L'Art*, about the bust of a woman belonging to the Museum of Berlin; the discussion had caught the attention even of the non-specialists, and had caused the reproduction, in various stages, besides the marble in Berlin, of the bust of Isabella of Aragon in the Louvre (fig.**4.5**), that of Battista Sforza from Bargello and the Beatrice of Aragon then belonging to the Dreyfuss collection. According to the tastes of the French experts Laurana's too abstract geometry was counterpoised by Desiderio da Settignano's work which was so full of vitality and richness of expression, according to the old prejudice of Florentine superiority: in Laurana "lowered eyelids, mouths closed, smooth flesh, surfaces left undefined, stylised forms" were seen as "signs of sculptural incapability" (Michel, Muntz, Molinier 1902, pp. 37-44). From the point of view of Italian art criticism, Adolfo Venturi's intelligence caught the disconcerting poetry which sprang from the "insistence in smoothing, in making the individual features disappear": in the Eleonor of Aragon from the Museum of Palermo, defined by him as "a fine bust, extremely pure," Venturi was mesmerised by characteristics that Modigliani would have liked: "eyes cut like a mask, the eyebrows just traced as if by a thread" (Venturi 1908, pp. 1031 and 1040).
This distinction between Desiderio da Settignano's expressive Realism and Laurana's inexpressive abstraction (the latter was more or less seen as negative at that time) is at the base of Modigliani's partiality to this latter type of stylistic mode. Modigliani seemed to be attracted to an object-sculpture which no longer alluded to the vital presence of a physical person (he certainly knew for a fact that Battista Sforza's aristocratic detachment from worldly goods was due to the bust having originated from a funeral mask), however it states its essential plastic form.
A marble which, for nineteenth century sculpture, had represented a model of strict linear purism (its plaster mould was present, as a warning about the supremacy of style, in the sculptor's studio shown by Edouard Dantan in his *Le moulage sur nature* in 1887, fig. **4.6**) it became useful, in full twentieth century Modernism, when the question of abstract geometric volumes returned to the sculptors' agendas. Significantly, the mould of the Isabella of Aragon in the Louvre was situated in an important place in Amadeo de Souza Cardoso's apartment (fig. **4.7**), the Portuguese artist who was tied to Modigliani by a close friendship that coincided for the latter, with the years of his research into sculpture.

Flavio Fergonzi

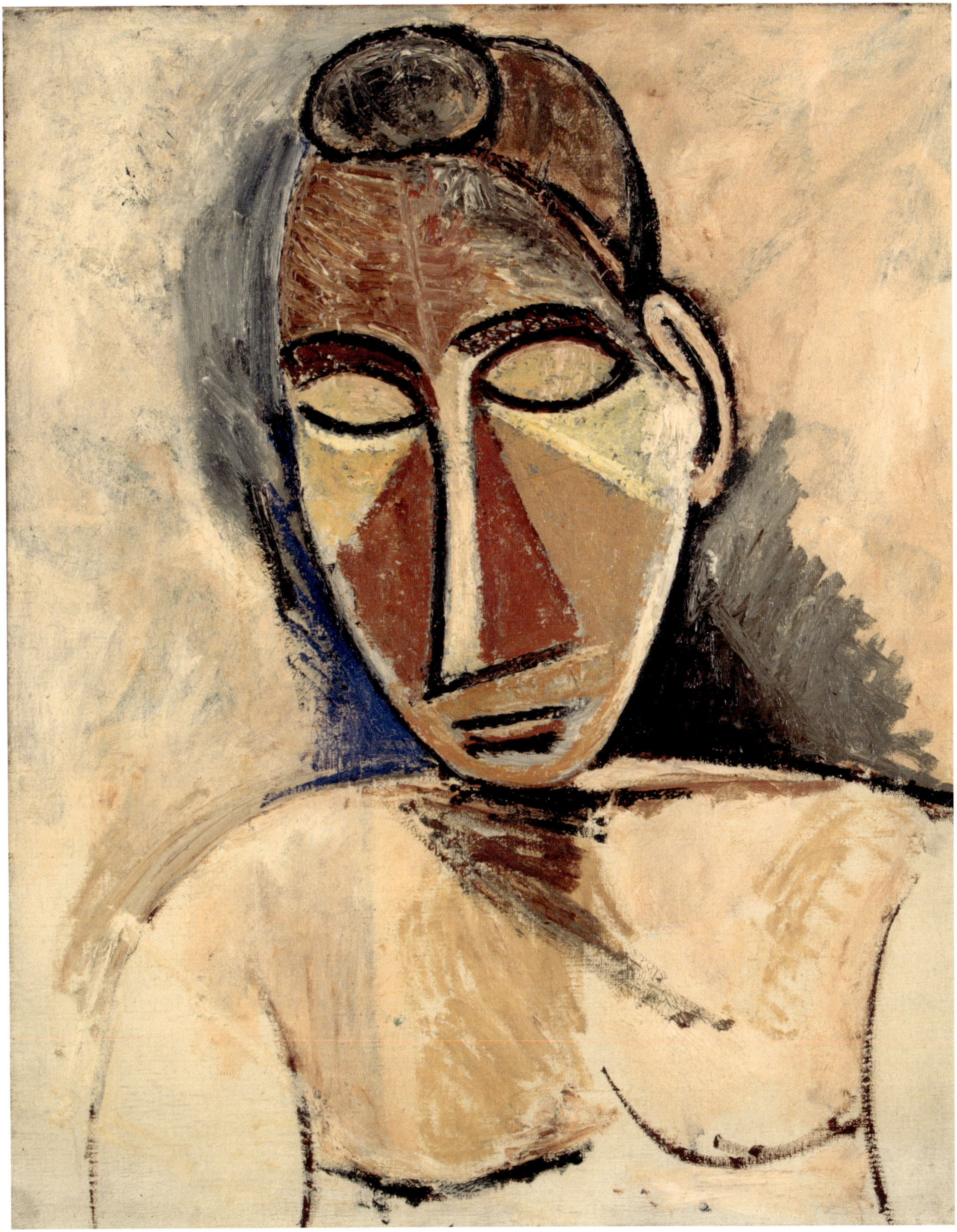

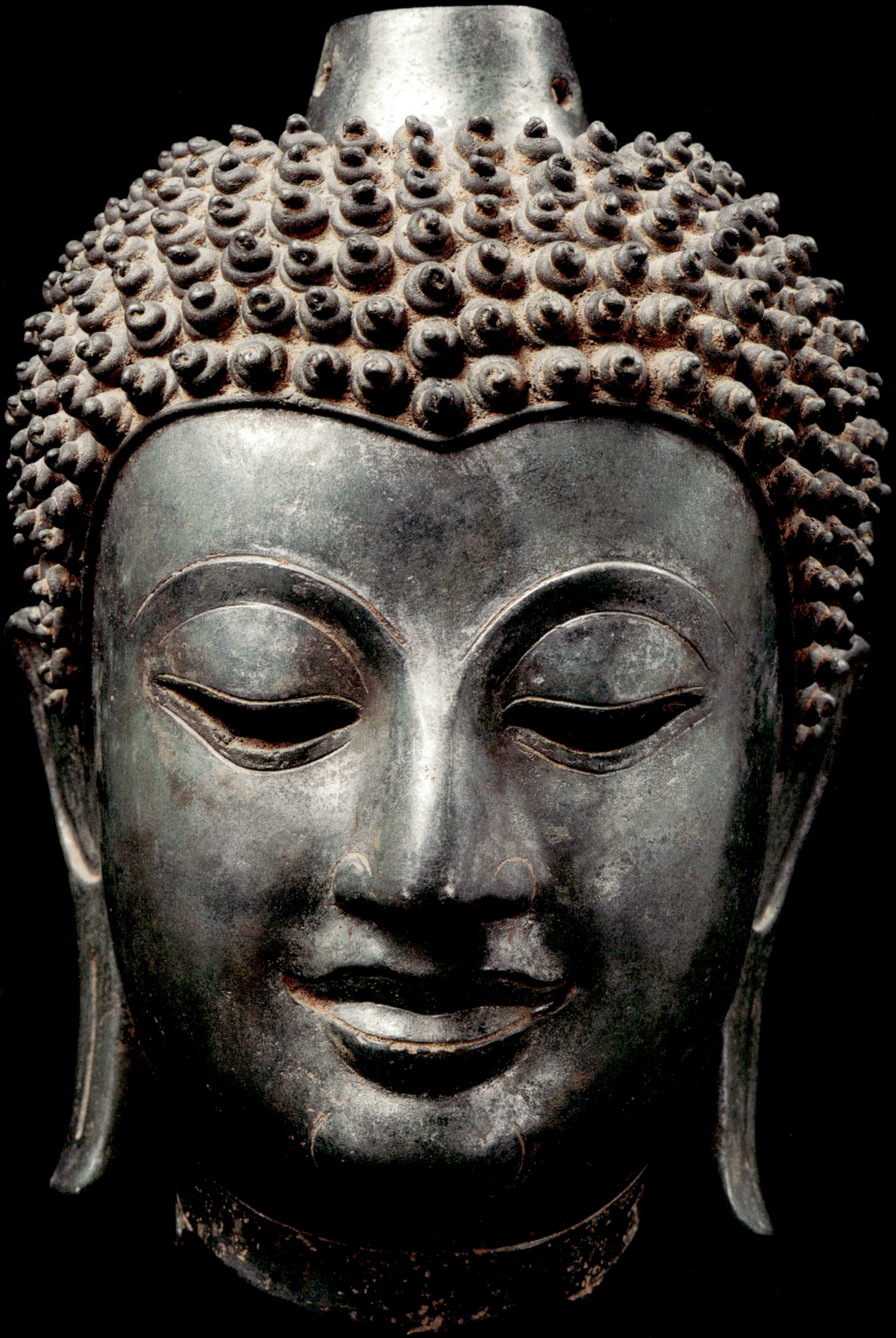

Section 5
Archaic Smiles and Oriental Faces

The first accounts regarding Modigliani's sculptural work all agree on the use of models inspired by the most varied sources: Egyptian art, archaic Greek art, African fetishes and masks. The Russian poetess Anna Achmatova, who was often in Modigliani's company in 1911, remembered: "At that time Modigliani was enthusiastic about Egypt. He used to take me to the Louvre to see the Egyption section, assuring me that 'tout le reste' was not worthy of attention. He drew my head with the adornments of the Egyptian queens and seemed to be completely bewitched by the great Egyptian art. [...] This period of Modigliani's is now called 'periode nègre'". That his admiration for Egypt should be overlapped by the attraction of African art is a typical error of those early and most confused phases of his attention to "primitive" art, however expressed. Other accounts, like Paul Alexandre's (Alexandre 1993, p. 63), remembered his eager visits to the Museum of the Trocadéro, where it seems that Modigliani favoured "the exhibition of Angkor, in the west wing."

Already in the 1920's the most varied directions that Modigliani took towards extra-European traditions had become commonplace in critical literature, if it is true that in 1929 Pfanstiel counted among the possible sources, neither without too many distinctions nor plausible comparisons, Egyption, Hindu, Khmer and Ivory Coast art. The strong analogies with art from archaic Greece were first noticed by Alphonse Basler (Basler 1931, p. 10), who retraced them to a vaster mixture of African and oriental influences, and much later by Werner in his first systematic study of Modigliani as a sculptor (Werner 1962, p. 31).

From this point of view, *Head* XII (cat. **24**) is the most interesting example – and perhaps the most difficult to interpret – of that behaviour of candid syncretism that Modigliani always maintained with regard to his sources. The necessity to achieve a stylistically efficient synthesis, able to mediate the different incentives towards a modern idiom (the models of Brancusi, Picasso, Derain that have been discussed in the first two sections) and towards a recovery, more mysterious than explicit, of a completely Classic measure urged the sculptor towards very confident choices, which could be discussed in critical literature with open admiration just as much as with explicit disapproval.

In fact, it was an ambitious programme, substantially set apart from the most radical tensions of the avant-garde; a project which aimed at a choice of ancient and modern designs, to be decanted during the process of stylistic purification. This use of formal elements deriving from archaic Greek art, from Indochinese and African sculpture could exist together, only at the cost of a complete sedimentation of the patterns and local jargon, in the sight of a distilling expression which could unite the various accents and normalise them in a composed and exemplary stylisation.

Head XII seems to be a sculpture of archaic taste, contaminated by figurative allusions of Oriental flavour. It is, in fact, the convergence of two studies inspired by the same number of models available in the Parisian museums. The Louvre offered a huge repertoire for Classic and Egyptian art and the Guimet for Oriental art, both able to trigger memories that the young Modigliani had of decisive viewings in Florence, Venice, Rome and Naples.

For this reason, the first comparative test is the admirable *Kouros Milani* in the Archaeological Museum of Florence (cat. **29**). The Kouros in Florence had, in fact, been bought by Luigi Adriano

Head of Buddha
XV-XVI century, Lanna, Thailand,
bronze, 22 x16 x 17 cm.
Paris, Musée Guimet
(cat. **25**)

Amedeo Modigliani
Head, 1912,
stone, 58 x 12 x 16 cm.
Paris, Centre Georges Pompidou,
Musée National d'art moderne /
Centre de création industrielle
(cat. **24**)

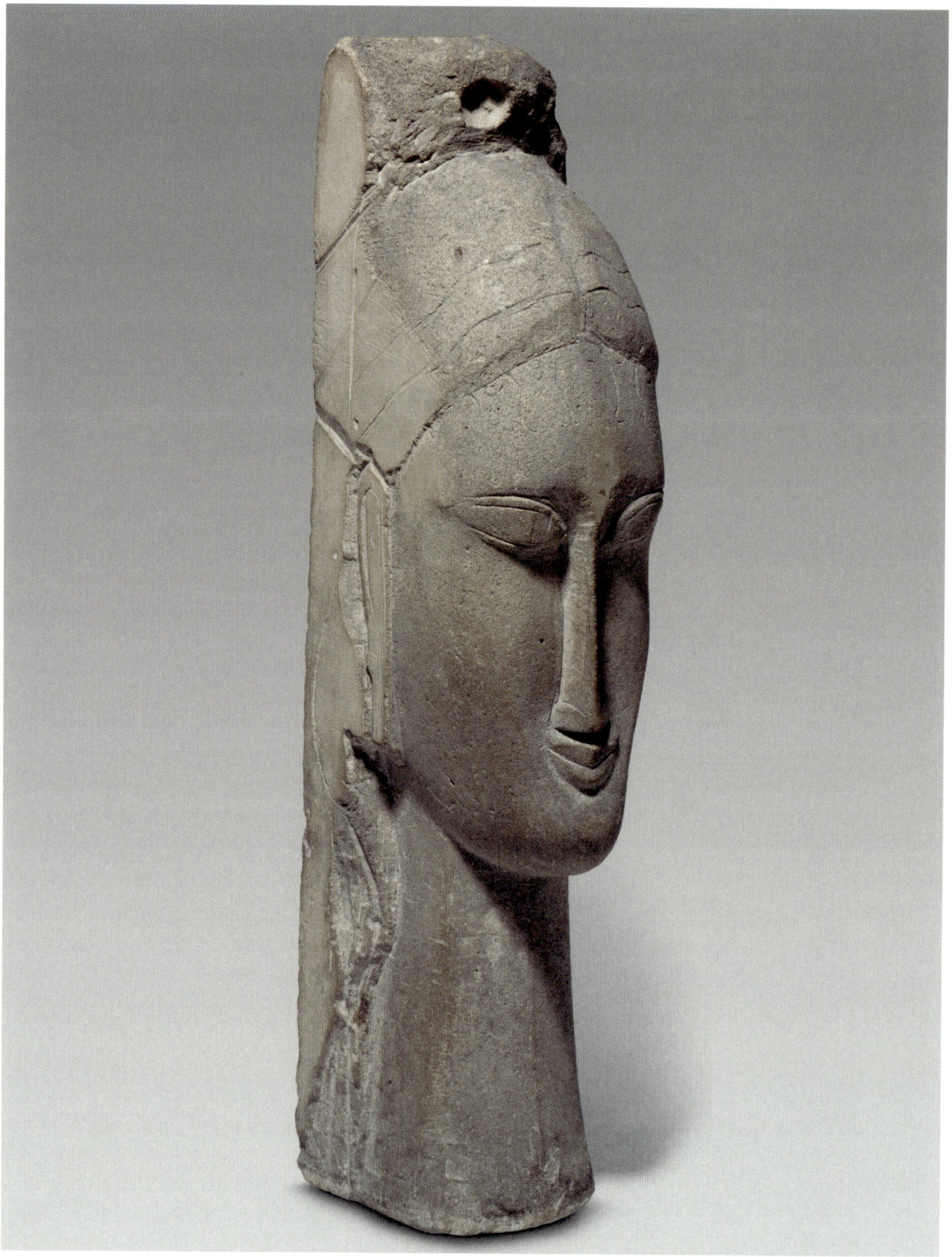

Milani, the first director of the Museum, together with the headless "Apollino", for the room dedicated to Greek and Roman sculpture. Despite the incomplete condition of one and the integration of the other (in particular parts of the nose and chin), they are both exceptional testimony of archaic Greek sculpture. The male nude figure (kouros) and the draped female one (kore), like the fragmentary heads (exemplified here by the *Athena* from Agrigento, cat. **30**) could offer sculptors efficient solutions for a non-academic Classicism: the compelling frontality of the figure, the elongated face, the aloofness of the "archaic smile" just hinted at, the deep almond shaped eyes, the rich decorative repertoire of the hairstyle, like the extremely elaborate curls of the *Kouros Milani*, which fall onto the shoulders. Such a figurative repertoire denoted a Classic and substantially timeless measure, beyond the grasp of learned or antique forms of retrieval; instead these models were able to diffuse a disturbing effect and to impress for their surprising plasticity.

The sculpture in Florence and the head of *Athena* from Agrigento sum up all the potential that archaic Greek sculpture could offer Modigliani and that could be found once again in the examples known of in Paris, like the famous Kouros in the Louvre. Some of the drawings belonging to Alexandre make it easier to understand the process of assimilation of such patterns and their flow into themes coming from other sources. In certain drawings (Alexandre 1993, Nos. 215-18) we can find the "archaic smile" of the kouros in a stylised head in accordance with the Ivory Coast Fang type masks; in some cases the contamination is such that the pendant earrings that can be seen in many drawings of female heads are transformed into the elongated lobes of the Buddhist sculptures: yet other drawings (like No. 135, fig. **5.1**, inconceivably called "caryatid", and No. 141), propose the model of the closed and related figure of the kouros with the grafting of a sculptural head in generic *nègre* style, so it seems that the male caryatids (Nos. 136-141) really seem to be the development of a theme studied on the archaic status.

It is a circulation and a contamination of sources and models more than open, shameless: and which the attention to Oriental art only helped to increase, in a moment in which, thanks also to the contributions of historical art research and some formidable additions to collections in museums, the notion itself of an unaltered Classicism was undermined. During the same years that Modigliani was meticulously refining his own sculptural style, the academic world had been confused by the question of the Greek-Buddhist sculpture from Gandhara. This name (ideological and Eurocentric, now obsolete) was designated for art that had developed from the I century BC until about the VII century, in the region of the same name found between Pakistan and Afghanistan (Verardi 2005, p. 507). A large amount of figurative testimony from this area documented a clear phenomenon of adaption of Hellenistic and Roman styles with Buddhist contents. Certainly, it was, as the Sinologist Raphaël Petrucci wrote in one of the first popular articles on the subject, "d'un conflit d'éléments et d'un mélange complexe dont nous pouvons débrouiller en partie les unités essentielles" (Petrucci 1911, p. 179). This could have been sufficient on one hand to spark up rather rash hypotheses about a classic influence able to push itself as far as the extreme regions of Indochina and Java; on the other to spread, instead of an approximate and superficial "Orientalism", an idea of continuity and transmission of unique roots of Greek, Christian and Buddhist art. Without speaking about a conscious and demonstrable imitation, it was however possible to observe at least a chain of analogies (Foucher 1905, p. 787).

It is difficult to think about Modigliani busy consulting the records of research institutes, the bulletins of the archaeological digs or the heavy tomes on antique learning; but even a straightforward sample of the press of the time, not necessarily the most specialised, and a verification of the exhibition programmes of the museums seem to be able to confirm the propagation of the question. On the other hand, right at the beginning of 1912, the rooms dedicated to "bouddhique ellenisante" art were opened at the Louvre, in the Galerie du Bord de L'Eau, with works coming from the explorations of Paul Pelliot and Fouché. The two collections seemed to be able to form two links of a historical chain which, as a critic of the time wrote with a certain exaggeration, told the story of the influences of Greek art on "Chinese" art *sic et simpliciter* (Dimier, 1912b). Apart from these inaccuracies, due mainly to the rather approximate knowledge of the facts, and an unrestrainable Eurocentric nature, if not chauvinist, it therefore seemed possible to lead a whole course of Middle and Far Eastern artistic traditions into a scheme of historical development which was not without some parallels with western tradition. Surprising matches were abundant, amazing analogies multiplied. In front of the riches of the dowry and the jewels of a female head found during an excavation in the Hadrian city of Antinoé, Émile Guimet personally observed that "on dirait voir un portrait peint par Ingres en 1928" (Guimet 1914, p. 26).

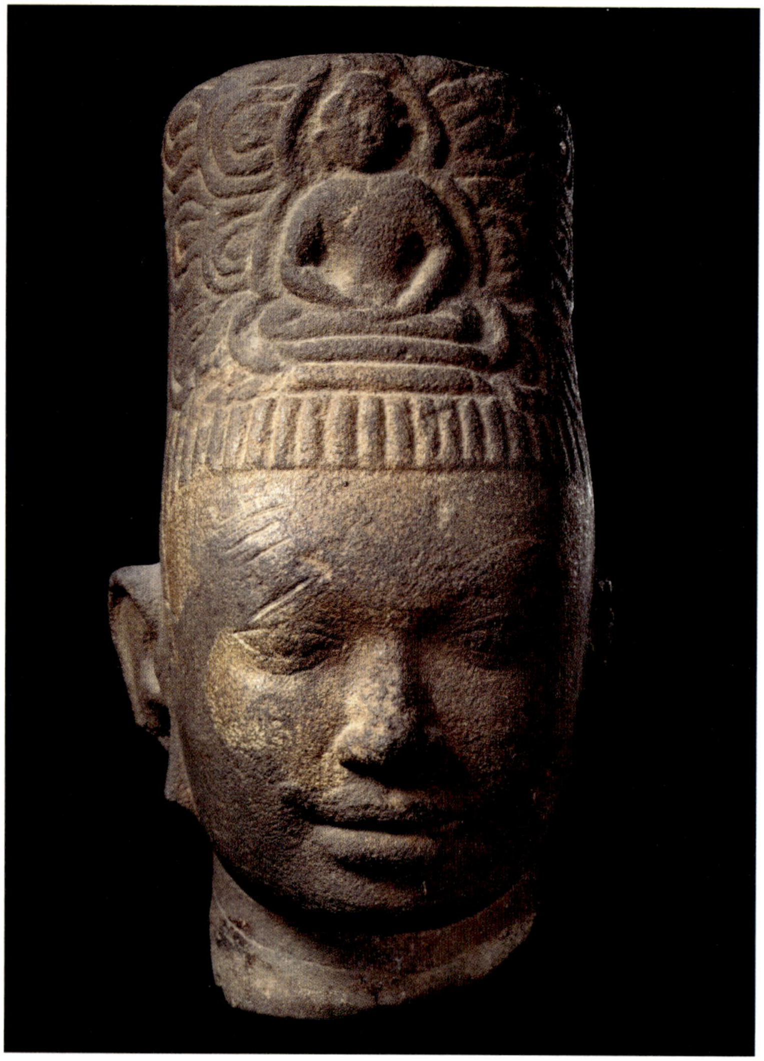

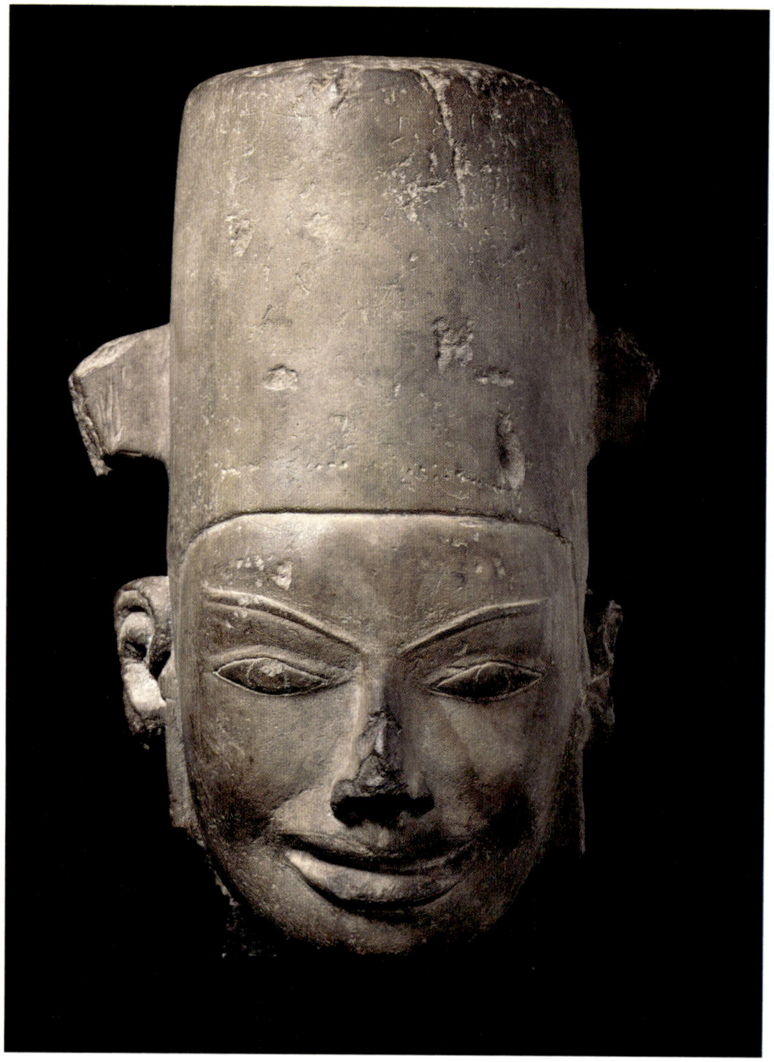

Head of Bodhisattva Avalokiteshvara,
VII-VIII century, Far Eastern art,
grés, 22 x 11.5 x 12.5 cm.
Paris, Musée Guimet
(cat. **27**)

Vishnu
VII-VIII century, Far Eastern art,
grés, 26 x 18.5 x 15 cm.
Paris, Musée Guimet
(cat. **26**)

A selection of Greek-Buddhist works and Chinese sculptures exhibited at the Musée Cernuschi was presented assuring that "Quelques connaisseurs, dont le goût s'était formé par la culte du *Trecento* et de l'art gothique, perçurent aussitôt des affinités nombreuses entre les œuvres de ces époques et celles qui venaient de se révéler en Chine" (Paris, 1913, p. X). It is feasible that the discontinuous and erratic nature of Modigliani's stylistic research could have found here, even though indirectly, or even through hearsay, a good confirmation of the idea of a dilated Classicism, when not eccentric, through the lens that at the same time was equally focusing the European and Asian "primitives". In this way he reflected that confident taste that seemed to focus the attention on the savouring of drawing inspiration from aestheticism, although historically misleading, of the eighteenth and nineteenth century *cabinets* (Cordier 1910).
For all of these reasons, the set of three Cambodian and Thai heads from the Guimet Museum (cats. **25-28**) should be seen as a supplementary dossier for a comparison with the archaic rendering of the faces. In these faces Modigliani was inclined to trace physiognomic features of an artificial and almost unnatural stereotype, like those observed in archaic Greek sculpture. Even more, in general, these approaches meant to support that idea, followed by Modigliani for a long time, of a varied style which through the purification of the sculptural material could lead to finding once again a mythical archetypal Classicism, even before the "humanistic" and regulated universality of the ideal Classic form.
The impact that the style of the Angkor artistic culture had on Modigliani can be measured even more by observing works like the statue of female divinity (fig. **5.2**) which arrived at the Museum

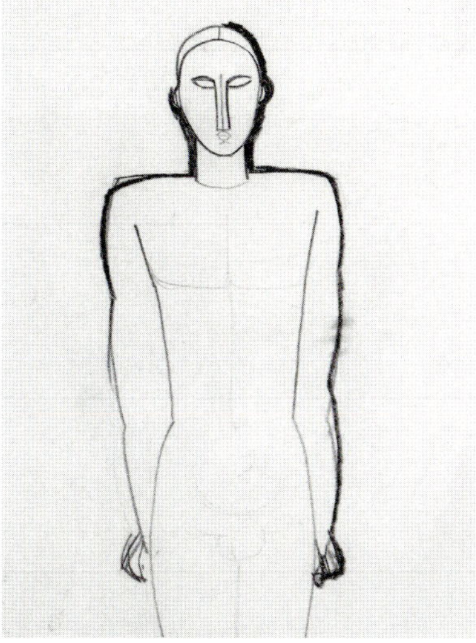

5.1. Amedeo Modigliani
Male Caryatid, 1911-1912,
grease pencil. Private collection

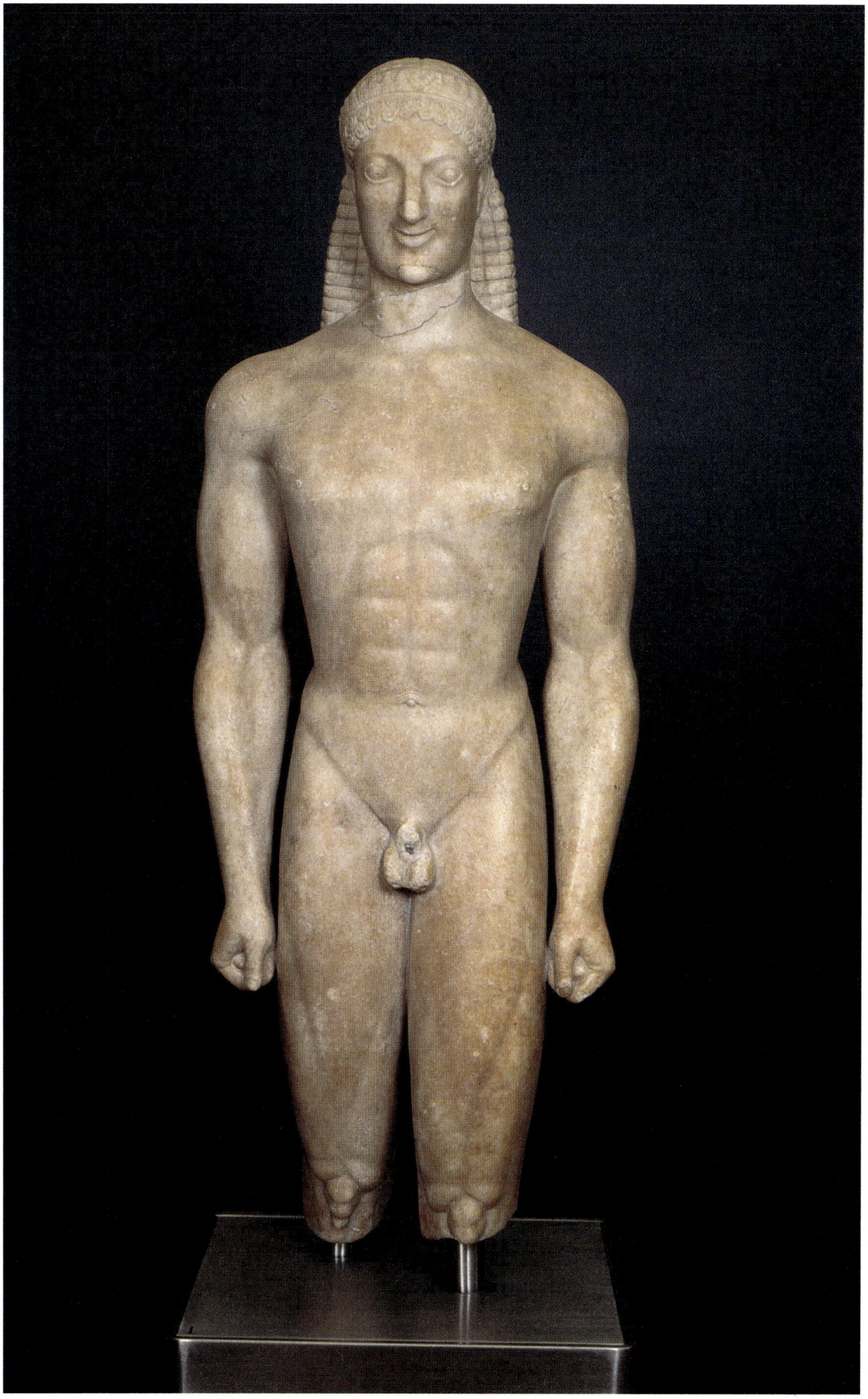

Statue of Kouros - "Apollo" Milani,
530 BC, Attic production,
white marble, h. 139 cm.
Florence, Museo Archeologico
Nazionale
(cat. **29**)

Head of Helmeted Athena,
V century BC, painted terracotta,
h. 23 x 12.5 x 17 cm.
Agrigento, Museo Archeologico
Regionale P. Griffo
(cat. **30**)

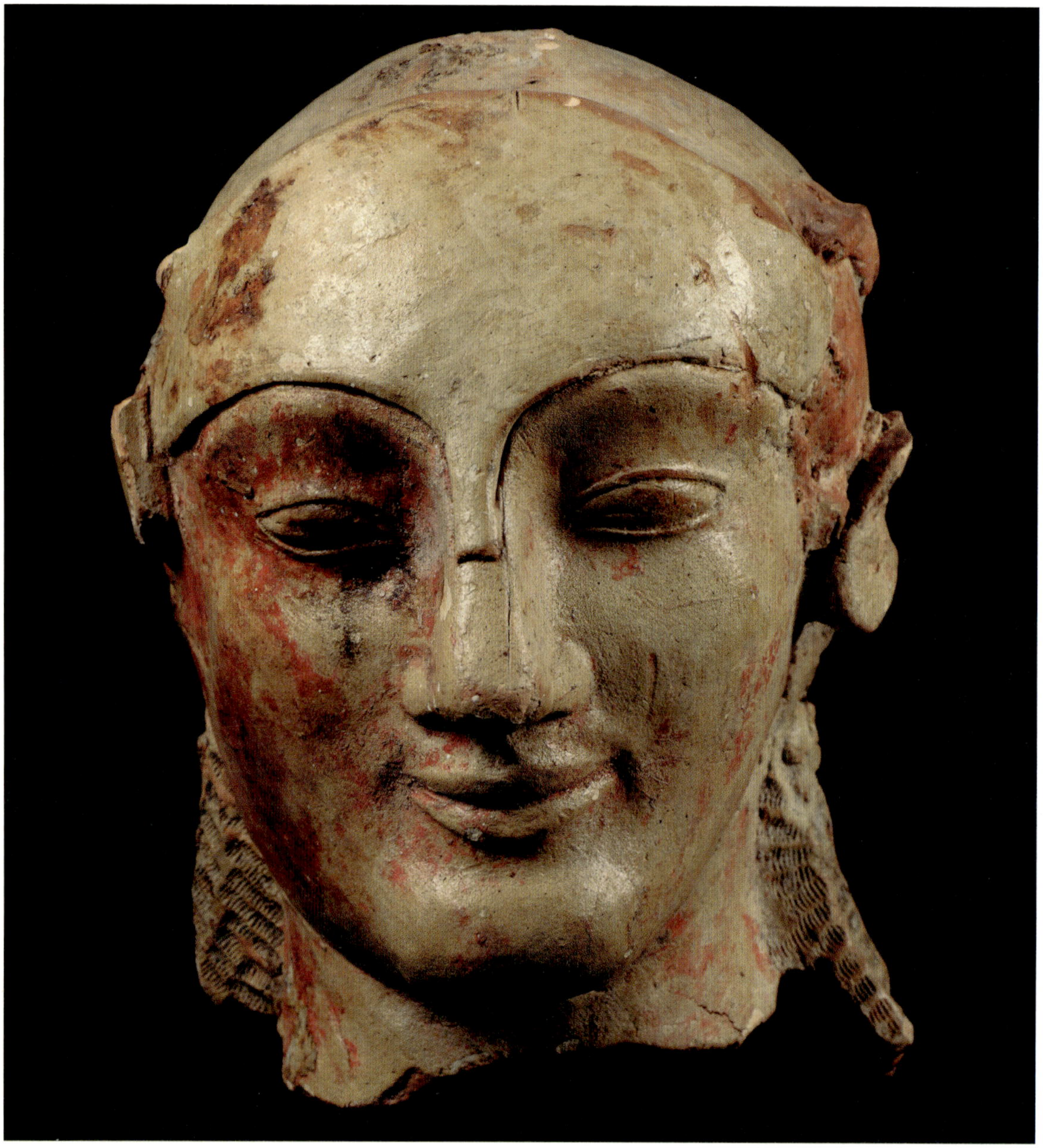

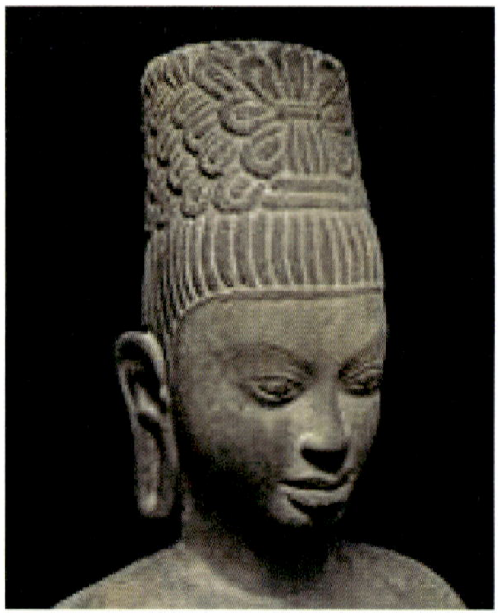

5.2. Pre-Angkor art from Cambodia, Female divinity, VIII century, detail. Paris, Musée Guimet.

Head of female divinity,
end VII-beginning VIII century,
Cambodia,
grés, 29 x 13.8 x 7 cm
Paris, Musée Guimet
(cat. **28**)

of Trocadéro in 1896 as a gift from Adhémar Leclère, *resident de France* in the Indochinese countries until 1911 and founder of the Ethnologic Society in Paris. It is a full figure that has a spectacular impact (height 136 centimetres), that before being transferred to the Guimet, dominated in the room of the so-called "Indochinese Museum" at the Trocadéro. Modigliani must have taken this into account both for the sculptural heads (like *Head* XVI, which seems to exactly repeat the hair in parallel tresses), and for the flared shapes of the Canberra *Caryatid*.
Besides that warm pictorial quality and the texture of the stoneware, these works were impressive for the rigorous symmetry of the face, the almost calligraphic description of the hair and above all the disturbing sense of the motionless smile associated with heavy closed eyelids: a fluctuation between realism and the abstract that confirmed the ambiguous fascination of these works.

Alessandro Del Puppo

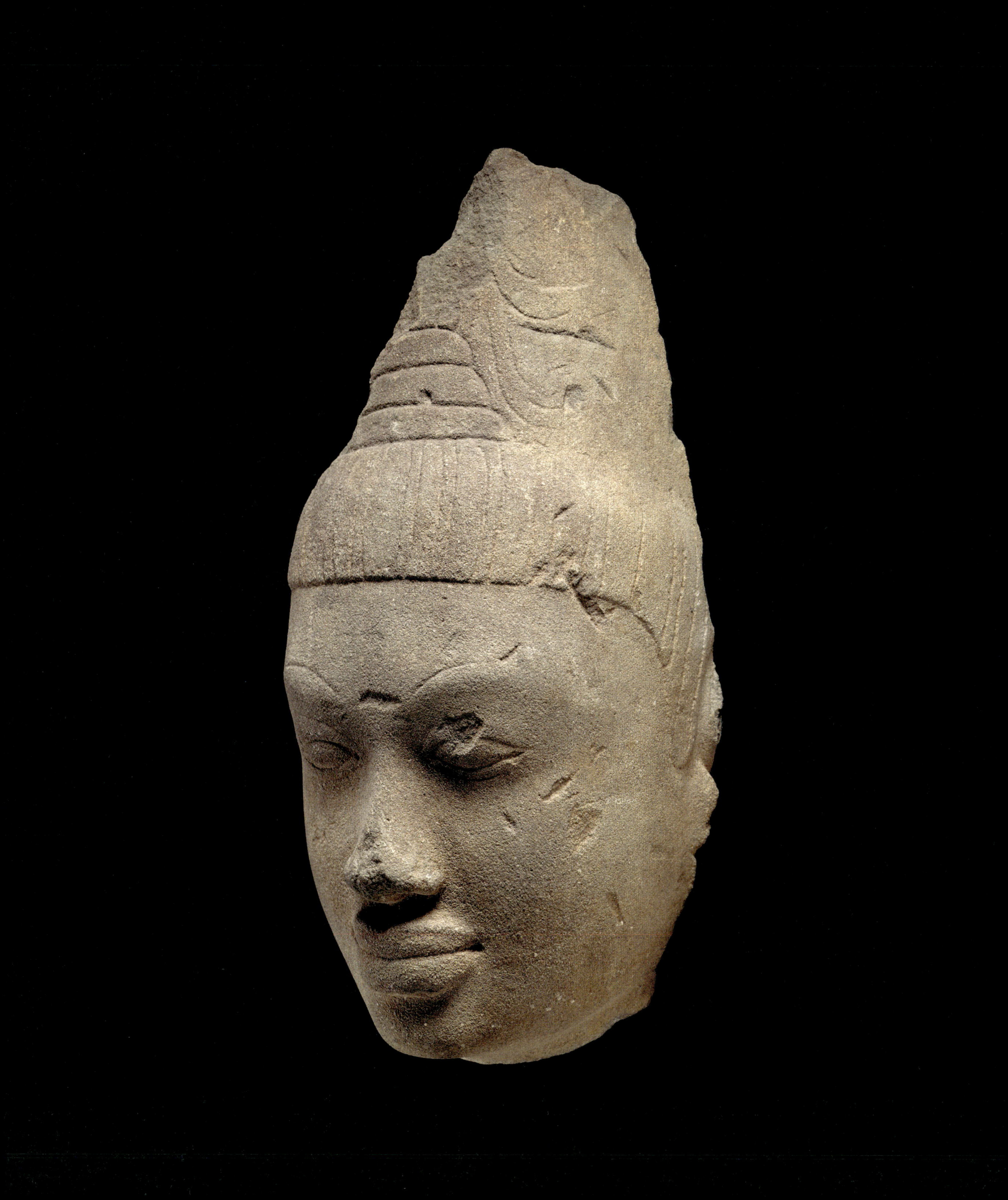

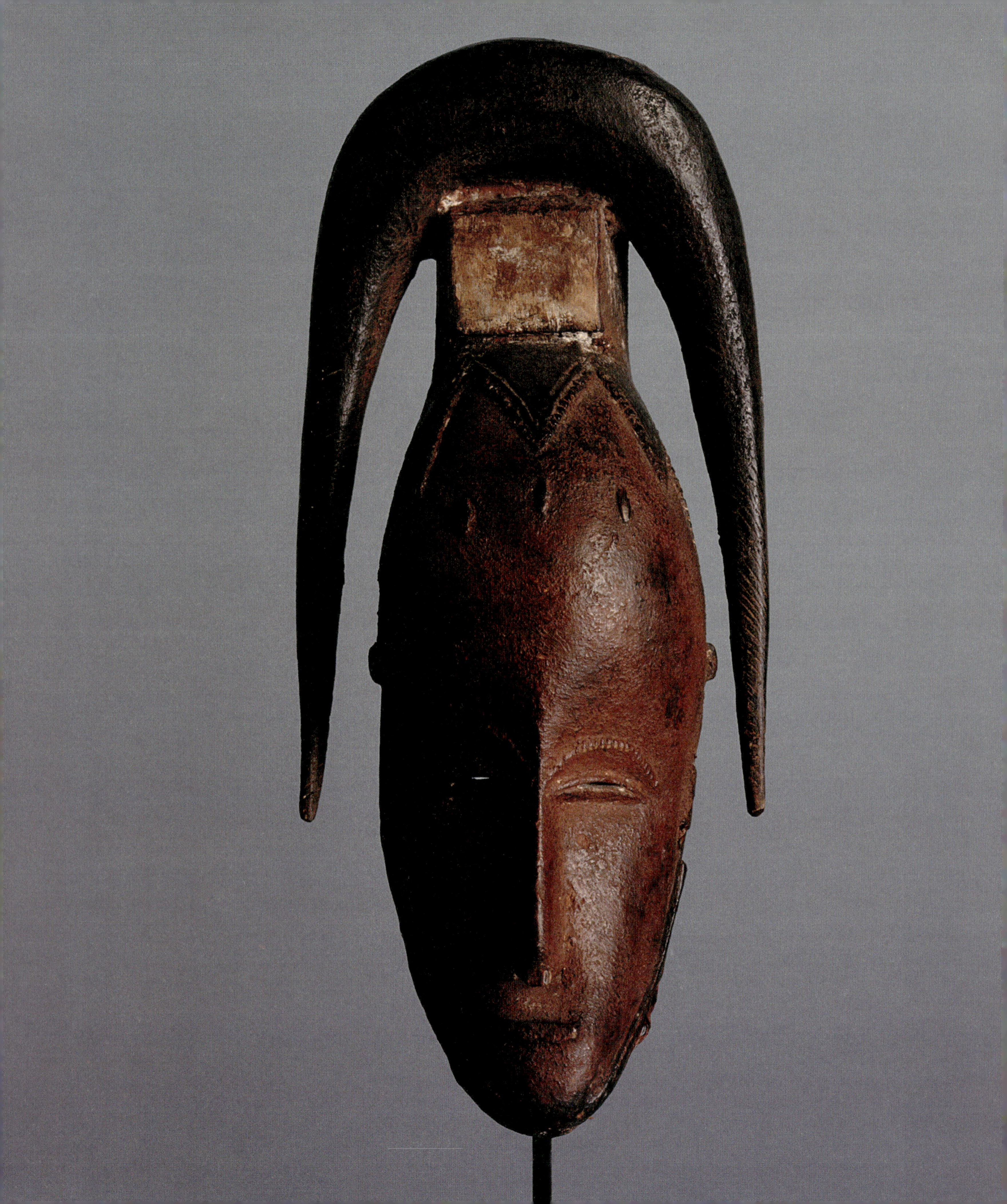

Section 6

The Sculptured Heads and the Parisian Suggestions of Tribal Art

Some of Modigliani's sculptures, documented here by two magnificently finished examples like *Head* XX from Philadelphia and *Head* XXIV from London (cats. **31-32**), present – although with the usual mixture of ancient and modern sources – formal elements clearly inspired by African masks.
Primitivism – or rather, for lack of a more appropriate term, that vast movement of modernist attention to works of art coming from extra-European culture – is undoubtedly one of the most characteristic traits of artistic research in the first decade of the XX century.
Before modern historiography tried to put some order to such a complex and crucial event, largely nourished by a great part of the historical avant-garde of that time, the phenomenon seemed rather confused, above all for the artists of that period: controversial chronologies, uncertain geographic provenance and the real function of the objects, the extremely generic names of the tribes, when not completely fanciful. Many fetishes were made from perishable materials (grass, resin, cotton) and were produced almost in series by an artisan procedure: they were of a much more recent date than their roughly made archaic manufacture would make them seem; the apparent invariability and absence of author (at least, in the western and modern concept of the term) increased their mythical nature, to the point where the fascination of these works seems inversely proportional to the knowledge of their owners.
From the artists' point of view, which was certainly not that of ethnographers and explorers, there was a rough distinction which was rather efficient for their use. In Oceanic art, especially in the form divulged by Paul Gauguin there was the desire to read the representation of a pure and uncontaminated nature, a sense of beauty and love. On the other hand African art appeared as the reign of magic, of the evil and mysterious sense of things.
Quite soon, however, with the intensification of the diffusion of the objects and the increase of specific knowledge, the appreciation of *art nègre* could be founded on various criteria of interpretation. A magic-cathartic reading encouraged in some authors (Picasso in 1907 and German painters such as Nolde and Kirchner) the expressive deformation of the faces and their rendering in terms of dramatic psychological depth. The recognition of a coldly logical function enabled the appreciation in primitive objects of the ideographic reduction and transcription of forms into abstract figures, "raisonnables" according to Picasso's definition (who would draw the consequences for his constructions in a variety of materials like the *Guitar* of 1912). Between these two extremes there was a milder taste that favoured essential linearity, elegant stylisation and the volumetric counterpoint of Gabon and Ivory Coast masks.
Modigliani's attention to African art must be traced back to this line in particular, indicated by all the testimony. Gustave Coquiot wrote about it in a page of his *Peintres maudits* (Coquiot 1924, p. 104): "un jour il me montra de la sculpture, modelée tout à fait sous l'influence de la sculpture nègre, collectionnée dans certains ateliers – et chez quelques critiques d'art." André Salmon (Salmon 1926, p. 18) more appropriately recognised the

Mask (Gu)
XIX-XX century
Guro, Ivory Coast
wood, pigments, rope, h. 44.1 cm.
New York, The Metropolitan Museum of Art, donated by Gertrud A. Mellon, in memory of Dr. Robert Goldwater, 1977 (1977.457)
(cat. **34**)

Amedeo Modigliani
Head of a Woman, 1912
limestone, 70.5 x 23.5 x 7.6 cm.
Philadelphia, Philadelphia Museum of Art, donated by Mrs. Maurice J. Speiser in memory of her husband, 1950
(cat. **31**)

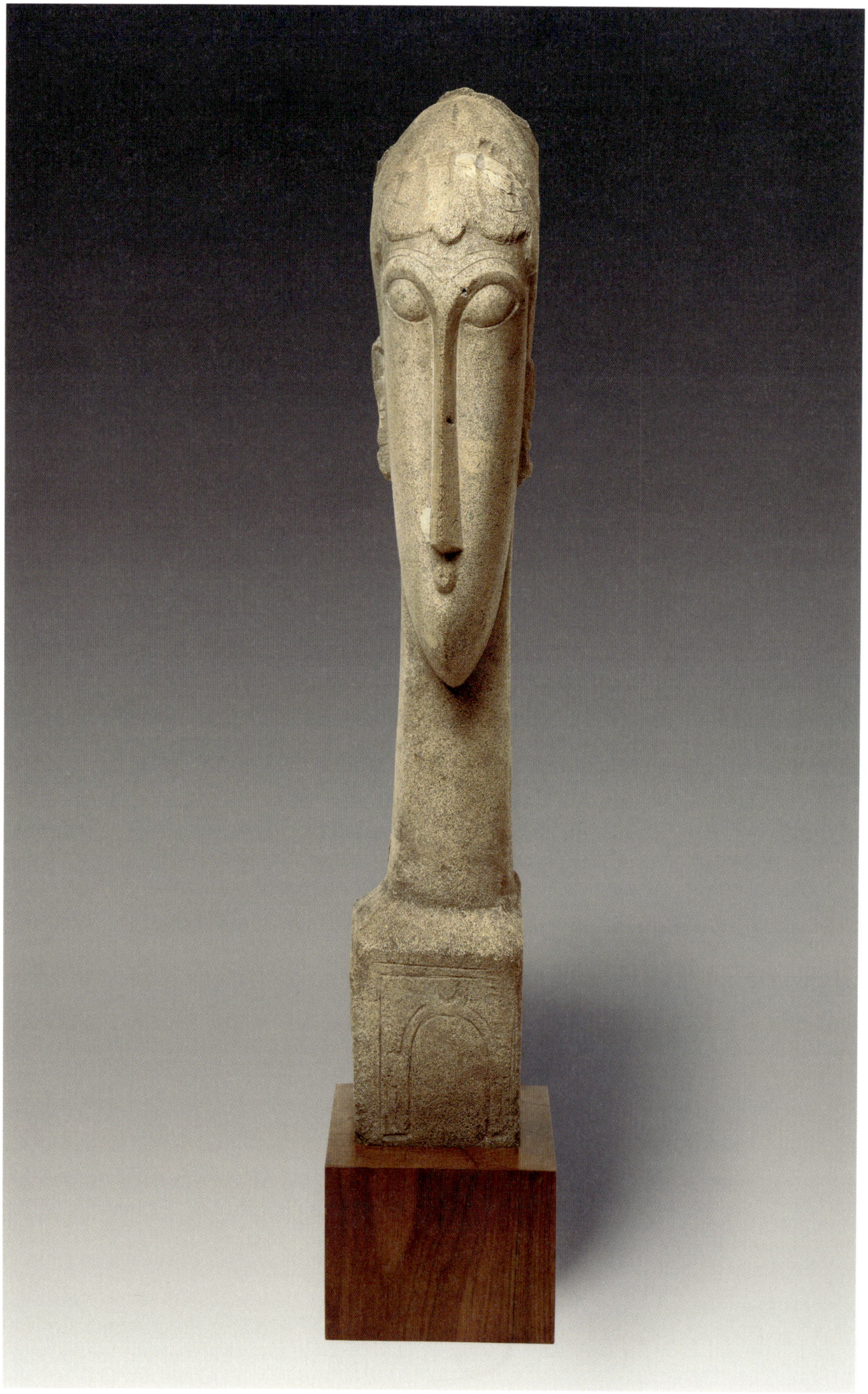

Amedeo Modigliani
Head, 1911-1912 ca.
limestone, 89.2 x 14 x 35.2 cm.
London, Tate: transferred
from the Victoria & Albert Museum
1983
(cat. **32**)

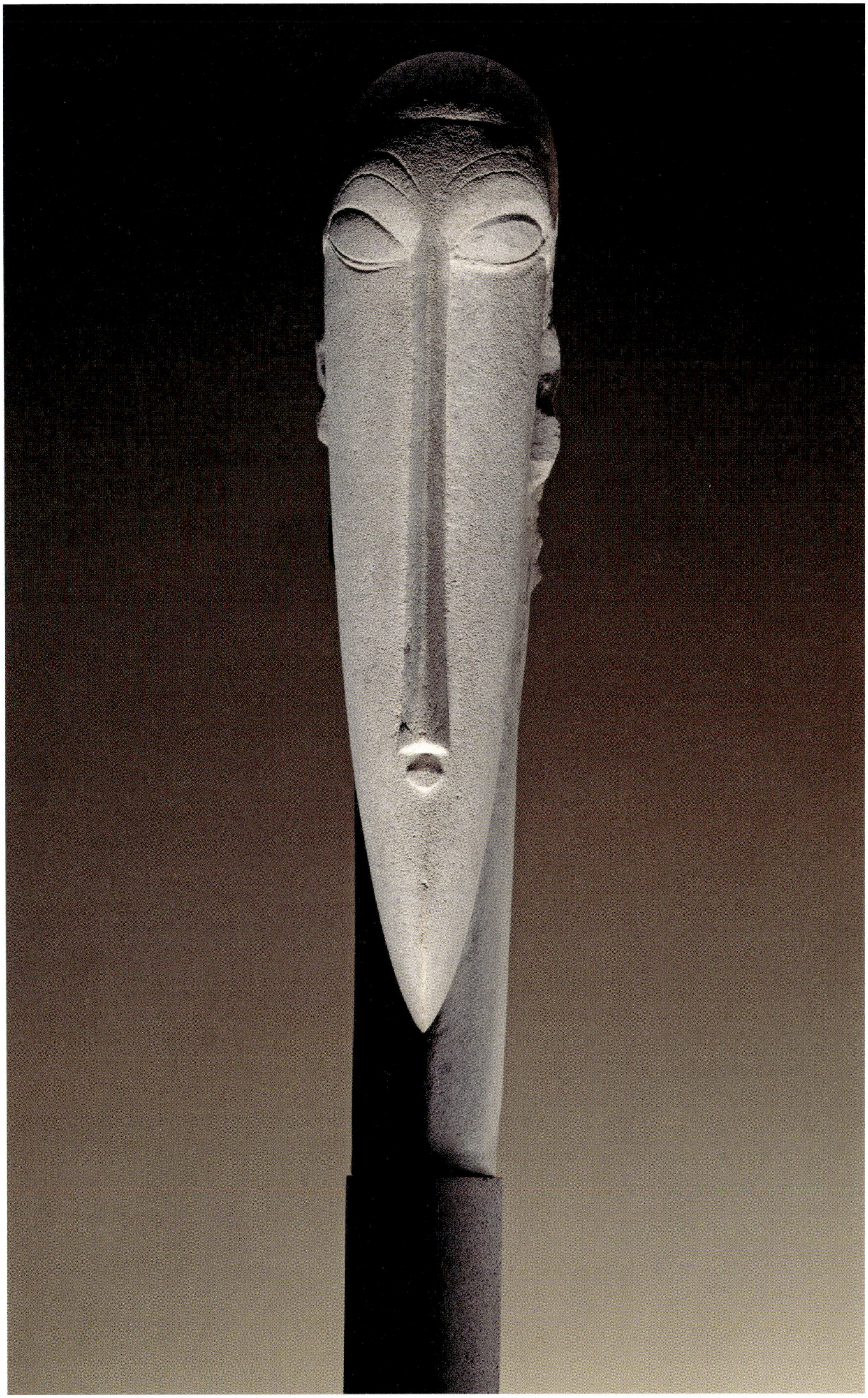

Mask
Fang, Gabon
wood, 34 x 21.5 x 15.6 cm.
Paris, Musée du quai Branly
(cat. **35**)

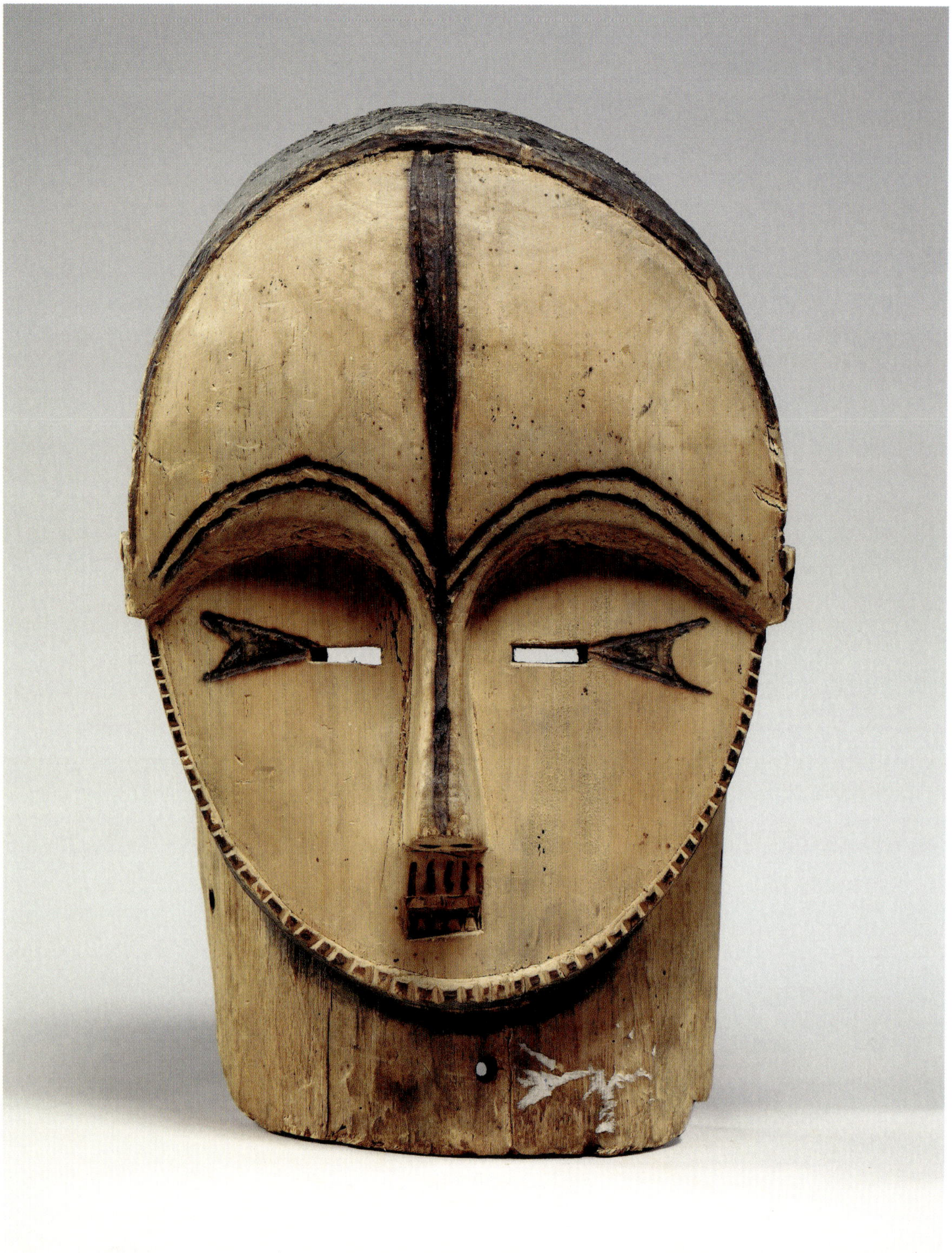

work of stylistic purification and the capacity of the sculptor to read the intuitive and original forms of African art as a resource for a renewed classicism ("Modigliani doit aux nègres eux-mêmes qu'il ne découvrit pas le premier. Mais, des premiers, il sut faire, à travers la statuaire nègre, œuvre mère, la révision de tout le classicisme").
Paul Guillaume's taste could be found in this moderate Primitivism, which turned away from the most frightening and deformed fetishes, favouring moderate and inoffensive forms. In the summer of 1912, before showing Modigliani's works in his gallery, Guillaume was working in Paris to promote *art nègre,* there was a special society of which he was the

Mask
Guro, Ivory Coast
carved wood and monkey hair,
h. 26 x 14,5 x 12 cm.
London, The British Museum
(cat. **33**)

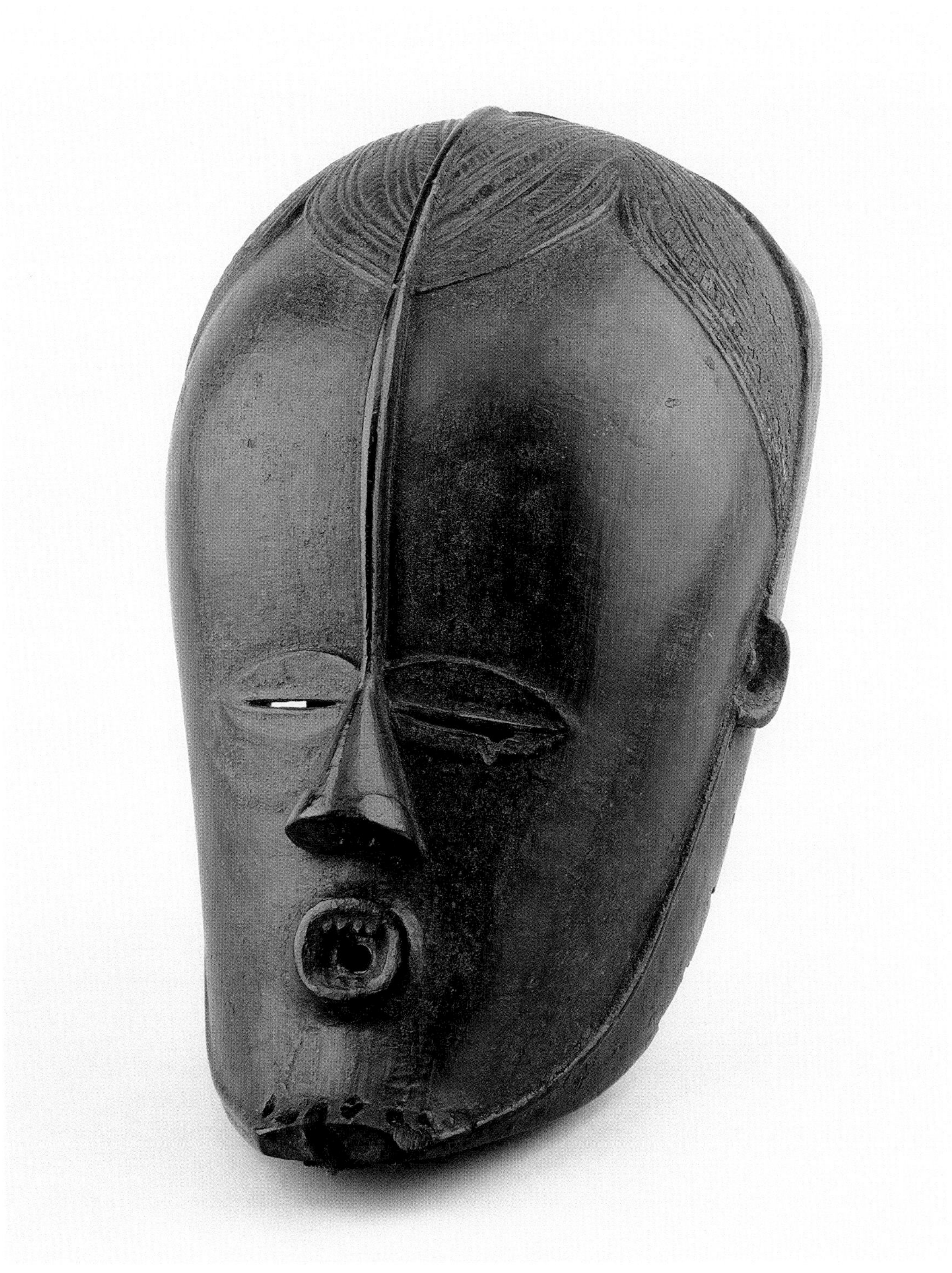

director and exhibitions of African art were planned (*Les Annales coloniales*, 14th July 1912; *La Vie*, 21st September 1912).
From being a simple curiosity to be hung on the walls of the ateliers (as can be seen in the famous photos of the Picasso, Derain and Brancusi studios), African art – or at least, in its most reassuring version – was preparing to enter the circuits of merchandise. Subtracted from the descriptive system of the ethnographic collections, this particular production could be inserted in a line reflecting modern taste and evaluated in its exquisitely formal aspects.

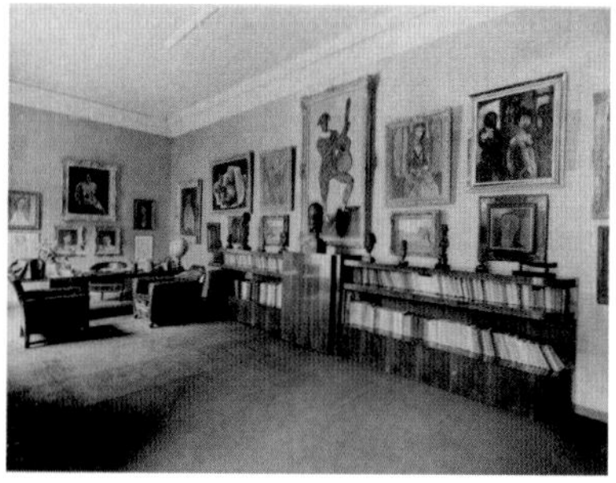

6.1. Paul Guillaume's apartment in avenue Foch, around 1930: Modigliani's paintings and the collection of African art. In the centre of the bookcase, the head of Fang Byeri reliquary, Gabon.
Paris, Musée de l'Orangerie

A very eloquent example of this taste is a type of Fang head used for the Byeri rite, the culture of the ancestors that foresees the preservation of the bones in containers surmounted by reliquary heads, in wood and metal which acted as guardians of the remains. The ritual nature of these objects passed into second place compared to the appreciation of collectors for the synthetic rendering of the form (an almost spherical skullcap grafted onto a long neck), the smoothness, the abstraction of every naturalism. A sculpture of this kind, previously belonging to Paul Guillaume's collection (fig. 6.1), was reproduced for the beginning of the volume *Sculpture nègres*, a lavish publication, accompanied by 24 photographic tables, edited in 1917 by the gallery owner himself in 63 very rare copies, in the explicit attempt to convert the fetishes of the *marché aux puches* into appetising works of art for the Parisian market. Guillaume took care, in fact, to guarantee the pleasant and inoffensive quality of the works he had chosen, with reasonings, that, apart from the lack of expertise, were on the verge of racial insolence: "C'est le plus souvent dans le bois que les artisans nègres taillent leurs divinités; cette matière offrant à l'expression plastique plus de docilité, cela était d'une grande importance chez ces races nonchalantes accoutumées à l'oisiveté voluptueuse et à la contemplation méditative." If the commercial nature of the volume was not concealed, the introductory text by Guillaume Apollinaire confirmed the purely stylistic and formal reasons for this success, and how much the artists' recent interest was "au point du vue purement artistique et en faisant abstraction du caractère surnaturel."
The formalities of Modigliani's Primitivist assumptions appear to be in perfect agreement with the lines of moderate Primitivism promoted by Guillaume.
The elongated lines of the face derive from models which can be traced back to the Guro culture, from the Ivory Coast. In particular, the exhibit at the Metropolitan Museum of New York (cat. **34**) is a sure term of comparison for the articulation between the concave and convex forms of the forehead, of the cheeks and chin, for the long thin nose, for the slit eyes.
On the whole, these characteristics are common to the group of sculptures XVI-XXIV – the heart, we can say, of Modigliani's work – even though mixed with other stylistic and diversified solutions with precise variants in three particular areas. Modigliani applied a system of variations and alterations to the fixed pattern of the elongated face, solemn, with rigid symmetry, concentrating on the area of the eyes and the grafting of the nose, on the decorative finishing of the hair and on the execution of the mouth which from the "archaic" smile contracts to a simple cylinder shape, in a geometric condensation that betrays another primitive source, still from the Ivory Coast, Grebo art.
If the Guro and Grebo masks could be intended as a vigorous plastic and volumetric solution, the Fang heads (from Gabon) suggested instead flatter and more simplified forms and a treatment of the surfaces that could be read as graphical and pictorial motifs (fig. **6.2**). It is for this reason that such objects, originating from the region of the Ivory Coast and commercially widespread were favoured by the artists. In fact, the mask bought by Maurice de Vlaminck and then sold to André Derain (fig. **6.3**) belonged to this kind, that has in some ways become the icon of Parisian Primitivism. The semi-circular joint between the arches of the eyes and the rod-like nose, which designs the face with an elegant decorative inflection, in fact, became an extraordinarily successful solution in the painting of Matisse, Derain, Picasso. This type of sculpture easily entered the norm of moderate *art nègre* promoted by Paul Guillaume. Besides owning a similar sculpture himself (today in the Museum of Quai Branly), Guillaume presented an example bought by Pablo Picasso at the crucial *Exposition d'art nègre* and in the volume, edited by Henri Clouzot and André Level *L'art nègre et l'art océanien* (Clouzot, Level 1919), which was published on that occasion to re-launch the fashion of tribal sculpture on the Parisian post-war market.

Head of the Guardian of the reliquary
Fang, Gabon,
wood, cm 46.7 x 14.5 x 14.2 cm.
Paris, Musée du quai Branly
(cat. **36**)

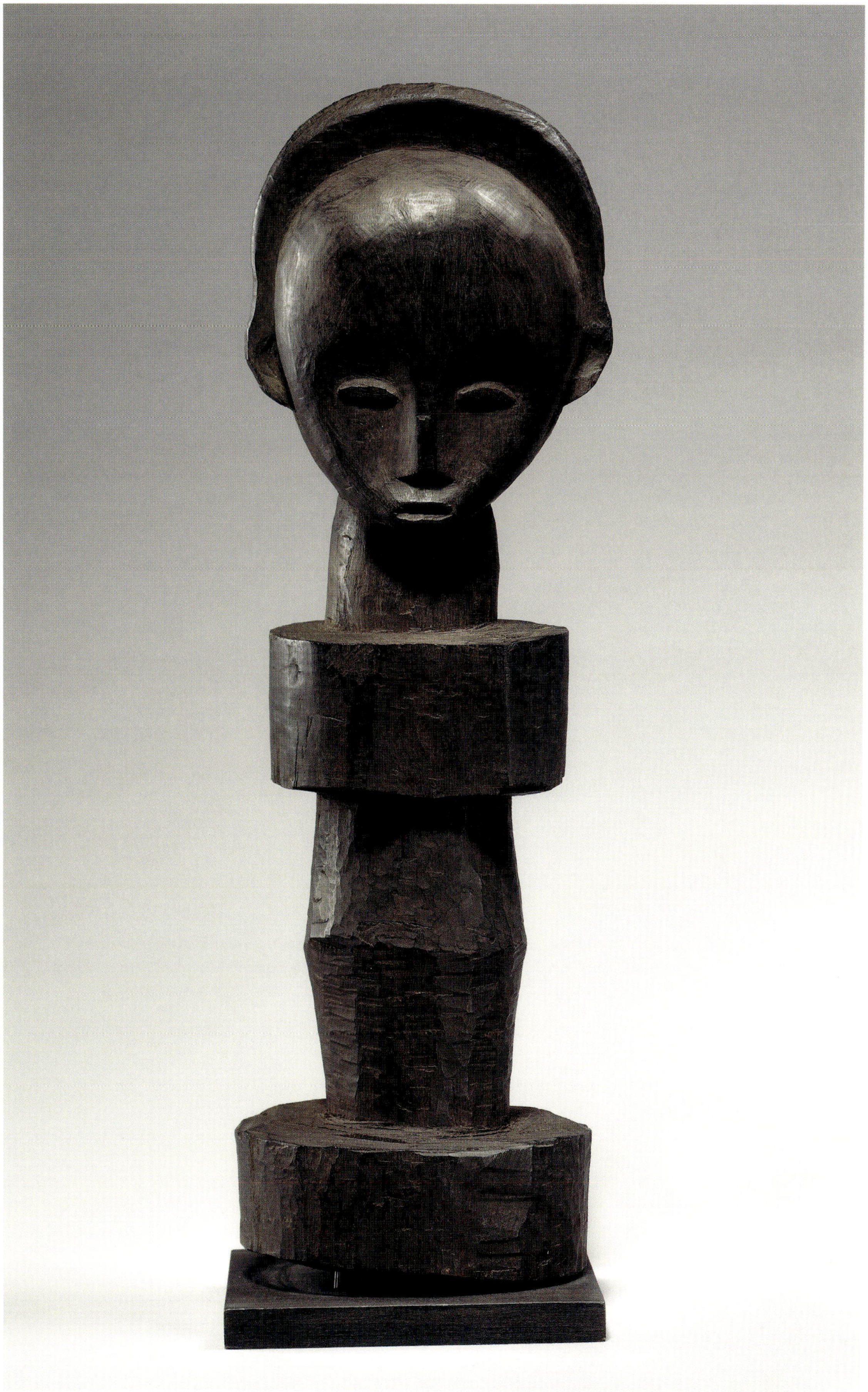

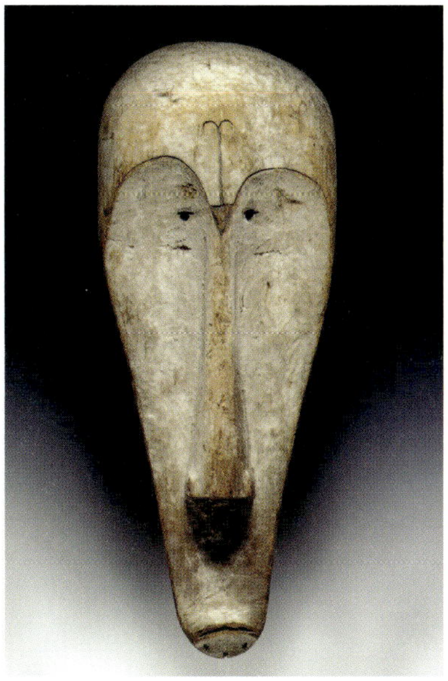

6.2. Fang, Gabon. *Ngil Mask*. Berlin, Staatliche Museen zu Berlin, Ethnologisches Museum

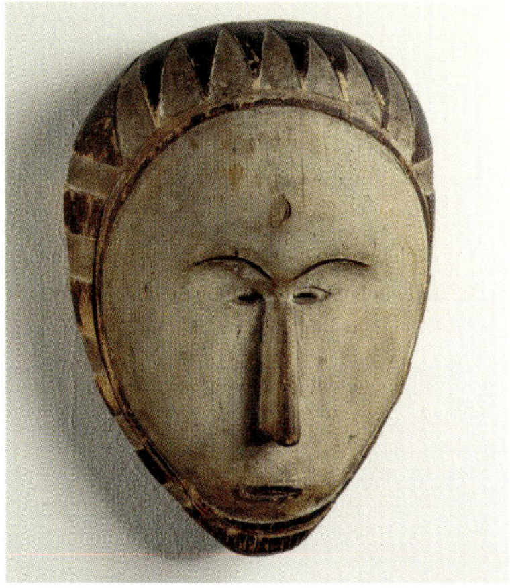

6.3. Fang, Gabon mask arrived in france before 1906. Formerly André Derain collection. Paris, Centre Georges Pompidou, Musée National d'art moderne

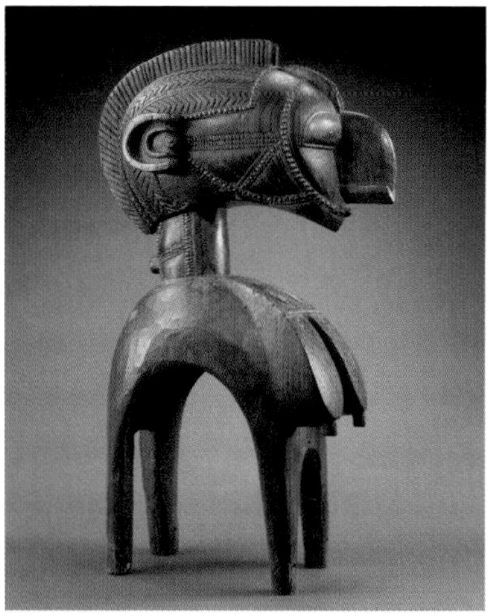

6.4. Nimba mask, New Guinea.
Paris, Musée du quai Branly

An exemplary case of the circulation of these models can be found in *Girl Full of Love* (cat. **37**) by Arturo Martini. This is a sculpture in plaster (with a variant in glazed terracotta), modelled on direct emulation of Modigliani's heads which Martini was able to see for himself at the Salon d'Automne in 1912, where the young Italian from Treviso was present with a series of engravings, together with Gino Rossi's Breton paintings.
The undoubtedly *nègre* taste in Martini's sculpture, with obvious typological deductions from the Nimba and Fang models appears to be a case of indirect quotation, more indirectly from Modigliani's work – as shown in the detail of the long neck – than from a direct knowledge of the primitive object; even though Martini could certainly have been able to benefit from the influence of the works still exhibited in the African rooms of the Trocadéro (fig. **6.4**). Compared to the calm passivity of Modigliani's heads, Martini's stands out for the decisive and brazen set of the jaws, for the intense expression of the face and the accentuated naturalism, made even more explicit by the crudely allusive title.

Alessandro Del Puppo

Arturo Martini
Young Girl Full of Love, 1913
plaster, 37 x 19 x 28 cm
Treviso, Museo di Santa Caterina
(cat. **37**)

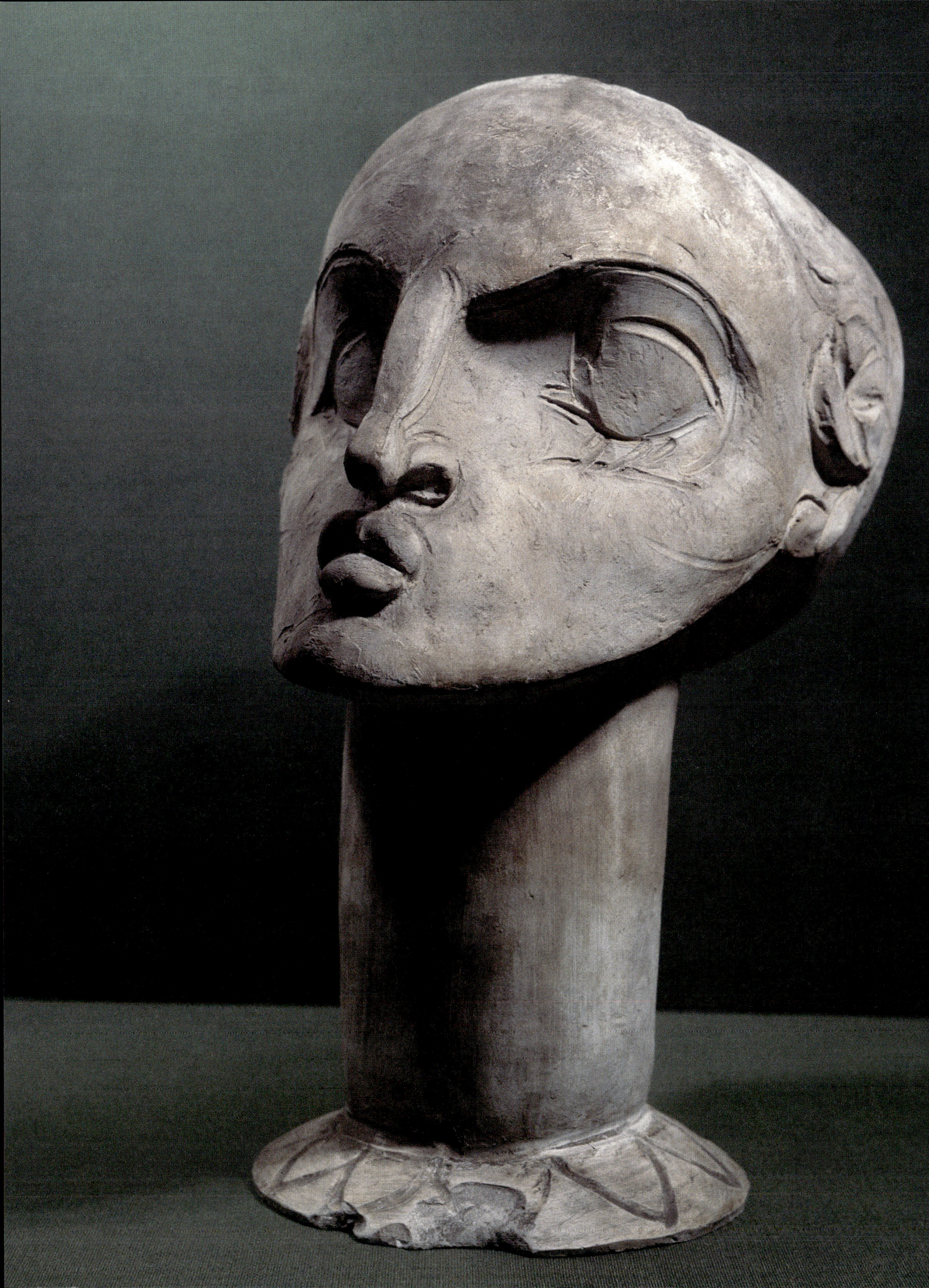

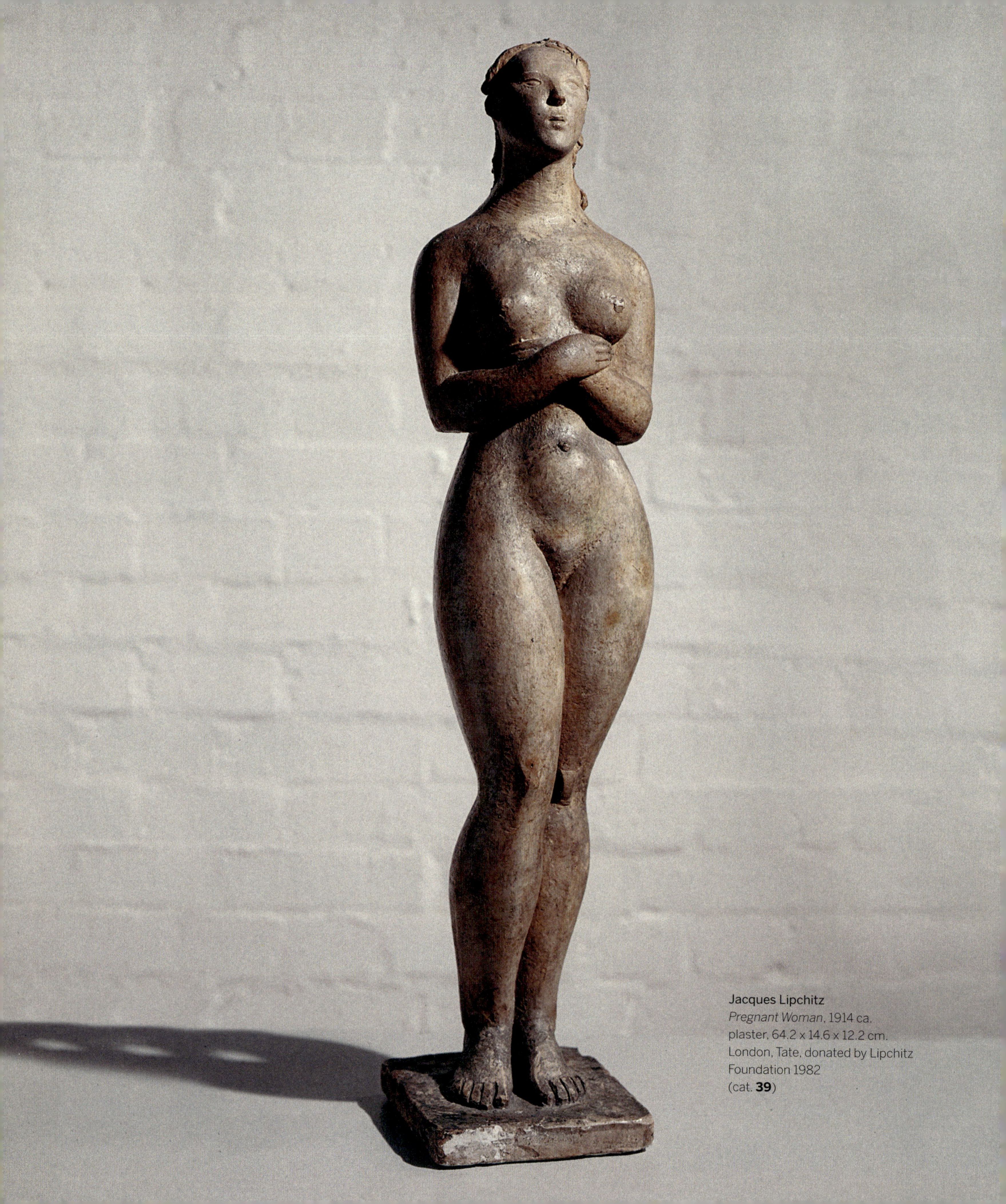

Jacques Lipchitz
Pregnant Woman, 1914 ca.
plaster, 64.2 x 14.6 x 12.2 cm.
London, Tate, donated by Lipchitz Foundation 1982
(cat. **39**)

Section 7
The Standing Figure: Primitivist Influences

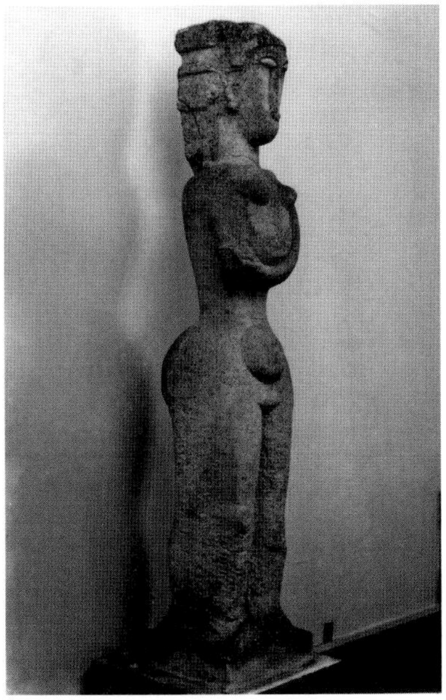

7.1. Amedeo Modigliani
Caryatid, 1911-1912.
Canberra, The National Gallery of Australia. Ceroni XI

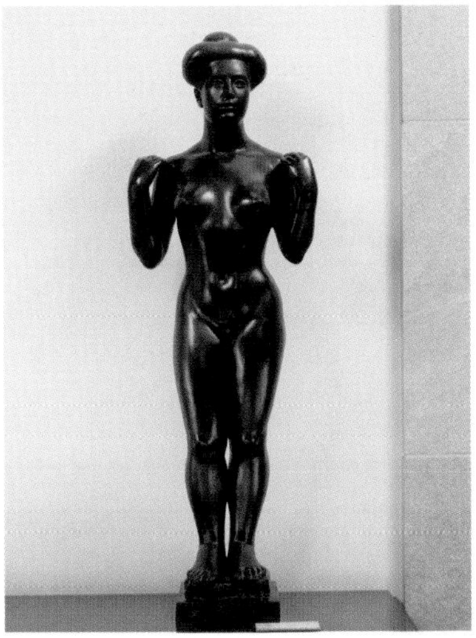

7.2. Aristide Maillol
Baigneuse aux bras relevés, 1900.
Paris, Musée d'Orsay

As has already been seen, his study of sculptural heads led Modigliani to a triple comparison with the development of post-Rodin plastic art, with the tradition of direct carving, with the Renaissance-like type of bust and finally with the models of Primitive, archaic and Oriental arts.

The realisation of the *Caryatid,* today in Canberra (fig. **7.1**) – an exceptionally interesting *unicum* in his repertoire, and we can only deplore its absence here – obliged Modigliani to measure himself against the full figure. In this way another two important questions were opened up: the subject of the standing figure with its autonomous plastic tradition and consequently, an idea of full height sculpture, no longer as a "decorative piece," according to the precepts of 1912, but rather a monumental size on an architectonical scale.

This line of research intercepted a pattern which was very widespread in the work of many sculptors' who tended towards the translation of some formal aspects of Primitivism, not so much in terms of expressive intensification or psychological enquiry of the head-portrait, but rather in terms of the review of the canonical proportions of the full figure. In fact, moving the attention from the face to the body, from physiognomy to anatomy, meant eliminating the most radical forms of deformation and, together with these, the overtones and the excess of expression, conveying instead more composed and controlled patterns of structural articulation – although derived from "anti-Classic" examples – to the Classic typology of the monumental figure or group. It is not by chance that this was the solution favoured by the "pure" sculptors, some of whom are grouped in this section, contrary to those painters-sculptors who, from Gauguin to Derain up to Picasso and with the only exception of Matisse, often chose the first course.

To challenge oneself with the full figure meant, first of all, reckoning with the renewal of the canons by August Maillol in his series of female statues of immobile Classicism that had brought him such success during the first decade of the century (fig. **7.2**).

Among all the young artists who struggled with the theme of the full figure and Classic continuity, the Russian sculptor Alexander Archipenko (1887-1964) was among the most interesting. After early studies in Moscow and Kiev, Archipenko moved to Paris in 1908, enrolling at the École des Beaux Arts. However, he soon rejected academic teaching as well as the influence of Rodin, moving instead towards Synthetic Primitivism, thanks also to the use of direct carving of stone, with works that already in 1909 showed Brancusi's influence. However, his faithfulness towards Classic typology can be observed in his regular participation in the Parisian exhibitions. One group, *Adam and Eve* peppered with a clear allusion to Javanese bas-reliefs, was presented at the Salon des Indépendants in 1910 (fig. **7.3**); a marble *Maternity* with composed and compact forms, was exhibited at the Salon d'Automne in 1911; a *Repos* that proposed a female nude reclining in a variation of nonchalant formal articulation, confirming the attention to a Classic theme, was sent to Amsterdam in 1912.

A large and ambitious *Venus* caused a sensation at the Indépendants in 1912, for the large and essential form of the figure, the full and elegantly rhythmic volume with geometric simplification of the muscular masses, displayed in a mannered torsion but sufficiently

Alexander Archipenko
Family Life, 1912 (2007)
posthumous bronze,
57 x 33 x 23.2 cm.
Bearsville, New York,
The Archipenko Foundation
(cat. **40**)

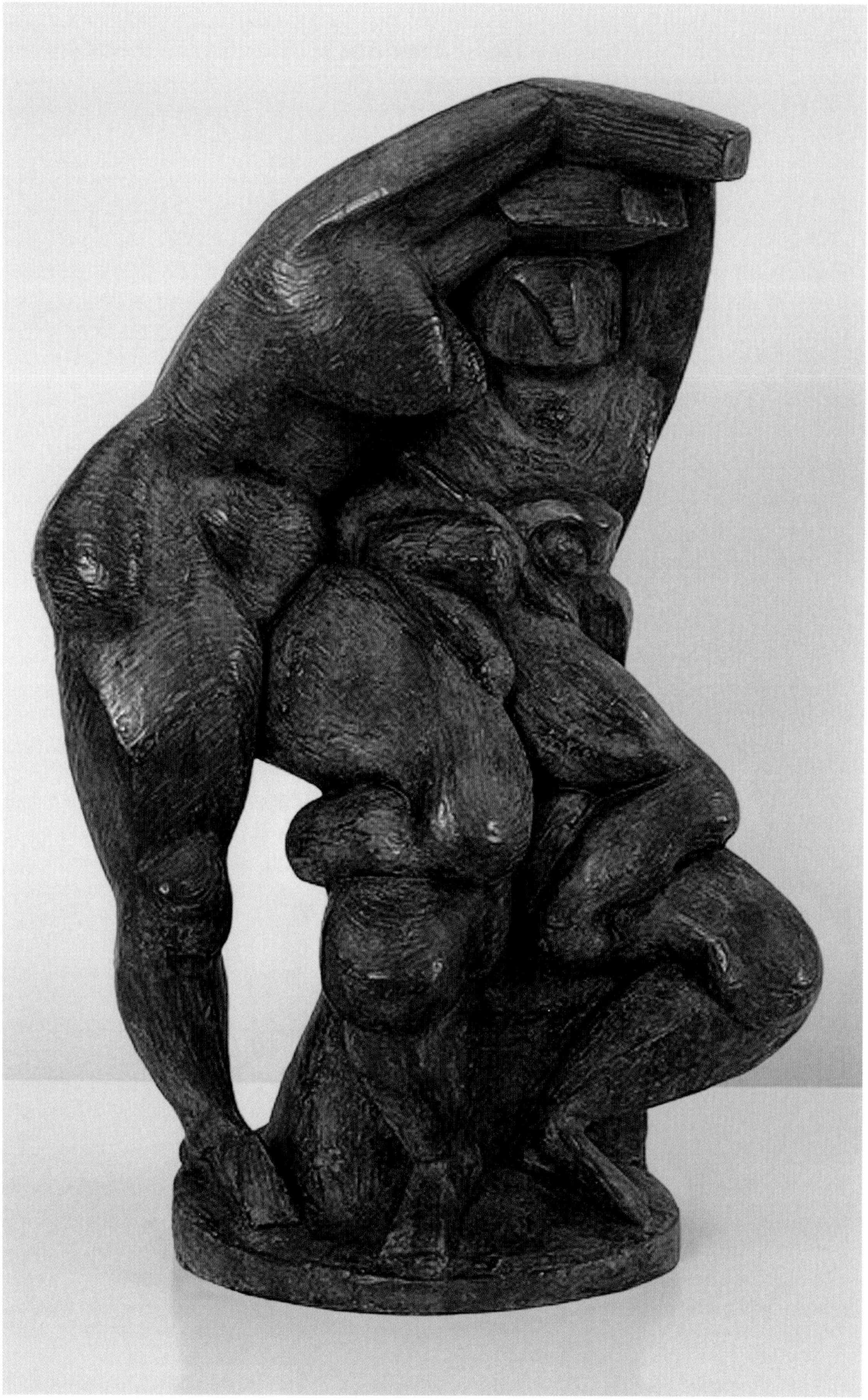

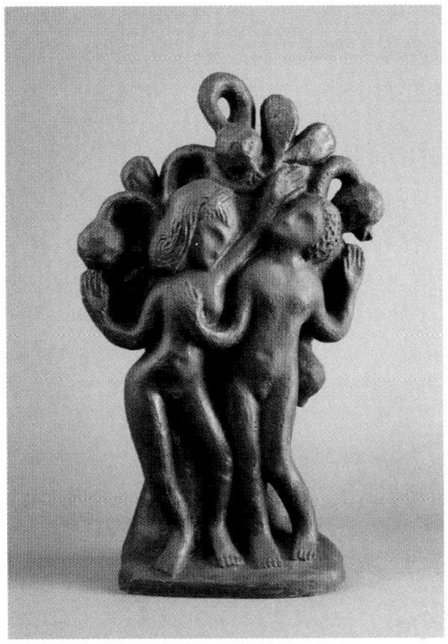

7.3 Alexander Archipenko
Adam and Eve (*Les Grenades*), 1909.
Saarbrüken, Saarland Museum

contorted to be able to enter the author's name in the group – of rather ambiguous denomination – of the "Cubist" sculptors.

Together with Brancusi's masterpieces like the *Musée endormie,* the *Prométhée* and above all the *Baiser* ("dont l'architecture est calme et puissante"), Roger Allard, a critic of Modernist taste mentioned Archipenko's *Venus* as being "surtout remarquable par l'ampleur des mesures et aussi par une ferveur sensuelle et un lyrisme très personnels" (Allard 1912).

The *Salomé* in cement (cat. **38**) was instead exhibited at the Salon d'Automne in 1912 with the title *Baigneuse.* The work quite evidently repeated the solution of the *Venus*, in this way introducing a modern solution to the Classic figure, however, without losing the pathos of the monumental size and the symbolic-literary theme. Nevertheless, the author could not avoid the destiny of being mocked: the nude from "l'homme qui comprend les femmes," transposed into a caricature-like form, shared the humorous *La vie parisienne* (fig. **7.4**) with two of Modigliani's heads.

Archipenko presented a smaller group of three figures in plaster at that same Salon, *Family Life* (cat. **40**). The following year the work was destined to the influential Armory Show in New York. In the complex articulations of the figures, where the abrupt joints of the limbs stand out, a moment of extreme syntax of the modelling can be observed: an exasperation of the volumetric and plastic production which would find a temporary resolution in the Polimateric, coloured sculptures that caused some amazement in Paris in 1914.

The career of Jacques Lipchitz (1891-1973), a Lithuanian, nationalised French, is similar to Archipenko's not only due to the common destiny of émigré but also to their academic preparation, with studies carried out at the École and the Académie Julien, signs of which appear in his very early works like the *Femme enceinte* of 1912 (cat. **39**; cf. Paris 2009, No. 71). These academic modes were soon put to one side after meeting Picasso, Gris and Max Jacob, thanks to this meeting Lipchitz approached Cubist modes, faceted forms, volumes returned to intertwining plastic planes, infraction of the sculptural block and the compositional unit.

The influence of primitive statues continued to move behind all these results, even though in a more filtered and composed way. For this reason the examples of Fang reliquaries that are present here (cats. **41-44**) have the task of documenting a possible model for the anti-academic study of the full figure. In these small sculptures, very widespread in the Parisian ateliers, instead of being taken as an inviolable unit, the human body was disassociated in its parts and considered as a group of distinct units which were assembled, favouring a system of formal dissonances rather than the homogeneity of the figure.

The articulations jutted out from the trunk in a sort of "eight" shape, it was easily articulated in unconventional forms or could be transformed into a decorative rhythm. The preparatory drawings for the great *Caryatid* (Alexandre 1993, Nos. 144-147) showed evidence of this simplification, showing the path that led Modigliani from an appreciation for the elementary syntax of African statues to the architectonical compactness of the *Caryatid,* without neglecting explicit primitive and archaic accents.

With Brancusi's *Adam and Eve* (cat. **45**) the trajectory of the primitive influence achieves an absolutely formal rarefaction and, at the same time, a stronger condensation of the motif (cf. Paris 1995, No. 58).

The work impresses for the almost totem-like display of the amphibian figure that emerges from the wonderful decorative modelling of the base as a peremptory declaration. In this formal statement, the old problem of the overlapped figures is resolved in an ideographic reduction of the sexual organs, generating a disturbing graft, a real visual shock, which exploits the ambivalence of formal choices. The carved spherical modules of the head recall the decorative simplicity of earlier works like the *Cup* of 1915: the thick lips represent the

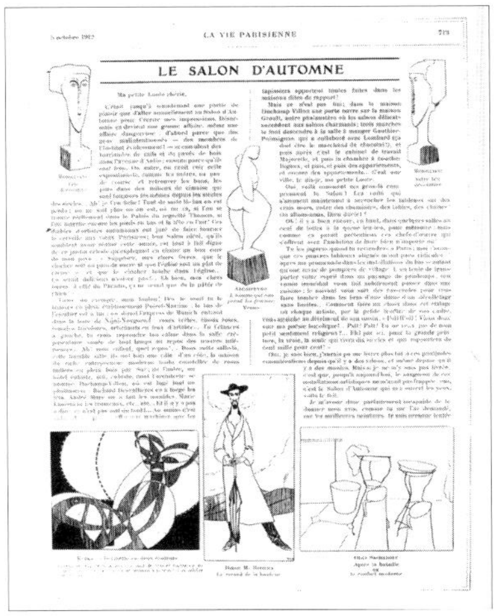
LA VIE PARISIENNE

LE SALON D'AUTOMNE

7.4 *La vie parisienne*,
5th October 1912

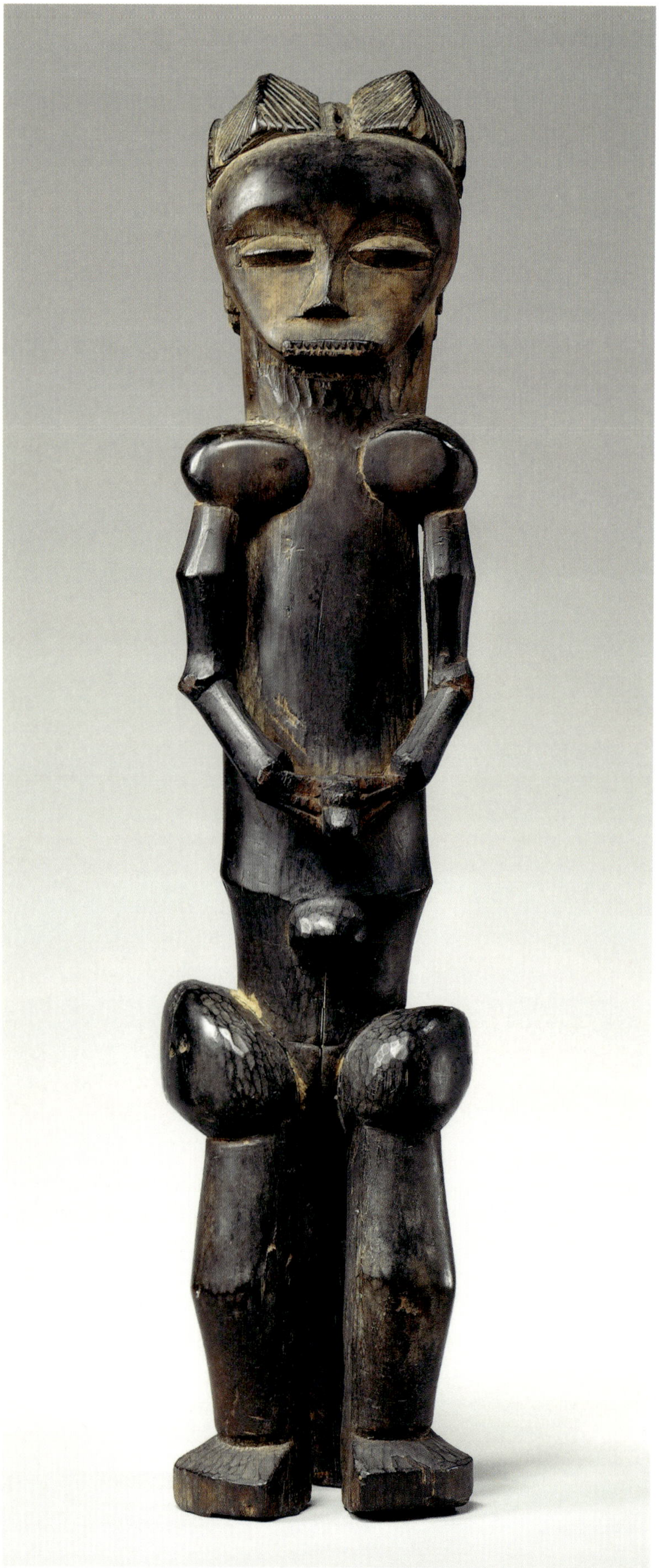

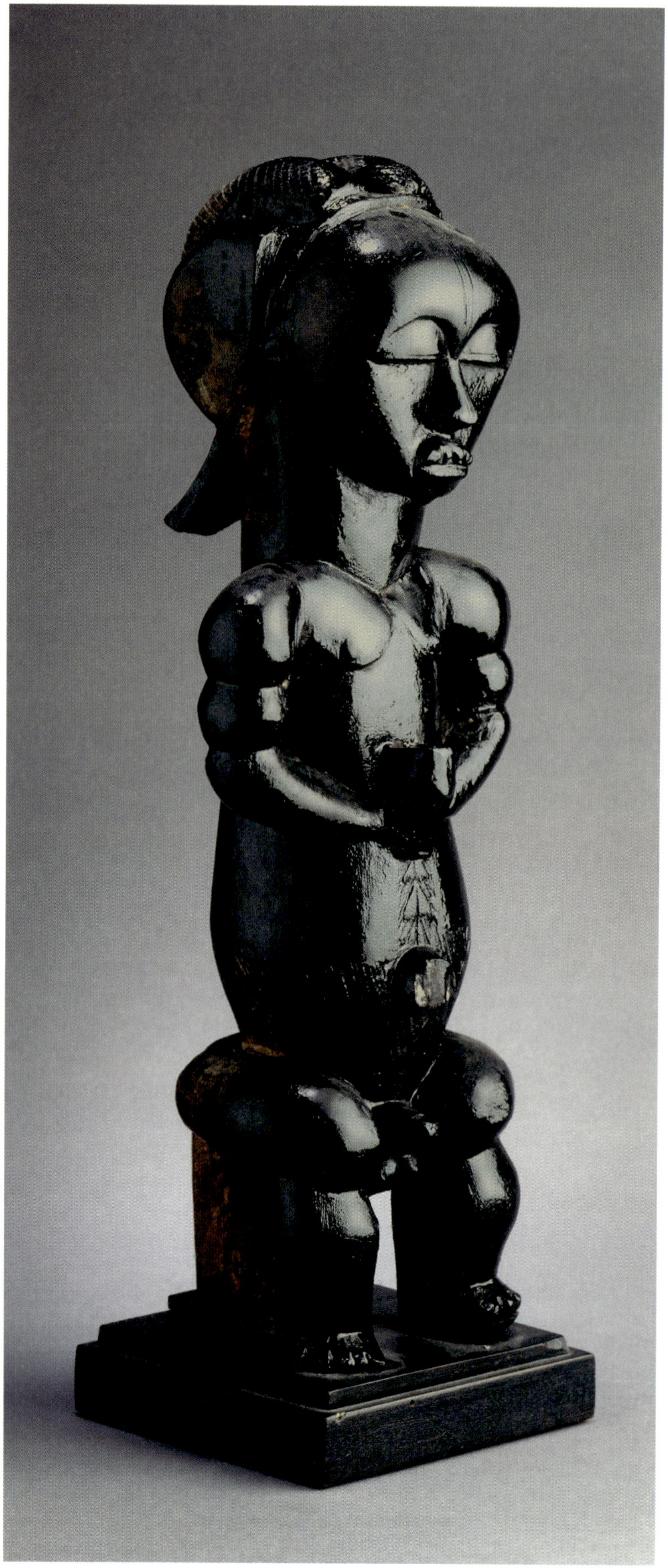

Figure of the Eyima Byeri Reliquary
Fang, Gabon,
wood, 61.8 x 14.2 x 14.7 cm.
Paris, Musée du quai Branly
(cat. **41**)

Statue of Byeri Reliquary
Fang, Gabon,
wood, 38 x 13 x 10 cm.
Marseilles, Musée d'Arts Africains,
Océaniens, Amérindies
(cat. **43**)

Figure of the Eyima Byeri Reliquary
Fang, Gabon,
wood, 59 x 17 x 15 cm.
Marseilles, Musée d'Arts Africains,
Océaniens, Amérindies
(cat. **44**)

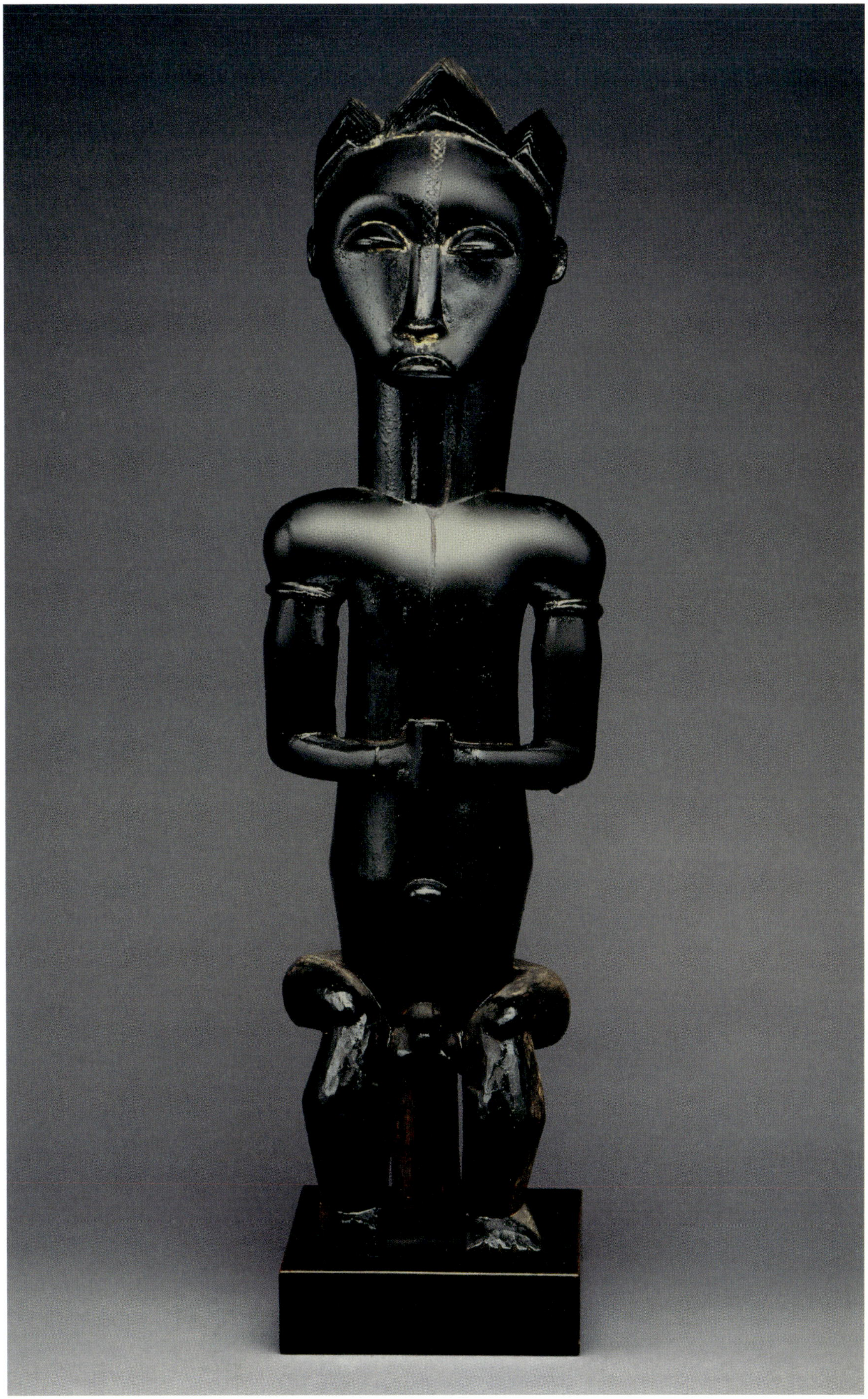

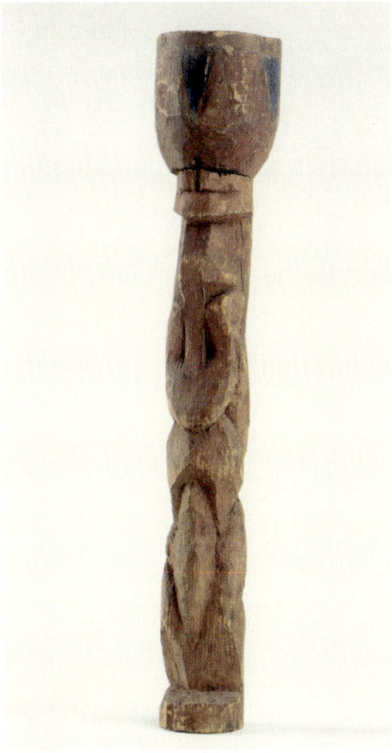

7.5. Pablo Picasso
Standing Figure, 1907.
Paris, Musée Picasso

Figure of the Guardian of Skulls
Ngumba, Cameroon, 1894
wood, h. 72 cm.
Berlin, Ethnologisches Museum
(cat. **42**)

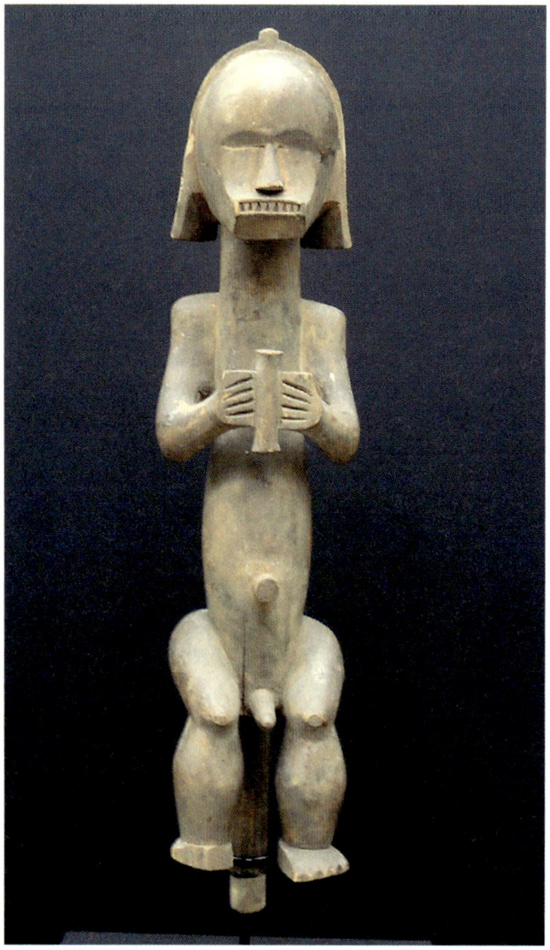

sensual evidence of a coloured woman; the spherical cup of the breasts grafted on to the neck suggests an erotic element of disturbing reversibility. Beneath the voluminous wooden diaphragm, the figure of Adam appears as the essence of the motifs that Brancusi had already studied with his *Caryatid* in 1914, at the same time as Modigliani's versions on the same theme. Adam's torso has the symmetric decorative motif of the rhomboidal overlapped volumes, initially intended in stone for some versions of the Maiastra and completed in *The Endless Column*, the neck is a cylinder with grooved horizontal cuts, a direct quotation of African anthropomorphic statues; the head seems to be bent beneath the weight it has to carry.

Henri-Pierre Roché who was the first owner of this work, called it *Adambase* to underline the double and ambiguous nature of the base. Instead Brancusi explained his work with these words: "Eve is above because it is her task to perpetuate life. She is enchanting and innocent. She represents fertility, a bud that is opening up, a flower which bears fruit. Adam, underneath, works the earth, he toils and sweats."

The theme of the group of figures finds here an almost definitive resolution which is of spectacular impact, beyond which there can only be the re-launching of Surrealist Primitivism, of Polimateric experimentation, with the works of Giacometti, Arp and Moore; the new and completely modern course of sculpture in the twentieth century.

Alessandro Del Puppo

Constantin Brancusi
Adam and Eve, 1921
chestnut and oak wood,
238.8 x 47.6 x 46.4 cm.
New York, Solomon R. Guggenheim Museum
(cat. **45**)

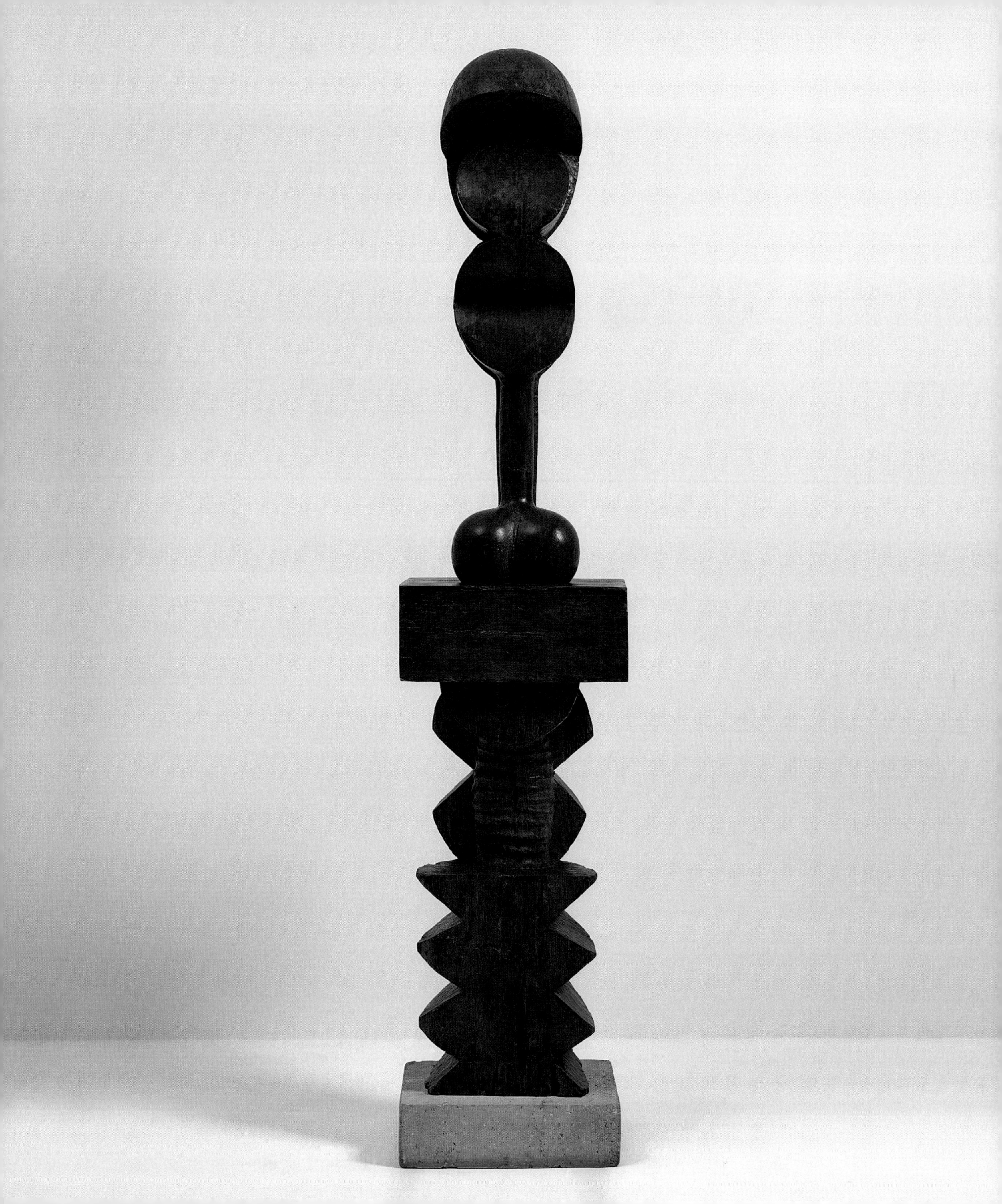

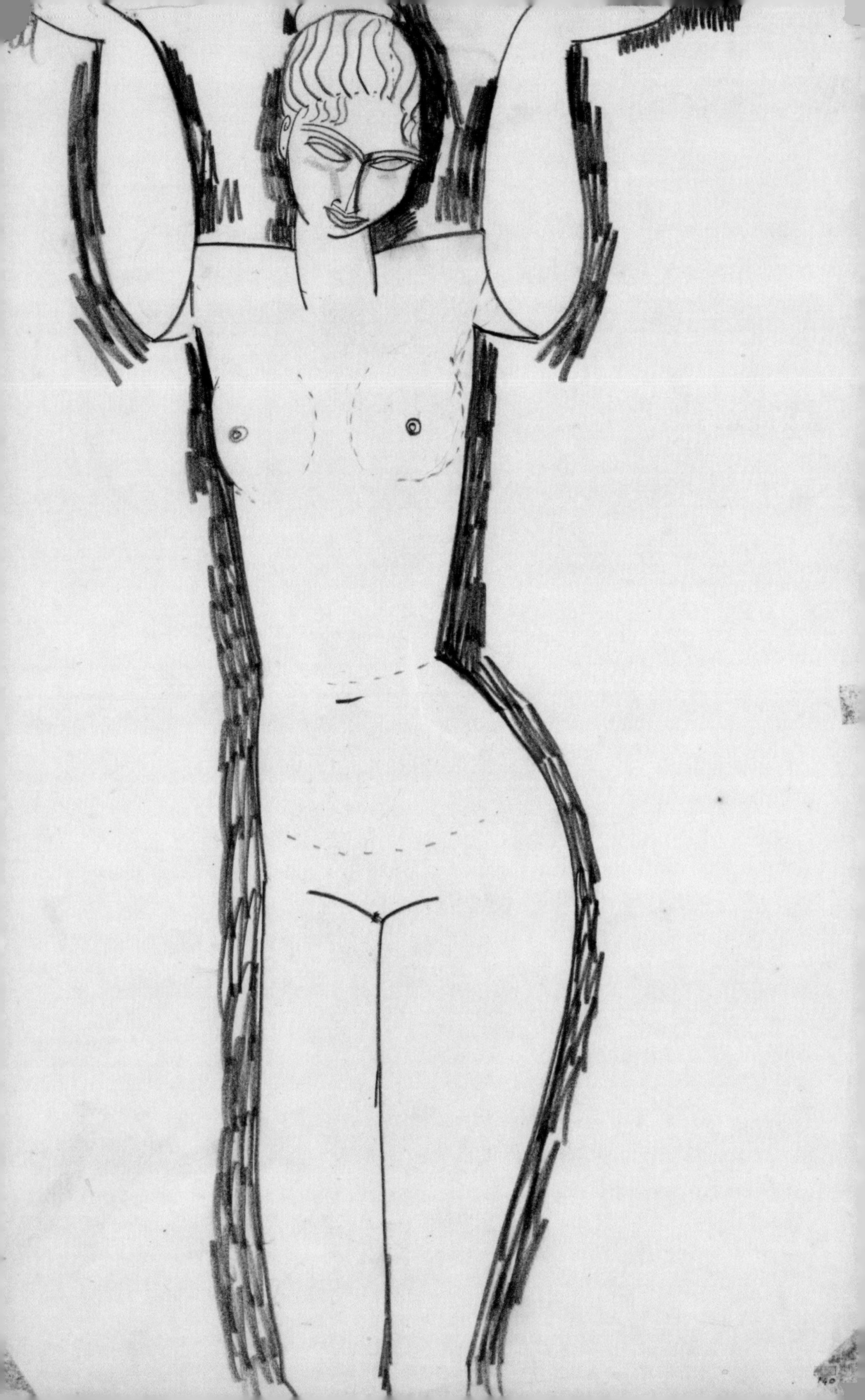
140

Section 8

From Standing Figures to Caryatids

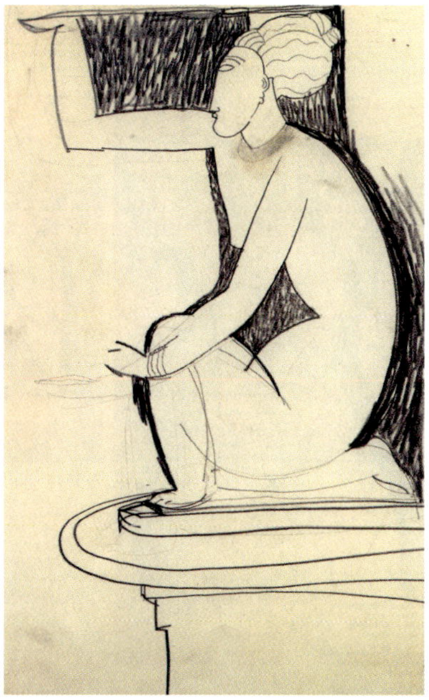

8.1. Amedeo Modigliani
Caryatid Kneeling on Shelf Base
[1911-1912], pencil on paper.
Private collection

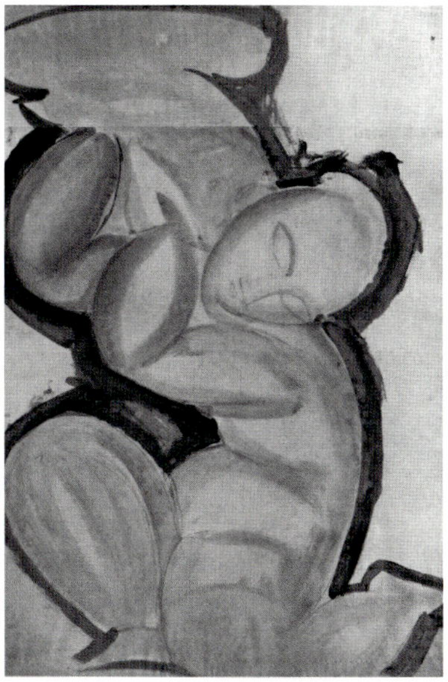

8.2. Amedeo Modigliani
Kneeling Caryatid, 12th September 1914, pencil and watercolour on paper.
Private collection

Amedeo Modigliani
Caryatid, 1910-1911
pencil on paper, 43 x 26 cm.
Private collection
(cat. **47**)

The graphic studies carried out by Modigliani that can be linked to the two sculptural *Caryatids* that are known today (XI and XXV) cover a stylistic and typological period of time that is much longer than that of the drawings of heads. Modigliani drew simple standing figures (cats. **46, 48**), seen from the front or in profile, both with or without a trabeation supported by their arms (cat. **47**); either kneeling or sitting (cats. **49-56**), sometimes connected to the architectonical container for which they were foreseen (fig. **8.1**); at other times, represented while carrying out a gesture of torsion (cats. **58-59**), even lifting a vase: in the latter the meaning itself of the caryatid as a figure that statically makes an effort and is compressed by the weight of the architecture is completely cancelled out. There are drawings where the figure is only outlined in pencil, others roughly shaded and others again which are cleverly carried out in watercolour. Furthermore their chronological extension is, as far as it is possible to reconstruct at this point in the research, longer than that of the heads: the date "2 juillet 911" can be read on a sheet which belonged to Paul Alexandre (Alexandre 1993, No. 44) while one of the caryatids with the typical sickle shaped curved limbs (Ceroni 1965, No. 121: fig. **8.2**) is dated and dedicated by Modigliani to "my friend Coria" 12th September 1914.

A first approximate division can be made between the preparatory drawings for the *Caryatid* sculpture, in Canberra today (XI), which study a standing figure and those that study a sitting Caryatid, today at the Museum of Modern Art in New York (XXV). Even though, while Modigliani was alive, the two sculptures were never exhibited and we have no certain elements to ascertain a date, no doubt should remain concerning their sequence (and therefore that of their relative preparatory drawings). Paul Alexandre said that Modigliani left him a large selection of graphic studies on sculptures before leaving for Italy in April 1913; if in this selection there is not the presence of the sitting caryatids that can be stylistically referred to *Head* XXV, the studies for this should, rationally, be collocated after Modigliani's return to Paris, in June 1913.

However, this first division does not solve the problem concerning the significance that all these drawings had. Differently from the drawings of heads, their nature as preparatory studies for sculptures cannot always be documented. For example, in the sequence presented in this exhibition, a standing figure without any determination of sex can take on the aspcct of a graceless Primitivist puppet (cat. **46**); or a kneeling female figure can be profiled with a graceful, calligraphic rotation of the bust (cats. **50**, **52**); or in the last watercolours, the forms are compacted so much up to the point of seeming like a kind of column (cats. **61-62**).

The most important gap is not that which separates the series of kneeling figures from the standing ones, as much as that, which over time, modifies the plastic reasoning implied by the representation of the body of the caryatid. If we take a *Kneeling Caryatid* like the one exhibited here (cat. **55**) given by Modigliani to Jacob Epstein, and the watercolour one which is at the Tate today (cat. **59**), the crucial transition does not

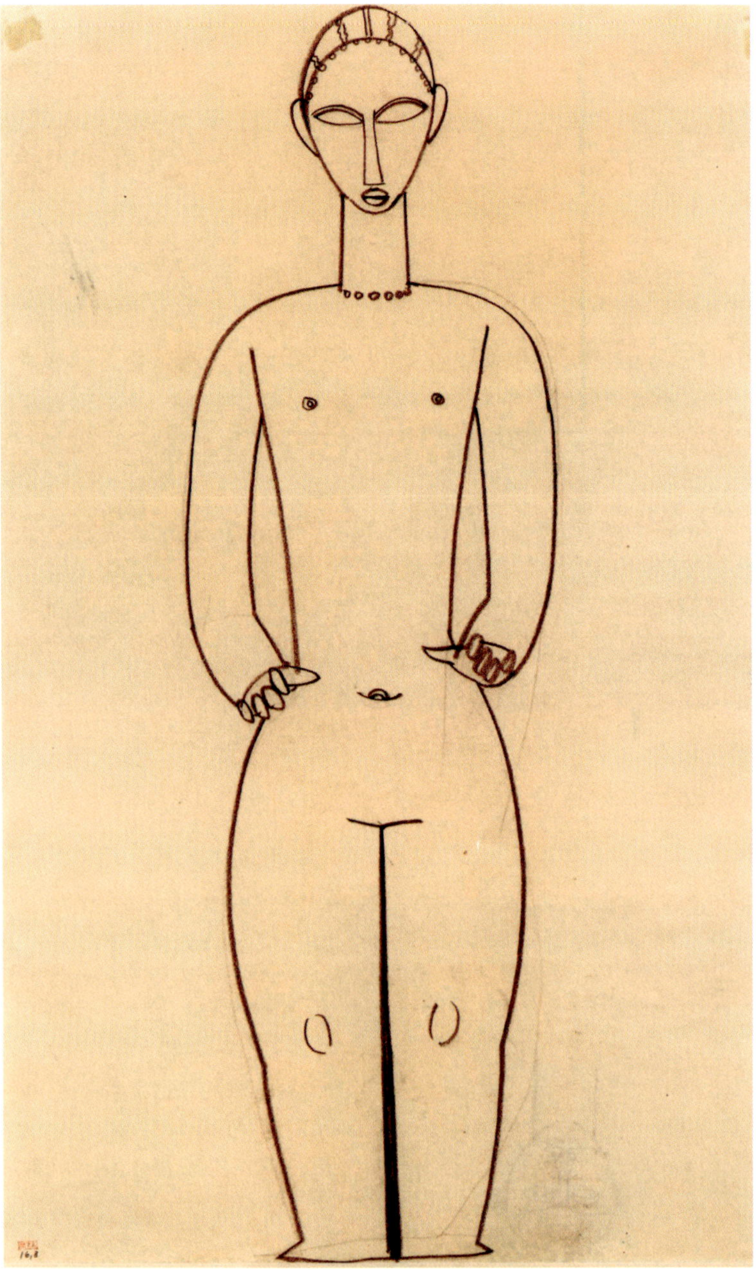

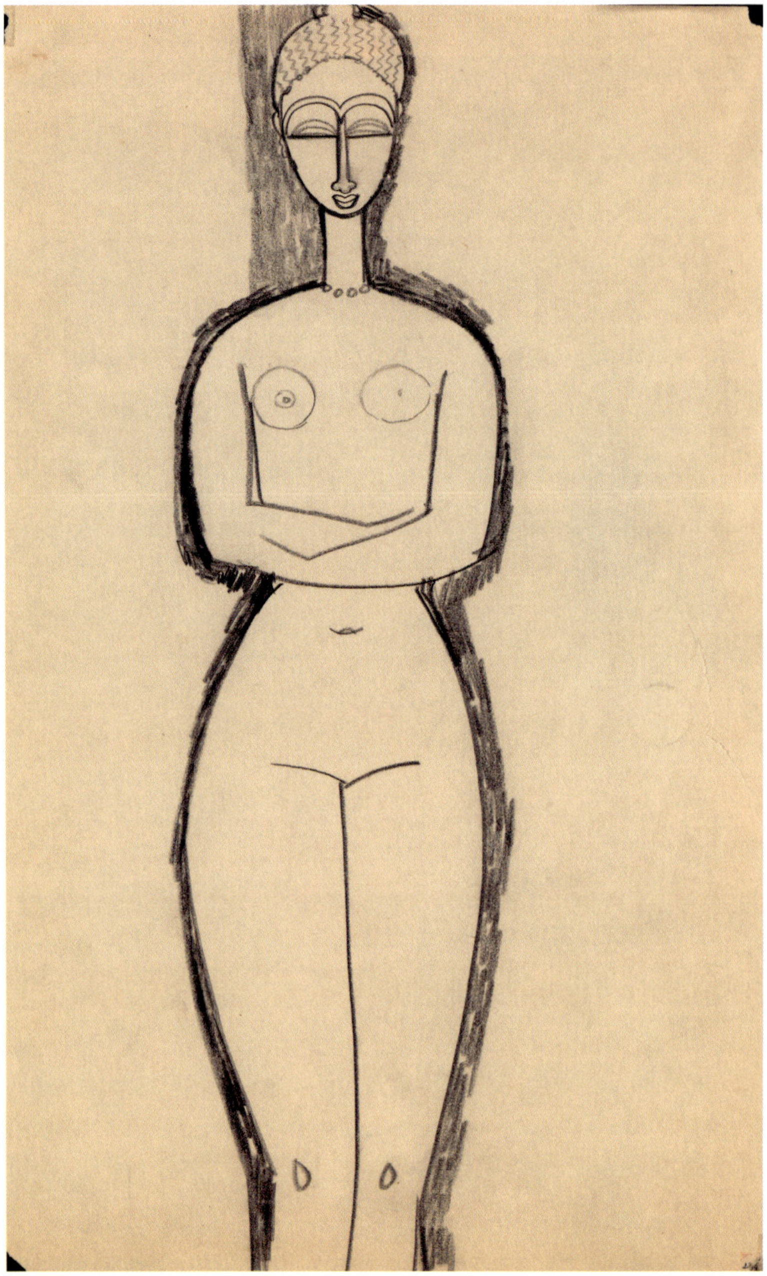

Amedeo Modigliani
Hermaphrodite, 1910-1911,
pencil on paper, 43 x 26.7 cm.
Milan, private collection,
courtesy Giulio Tega,
(cat. **46**)

Amedeo Modigliani
Standing Nude Woman, 1910-1911,
pencil on paper, 43 x 26.5 cm.
Private collection
(cat. **48**)

concern the posture. From the identification of a precise and simple linear scheme into which the figure is forced there is the passage to the drawing in the Tate, to the accentuation of the torsional gesture: Modigliani's aim was to compose the body as if it were a harmonious whole with rounded or tapered volumes: he emphasised the purely decorative values of the arabesque, going beyond the plastic logic of *Caryatid* XXV. It is very likely that, having realised this sculpture, Modigliani wanted to continue a series of graphic research that would increase the effect of elegant volumetric abstraction, and at the same time, would bring back some sensuality to the female nude. In the final results Modigliani reached those extraordinary large sheets on which he profiled the female figure (reduced to a superimposed light shape only outlined, just hinted at) against the watercolour background, in a way that knows no comparison except for Rodin's last watercolour drawings.
Modigliani's contemporaries soon realised the exceptionality of Modigliani's graphic caryatids, starting with the design of XXV. Discussing the subject of a line as a means

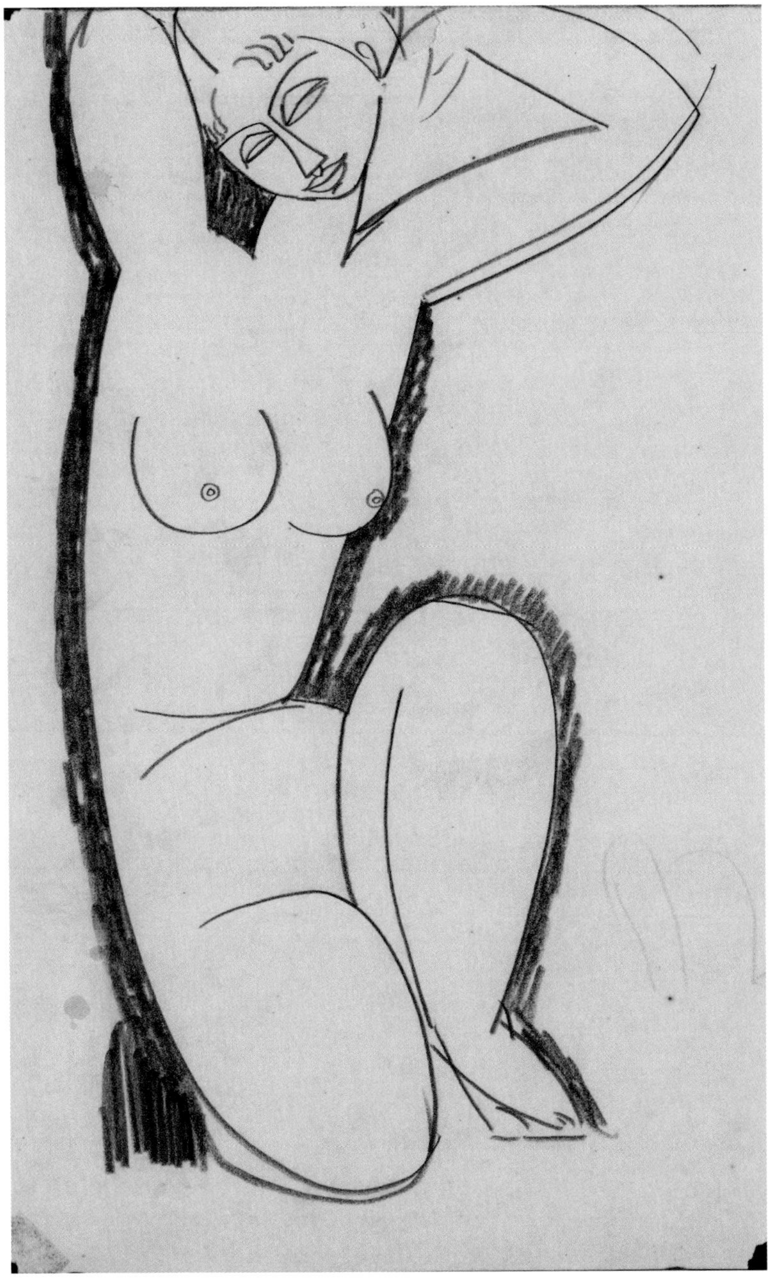

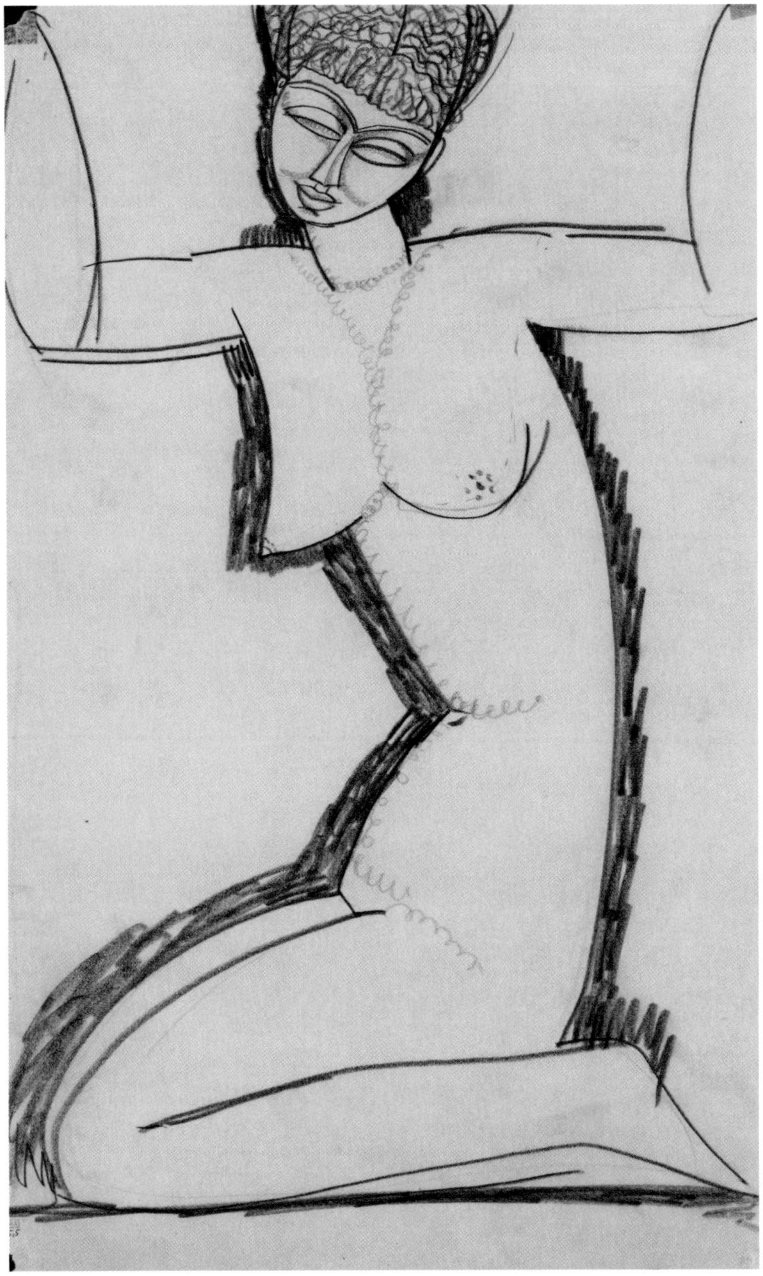

Amedeo Modigliani
Kneeling Caryatid, 1910-1911,
pencil on paper, 42.5 x 26.5 cm.
Private collection
(cat. **51**)

Amedeo Modigliani
Kneeling Caryatid, 1910-1911,
pencil on paper, 43 x 26.5 cm.
Private collection
(cat. **50**)

of modern artistic expression, in an article dated 1919, Roger Fry reproduced one of these caryatids (this has now been lost), fig.**8.3**, as an example of the process, typical to sculptors, of reducing the variety of the forms represented to their common denominator. However, if it was true that "His [Modigliani's] notion of plasticity appears here as uniform and unvaried" and "its effect is got by the arrangement of a number of essentially similar units," the play did not seem to him too cold and intellectual: "The beautiful variety and play of his surfaces is one of the remarkable things about Modigliani's art, and shows that his sculptor's sense of formal unity is crossed with a painter's feelings for surfaces" (Fry 1919, p. 69).
If Modigliani's drawings with caryatids as the subject, carried out from 1911 to 1914 (and perhaps later) are lined up next to one another, it is impressive to observe the range of stylistic references that accompany his work. In this process of assimilation, that I have tried to reconstruct in my introductory essay, Modigliani effectively mastered the language of sculptural modernity. He started off from the Liberty style

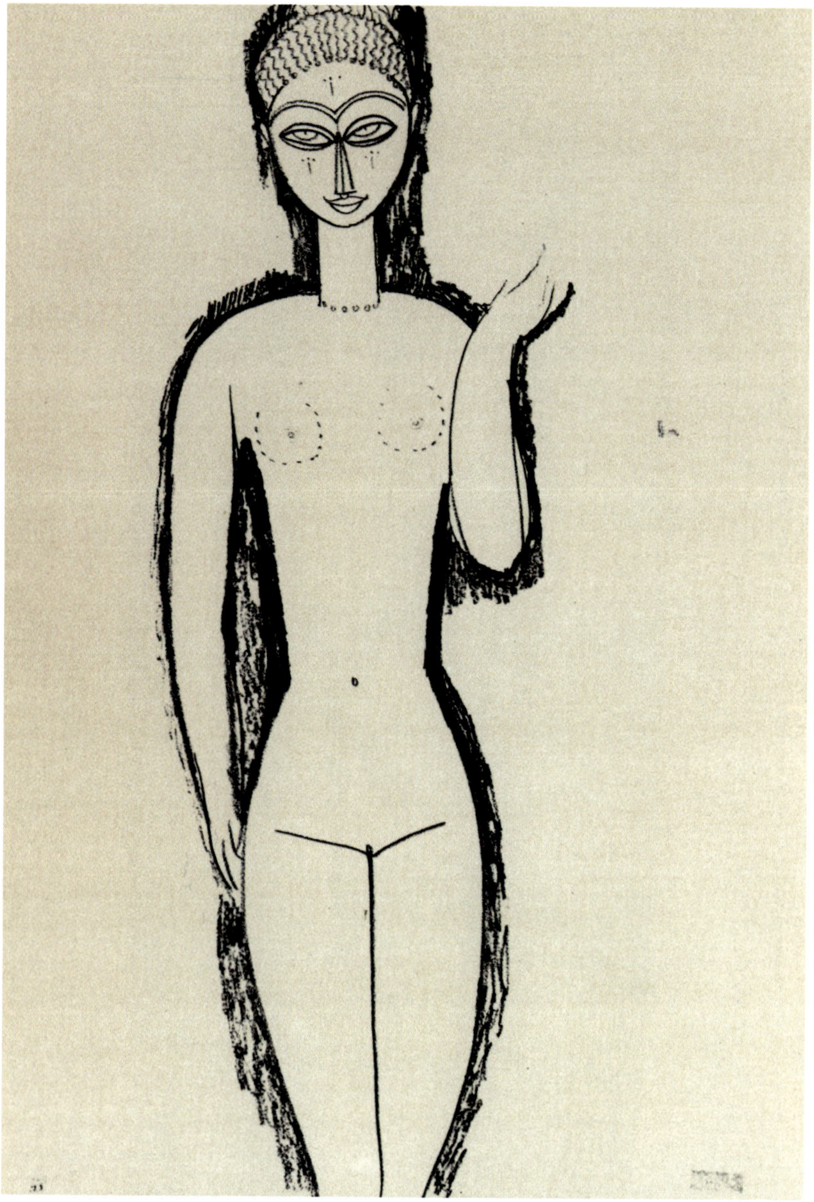

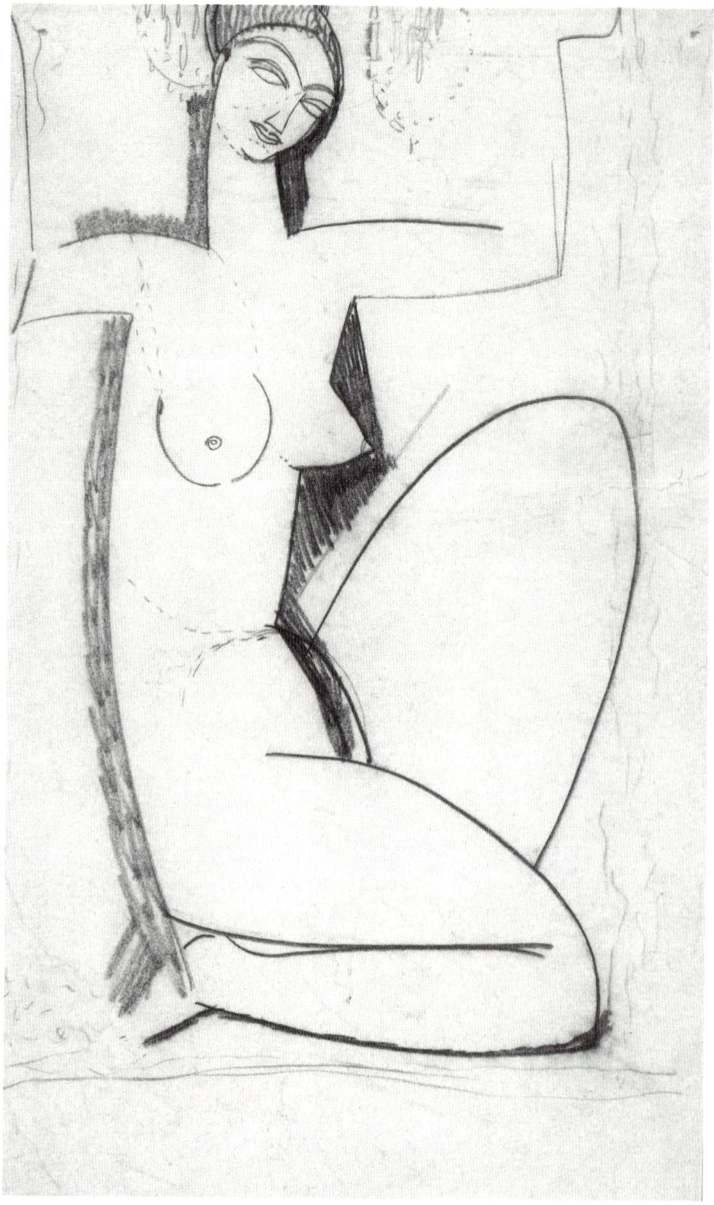

Amedeo Modigliani
Standing Nude, 1910-1911,
pencil and charcoal on paper,
43 x 26 cm.
Private collection

Amedeo Modigliani
Caryatid, 1913,
pencil on paper, 39.7 x 25.7 cm.
Dijon, Musée des Beaux-Arts
de Dijon
(cat. **52**)

elegance of his first studies, originating from poses taken up by his mistress, Anna Achmatova; then he found, without too many contradictions, a support in the Egyptian sculptures in the Louvre when he began studying the Canberra *Caryatid*: he grafted Primitivism onto this stylisation (with the decisive mediation of Picasso), Orientalism and even rhythms deriving from the most essential of Maillol's sculptures. The sinuous curved line of the first graphic caryatids that developed starting with *Caryatid* XXV seems to dialogue with that of Boccioni's drawings presented at the Galerie de la Boëtie during the summer of 1913; while the pose, and extreme caryatid watercolour plastic character, reduced to pure and abstract volumes, would seem to be a reaction to the problems raised by Constantin Brancusi's *Princesse X* (fig. **8.4**, which, however, is from 1915 and I believe opens up a question for the dating of these Modigliani drawings).
In the present stage of studies the question of the contemporaneity between the last graphic caryatids and the pictorial portraits of 1914 and 1915 remains unresolved, dominated by completely different formal problems. The real result of the long season of research regarding the theme of the kneelinging female figure in various phases

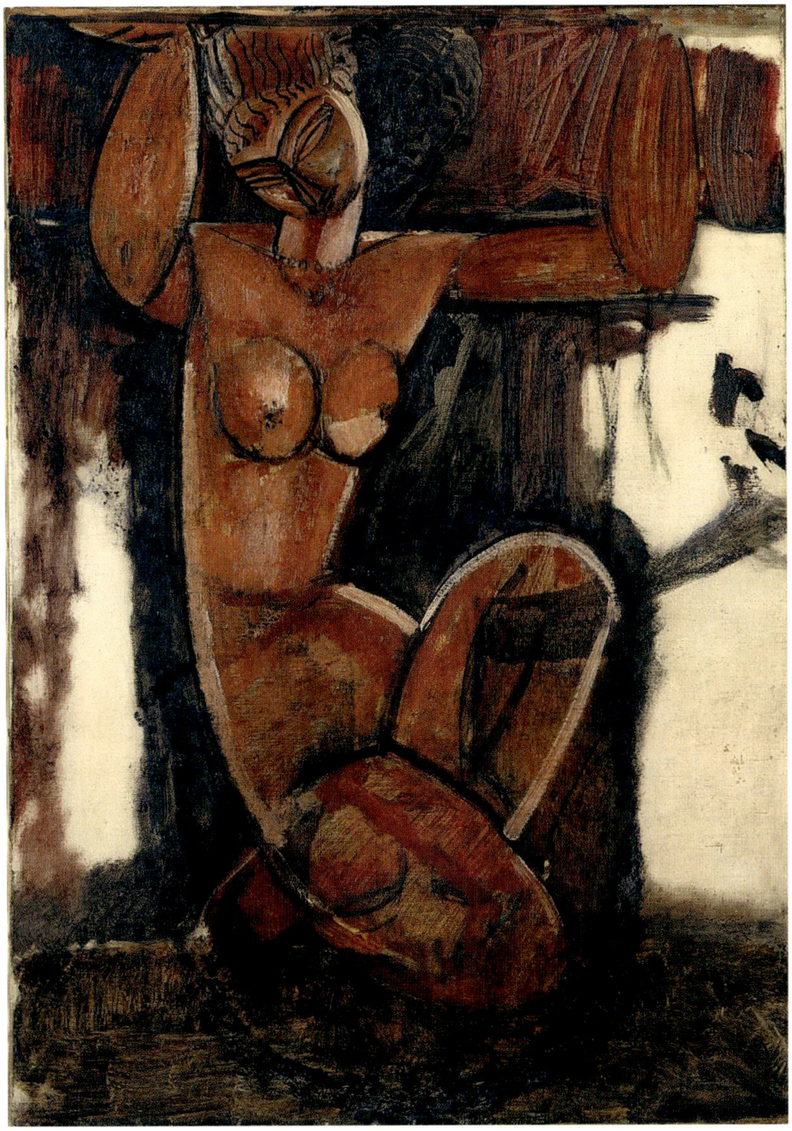

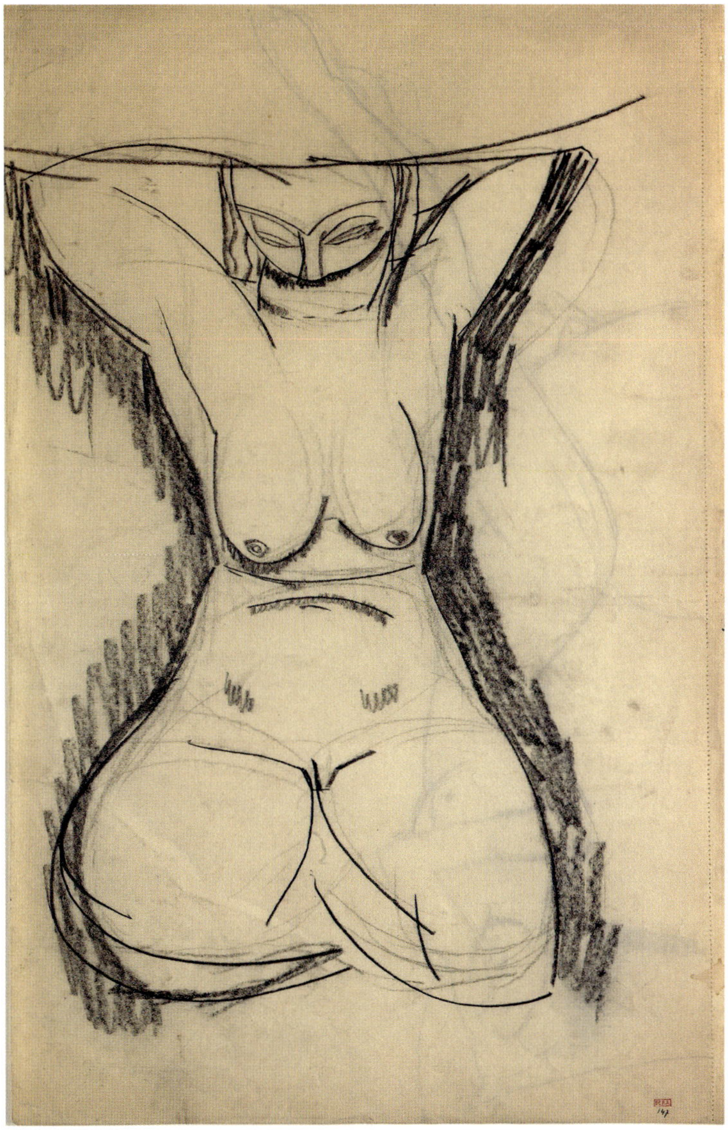

Amedeo Modigliani
Caryatid, 1911-1912 ca.,
oil on canvas, 72.9 x 50.1 cm,
Düsseldorf, Kunstsammlung
Nordrhein-Westfalen
(cat. **49**)

Amedeo Modigliani
Monumental Caryatid, kneeling, from the front, arms raised behind the head, bent forward,
black pencil on paper, 43.1 x 27.7 cm.
Rouen, Musée des Beaux-Arts,
donated by Blaise Alexandre, 2001
(cat. **54**)

was only achieved with the 1917 nudes: in the first monographic article dedicated to the artist, Francis Carco had already recalled this link between caryatids and nudes, singling out the crucial passage in Modigliani's abandoning of a drawing inspired by a sculptural thought, that was significant in a spatial sense: "Alors [that is, about 1913] qu'il traitait dans des roses et des noirs des figures tourmentées, son dessin supprimait peu à peu les lignes. Il suggérait. Il retenait dans une écriture châtiée, les éléments d'un style émouvant et noble" (Carco 1919, p. 206).

Flavio Fergonzi

Amedeo Modigliani
Kneeling Nude, 1910-1911
grease pencil on paper, 43 x 26.5 cm.
Private collection
(cat. **53**)

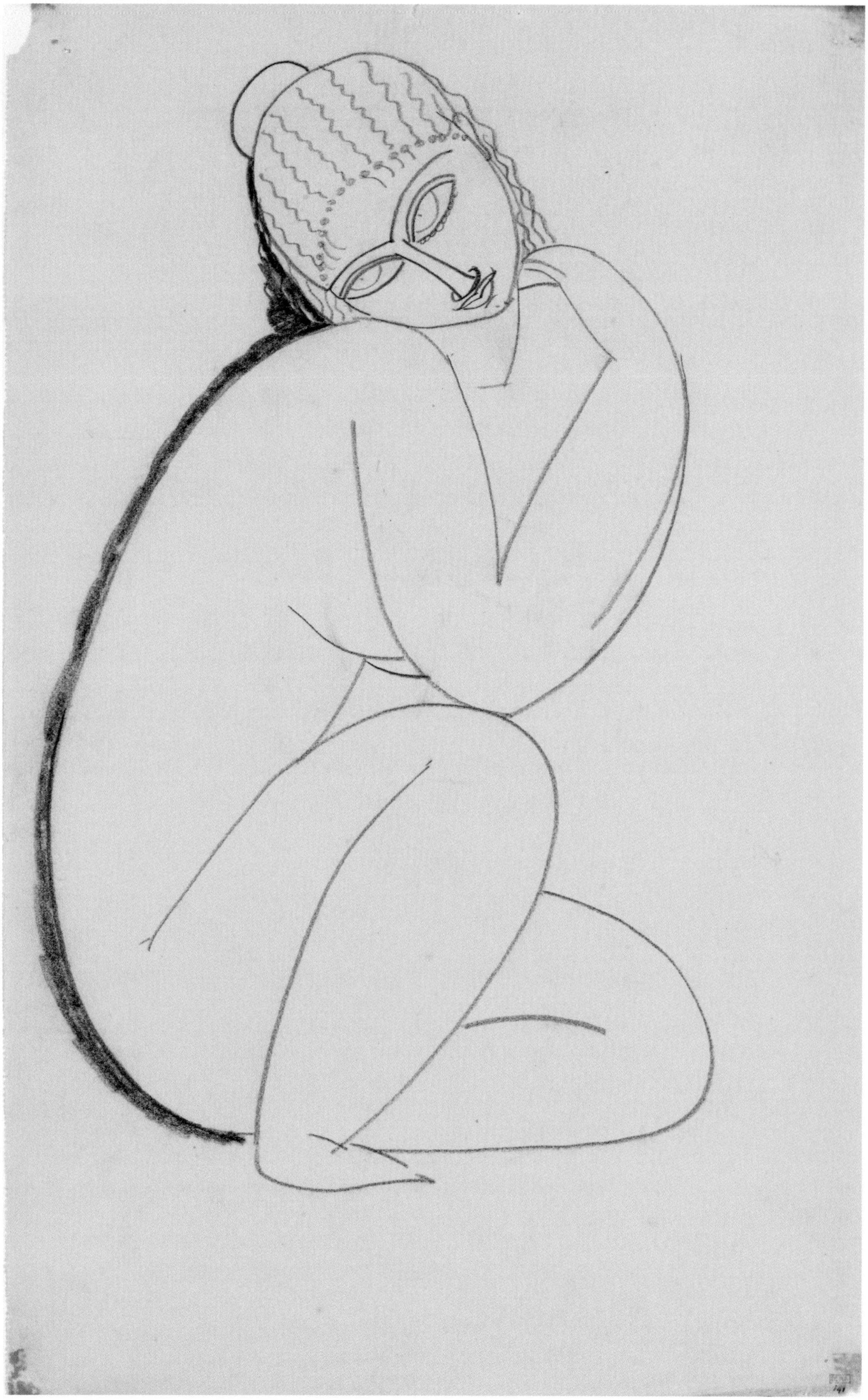

Amedeo Modigliani
Caryatid, 1913-1914,
pencil and chalk on paper,
55 x 41.5 cm.
Walsall, The New Art Gallery Walsall
(cat. **55**)

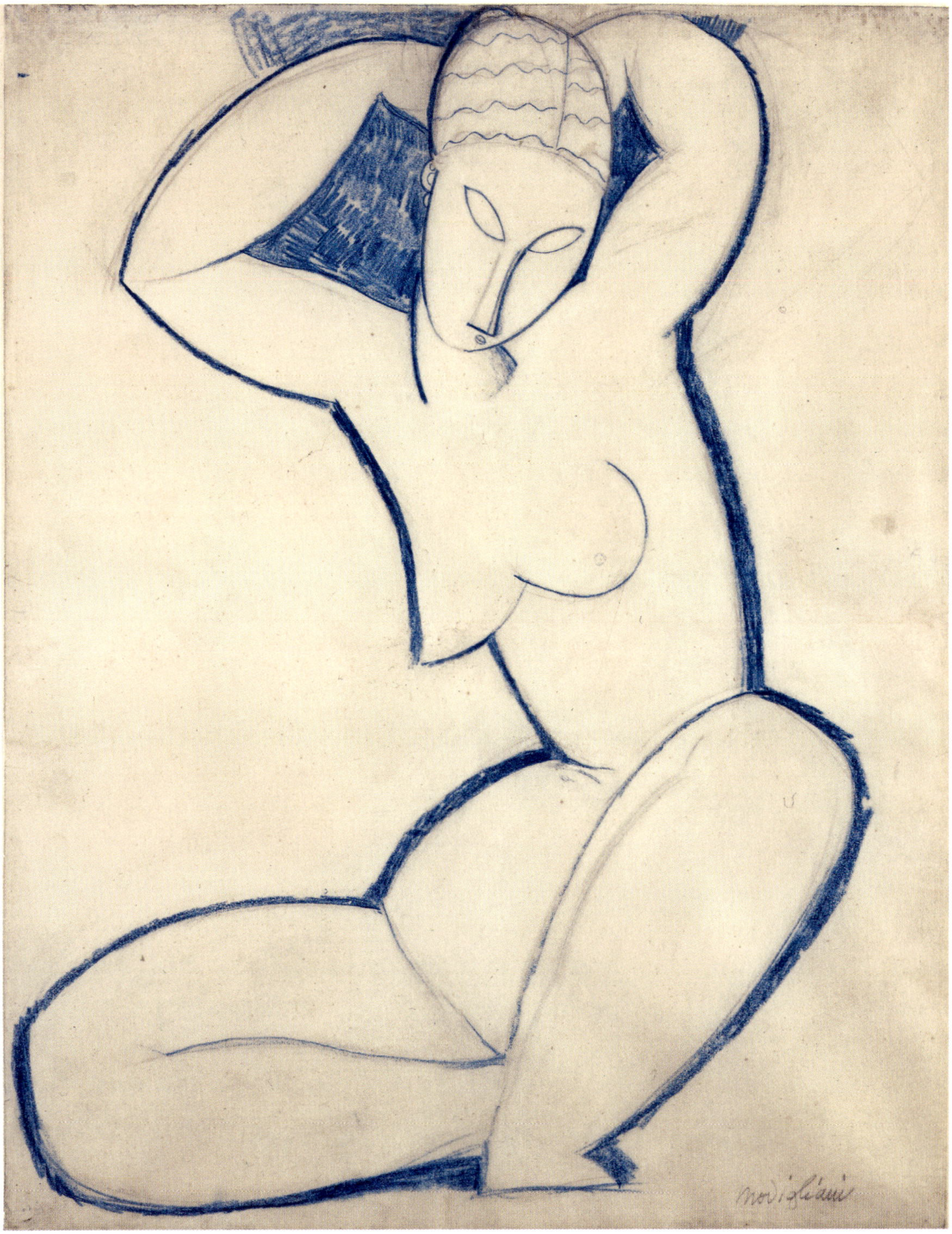

Amedeo Modigliani
Anadyomene, 1914
Graphite and carved lines with relief, on fine white woven paper,
33.9 x 26.5 cm.
Princeton, Princeton University Art Museum, legacy of Dan Fellows Platt
(cat. **56**)

Amedeo Modigliani
Figure, 1914,
drawing and watercolour on paper,
h. 34 cm.
Private collection, courtesy Amedeo Porro arte moderna e contemporanea, Milan
(cat. **57**)

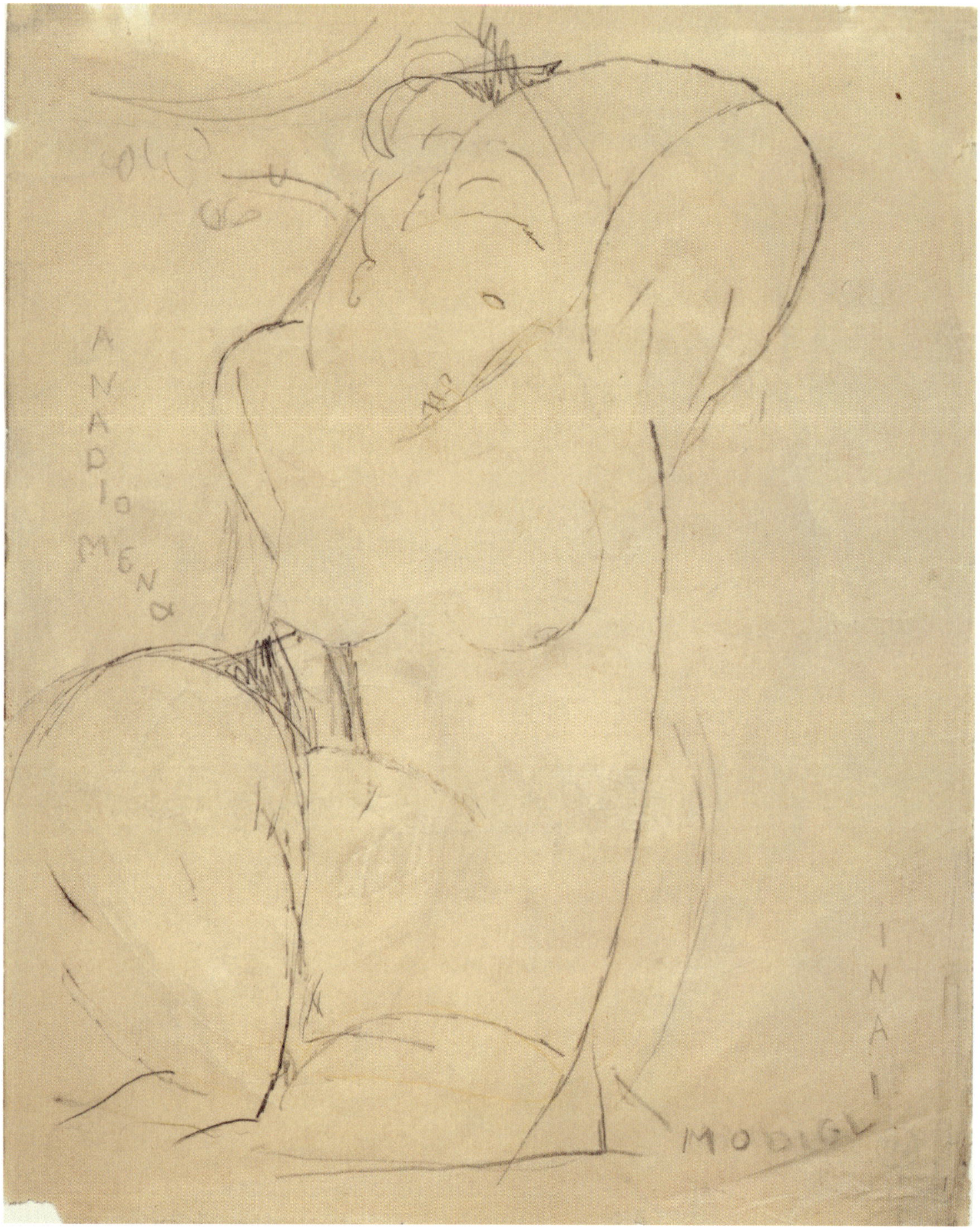

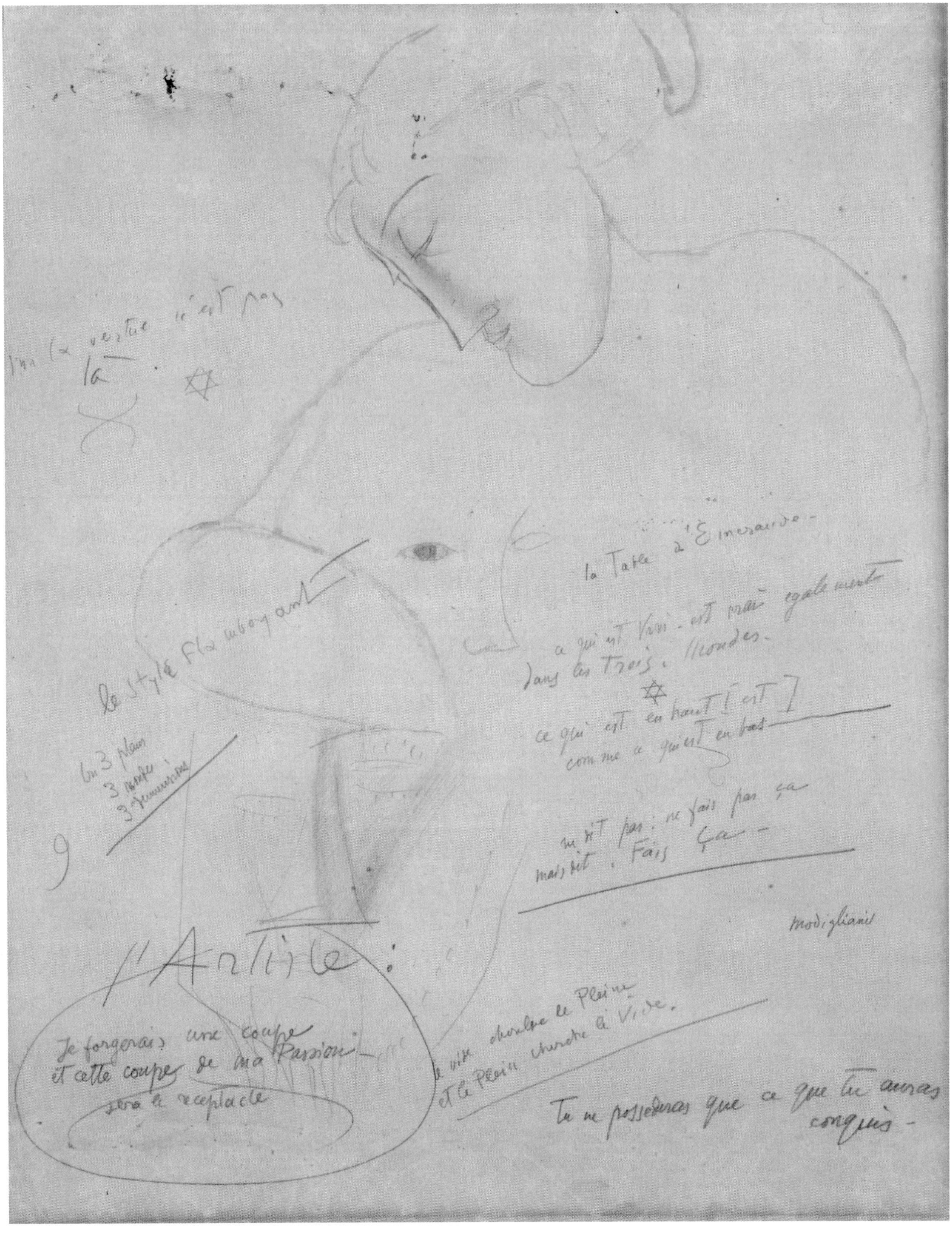
le style flamboyant
la Table d'Émeraude -
ce qui est Vrai - est vrai également dans les Trois. Mondes.
ce qui est en haut [est] comme ce qui est en bas
ne dit pas: ne fais pas ça mais dit. Fais ça -
modigliani
l'Artiste:
Je forgerais une coupe et cette coupe de ma Passion - sera le receptacle
le vide cherche le Plein et le Plein cherche le Vide.
Tu ne posséderas que ce que tu auras conquis -

Amedeo Modigliani
Cariatide, circa 1913
pencil and watercolour on paper,
55.9 x 45.1 cm.
France, private collection
(cat. **58**)

Amedeo Modigliani
Caryatid with Vase, 1914 ca.,
watercolour on paper,
63.3 x 48.1 cm.
London, Tate, legacy
of Mrs. A. F. Kessler, 1983
(cat. **59**)

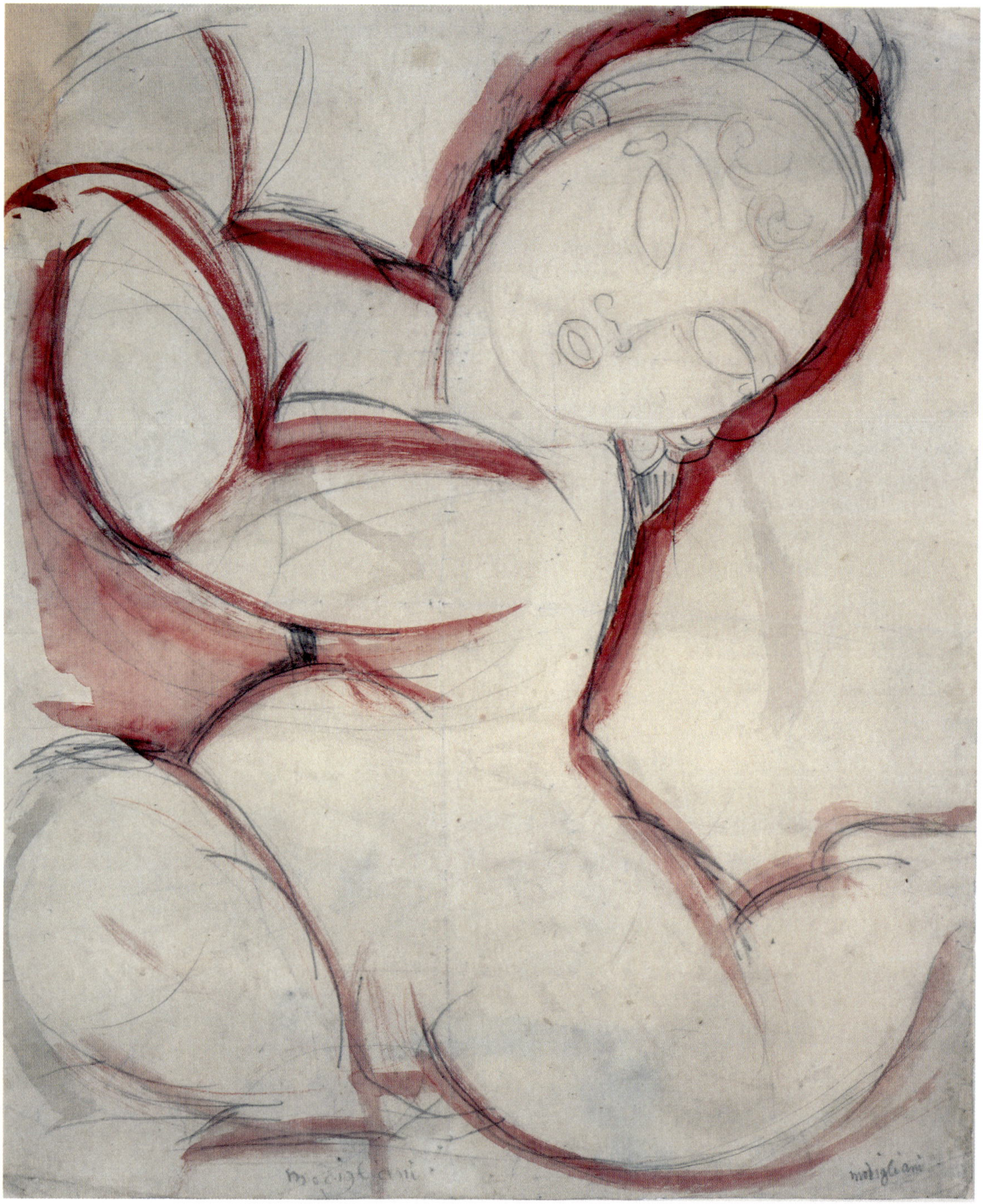

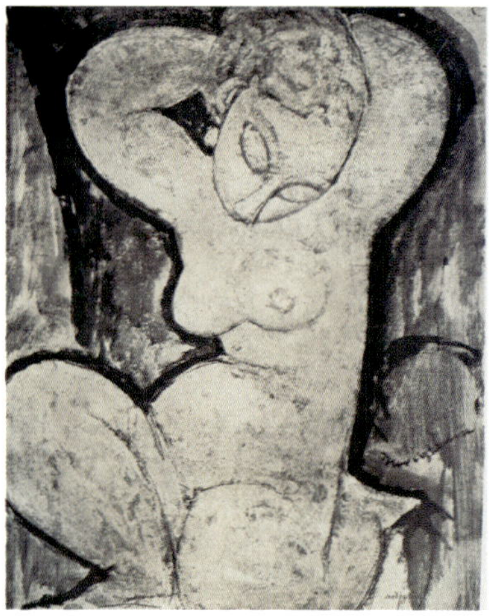

8.3. Amedeo Modigliani
Kneeling Caryatid [1913-14],
in *The Burlington Magazine*, London,
1919. This work has been lost

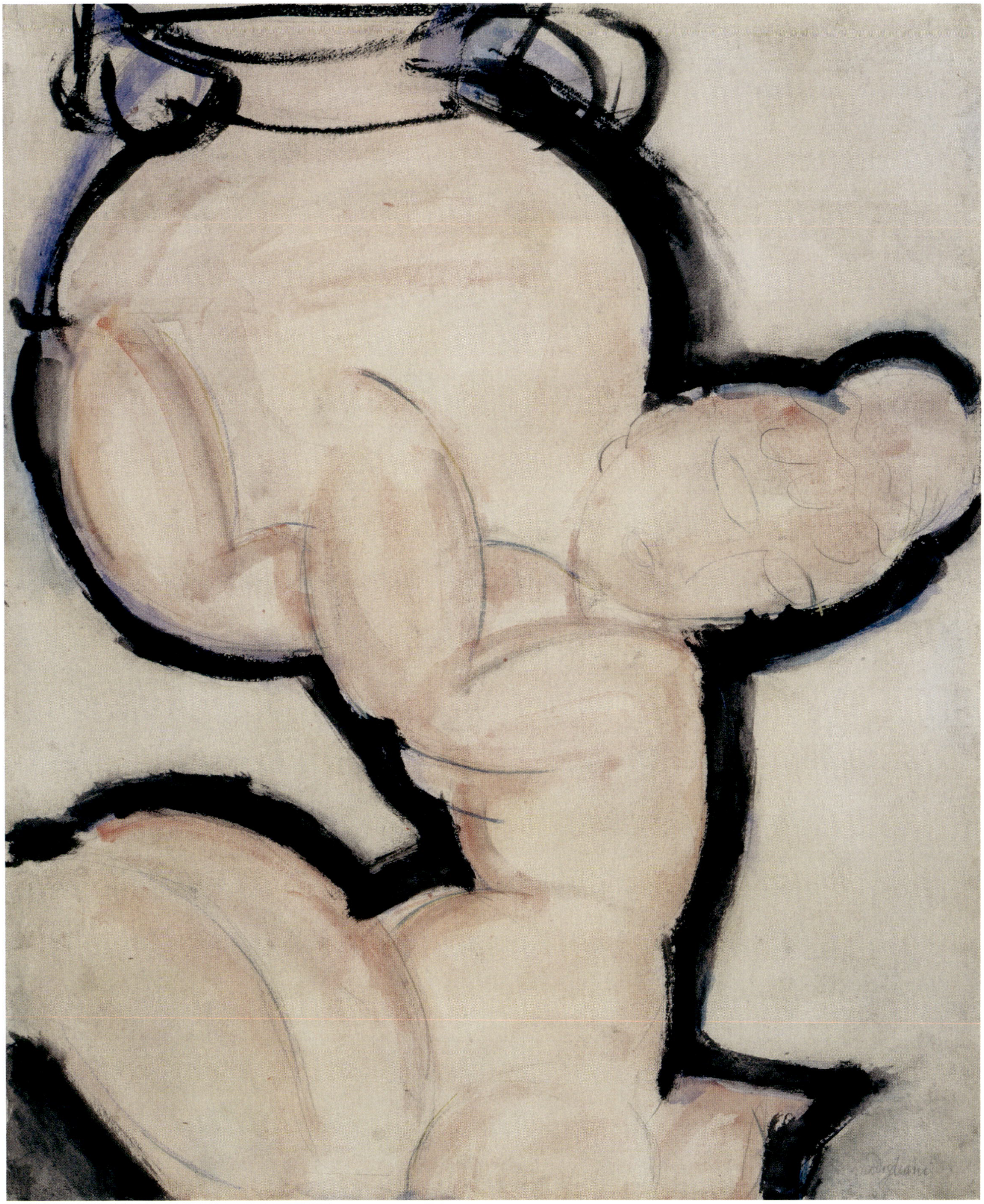

Amedeo Modigliani
Caryatid, 1915,
tempera on woven paper,
67 x 42 cm.
Private collection, courtesy Claudia Gian Ferrari Studio di Consulenza per il '900 Italiano, Milan
(cat. **61**)

Amedeo Modigliani
Caryatid, 1914,
tempera on card, 90 x 70 cm.
Private collection
(cat. **62**)

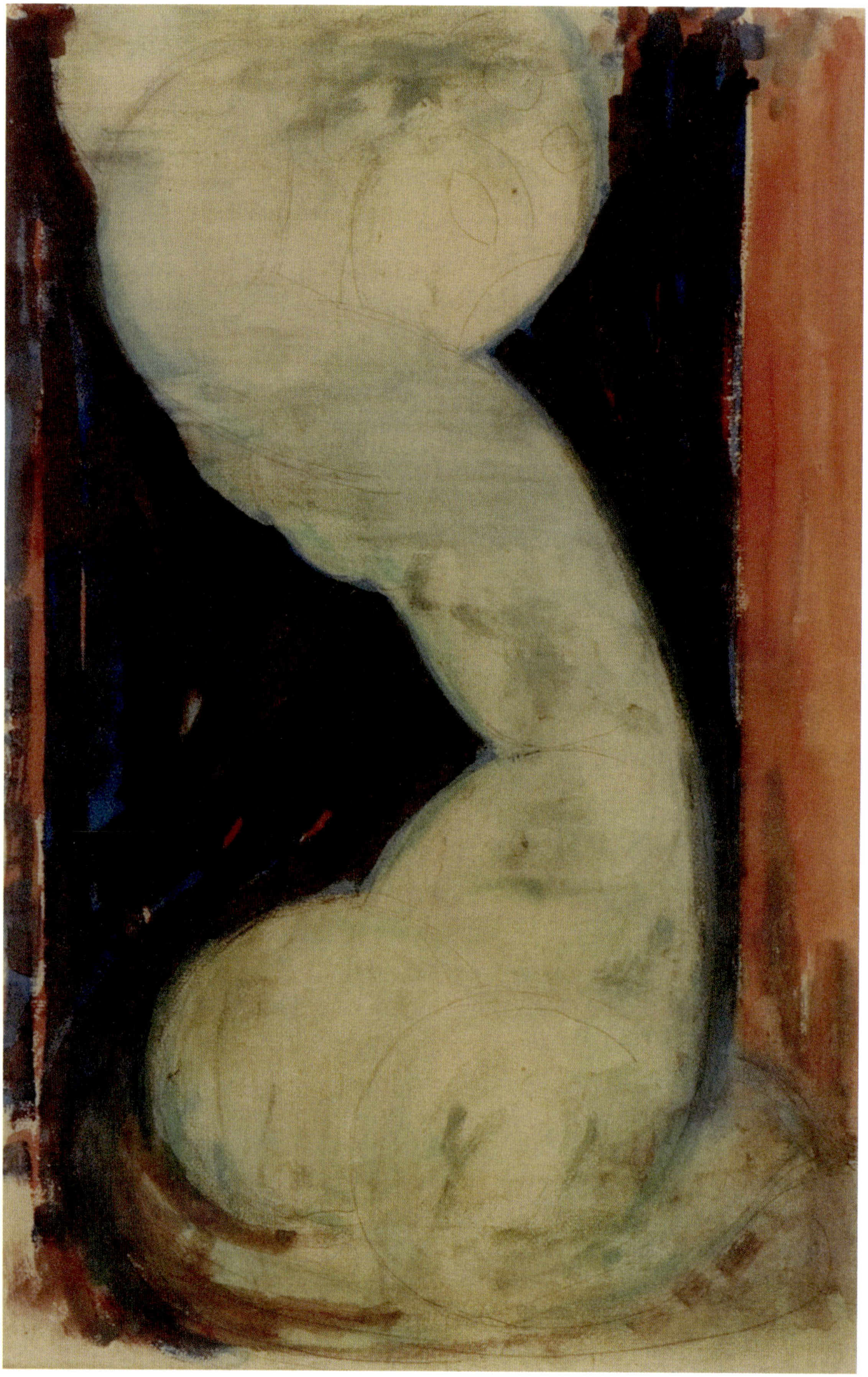

8.4. Constantin Brancusi
Princess X, 1915-1916, silver salt print.
Paris, Centre Georges Pompidou, Musée National d'art moderne

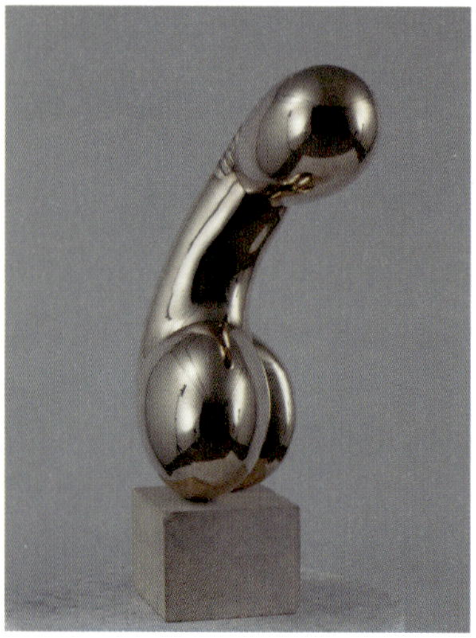

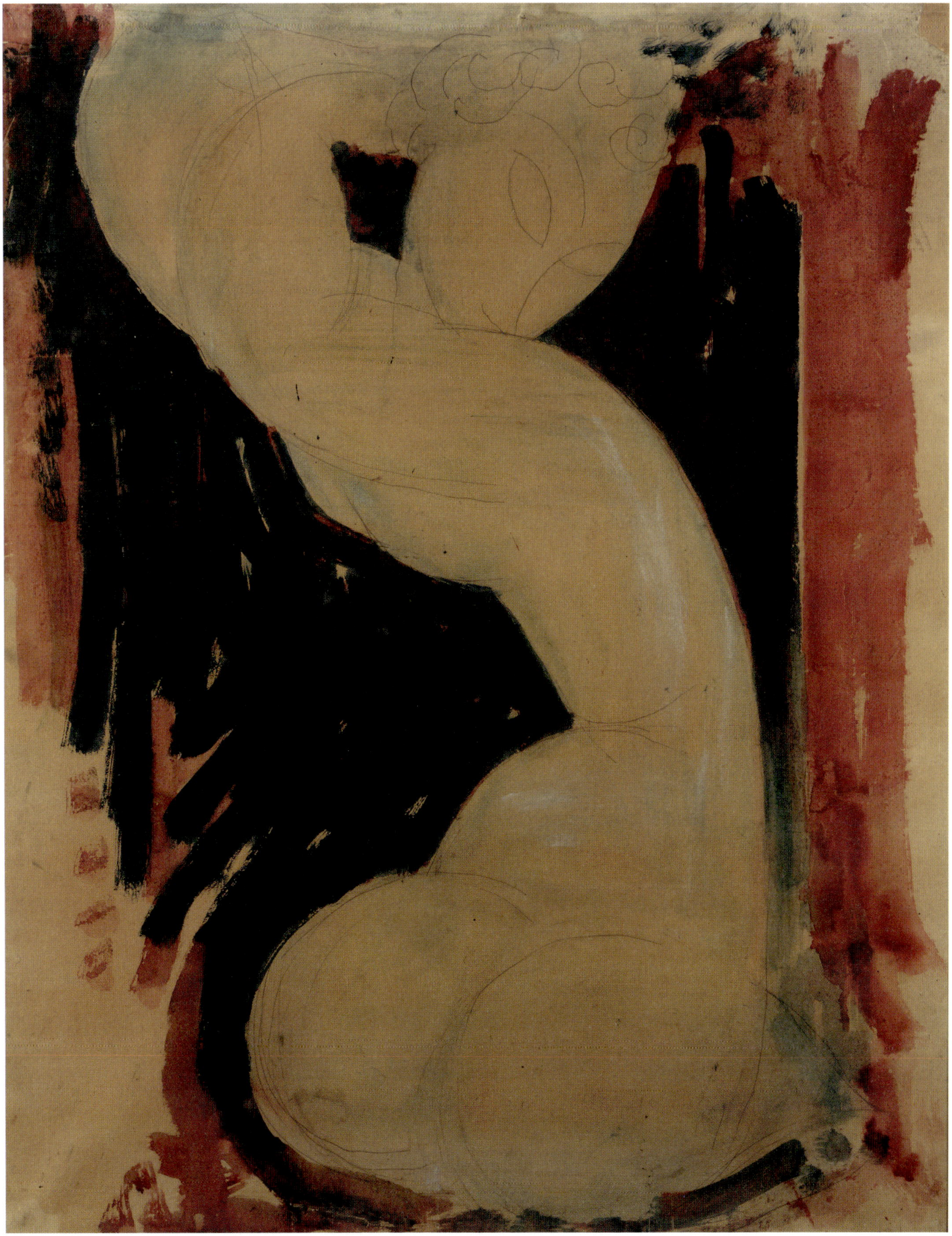

Amedeo Modigliani
Caryatid, 1914-1915,
tempera on woven paper, 49 x 32 cm.
Private collection, courtesy Claudia
Gian Ferrari Studio di Consulenza
per il '900 Italiano, Milan
(cat. **60**)

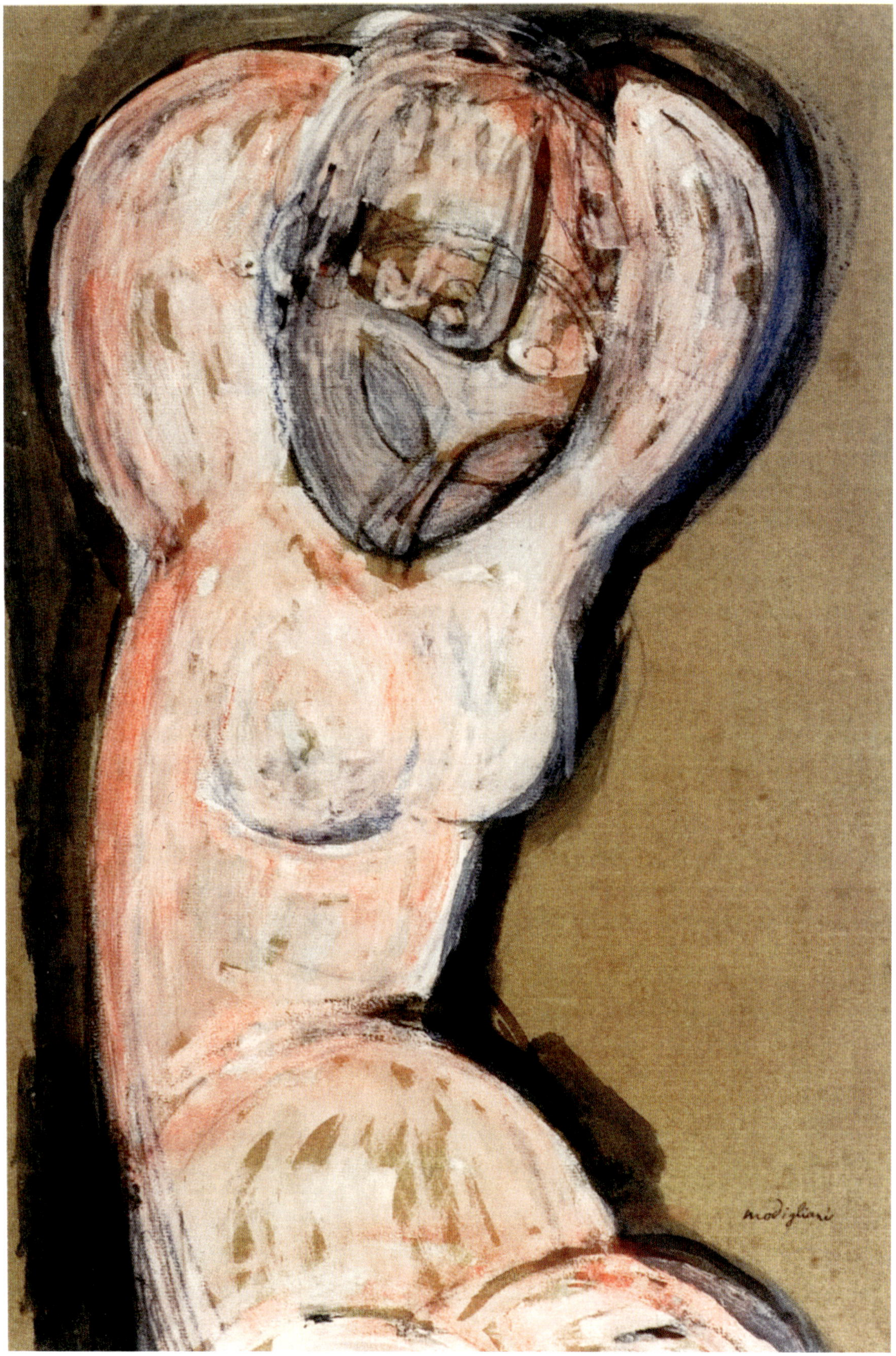

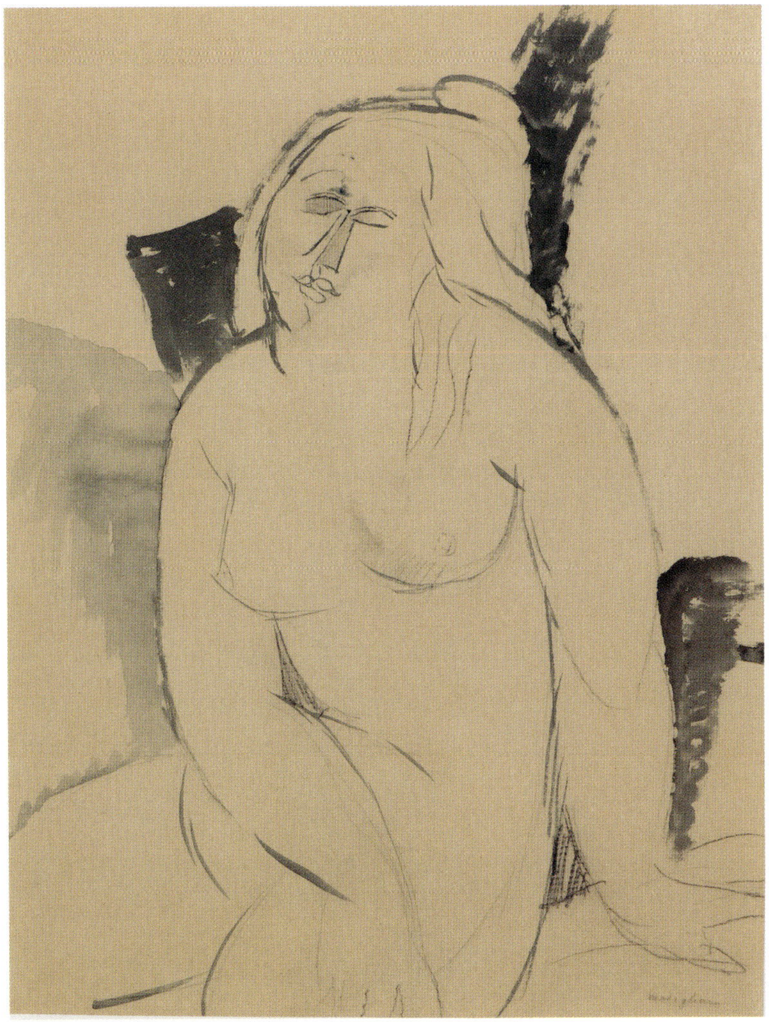

Amedeo Modigliani
Female Nude,
watercolour and pencil on paper,
54.5 x 42 cm.
Private collection,
courtesy Galleria Tega, Milan
(cat. **63**)

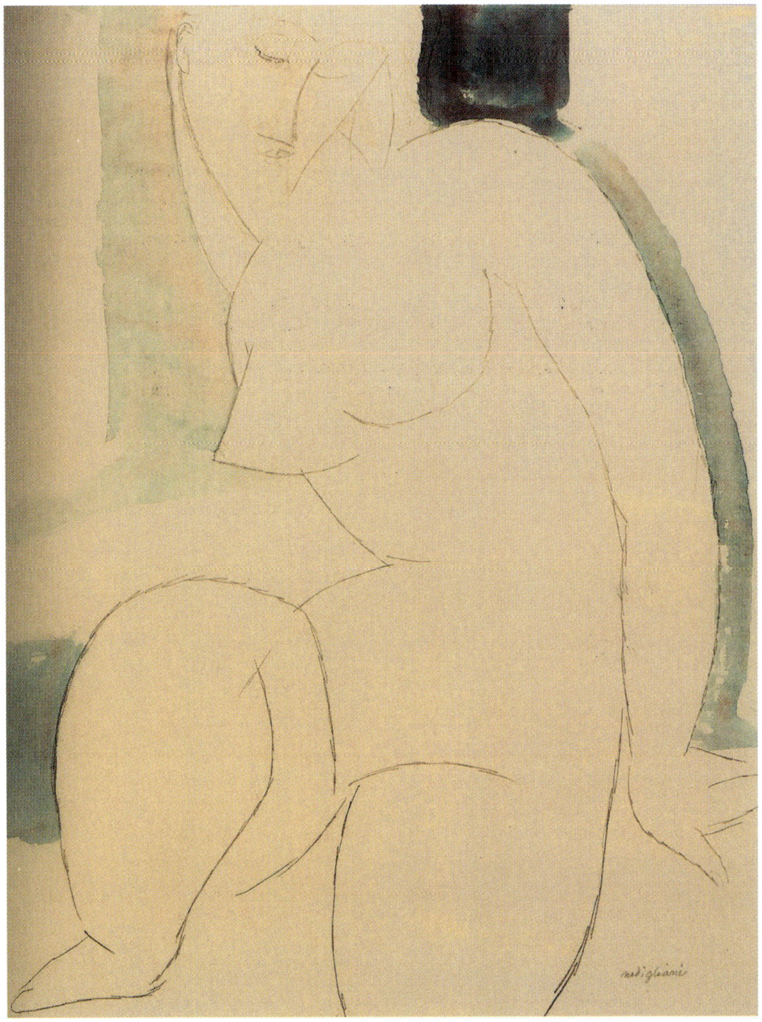

Amedeo Modigliani
Seated Nude, 1914,
pencil and watercolour on paper,
54.3 x 43.5 cm.
Private collection,
courtesy Galleria Tega, Milan
(cat. **64**)

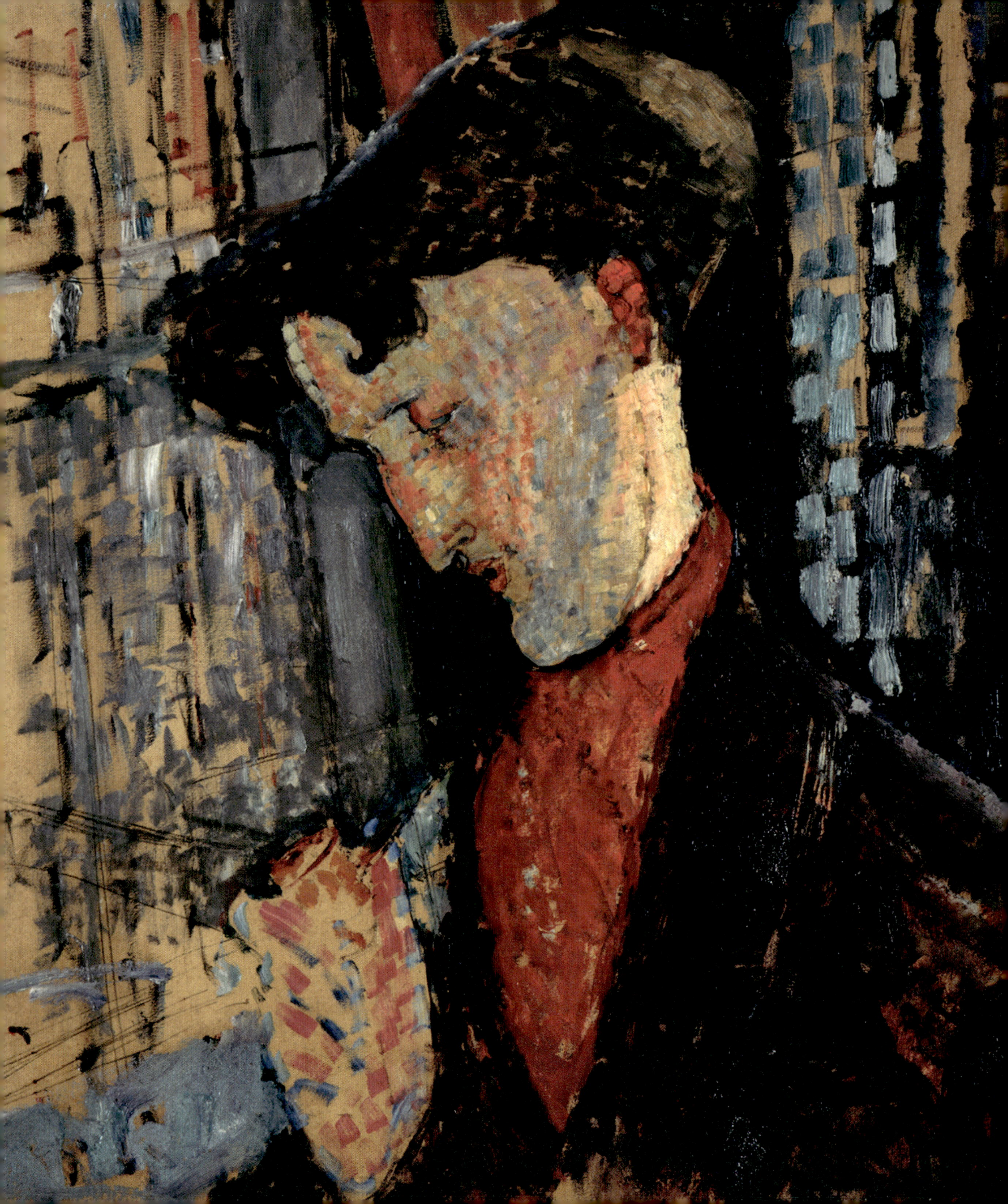

Section 9
Painting as a Development of the Sculptural Heads

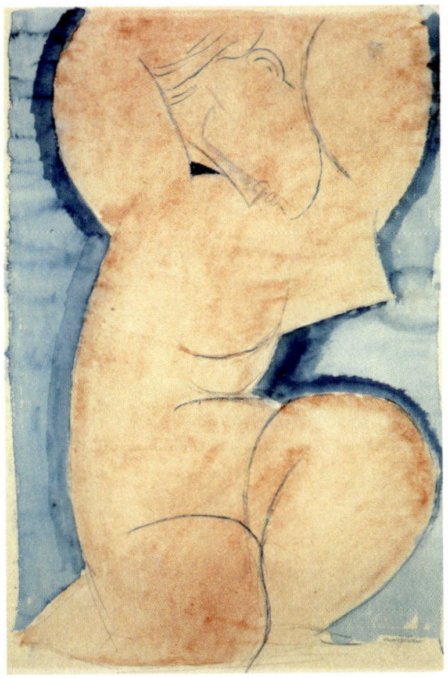

9.1. Amedeo Modigliani
kneeling Caryatid, 1913,
pencil and watercolour on paper.
Chicago, The Art Institute, Amy
McCormick Memorial Collection

Amedeo Modigliani
Portrait of the Painter Frank Haviland,
1914, oil on cardboard, 73 x 60 cm.
Gianni Mattioli Collection
Long term deposit with the Peggy
Guggenheim Collection, Venice
(cat. **65**)

Some considerations about the contribution that Modigliani's sculptural research made to his later (1914-1919) season of painted portraits must start from the following simple observation. The paintings – portraits or figures – painted by Modigliani up to 1909 (and exhibited until 1910) in a Post-Impressionist style, or more specifically in Cézanne style, intended to connect the figure and the space surrounding it through a process of reciprocal interaction of chiaroscuro and tone. In the portraits painted from 1914 onwards this preparation became completely overshadowed. The various planes of the posing figure (the nose, face, neck, hair, clothes) and those of the surroundings (the background, the floor when in view, the various recognisable objects in the room) are represented as if they were not spatially related to one another, often surrounded by a line to isolate them: in this way the elegance of the profiles is accentuated, the skill of interlocking things, the balancing of the decorative arrangement. The process of synthesis of the planes and the elimination of the spatial junctions, experimented by Modigliani in his sculptures (and above all, the long graphic phase of his sculpture), is carried into his painting in this way. It determines that trace of distance from reality which can be optically perceived that makes Modigliani's portraits so appealing, as if they show figures stripped of their material reality, ready to entrust their interior, spiritual world to the spectator.
Furthermore, as has been observed in the previous section, the crucial turning point which came about with *Caryatid* XXV contributed to deflecting the relative graphical studies away from formal purely sculptural problems: the purity of the arabesque in itself was valorised by Modigliani and made his own in his paintings of nudes from 1916-1917.
In this short anthology of paintings our intention is to put together a sample of Modigliani's pictorial portraits which continue the considerations he began in his sculptures: not so much as to show literal debts from sculptural precedents, as to sum up the different ways in which the continuity between sculpture and painting was shown.
Let us take *Portrait of Frank Haviland,* 1914 (cat. **65**), a figure who was important for leading Modigliani towards the fashion of tribal sculpture (Basler 1931, pp. 10-11; Wayne 2002, p. 47). It is clear that due to the flatness of the drawing, the aristocratic elegance of the shape of the face and the use of the expressive resource of Pointillism, at first sight this portrait does not seem to be the work of an artist who had made sculpture his main interest for two years. However, if you put it next to the Princeton drawing exhibited here at number (**56**); or the one from a private collection here at number (**57**); or better still the watercolour with *Caryatid* from 1913-14 (fig. **9.1**), today at the Art Institute of Chicago (Patani 1992, No. 179), it can be seen how this portrait owes much to solutions which were elaborated during his months of work on sculptures. Modigliani could have attained the completely new choice of absolute profile, with the hair gathered at the nape of the neck in a compact mass, from the same preparatory drawings for the sculptural heads. However, some solutions that typically characterise the posing model (elegant and melancholic inclination of the face, the high setting of the ear, the profile of the lips and chin) and above all the unnatural placing of the head on the body, without any spatial mediation, lead back to the afore-mentioned caryatids. The *Portrait of Frank Haviland*, in this way represents an important point in the catalogue of

Amedeo Modigliani
Self-Portrait as Pierrot, 1914,
oil on cardboard, 43 x 27 cm.
Copenhagen, Statens Museum
for Kunst
(cat. **66**)

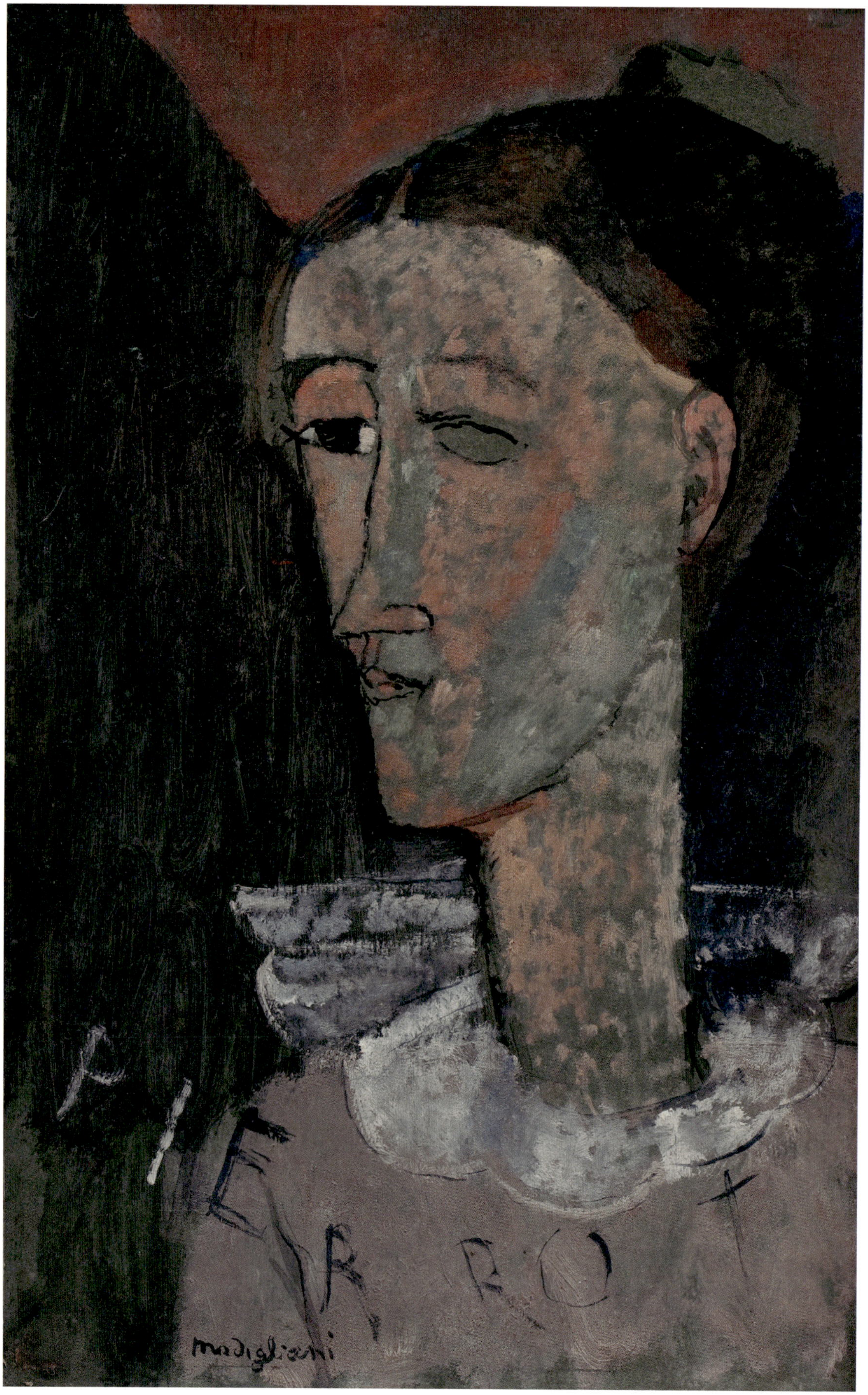

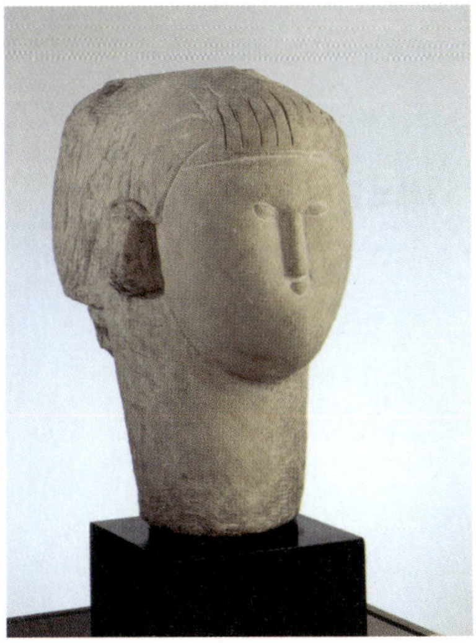

9.2. Amedeo Modigliani
Head, 1911-1913.
Gwendolyn Weiner Collection. Ceroni I

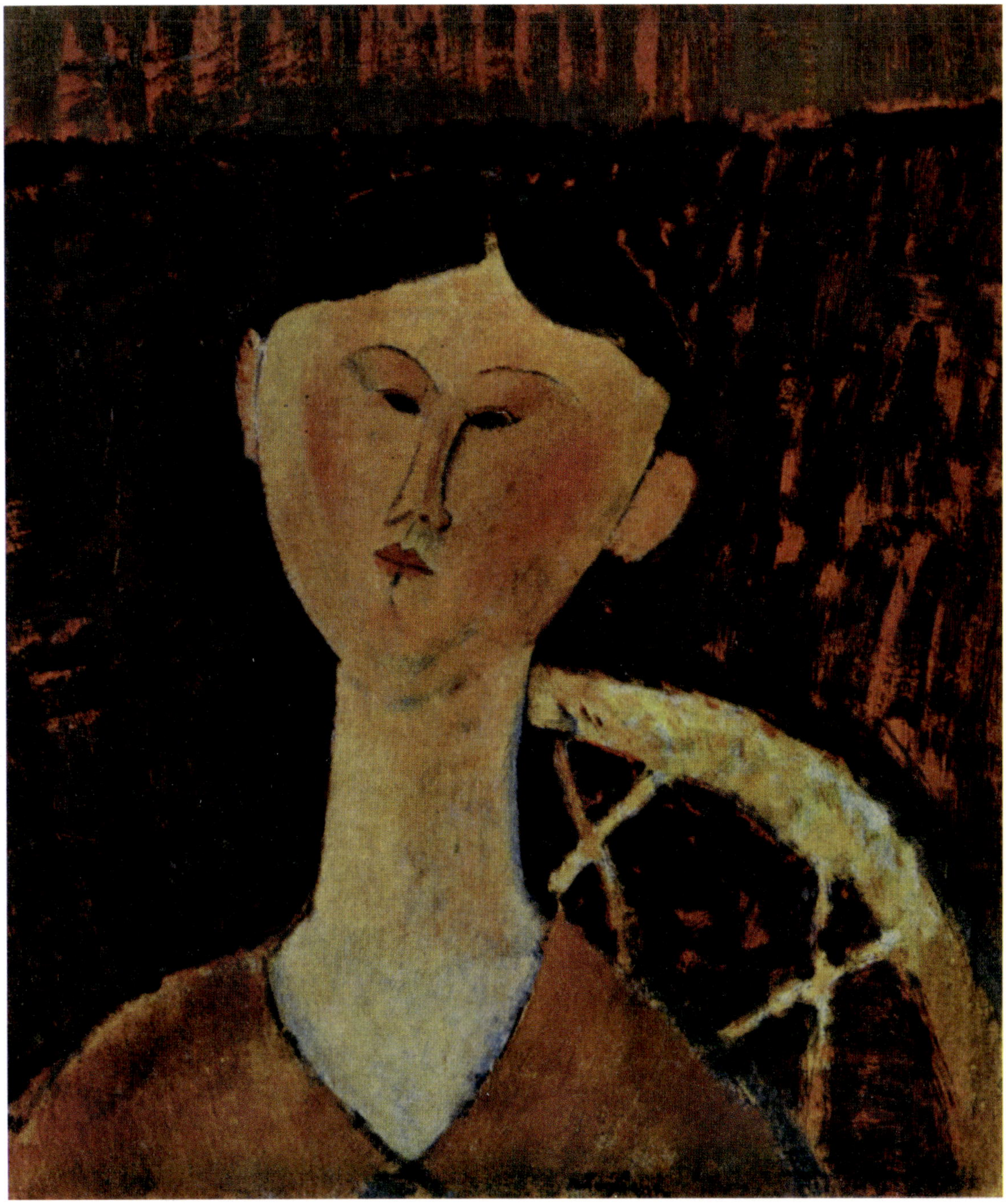

9.3. Amedeo Modigliani
Beatrice Hastings' Portrait, 1915.
Toronto, Art Gallery of Ontario,
gift by Sam and Ayala Zacks

Modigliani painter: he seems to have appropriated a repertoire of stylisations which he studied for a long time during his graphic training for the sculptures and which at the same time open up for the first time to an elegance of lines that recall fourteenth and fifteenth century Tuscan painting.
In *Pierrot* in Copenhagen (cat. **66**) and in *Portrait of Leon Indenbaum* (cat. **68**) the attention to sculptural solidity is more evident. Here Modigliani plays the card of contrast between the spatial vagueness of the background and the precise plastic identification of the head, represented as a perfect form in chiaroscuro, of almost tactile evidence. These two heads are placed in the space of the painting like a sculpture in a showroom, with a mixture of lack of naturalness, enigmatic expression and disorientation.
One cannot help noticing the link between *Woman with Red Hair* from the Orangerie in Paris (cat. **67**) and the two sculptural heads which are classified at the beginning of the Ceroni

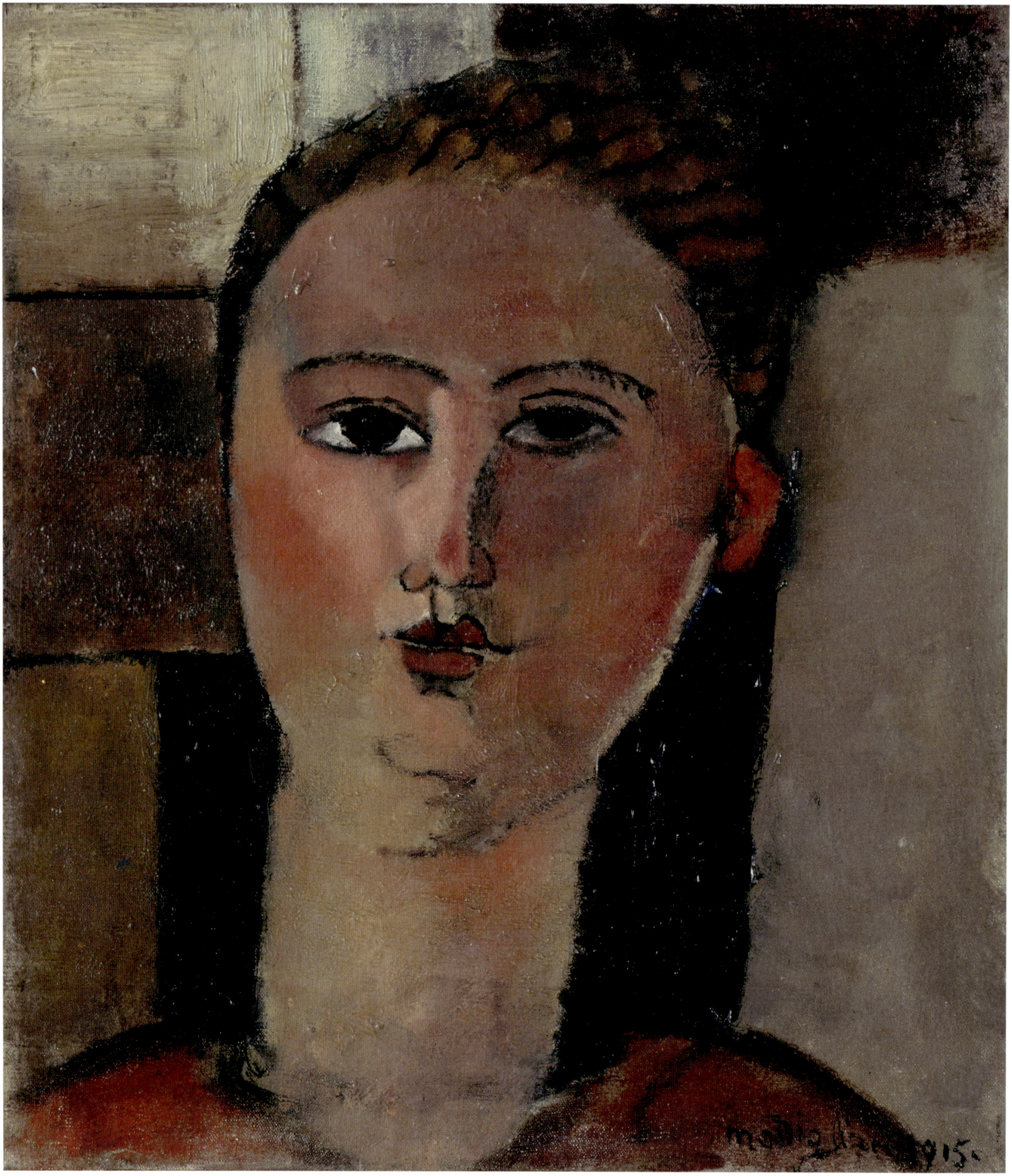
modigliani 1915

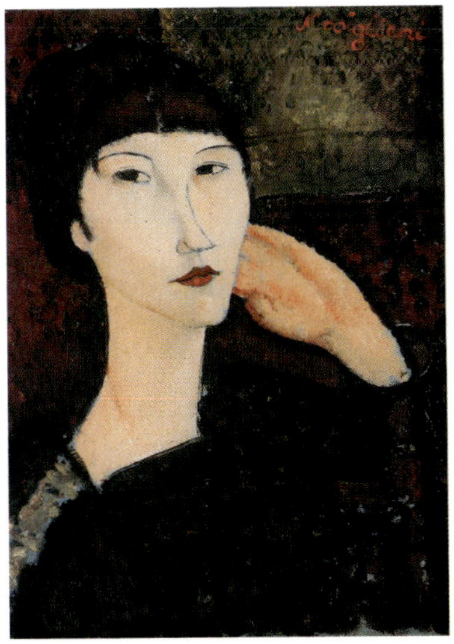

9.4. Amedeo Modigliani
Adrienne, 1917. Washington, DC, National Gallery of Art, Chester Dale Collection

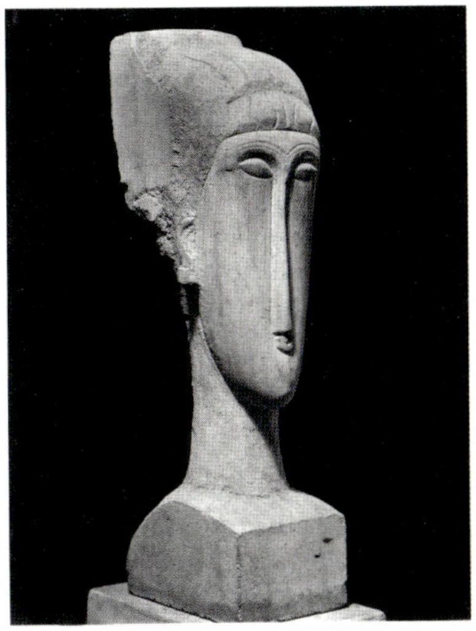

9.5. Amedeo Modigliani
Head, 1911-1912.
Private collection. Ceroni XXII

catalogue (I fig. **9.2** and II, but perhaps chronologically later than the more elongated heads): the only ones that present rounded forms and a treatment of the surfaces which seems to suggest a sort of plastic expansion of the volume. In the painting the tri-dimensional representation of the head is entrusted to a particular use of colour: without using chiaroscuro, Modigliani determines the two spatial edges of the oval of the face (to the right the plane of the cheek, to the left the *decalage* along the profile underneath the ear) using two simple red highlights. The slight dissymmetry of the eyes, the mouth and the chin, in contrast, direct the attention to the perfectly stereometric visual plan that Modigliani started from, derived from his sculptures. In this phase Modigliani carried out an open game of visual recall between the profiles of the head, that are solidly plastic and the background details, painted with very flat strokes. Here this visual link comes about by contrast: against a chess board-like background the curve (and rounded plane) of the face stands out. In another portrait where there is another clearly ovoid head, *Beatrice Hastings* from the Museum of Toronto (fig. **9.3**, Ceroni 1970, No. 79), the curve of the face is instead reaffirmed in the curve of the chair back and then once again in the curve of the shoulder, in a sort of homage to Ingres' linear rhythms, perhaps specifically to the *Marie Rivière* in the Louvre.
It seems to me that the next step is the recovery of a certain expressive character, almost caricature-like, of the sculptural heads, however, it has not been possible to document this here. If we try to put next to each other *Adrienne* from Washington (fig. **9.4**), which wavers between 1915 and 1917 (National Gallery of Art, Chester Dale Collection: Ceroni 1970, No. 64) and *Head* XXII (fig. **9.5**), it is possible to see how Modigliani managed to find certain accentuations once again, of Egyptian and Negroid traces, in the living reality of the model, and he instilled them into the portrait genre: especially when the linear stylisation accentuated the lyrical sense, no longer that brutally spatial one of deformation.
The Modigliani who in 1917 captured the features of the painter and gallery owner Elena Povolozky (cat. **69**) in a portrait; (Brunner 2006, p. 152) had by then overturned the sense of that absolute frontality which five years earlier had allowed him to study the proportions between the parts of a head. Here the sought after lack of expression in sculpture had become an investigation of the interior movement of the subject of the portrait, between interior concentration and suspended melancholy.

Flavio Fergonzi

Amedeo Modigliani
Woman with Red Hair, 1915
oil on canvas, 42 x 36 cm.
Paris, Musée de l'Orangerie, Jean Walter and Paul Guillaume Collection
(cat. **67**)

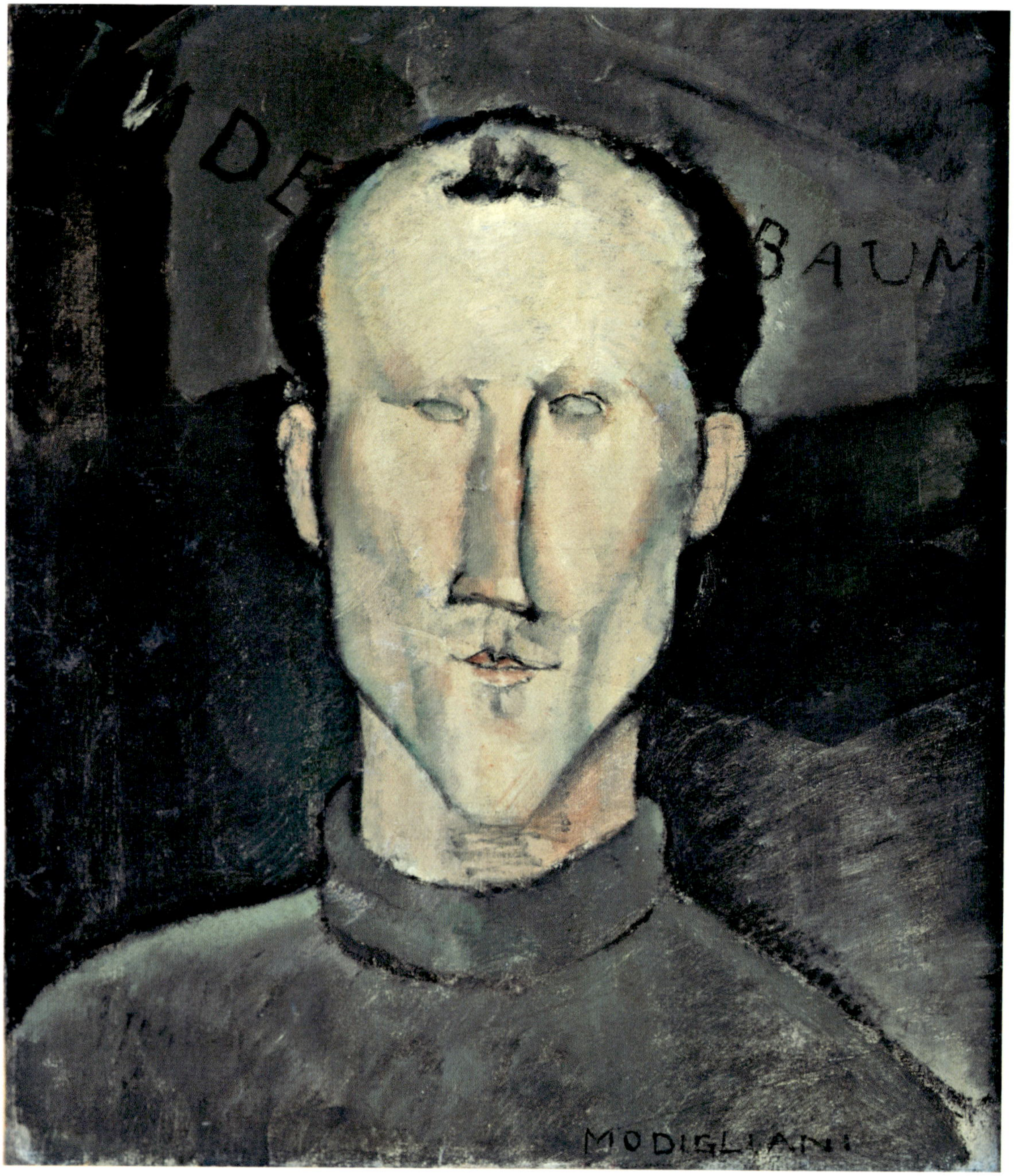

Amedeo Modigliani
Portrait of Léon Indenbaum, 1916,
oil on canvas, 54.6 x 45.7 cm.
The Henry and Rose Pearlman
Foundation, long term loan to
Princeton University Art Museum
(cat. **68**)

Amedeo Modigliani
Elena Povolozky, 1917,
oil on canvas, 64.77 x 48.57 cm.
Washington DC,
The Phillips Collection
(cat. **69**)

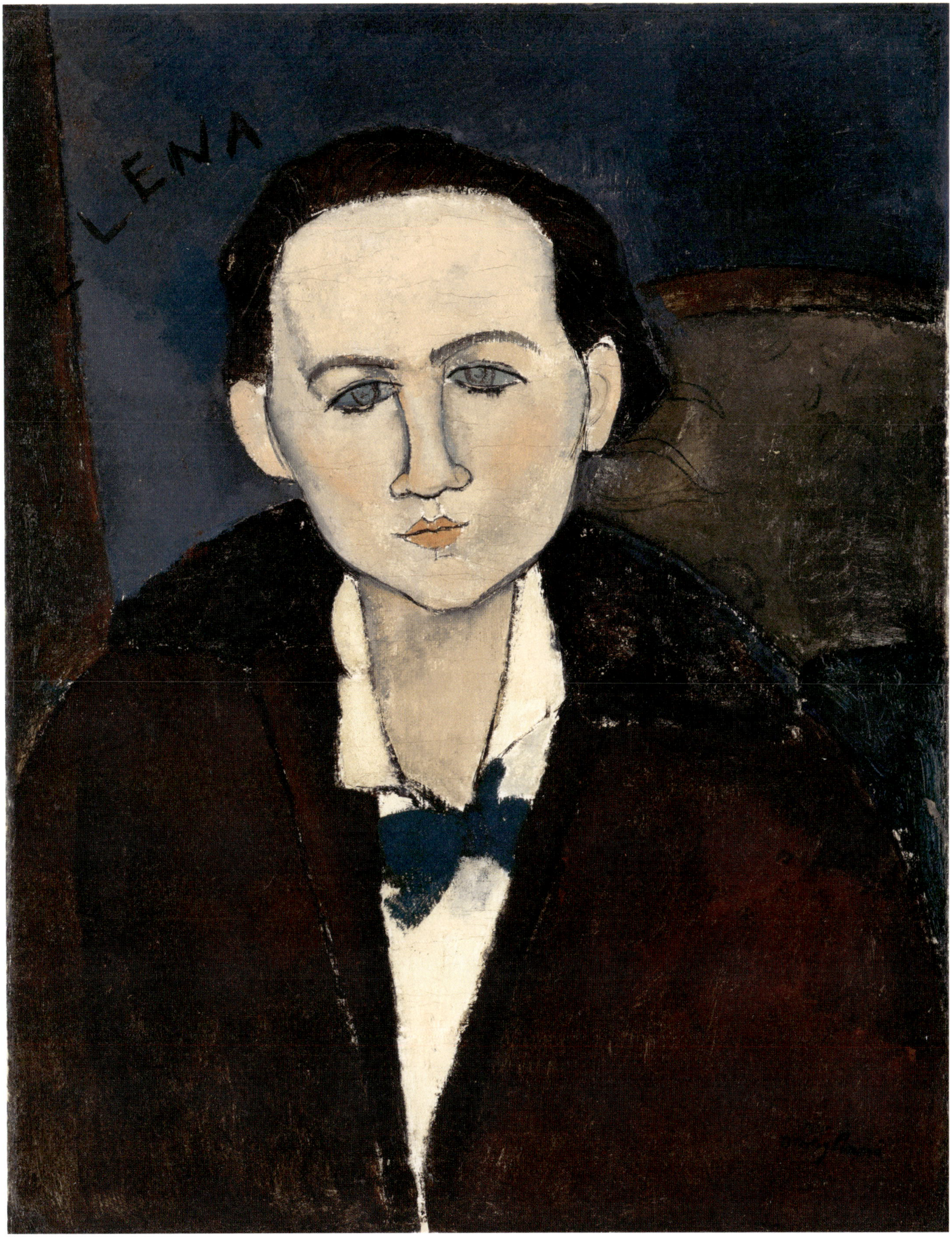
LENA

Entries

Head
1911-1913
cat. 7

Stone, 47 x 25 x 30 cm
Paris, Centre Georges Pompidou, Musée d'art moderne, purchased in 1950

Exhibitions:
Rome 1951-1952; Marseilles 1958; Liège 1980, No. 63; Paris 1981, No. 221; Livorno 1984, No. 4; Martigny 1990, No. 14; New York 2004, No. 9.

Bibliography:
Carli 1952, No. 26; Dorival 1950, pp. 165-7; Werner 1960-61, p. 70; Werner 1962; Patani 1992.

Ceroni III

This *Head* is part of a set of three sculptures classified in the first numbers in the Modigliani catalogue, even though there are no certain elements which make it possible to attribute them to his beginnings as a sculptor. The experimental nature of this work is however clearly shown in the incompleteness of the carving, in the many details which are just hinted at, in the evident uncertainties in the volumetric definition of the block. The author's still uncertain approach is confirmed by the presence, on the back of the sculpture, of the outline of a face which has been left largely unfinished.
This is a stone parallepiped , with an almost square base, worked in three distinct bands. A rather rudimental hairline has been chiselled in the upper part; the face has been obtained on the same level, carving the thin lines that draw the outlines of the eyes and eyebrow arches; while the volume of the nose has been obtained by a slight depression of the cheeks to emphasise the triangular and squashed planes of the nostrils. This seems to be a solution which was forced by what was, evidently, a *défaillance* in the control of the sculptural block: reason for which the work was abandoned, once it had been understood that it was impossible to carry it out adequately following the right profile, after having moved back the base of the neck, hinting at a decorative arch motive along the base. From a stylistic point of view, however, it is necessary to remember that similar solutions appear in André Derain's stone sculptures which were only a little earlier, like the *Head* thought to be 1912-1914 (fig. **1**; cf. Madrid 2008, cat. 28) which is a good model for comparison (and, it can be said in passing, a possible term of comparison with one of the controversial heads today deposited with the Superintendence of Pisa). Furthermore, perhaps here for the first time we can see the small mouth, shaped with that smile which, at the same time, has a hint of archaic and oriental that would be further developed in *Heads* IX and XII.
During the progress of Modigliani sculptor, *Head* III appears as an intermediate solution between the monolithic block, almost absolutely abstract, of *Head* II and the more accurate modelling of the more complete heads that followed. This is one of the few works which is documented by photographs of the time, it is impressive for the massive consistency of the block, only just articulated with prominent nose and hair, with a clear correspondence to the alarmingly modern solutions of the Cycladic heads (like those at the Louvre, which were admitted in 1873; fig. **2**); however it can also be usefully compared, on another level, to the rigorous syntax of *La sagesse de la terre* (1909, Bucharest, Museum of Art), the first work where Brancusi makes use of the final polishing of the stone, to obtain a shiny smooth surface.
From this point of view, *Head* I, with its full and well defined volume and the harmonious connection between the mass of the head, the tapered neck and the block of hair which becomes the base of the caryatid, appears as the fulfilment of this set of three.

Alessandro Del Puppo

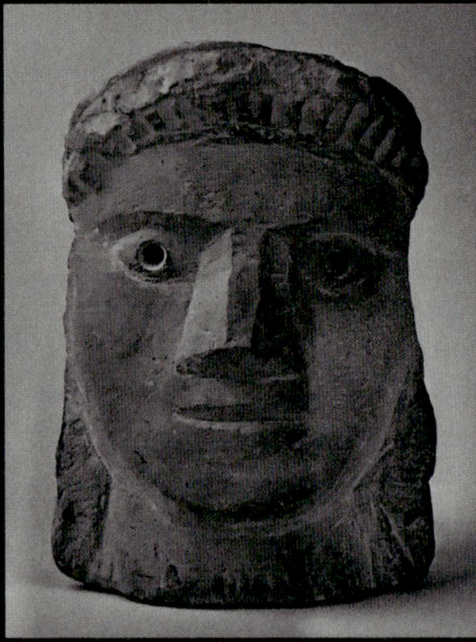

1. André Derain
Head, 1912. Valencia, Institut Valencià d'Art Modern

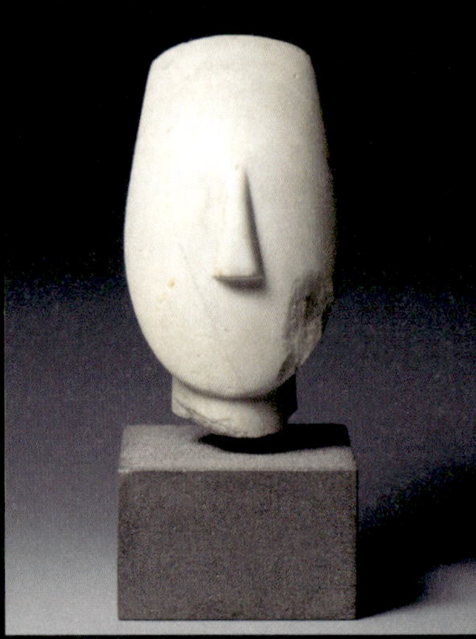

2. Cycladic art, Head of a large female statuette belonging to the category "idols with folded arms," 2700-2300 BC.
Paris, Musée du Louvre

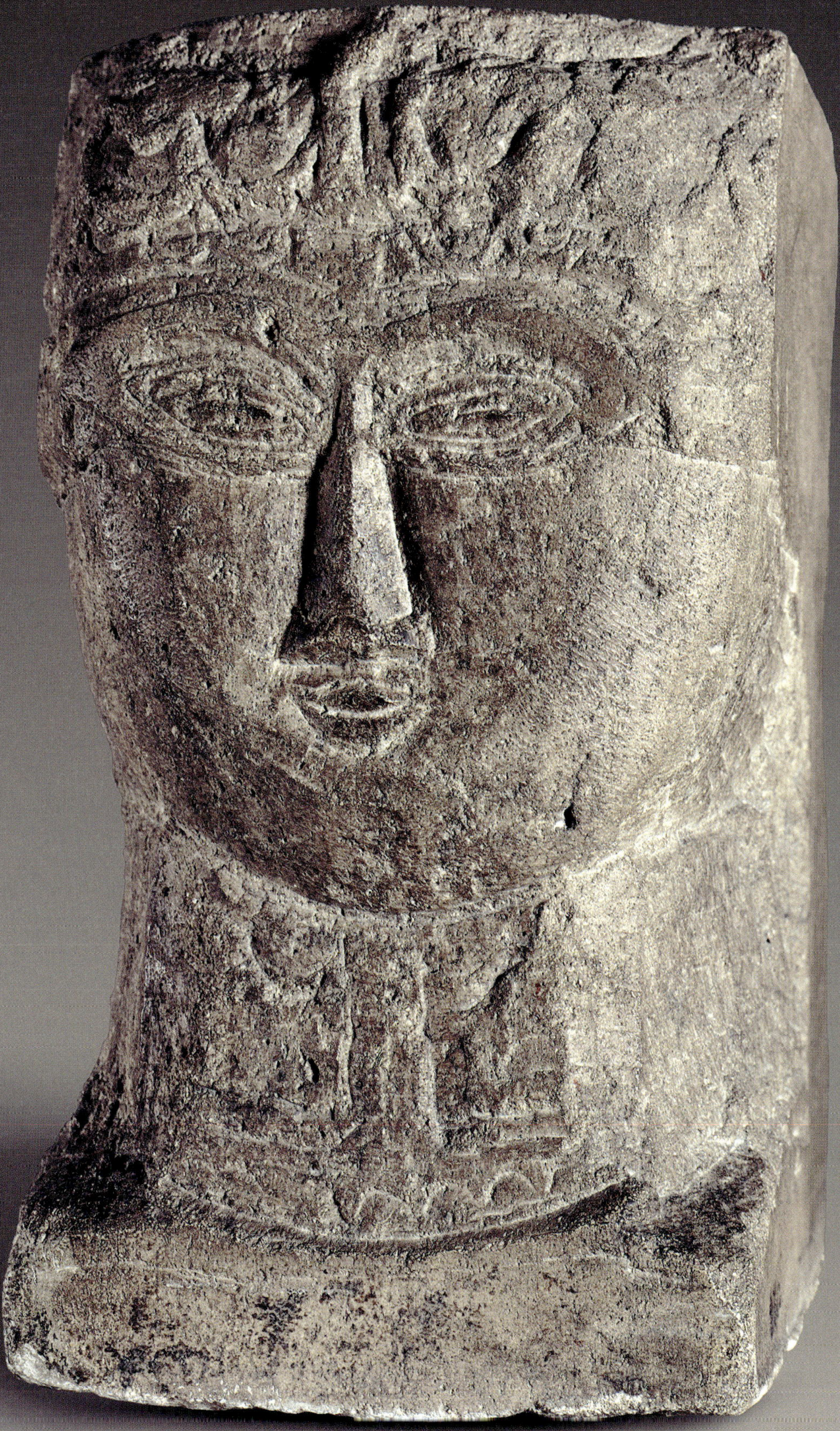

Head, 1911-1912
cat. 9

limestone, 41,8 x 12,5 x 17 cm
Princeton, The Henry and Rose Pearlman Foundation, long-term loan to the Princeton University Art Museum

Exhibitions:
New York 2004, No. 10

Bibliography:
Werner 1962, Nos. 36-37;
Patani 1992, No. 6.

Ceroni V

Although it appears among those more problematic stones as far as the work is concerned, with motifs quickly obtained with a rough chiselling, largely unfinished parts and the few detailed features compromised by the erosive effects of the poor quality stone, the Princeton *Head* shows some very interesting feature. It is, in fact, possible to link it to another two *Heads* (VI and XII) which show common solutions, even if better carried out: the positioning of the face in the middle of the block, which leaves about a third of the volume above and below the face: the modelling of the slightly concave face which signals a first form of evolution compared to the flat and frontal surfaces of other contemporary stones (like head IV in Toronto or VIII in Harvard); the almond shaped eyes, with explicit reference to models of Khmer sculpture (confirmed in the Princeton head, by the elongated right ear just hinted at by a chiselled line); the rough hewing of the base and top part compared to the smoothness of the face.
The presence of a circular blank space at the summit of the block is common to both *Heads* V and XII and is difficult to interpret: just a hint at a decorative pattern, or rather a portion of stone that was difficult to work or – if you want to give in to a highly cultured interpretation – an allusion to the seals of certain headdresses that can be seen on some Egyptian heads, like in the statue of Nefertiti in Berlin (fig. **1**) or the portrait of Akhenaton in the Louvre (fig. **2**): an enchanting limestone bust from the Egyptian Department of Antiquities which Modigliani must certainly have seen and borne in mind, also for later heads, like *Head* XXI.
This work is one of Modigliani's fifteen sculptures which are present today in American public and private collections. It is part of the conspicuous collection of European Post-Impressionist works from the Henry and Rose Pearlman Foundation: a collection which includes, apart from Modigliani's sculptures and drawings, paintings by Vincent van Gogh, Paul Cézanne, Henri de Toulouse Lautrec and Chaïm Soutine.

Alessandro Del Puppo

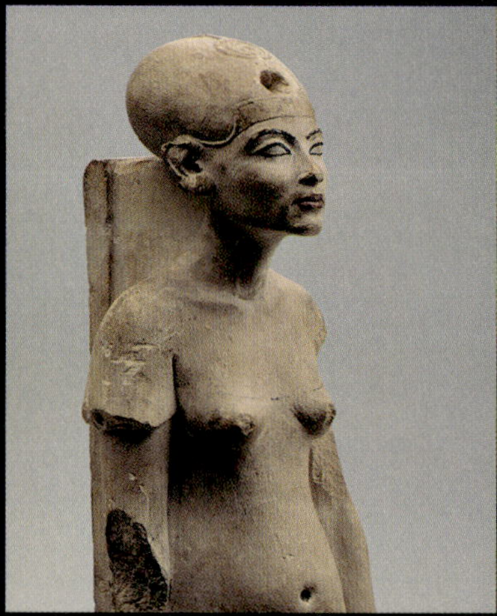

1. Egyptian art, Reign of Aménophis IV-Akhénaton (1353-1337).
Statue of Queen Nefertiti in standing pose. Berlin, Ägyptisches Museum und Papyrussammlung

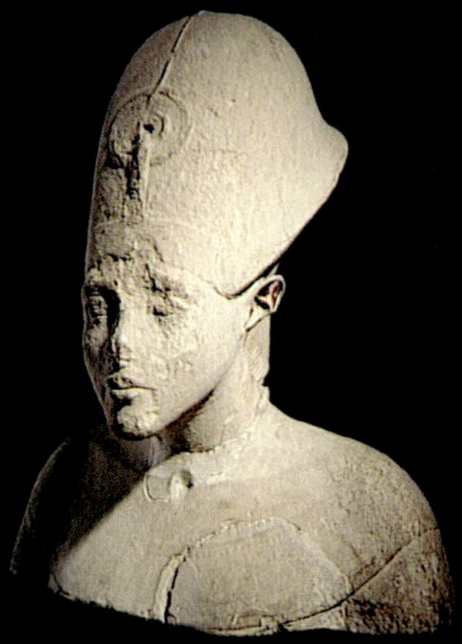

2. Egyptian art, 18th Dynasty (1550-1295). Bust of Pharaoh Akhénaton surmounted by the blue crown. Paris, Musée du Louvre

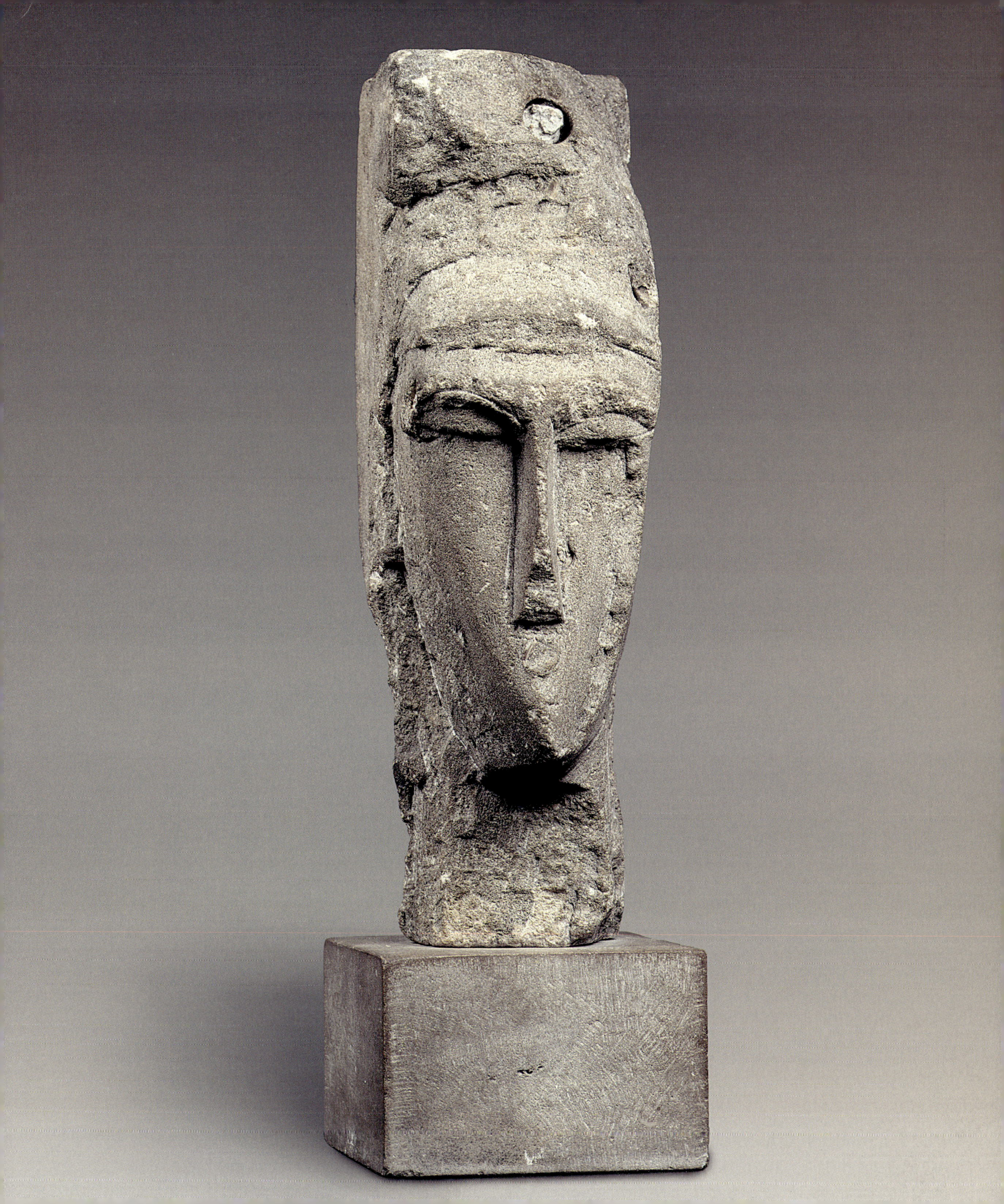

Head, 1911-1912
cat. 8

stone, 49,5 x 18,4 x 22,8 cm
Washington, Hirshhorn Museum and Sculpture Garden, Smithsonian Institution, donated by Joseph H. Hirshhorn, 1966

Exhibitions: New York 1953-1954; New York 1963; Düsseldorf 1991, No. 93; Buffalo 2002-2003, No. 46; New York 2004, No. 12.

Bibliography:
di San Lazzaro 1953, No. 4; Descargues 1951, No. 13; Werner 1962, No. 41; Patani 1992, No. 10.

Ceroni VII

To all evidence this *Head* also belongs to the series of works (catalogued by Ceroni at numbers I-VI and X) characterised by an explicit experimental intention, often carried out roughly and incomplete: works to be considered more as documents of a long and tiring apprenticeship of sculpting technique than finished works. These are the reasons for the relatively recent success of this stone. It was published for the first time in the monograph by Pierre Descargues in 1951 and quickly arrived on the American market, through the Curt Valentin Gallery of New York, which exhibited it in 1954. The *Head* was finally approved by Werner in 1962 (Werner 1962) and passed to the Ceroni canons (besides the monograph by Elsen in 1974), as an example of the still largely experimental vocation of sculptural techniques: even though there was no lack of more or less implicit references to later and much more certain stylistic techniques. The shape of the oval of the face and the double lines which mark the arches of the eyes (in accordance with the prototypes of the Ivory Coast Guro masks) in fact, recall *Head* XIII; the elongated lines of the nose, with the trapezoidal grafting of the nostrils are those already found in sequence XIII-XVII (many of which were presumably exhibited at the Salon d'Automne of 1912); the circular everted volume of the mouth is a *nègre* stylistic element (drawn from the widespread circulation of masks), here only hinted at but which is completed in *Heads* XIII and XVI. It is clear that, regarding all these later examples, the rough workmanship of the surface is due to the abandonment of the work at an intermediate stage.
In some studies of full figure male caryatids and half figure female ones (Alexandre 1993, Nos. 137-138 and 253-255) it is possible to find traces of common elements, like the doubling of the eyebrow arches and the cruciform setting of the horizontal ocular axis with the vertical one of the nose.

Alessandro Del Puppo

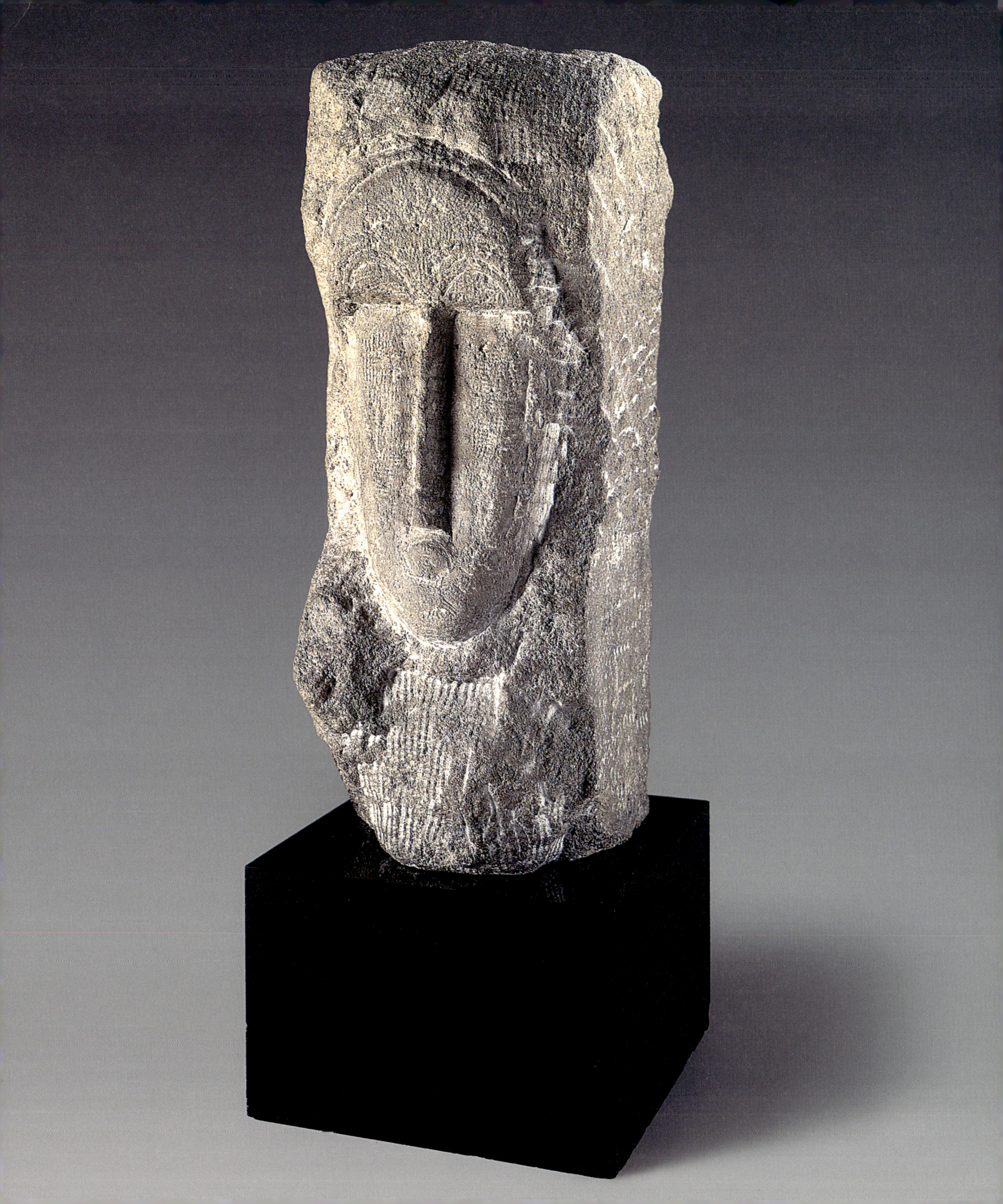

Head, 1911-1912
cat. 24

stone 58 x 12 x 16 cm
Paris, Centre Georges Pompidou, Musée National d'art moderne

Exhibitions:
Paris 1950; Rome 1951-1952; Düsseldorf 1991, No. 94; New York 2004, No. 15.

Bibliography:
Salmon 1926, No. 50; Basler 1928, p. 38; Dorival 1949; Dorival 1950; Werner 1962, Nos. 5-8; Patani 1992, No. 18.

Ceroni XII

This *Head* is, together with XXIV in London, Modigliani's most successful sculptural work, for the purposely ambiguous stylisation between the models of ancient Greek art and Oriental art; for the important museum collocation and the abundant exhibitive and editorial events; and finally, for the richness (and the complexity) of the possible references. It was the property of Paul Guillaume (Salmon 1926) and the first to be included in a systematic study of modern sculpture (Basler 1928), among the few which were objects of specific writings (Dorival 1949). However, this rich documentation does not seem to be sufficient to disentangle the sense of this work which is an exception. In fact, it is one of the four female *Heads* carried out by Modigliani (the others are VIII-X, besides naturally, the Canberra *Caryatid*); the only one which exclusively proposes attributions that are of "Oriental" taste (IX is comparable but it appears as a transitional solution; VI is incomplete); it is the only one that is signed (top right, in lower case italics as can be read on his paintings: "modigliani").
The most surprising aspect of this sculpture, so alienating as to cause some disturbance, is the continuous enigmatic oscillation between two striking references: that of archaic sculpture and that of Cambodian sculpture. These two paths lead respectively to the Louvre Museum and the Guimet Museum. At the Louvre there were two possible sources during the years in which Modigliani visited it: one is the famous fifth century Kouros (fig. **1**), which was added to the collections of the museum in 1910 and immediately became a fundamental bridge between the archaic Mediterranean culture and the Greek Classics. In this work Modigliani could find confirmation of the visual information that he had already acquired during his early academic training and his stays in Florence. From this point of view the *Kouros Milani* in the Museo Nazionale in Florence (cat. **29**) became an almost compulsory term of comparison, and at the same time added to a circle of stimulations which found confirmation in Etruscan terracotta, in the female face in the *Sarcophagus of the Spouses* in the Louvre (fig. **2** Schmalenbach 1990, p. 10, refers instead to a Kouros in the Museum of Berlin).
Another two works in the Louvre could have given the same stimulations, still referring to the detail of the stereotyped smile: the head of the famous *Rampin Horseman* (fig. **3**), belonging to the legacy of Georges Rampin of 1896, and – in the room dedicated to the ancient Cypriot production – a fragmentary figure but of great impact (height 98 cm) of an offering bearer (fig. **4**), which was added after the historical Edmond Duthoit exploration in 1865 and a term of comparison for the subtle mind, the modulation of the eyeballs and the undefined smile, also for *Heads* XVII and XXIII.
The serene smile, the composed nobility and the haughty beauty of these heads are characteristics of which Modigliani could find confirmation in certain Buddhist heads of the Gupta era (IV-VI century BC) that could be admired at the Guimet Museum. Recognisable for the meditative pose and the heavy lowered eyelids, such sculptures are documented here by three Cambodian heads in stoneware and a more recent bronze (cats. **25-28**). These are central works in the exhibition path of the Guimet and have been since their first display (cf. De Milloué 1883, p. 76 and following); these works are of great beauty and seem to simulate an enchanting and almost supernatural incarnation.

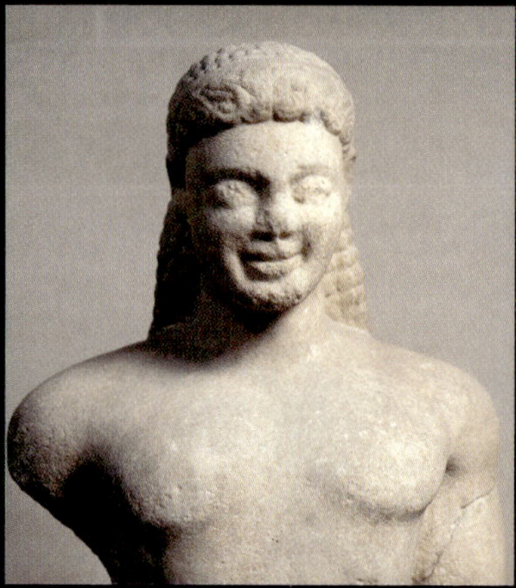

1. Kouros known as *Kouros of Paros*, circa 540 BC. Paris, Musée du Louvre

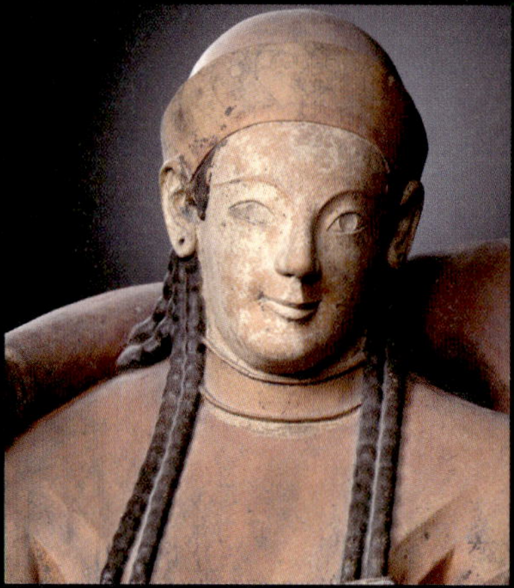

2. Etruscan art, *Sarcophagus of the Spouses*, couple on funeral bed / detail of the female figure.
Last quarter of VI century BC.
Paris, Musée du Louvre

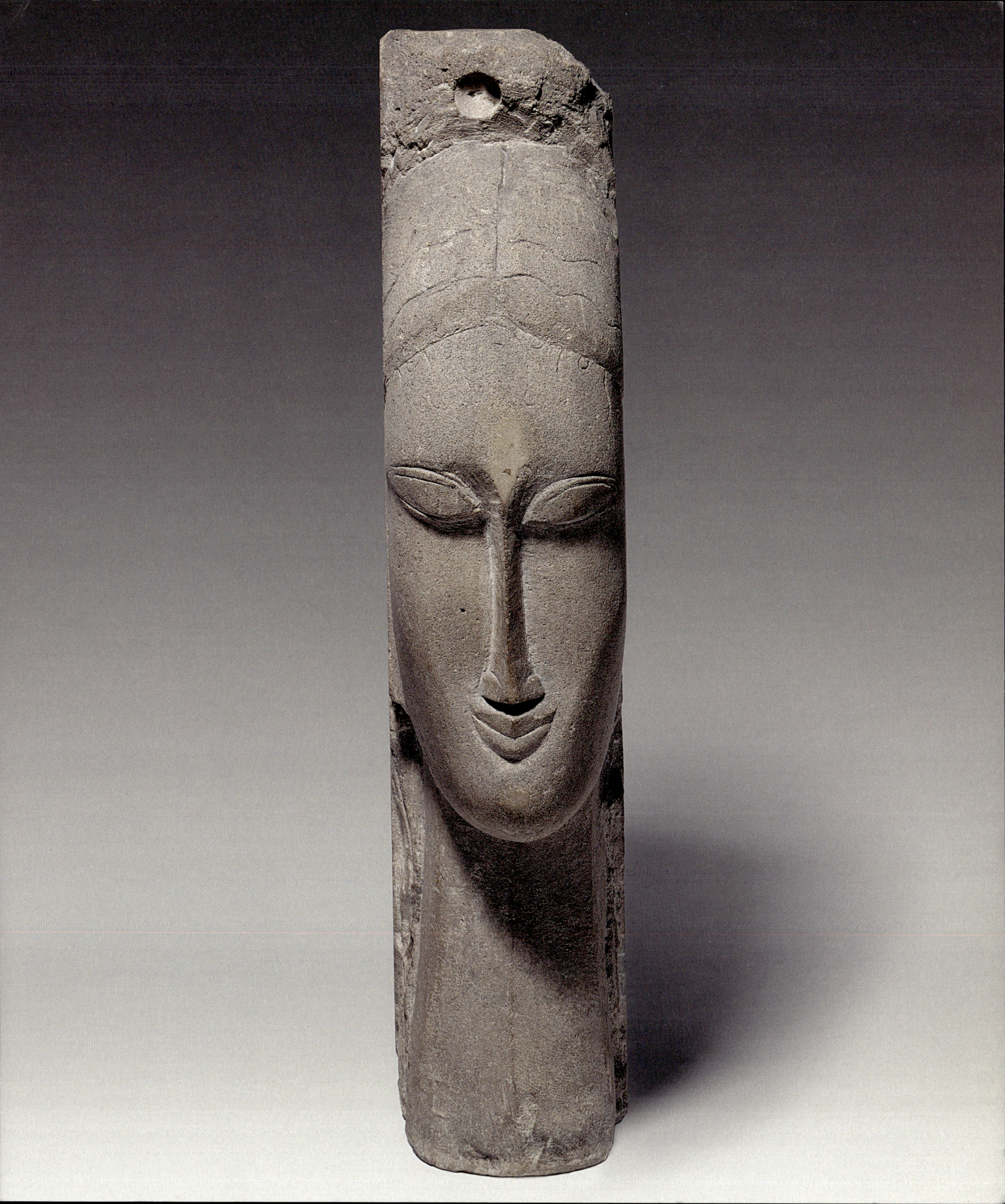

To these two explicit physiognomic deductions, alluding to two opposing cultural traditions, there is the addition of the modelling of the whole face, which proceeds along sinuous and elongated lines, along welcoming profiles and sweetly concave and convex planes. It is difficult to say if this is a recollection, strongly filtered stylistically, of the more elegant Fang masks; however, it is clear that the result, on the whole, offers a complete compositional harmony and an unmistakeable exotic grace. In the corpus of Modigliani's sculptures, *Head* XVIII is that which undoubtedly shows the most common traits, even though with a naturalistic and realistic accentuation of the male physiognomy. Some drawings seem to be associated with *Head* XII: two drawings of mediocre quality belonging to Paul Alexandre (Nos. 215, 218) and, from the same collector, a study of a head with the detail of the archaic smile (Patani 1992, No. 72), as well as two female heads in profile which belonged to Paul Guillaume (Patani 1992, Nos. 86 and 129); on the other hand the Masurel drawing of Villeneuve d'Ascq should be considered spurious, or at best a clumsy *d'après* (Patani 1992, No. 121).

Alessandro Del Puppo

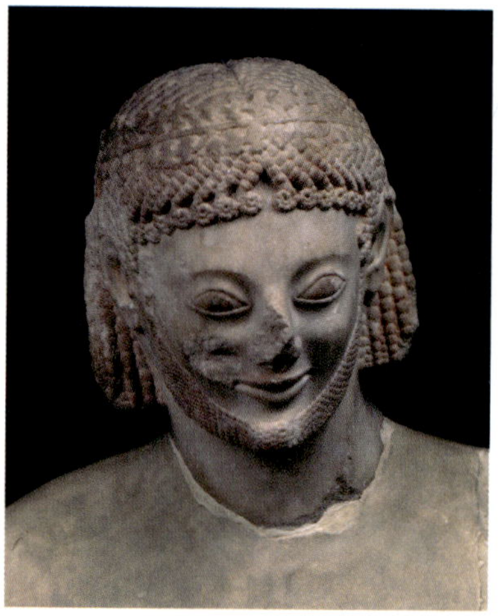

3. *Rampin Horseman*, marble head integrated with moulds of a torso of a horseman and the neck of his horse conserved at the Museum of the Acropolis in Athens, just after 545 BC. Paris, Musée du Louvre

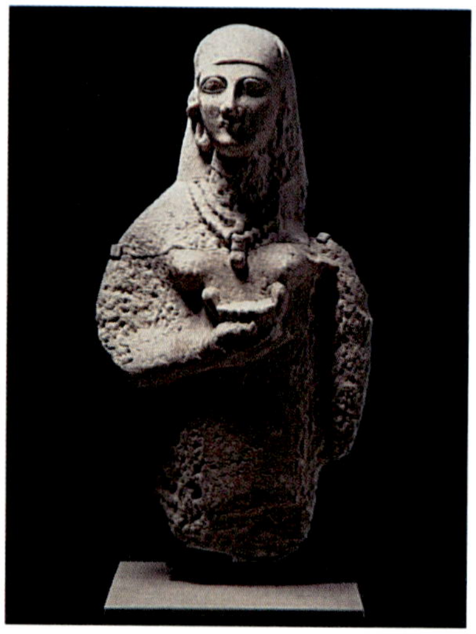

4. Archaic Cypriot Art, *Statue of Offering Bearer*, circa 600 BC. Paris, Musée du Louvre

Head, 1911-1912
cat. 22

limestone,
height 65.4 x 17.1 x 21.3 cm
Minneapolis (Minnesota), The Minneapolis Institute of Art, donated by Mr. and Mrs. John Cowles

Exhibitions:
Paris 1912d, Nos. 1215 or 1216 or 1217?; Paris 1925, No. 35; Winnipeg 1987, p. 212.

Bibliography:
Vente Drouot 1930, No. 15; Descargues 1951, table 1; Werner 1962, tables 52, 53, 87; Ceroni 1965, No. XVI, p. 25 and tables 72, 75; Patani 1992, No. 11.

Ceroni XVI

The first evidence of this *Head* can be found in the famous photograph that shows it placed, without a base, on a narrow shelf (fig. **1**): in the photograph it is next to *Head* "A" (former Lévy collection) and collocated in front of a drawing, fixed to the wall with two pins, which can be identified as the one published in Alexandre 1993, No. 126 (which still shows the marks left by the pins). The photograph is traditionally referred to (Modigliani 1958, pp. 63-64) the organisation of an exhibition which was supposedly held by Modigliani in the studio of Amadeo de Souza Cardoso in March 1911. In the essay in this catalogue I have tried to question this well established hypothesis, preferring instead to attribute the photograph as having been taken by an anonymous photographer (perhaps Souza Cardoso himself, among whose papers the photograph was found: Ferreira 1995, p. 73) in Modigliani's studio at the Cité Falguière, perhaps in 1912. In the same series of photographs at least two of the *Heads* represented ("A" and Ceroni XV) were exhibited at the Salon d'Automne in 1912 and appear either completed or nearly so. In the photograph in object this *Head* in particular, *Head* XVI, seems incomplete compared to the state in which it is known today. For how much the not very good black and white definition of the photograph allows us to establish, Modigliani had still not finished the motif of the hair above the fringe and the area beneath the forehead: only at a later moment would he have attributed a strong relief to the eyebrow arches and the almond eyes, by means of a more accentuated carving of the forehead and the temples. That Modigliani left the decision about these decorative details only to the end of the work may mean that he wanted to harmonise with those of the *Heads* that he intended to exhibit near to each other.

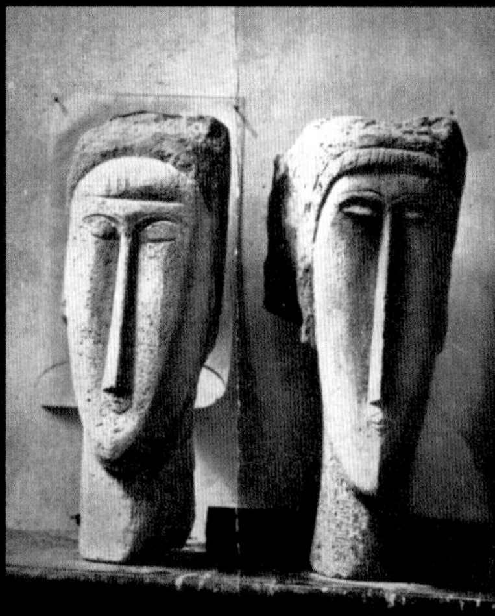

1. Anonymous photographer
Heads (1911-1912) by Amedeo Modigliani (Ceroni XVI and *Head* "A"). Lisbon Fundação Calouste Gulbenkian, Archive Amadeo de Souza Cardoso

From the photographs of the exhibition, from photographs of that period, from drawings and caricatures of the *Heads* presented at the Salon d'Automne in 1912 we know that they were exhibited on cubic bases. Today we can definitely identify five of those seven *Heads* (XV, XXI, XIII, "A", "B"); for the remaining two the choice should be among the four that present this base (XVI, XVII, XX, XXIV) and it is therefore very probable that this *Head* was exhibited in Paris in October 1912.
Within an established module, Modigliani was searching for maximum variety and maximum monumentality. As far as the monumentality of this *Head* is concerned, with its dimension of 65 cm, it carried out its task perfectly. It was, in fact, a different format from that of the traditional sculptural head of Rodin or post-Rodin tradition: exhibited in a Salon the stone recalled, for its impressiveness, the architectonic destination for which it was originally conceived (the "Temple of Love" which Paul Guillaume would later remember) and it generated some bewilderment in its observers.
Reasoning on the drawings from the Paul Alexandre collection it seems obvious how the Ceroni XVI is an evolution of the form and in a certain sense model put into being in *Head* XIII (Alexandre 1993, No. 97), and fundamental starting point, on the way to defining new harmonies, towards *Heads* XIX and "A" (Alexandre 1993, Nos. 123, 124, 126).
The stone does not seem to have been purchased by collectors (John, Roworth, Malpel, Köhler) who were interested in Modigliani sculptor quite early on. So, it remained in Paul Guillaume's possession, who after the artist's death sent it to the important Modigliani exhibition at the Galerie Bing, in 1925. Five years later, in April 1930, the *Head* went up for auction at the Hôtel Drouot.
In November 1950 John Cowles bought the sculpture from the Buchholz Gallery in New York and donated it to the Minneapolis Museum of Art in 1962.

Flavio Fergonzi

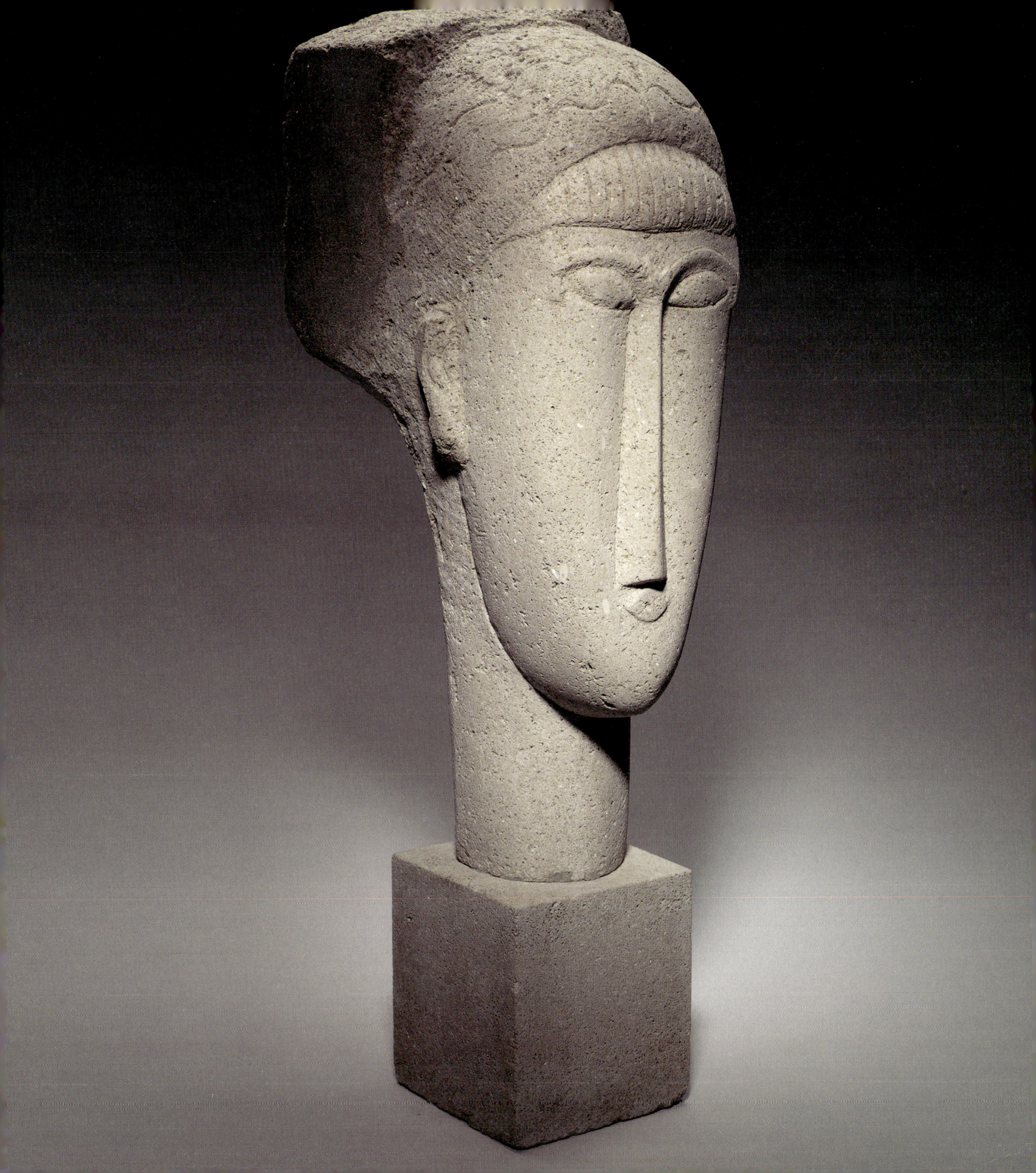

Head, 1911-1912
cat. 20

stone, height 65 x 19 x 24 cm
Washington, National Gallery of Art, Chester Dale Collection

Exhibitions:
Philadelphia 1943, No. 20; Cleveland-New York 1951, p. 22; Toronto 1981-82, No. 68; Venice 1989, pp. 360,742; New York 2004, pp. 101 and 207, fig. 16.

Bibliography:
Dale 1929, No. 50; Lipchitz 1952, p. 6; Werner 1962, figs. 38, 39, 87; Ceroni 1965, No. XVII, p. 25, fig. 74; Lanthemann 1970, p. 143, No. 316; Patani 1992, No. 5.

Ceroni XVII

Ambrogio Ceroni's catalogue (Ceroni 1965, p. 25, tables 72-73) wrongly identifies this *Head* (XVII) with the one shown while work was ongoing in the old photograph discussed in the previous number, that *Head* which is in reality *Head* "A" of the former Lévy collection. As in the photograph *Head* "A" is placed next to, and in the same phase of finishing as *Head* XVI, this has caused, in the sequence of the Ceroni catalogue, the collocation of XVII at the number immediately following *Head* XVI. Despite this error, the hypothesis of the succession between the two sculptures (XVI and XVII) is more than plausible as far as style is concerned: the substantial similarity of formal solutions makes Alfred Werner's sequence a little risky as he placed an interval of six numbers (inserting the very different Ceroni I, II and IX) between the *Head* in Washington today and the one which is now in Minneapolis, even anticipating the Washington *Head* (Werner 1962, tables 39, 52-53). The hypothesis of an anticipation of XVII before XVI is still sustained, without giving any kind of explanation, in Osvaldo Patani's general catalogue (Patani 1992, Nos. 5, 11; with *Heads* V, VIII, IX, VI, VII in the interval between them); while Schuster's often quite imaginative sequence has given *Head* XVI the role of predecessor to XVII (Schuster-Pfannstiel [1986], p. 88, with the interval of Ceroni's XIX).
The *Head* from the Chester Dale collection is a refined consequence of Modigliani's values experimented in *Head* XVI (and before reaching the linear abstraction of *Head* "A"). Compared to the previous one, the shape of the face is elongated, becoming more stylised also thanks to the clear closure of the hair at ear level; the chin becomes more impressive, emphasising its anti-naturalist essence of a perfectly polished solid. To balance this drift towards a pure form, some particulars are defined by new graphic elements: the nostrils are marked with two lunettes in relief at the base of the nose; the mouth is protruding like those of the African masks; the eyes are two almonds in relief with a different slant, this is a particular which represents the clearest infraction of the stereometry of the whole catalogue of Modigliani's sculptural heads.
Even the proof from the drawings belonging to Paul Alexandre seems to confirm this. Although no study which can be closely related to *Head* XVII has survived, it is in the graphic developments starting from *Head* XVI (Alexandre 1993, Nos. 97, 120, 125-126) that patterns can be found (the elongation of the oval, the highlighted nostrils, the design of the fringe) which were destined to flow into this *Head*. As in the case of *Head* XXI, some solutions were found by Modigliani directly on the stone, without any evidence of previous graphic elaboration.
The *Head* was reproduced for the first time in the book on Modigliani published in New York in 1929 by the editor Alfred Knopf and prefaced by Maud Dale (Dale 1929, No. 50), Chester Dale's wife, he was a rich New York stock broker and a very active collector of European art of the XIX and XX centuries: in the caption to the illustration in the book the *Head* was said to belong to the collector Maurice Speiser, a Philadelphian lawyer who had defended Brancusi in the famous case against the United States government for having taxed the importation of *Bird in Space*, which was not considered a work of art by New York customs officials. However, according to Chester Dale's papers, the *Head* was already in his collection in 1928, and was exhibited with that collection at the Philadelphia Museum of Art in 1943 (Philadelphia 1943, No. 20).

Flavio Fergonzi

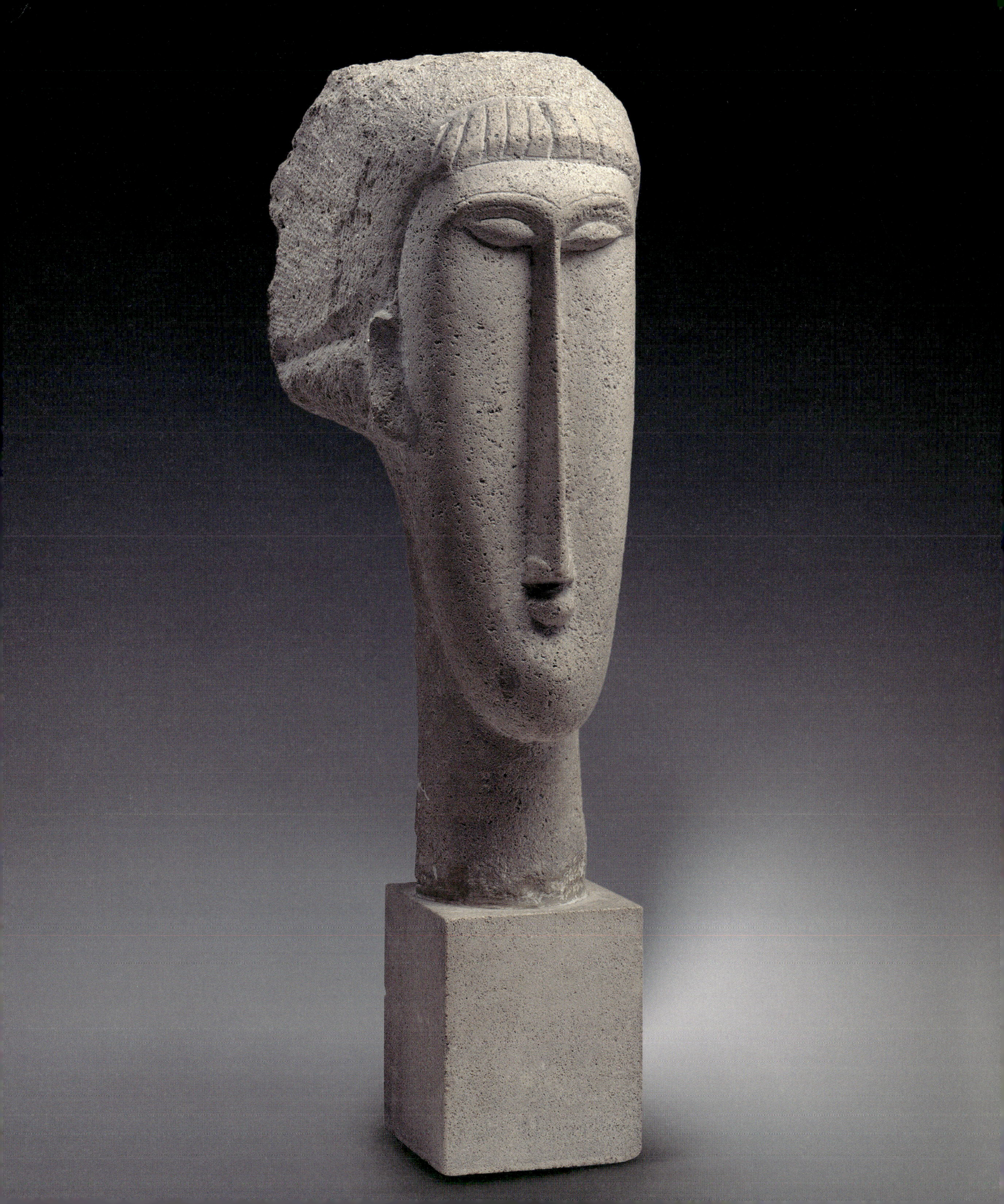

Head, 1911-1912
cat. 31

limestone, 70.5 x 23.5 x 7.6 cm.
Philadelphia, The Philadelphia Museum of Art,
donated by Mrs. Maurice J. Speiser in memory of her husband, 1950

Exhibitions:
Cleveland-New York 1951; Düsseldorf 1991, No. 97; Buffalo 2002-2003, No. 44; New York 2004, No. 13; Bonn 2009, No. 24.

Bibliography:
Revista Nova 1914, p. 11; Dale 1929, No. 50; Pfannstiel 1929, pp. 82, 86; *A Review of the Year 1949-1950*, pp. 107-119; Soby 1954, p. 17; Roy 1958, p. 52, Werner 1962, Nos. 20-22, Patani 1992, No. 21

Ceroni XX

Together with XXIII, it is the tallest *Head* among those which were probably exhibited as a decorative ensemble at the Salon d'Automne in 1912. It certainly belongs to the works which can be attributed to stylistic maturity and achievement of a complete and certain result, comparable to another ten works in the catalogue (XIII-XXII, XXIV) where the mixture of the various visual contributions (the cylinder type mouths of the Nimba sculptures; the *quart de brie* nose of the Fang masks; the elongated lobes of the Buddhist statues, the full and dilated eyeballs, as in Brancusi's *Mademoiselle Pogany*), reached a full synthesis, able to blend the various sources in the harmony of a plastic language controlled by certainty and measure. At the same time, Modigliani reached that perceptive dissociation between frontal vision, becoming continuously thinner and Manneristically tense, and side vision that develops the profiles of the face in silhouette with more complex rhythm and musical graphic elements, perfected using many preparatory drawings.
Contrary to many of these works, however, this one from Philadelphia maintains the original stone base, which is a single block with the neck: on the front part as a decorative theme it presents an arch with semi-circular motifs hinted at along the sides and, more clearly on the top. In this solution it is difficult not to see a clear reference to decorative motifs that Constantin Brancusi was perfecting, in an original combination of Romanian folklore patterns with Classical typology. This is a path that began with the theme of the close-set eyes, in *Kiss* 1910 in stone and following repetitions which can be found on the wooden bases of certain sculptures from 1912 (like the *Muse* in marble at the Guggenheim in New York) and in following works (like the wooden base, sculpted with the same patterns, of the now famous *Madame L.R.*, 1914; fig. **1**) that culminated, on a monumental scale, in the decorative themes of the *Gate of the Kiss* in Tirgu Jiu, which was carried out in 1937. It is probable that, alluding to a similar very recognisable decorative scheme Modigliani desired, in some way, to pay homage to his sculptor friend who was among the first to guide him towards direct carving of stone.
As already seen in other cases (above all *Head* XII), also here the subject of the head is a contaminated place between contemporary allusions and reminiscences. In fact, it is plausible that the wavy hairline can be compared to the almost stereotype solution of Etruscan sculpture; with regards to this it is possible to mention the male figure of the *Sarcophagus of the Spouses* from Cerveteri (Rome, Museo di Villa Giulia, fig. **2**) and above all the *Sarcophagus of the Spouses* in the Louvre, a probable iconographic reference also for *Head* XII.
The sculpture had great success. Together with the *Head* in Karlsruhe today, it was bought by the art critic and collector Charles Malpel certainly before 1914, year in which they were both published in *Revista Nova* in Barcelona, a magazine dealing with Catalan Modernism, with the mention of the owner. Malpel (1874-1926) is still a figure of some interest: he was a lawyer at the Court in Toulouse and inherited his father's property, investing then in vine-growing. He moved to Paris in Rue Clichy 26, and had his portrait painted together with his wife Marie by Kees Van Dongen in 1907 (Rotterdam 1996-1997, p. 240). There is a

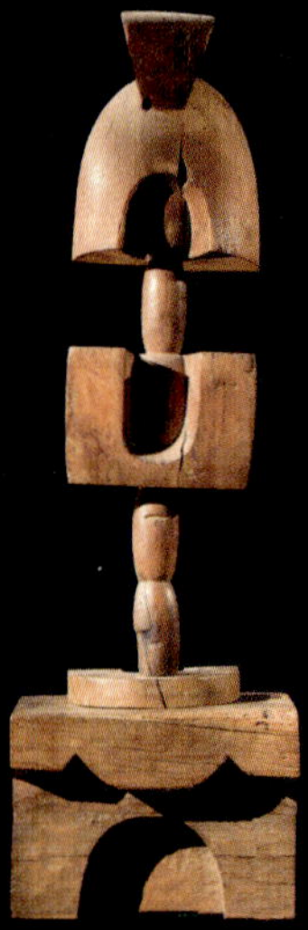

1. Constantin Brancusi
Madame L.R., 1914.
Private collection

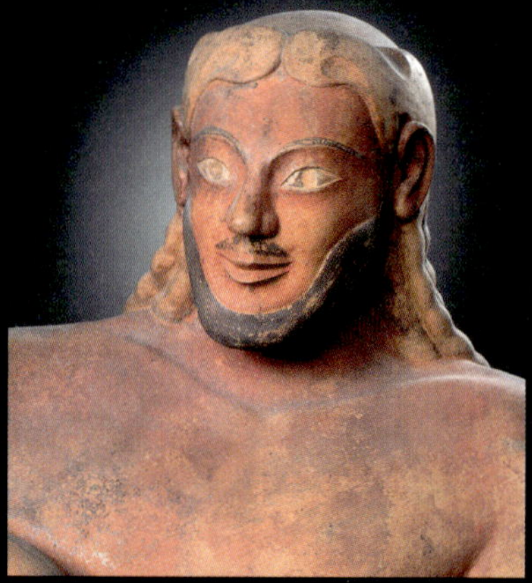

2. Etruscan art, *Sarcophagus of the Spouses*, couple on funeral bed / detail of the female figure.
Last quarter of VI century BC.
Paris, Musée du Louvre

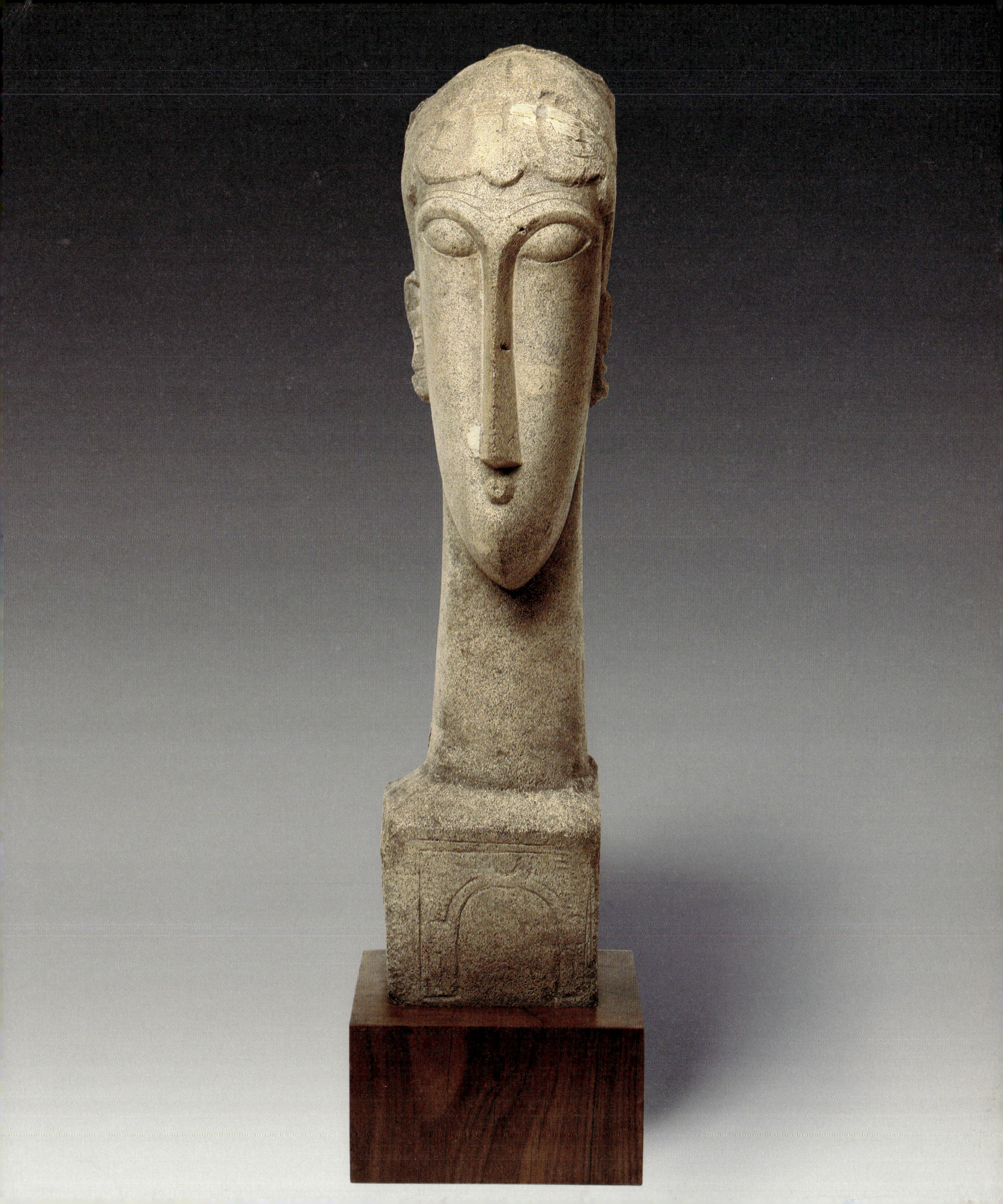

large collection, dated 1910, in two volumes, of his speeches and reviews on modern art, published by Grasset, entitled *Notes sur l'art d'aujourd'hui et peut-être de demain*. In 1914 he stipulated an exclusive contract with Marc Chagall, for a year and a half, for his entire production; other relationships that he had with painters who immigrated to Paris and were active in Montparnasse are also documented (Haršav 2004, p. 217).
The head in Philadelphia was the first to travel across the Ocean: there is documentation regarding its showing at an exhibition of modern sculpture at the Modern Gallery of Marius de Zayas, in New York in 1916 (de Zayas 1996, pp. 99, 139). Thanks also to its characteristics of immobility and almost impersonal stylistic purification, the work became a decisive term of comparison in modernist historiography and in that of Modigliani.
Some important Alexandre drawings can be associated with the sculpture: a three quarter head, before April 1913, that can be compared to an incomplete sheet, in grease pencil: a frontal head, with circular fringe and earrings; finally, a study in blue pencil with the same decorative pattern at the hairline (Alexandre 1993, Nos. 164, 173, 182 and 239 respectively); a possible congruence has been pointed out with the two drawings showing profile view heads (241, 187, 188).

Alessandro Del Puppo

Head, 1912-1913
cat. 32

limestone, 89.2 x 14 x 35.2 cm
London, The Tate Gallery

Exhibitions:
Venice 1930; Rome 1951-1952; Paris 1981, No. 225; Leghorn 1984, No. 13; Düsseldorf 1991, No. 100; London 2006, No. 1; Madrid 2008, No. 16; Bonn 2009, No. 21.

Bibliography:
Pfannstiel 1929, No. 86b; Carrieri 1950, No. 111; Carli 1952, Nos. 28-29; Werner 1962, Nos. 32-33; Patani 1992, No. 22.

Ceroni XXIV

This is the first of Modigliani's works to be acquired by a public collection. It entered the Victoria & Albert Museum of London in 1922, donated by the South African painter Edward Roworth, pupil of the Slade School of Art in London between 1911 and 1914, he had in turn bought it directly from Modigliani's studio in Paris. Promptly exhibited at the Whitechapel Gallery in that same year, it was mistaken by the local press as a "Futurist" work, a quite common expression used to mock a provocatively modern work (Wayne 2006, p. 65). It was also his first sculpture that could be seen in Italy, together with *Head* IX, during the retrospective exhibition curated by Lionello Venturi at the *Biennale di Venezia* in 1930, an exhibition which started off the sensational Modigliani "affair."
Both for its precocious destination to museums and for the exceptional formal quality, over the years the work has achieved a formidable bibliographic success. It is by far the Modigliani sculpture which has circulated the most and had the most visual exposure, it has also become the focus point of nearly all the monographs on the author, but also of a great part of the historiography on twentieth century sculpture (Giedion-Welker 1937, Read 1964, Hammacher 1969, Elsen 1974, Krauss 1977) and on the Modernist tradition (like the Parisian exhibition in 1960, *Les sources du XX siècle*, No. 463).
Furthermore, thanks to the ease with which it was possible to set the smooth surfaces of the Modigliani style modelling near the more refined and purified results of certain tribal sculptures, the sculpture became one of the most classic examples of Primitivist derivation, thus gaining space in all the bibliographies regarding the subject, starting with Robert Goldwater's study (he owned a Guro mask that we propose here for its surprising correspondence; fig. **1**), up to the now historical exhibition *Primitivism and Modern Art* organised by William Rubin (New York, 1984) where there was the exciting comparison, which has become a canon and taken up by us again here, with a Guro mask from the Ivory Coast.
Its status as classic Modigliani style, almost a supreme synthesis of the qualities which were gradually explored in the previous works, was confirmed by Ceroni himself, who placed sculpture XXIV ideally at the top of the sequence of *Heads*. It can be thought, or better, precisely for the combined reasons of its perfection of style and its sale, that it was carried out after the presentation of seven *Heads* at the Salon d'Automne in 1912. Its nature as a work destined to close the cycle can therefore motivate a chronological shift of a year or two compared to the tight limit (1911-1912) proposed by Ceroni.
In any case, it is clear that this is a work which contends, together with *Head* XXI in the Guggenheim, the award for Modigliani's most beautiful sculpture. In fact, here the author reaches the limit of rarefaction; frontally, the sculpture appears as a stone blade, narrowing to the chin down an uncompromising vertical axis, strengthened by the clear profile and confirmed by the nose, by the graphic insertions on the eyeballs, on the forehead and the skull-cap, by the microscopic mouth. More than carved from the substance, the single physiognomic elements seem to be inscribed or engraved on it, in an elegant and fierce deformation, in an alluring and Mannered frontality.

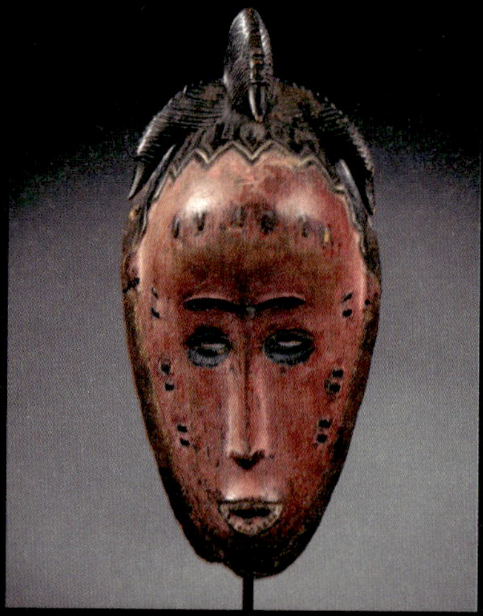

1. Ivory Coast, *Guro Mask*.
New York, The Metropolitan Museum of Art, The Michael C. Rockefeller Memorial Collection.
Gift of Robert Goldwater, 1961

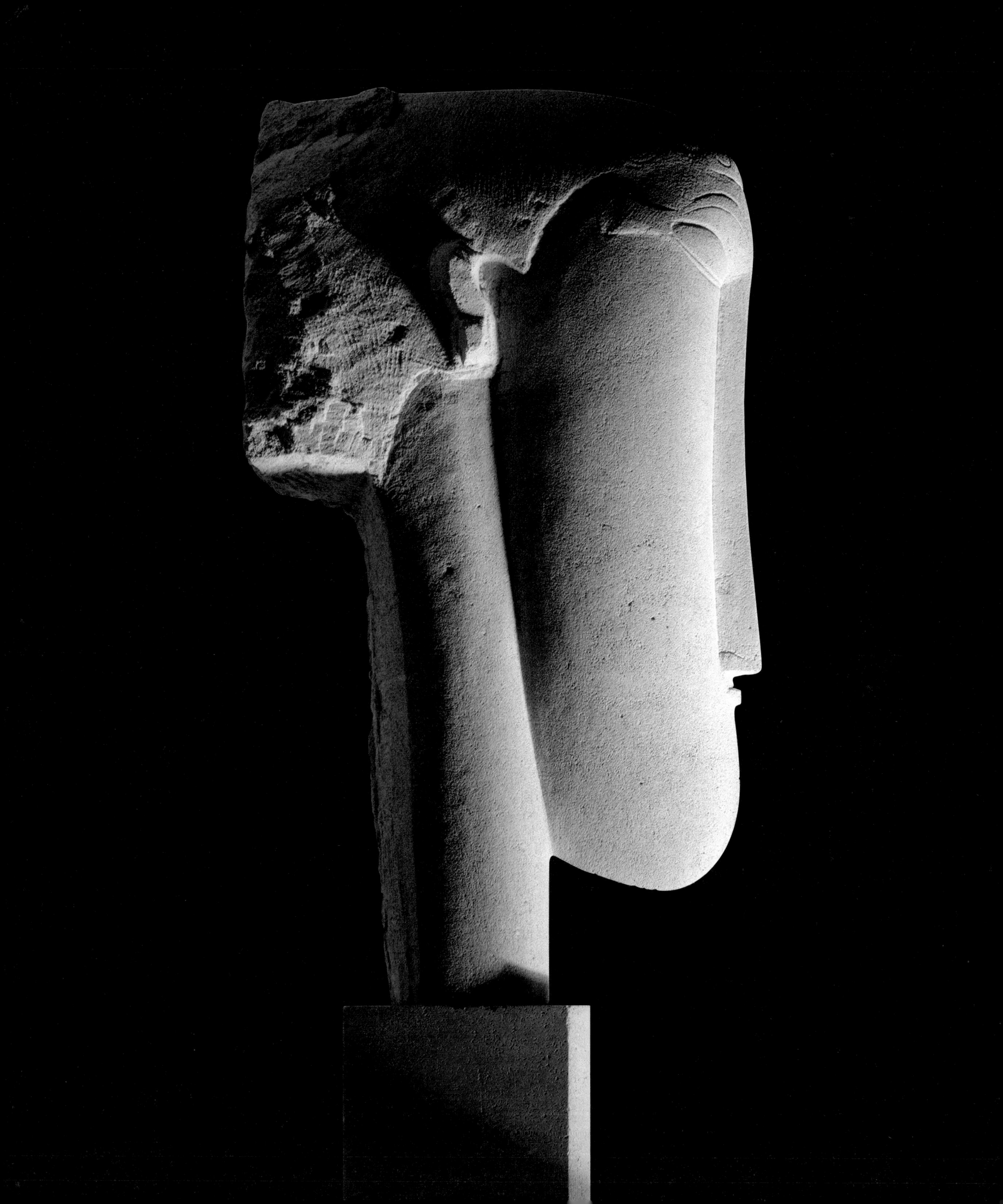

Seen in profile, like the others which can be attributed to this final phase (XVIII, XX, XXII), a real visual dissociation is underway: here profiles acquire a harmony which is not due to the plastic and volumetric proportion with the front part, but rather to an autonomous development of an arabesque. More than a complete three-dimensional and sculptural development in the strict sense, the *Head* appears as the projection of two pictorial surfaces studied separately and then put together on two inflexible levels of the stone block. This process can be deduced from the work sheets. The profiles are, in fact, perfected in the sequence of Alexandre drawings Nos. 189-209, numerically the most, to testify a crucial phase of work. The first drawings (Nos. 189-192) concentrate on the connection between the *quart de brie* nose and the strong semi-circular chin: a second *tranche* develops the theme of the horizontal development of the caryatid head (Nos. 193 and following). The frontal vision is deduced from sheets 240-241, with the typical eyes extended to the edges of the face and the long stylised rod of the nose, in an almost cruciform scheme, confirmed by the broken lines which mark the symmetric bilateral axis of the chin (Nos. 184, 232, 239-240). Its nature as bridge-work between the plastic research and the consequent redefinition of the pictorial style, can be found in the comparison between *Head* XXIV and *Portrait of Frank "Burty" Haviland* (cat. **65**) where a sort of pictorial paraphrasing of the patterns present here can, in fact, be found.

Alessandro Del Puppo

Amedeo Modigliani
Biographical notes

1884 he was born on 12th July in Livorno, the last of four children. His father Flaminio was Jewish from Livorno, he traded in wood and coal. His mother, Eugenia Garsin, a very important figure when learning about Modigliani's early years, was an educated woman who descended from a banking family. When Modigliani was born the family was in a very serious financial situation.

1886 Eugenia started writing a diary, where for a long time she wrote about all the family affairs. Modigliani's childhood and early adolescence were marked by continuous illness which would affect his health for the rest of his life. Perhaps it was also for this reason that he showed very little interest in his studies. However he was very fond of reading works by authors who were very modern at that time, like Baudelaire and Nietzsche, although he did not neglect the Italian classics, such as Dante.

1898 He became seriously ill with typhoid. The account of those terrible days of his illness is noted in his mother's diary. It was in those circumstances that Eugenia, understanding in her son's delirium caused by fever, that he wanted to dedicate himself to art, decided that once he was better, Amedeo would be allowed to follow artistic studies.

1899 When he was fifteen, he began having lessons at Guglielmo Micheli's studio in Livorno, he was formerly one of Fattori's students: there were other young talents there with him: Benvenuto Benvenuti, Oscar Ghiglia, Llewelyn Lloyd, Gino Romiti.

1900 He made a long trip with his mother to the central part of southern Italy, in the hope of improving the rather precarious conditions of his health. It was his uncle who covered all the expenses. He visited Naples, Capri, Amalfi, Rome, Florence and they arrived in Venice. It was in this period that the desire to become a sculptor was born in him.

1902 According to Gino Romiti's testimony, the young Amedeo moved to Pietrasanta and Carrara to realise some sculptures. On 7th May he was in Florence, where he enrolled at the Scuola Libera di Nudo, where Fattori taught.

1903 He moved to Venice and on 19th March he enrolled at the Scuola Libera di Nudo at the Istituto di Belle Arti. He met Umberto Boccioni, Guido Cadorin, Guido Marussig, Fabio Mauroner, Ardengo Soffici. Mauroner introduced him to engraving techniques and Vittorio Pica's worthy editions *Attraverso gli albi e le cartelle*. During this period the young artist from Livorno painted nudes and portraits.

1905 His mother gave him the *Ballad of Reading Gaol* by Oscar Wilde, maximum exponent of English aestheticism, where the author tells of his experience in Reading Gaol (1895-1897), after being found guilty of sodomy. At the Biennale d'Arte in Venice (1903 and 1904) he had the opportunity of getting to know Symbolist painting and Auguste Rodin's sculptures.

1906 He left for Paris with a letter of recommendation signed by Ortis de Zarate, the painter of Chilean origin who was born in Como in Italy. The letter was addressed to the Polish-Jewish sculptor Granowski. Modigliani attended the courses of nudes at the Académie Colarossi, founded by Filippo Colarossi in opposition to the École des Beaux Arts. At the Académie, which had the particularity of also accepting women, his future wife Jeanne Hébuterne also studied painting.

1907 Thanks to the painter Henri Doucet, he met the doctor, collector and great friend to the artists, Paul Alexandre. As Alexandre remembered, Doucet had met Modigliani in a famous Parisian bistrot, the *Lapin Agile*. Touched by Modigliani's terrible depression caused by the fact that he had been obliged to give up his studio, Doucet invited him to the house in rue Delta, where Paul Alexandre rented rooms to many young artists. The relationship between Modigliani and Alexandre was immediately of great friendship. Together they visited the Parisian museums, exhibitions, artists' studios. At the Salon d'Automne there was a retrospective of Cézanne and Modigliani also exhibited seven works, almost all drawings.

1908 Modigliani participated for the first time at the Salon des Indépendants: he exhibited five paintings and a drawing.

1909 He returned to Livorno for some months, as can be seen in his mother's letter dated 3rd July. He painted *Begger of Livorno.* Disappointed by the very provincial atmosphere of the Tuscan city, he returned to Paris and moved to the Cité Falguière, renting a studio near Constantin Brancusi's.

1910 Following Guillaume Apollinaire's advice he exhibited six works at the Salon des Indépendants. He dedicated himself to sculpture but did not abandon painting.

1911 He spent a short time in Normandy. According to a note sent from Brancusi to Paul Alexandre, on 5th March Modigliani exhibited some of his sculptures in Amadeo Souza Cardoso's studio, a Portuguese painter who lived in rue du Colonel Combes. Brancusi helped to organise the exhibition. Modigliani exhibited sketches, gouaches and five sculptures, documented by some photographs. In the spring he exhibited at quai d'Orsay at the Salon des Indépendants, a caryatid, a head and four drawings. At the same Salon, besides a retrospective dedicated to Henri Rousseau, the first review of Cubism took place: Picasso and Braque were noticeably absent.

1912 This was certainly the most important year for his activity as a sculptor: he exhibited seven sculptures all indicated as *Tête, ensemble decoratif* at the X edition of the Salon d'Automne (1st October-8th November), which was held at the Grand Palais des Champs-Elysées.

1913 From the end of April to mid June, for the second time since he had moved to Paris, he went back to Italy. Before leaving for Livorno he handed his sculptures over to Paul Alexandre. From Italy he wrote to his doctor friend to remind him to

pick up one of his sculptures from Brancusi's studio. In Livorno, the legend was born about the sculptures being thrown into a ditch: *vox populi* affirmed that some of his friends had found him a studio with a lot of blocks of stone and Modigliani not being able to extract anything from them, disappointed, he threw them into a ditch, the Fossa Reale.
It is certain that during this stay he visited the Carrara quarries, that really impressed him and urged him to write: "I only want to sculpt with marble." He returned to Paris, to the Cité Fulguière. He met Jacques Lipchitz, Max Jacob, Chaïm Soutine.

1914 Through Max Jacob he met Paul Guillaume who began buying his works and got him a studio in rue Ravignan. He met the English poetess Beatrice Hastings who was his inspiration and model until 1916: he realised ten oil portraits of her and many drawings. His works were exhibited at the Whitechapel Art Gallery in London: he presented a drawing and the stupendous *Head*, previously bought in Paris by the artist Edward Roworth, this is now in the Tate Gallery.
Due to the general mobilisation, on 2nd August Paul Alexandre was assigned to an infantry battalion. He took part in the war until demobilisation, which was just shortly before Modigliani's premature death. The two friends never met again.

1915 Modigliani participated in the exhibition organised by Paul Guillaume in rue Huyghens 6, with Ortis de Zarate, Pable Picasso, Moïse Kisling, Hentri Matisse.

1916 His health got worse, also because of drug and alcohol abuse. He met the poet Léopold Zborowski, who began buying and selling his works and let him have a room in his apartment ın rue Joseph Bara 3. Critics like Apollinaire and Salmon began appreciating his work.
In March he exhibited two *Heads* at the *Exhibition of Sculpture* at the Marius de Zayas's Modern Gallery in New York.

1917 He met the painter Jeanne Hébuterne, a pupil at the Académie Colarossi, who left her family for him and shared his rather modest studio in rue de la Grande-Chaumière.
From 3rd to 30th December Zborowski organised his first personal exhibition at the Galerie Berthe Veill, (*Peintures et des Dessins de Modigliani*).
According to his daughter Jeanne, his nudes were accused of offending public decency and the police closed down the exhibition. No paintings were sold. It was a period of hard work, Modigliani drew a lot and above all he did so in the cafés. He often did portraits of people who just happened to be next to him. Nina Hamnett recalled that he sold his work for little or nothing and remembered that Modigliani used to repeat: "I am Modigliani, a Jew, 5 francs", to convince people to buy his drawings.

1918 He was by now affirmed as a painter but his health continued to deteriorate. With his wife pregnant with their first daughter, he moved to Nice and then Cagnes where he spent the winter. On 29th November his little daughter Jeanne was born. In Nice Modigliani met Paul Guillaume again, as well as the Russian painter Leopold Survage, the Swiss poet Blaise Cendrars who was in contact with the Futurists and in particular with Sonia Delaunay. In his correspondence with Léopold Zborowski, Modigliani continuously asked him to send money because of his difficult economic situation.

1919 He was in Cagnes for some months, as the painter Osterlind's guest, in the villa La Riante. He caught the Spanish flu. He worked a lot, he met Auguste Renoir whom he did not appreciate however. On 31st May he returned to Paris, Jeanne was pregnant again. In September Zborowski organised an exhibition with some of his works at the Hillary Gallery in London. It was a success: Modigliani sent the newspaper cuttings to his mother.
The tuberculosis got worse.
He exhibited at the Salon d'Automne.

1920 Modigliani died on 24th January of tubercular meningitis. Two days later, his wife who was nine months pregnant, committed suicide by throwing herself from the fifth floor of her home.

Catalogue of Works in the Exhibition

Section 1

1. Joseph Antoine Bernard
Straining Towards Nature, ca. 1907.
Lens stone, 32 x 29 x 31.5 cm
Paris, Musée d'Orsay

2. Joseph Antoine Bernard
Modern Sphinx, 1908
Asian marble, 34 x 21.5 x 30 cm
Saint Rémy les Chevreuses, Fondation de Coubertin, donated by Jean Bernard, 1985

3. Elie Nadelman
Classical Head, ca. 1909
marble, 32.1 x 21.3 x 22.7 cm
Washington DC, Hirshhorn Museum and Sculpture Garden, Smithsonian Institution, donated by Joseph H. Hirshhorn, 1966

4. Wilhelm Lehmbruck
Bust of a Kneeling Woman, 1911
chamotte, 48 x 48 x 36 cm
Vienna, Belvedere

5. Wilhelm Lehmbruck
Mother and Child, 1917-1918
artificial stone, 53 x 34 x 17.5 cm
Hamburg, Hamburger Kunsthalle

Section 2

6. Constantin Brancusi
The Kiss, 1907-1908
Marne stone, 28 x 26 x 21 cm
Muzeul de Arta, Craiova – Romania (The Art Museum of Craiova)

7. Amedeo Modigliani
Head of a Woman, 1911-1913
stone, 47 x 25 x 30 cm
Paris, Centre Pompidou, Musée National d'art moderne / Centre de création industrielle (Ceroni III)

8. Amedeo Modigliani
Head, 1911-1912
stone, 49.5 x 18.4 x 22.8 cm
Washington DC, Hirshhorn Museum and Sculpture Garden, Smithsonian Institution, donated by Joseph H. Hirshhorn, 1966 (Ceroni VII)

9. Amedeo Modigliani
Head, 1911-1912
limestone, 41.8 x 12.5 x 17 cm
The Henry and Rose Pearlman Foundation on long term loan to Princeton University Art Museum (Ceroni V)

10. Ossip Zadkine
Head with Lead Eyes, 1919
stone encrusted with original lead, 50 x 23 x 23 cm
Paris, Musée Zadkine de la Ville de Paris

11. Henri Laurens
Woman with Earrings, 1921
stone, h. 40 cm, 13 x 9.3 cm
Berne, Kunstmuseum, Hermann and Margit Rupf Foundation

12. Amedeo Modigliani
Portrait of Pablo Picasso, 1915
oil on cardboard, 34.2 x 26.3 cm
Russia, private collection

13. Ossip Zadkine
Head of a Man, 1918, stone, 34 x 19 x 18 cm. Paris, Musée Zadkine de la Ville de Paris

Section 3

14. Amedeo Modigliani
Head of Caryatid, 1910-1911
blue pencil on paper, 43 x 17 cm
Verona, courtesy Galleria dello Scudo

15. Amedeo Modigliani
Head and Shoulders from Front, Fringe, 1911-1912
black pencil on paper, 42.8 x 26.5 cm
Rouen, Musée des Beaux-Arts, donated by Blaise Alexandre, 2001
Musées de la Ville de Rouen

16. Amedeo Modigliani
Head surmounted by architectural element – sketch for the same figure upside down, 1911-1912
pen and black ink on paper, 20.9 x 26.7 cm
Rouen, Musée des Beaux-Arts, donated by Blaise Alexandre, 2001
Musées de la Ville de Rouen

17. Amedeo Modigliani
Head, 1910-1911
pencil on paper, 43 x 26.5 cm
Private collection

18. Amedeo Modigliani
Head, 1912
pencil on paper, 43 x 26.5 cm
Private collection

19. Amedeo Modigliani
Profile of Head, 1911
grease pencil on paper, cm 43 x 26.5
Private collection

Section 4

20. Amedeo Modigliani
Head of a Woman, 1911-1912
limestone, 65 x 19 x 24 cm
Washington DC, National Gallery of Art, Chester Dale Collection 1963 (Ceroni XVII)

21. Francesco Laurana
Bust of Battista Sforza, 1475 ca.
marble, h. 49 cm
Florence, Museo Nazionale del Bargello

22. Amedeo Modigliani
Head of a Woman, 1911-1912
limestone, 65.4 x 17.1 x 21.3 cm
Minneapolis, Minneapolis Institute of Arts, donated by Mr. and Mrs. John Cowles (Ceroni XVI)

23. Pablo Picasso
Female Nude, 1907
oil on canvas, 61 x 47 cm
Saint Petersburg, The State Hermitage Museum

Section 5

24. Amedeo Modigliani
Head, 1911-19122
stone, 58 x 12 x 16 cm
Paris, Centre Georges Pompidou, Musée National d'art moderne / Centre de création industrielle (Ceroni XII)

25. *Head of Buddha*
XV-XVI century, Lanna, Thailand
bronze, 22 x 16 x 17 cm
Paris, Musée Guimet

26. *Vishnu*
VII-VIII century, Far Eastern art
grés, 26 x 18.5 x 15 cm
Paris, Musée Guimet

27. *Head of Bodhisattva Avalokiteshvara*
VII-VIII century, Far Eastern art
grés, 22 x 11.5 x 12.5 cm
Paris, Musée Guimet

28. *Head of female divinity*
end VII-beginning VIII century, Cambodia

grés, 29 x 13.8 x 7 cm
Paris, Musée Guimet

29. *Statue of Kouros - "Apollo" Milani*
530 BC, Attic production
white marble, h. 139 cm
Florence, Museo Archeologico Nazionale

30. *Head of Helmeted Athena*
V century BC,
painted terracotta,
h. 23 x 12.5 x 17 cm
Regional Council for Cultural Heritage and Sicilian Identity, Museo Archeologico Regionale P. Griffo di Agrigento

Section 6

31. Amedeo Modigliani
Head, 1911-1912
limestone, 70.5 x 23.5 x 7.6 cm
Philadelphia, Philadelphia Museum of Art, donated by Mrs. Maurice J. Speiser in memory of her husband, 1950 (Ceroni XX)

32. Amedeo Modigliani
Head, 1912-1913 ca.
limestone, 89.2 x 14 x 35.2 cm
London, Tate: transferred from the Victoria & Albert Museum 1983, (Ceroni XXIV)

33. *Mask*
Guro, Ivory Coast
carved wood and monkey hair,
h. 26 x 14,5 x 12 cm
London, The British Museum

34. *Mask (Gu)*
XIX-XX century
Guro, Ivory Coast
wood, pigments, rope, h. 44.1 cm
New York, The Metropolitan Museum of Art,
donated by Gertrud A. Mellon,
in memory of Dr. Robert Goldwater,
1977

35. *Mask*
Fang, Gabon
wood, 34 x 21.5 x 15.6 cm
Paris, Musée du quai Branly

36. *Head of the Guardian of the Reliquary*
Fang, Gabon
wood, cm 46.7 x 14.5 x 14.2 cm
Paris, Musée du quai Branly

37. Arturo Martini
Young Girl Full of Love, 1913
plaster, 37 x 19 x 28 cm
Treviso, Museo di Santa Caterina

Section 7

38. Alexander Archipenko*
Salome, 1912
cement, h. 102.9 cm
Switzerland, Rietberg Museum
*not present in the exhibition

39. Jacques Lipchitz
Pregnant Woman, 1914 ca.
plaster, 64.2 x 14.6 x 12.2 cm
London, Tate, donated by Lipchitz Foundation 1982

40. Alexandr Archipenko
Family Life, 1912 (2007)
posthumous bronze,
57 x 33 x 23.2 cm
Bearsville, New York,
The Archipenko Foundation

41. *Figure of the Eyima Byeri Reliquary*
Fang, Gabon
wood, 61.8 x 14.2 x 14.7 cm
Paris, Musée du quai Branly

42. *Figure of the Guardian of Skulls*
Ngumba, Cameroon, 1894
wood, h. 72 cm
Berlin, Ethnologisches Museum

43. *Figure of the Eyima Byeri Reliquary*
Fang, Gabon
wood, 38 x 13 x 10 cm
Marseilles, Musée d'Arts Africains, Océaniens, Amérindies

44. *Figure of the Eyima Byeri Reliquary*
Fang, Gabon
wood, 59 x 17 x 15 cm
Marseilles, Musée d'Arts Africains, Océaniens, Amérindies

45. Constantin Brancusi
Adam and Eve, 1921
chestnut and oak wood,
238.8 x 47.6 x 46.4 cm
New York, Solomon R. Guggenheim Museum

Section 8

46. Amedeo Modigliani
Hermaphrodite, 1910-1911
pencil on paper, 43 x 26.7 cm
Private collection, courtesy Galleria Tega, Milan

47. Amedeo Modigliani
Caryatid, 1910-1911
pencil on paper, 43 x 26 cm
Private collection

48. Amedeo Modigliani
Standing Nude Woman, 1910-1911
pencil on paper, 43 x 26.5 cm
Private collection

49. Amedeo Modigliani
Caryatid, 1911-1912 ca.
oil on canvas, 72.9 x 50.1 cm
Düsseldorf, Kunstsammlung Nordrhein-Westfalen

50. Amedeo Modigliani
Kneeling Caryatid, 1910-1911
pencil on paper, 43 x 26.5 cm
Private collection

51. Amedeo Modigliani
Kneeling Caryatid, 1910-1911
pencil on paper, 42.5 x 26.5 cm
Private collection

52. Amedeo Modigliani
Caryatid, 1913
pencil on paper, 39.7 x 25.7 cm
Dijon, Musée des Beaux-Arts de Dijon

53. Amedeo Modigliani
Kneeling Nude, 1910-1911
grease pencil on paper, 43 x 26.5 cm
Private collection

54. Amedeo Modigliani
Monumental Caryatid, kneeling, from the front, arms raised behind the head, bent forward.
black pencil on paper,
cm 43.1 x 27.7
Rouen, Musée des Beaux-Arts,
donated by Blaise Alexandre, 2001

55. Amedeo Modigliani
Caryatid, 1913-1914
pencil and chalk on paper,
55 x 41.5 cm
Walsall, The New Art Gallery Walsall

56. Amedeo Modigliani
Anadyomene, 1914
graphite and carved lines with relief, on fine white woven paper,
33.9 x 26.5 cm

Princeton, Princeton University Art Museum, legacy of Dan Fellows Platt

57. Amedeo Modigliani
Figure, 1914
drawing and watercolour on paper
h. 34 cm
Private collection, courtesy Amedeo Porro arte moderna e contemporanea, Milan

58. Amedeo Modigliani
Caryatid, 1913 ca.
pencil and watercolour on paper, 55.9 x 45.1 cm
France, private collection

59. Amedeo Modigliani
Caryatid with Vase, 1914 ca.
watercolour on paper, 63.3 x 48.1 cm
London, Tate: legacy of Mrs. A. F. Kessler, 1983

60. Amedeo Modigliani
Caryatid, 1914-1915
tempera on woven paper, 49 x 32 cm
Private collection, courtesy Claudia Gian Ferrari Studio di Consulenza per il '900 Italiano, Milan

61. Amedeo Modigliani
Caryatid, 1915
tempera on woven paper, 67 x 42 cm
Private collection, courtesy Claudia Gian Ferrari Studio di Consulenza per il '900 Italiano, Milan

62. Amedeo Modigliani
Caryatid, 1914
tempera on card, 90 x 70 cm
Private collection

63. Amedeo Modigliani
Female Nude
watercolour and pencil on paper, 54.5 x 42 cm
Private collection, courtesy Galleria Tega, Milan

64. Amedeo Modigliani
Seated Nude, 1914
pencil and watercolour on paper, 54.3 x 43.5 cm
Private collection, courtesy Galleria Tega, Milan

Section 9

65. Amedeo Modigliani
Portrait of the Painter Frank Haviland, 1914
oil on cardboard, 73 x 60 cm
Gianni Mattioli collection
Long term deposit with the Peggy Guggenheim collection, Venice

66. Amedeo Modigliani
Self-Portrait as Pierrot, 1914
oil on cardboard, 43 x 27 cm
Copenhagen, Statens Museum for Kunst

67. Amedeo Modigliani
Woman with Red Hair, 1915
oil on canvas, 42 x 36 cm
Paris, Musée de l'Orangerie, Jean Walter and Paul Guillaume Collection

68. Amedeo Modigliani
Portrait of Léon Indenbaum, 1916
oil on canvas, 54.6 x 45.7 cm
The Henry and Rose Pearlman Foundation, long term loan to Princeton University Art Museum

69. Amedeo Modigliani
Elena Povolozky, 1917
oil on canvas, 64.77 x 48.57 cm
Washington DC, The Phillips Collection

70. Amedeo Modigliani
Sculptural Head, 1910-1911
grease pencil on paper, 43 x 19 cm
Courtesy Guido Guastalla

71. Amedeo Modigliani
Original letter, that accompanies the Sculptural Head drawing, 1910-1911, ink on paper, 18 x 21 cm
Courtesy Guido Guastalla

Bibliography of the Essays and Entries in Catalogue

A Review of the Year 1949-1950
A Review of the Year. Presented at the Annual Meeting on June 12, 1950, in The Philadelphia Museum Bulletin, 226, 1949-1950, pp. 107-119.

Achmatova 1964
A. Achmatova, *I miei incontri con Modigliani*, in *L'Europa letteraria*, 27, March 1964.

Achmatova 1973
A. Achmatova, *Young in Paris and Headed Toward Fame*, edited by O. Carlisle, in *Vogue*, August 1973, p. 146.

Achmatova 1990
A. Achmatova, *Poem without a Hero, 1940-62* in Schmalenbach 1990.

Achmatova 2004
A. Achmatova, *Amedeo Modigliani e altri scritti*, edited by E. Bazzarelli, SE, Milan 2004.

Adam 1906
P. Adam, *Vues d'Amérique*, Paul Ollendorff, Paris 1906.

Adam 1910
P. Adam, *Dix ans d'art français*, Albert Méricant, Paris 1910.

Ahlers-Hestermann 1918
F. Ahlers-Hestermann, *Der Deutsche Kunstlerkreis des Café du Dôme in Paris*, in *Kunst and Kunstler*, 16, 1918.

Alexandre 1922
A. Alexandre, *La vie artistique. Jeunes et autres*, in *Le Figaro*, 15 fevrier 1922.

Alexandre 1993
Modigliani inconnu: témoignages, documents et dessins inèdits de l'ancienne collection de Paul Alexandre, par N. Alexandre, A. Michel, Paris 1993 (Italian edition *Modigliani, testimonianze, documenti e disegni inediti provenienti dalla collezione del dottor Paul Alexandre*, edited by N. Alexandre, U. Allemandi, Turin 1993.

Alexandre, Bakhu s 2002
N. Alexandre, D. Bakhu s, *Catalogue*, in *Amedeo Modigliani. Peintures et dessins provenant de la collection de Paul Alexandre conservés au musée des Beaux-Arts de Rouen*, Musee des beaux-arts, Cabinet des dessins, Rouen 2002.

Allard 1911
R. Allard, *Exposition à la Galerie d'art ancien et d'art contemporain*, in *La Revue Indépendante*, décembre 1911.

Allard 1912a
R. Allard, *Salon des Indépendants-La sculpture*, in *La Revue de France et des pays français*, 2, mars 1912, pp. 67-73.

Allard 1912b
R. Allard, *Le Salon des artistes Indépendants*, in *La Côte*, 8 mars 1912, p. 3.

Allard 1912c
R. Allard, *La vie artistique. Le Salon d'Automne*, in *La Côte*, 7 octobre 1912, p. 3.

Allard 1912d
R. Allard, *La vie artistique. Le Salon d'Automne*, in *La Côte*, 14 octobre 1912.

Allard 1912e
R. Allard, *untitled article*, in *La Côte*, 19-20 octobre 1912, p. 5.

Anti 1922
C. Anti, *Mostra di arte negra*, in Venice 1922, p. 41.

Amadeo de Souza Cardoso 2007
Amadeo de Souza Cardoso, fotobiografia, Assirio & Alvim, Lisboa 2007.

Apollinaire 1912a
G. Apollinaire, *Le Salon des Indépendants*, in *L'Intransigeant*, 3 avril 1912, in Apollinaire 1960, p. 294.

Apollinaire 1912b
G. Apollinaire, *Salon d'Automne*, in L'*Intransigeant*, 2 octobre 1912, in Apollinaire 1960, p. 332.

Apollinaire 1913a
G. Apollinaire, *La sculture d'aujourd'hui*, 7 juin 1913 (unpublished), in Paris 1993, pp. 136-137.

Apollinaire 1913b
G. Apollinaire, *Première exposition de sculpture futuriste du peintre et sculpteur futuriste Boccioni*, in *L'Intransigeant*, 21 juin 1913, in Apollinaire 1960, pp. 409-411.

Apollinaire 1913c
G. Apollinaire, *Méditations esthétiques. Les peintres cubistes*, Paris 1913.

Apollinaire 1914
G. Apollinaire, *Le sculpteur Lehmbruck*, in *Paris Journal*, 26 juin 1914, in Apollinaire 1960, p. 500.

Apollinaire 1917
Sculpture nègres. 24 photographies précédées d'un avertissement de Guillaume Apollinaire et d'un exposé de Paul Guillaume, Paul Guillaume, Paris 1917.

Apollinaire 1960
G. Apollinaire, *Chroniques d'art 1902-1918*, edited by L.C. Breunig, Gallimard, Paris 1960 [2002].

Apollinaire 1988
G. Apollinaire, *Apollinaire on Art: Essays and Reviews 1902-1918*, edited by L.C. Breunig, Da Capo Press, New York 1988.

Apollinaire 1993
G. Apollinaire, *Oeuvres en prose complètes*, edited by P. Caizergues, M. Décaudin, Gallimard, Paris, 1993.

Apollinaire 2009
G. Apollinaire, *Correspondance avec les artistes: 1903-1918*, edited by L. Campa, P. Read, Gallimard, Paris 2009.

Aragon 1930
L. Aragon, *La peinture au défi*, in Paris 1930.

Au Salon d'Automne 1912a
Au Salon d'Automne, in *L'Illustration*, 12 octobre 1912.

Au Salon d'Automne 1912b
Au Salon d'Automne. Maîtres Cubes, in *Comœdia Illustré*, 20 octobre 1912, p. 62.

Auf der Heyde 2009
A. Auf der Heyde, *Ivan Meštrovi : "Lo scultore del popolo serbo,"* in G. Bacci, M. Ferretti, M. Fileti Mazza (edited by), *Emporium*.

Parole e figure tra il 1895 e il 1964, Edizioni della Normale, Pisa 2009, pp. 465-490.

Balas 1981
E. Balas, *The art of Egypt as Modigliani stylistic source*, in *Gazette des Beaux Arts*, février 1981, p. 87.

Balas 1987
E. Balas, *The Unbuilt Architecture of the Early Modern Sculptors*, in *Gazette des Beaux Arts*, 1426, November 1987, pp. 181-190.

Balas 1998
E. Balas, *Joseph Csáky. A pioneer of Modern Sculpture*, America Philosophical Society, Philadelphia 1998.

Baldelli 2007
F. Baldelli, *Tino di Camaino*. Documented appendix edited by C. Carmi, S. Felicetti, Selective Art Edizioni, Morbio Inferiore 2007.

Barber 1990
R. Barber, *Classical: Discovery, Research and Presentation, 1890-1930*, in London 1990, pp. 391-411.

Barth 1997
A. Barth, *Alexander Archipenkos plastisches oeuvre*, Peter Lang, Frankfurt 1997.

Basler 1928
A. Basler, *La sculpture moderne en France*, Crès, Paris 1928.

Basler 1931
A. Basler, *Modigliani*, Crès, Paris 1931.

Baudelaire 1859
Ch. Baudelaire, *Le peintre de la vie moderne* [1859], in Id., *Scritti sull'arte*, Einaudi, Torino 1981, pp. 290-291.

Bazile 1912
G. Bazile, *Oscar Wilde prisonnier de la Préfecture de la Seine*, in *Comœdia*, 9 octobre 1912, p. 2.

Beattie 1983
S. Beattie, *The new sculpture*, Yale University Press, New Haven-London 1983.

Beausire 1988
A. Beausire, *Quand Rodin exposait*, Editions Musée Rodin, Paris 1988.

Bégain 1995
G. Bégain, *Musée National des Arts Asiatiques Guimet. Les peintures du bouddisme tibétain*, Réunion des Musées Nationaux, Paris 1995.

Bell 1922
C. Bell, *Negro sculpture*, in *Since Cézanne*, Harcourt-Brace and Company, New York 1922, pp. 113-118.

Benton *et al.* 2003
C. Benton *et al.*, *Art déco 1910-1939*, Bulfinch, Boston-London 2003.

Burgess 1910
G. Burgess, *The Wild Men in Paris*, in *Architectural Record*, 5, May 1910, pp. 401-414.

Bertelli 1989
C. Bertelli, *Modigliani, l'italiano cosmopolita*, in London 1989, pp. 57-60.

Blackmun Visonà *et al.* 2001
M. Blackmun Visonà *et al.*, *A history of art in Africa*, Harry H. Abrams, New York 2001.

Blanc 1867
Ch. Blanc, *Grammaire des Arts du dessin* [1867], vol. I, Paris 1885.

Blanc s.d.
Ch. Blanc, *La Sculpture*, Librairie Renouard, Henri Laurens Editeur, Paris s.d.

Blau, Troy 1997
E. Blau, N.J. Troy, *Architecture and cubism*, MIT Press, Cambridge (Massachusetts)-London 1997.

Boas 1911
F. Boas, *The Mind of Primitive Man*, The MacMillan Company, New York 1911.

Bozo 1986
D. Bozo, *Préface*, in Paris 1986b, p. 6.

Braun 2004
E. Braun, *The Faces of Modigliani. Identity Politics under Fascism*, in New York 2004, pp. 25-41.

Braun 2006
E. Braun, *Carnal Knowledge*, in London 2006, pp. 45-63.

Breton 1965
A. Breton, *Pablo Picasso. 80 carats... mais une ombre*, in *Le Surréalisme et la peinture* [1928], Gallimard, Paris 1965, pp. 116-118.

Brunner 2006
K. Brunner, *Biographies of Modigliani's Models*, in London 2006, pp. 148-153.

Bullen 2003
J.B. Bullen, *Great British Gauguin, His Reception in London 1910*, in *Apollo*, 500, October 2003, pp. 3-12.

Burnham 1968
J. Burnham, *Beyond Modern Sculpture. The Effects of Science and Tecnology on the Sculpture of this Century*, The Penguin Press, London 1968.

Bushell 1910
S.W. Bushell, *L'art chinois*, Laurens, Paris 1910.

Canudo 1908
R. Canudo, *La torre del lavoro e della libertà di Augusto Rodin*, in *Vita d'Arte*, I, 1, 1908.

Caprile 2006
R. Caprile, *Cariatidi*, in Rome 2006, pp. 213-219.

Carco 1919
F. Carco, *Modigliani*, in *L'Eventail*, 15 juillet 1919, pp. 201-209.

Carli 1952
E. Carli, *Amedeo Modigliani. Con una testimonianza di Jean Cassou*, De Luca, Roma 1952.

Carnduff Ritchie 1952
A. Carnduff Ritchie, *Sculpture of the Twentieth Century*, The Museum of Modern Art, New York 1952.

Carrieri 1950
R. Carrieri, *12 opere di Amedeo Modigliani*, Edizioni del Milione, Milan 1950.

Cellini [1558-1566] 1991
B. Cellini, *La vita* [1558-1566], edited by C. Cordié, Mondadori, Milan 1991.

Ceroni 1958
A. Ceroni (edited by), *Amedeo Modigliani, peintre*, suivi des "souvenirs" de L. Czewchoska, Edizioni del Milione, Milan 1958.

Ceroni 1965
A. Ceroni (edited by), *Amedeo Modigliani, dessins et sculptures avec suite du catalogue illustré de peintures*, Edizioni del Milione, Milan 1965.

Ceroni 1970
A. Ceroni (edited by), *I dipinti di Modigliani*. Presentation by L. Piccioni. Critical and philological apparatus by di A. Ceroni, Rizzoli, Milan 1970.

Chanson Madécasses 1920
Chanson Madécasses, traduit par Évariste Parny, Èditions de la Nouvelle Revue Française, Paris 1920.

Chavannes 1913
E. Chavannes, *Mission archéologique dans la Chine Septentrionale*, Ernest Leroux, Paris 1913.

Chevillot 2009
C. Chevillot, *Forme close avant éclatement*, in Paris 2009, pp. 159-165.

Cladel 1908
J. Cladel, *Auguste Rodin. L'Oeuvre et l'Homme*, Libraire nationale d'art et d'histoire G. van Oest & C., Bruxelles 1908.

Clouzot, Level 1919
H. Clouzot, A. Level, *L'art nègre et l'art océanien. 40 planches hors texte*, Devambez Editeur, Paris 1919.

Collection de M. Charles Vignier 1913

Collection de M. Charles Vignier consistant en sculptures, peintures et objets d'art anciens de l'Asie, ainsi qu'en quelques pièces d'art égyptien, d'art nègre et d'art aztèque, exposées du 16 Mai au 15 Juin 1913, dans la galerie Levesque&C., 190, Faubourg Saint-Honoré.

Coquiot 1924
G. Coquiot, *Des peintres maudits*, Delpeuch, Paris 1924.

Cordier 1910
H. Cordier, *La Chine en France au XVIIIème siècle*, Laurens, Paris 1910.

Cork 1988
R. Cork, *David Bomberg*, The Tate Gallery, London 1988.

Cottington 1997
D. Cottington, *The Maison Cubiste and the Meaning of Modernism in pre-1914 France* in Blau, Troy 1997, pp. 17-40.

Coup d'œil aux Expositions 1922
Coup d'œil aux Expositions, in *Journal des Débats*, 26 fevrier 1922, p. 2.

d'Ivray 1911
J. d'Ivray, *Les fouilles de Kom-E-Chougafa*, in *L'Art Décoratif*, XXV, janvier-juillet 1911, pp. 250-251.

Daix 1979
P. Daix (text by), *Le cubisme de Picasso. Catalogue raisonné de l'œuvre peint, 1907-1916 par P. Daix, J. Rosselet*, Ides et Calendes, Neuchatel 1979.

Dale 1929
M. Dale, *Modern Art: Modigliani*, A. Knopf, New York 1929.

de Colombier 1920
P. de Colombier, *Notes d'art. La Jeune Peinture française*, in *Revue critique des idées et des livres*, 25 juillet 1920.

de Macedo 1959
D. de Macedo, *Les deux Amadeo. Amadeo Modigliani et Amadeo de Souza Cardoso*, Edições Panorama, Lisbonne 1959.

De Milloué 1883
L. De Milloué, *Catalogue du Musée Guimet*, Impr. Pitrat aine, Lyon 1883.

De Seidlitz 1911
W. De Seidlitz, *Les estampes japonais*, Hachette, Paris 1911.

de Zayas 1996
M. de Zayas, *How, When, and Why Modern Art Came to New York*, MIT Press, Cambridge (Massachusetts) 1996.

Denis 1905
M. Denis, *Aristide Maillol*, in *L'Occident*, November 1905, in Denis 1912, pp. 227-236.

Denis 1912
M. Denis, *Théories 1890-1910. Du symbolisme et de Gauguin vers un nouvel ordre classique*, Bibliothèque de l'Occident, Paris 1912.

Descargues 1951
P. Descargues, *Amedeo Modigliani 1884-1920*, Braun, Paris 1951.

di San Lazzaro 1953
G. di San Lazzaro, *Modigliani*, Les Editions du Chêne, Paris 1953.

di San Lazzaro 1957
G. di San Lazzaro, *Modigliani-Portraits*, Fernand Hazan, Paris 1957.

Dimier 1912a
L. Dimier, *Chronique artistique*, in *L'Action Française*, 10 octobre 1912, p. 4.

Dimier 1912b
L. Dimier, *Chronique artistique*, in *L'Action Française*, 13 octobre 1912, p. 4.

Doni [1552] 1863
A.F. Doni, *I marmi* (1552), edited by P. Fanfani; with the author's life written by da S. Bongi, 2 vols., Barbera, Florence 1863.

Dorival 1949
B. Dorival, *Sculptures de peintres: Musée d'Art Moderne*, in *Musées de France*, 1949, pp. 263-271.

Dorival 1950
B. Dorival, *Trois oeuvres de Modigliani*, in *Bullettin del Musée de France*, 7, septembre 1950, pp. 165-167.

Dorival 1974
B. Dorival, *Les Omissions d'Archipenko et de Lipchitz*, in *Bulletin de la Société de l'histoire de l'art francais*, 1974, pp. 201-220.

Dormoy 1922
M. Dormoy, *L'Enseignement du Maitre Sculpteur Antoine Bourdelle*, in *Mercure de France*, I-V, 1922, pp. 684-702.

Downing 1963
G.E. Downing, *Alfred Werner. Modigliani the Sculptor*, in *Art Journal*, 1, 1963, pp. 88, 90.

Duchamp-Villon 1912
R. Duchamp-Villon, *Les Arts. Enquête sur la Sculpture de plein air*, in *Gil Blas*, 17 septembre 1912, p. 4.

Dujardin-Beaumetz 1913
E. Dujardin-Beaumetz, *Entretiens avec Rodin*, Paul Dupont, Paris 1913.

Dumond Wilden 1914
J. Dumond Wilden, *Le plus grand sacrifice*, in *Revista Nova*, I, 20, 20 agosto 1914.

Ede 1971
H.S. Ede, *Savage Messiah: a Biography of the Sculptor Henri Gaudier-Brzeska*, Gordon Fraser, London 1971.

Ede 1987
H.S. Ede, *Savage Messiah: a Biography of the Sculptor Henri Gaudier-Brzeska*, Gordon Fraser, London 1987.

Eli Nadelmann 1913
Eli Nadelmann, in *Gil Blas*, 1 juin 1913, p. 3.

Elsen 1965
A.E. Elsen, *Rodin: Readings on His Life and Work*, Englewood Cliffs, Prentice-Hall, New Jersey 1965, p. 146.

Elsen 1969
A.E. Elsen, *The Partial Figure in Modern Sculpture from Rodin to 1969*, Baltimore Museum of Art, Baltimore 1969.

Elsen 1974
A.E. Elsen, *Origins of modern sculpture: Pioneers and Premises*, George Braziller, New York 1974.

Epstein 1931
J. Epstein, *The Sculptor Speaks. Jacob Epstein to Arnold L. Haskell*, Heinemann, s.l. 1931.

Epstein 1940
J. Epstein, *Let there be sculpture*, G.P. Putnam's Sons, New York 1940.

Epstein 1955
J. Epstein, *An Autobiography*, New York 1955.

Expositions et Concours 1920
Expositions et Concours de *La Chronique des Arts et de la Curiosité*, 12, 30 juin 1920, p. 108.

Faivre 1912
A. Faivre, *Chez les futuristes c'est peut-être les Balkans*, in *Le Figaro*, 3 octobre 1912.

Fels 1921
F. Fels, *Pariser Kunstchronik*, in *Das Kunstblatt*, 3, 1921, pp. 92-94.

Fenellosa 1914
E.F. Fenellosa, *L'art en Chine et au Japon*, Hachette, Paris 1914.

Ferreira 1995
P. Ferreira, *Amadeo de Souza Cardoso peintre portugais 1887-1919*, Centre Culturel C.Gubelkian, Paris 1995.

Flam, Deutch 2003
J. Flam, M. Deutch, *Primitivism and Twentieth Century Art. A Documentary History*, University of California Press, Berkley-Los Angeles 2003.

Foucher 1905
A.A. Foucher, *L'art gréco-bouddique du Gandhara. Étude sur les origines de l'influence classique de l'art*

bouddique de l'Inde et de l'Extrême Orient, 2 voll., Imprimerie Nationale, Ernest Leroux, Paris 1905.

Franchi 1947
R. Franchi, *Modigliani*, Arnaud Editore, Florence 1947.

Fry 1910
R. Fry, *Bushman Paintings*, in *The Burlington Magazine*, March 1910, pp. 334-338.

Fry 1919
R. Fry, *Line as a means of expression in modern art*, in *The Burlington Magazine*, February 1919, pp. 62-69.

Fry 1920
R. Fry, *Negro sculpture*, in *Vision and design*, Chatto and Windus, London 1920, pp. 65-68.

Gautherie-Kampa 1993
A. Gautherie-Kampa, *Le Cercle des artists du Café du Dôme 1903-1904*, doctoral thesis, Institute d'Histoire de l'Art, Université Lumiere Lyon 2, Lyon 1993.

George 1922
W. George, *Joseph Bernard*, in *L'Amour de l'Art*, 1922, pp. 173-175.

George 1925
W. George, *Modigliani*, in *L'Amour de l'Art*, octobre 1925.

Giedion-Welcker 1937
C. Giedion-Welcker, *Moderne Plastik: Elemente der Wirklichkeit; Masse und Auflockerung*, Girsberger, Zürich 1937.

Giraudon 1992
C. Giraudon, *Paul Guillaume et les peintres du XXe siècle. De l'Art nègre à l'Avant-garde*, La Bibliothèque des Arts, Paris 1992.

Golding 1959
J. Golding, *Le Cubisme* [1959], René Julliard, Paris 1968, pp. 228-229.

Golding 1985
J. Golding, *Unique Forms of Continuity in Space*, Tate Gallery, London 1985.

Goldwater 1938
R. Goldwater, *Primitivism in Modern Art*, Harper, New York 1938.

Gonzáles 1931-1932
J. Gonzáles, *Picasso et les cathédrales. Picasso sculpteur* [1931-1932], IVAM, Centro Julio Gonzáles, Valencia.

Gopnik 1983
A. Gopnik, *High and Low: Caricature, Primitivism and the Cubist Portrait*, in *Art Journal*, XLIV, 4, 1983, pp. 371-376.

Grey 1920
R. Grey, *Modigliani*, in *L'Action*, 6, 1920, pp. 49-53.

Gronkowksi 1920
C. Gronkowksi, *La réouverture du Musée Cernuschi et les théories nouvelles sur l'Art Chinois primitif*, in *La Renaissance de l'Art Français et des industries de luxe*, III, 1920, pp. 464-467.

Guastalla 2006
S. Guastalla (with critical text by), *Jacob Modigliani Picasso. Gouaches, disegni, incisioni*, Graphis Arte, Livorno 2006.

Guillaume 1920a
P. Guillaume, *Deux Peintres: Modigliani, Utrillo*, in *Les Arts à Paris*, 6, November 1920, pp. 1-2.

Guillaume 1920b
P. Guillaume, *"Les Art à Paris" à Londres*, in *Les Art à Paris*, 7, décembre 1920, p. 2.

Guillaume 1953
Ricordo di Paul Guillaume a Gotthard Jedlicka in Jedlicka 1953, pp. 33-34.

Guimet 1914
É. Guimet, *Les portraits d'Antinoé au Musée Guimet*, Hachette, Paris 1914.

Hamel 1920
M. Hamel, *La jeune peinture française*, in *Les Arts*, 185, 1920, p. 24.

Hammacher 1971
A.M. Hammacher, *L'évolution de la sculpture moderne. Tradition et innovation*, Editions Cercle d'art, Harry H. Abrams, Paris, New York 1971.

Hammacher 1984
A.M. Hammacher, *Amedeo Modigliani*, in Livorno 1984, pp. 43-49.

Haršav 2004
B. Haršav, *Marc Chagall and His Times: a Documentary Narrative*, Stanford University Press, Stanford (California) 2004.

Haskell 2003
B. Haskell, *Elie Nadelman: Sculptor of Modern Life*, Whitney Museum of American Art, New York 2003.

Haskell, Penny 1981
F. Haskell, N. Penny, *Taste and the Antique: The Lure of Classical Sculpture, 1500-1900*, Yale University Press, New Haven-London 1981.

Hausenstein 1918
W. Hausenstein, *Albert Weisgerber*, Piper, Münich 1918, p. 8, in Gautherie-Kampa 1993, p. 76.

Hildebrand 1907
A. Hildebrand, *The Problem of Form in Painting and Sculpture*, translated by M. Meyer, R.M. Ogden, G.E. Stechert & Co., New York 1907.

Hourcade 1912a
O. Hourcade, *Le mouvement pictural. Verse un école française de peinture*, in *La Revue de France et de Pays Français*, 5, juin 1912, pp. 254-258.

Hourcade 1912b
O. Hourcade, *Au Grand-Palais. Vernissage du Salon d'Automne- Impressions d'ensemble*, in *Paris Journal*, 30 septembre 1912, p. 1.

Hourcade 1912c
O. Hourcade, *Le Salon d'Automne. Salle XI*, in *Paris Journal*, 30 septembre 1912, p. 2.

Hourcade 1912d
O. Hourcade, *Le Salon d'Automne. Salle III*, in *Paris Journal*, 1 octobre 1912, p. 3.

Humbert 1994
J.M. Humbert, edited by, *Egyptomania*, Réunion des musees nationaux, Paris 1994.

I Remember Modigliani 1951
I Remember Modigliani. Jacques Lipchitz as Told to Dorothy Seckler, in "Art news," 1951, pp. 26-30.

Ivan Mestrovich 1919
Ivan Mestrovich. A Monograph, Williams and Borgate, London 1919.

Jamot 1912
P. Jamot, *La "suite indienne" de M. Albert Besnard*, in *Gazette des Beaux Arts*, 660, juin 1912, pp. 437-449.

Jedlicka 1953
G. Jedlicka, *Modigliani 1884-1920*, Rentsch, Erlenbach-Zürich 1953.

Jianou, Dufet 1975
I. Jianou, M. Dufet, *Bourdelle*, Arted, Paris 1975.

John 1954
A. John, *Chiaroscuro. Fragments of autobiography*, Jonathan Cape, London 1954.

Jullian *et al.* 1989
R. Jullian, J. Bernard, L. Stoenesco, P. Grémont Gervaise, *Joseph Bernard*, Fondation de Coubertin, Saint-Rémy-les-Chevreuses 1989.

Kahn 1911
G. Kahn, *Art moderne*, in *Le Mercure de France*, 16 décembre 1911, p. 846.

Kahn 1912
G. Kahn, *untitled article*, in *Le Mercure de France*, 1 novembre1912, pp. 178-182.

Kessler 2004
H. Kessler, *Das Tagebuch*, edited by C. Schäfer, G. Biedermann, Klett Cotta, Stuttgart 2004.

Kirstein 1948
L. Kirstein, *The Sculpture of Elie Nadelman*, The Museum of Modern Art, New York 1948.

Kirstein 1973
L. Kirstein, *Elie Nadelman*, Eakins Press, New York 1973.

Klein 2002
H. Klein, *Vicenc Kramà, un théoricien et collectionneur du cubisme à Prague*, Réunion des musées nationaux, Paris 2002.

Krauss 1977
R. Krauss, *Passages in Modern Sculpture*, Thames and Hudson, London 1977.

Kropmanns 1999
P. Kropmanns, *The Gauguin Exhibition in Weimar in 1905*, in *The Burlington Magazine*, January 1999, pp. 24-31.

La Brosse 1912
La Brosse, *Courrier des Arts. J.A. Csáky*, in *Paris Journal*, 27 septembre 1912, p. 4.

La tombe d'Oscar Wilde 1911
La tombe d'Oscar Wilde, in *Gil Blas*, 18 November 1911, p. 2.

Lanthemann 1970
J. Lanthemann, *Modigliani 1884-1920: Catalogue Raisonné*, Barcelona 1970.

Lariot 1913
V. Lariot, *L'Art immoral*, in *Montjoie!* , 4, 29 mars 1913, p. 6.

Laude 1968
J. Laude, *La peinture française (1905-1914) et "l'art nègre". Contribution à l'étude des sources du fauvisme et du cubisme*, Klincksieck, Paris 1968.

Laughing Torso 1932
Laughing Torso. Reminiscences of Nina Hamnett, Constable Co., London 1932.

Le Normand Romain 2009
A. Le Normand Romain, *"Rodin n'a pas d'élèves,"* in Paris 2009, pp. 105-109.

Le Salon d'Automne 1912a
Le Salon d'Automne, in *Comœdia*, 30 septembre 1912, p. 1.

Le Salon d'Automne 1912b
Le Salon d'Automne, in *La Vie parisienne*, 5 octobre 1912, p. 713.

Le Théâtre des Champs-Elysées 1912
Le Théâtre des Champs-Elysées entièrement construit en ciment armé, in *Gil Blas*, 29 février 1912.

Lecombre 1994
S. Lecombre, *Zadkine. L'œuvre sculpté*, Paris-musées, Paris 1994.

Les arts plastiques 1913
Les arts plastiques, in *Montjoie!*, 9-10, 14-19 juin 1913, p. 12.

Les Arts. Modigliani 1922
Les Arts. Modigliani, in *L'Europe Nouvelle*, 25 février 1922, p. 243.

Les beaux-arts, A travers les expositions 1922
Les beaux-arts, A travers les expositions, in *Revue critique des idées et des livres*, mars 1922, p. 185.

Level 1959
A. Level, *Souvenirs d'un collectionneur*, Paris, Alain Mazo, 1959.

Levinson 1925
A. Levinson, *Joséphine Baker et la "Revue nègre,"* in *L'Art vivant*, 21, 1 novembre 1925.

Licini 1934
O. Licini, in *L'Orto* [1934], in Verona 1984-1985, p. 106.

Lipchitz 1954a
J. Lipchitz, *Amedeo Modigliani, 1884-1920,* Flammarion, Paris 1954.

Lipchitz 1954b
J. Lipchitz, *Amedeo Modigliani, 1884-1920*, Abrams, New York 1954.

Lipchitz 1958
J. Lipchitz, *Amedeo Modigliani*, Garzanti, Milano 1958.

Lipchitz 1972
J. Lipchitz (con H.H. Arnason), *My Life in Sculpture*, The Viking Press, New York 1972.

Lloyd 1991
J. Lloyd, *German Expressionism: Primitivism and Modernity*, Yale University Press, New Haven-London 1991.

Locke 1924
A. Locke, *Note on African Art*, in *Opportunity. Journal of Negro Life*, May 1924, pp. 134-138.

Marani 1999
P. Marani, *Leonardo. Una carriera di pittore*, Motta, Milan 1999.

Marcadé 1979
J.C. Marcadé, *L'Avant-Garde Russe et Paris*, in *Cahiers du Musée national d'Art moderne*, octobre-décembre 1979, pp. 174-183.

Marchilac 2007
F. Marchilac, *Joseph Csáky du cubisme historique à la figuration réaliste catalogue raisonné des sculptures*, Les Éditions de l'Amateur, Paris 2007.

Maspero 1908
G. Maspero, *Causerie d'Egypte*, Guilmoto, Paris 1908.

Maspero 1912
G. Maspero, *Egypte*, Hachette, Paris 1912.

Maspero 1913
G. Maspero, *Essais sur l'art égyptien*, Guilmoto, Paris 1913.

Matisse 1908
H. Matisse, *Note di un pittore* (1908), in *Scritti e pensieri sull'arte*, collected and annotated by D. Fourcade, Einaudi, Turin 1979, pp. 3-14.

Mattarella 2006
L. Mattarella, *Alla ricerca della forma perfetta. Modigliani e le donne*, Rome 2006, pp. 99-111.

Megged 1984
M. Megged, *Modigliani: l'enigma*, in Livorno 1984, pp. 50-59.

Meidner 1943
L. Meidner, *The Young Modigliani: Some Memories*, in *The Burlington Magazine*, April 1943, pp. 87-91.

Melani 1912
A. Melani, *Scultura italiana antica e moderna*, Hoepli, Milan [1912].

Mercereau 1911
A. Mercereau, *Critique et notes. Exposition de l'art contemporain*, in *Vers et Prose*, octobre-décembre 1911.

Messina 1994
M.G. Messina, *Le muse d'oltremare. Esotismo e primitivismo nell'arte contemporanea*, Einaudi, Turin 1994.

Messina 2004
M.G. Messina, *Una visione imperiosa": l'ordine del giorno a Paris fra 1907 e 1908*, in *Ricerche di Storia dell'Arte*, 81, 2004, pp. 23-36.

Meyers 2006
J. Meyers, *Modigliani: a Life*, Duckworth, London 2006.

Michaelsen 1977
K.J. Michaelsen, *Archipenko: a Study of the Early Works, 1908-1920*, Garland Publications, New York 1977.

Michel, Muntz, Molinier 1902
A. Michel, E. Muntz, E. Molinier, *Tribune des Arts. La Question Laurana*, in *Les Arts*, I, 4, mai 1902, pp. 37-44.

Migeon 1908
G. Migeon, *Au Japon; promenades aux sanctuaires de l'art; ouvrage illustré de 68 gravures tiré hors texte*, Hachette, Paris 1908.

Miller 1995
S. Miller, *Brancusi. A survey of his work*, Oxford University Press, Oxford 1995.

Modigliani 1958
J. Modigliani, *Modigliani senza leggenda*, Vallecchi, Florence 1958.

Modigliani 1990
J. Modigliani, *Modigliani: une Biographie*, Adam Biro, Paris 1990.

Modigliani 2004
Modigliani, presentation by L. Piccioni (special edition for the *Corriere della Sera*) Rizzoli, Skira, Milan 2004.

Modigliani 2005
J. Modigliani, *Modigliani, mio padre*, edited by Ch. Parisot, Abscondita, Milano 2005.

Modigliani 2006
A. Modigliani, *Le lettere*, edited by E. Pontiggia, Abscondita, Milan 2006.

Montserrat 2002
D. Montserrat, *Ninety years of Nefertiti*, in *Apollo*, 485, 2002, pp. 3-8.

Morice 1910
Ch. Morice, *Le Salon de la Société Nationale des Beaux-Arts*, in *Mercure de France*, 1 mai 1910, pp. 157-163.

Nadelman 1974
E. Nadelman, [*Declaration*], in Elsen 1974, p. 122.

Neugass 1934
F. Neugass, *Les sources de l'art de Amadeo Modigliani*, in *L'Art et les artistes*, XXVIII, 1934, pp. 330-335.

Ojetti 1912
U. Ojetti, *La decima Esposizione d'arte a Venezia*, Istituto Italiano d'Arti Grafiche, Bergamo 1912.

Opinions sur l'art nègre 1920
Opinions sur l'art nègre, in *L'Action*, I, 2, 1920, pp. 23-28.

Pach 1913
W. Pach, *A Sculptor's Architecture*, New York 1913, in *The Armory Show-International Exhibition of Modern Art 1913*, Pamphlets-Arno Press, New York 1972, vol. II, pp. 7-21.

Pach 1924
W. Pach, *Raymond Duchamp-Villon*, Imprimé pour John Quinn et ses amis, Jacques Povolozky Editeur, Paris 1924.

Parigoris 1988
A. Parigoris, *Les constructions cubistes dans "Les Soirées de Paris". Apollinaire, Picasso et les clichés Kahnweiler* , in *La Revue de l'Art*, IV, 82, 1988, p. 61-74.

Parisot 2005
Ch. Parisot, *Modigliani*, Gallimard, Paris 2005.

Parisot 2006
Ch. Parisot, *Modigliani: la vita, le opere*, Delfino-Carte segrete, Sassari-Rome 2006.

Parisot 2008
Ch. Parisot, *Modigliani, l'artiste italien*, in Caserta 2008, pp. 23-94.

Parisot 2010
Ch. Parisot, *La vie d'artiste*, in *Modigliani. Dal Classicismo al Cubismo*, Palestrina, Museo Archeologico Nazionale, 24th June-10th September 2010, catalogue of the exhibition edited by C. Strinati *et al.*, Edizioni Casa Modigliani, Rome 2010, pp. 25-38

Patani 1992
O. Patani, *Amedeo Modigliani. Catalogo generale. Sculture e disegni 1909-1914*, Leonardo, Milano 1992.

Patani 1994
O. Patani, *Amedeo Modigliani. Catalogo generale: disegni 1906-1920 con i disegni provenienti dalla collezione Paul Alexandre (1906-1914)*, Leonardo, Milan 1994.

Petrucci 1911
R. Petrucci, *L'Art Bouddique en Extrême Orient d'après des découvertes récentes*, in *Gazette des Beaux-Arts*, 651, septembre, 1911, pp. 177-192.

Pfannstiel 1929
A. Pfannstiel, *Modigliani*, Éditions M. Scheur, Paris 1929.

Piccioni 2004
L. Piccioni, *Esplosione di canto*, in *Modigliani* 2004, pp. 7-23.

Porter 1937
J.A. Porter, *The Negro Artist and Racial Bias*, in *Art Front*, July-August 1937, pp. 8-9.

Pottier 1909
E. Pottier, *Les terres cuites de Tanagre*, in *Gazette des Beaux-Arts*, series IV, I, 1909, pp. 21-33.

Pound 1992
E. Pound, *Henri Gaudier Brzeska*, Tristram, Auch 1992.

Ragghianti 1959
C.L. Ragghianti, *Revisione di Modigliani*, in *Sele Arte*, VII, 40, 1959.

Read 1964
H. Read, *Modern Sculpture. A concise history*, Thames and Hudson, London 1964.

Reinach 1897
S. Reinach, *Répertoire de la Statuaire Greque et Romaine*, vol. I (*Clarac de poche*), E. Leroux, Paris 1897.

Rhodes 1994
C. Rhodes, *Primitivism and Modern Art*, Thames and Hudson, London 1994.

Roches 1912
F. Roches, *Le Salon d'Automne*, in *L'Art Décoratif*, II, 1912, p. 342.

Rodin 1904a
A. Rodin, *La Leçon de l'Antique*, in *Le Musée*, vol. I, 1904, pp. 15-18.

Rodin 1904b
A. Rodin, *Une Statue de Femme au Musée de Naples*, in *Le Musée*, vol. I, 1904, pp. 116-120.

Rodin 1904c
A. Rodin, *La Tête Warren*, in *Le Musée*, vol. I, 1904, pp. 298-301.

Rodin 1905
A. Rodin, *Le Parthénon et les Cathédrales*, in *Le Musée*, vol. II, 1905, pp. 66-68.

Rodin 1910
A. Rodin, *Vénus, à la Vénus de Milo*, in *L'Art et les Artistes*, mars 1910.

Rodin 1911
A. Rodin, *L'Art. Entretiens réunis par Paul Gsell*, Grasset, Paris 1911 (Italian edition A. Rodin, *L'Arte. Conversazioni raccolte da Paul Gsell*, Reverdito, Trento 1911).

Roger-Marx 1912
C. Roger-Marx, *La comédie artistique au Salon d'Automne. Maîtres cubes*, in *Comœdia Illustré*, 20 octobre 1912.

Rosenblum 1970
R. Rosenblum, *Transformation in Late Eighteenth Century Art*, Princeton University Press, Princeton 1970.

Rosenthal 1912
L. Rosenthal, *Les Salons des 1912*, in *Gazette des Beaux Arts*, II, 1912, pp. 35-62.

Roy 1958
C. Roy, *Modigliani*, in *Le goût de notre temps*, vol. 23, Editions d'Art Albert Skira, Genève 1958.

Rowell 1995
M. Rowell, *Brancusi and Drawing*, in Paris 1995, pp. 286-299.

Rubin 1985
W. Rubin, *Primitivismo modernista. Un'introduzione*, in *Primitivismo nell'arte del 20. secolo: affinità fra il tribale e il moderno,* edited by W. Rubin, 2 vols., Mondadori, Milan 1985.

Rumpf 1953
A. Rumpf, *Archaeologie, I*, 1953.

Salmon 1910
A. Salmon, *Le Salon de la Société Nationale des Beaux -Arts*, in *Paris Journal*, 14 avril 1910, p. 2.

Salmon 1911a
A. Salmon, *Le Salon d'Automne*, in *Montjoie!*, novembre-décembre 1911.

Salmon 1911b
A. Salmon, *Courrier des ateliers*, in *Paris Journal*, 14 décembre 1911, p. 4

Salmon 1912
A. Salmon, *Courrier des ateliers*, in *Paris Journal*, 16 mars 1912, p. 4.

Salmon 1914
A Salmon, *Elie Nadelman*, in *L'Art decorative*, mars 1914, pp. 107-114.

Salmon 1919
A. Salmon, *La Jeune Sculpture française*, Albert Messein, Paris 1919.

Salmon 1926
A. Salmon, *Modigliani. Sa vie et son oeuvre*, Éditions des Quatre Chemins, Paris 1926.

Salmon 1958
A. Salmon, *Le vie passionnée de Modigliani*, Intercontinentale du Livre, Paris 1958.

Sarti 1921
C.G. Sarti, *Après l'exposition Amedeo Modigliani*, in *Don Quiquote*, 22 janvier 1921.

Schaub-Koch 1933
E. Schaub-Koch, *Modigliani*, Mercure universel, Lille, Paris 1933.

Scheiwiller 1927
G. Scheiwiller, *Amedeo Modigliani*, Hoepli, Milan 1927.

Schmalenbach 1990
W. Schmalenbach, *Amedeo Modigliani: Paintings, Sculptures and Drawings*, Prestel, Münich 1990.

Schmalenbach 2006
W. Schmalenbach, *I ritratti*, in Rome 2006, pp. 43-63.

Schnell 1980
W. Schnell, *Der Torso als problem des modernes kunst*, Mann Verlag, Berlin 1980.

Schnell 2009
W. Schnell, *Quelques réflexions sur la gestuelle, l'exemple de l'Agenouillée de Wilhelm Lehmbruck, héritière de Ferdinand Hodler*, in Paris 2009, pp. 197-203.

Schuster, Pfannstiel 1986
B. Schuster, A.S. Pfannstiel, *Modigliani: a study of his sculpture*, Namega corporation, Jacksonville 1986.

Sculpture futuriste 1912
Sculpture futuriste, in *Paris Journal*, 28 septembre 1912, p. 3.

Segalen 1995
V. Segalen, *Essai sur l'exotisme, une esthétique du divers*, Bibliothèque artistique et littéraire, Fontfroide 1995.

Serstevens 1912a
A. Serstevens, *Considérations sur le Salon de la Nationale. La Sculpture*, in *Comœdia*, 4 juin 1912, p. 2.

Serstevens 1912b
A. Serstevens, *Les sculptures décoratives d'Emile Bourdelle pour le Théâtre des Champs-Elysées*, in *Comœdia*, 29 décembre 1912, pp. 1-2.

Silber 1986
E. Silber, *Primitivism and the Avant-Garde*, in Ead., *The sculpture of Epstein with a complete catalogue*, Phaidon, Oxford 1986, pp. 23-26.

Silhouettes-Emile Antoine Bourdelle 1912
Silhouettes-Emile Antoine Bourdelle, in *Paris Journal*, 21 août 1912, p. 4.

Silver, Golan 1985
K.E. Silver, R. Golan, *The Circle of Montparnasse: Jewish artists in Paris, 1905-1945*, Universe Books, New York 1985.

Simon 1994
M. Simon, *La Sculture d'André Derain ou "la matière est la vertu des formes,"* in Paris 1994-1995, pp. 313-321.

Soby 1954
J.T. Soby, *Modigliani*, The Museum of Modern Art, New York 1954.

Soffici 1954
A. Soffici, *Il salto vitale*, Vallecchi, Florence 1954.

Spies 1983
W. Spies, *Picasso. Das plastische Werk*, Stuttgart, Gerd Hatje 1983.

Spies 2000
W. Spies, *Picasso Sculpteur. Catalogue raisonné des sculptures*, Centre Georges Pompidou, Paris 2000.

Stoermer 1931
C. Stoermer, *Erinnerungen an Modigliani*, in *Der Queerschnitt*, Juni, 1931, pp. 13-14.

Strachan 1976
W.J. Strachan, *Towards Sculpture. Maquettes and Sketches from Rodin to Oldenburg*, Thames and Hudson, London 1976.

Strinati 2010
C. Strinati, *Modigliani dal Classicismo al Cubismo*, in *Modigliani. Dal Classicismo al Cubismo*, Palestrina, Museo Archeologico Nazionale, 24th June-10th September 2010, catalogue of the exhibition edited by C. Strinati *et al.*, Edizioni Casa Modigliani, Rome 2010.

Sweeney 1935
J.J. Sweeney, *African Negro Art*, The Museum of Modern Art, New York 1935.

Tagliapietra 2002
F. Tagliapietra, *Amedeo Modigliani a Venezia 1903-1905*, in *Arte documento*, 16, 2002, pp. 230-241.

Torgovnick 1990
M. Torgovnick, *The Politic of Roger Fry's Vision and Design*, in *Gone Primitive: Savage Intellects, Modern Live*, The University of Chicago Press, Chicago 1990, pp. 85-104.

Valentiner 1935
W.R. Valentiner, *Tino di Camaino. A Sienese Sculptor of the Fourteenth Century*, Pegasus press, Paris 1935.

Vanderpyl 1920
Vanderpyl, *Salons et Expositions*, in *Le Petit Parisien*, 26 décembre 1920.

Vauxcelles 1910
L. Vauxcelles, *Y-a-t-il une Renaissance de l'Idéal classique?*, in *Gil Blas*, 30 septembre 1910, p. 3.

Vauxcelles 1912a
L. Vauxcelles, *Enquête sur la sculpture de plein air*, in *Gil Blas*, 7 septembre 1912, p. 4.

Vauxcelles 1912b
L. Vauxcelles, *untitled article*, in *Gil Blas*, 12 septembre 1912.

Vauxcelles 1912c
L. Vauxcelles, *Le Salon d'Automne. Rotonde de l'avenue d'Antin. M. Joseph Bernard*, in *Gil Blas*, 30 septembre 1912, p. 3.

Vauxcelles 1912d
L. Vauxcelles, *Le Salon d'Automne. Salle XI*, in *Gil Blas*, 30 septembre 1912, pp. 2-3.

Vauxcelles 1912e
L. Vauxcelles, *La jeune peinture française*, in *Gil Blas*, 21 octobre 1912.

Vauxcelles 1912f
L. Vauxcelles, *Les Arts-Discussion*, in Gil Blas, 22 octobre 1912, p. 4.

Vente Drouot 1930
Vente Hôtel Drouot, Paris, 14 juin 1930.

Venturi 1908
A. Venturi, *Storia dell'Arte Italiana. VI. La Scultura del Quattrocento*, Hoepli, Milano 1908.

Venturi 1930
L. Venturi, *Mostra personale di Amedeo Modigliani*, in Venezia 1930, pp. 116-118.

Verardi 2005
G. Verardi, *Gandhara*, in *Enciclopedia archeologica. Asia*, Istituto della Enciclopedia italiana, Roma 2005.

Vildra 1913
Ch. Vildra, *Les ensemble décoratifs au Salon d'Automne*, in *L'Effort Libre*, 3, décembre 1913, pp. 175-178.

Vogel 1908
P. Vogel, *Études de sculpture bouddhique*, in *Bulletin de l'Ecole française d'Extrême-Orient*, 8, 1908, pp. 487-500.

Vorobev 1974
Marevna [Vorobev], *The Painters of La Ruche*, translated by N. Heseltine, MacMillan, New York 1974.

Wayne 2002
K. Wayne, *Modigliani and the Artists of Montparnasse*, Harry N. Abrams, in association with the Albright-Knox Gallery Buffalo, New York 2002.

Wayne 2006
K. Wayne, *Modigliani and England*, in London 2006, pp. 65-73.

Werner 1960-61
A. Werner, *Modigliani as a sculptor*, in *Art Journal*, 2, Winter, 1960-1961, pp. 70-78.

Werner 1962
A. Werner, *Modigliani Sculpteur*. Adaption française de F.et J. Bruschweiler, Nagel, Génève1962.

Westheim 1921
P. Westheim, *Der Maler malt Kunstprobleme*, in *Das Kunstblatt*, 1921, third to last number, pp. 289-295.

Wiese 1923
E. Wiese, *Alexander Archipenko*, Junge Kunst, vol. 4, Lipsia 1923.

Wilenski 1932
R.H. Wilenski, *The meaning of modern sculpture*, Stokes, New York 1932.

Zadkine 1968
O. Zadkine, *Le Maillet et le Ciseau. Souvenirs de ma vie*, Albin Michel, Paris 1968.

Zervos 1942
Ch. Zervos, *Pablo Picasso, Œvres de 1906 à 1912*, vol. II, *Cahiers d'art*, Paris 1942.

Zöllner 2004
F. Zöllner, *Leonardo da Vinci 1452-1519. The complete paintings*, Taschen, Köln 2004.

Exhibitions Related to the Essays and Entries in Catalogue

Paris 1905
Société du Salon d'Automne. Catalogue des ouvrages de peinture, sculpture, dessin exposés au Grand Palais des Champs-Elysées, Paris, Grand Palais, 18th October - 25th November 1905, catalogue of the exhibition, Paris 1905.

Paris 1906
Société du Salon d'Automne. Catalogue des ouvrages de peinture, sculpture, dessin exposés au Grand Palais des Champs-Elysées, Paris, Grand Palais, 6th October - 15th November 1906, catalogue of the exhibition, Paris 1906.

Paris 1908a
Salon des Indépendants. Catalogue de la 24e exposition, Paris, Jardin des Tuileries, Serres de l'Orangerie, 20th March - 2nd May 1908, catalogue of the exhibition, Société des artistes indépendants, Paris 1908.

Paris 1908b
Société du Salon d'Automne. Catalogue des ouvrages de peinture, sculpture, dessin exposés au Grand Palais des Champs-Elysées, Paris, Grand Palais, October-November 1908, catalogue of the exhibition, Dupont, Paris 1908.

Paris 1910
Le goût chinois en Europe au XVIIIe siècle, Paris, Musée des Arts Décoratifs, June-October 1910, catalogue of the exhibition, Paris 1910.

Paris 1911a
27e Exposition. Société des Artistes Indépendants, Paris, Quai d'Orsay (Pont de l'Alma), 21st April - 13th June, Paris 1911.

Paris 1911b
Catalogue de Cent Peintures originels de l'Ecole Ukiyo-e composant la collection Fokuba, Paris, Musée des Arts Décoratifs, 24th February - 19th March 1911, catalogue of the exhibition, Boudin, Paris 1911.

Paris 1911c
La chinoiserie en Europe au XVIIIe siècle, Paris, Musée des Arts Décoratifs, catalogue of the exhibition, Librairie centrale des Beaux-Arts, Paris 1911.

Paris 1912a
Exposition d'estampages d'anciennes sculptures chinoises, Paris, Musée des Arts décoratifs, catalogue of the exhibition, 11th January - 12th February 1912, Paris 1912.

Paris 1912b
Exposition de peintures chinoises anciennes, Paris, Musée Cernuschi, April-May 1912, catalogue of the exhibition, Marty, Paris 1912.

Paris 1912c
Section d'Or, Paris, Galerie La Boëtie, October 1912, catalogue of the exhibition, Paris 1912.

Paris 1912d
Société du Salon d'Automne. Catalogue des ouvrages de peinture, sculpture, dessin exposés au Grand Palais des Champs-Elysées, Paris, Grand Palais, 1st October-8th November 1912, catalogue of the exhibition, Kugelmann, Paris 1912.

Paris 1913
4° Exposition des Arts de l'Asie. Art Bouddique. Catalogue sommaire, Paris, Musée Cernuschi, catalogue of the exhibition, Paris 1913.

London 1914
Whitechapel Art Gallery: Twentieth Century Art. A Review of Modern Movements. Summer Exhibition, London, Whitechapel Art Gallery, May-June 1914, catalogue of the exhibition, London 1914.

Paris 1914
Exposition des œuvres de Wilhelm Lehmbruck, Paris, Galerie Levesque, 20th-30th June 1914, catalogue of the exhibition with the preface by A. Salmon, Paris 1914.

Paris 1916
Lyre et Palette, Paris 1re Exposition. Kisling, Matisse, Modigliani, Ortiz de Zarate, Picasso. Sculptures nègres, Paris, Lyre et Palette, November-December 1916, catalogue of the exhibition, Paris 1916.

Venice 1922
XIII Esposizione Internazionale d'Arte della città di Venezia, Venice, Giardini della Biennale, 15th April - 31st October 1922, catalogue of the exhibition, Bestetti&Tumminelli, Roma 1922.

Paris 1925
Modigliani, Paris, Galerie Bing & Cie, November 1925, catalogue of the exhibition, Paris 1925.

Paris 1930
Les collages, Paris, Galerie Goermans, March 1930, catalogue of the exhibition, Hermann, Paris 1930.

Venice 1930
XVII Esposizione Biennale Internazionale d'Arte. Catalogo, Venice, Giardini di Castello, 4th May - 2nd November 1930, catalogue of the exhibition, Ferrari, Venezia, 1930.

Philadelphia 1943
Paintings from the Chester Dale collection, The Philadelphia Museum of Art, Philadelphia 1943.

Paris 1950
Exposition d'Art Moderne Italien, Paris, Musée National d'Art Moderne, May-June 1950, catalogue of the exhibition, Presses artistiques, Paris 1950.

Cleveland-New York 1951
Modigliani: Paintings, Drawings, Sculpture, Cleveland, Cleveland Museum of Art; New York, The Museum of Modern Art, 1951, catalogue of the exhibition with a presentation by J.Th. Soby, The Museum of Modern Art, New York 1950.

Rome 1951-1952
VI Quadriennale Nazionale d'Arte, Rome, Palazzo delle Esposizioni, December 1951 - April 1952, catalogue of the exhibition, De Luca, Rome 1952.

New York 1953-1954
Sculptures and Sculptors, Drawings, New York, Curt Valentin Gallery, 22nd December1953 - 24th January1954, catalogue of the exhibition, New York 1954.

Marseilles 1958
Modigliani, Marseilles, Musée Cantini, 10th June - 27th July 1958, catalogue of the exhibition, Presses municipales, Marseilles 1958.

Paris 1960-1961
Les sources du XXe siècle: les arts en Europe de 1884 à 1914, Paris, Musée National d'Art Moderne, 4th November 1960 - 23rd January 1961, catalogue of the exhibition, Les Presses Artistiques, Paris 1961.

New York 1963
Artist and Maecenas. A tribute to Curt Valentin, New York, Marlborough-Gerson Gallery, November-December 1963, catalogue of the exhibition, New York 1963.

Duisburg 1965
Pariser Begegnungen, 1904-1914, Duisburg, Wilhelm-Lehmbruck-Museum der Stadt, 16th October-28th November 1965, catalogue of the exhibition, Graphische Kunstanstalt, Recklinghausen 1965.

Paris 1966-1967
Hommage à Pablo Picasso (dessins, gouaches, papiers collés, sculptures), Paris, Musée du Petit Palais, November 1966-February 1967, catalogue of the exhibition edited by J. Leymarie, RMN, Paris 1966.

Paris 1978
Lipchitz: œuvres de Jacques Lipchitz (1891-1973), Paris, Musée National d'Art Moderne-Centre George Pompidou, catalogue of the exhibition edited by N. Barbier, Centre Georges Pompidou, Paris 1978.

Liege 1980
Modigliani, Liege, Musée Saint-Georges, 18th October-14th December 1980, catalogue of the exhibition, Liege 1980.

Paris 1981
Amedeo Modigliani 1884-1920, Paris, Musée d'Art Moderne de la Ville de Paris, 26th March - 28th June 1981, catalogue of the exhibition, Musée d'Art Moderne de la Ville de Paris, Paris 1981.

Toronto 1981-1982
Gauguin to Moore. Primitivism in Modern Sculpture, Toronto, Art Gallery of Ontario, 7th November 1981 - 3rd January 1982, catalogue of the exhibition edited by A.G. Wilkinson, Art Gallery of Ontario, Toronto 1981.

Livorno 1984
Modigliani, gli anni della scultura, Livorno, Museo Progressivo d'Arte Contemporanea, 1st July - 9th September 1984, catalogue of the exhibition edited by D. Durbé, V. Durbé, P. Vivarelli, Mondadori, Milan 1984.

New York 1984
"Primitivism" in 20th century art: affinity of the tribal and the modern, New York, Museum of Modern Art, catalogue of the exhibition edited by W. Rubin, New York Graphic Society Books, Boston 1984.

Verona 1984-1985
Modigliani: dipinti e disegni; incontri italiani 1900-1920, Verona, Galleria dello Scudo, 25th November 1984 - 31st January 1985, catalogue of the exhibition edited by O. Patani, Mazzotta, Milan 1984.

Paris 1986a
La Sculpture française au XIXe siècle, Paris, Galeries Nationales du Grand Palais, April-July 1986, catalogue of the exhibition edited by A. Pingeot, Réunion Musées Nationaux, Paris 1986.

Paris 1986b
Qu'est-ce que la sculture?, Paris, Centre Pompidou, Musée National d'Art Moderne, 3rd July - 13th October, catalogue of the exhibition edited by M. Rowell, Èditions du Centre Pompidou, Paris 1986.

Winnipeg 1987
Break Up of Tradition. Traditions et Ruptures, Winnipeg, Winnipeg Art Gallery, August-October 1987, catalogue of the exhibition edited by L. d'Argencourt, Goose Lane Editions, Fredericton 1987

Paris 1988
Le Japonisme, Paris, Galeries nationales du Grand Palais, 17th May - 15th August 1988, catalogue of the exhibition, Ministère de la culture et de la communication-Editions de la Réunion des musées nationaux, Paris 1988.

London 1989
Arte italiana del XX secolo: pittura e scultura 1900-1988, London, Royal Academy of Arts, 14th January - 9th April 1989, catalogue of the exhibition edited by N. Rosenthal, G. Celant, Royal Academy of Arts-Leonardo, London-Milan 1989.

Venice 1989
Arte Italiana. Presenze 1900-1945, Venice, Palazzo Grassi, 30th April-5th May 1989, catalogue of the exhibition edited by P. Hulten, G. Celant, Bompiani, Milan 1989.

London 1990
On classic ground: Picasso, Léger, de Chirico and the New Classicism 1910-1930. London, Tate Gallery, 6th June - 2nd September 1990, catalogue edited by E. Bowling, J. Mundy, Tate Gallery, London 1990.

Düsseldorf 1991
Amedeo Modigliani Malerei, Skulpturen, Zeichnungen, Düsseldorf, Kunstsammlung Nordrhein-Westfalen, 19th January - 1st April 1991, catalogue of the exhibition edited by W. Schmalenbach, Prestel-Verlag, Munich 1990.

Martigny 1990
Modigliani, Martigny, Fondation Pierre Gianadda, 19th June - 28th October 1990, catalogue of the exhibition edited by D. Marchesseau, Martigny, Fondation Pierre Gianadda, Martigny 1990.

Paris 1993
Apollinaire, critique d'art, Paris, Pavillon des arts, 2nd February - 9th May 1993, catalogue of the exhibition, Paris Musées-Gallimard, Paris 1993.

Venice 1993
Modigliani: testimonianze, documenti e disegni inediti provenienti dalla collezione del dottor Paul Alexandre, Venice, Palazzo Grassi, edited by N. Alexandre, Allemandi, Turin 1993.

Paris 1994-1995
André Derain, Le Peintre du "trouble moderne", Paris, Musée d'Art Moderne de la Ville de Paris, 18th November 1994 - 19th March 1995, Paris-Musées, Paris 1994.

Paris 1995
Constantin Brancusi: 1876-1957, Paris, Musée National d'Art Moderne-Centre George Pompidou, 14th April - 21st August 1995, catalogue of the exhibition edited by F. Taja Bach, M. Rowell, A. Temkin, Gallimard-Centre Pompidou, Paris 1995.

Rotterdam 1996-1997
Van Dongen retrouvé, l'œuvre sur papier, 1895-1912, Rotterdam, Museum Boijmans Van Beuningen, 2nd November 1996 - 5th January 1997, catalogue of the exhibition edited by A. Hopmans, Réunion des musées nationaux, Paris 1997.

Rouen 1999
Duchamp-Villon sculpteur 1876-1918, Rouen, Musée de beaux-arts, 20th February - 24th May 1999, catalogue of the exhibition edited by B. Ajac, M. Pessiot, Éditions du Centre Pompidou-Réunion des Musées Nationaux, Paris 1998.

Châteauroux 2000
La Section d'or, 1912, 1920, 1925, Châteauroux, Musées de

Châtcauroux, 21st September - 3rd December 2000, catalogue of the exhibition edited by C. Debray, F Lucbert, Editions du Cercle d'art, Paris 2000.

Venice 2000
Modigliani e i suoi. Jeanne Hébuterne, André Hébuterne, Georges Dorignac, Amedeo Modigliani, Venice, Fondazione Giorgio Cini, Isola di San Giorgio Maggiore, October-December 2000, catalogue of the exhibition edited by Ch. Parisot, Edizioni Canale Arte, Borgaro Torinese 2000.

Paris 2000
Picasso sculpteur, Paris, Centre George Pompidou, Musée National d'Art Moderne, 7th June - 25th September 2000, Èditions du Centre Pompidou, Paris 2000.

Buffalo 2002-2003
Modigliani & the artists of Montparnasse, Buffalo, New York, Albright-Knox Art Gallery, 19th October 2002 - 12th January 2003, catalogue edited by K. Wayne, Harry N. Abrams in association with the Albright-Knox Art Gallery, New York-London 2002.

Milan 2003
Amedeo Modigliani: l'angelo dal volto severo, Milan, Palazzo Reale, 21st March - 6th July 2003, catalogue of the exhibition edited by M. Restellini, Skira, Geneva-Milan 2003.

New York 2003
Elie Nadelman. Sculptor of Modern Life, New York, Whitney Museum of American Art, 3rd April - 20th July 2003, catalogue of the exhibition, Whitney Museum of American Art, New York 2003.

Paris 2004
Primitifs français: découvertes et redécouvertes, Paris, Musée du Louvre, 27th February -17th May 2004, catalogue of the exhibition edited by D. Thiébaut, P. Lorentz, F.R. Martin, Réunion des Musées Nationaux, Paris 2004.

Andorra 2004
Modigliani al cor de Paris. Itineraris d'artistes, Andorra La Vella, Sala d'exposicions del Govern d'Andorra, April-May, catalogue of the exhibition edited by Ch. Parisot, Govern d'Andorra, Andorra La Vella 2004.

New York 2004
Modigliani Beyond the Myth, New York, The Jewish Museum, May-September 2004, catalogue of the exhibition edited by M. Klein, Yale University Press, New Haven-London 2004.

Rome 2006
Modigliani, Rome, Complesso del Vittoriano, February-June 2006, catalogue of the exhibition, edited by R. Chiappini, Skira, Geneva-Milan 2006.

London 2006
Modigliani and His Models, London, Royal Academy of Arts, July-October 2006, catalogue of the exhibition, edited by S. Fraquelli, N. Rosenthal, Royal Academy of Arts, London 2006.

Ferrara 2006-2007
André Derain, Ferrara, Palazzo dei Diamanti, 24th September 2006 - 7th January 2007, catalogue of the exhibition, edited by I. Monod-Fontaine, Ferrara Arte, Ferrara 2006.

Lisbon 2006-2007
Amadeo de Souza Cardoso: diálogo de Vanguardias, Lisbon, Centro de Arte Moderna José de Azeredo Perdigão, 15th November 2006 - 14th January 2007, catalogue of the exhibition edited by H. de Freitas, Fundação Calouste Gulbenkian, Lisbon 2006.

Rome 2007
Modigliani e la spiritualità africana, Rome, Palazzo Taverna, 25th October - 23rd November 2007, catalogue of the exhibition with texts by S. Buisson, Ch. Parisot, Carte Segrete, Rome 2007.

Madrid 2008
Modigliani y su tiempo, Madrid, Museo Thyssen-Bornemisza, Fundacion Caja Madrid, 5th February - 18th May 2008, catalogue of the exhibition edited by F.C. Serraller, Museo Thyssen-Bornemisza-Fundacion Caja Madrid, Madrid 2008.

Caserta 2008
Modigliani, l'artiste italien. Caserta, Belvedere di San Leucio, 1st June - 24th July 2008, catalogue of the exhibition edited by V. Goriinov, C. Filippini, Ch. Parisot, Cairo Publishing, Milan 2008.

Paris 2009
Oublier Rodin?: la sculpture à Paris, 1905-1914, Paris, Musée d'Orsay, 10th March - 31st May 2009, catalogue of the exhibition, Hazan, Paris 2009.

Bonn 2009
Amedeo Modigliani: ein Mythos der Moderne, Bonn, Kunst und Ausstellungshalle der Bundesrepublik Deutschland, 17th April - 30th 2009, catalogue of the exhibition edited by C. Vitali, DuMont, Cologne 2009.

London 2009-2010
Wild thing: Epstein, Gaudier-Brzeska, Gill, London, Royal Academy of Arts, 24th October 2009 - 24th January 2010, catalogue of the exhibition edited by R. Cork, Royal Academy of Arts, London 2009.

Palestrina 2010
Modigliani. Dal Classicismo al Cubismo, Palestrina, Museo Archeologico Nazionale, 24th June - 10th September 2010, catalogue of the exhibition edited by C. Strinati *et al.*, Edizioni Casa Modigliani, Rome 2010.

Silvana Editoriale

Produced by
Arti Grafiche Amilcare Pizzi Spa

Direction
Dario Cimorelli

Art Director
Giacomo Merli

Copy Editor
Clelia Palmese

Layout
Donatella Ascorti

Production Coordinator
Michela Bramati

Editorial Assistant
Elena Piaggesi

Iconographic office
Deborah D'Ippolito, Alessandra Olivari

Press office
Lidia Masolini, press@silvanaeditoriale.it

Silvana Editoriale Spa

via Margherita De Vizzi, 86
20092 Cinisello Balsamo, Milano
tel. 02 61 83 63 37
fax 02 61 72 464
www.silvanaeditoriale.it

Reproductions, printing and binding by
Arti Grafiche Amilcare Pizzi Spa
Cinisello Balsamo, Milan

Printed
December 2010

Photo Credits

© 2010 Digital Image Museum Associates/LACMA/Art Resource NY/Scala, Firenze
© 2010 Estate of Alexander Archipenko/Artists Rights Society (ARS), New York/SIAE Rome
© 2010 Foto Scala, Florence/BPK,Bildagentur fuer Kunst, Kultur und Geschichte (photo by Martin Franken), Berlin
© 2010 Image copyright The Metropolitan Museum of Art/Art Resource/Scala, Florence
© 2010 Musee du quai Branly (photo by Hughes Dubois) Scala, Florence
© Belvedere, Vienna
© BPK, Berlin, Dist. RMN / Jürgen Liepe, Paris
© E.O. Hoppé/CORBIS, Milan
© Fondation de Coubertin, Saint-Rémy les Chevreuse
© Hamburger Kunsthalle / BPK (photo by Walford/Dunkelberg), Berlino
© Philippe Ladet / Musée Zadkine / Roger-Viollet, Paris
© Pierre Joffre / Musée Zadkine / Roger-Viollet, Paris
© RMN (Collection Georges Pompidou) / Adam Rzepka, Paris
© RMN (Collection Georges Pompidou) / Bertrand Prévost, Paris
© RMN (Collection Georges Pompidou) / Droits réservés, Paris
© RMN (Collection Georges Pompidou) / Georges Meguerditchian, Paris
© RMN (Collection Georges Pompidou) / Jacqueline Hyde/ Philippe Migeat, Paris
© RMN (Collection Georges Pompidou) / Jean-Claude Planchet, Paris
© RMN (Musée de l'Orangerie) / Madeleine Coursaget / Hervé Lewandowski, Paris
© RMN (Musée d'Orsay) / Hervé Lewandowski (Bernard Joseph Antoine), Paris
© RMN (Musée Guimet) / Thierry Ollivier / Michel Urtado, Paris
© RMN (Musée Picasso) / Thierry Le Mage, Paris
© RMN / Béatrice Hatala, Paris
© RMN / Daniel Arnaudet, Paris
© RMN / Franck Raux, Parigi
© RMN / François Vizzavona, Paris
© RMN / Gérard Blot / Hervé Lewandowski / René-Gabriel Ojéda, Paris
© Tate, London 2010, London
© The Garman Ryan Collection, The New Art Gallery Walsall, Walsall
© The Israel Museum, Jerusalem
© The Phillips Collection, Washington DC
© The Solomon R. Guggenheim Foundation (photo by David Heald), New York
© The Trustees of the British Museum, London
Ägyptisches Museum und Papyrussammlung, Berlin
Aichi Prefectural Museum of Art, Nagoya
Archipenko Foundation, New York
Art Gallery of Ontario, Toronto
Biblioteca de Catalunya, Barcelona
Casa Buonarroti, Florence
Christie's Image Limited 2010
Courtesy Claudia Gian Ferrari - Studio di Consulenza per il '900 Italiano, Milan
Courtesy Galleria Tega (photo by Ares and Carlo Pedroli), Milano
Courtesy of Palm Springs Art Museum (photo by Mark Stephenson), Palm Springs
Courtesy of the Philadelpia Museum of Art, Philadelphia
Courtesy Studio Guastalla, Milan
Fundação Calouste Gulbenkian, Archive Amadeo de Souza Cardoso, Lisbon
Harvard Art Museum, Cambridge
Hirshhorn Museum and Sculpture Garden (photo by Lee Stalsworth), Washington
Image courtesy of the Board of Trustees, National Gallery of Art, Washington
Institut Valencià d'Art Modern, Valencia
Kunsthalle, Karlsruhe
Kunstmuseum - Kupferstchkabinett, Basilea
Kunstmuseum Bern, Berne
Kunstsammlung Nordrhein-Westfalen, Düsseldorf
Latner Family Art Collection, Toronto
Minneapolis Institute of Arts, Minneapolis
Modigliani Institut Archives Légales, Paris-Rome
Musée des Arts Africains, Océaniens et Amérìdiens (photo by Gerard Bonnet), Marseilles
Musée des Beaux-Arts de Djion (photo by François Jay), Djion
Musées de la Ville de Rouen (photo by Catherine Lancien), Rouen
Museo archeologico regionale, Agrigento